Industrial-Organizational Psychology

Industrial-Organizational Psychology

John B. Miner

The State University of New York at Buffalo

McGraw-Hill, Inc.

New York   St. Louis   San Francisco   Auckland   Bogotá   Caracas
Lisbon   London   Madrid   Mexico   Milan   Montreal   New Delhi
Paris   San Juan   Singapore   Sydney   Tokyo   Toronto

Industrial-Organizational Psychology

Copyright © 1992 by McGraw-Hill, Inc. All rights reserved. Printed in the United States of America.
Except as permitted under the United States Copyright Act of 1976, no part of this publication may be
reproduced or distributed in any form or by any means, or stored in a data base or retrieval system,
without the prior written permission of the publisher.

1 2 3 4 5 6 7 8 9 0 DOC DOC 9 0 9 8 7 6 5 4 3 2 1

ISBN 0-07-042440-3

This book was set in Palatino by The Clarinda Company.
The editors were Christopher Rogers and James R. Belser;
the designer was Wanda Siedlecka;
the production supervisor was Denise L. Puryear.
R. R. Donnelley & Sons Company was printer and binder.

Library of Congress Cataloging–in–Publication Data

Miner, John B.
    Industrial–organizational psychology/John B. Miner.
        p.   cm.
    Includes bibliographical references and index.
    ISBN 0-07-042440-3
    1. Psychology, Industrial.   2. Oganizational behavior.
I. Title.
HF5548.8.M497   1992
158.7—dc20   91–16818

About the Author

John B. Miner is Donald S. Carmichael Professor of Human Resources at the State University of New York at Buffalo where he also chairs the Department of Organization and Human Resources, serves as faculty director of the Center for Entrepreneurial Leadership, and holds an appointment in the Department of Psychology. Previously he has served on the faculties of the University of Oregon, University of Maryland, and Georgia State University; he also has held visiting, part-time or research appointments at Princeton University, Georgia Institute of Technology, Brooklyn College, Columbia University, the University of Pennsylvania, the University of California at Berkeley, and the University of South Florida. His teaching has extended over a number of different areas related to organizations and their functioning and human resource management. He has taught undergraduate and graduate industrial-organizational psychology courses on numerous occasions at several different universities.

John Miner has had considerable experience as an I/O psychology practitioner. He spent several years directing psychological research activities at the Atlantic Refining Company, and several more as an internal consultant in psychology with McKinsey and Company in both its San Francisco and New York offices. His own consulting practice extending over many years focused initially on managerial and professional selection and development research, later on activities related to serving as an expert witness in equal employment opportunity cases, and most recently on psychological assessments of top executive team members. He heads Organizational Measurement Systems Press which publishes psychological testing materials.

In the professional associations John Miner has been particularly active with the Society for Industrial and Organizational Psychology, the American Psychological Association, and the Academy of Management. He has served the latter as its president and as editor of the *Academy of Management Journal*. He has published over forty textbooks, professional books, and research monographs, over one hundred articles, and some ten different psychological tests or testing materials. Among his books, those having particular relevance for industrial-organizational psychology are *Studies in Management Education* (1965), *Personnel Psychology* (1969), *Intelligence in the United States* (1973), *Motivation to Manage* (1977), *Employee Selection within the Law* (1978), *Theories of Organizational Behavior* (1980), *Theories of Organizational Structure and Process* (1982), and *Organizational Behavior: Performance and Productivity* (1988). His articles have appeared in a wide range of professional and scholarly publications, with particular concentration in the *Journal of Applied Psychology* and *Personnel Psychology*.

John Miner received a masters degree in psychology from Clark University and both undergraduate and doctoral degrees in psychology from Princeton University. He has been licensed as a psychologist at various times in the past in Oregon and Georgia, and is currently licensed in the state of New York.

Contents

19
Training and Development   521

20
Safety Psychology and Industrial
Clinical Psychology   556

Case Problems

List of Boxes

Preface

In recent decades, industrial-organizational psychology has been changing rapidly. Twenty-five years ago the textbooks carried titles such as *Industrial Psychology* and *Personnel and Industrial Psychology*. Their content concentrated heavily on personnel matters, with a smattering of organizational psychology and human factors psychology. Consumer psychology and applications of psychological knowledge to marketing might or might not be covered.

What the field now has come to can be illustrated with reference to a survey of 427 psychologists teaching courses in industrial-organizational psychology. This survey preceded the writing of this book and in a number of respects helped to guide its development. The most striking aspect of the responses was what these psychologists had to say about organizational psychology. Roughly 55 percent taught a course that was equally balanced between organizational and personnel content. Another 30 percent emphasized organizational psychology more than personnel psychology. Only about 15 percent were following the prevailing practice of twenty-five years before. In this book the balance between organizational and personnel content is roughly equal, although there is one more chapter in the organizational part. The part of the book dealing with organizational psychology is placed first to reflect the predominant emphasis in courses at the present time. As indicated in Chapter 1, there is a logical rationale for this placement as well. However, some professors may wish to take up personnel psychology first. The

material is presented so as to facilitate doing this.

The survey yielded mixed results regarding human factors and engineering psychology. A slight majority of the respondents gave little or no attention to this subject in their courses. Either they considered it more appropriately taught elsewhere in the curriculum, or they felt that they had insufficient time to include it. Clearly, the time devoted to human factors subject matter in industrial-organizational psychology courses has declined sharply over the past twenty-five years; new developments in personnel-related areas and the burgeoning of the field of organizational psychology have simply pushed it to the periphery. Reflecting this trend, and in order to cover all that is needed in the key organizational and personnel areas, this book does not contain a separate, chapter-length treatment of human factors and engineering psychology. Content from this area is included at various points, however, throughout the book. This is true in particular of the discussion of work redesign in Chapter 4, of work and stress in Chapter 6, of work redesign and sociotechnical interventions in Chapter 11, of job analysis in Chapter 13, and of safety psychology and the work context in Chapter 20.

Consumer psychology has never been part of the standard fare in industrial-organizational psychology. The survey results indicate that it still is not. Just over 70 percent of the professors give little or no attention to this subject. There are a number of reasons for this, including the rise of consumer behavior and consumer psychology as a separate and distinct field of its own. In any event, this book follows prevailing practice and accordingly devotes little space to this topic.

Twenty-five years ago legal considerations would hardly have been mentioned in a book such as this. Today they are entwined with almost every aspect of the field. The practice here has been to consider relevant legal constraints and methods of dealing with them as appropriate throughout the book. Chapter 12 in particular is concerned with fair employment practices law and its relationship to psychology. The statistical appendix presents various statistical approaches in the context of their relevance for dealing with legal issues.

One factor that has changed very little over the years is the importance of research and research design, including statistical analysis, to industrial-organizational psychology. The field not only uses knowledge gained from research as its stock in trade, it is one of the few social science disciplines where normal professional practice actually involves the conduct of applied research. Accordingly, it should not come as a surprise that substantial attention is given to research procedures and results in this book. In general, the approach has been to take up appropriate research designs as the need to do so emerges. However, Chapters 16 and 19 both contain major segments dealing with research design, and statistics receive special attention in the appendix. Furthermore, among the 100 boxes scattered throughout the book, fifty-eight present actual research studies conducted either in a field setting or in the laboratory. Many more exhibits present the results of research studies.

■ THE ORGANIZATION OF THE BOOK

As noted, organizational psychology comes first, after the introductory chapter. The approach in presenting this material is the common one of moving from aspects of the individual, to groups, and finally to the organizational level, thus dealing with increasing degrees of social complexity. At the individual level, Chapter 2 takes up cognitive processes such as learning, intelligence, and individual decision making. Then there are two chapters dealing with individual motivation, a core aspect of organizational psychology. Chapter 5 considers attitudes, commitments, and values; job satisfaction has long been of major concern to industrial-organizational psychologists. The concluding chapter among those dealing with factors within the individual focuses on human personality, with particular attention to emotional stress.

Chapters 7 and 8 move to the next higher level, dealing with group processes and group decision making, respectively. Chapters 9 and 10 discuss leadership, another key area within organizational psychology. Leadership is both an aspect of group functioning and an organizational activity; as such, the subject bridges the two levels. Chapter 11 discusses issues of exclusively organizational concern.

Part Three takes up subject matter related to personnel and human resources practice. Chapters 12 and 13 form something of a unit. The first deals with the people who come into an organization. The second considers the jobs that they find there. Both subjects, individual differences and job analysis, form a backdrop for the chapters which follow. Chapters 14 and 15 are concerned with the evaluation of employee performance. It is important to understand how performance is graded at an early point, because information of this kind is used subsequently to select people for hiring and placement. The next three chapters focus on the process of bringing people into organizations and jobs: Chapter 16 takes up selection research designs in all their complexity; Chapter 17 deals with interviews, application blanks, references, and the like; and Chapter 18 discusses psychological testing. The remaining two

Industrial-
Organizational
Psychology

PART ONE Introduction

1

The Field of Industrial-Organizational Psychology

Consultant or Senior Consultant. Personnel Designs, Incorporated is a full-range human resources consulting firm with offices in Detroit, Houston, Stamford, and Hartford. Across the offices, Personnel Designs has one of the largest complements of Industrial-Organizational Psychologists in the nation. Our business spans a range of industry groups, including the manufacturing, electronics, retail, transportation, pharmaceutical, petroleum, health care and entertainment industries. We work in both the public and private sectors. We are seeking Ph.D. or Master's level I-O psychologists who have strong writing, presentation, psychometric and statistical skills. Initial job duties would depend upon previous experience, and would include participation in a range of activities associated with the construction and implementation of selection systems (e.g., test development, test validation, interview construction and training, assessment center design), performance appraisal systems, career developmental programs, compensation programs, and attitude surveys. Advancement potential within the firm, commensurate with performance and on-going development of skills. Salary competitive. Send resume to: Dr. John D. Arnold, Vice President, Personnel Designs, Incorporated, P.O. Box 36778, Grosse Pointe, MI 48236.

Human Resources Research Interns. BellSouth Corporation, a leader in the telecommunications and information industry, is currently accepting applications for Pre-Doctoral (3rd and 4th Year) Industrial/Organizational Psychology internships. These positions provide an excellent opportunity to conduct applied research, develop various human resources programs, and gain insight into the environment of a major corporation while interacting with a large staff of I/O Psychologists. The internships are full time and are normally six months in duration. All positions are located in Atlanta, Georgia, with several internships becoming available January and July.

Qualified applicants should be enrolled in an I/O Psychology doctoral program, and have completed a Master's degree or equivalent (i.e., admitted to doctoral candidacy). Applicants should possess strong research and analytical skills as well as good written communication skills. Expertise in computer skills (SAS, SPSS, PC) is highly desirable.

Interested graduate students are invited to submit a cover letter, vita, and two letters of recommen-

dation to: Dan Whitenack, Ph.D., Human Resources Research, BellSouth Corporation, 1155 Peachtree Street, N.E., Room 13D03, Atlanta, Georgia 30367–6000.

Industrial/Organizational Psychology. A tenure-track faculty position (Assistant Professor) is available at the Illinois Institute of Technology in Chicago beginning Fall 1991. Responsibilities include teaching undergraduate and graduate level courses, and supervision of Masters and Ph.D. theses. Qualified applicants should have a strong interest in personnel psychology and a commitment to an active ongoing research program. A Ph.D. is required and field experience is desirable. Send vita, three letters of recommendation and a sample of research papers to: Dr. Roya Ayman, Director, I/O Program, Department of Psychology, Illinois Institute of Technology, Chicago, IL 60616. Recruitment will continue until a suitable candidate is found. IIT is an equal opportunity/affirmative action employer, M/F/V/H.

Industrial/Organizational Psychologist. Mervyn's, a $4 Billion retail store division of Dayton Hudson Corporation, is seeking a Ph.D. with 1–5 years experience to contribute to our Management Development and Organizational Development challenges. Must have organizational experience/savvy, creative design skills, and internal consulting capability. Accountabilities will include Performance Management, Career Development, Human Resource Planning and Survey Feedback; the design of HR systems such as selection and performance appraisal; consulting on structure and process; and oversight of ongoing test validation. This can be an exciting professional opportunity, located in the San Francisco Bay Area. Qualified applicants please send a resumé to: Richard M. Vosburgh, Ph.D., Vice President, Human Resources, Mall Stop C09A, Mervyn's, 25001 Industrial Boulevard, Hayward, CA 94545. Mervyn's is an equal opportunity employer.

Industrial/Organizational Psychology. The Ohio State University Department of Psychology announces a tenure-track position at the Assistant Professor level in the I/O program effective Autumn, 1991. Preference will be given candidates with excellent research credentials who a) possess strong expertise in one or more of the related fields of COGNITIVE, QUANTITATIVE, OR SOCIAL psychology and b) have a clear commitment to the study of behavior in an organizational context. Areas of particular interest are decision and group processes (including bargaining, negotiations, mediation, and conflict resolution), social attitudes, social cognition, performance modeling, formal models of complex behavior in organizations, and psychometrics and measurement theory. However, the specific area is less important than the degree of commitment to a program of basic research on issues relevant to either individual or group behavior in organizations. In addition to their research, candidates will be expected to contribute to the program both at the advanced undergraduate and graduate levels of instruction. Applicants should send a vita, a cover letter noting their current scholarly interests and three letters of recommendation to: Dr. Robert Billings, Chair, I/O Search Committee, Department of Psychology, The Ohio State University, Columbus, Ohio 43210. To receive full consideration, materials should be posted by November 30, 1990. An Equal Opportunity Employer.

Consulting Intern. Development Dimensions International, a world leader in human resource management, consulting, assessment, development, and training, is seeking post-masters candidates with backgrounds in industrial psychology, personnel management, or applied social psychology who are interested in an exciting and challenging 4–6 month internship. Candidates must have an interest in a consulting career, possess effective oral and written communication skills, and have a strong quantitative background. Projects may include conducting a job analysis, evaluating the validity and adverse impact of selection programs, designing and implementing a new selection system, and/or conducting research investigations in these areas. Send cover letter and résumé/vita to Susan Cohen, Development Dimensions International. P.O. Box 13379, Pittsburgh, PA 15243. Equal Opportunity Employer.

These position announcements provide an introduction to the kinds of things industrial-organizational (I/O) psychologists do. They are from a publication called *The Industrial-Organizational Psychologist,* which publishes items dealing with professional practice in the field (Lindell, 1990, 1991). The chapters of this book provide detailed coverage of the various duties and activities noted in these position announcements.

Industrial-organizational psychology is first of all a subfield within psychology, as are experimental psychology, clinical psychology, social psychology, and many other subfields. Within the American Psychological Association (APA) its interests are represented primarily by the Society for Industrial and Organizational Psychology (which publishes *The Industrial-Organizational Psychologist*). Other divisions of the APA with interests that are to varying degrees similar are the Division on Evaluation and Measurement, the Society of Personality and Social Psychology, the Division of Applied Experimental and Engineering Psychologists, the Division of Consumer Psychology, and the Division of Consulting Psychology. Recently the Society for Industrial and Organizational Psychology has also affiliated with the American Psychological Society, which is a new professional organization designed to emphasize the scientific aspects of psychology (Hakel, 1988; Schmitt & Howard, 1989). As a component of psychology, **industrial-organizational psychology** is concerned with the application of psychological science, and thus its theory and research, to the problems of human organizations and in particular to the utilization of human resources within organizations.

Originally the field of industrial-organizational psychology was known as *industrial psychology* and was concerned almost entirely with certain areas within human resource (or personnel) management; thus for all practical purposes the term *industrial psychology* was synonymous with *personnel psychology.* More recently the word *organizational* has been added to reflect an increasing concern with aspects of organizational functioning that extend beyond human resource utilization. This organizational psychology developed in close relation to, and in fact as part of, organizational science as a whole. Thus, to understand fully what industrial-organizational psychology is today, it is necessary to understand its relations to both human resource management and organizational science.

■ RELATIONS TO HUMAN RESOURCE MANAGEMENT

□ What Is Human Resource Management?

Human resource management may be defined as the process of developing, applying, and evaluating policies, procedures, methods, and programs relating to the individual in the organization. The human resource function is concerned with the management of the human resources of an organization, in contrast to its material or financial resources. Human resource management, like industrial-organizational psychology, is both an area of practice within an organization and a body of knowledge that may be developed and taught. The term *human resources management* has now largely replaced the older term, *personnel management.*

Exhibit 1-1 provides an overview of the programs and activities in which human resource units are most likely to be involved. Whether a particular activity will be performed by a human resource unit in a specific organization depends on a number of factors. Some firms, especially smaller ones, simply do not have formal procedures for career planning and development, college recruiting, and the like. Others may locate activities such as union and labor relations or skill training outside the human resource function,

in a legal department or manufacturing, for instance. These differences in whether certain programs and activities are needed, viewed as useful, and considered an appropriate human resource function account for the frequency variations noted in Exhibit 1-1. However, these lists taken as a whole provide a good summary statement of human resource management's subject matter.

A somewhat different approach to the same problem is taken in Exhibit 1-2. Here human resource management is viewed as pursuing the same goals as the rest of the organization, and as operating under constraints that limit the alternative strategies that may be followed at a given time. Human resources are taken into the organization, acted upon via various activities and programs (called *mediators*), with the result that a continuous stream of output behaviors is emitted. In this way the organization creates products and supplies services to its employees as well as its customers. Mediators may vary in terms of the type of goal they serve best; whether they utilize a functional process or the structure of the organization to achieve their ends; and whether the primary objective is to improve upon the human capabilities existing at the time of hiring, merely to sustain those capabilities, or to correct performance deficiencies and thus control them. The objective of Exhibit 1-2 is not only to portray the various activities of human resource management, but to show how they relate to one another.

□ How Does Psychology Fit In?

Human resource management as a field has developed its knowledge base in part internally and in part through contributions from other disciplines—sociology, economics, engineering, law, medicine, education, journalism, and of course psychology. A survey of human resource managers requested information on the areas within the function

Exhibit 1-1   Programs and Activities in Which Human Resource Units Report Considerable Involvement

Reported to Be Part of the Work of the Human Resource Department in:			
Over 90% of the Companies	80–89% of the Companies	70–79% of the Companies	60–69% of the Companies
Personnel records and reports	Personnel research	Health and medical services	Union and labor relations
Recruiting, interviewing, and hiring	Supervisory training	Retirement counseling	Community relations and fund drives
Promotions, transfers, and separations	Recreational and award programs	Employee communications and publications	Relocation services
Equal employment opportunity	Pensions and profit sharing	Preemployment testing	Skill training
Wage and salary administration	Nonmanagement performance evaluation	Executive compensation	Organization development
Induction and orientation of new employees	Management development	Counseling and employee assistance	College recruiting
Grievances and discipline	Tuition aid and scholarships	Management appraisal	Productivity and motivation
Insurance benefits	Safety management		Career planning and development
Handling unemployment compensation			
Job evaluation			
Handling workers' compensation			
Vacation and leave processing			
Human resource planning			

Source: Adapted from Bureau of National Affairs. (1983, May 26). ASPA-BNA survey no. 46—Personnel activities, budgets, and staffs. *Bulletin to Management*, p. 3.

where industrial-organizational psychologists could contribute the most (Cederblom, Pense, & Johnson, 1984). More than half mentioned management development, employee motivation, morale and job satisfaction, management selection, employee training, productivity, performance appraisal, and employee selection. Slightly fewer noted designing work conditions and designing organizational structures. About 30 percent viewed labor relations as an area for contributions.

Because practicing industrial-organizational psychologists are often housed in a personnel research unit, it is entirely possible that they might use their research skills to solve problems within any area of human resource management (Rassenfoss & Kraut, 1988). In actuality, however, psychological skills and knowledge have tended to develop in certain directions and not others. Within Exhibit 1–2 the areas of psychological focus may be described as follows:

The *input processes* of interviewing, testing, hiring and placement of new employees; recruiting to a much lesser degree

The primarily *productivity-oriented functional mediators* of management development, training, safety management, and the techniques of performance control derived from industri-

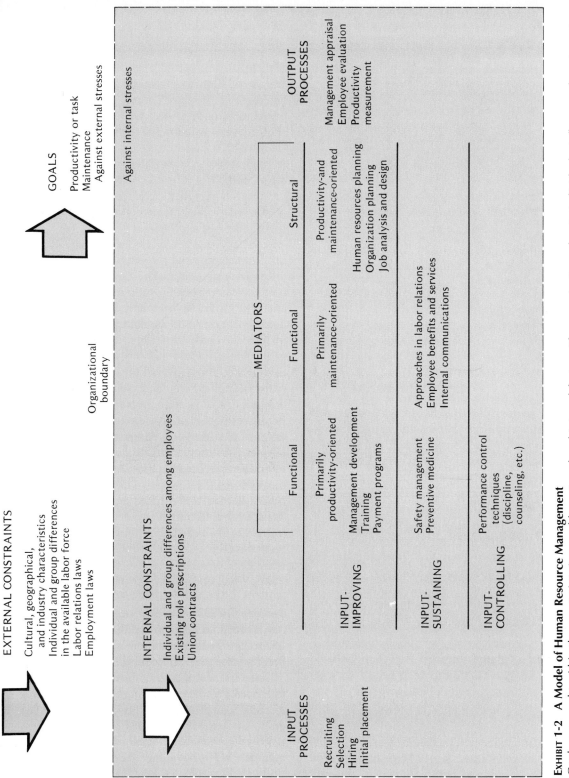

EXHIBIT 1-2 A Model of Human Resource Management
Goals are sought within the constraints imposed by external and internal factors. The organization takes in individuals, influences them in various ways, and obtains benefits in the form of products and services that can be sold.

7

al clinical psychology; payment programs and preventive medicine to a much lesser degree

The primarily *maintenance-oriented functional mediators* associated with internal communications; approaches in labor relations, and employee benefits and services to a much lesser degree

The *structural mediators* of organization planning, and job analysis and design; human resource planning to a much lesser degree

The *output processes* of management appraisal and employee evaluation; productivity measurement to a much lesser degree

Since a major concern of industrial-organizational psychologists is to develop and use measures of various kinds, such as tests, scales, questionnaires, indexes, and surveys, another approach to identifying the scope or domain of the field is to consider the variety of these instruments. Exhibit 1-3 does just that. It is apparent that a wide range of characteristics has been measured.

Finally, Exhibit 1-4 profiles the views of psychologists employed in business firms and in consulting. Scores of 4 and above reflect a view that the area is important to varying degrees; only personnel selection and placement, and performance appraisal techniques, receive ratings in the moderately important to very important range. In contrast, consumer behavior and human–machine interaction are not considered by these industrial psychologists to be at all important.

■ RELATIONS TO ORGANIZATIONAL SCIENCE

□ What Is Organizational Science?

Organizational science is a discipline that has emerged quite recently, primarily within colleges of business and management. Its sub-

ject matter is the study of organizations and their functioning, and what individuals do in and in relation to organizations. Although it has been concerned more frequently with business organizations than other types, it certainly is not restricted in this respect; government, for instance, is a common concern. A major thrust within the discipline is the achievement of improved performance and productivity from individuals, from groups, and from organizations as a whole (Kopelman, 1986; Miner, 1988).

This organizational science is often divided into two components—one micro and the other macro—although the dividing line tends to vary from one application to another and considerable overlapping is often evident. However, it is common practice to include at least the individual and small-group levels of functioning within the micro designation, and to label this subfield **organizational behavior.** The macro component of organizational science, in contrast, deals with organizational structure and process and covers organizationwide concepts and organization–environment interactions. Intergroup relationships occupy a middle ground, and may be handled within either the micro or macro subfield. Examples of major contributions at the micro and macro levels may be found in Miner (1980) and Miner (1982), respectively.

□ How Does Psychology Fit In?

The distinction between micro and macro organizational science is important, but it is probably emphasized more than it should be because the two subfields derive from different disciplinary origins. From its beginnings the micro component, organizational behavior, has been strongly influenced by psychologists. A large proportion of the theories, research, and techniques of organizational behavior have been contributed by organizational psychology. This work has dealt with

EXHIBIT 1-3 A Picture of Industrial-Organizational Psychology's Scope as Depicted by a Sampling of Its Measures*

Types of Dimensions Measured	Examples and References
Employee needs	Job Choice Exercise—Adrain M. Harrell & Michael J. Stahl (1981). A behavioral decision theory approach for measuring McClelland's trichotomy of needs. *Journal of Applied Psychology, 66*, 242–247.
Group-level attitudes and perceptions	Group Cohesiveness Measure—Ralph M. Stogdill (1965). *Manual for group dimensions descriptions.* Columbus, OH: Bureau of Business Research, Ohio State University.
Job involvement	Job and Work Involvement Scales—Rabindra N. Kanungo (1982). Measurement of job and work involvement. *Journal of Applied Psychology, 67*, 341–349.
Job satisfaction	Job Descriptive Index—Patricia C. Smith, Lorne M. Kendall, & Charles L. Hulin (1969). *The measurement of satisfaction in work and retirement.* Chicago: Rand McNally.
Job/task complexity	Multimethod Job Design Questionnaire—Michael A. Campion & Paul W. Thayer (1985). Development and field evaluation of an interdisciplinary measure of job design. *Journal of Applied Psychology, 70*, 29–43.
Leadership	Least Preferred Co-worker Scale—Fred E. Fiedler (1967). *A theory of leadership effectiveness.* New York: McGraw-Hill.
Organizational climate	Creativity Climate Measure—Calvin W. Taylor (1972). *Climate for creativity.* Elmsford, NY: Pergamon Press.
Organizational commitment	Organizational Commitment Questionnaire—Lyman W. Porter, Richard M. Steers, Richard M. Mowday, & P. V. Boulian (1974). Organizational commitment, job satisfaction, and turnover among psychiatric technicians. *Journal of Applied psychology, 59*, 603–609.
Organizational communication	Organizational Communication Questionnaire—Karlene H. Roberts & Charles A. O'Reilly (1974). Measuring organizational communication. *Journal of Applied Psychology, 59*, 321–326.
Perceived stress	Life Experiences Survey—Irwin G. Sarason, J. Johnson, & J. Siegel (1978). Assessing the impact of life change: Development of the Life Experiences Survey. *Journal of Consulting and Clinical Psychology, 46*, 932–946.
Role ambiguity and conflict	Job Related Tension Index—Robert L. Kahn, Donald M. Wolfe, Robert P. Quinn, & J. Diedrick Snoek (1964). *Organizational stress: Studies in role conflict and ambiguity.* New York: Wiley.
Union-related measures	Union and Management Attitudes toward Each Other—Ross Stagner, W. E. Chalmers, & Milton L. Derber (1958). Guttman-type scales for union and management attitudes toward each other. *Journal of Applied Psychology, 42*, 293–300.
Protestant work ethic	Survey of Work Values—Stephen Wollack, J. G. Goodale, Jon P. Wijting, & Patricia C. Smith (1971). Development of the Survey of Work Values. *Journal of Applied Psychology, 55*, 331–338.

*This listing does not include measures used to assess applicant characteristics such as mental aptitude tests and personality inventories.

Source: Kenneth P. DeMeuse (1986). A compendium of frequently used measures in industrial/organizational psychology. *The Industrial-Organizational Psychologist, 23*(2), 53–59.

EXHIBIT 1-4 **Importance of Knowledge in Various Areas* for Industrial-Organizational Practice as Judged by Existing Practitioners**

Content Area	Mean Rating	Content Area	Mean Rating
Personnel selection and placement	5.3	Learning principles	4.2
Performance appraisal techniques	5.1	Group dynamics	4.1
Job analysis	4.9	Attitude and value formation	4.0
Legal issues	4.8	Pay and compensation systems	3.8
Ethical issues	4.8	Personality theories	3.8
Training and development techniques	4.7	Decision-making strategies	3.7
Motivation principles	4.6	Conflict management techniques	3.5
Organization development	4.4	Labor relations	3.2
Organization theory	4.4	Stress-management techniques	3.1
Leadership theories	4.2	Consumer behavior	2.6
Quality of work life (job satisfaction)	4.2	Human–machine interaction	2.5

*The areas were rated on a 6-point scale from 1 (very unimportant) to 6 (very important).

SOURCE: Adapted from Mark Wesolowski & Hubert S. Feild (1987). Recruiting and selecting Ph.D. I/O graduates by business and consulting organizations. *The Industrial-Organizational Psychologist, 25*(1), 17–21.

learning, intelligence, individual decision-making, motivation, attitudes, values, personality—in short, all the aspects of individuals that psychologists study—but with a central focus on work and organizations. It also has dealt with work groups, their leadership, and organization development—the latter often penetrating rather deeply into the realm of macro organizational science.

Macro organizational science, in contrast, has been influenced to a large degree by sociology, with additional contributions from political science and economics, and even history and anthropology. Organizational psychologists have not been totally inactive here, but other disciplines have had a greater impact. Thus, viewing organizational science in its totality, industrial-organizational psychology accounts for only part of the whole, just as it does within human resource management.

In short, industrial-organizational psychology occupies a substantial area within both human resource management and organizational science. It brings important theoretical approaches and research contributions to

both. Above all else, it is a component of psychology; that is its home discipline.

■ CAREERS IN INDUSTRIAL-ORGANIZATIONAL PSYCHOLOGY

Industrial-organizational psychology offers a wide range of career opportunities, in large part because the field represents the application of psychological science to organizational functioning wherever and however useful applications may emerge. In just five years the field experienced a growth rate of 24 percent, as compared with a growth rate of less than 15 percent for psychology as a whole (Howard, 1986). The Society for Industrial and Organizational Psychology has projected a series of books under the umbrella title of Frontiers of Industrial and Organizational Psychology. The first of these to appear was *Career Development in Organizations* (Hall, 1986). Clearly, career opportunities and career growth are important considerations within industrial-organizational psychology these days.

☐ Industrial-Organizational Psychology in the Context of Psychology

Compared to psychology as a whole, the industrial-organizational subfield is not very large, although it is growing. Roughly 5 percent of psychologists in the United States identify industrial-organizational as their major field. This percentage is exceeded by clinical, counseling, educational, and school psychology. The major employment settings for industrial-organizational psychologists are universities, consulting firms, business organizations, and government. Among psychologists involved in research activities, industrial-organizational psychologists represent 7 percent; thus there is a disproportionately high involvement in research, with a lesser involvement in education and health services (Stapp, Tucker, & Vanden Bos, 1985). This reflects the major orientation of industrial-organizational psychology toward personnel research.

☐ Primary Employment Settings

This chapter began with a listing of six employment advertisements. Two were for university faculty positions—one at Ohio State University and the other at Illinois Institute of Technology. Two more positions were with corporations—Mervyn's and BellSouth. The other two positions were with Development Dimensions and Personnel Designs, both major psychological consulting firms. As indicated in Exhibit 1-5, the distribution of these advertisements closely parallels actual employment figures for industrial and organizational psychologists (Howard, 1990).

Colleges and Universities. As in other faculty positions, people involved in industrial-organizational psychology pursue some mix of teaching, research, and service (committee

EXHIBIT 1-5   Where Are Industrial-Organizational Psychologists Working?

Employment Setting	Percent
Colleges and universities	36
Consulting	28
Business firms	24
Government	7
Health services	5

SOURCE: Ann Howard (1986). Characteristics of society members. *The Industrial-Organizational Psychologist,* *23*(3), 46.

work, administration, giving speeches, etc.). In major universities the emphasis is more likely to be on research that can be published, with teaching and service taking secondary roles. In other institutions teaching is more time-consuming and receives greater emphasis. Faculty positions in organizational behavior or human resource management within psychology departments and business schools differ in that one is surrounded by different disciplines—psychologists in the one instance, and economists and other business specialties in the other. Yet beyond that there are few major differences; the emphasis on publication and research is characteristic in both settings (Thayer, 1984).

Consulting. Many industrial-organizational psychologists on university faculties do consulting, but we are concerned here with full-time consultants—as solo private practitioners, in psychological consulting firms, as members of firms that offer a broader spectrum of services such as human resource management as a whole, or within general management consulting firms such as McKinsey and Company or Booz, Allen, Hamilton. Whatever the setting, consultants may specialize quite narrowly, by offering a certain type of management development program or utilizing certain approaches to assessing candidates for employment and promotion, or they may range over the whole gamut of industrial-organizational psychology's techniques and skills. Management Decision Systems, for example, has ten internal people and twelve to fifteen associates who are primarily university professors; it operates across the spectrum in the human resources area. Included are selection and assessment work, survey work, the design of training programs, some executive resources work, and so forth.

Most consulting is very much a feast-or-famine matter, in part because clients are willing to pay for it when business is up and less willing when business is down. In any event, success requires giving clients what they want so that they will come back for more, and doing a certain amount of marketing of one's services. Given that, the future in psychological consulting appears to be bright. As the head of Management Decision Systems puts it:

> I think the future is very positive in consulting for those people who take a client orientation and use practical problem solving in their approach to what they do. I think there is going to be more dependence on consultants in organizations as the whole area of human resources gets more complex. I think we are going to see more legislation in areas where consultants will be called on to make a contribution (Hinrichs, 1984, p. 23).

Industry. Box 1-1 describes the AT&T approach to utilizing industrial-organizational psychologists that emerged after divestiture. The function clearly was downsized, but it remained large compared to most firms. In many companies a single psychologist would be involved in all of the activites noted. Thus, the description taken as a whole provides a good overview of what psychologists do in industry. Note that there is a heavy emphasis on aspects of selection, placement, and promotion; this is quite typical. Note also that all

the psychologists mentioned have doctoral degrees; this too is typical.

Another point about working in industry is that if a psychologist wants to move up, he or she will rapidly hit a point where the work is no longer primarily psychological in nature (Howard, 1984). The higher-level positions are in human resource management generally, not in industrial-organizational psychology itself. At AT&T during the time covered by Box 1-1, the senior vice president for personnel was a psychologist. Psychology is a good career starting point in many firms. But moving upward means moving away from professional activities per se and into a more managerially oriented type of work. Success in this work requires a strong desire to manage (Miner, 1976).

□ Licensing and Certification Issues

The practice of professional psychology in any area has been increasingly circumscribed and defined as state after state has passed laws related to practice. These laws may restrict the use of certain techniques and procedures, as in the case of licensing, or they may restrict the use of the title *psychologist*, as in the case of certification. The primary impetus for the laws came from clinical psychology and related to the provision of health-care services to the public. Industrial-organizational psychological practice became regulated as part of the overall movement within psychology to seek legislative definition.

At the present time industrial-organizational psychology is covered under most state laws, but not all. Some states exempt practice in business organizations, in addition to the usual exemptions for academics and government employees. There is considerable variation from state to state, and in fact the Society for Industrial and Organizational Psychology has argued frequently for a total exclusion of the field from state legislation (Howard & Lowman, 1982, 1985). It seems

BOX 1-1 I/O PSYCHOLOGY IN PRACTICE

Industrial-Organizational Psychology at AT&T after Divestiture

As the Bell System was dismantled by the courts and the old operating companies went their separate ways, major changes in the utilization of industrial-organizational psychologists occurred. In 1981 some thirty psychologists could be identified at AT&T. By 1984 this number was down to seventeen. These psychologists within the AT&T corporate headquarters worked within a number of groups and carried out a variety of functions:

Human resource studies. This group was under the stewardship of Ann Howard (Ph.D., University of Maryland). It conducted longitudinal research for many years which led to the use of the assessment center, improved selection standards, and management development programs.

Management staffing, development, and education. Directed by Richard Campbell (Ph.D., Ohio State University), a major goal of this group was to guide the corporation in identifying and developing high-potential managers. The group had a heavy policy and program implementation role with a strong research and development effort behind it. The R&D function was managed by Joel Moses (Ph.D., Baylor University).

Management employment. Psychologists in this unit devoted their energies to the development and validation of entry-level selection procedures for a variety of jobs in the AT&T entities, including general management, sales and marketing positions, and some technical specialties.

Employment policies and systems. This group, managed by Mary Tenopyr (Ph.D., University of Southern California), provided research, development, and administrative support for valid, legally defensible selection procedures for nonmanagement, and selected management, jobs.

Work relationships. Tapas Sen (Ph.D., Johns Hopkins University) was manager of this quality-of-work-life (QWL) group. They conducted attitude surveys in all the AT&T entities and assisted in the development of entity-specific survey instruments. They analyzed trends in employment attitudes and values, provided expertise and leadership in the area of union–management cooperation, and integrated survey findings and QWL experiences to enhance the satisfaction and effectiveness of employees at all levels.

Employment administration. Psychologists in this unit had the mission of developing uniform employment policies and consolidating employment resources across the AT&T entities for management and nonmanagement employees.

The senior vice president for personnel at AT&T was a psychologist—H. Weston Clarke (Ph.D., Ohio State University).

SOURCE: Joel Moses (1981). I/O psychologists at AT&T. *The Industrial-Organizational Psychologist, 18*(3), 46–47. Manuel London (1984). Whither goest the AT&T psychologists? *The Industrial-Organizational Psychologist, 21*(2), 39–43.

---

that legal coverage should be most appropriate for those engaged in consulting who provide services to the general public. A particularly strong case for legislation can be made with regard to the practice of industrial clinical psychology. Activities such as individual assessment and counseling, interpretation of individual test scores, and training which borders on group psychotherapy most closely approximate the health-care services that were the reason psychology became involved in seeking legislation initially.

Actually, fewer than 50 percent of all industrial-organizational psychologists are licensed or certified at the present time, and a disproportionate number of these individuals are engaged in the practice of industrial clinical psychology.

■ THEORY AND RESEARCH

Industrial-organizational psychology is both a science and a practice. We have considered the practice, which often involves applied research, at some length. Now we turn to the scientific aspects of the field, and to a more explicit statement of how theory and research relate to it.

□ Theory

A **theory** is a generalization that specifies relationships between factors; it is an attempt to make sense out of empirical observations that do not contain any inherent and obvious logic. A sound scientific theory should be as simple as possible, logically consistent within itself and with other known facts, and constructed so that it is clear exactly what must be done to confirm or disprove it. In addition, it should:

Aid understanding and prediction, thus enabling practitioners more easily to anticipate and influence events.

Specify the boundaries within which the theory applies.

Direct research efforts toward socially important matters and relationships that are significant for society.

Provide a degree of value beyond that of the specific research used to test it. Thus, if a limited number of **hypotheses** (tentative propositions advanced to explain something that is not understood) derived from a theory are confirmed by research, a much larger body of

knowledge should become available for purposes of understanding, predicting, and influencing events.

Most theories in industrial-organizational psychology are stated verbally, although a few are set forth in mathematical terms as well. At present these theories are most likely to operate within rather narrow boundaries. Each applies only in a limited set of situations, in contrast to the grand theories of the past, which often tried to encompass too much and ended by in fact accomplishing very little.

Box 1-2 describes an analysis made of theories generally in organizational science. It appears that the psychological theories have fared very well at the hands of research, both in terms of their validity or correctness and their contributions to practice. Many of these theories are treated in depth in the following chapters.

□ Research

Some research in industrial-organizational psychology is conducted to test the truth of hypotheses derived from theories. On occasion such theory testing involves comparing alternative hypotheses to see which one offers a more precise explanation of observed phenomena (Dansereau, Alutto, & Yammarino, 1984). Other research has little if any relation to theory, but rather is conducted to evaluate existing or proposed practices. This latter type of research, which confirms whether or not a given practice accomplishes its intended purpose, supplies useful information but does not provide the broad understanding that theory testing does. An example of practice-related rather than theory-related research is described in Box 1-3, which deals with psychological evaluation at McKinsey and Company. Because of certain unique aspects of this particular firm, psychological evaluations did not work well there. More encouraging results have been obtained in other settings.

Research methodology is a complex field, the study of which requires considerable mathematical knowledge. Over the years a number of research methods have been developed, all of which are aimed at ensuring that valid conclusions can be drawn—that measures are precise, the number of people studied adequate, alternative interpretations of the findings ruled out, and the like. Several years ago the Society for Industrial and Organizational Psychology commissioned the writing of a multivolume series on innovations in methodology for studying organizations. These books, with titles such as *Making It Happen: Designing Research with Implementation in Mind* (Hakel, Sorcher, Beer, & Moses, 1982) and *What to Study: Generating and Developing Research Questions* (Campbell, Daft, & Hulin, 1982), represent a useful source of information on research approaches in the field. In this book research issues are discussed at many points in connection with the presentation of actual studies and as appropriate to specific subject matters. A statistical appendix describes the various statistical procedures and techniques often used. Because both the science and the practice of industrial-organizational psychology are closely tied to research, the field has a special concern with matters of research design, measurement, and statistical analysis of data.

Although much research in industrial-organizational psychology is conducted out in the field with the people actually working at the job which is under study, there is a sizable body of **laboratory research** as well. This latter is conducted in a more isolated setting which simulates the phenomenon under study and simplifies it as well. Often the subjects are college students who have not met previously, the time span of study is short, and the task is lacking in complexity. The goal is to eliminate confounding factors so that it is relatively easy to determine what is causing what. Box 1-4 provides an example of this type of research. The study was carried out in the Department of Management at the University of Tennessee.

Comparisons of research results obtained in field settings and in the laboratory indicate that in many areas of study the findings are virtually identical (Locke, 1986). This is true in areas such as job satisfaction and performance appraisal, for instance, and in aspects of motivation such as setting performance goals. Yet there are areas where different results have been obtained as well, presumably because field settings naturally contain certain aspects that have not been incorporated in the laboratory research.

☐ Scientific Values

A major strength of industrial-organizational psychology has been its capacity to incorporate social science research into the functioning of ongoing organizations, especially in the business sector. No other social science discipline has done this as well. Yet on occasion the values of science do come into conflict with the action and efficiency orientations that characterize many managers. This is clearly demonstrated in Box 1-5.

A major difficulty is that scientists are taught to be cautious and skeptical. They remain neutral until a convincing body of evidence is developed to support a theory; this is the essence of scientific objectivity. Accordingly, because decisions are based on controlled research and substantiated theory, not on hunch and bias, "I don't know" is not only an acceptable answer to a question, but often a highly valued one. By admitting that adequate knowledge to make a decision is lacking, scientists leave the matter open to further research. From the scientist's viewpoint, the greatest error is the one that occurs when inadequate or insufficient information is interpreted in such a way that an unsolved problem is considered

BOX 1-2   RESEARCH IN I/O PSYCHOLOGY

How Industrial-Organizational Psychology's Theories Have Fared

An idea of how well theories based in industrial-organizational psychology are doing, relative to theories in organizational science as a whole, may be obtained from an analysis of thirty-two major theories dealing with aspects of organizational functioning. This analysis categorized the theories, eighteen of which were developed by psychologists, in terms of their estimated scientific validity and their estimated usefulness in application.

Estimated **scientific validity** was a rating made by the author to indicate whether good theory, and thus improved understanding and prediction regarding organizations, had been obtained. The key to this rating was the extent to which research tests had been carried out and had supported the theory. A high rating was given if substantial segments of the theory had been supported by subsequent research. A mixed rating was given if the research evidence was conflicting. A low rating was given if the research evidence was primarily nonsupportive, or if the theory had not generated the necessary research in spite of the elapse of sufficient time to permit studies to be conducted. In cases of the latter type, highly abstract or imprecise definitions often made appropriate testing difficult if not impossible.

The estimated **usefulness in application** rating also made by the author dealt with the extent to which the theory had contributed applications that could be put to use in practice to achieve stated goals. The key here was not how much use had been made of these applications in prac-

tice, but whether the applications had been subjected to research evaluation and shown to work to produce their intended objectives. A high rating was given if an application has been generated and shown to produce the intended result. A questionable rating was given if there was some doubt regarding either the real usefulness of any application or the extent to which it had in fact derived from the underlying theory. A low rating was given when the theory clearly had not contributed to practice in any meaningful way, either because applications were not generated or because those that were generated had proved essentially useless.

From the above matrix it can be seen that psychological theories have fared very well on both dimensions. The seven theories with high usefulness in application were all developed by psychologists, and nine of the eleven theories with high scientific validity had similar origins. The four high–high theories in the upper right corner are all psychological theories of motivation. Only one of the five low–low theories in the lower left corner comes form psychology.

SOURCE: John B. Miner (1984). The validity and usefulness of theories in an emerging organizational science. *Academy of Management Review, 9,* 297–302. John B. Miner (1984). The unpaved road over the mountains: From theory to applications. *The Industrial-Organizational Psychologist, 21*(2), 9–20. See also John B. Miner (1990). The role of values in defining the "goodness" of theories in organizational science. *Organization Studies, 11,* 161–178.

solved. Errors of this kind block scientific progress.

Managers, however, are constantly faced with the need to make decisions on the basis of insufficient information. Often the cost of obtaining more information is considered excessive, so managers must accumulate as much data as they can in the time available

and then plunge ahead. Such decisions can be very risky, but if time or the budget does not allow judgment to be deferred, managers must simply do the best they can with whatever information is on hand.

These differences in decision-making modes can result in considerable misunderstanding and hinder the application of theory

A Usefulness-Validity Matrix in Terms of Primary Disciplinary Origin of the Author and Subject Matter of the Theory for Thirty-Two Major Theories Dealing with Organizations

	Scientific Validity		
	Low	**Mixed**	**High**
Usefulness in Application — High	1 psychology theory in the field of organization development	2 psychology theories: 1 in motivation and 1 in organization development	4 psychology theories, all in motivation
Usefulness in Application — Questionable	2 psychology theories: 1 in motivation and 1 in leadership; 1 organizational behavior theory in organization developement; 1 social sciences theory in organization development; 1 engineering theory in structuring	1 psychology theory in leadership; 1 organizational behavior theory in organization development; 1 history theory in structuring; 1 economics theory in leadership	2 psychology theories: 1 in motivation and 1 in leadership; 1 law theory in structuring
Usefulness in Application — Low	1 psychology theory in motivation; 3 sociology theories: 2 in structuring and 1 in organization development; 1 industrial relations theory in leadership	2 psychology theories in organization development; 1 organizational behavior theory in leadership; 1 sociology theory in structuring	3 psychology theories: 1 each in motivation, leadership and organization development; 1 political science theory in structuring

and research. Experienced industrial-organizational psychologists, however, seem to be able to deal with these problems without compromising their scientific values. Unfortunately, it does not appear easy to teach these skills in avoiding value clashes. It seems that most psychologists must learn the way on their own.

■ BRIEF HISTORY OF INDUSTRIAL-ORGANIZATIONAL PSYCHOLOGY

Industrial-organizational psychology is not very old—certainly less than 100 years—and one might be tempted to dismiss its history as being too short to deserve attention. In

BOX 1-3   RESEARCH IN I/O PSYCHOLOGY

Did Psychological Evaluations at McKinsey and Company Result in the Hiring of Better Consultants?

For a number of years, McKinsey and Company, a large international consulting firm, had been using outside psychological consulting organizations to evaluate candidates for its beginning consulting positions. Each candidate went to a psychologist's office to be tested and interviewed. McKinsey subsequently received a written report describing the candidate's test results and making a hiring recommendation on a scale ranging from "a clearly outstanding candidate" to "definitely not recommended." Each of these evaluations cost several hundred dollars, and the influx of new employees was such that the firm was spending well over $100,000 a year on them.

A question arose as to whether the evaluations were worth their cost. Did the firm get better consultants if it followed the psychologists' recommendations? It was possible to check this hypothesis, because some people who were not recommended were subsequently hired on the basis of other considerations, and because the psychologists' reports were kept on file. The psychologists' recommendations at the time of hiring were compared with various measures of how well the consultants had actually performed on the job. Performance ratings, salary increases, promotions, and length of employment were all used as measures of success. Five different studies were carried out in separate offices of the firm.

The results of the research were clear-cut: No matter which measure of success was applied or which group of consultants was studied, there was not a single study in which the consultants whom the psychologists had recommended for hiring were found to be more successful on the job than those who had been hired despite an unfavorable rating. This was an unexpected finding, and it took a while for the management of the firm to act on it. However, McKinsey ultimately discontinued the use of psychological evaluations, at considerable saving and with no loss in the overall efficiency of its consultants. For this particular firm, psychological evaluations of potential employees were not useful—a fact that was brought to light as a result of research.

SOURCE: Based on John B. Miner (1970). Psychological evaluations as predictors of consulting success. *Personnel Psychology, 23,* 383–405.

---

fact, industrial-organizational psychology has tended to ignore its history and the historical context in which it developed, sometimes to its detriment (Nord, 1982). Yet the present often takes on new meaning when viewed in relation to the past.

☐ Beginnings

The origins of industrial psychology have been a matter for some debate; it is not possible to attribute the field's creation to a single individual (Stagner, 1982). The following quotation illustrates the point:

An examination of the origins of industrial and organizational psychology reveals two names, Walter Dill Scott and Hugo Münsterberg, that stand out as the most frequently mentioned and widely acknowledged candidates for having "fathered" this field. Rather than engaging in an interesting but irrelevant discussion as to which of the two deserves the honor, it should be sufficient to recognize the prominant role each of them played. . . . If one had to pick a date to mark the founding of I/O psychology, a good choice would be December 20, 1901. On that date, Scott, a psychology professor at Northwestern University, addressed a group of advertising professionals and outlined the potential

BOX 1-4   RESEARCH IN I/O PSYCHOLOGY

An Example of Laboratory Research—Studying Performance Appraisal with College Students at the University of Tennessee

One of the more consistent findings from research carried out within organizations is that when employees rate their own performance, the results are not the same as when they are rated by their supervisors. One hypothesis regarding this result is that while supervisors have a wealth of information regarding the performance of all those who report to them, their subordinates must rate their own performance in a vacuum, with little or no comparative performance information available to them. Since the superior and self ratings are carried out in different information contexts, it is not surprising that they exhibit very little relation to one another.

To test this hypothesis, undergraduate students who reported to a large behavioral laboratory were given the task of proofreading typewritten material containing numerous errors for thirty minutes. Certain students were chosen randomly to serve as supervisors. These "supervisors" reviewed the work of a group of other students and rated their performance. Half of the students who were doing the proofreading merely rated their own performance afterward, without knowledge of how others had done. The other half were given eight minutes to look over and review the work of four other proofreaders before making their self-ratings.

As in the field setting, there was little or no relationship between the two types of ratings when the proofreaders had no knowledge of how others were doing. But when the proofreaders had the comparative performance information, the results changed; now the ratings of their supervisors were much more closely aligned with their own. The relationships were still not terribly high, but they were well above those found when comparative performance information was denied. Thus the hypothesis was supported.

SOURCE: Jiing-Lih Farh & Gregory H. Dobbins (1989). Effects of comparative performance information on the accuracy of self-ratings and the agreement between self- and supervisor ratings. *Journal of Applied Psychology, 74,* 606–610.

---

contributions of psychology to the field of advertising. Over the next several years, Scott published several articles and books that elaborated a psychological theory of advertising and provided guidelines for its application. . . . He later expanded the domain of his interests to include a wider range of business concerns. . . . Scott's writings on advertising influenced the work of the other "founding father" of industrial psychology, Hugo Münsterberg. After emigrating to the United States from Germany in 1892, Münsterberg directed the psychological laboratory at Harvard and began to explore seriously the application of psychological principles to practical problems (Mankin, Ames, & Grodsky, 1980, p. 1).

Although Scott's publications in the area of advertising preceded Münsterberg's works, the latter focused more centrally on what have become major concerns of industrial-organizational psychology. Münsterberg (1913) developed an extremely active interest in seeking out ways in which psychology could be applied to business and industry, and he wrote extensively expounding his views. He was also able to put a number of his ideas to good use within several firms in the Boston area. His most famous study involved the development of a selection test for operators of electric streetcars. Münsterberg placed a strong emphasis on empirical

BOX 1-5   I/O PSYCHOLOGY IN PRACTICE

How Researchers' and Managers' Values Can Clash

A young psychologist received the following memo from the chief executive of a company when he began working with the company as a consultant. It came as a sharp contrast to the strong research values the young man had been taught during his professional training.

> Since I will not be here when you start your consulting program, I am passing along some thoughts for your consideration as you start the work. Then I'll look forward to discussing these and other points when I get back.
>
> We are delighted that you are going to be with us and are looking forward to getting some real benefits from your assistance; and that is the main purpose of these comments. These suggestions are designed to help get us full value for what I feel is a very handsome compensation.
>
> 1. I hope that your objective will be productivity for us rather than gathering research material for yourself. Naturally we would hope that you would get some benefit from the work that might be useful in your teaching and writing, but we hope that this will be clearly a by-product.
>
> 2. This approach leads directly to emphasizing that we hope you will be doing consulting rather than research. In other words, we hope that you will take a decision-making approach rather than a research approach. I am led to offer this suggestion by the proposal that you made which contained the fifty paired individuals. That was a research approach and, in my opinion, unnecessarily extensive. I know that you have agreed to cut it down in scope and time, but believe it should be reduced even further.
>
> In fact, if you will take a decision-making approach rather than a research approach, you will be able to get that first project done in a couple of months and come up with thoroughly reliable results for our purposes. In fact, we would expect to have a large element of your own judgment and we do not expect—nor do we want to pay for—research results to support your judgment.
>
> 3. Therefore, I believe we should get agreement with you as to the differences between the decision-making approach and the research approach. I suggest that you discuss these differences in approach with some of the other managers, as I am sure it will be helpful throughout your work. In view of the use that we plan to make of your findings and recommendations, we are quite confident that the decision-making approach is all that the situation calls for.
>
> 4. We hope that you will do all of your work for us on an action-oriented basis, i.e., that you come up with recommendations on things that we should do, stop doing, or change. The decision-making approach is geared to action.
>
> I look forward to getting together with you as soon as I can after my return. By that time you will be well into the work and we will have a better basis for discussion.

Ultimately the young psychologist to whom the memo was addressed was fired. The problems created by conflicting values proved too great.

---

analysis and statistical validation, an emphasis that remains evident in industrial-organizational psychology today.

A third individual who has on occasion been considered a "father" of industrial psychology is James McKeen Cattell. Cattell, like Münsterberg, was initially trained in Germany. By 1890 he had coined the term "men-tal test" and assumed the chair of the psychology department at Columbia University. During his years at Columbia he actively encouraged research and interest in the applications of psychology to practical problems. In his later years he founded the Psychological Corporation, a consulting firm providing psychological services to industry and a major publisher of psychological tests.

World War I

Many of the most historically significant contributions of industrial psychology came during World War I. The U.S. Army was faced with the problem of deciding what to do with the millions of men being drafted into service. Which ones should go to Officer Candidate School, and which ones should get technical training? A special committee of psychologists constructed a short intelligence test known as the Army Alpha. Based on an experimental instrument being developed by Arthur Otis, a Cleveland psychologist, the Alpha was the first group intelligence test and a milestone in the methodology of psychological test construction.

During the course of administering the Army Alpha, it became apparent that a surprisingly large number of recruits were scoring at the zero point or very close to it. Investigation revealed that many of these individuals were illiterate and that Army Alpha presumed a certain amount of literacy. This led to the construction of a second test, Army Beta, designed specifically to provide information regarding the intelligence of those who were not able to read and write well enough to complete Army Alpha. The new instrument proved invaluable as an aid in the placement of less well-educated recruits. It subsequently found wide usage in the postwar years in the testing of immigrants who came to the United States with little knowledge of the English language.

The Interval between the Wars

As a result of steadily increasing growth prior to World War I, the success of the Army human resource program, and the general business boom, industrial psychology grew rapidly during the 1920s. Many companies added human resource departments for the first time, and a number of colleges and universities began to offer training in the area. Psychological consulting firms began to appear, one of the first being the Scott Company, which was formed by a group of people who had worked on the Army Alpha and Beta during the war years.

Toward the end of the 1920s, a series of experiments began at the Hawthorne plant of the Western Electric Company, near Chicago, that was to extend over several years and to have a substantial impact. Briefly, these experiments, which have been described and discussed at length in other publications (Roethlisberger & Dickson, 1939; Cass & Zimmer, 1975) were initiated in order to study the effects of physical factors such as lighting and ventilation on worker productivity. As time went on, however, it began to seem increasingly likely that productivity was affected primarily by the emotional states of the employees; by their relationships with other people, particularly those with whom they worked; and by the amount and kind of attention they received from superiors.

These conclusions came to fuel what has since been called the **human relations** movement in American industry, which served both to promulgate humanist values and to initiate the field now called *organizational behavior*. It is important to recognize, however, that none of those involved in the Hawthorne research were psychologists by training. Where these studies have influenced industrial-organizational psychology, it has been primarily via the organizational science route, although aspects of human resource management have been involved as well.

These studies, which extended over a number of years, had a major impact in developing a primarily work group-based and ultimately organizational approach to psychological analysis. More recently the studies have been brought into serious question, but not before exerting a substantial effect on organizational science as a whole (Franke & Kaul, 1978).

☐ World War II

As in World War I, psychologists during World War II were called upon to help solve the problems of the Armed Forces in the placement of the vast numbers of draftees and volunteers; the task had become much more complex because of the tremendous increase in the number of technical specialties. The result was a great variety of psychological tests developed to aid in the process of allocating individuals to training programs and to specific duty assignments; many of these tests were later adapted for industry use. Military researchers also did considerable work in the applied science of learning and in human engineering as they sought better ways of designing military equipment and more effective ways of teaching people how to use it. Many of the techniques introduced by the Armed Services subsequently found their way into the business world and had a profound influence on industrial training and management development.

To meet the need for effective utilization of personnel in the United States, the War Manpower Commission was established to find ways of locating, training, and assigning people with appropriate skills not only for the military, but also for civilian government agencies, business, and agriculture. A major problem was how to train the large numbers of individuals who flocked into the defense plants, many of them women and older people with no factory experience, so that they would become satisfactory workers within a relatively short period of time. The problem was complicated by the fact that there was a shortage of experienced instructors to provide training. The solution was the development of a program of **job instruction training (JIT)** sessions, conducted by the War Manpower Commission's Training within Industry Division, which were highly successful in training inexperienced trainers. The JIT guidelines, using some of the same principles of applied learning theory as were used by the military psychologists, were developed in considerable detail and became the basis of many industrial on-the-job training programs that are still in use.

The overall impact of World War II was that the scope of activities handled by psychologists increased substantially. Yet these activities were primarily those of human resource or industrial psychology, as they concentrated heavily in areas such as selection, placement, and training.

☐ The Recent Past

Since World War II, much of what has happened to industrial-organizational psychology has been determined by changes that affected the personnel and human resource field first. These include, in historical order, changes in labor legislation, the passage of civil rights laws, and the downsizing of many corporations as a consequence of increased international competition.

But there has been another, stabilizing process—the increasing development of research and research findings within both the industrial and the organizational components of the field. This research has followed the multiple branchings of human resource management, and of organizational science as well. There are increasingly new knowledges to be conveyed and new skills to be practiced. This is the real strength of the industrial-organizational psychology field—its commitment to research, and its capacity to stabilize itself over many changing conditions on a foundation of newly generated, research-based contributions.

Interpreting what the recent past means for the future involves so many uncertainties that it is unlikely to be fruitful. Yet one thing is certain. Industrial psychology started out as the application of psychological theories and applications to the problems of business and industry. It still does this to some degree. But what is really significant is that it has bridged the gap so that it now has begun to create its own theories and applications. In many instances it no longer needs to delve back into experimental and social psychology to achieve understanding. It has the needed theories at its own fingertips. This is a tremendous advance, earned at the expense of the substantial commitment to research that characterizes the field. It bodes well for the future.

■ ORGANIZATION OF THE BOOK

Until now the discussion has followed the industrial→organizational progression that characterizes the development of the field, the titles it utilizes (I, then O), and the weighting of practice. However, for purposes of presenting the knowledge of the field, this is not, at this time, the most useful approach. In science, research and ultimately much practice follow theory. Organizational psychology is the major source of theory within industrial-organizational psychology. Throughout much of its history, industrial (personnel) psychology developed practically devoid of theory, focusing rather on specific practical problems. Now, increasingly, the theories and concepts of organizational psychology are able to provide explanations and new approaches to industrial psychology. There is still much of industrial psychology that is entirely empirical and uninfluenced by the theories of organizational psychology, but the balance is shifting. That shift now appears to have attained sufficient proportions to justify an organizational→industrial progression.

After the introduction set fort in this single chapter of Part One, we turn in Part Two to the major concerns of organizational psychology. The discussion begins in Chapter 2 with cognitive factors—learning, intelligence, and individual decision making. This is a central area of psychology as a whole at the present time, and it is equally important for organizational psychology. Chapters 3 and 4 then deal with motivation and the methods of influencing it, including job redesign and rewards. In Chapter 5 we consider work attitudes, including job satisfaction, commitment, values, and ethics. The final chapter dealing with aspects of the individual is Chapter 6, which focuses on personality and emotions.

As the discussion moves on to the group level, we turn to group processes and techniques in Chapter 7 and to group decision making in Chapter 8. There are times when group approaches to decision making are more appropriate, and other times when the individual decision-making approaches considered in Chapter 2 are to be preferred. Leadership of a group is covered in two chapters—9 and 10—the first of which takes up the earlier theories of leadership style while the latter concentrates on theories at the cutting edge of leadership. Chapter 11 winds up the presentation of organizational psychology with a treatment of organization development and quality of work life.

In Part Three, Chapter 12 sets the stage for the discussion of industrial psychology by taking up the constraints that set limits on what may be done in dealing with human resources; special attention is given to legal factors and individual differences. Chapter 13 covers the scope and methods of job analysis. Practically everything that is done in industrial psychology relates back in one way or another to job analysis. In Chapter 14 and 15 the approaches used to evaluate the performances of managers and employees are considered; in industrial psychology this is often referred to as *criterion development*.

The next three chapters focus on the selection and placement of individuals—the input process. The logic of selection processes, including the research designs used, is set forth in Chapter 16. Employment interviews and similar techniques such as application blanks and references are considered in Chapter 17. Psychological testing is the subject of Chapter 18. Chapter 19 deals with training and development, including the widely emphasized topic of career development. Safety psychology and the performance control processes of industrial clinical psychology are treated in Chapter 20. The text ends with the Statistical Appendix.

KEY TERMS

Industrial-organizational psychology
Human resource management
Organizational science
Organizational behavior
Theory
Hypotheses

Scientific validity
Usefulness in application
Laboratory research
Human relations
Job instruction training (JIT)

SUMMARY

Industrial-organizational psychology is concerned with the application of psychological science to the problems of human organizations, and in particular to the utilization of human resources within these organizations. In this connection it is closely tied to *human resource management* on the one hand and to the *organizational behavior* component of *organizational science* on the other.

Careers in the field are concentrated almost equally in the academic world, where they are split between psychology departments and business schools, corporate human resource management, particularly in personnel research, and consulting of one kind or another. Only about 5 percent of all psychologists view the industrial-organizational component as their major field.

Industrial-organizational psychology is both science and practice, and *theory* and research play an important role in both. Within organizational science, organizational psychology has been a leader in generating theories that possess both *scientific validity* and *usefulness in application*. Within human resource management, industrial psychology has been a primary source of important research findings. Yet clashes can occur between the values of science and the exigencies of managerial realities. Industrial-organizational psychology has been extraordinarily successful among the social sciences in creating a research niche for itself within ongoing organizations. However, the divergent values involved do on occasion create frictions; they offer a major challenge to practice in the field.

The history of industrial-organizational psychology emphasized human resource applications in the early years, with Münsterberg and Cattell being the major contributors. Scott's initial contributions were in advertising and sales psychology, and only later included personnel components. Both World War I and World War II fostered major developments in personnel applications, while the intervening years saw the unfolding of the Hawthorne studies, which had such an impact on organizational psychology via the *human relations* movement. Psychology as a whole, human resource management, and organizational science continue to exert a major influence on the field. Yet what is most encouraging in the recent past is the tendency within industrial-organizational psychology to generate home-grown theories to deal with the organizational realities it faces. These theories and the research they generate represent the real future of industrial-organizational psychology.

QUESTIONS

1. What has been the role of the Hawthorne studies in the development of industrial-organizational psychology?

2. Where do industrial-organizational psychologists work, and in what proportions?

3. Who are the claimants to the position of father of industrial-organizational psychology, and what is the nature of their claims?

4. What are the various activities that are part of human resource management, and which of these contain substantial involvement on the part of industrial-organizational psychology?

5. How do the values of science come into conflict with the values of corporate management?

6. What is the status of industrial-organizational psychology with reference to licensing and certification by the states?

7. Why did World Wars I and II emerge as major influences in the development of industrial-organizational psychology? What contributions were made during these periods?

8. How does the micro–macro distinction in organizational science relate to industrial-organizational psychology?

9. Why is research particularly important to the practice of industrial-organizational psychology, and what roles does it play in the field?

10. How have the theories of industrial-organizational psychology fared at the hands of research testing their validity and usefulness? What types of theories have fared best?

CASE PROBLEM

DAVID D. ROBINSON, PH.D.
Industrial-Organizational Psychology Consultant

While completing his Ph.D. dissertation at Ohio State University, David Robinson took a part-time job with Ernst & Whinney, the national accounting firm. As one of its numerous services, this firm provided psychological consulting expertise to its clients. Subsequently David was offered a permanent position with the firm and moved to the Boise, Idaho, office. After three years there he was asked to move to the firm's Los Angeles office. Instead he decided to establish his own office as an independent psychological consultant and stay in Boise.

As his consulting practice developed, David took on a considerable variety of assignments:

1. *Job analysis.* This work often has been preliminary to other activities such as defining newly created positions, helping partners resolve role

conflicts, selecting personnel, training, compensation, and performance evaluation.

2. *Personnel selection.* This work involves development of criteria and the conduct of validation studies, as well as choosing the selection instruments to be used. It has on occasion required the development of assessment centers.

3. *Training program design.* This work focuses primarily on setting up training programs consistent with job requirements and existing training needs. It also involves evaluating the effects of training.

4. *Compensation system design.* This work is concerned with developing wage and salary programs. The method used is one that was developed within industrial-organizational psychology—the Position Analysis Questionnaire (McCormick, Jeanneret, & Mecham, 1972).

5. *Job performance evaluation systems.* This work has varied considerably in the extent of demand. It is currently on the upswing as a result of greater emphasis on deregulation and organizational downsizing.

6. *Expert witness work.* This work, for lawyers and their clients, ranges from testimony on the fairness of lineup procedures to the effects of alcohol on behavior, the reliability of eye-witness testimony to civil rights cases, the fairness of testing procedures, and such matters as the safety of various products and the employability of accident victims.

Over the years David has develop some firm opinions as to the pitfalls inherent in the kind of work he does. He has this to say:

An independent consultant must recognize the boundaries of his or her own expertise and arrange for the services of other professionals in bookkeeping, accounting, budgeting, tax, marketing, and advertising to name some of the most critical areas of business activity. . . . Perhaps the biggest pitfall is the idea that a small consultant can do much more than make a comfortable living from billing professional services on a time basis. Most beginners overestimate the number of billable (and collectable) hours available per year, and underestimate the hourly rate they should charge for their services. In a mature practice, no more than 1000 hours per year is typically billable. The other 1000 or so hours in a normal year are taken up with office administration, business development, continuing education, professional affairs, nonbillable correspondence and other writing, and a host of other time-consuming activities including vacation and sick leave. Consulting tends to be feast or famine. An independent consultant can make a good living and have an interesting career, but few of us become wealthy. . . . If I had a chance to do it all over again, I might look for a little bigger market, some local I/O colleagues, and higher levels of client awareness that problems can be solved through applications of I/O psychology.

SOURCE: Adapted from David D. Robinson (1987). A consultant's view of being a consultant: The small established consulting firm. *The Industrial-Organizational Psychologist, 24*(4), 43–52.

Questions

1. Does the type of work described appear interesting to you? Why, and in what aspects?
2. What frustrations does David Robinson appear to have experienced in his career as an industrial-organizational psychologist?
3. If David were to add another industrial-organizational psychologist to his firm to supplement his own knowledge, skills, and capabilities, what kinds of capabilities should he look for in the new person? Assume that his objective is to extend the range of assignments that his firm might undertake.

PART TWO Organizational Psychology

2

Cognitive Processes

The following questionnaire gets at various types of cognitive ways of thinking. There are no "right" or "wrong" responses to any of these items.

Part I. Circle the response that comes closest to how you usually feel or act.

1. Are you more careful about:
   A. people's feelings
   B. their rights

2. Do you usually get on better with:
   A. imaginative people
   B. realistic people

3. Which of these two is the higher compliment:
   A. a person has real feeling
   B. a person is consistently reasonable

4. In doing something with many other people, does it appeal more to you:
   A. to do it in the accepted way
   B. to invent a way of your own

5. Do you get more annoyed at:
   A. fancy theories
   B. people who don't like theories

6. It is higher praise to call someone:
   A. a person of vision
   B. a person of common sense

7. Do you more often let:
   A. your heart rule your head
   B. your head rule your heart

8. Do you think it a worse fault:
   A. to show too much warmth
   B. to be unsympathetic

9. If you were a teacher, would you rather teach:
   A. courses involving theory
   B. fact courses

Part II. Which word in the following pair appeals to you more? Circle A or B.

10. A. compassion
    B. foresight

11. A. justice
    B. mercy

12. A. production
    B. design

13. A. gentle
    B. firm

14. A. uncritical
    B. critical

15. A. literal
    B. figurative

16. A. imaginative
    B. matter-of-fact

Scoring Key. This key is to be used to diagnose your responses to the questionnaire. Count one point for each response on the four scales at right. Then, total the number of points recorded in each column. Instructions for classifying your scores are indicated below.

Sensation	Intuition	Thinking	Feeling
2 B_____	2 A_____	1 B_____	1 A_____
4 A_____	4 B_____	3 B_____	3 A_____
5 A_____	5 B_____	7 B_____	7 A_____
6 B_____	6 A_____	8 A_____	8 B_____
9 B_____	9 A_____	10 B_____	10 A_____
12 A_____	12 B_____	11 A_____	11 B_____
15 A_____	15 B_____	13 B_____	13 A_____
16 B_____	16 A_____	14 B_____	14 A_____
Totals_____	_____	_____	_____

Classifying Total Scores

Write *intuitive* if your intuition score is equal to or greater than sensation score. Write *sensation* if sensation is greater than intuition.

Write *feeling* if feeling is greater than thinking.

Write *thinking* if thinking is greater than feeling.

When thinking equals feeling, you should write *feeling* if a male and *thinking* if a female.

_____

_____

_____

_____

The resulting classifications yield four cognitive styles. These are ways in which a person approaches decisions, and types of decision-making contexts he or she prefers. The four cognitive groupings are as follows:

Sensation/thinkers. People who establish effective rules and regulations; decisive and excellent at making decisions that involve facts and figures; practical and logical; like structured, goal-oriented systems.

Sensation/feelers. Pragmatists who can deal with concrete problems methodically; tend to focus on the immediate situation; concerned with facts of a personal, human sort; like structured, people-oriented systems.

Intuition/thinkers. Architects of progress and ideas; intellectually ingenious and creative, but not implementers; have an abstract, impersonal, long-range conceptual focus; like impersonal planning systems.

Intuition/feelers. Make decisions in terms of personal feelings of others; tend to be concerned with new ventures of a broadly humanistic type; like loose, decentralized systems.

SOURCE: John W. Slocum & Don Hellriegel (1983). A look at how managers' minds work. *Business Horizons,* 26(4), 58–68.

Cognitive processes, of which cognitive styles are one aspect, have assumed an important role in psychology. **Cognitive processes** involve organizing information in our minds to help accomplish some desired end. Included are learning, memory, concept formation, problem solving, intelligence, and the use of language (Wortman & Loftus, 1988). Several of these processes have received substantial attention within organizational psychology, and are the subject of this chapter. Cognitive processes are in turn but one of a number of aspects of the individual that can influence performance. The first five chapters of Part Two deal not only with cognitive processes, but with various types of motivation, emotions, work attitudes, values, and personality. These concepts frequently overlap, but all focus on the individual. Later chapters on organizational psychology consider groups in organizations, group decision making, leadership, and organization development.

The list of individual factors omits one kind of factor that also can influence performance: physical factors such as physique, stature, handicaps, illness, health, strength, and attractiveness. With only a few exceptions, industrial-organizational psychology has not dealt with these matters. Much more frequently these are the concerns of medicine, biological science, and the health sciences generally. Research on these topics falls outside the normal scope of industrial-organizational psychology. It is important to recognize, however, that an extended treatment of individual influences on performance would include such physical influences.

We start our treatment of organizational psychology with a consideration of three cognitive processes that are closely interrelated: learning, intelligence, and individual decision making; all have played an important role in the development of organizational psychology.

What people bring to a job in terms of knowledge and skills is a consequence of learning. As they develop on the job by acquiring new knowledge and skills relevant to their work, that too is a function of learning. The most common and widely accepted definition of **learning** is that it is "a relatively permanent change, resulting from practice or experience, in the capability for responding" (Salmoni, Schmidt, & Walter, 1984). This change need not contribute to improved performance, however. Learning can produce myths, fictions, folklore, and outright errors on the job. It all depends on what is learned, in relation to expectations for job behavior.

In addition to learning, this chapter is concerned with **intelligence.** Intelligence represents a capacity or readiness for learning—an ability to learn and reason (Miner, 1973, pp. 4–5). The two concepts—learning and intelligence—are closely intertwined. Some people pick things up easily; they are often described as intellectually "quick." These people are more intelligent. Others take much longer to absorb new things, so that learning becomes a long-drawn-out struggle; these individuals are intellectually "slow."

The third component of this chapter is **individual decision making.** As a person mulls over alternative routes that might be followed to meet an objective, there comes a point when the person actually chooses a course of action. That is decision making. The decision selected is the one viewed, at the time the decision is made, as most likely to result in attainment of the objective (Harrison, 1989). This process is influenced in part by the related knowledge and skill the person has accumulated—that is, by prior learning. Decision making is also influenced by the person's intelligence—how quickly a course of action can be developed and evaluated, how many alternatives can be held in mind at once, and the like. It is because of these close ties among learning, intelligence, and decision making that they are treated together in this chapter. Knowing about one helps in understanding the others; all are cognitive in nature.

■ LEARNING

Learning often becomes important for performance through some type of training process, whether formal or informal. This training may be acquired by individuals in education-al institutions or through job experience. It also may be provided by a current employer. Box 2-1 describes how this last type of training is used to foster the attainment of organizational goals at IBM.

Not all change in people is a result of learning; thus the concepts and theories related to learning have only a limited zone of application. Changes in personality, emotions, motivation, and work attitudes have on occasion been described using terms and ideas from learning theory. However, it now seems apparent that treating these areas as part of learning theory is insufficient to account for human behavior in organizations.

Learning is involved in developing four different types of job skills (see Exhibit 2-1). Knowledge-based skills are of the kind typically developed in psychology courses; they involve acquiring knowledge or following a clearly specified method. Singular behavior skills, such as coming to work on time, setting specific goals for oneself, or operating a drill press, involve behaviors that can be structured and observed. Limited interpersonal skills are involved in activities such as orienting new employees, delegating responsibility, and providing feedback on performance to an individual. At the managerial level, social-interactive skills are required in order to manage conflict, utilize power effectively, negotiate a contract, and the like.

What Exhibit 2-1 shows is that a cognitive component, involving thinking, predominates in knowledge-based skills and that a behavioral component, involving acting out a prescribed role, predominates in singular behavior skills. In both of these cases, although more so in the former, concepts of learning are highly applicable. But as one moves to limited interpersonal skills and then to complex interactive skills, a noncognitive component becomes increasingly significant. This component is based on emotions, attitudes, values, personality characteristics, and other

BOX 2-1   I/O PSYCHOLOGY IN PRACTICE

The Strategic Role of Engineering Training at IBM

An important part of the IBM strategy for the 1970s and 1980s is vertical integration. More specifically, IBM is building robots to help build computers. Training has an important role to play in this strategy. IBM has increased its recruitment of mechanical and industrial engineers as well as electrical engineers for its training programs. IBM training programs help trainees develop robotics skills that cut across electrical, mechanical, and industrial engineering skills that are needed to help IBM realize its strategy.

Trainees are appraised on how well they can combine such skills as well as on many other dimensions. Trainees are rewarded in significant part on the basis of how well they can apply their learning and skills in the vertical integration robotics strategic area. This is not to suggest that a good electrical engineer who fits other IBM criteria would be rejected because of a difficulty with integrating electrical and mechanical engineering skills. Instead, and more to the point, the training programs can help locate, develop, and select trainees who have the particular skills, potential, and interests in the robotics area that are important for IBM's vertical integration strategy.

SOURCE: Reprinted from Richard P. Nielsen (1983). Training programs: Pulling them into sync with your company's strategic planning. *Personnel, 69*(3), 22.

---

qualities that are not easily affected by the acquisition of knowledge.

☐ Learning Concepts

What, then, are the concepts regarding learning that apply primarily to knowledge-based and singular behavior skills? We will consider five of them: motivation, reinforcement, knowledge of results, active practice and experiential learning, and transfer of training.

Motivation. Although a question may be raised as to whether all learning requires an incentive, there is no doubt that learning generally occurs when one is sufficiently motivated to acquire or sharpen a skill. As a typical example, an individual goes through an extensive apprenticeship involving technical school courses and on-the-job instruction in order to become a journeyman electrician. This learning may be stimulated by a desire to win acceptance among family members or peers, an intrinsic interest in the subject mat-

ter, a desire to enter what is perceived as a high-paying occupation, or by some other motive. People differ in the motives that spur them to action, even when the learning outcome is the same. What is constant, however, is that some strong incentive is involved. If this is not the case, learning can be expected to be minimal; our budding electrician would never achieve journeyman status.

Reinforcement. The **law of effect,** as formulated by Edward Thorndike, who served on the faculty of Columbia University for many years, states that behavior viewed as leading to reward or that satisfies a need tends to be learned and repeated; behavior that appears not to produce a reward, or leads to punishment, tends not to be repeated. Any event that increases the likelihood of a particular behavior is said to be **reinforcing.** Not all actions intended to be reinforcing, however, have the desired effect. A female manager may anticipate that praise for the efforts of a new male subordinate will bring about rapid

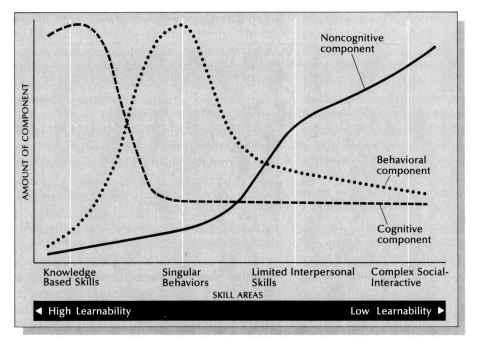

EXHIBIT 2-1   Relationships among Various Learning Components, Skill Areas, and Learnability
This diagram indicates the degree to which cognitive, behavioral, and noncognitive components enter into the acquisition of different types of skills.
SOURCE: Donald H. Brush & Betty Jo Licata (1983). The impact of skill learnability on the effectiveness of managerial training and development. *Journal of Management, 9*, 33.

learning of job duties. But the subordinate, out of a strong macho orientation, may reject the praise of his female boss as irrelevant or even a threat to his self-esteem, with the result that no positive reinforcement is perceived and no learning occurs. In such cases, if a reinforcing effect is to be achieved, it may be necessary to attribute the praise to someone else whom the subordinate does respect.

Knowledge of Results.   The process of feeding back information on the effectiveness of responses so that people have a clear picture of how well they are doing is referred to as **knowledge of results.** The provision of such information has been shown to have substantial value in conjunction with many training programs. Two typical examples are a program designed to reduce waste among textile

operators at Fieldcrest Mills, and a program to improve safety performance in departments such as crating, final assembly, and machine shop in a farm machinery manufacturing plant (McGehee & Thayer, 1961; Reber & Wallin, 1984). In these and other programs, trainees are more easily able to identify and focus on those areas where additional practice or instruction is needed. One of the advantages of computer-assisted instruction (CAI) is that knowledge of results is instantly available, as are learning materials appropriate to the student's needs (Schwade, 1985).

Active Practice and Experiential Learning.
By definition, learning requires practice and experience with the task. The central concept in **experiential learning** is that there should be **active practice** so that people can repeat-

edly do what they are expected to learn and thereby become proficient. Knowledge-based skills are best acquired by writing things down or repeating them orally; singular behavior skills are best learned by repeating correct actions many times.

The five central methods of experiential learning are simulations and games that model the work to be learned; exercises designed to facilitate movement through the learning experience; group interactions intended to instill group skills; role playing for the purpose of practicing new behaviors; and body movements like those used in stress-reduction and relaxation training (Walter & Marks, 1981).

Transfer of Training.   Unfortunately, what is learned in a training context may not carry over into the actual work situation and produce effective performance; **transfer of training** may fail to occur. In the military, for example, skills learned in basic training often evaporate under the stress of combat. To avoid this problem, instructors may design the learning experience so that there are identical elements in both training and actual job circumstances(Fotheringhame, 1986). The idea is to spark similar thoughts and feelings in the two situations so that transfer of learning occurs. Thus combat training may incorporate an infiltration course where trainees crawl under actual machine-gun fire.

A somewhat different approach, or at least one that has its origins in a quite different theoretical context, offers considerable promise. This procedure, which is illustrated in Exhibit 2-2, takes its lead from work that has been done to prevent reformed substance abusers such as alcoholics from relapsing. In essence, failure to transfer new learning to the job is viewed as a relapse that occurs in certain high-risk situations, as when time pressures intensify. By learning to anticipate these high-risk situations, and to cope with them when they do occur, workers can maintain their performance levels even under difficult circumstances.

☐ Identifying Learning Effects

How do we know if learning has occurred? The most common approach is to give a test after training and evaluate the results. However, it is always possible that those taking the test acquired the skills in question before entering the training program or through another means, such as on-the-job experiences. In such cases, trainees may test superbly, but the test results will have little to do with the effectiveness of the training procedure.

This whole matter of evaluating training programs to see if they are working has become increasingly complex, but the basic approach is still to use some type of pretest–posttest measurement with both experimental (trained) and control (untrained, but otherwise treated the same) groups (Latham, 1988; Wexley & Latham, 1981). Exhibit 2-3 shows how contrasting measurements were used to judge the effectiveness of a management course. In this instance, a pretest revealed that both the experimental and the control groups had virtually equal knowledge of management subject matter. The experimental group then took a lecture course in this subject, while the control group continued to do the same type of work as the experimental group but did not take the course. When the course ended, both groups were again tested—and this time the experimental group scored appreciably higher than the control group. Researchers were thus able to conclude that the training program was indeed effective.

☐ Single and Double Loop Learning

A set of learning concepts known as single and double loop learning differs substantially from those just considered. These concepts

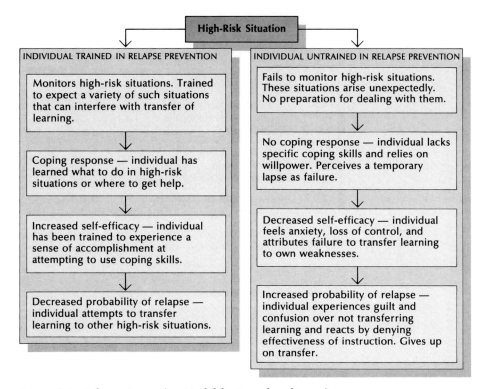

EXHIBIT 2-2   Relapse Prevention Model for Transfer of Learning
Training in relapse prevention can help individuals transfer new learning to actual high-risk situations, such as a sudden demand for increased output, instead of relapsing into former, ineffective responses that hinder performance.
SOURCE: Adapted from Robert D. Marx (1982). Relapse prevention for managerial training: A model for maintenance of behavior change. *Academy of Management Review, 7,* 434–436.

stem from sensitivity training, T-groups, and organization development, which we will consider later on. However, since learning is involved, it is relevant to note them here. At the same time it is important to understand that single and double loop learning do not have a great deal of research support. The ideas are interesting, deal with important issues, and are potentially useful, but we cannot be sure yet how correct they are. Also, although the processes involved are usually referred to as learning processes, it might be equally appropriate to view them as decision-making approaches.

The distinction between single and double loop learning is outlined in Exhibit 2-4.

Generally, decisions based on **single loop learning** are viewed as ineffective because they do not meet the requirements of the situation (a "mismatch" results). Decisions based on **double loop learning,** which involves a mental doubling back in order to question prevailing assumptions and the status quo—the governing variables of Exhibit 2-4—are more likely to "match" the overall needs of both the individual and the organization. Where single loop processes operate, the governing variables are not examined. These variables include a need to (1) achieve a specific purpose, (2) win at all costs, (3) avoid expressing negative emotions, and (4) emphasize only the rational aspects of a prob-

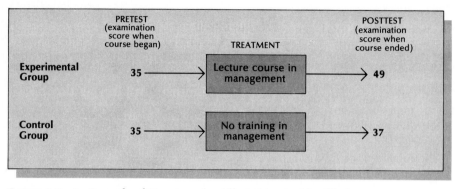

EXHIBIT 2-3   An Example of How Learning Effects May be Identified
This diagram shows the change in student performance on a seventy-five-item examination over the period of a single course. Note that the experimental group that had the
course increased its knowledge sharply, while the control group without the course
changed hardly at all.
SOURCE: Adapted from Eliot S. Elfner (1980). Lecture versus discussion formats in teaching a basic
management course. *Academy of Management Proceedings, 40,* 105–106.

lem. In sum, the individual focuses on controlling the situation, protecting his or her
position, and doing nothing to make others
angry. Performance suffers because many
important issues are not considered, including the good of the organization as a whole.

Under double loop conditions individuals
learn to go back and question governing variables. As a result, they come to substitute
more appropriate variables, which produces
an emphasis on (1) valid information, (2) free
and informed choice, and (3) internal commit-

ment to that choice. Individual defensiveness
is minimized, and those factors that are
important to the solution that is in the best
interests of the organization are brought out.
In single loop learning, the tendency is to
develop solutions for problems and errors
within existing norms. In double loop learning, response to error takes the form of
inquiry into the norms themselves.

For example, attempting to redesign a
product to make it conform more closely to
customer specifications involves single loop

EXHIBIT 2-4   The Single and Double Loop Learning Distinction
Single loop learning accepts the governing variables of prevailing assumptions and the
status quo as given, while double loop learning goes back further and questions these
governing variables.
SOURCE: Chris Argyris (1983). Usable knowledge for double-loop problems, in Ralph H. Kilmann,
Kenneth W. Thomas, Dennis P. Slevin, Raghu Nath, & S. Lee Jerrell (Eds.), *Producing useful knowledge for organizations,* p. 378. New York: Praeger.

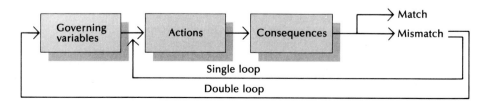

learning. Going beyond this to determine whether the product should continue to be manufactured at all involves double loop learning. In the latter instance, the issue involves overcoming defensiveness about having championed the product so that valid information and informed choice may prevail. The people involved must learn not to allow their own need to win at whatever cost and their need to appear omniscient stop them from identifying the central problem, developing solutions to it, implementing the solutions, and evaluating the effectiveness of the new course of action.

To replace single loop with double loop learning, some organizations sponsor seminars that utilize a form of group psychotherapy. An interventionist helps participants to recognize their personal defense mechanisms and question their assumptions, which in itself can be quite anxiety-producing. Participants then gradually learn to utilize double loop approaches. In the process, organizational goals should come to supersede individual goals. There is no question that this is an important need for organizational effectiveness, but we do not yet know how well the concepts of single and double loop learning work to produce the desired result (Argyris, 1982; Argyris & Schön, 1978).

■ INTELLIGENCE AND MENTAL ABILITIES

A number of theories of intelligence and concepts of intelligent functioning have been advanced. Many of these views fall within the framework of learning and involve cognitive processes (Sternberg, 1985). Often, intelligence is said to be based on the capacity or readiness for new learning. At the same time, intelligence is also said to involve the capacity to solve problems, to reason, and to achieve effective decisions. Thus, our discussion of intelligence serves to bridge the preceding

treatment of learning and the following consideration of individual decision making. From this standpoint, intelligence assumes an important position in the understanding of performance.

□ Development of Intelligence

Intellectual development occurs primarily in the early years and is largely complete for most people before they enter the work force. Yet it is helpful to know something about the processes of development in order to understand fully the role of intelligence in performance.

An individual's intelligence level is a consequence of both the external environment and internal characteristics (Fischer & Silvern, 1985). A rich environment—early and good schooling, a home where learning opportunities are readily available, and a highly differentiated social and physical setting—provides an ideal setting for the development of intelligence. At the same time, individual characteristics such as motivation to learn, the degree of anxiety experienced in learning contexts, and inherent ability are crucial as well. A rich environment is of little value if people do not or cannot use it to develop their intelligence.

In part at least, the internal factors in intellectual development appear to be genetically determined and exist at birth. Researchers have clearly established that intelligence unfolds through a series of stages. Each stage places an upper limit on intellectual capacity in the sense that certain approaches to learning and reasoning are not available at that stage, and restrictions are imposed on the speed of learning. To the extent that people fail to move through these stages to an adult level, the development of intelligence is capped—even within the richest of environments.

Intelligence is not a single entity. People often perform better in one area than another, and thus it is meaningful to speak in terms of multiple intelligences (Gardner, 1983). Both environmental opportunities and internal factors appear to account for these differences. If a person grows up in an environment where there are no musical instruments and music is rarely heard, musical ability is likely to be minimal. Likewise, if the individual develops an aversion to practicing music or a fear of performing, a lack of ability may result.

☐ Intelligence and Performance

That intelligence represents a major factor in the performance of many jobs can no longer be questioned (Gottfredson, 1986). Different jobs, however, require different skills, and consequently engage different types of intelligence or mental abilities.

Because environments are diverse and people may direct their learning efforts to any aspect of their environment, it is possible to identify a wide range of abilities (Weitzel, Dawis, & Mason, 1981). However, certain intellectual abilities appear to have much greater overall significance for job performance. In addition, more is known about the nature and measurement of some abilities than others. Of particular significance are:

Verbal ability—a knowledge of words and skill in their use

Numerical ability—skill in manipulating numbers

Mechanical ability—a capacity to manipulate mechanical objects and a knowledge of the principles that govern their operation

Spatial ability—skill in visualizing and relating objects in accordance with their shape and position in space

Some concept of social ability, defined in terms of skill in understanding and dealing with others, probably should be added. Managerial and sales jobs, in particular, seem to require this type of intelligence. However, no substantial body of research exists to assess the role of social ability in job performance.

On the other hand, researchers have documented a direct relationship between an individual's verbal abilities and that individual's occupational level. Exhibit 2-5, which takes its data from a representative sample of the employed U.S. population, reveals that verbal ability is of particular significance in the more highly skilled professional and managerial occupations. People without above-average verbal intelligence simply do not acquire these jobs. Among those who do become managers or professionals, verbal ability is apparently crucial in determining the level of performance. This is illustrated in Box 2-2, which describes a system designed to rate managers at International Telephone and Telegraph (ITT).

All jobs have what amount to minimum verbal ability demand levels, and these levels drop as one moves down the occupational scale from highly skilled to skilled to semiskilled work. At the unskilled level, verbal-intelligence requirements are often virtually nonexistent. Because verbal abilities are so crucial to occupational placement and performance, as well as educational placement and performance, measures of verbal ability now account for a considerable portion of most so-called general intelligence tests. Essentially, verbal communication, both written and oral, plays an important role in all segments of society. Accordingly, general intelligence continues to be a major contributor to job performance (Guion & Gibson, 1988).

Numerical, mechanical, spatial, and social abilities do not have the same pervasive influence. Each is important to certain types of work but matters little for a wide range of other jobs. For example, mechanical ability is very important in a number of production and maintenance jobs, but when the work

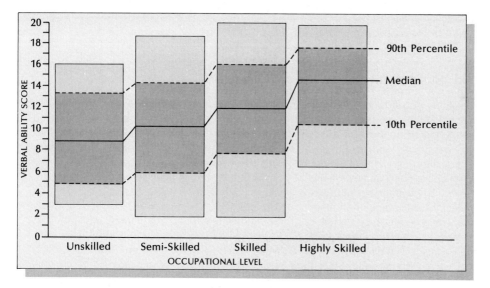

Exhibit 2-5   Verbal Ability at Different Occupational Levels
The 90th percentile point, the median score, and the 10th percentile point on verbal ability all rise steadily as one goes from the unskilled occupations to the semiskilled, to the skilled, and finally to the highly skilled.
Source: John B. Miner (1973). *Intelligence in the United States,* p. 128. Westport, CT: Greenwood Press.

involves selling insurance or teaching history, a person's level of mechanical ability matters little. Verbal ability, on the other hand, continues to play a role in the job performance of all but the least skilled members of the labor force. Some professional people, including writers, lawyers, and teachers, obtain and keep their jobs almost entirely on the basis of their verbal capabilities. Yet spatial ability is very important to the success of airplane pilots (Gordon & Leighty, 1988).

The proven relationship between intelligence and performance suggests that intelligence tests used for hiring and placement can make a considerable difference in overall company productivity. More than seventy years ago Atlantic-Richfield, like many other oil companies, began using tests to select the most intelligent employees it could find. The idea was that even though superior intelligence might not contribute much to performance in entry-level jobs, many new employ-

ees would eventually advance to high-level management positions, at which point the company's policy of stockpiling intelligence would pay off in improved performance and productivity.

☐ Dealing with Intellectual Influences on Performance

Where people lack the knowledge needed to perform a job well, learning can be facilitated through training programs. In many cases people recognize their own needs for increased knowledge or skills and seek out opportunities. Thus learning becomes part of personal career development.

Such learning is relatively easy, but intelligence acquisition presents major problems. To some degree, intelligence serves to limit and constrain learning, although attempts to increase intellectual abilities in adults have had some success (Pintrich, Cross, Kozma, &

BOX 2-2 RESEARCH IN I/O PSYCHOLOGY

Intelligence and Management Assessment at ITT

The Standard Telephone and Cables (STC) subsidiary of International Telephone and Telegraph (ITT) in the United Kingdom operates an assessment center to appraise lower- and middle-level managers, including those in manufacturing, engineering, finance, personnel, and marketing. The question at hand is whether a comprehensive measure of general intelligence of an essentially verbal nature would exhibit strong relationships to the management appraisal ratings—and thus to management success as measured.

The assessment center requires managers to perform various situational exercises over a two-day period. They are observed and subsequently rated on their performance by more senior managers in the company who have been trained for this purpose. The exercises used include:

In-tray exercise. This exercise simulates the in-tray of a senior manager in STC; almost all of the twenty-seven items were gathered from the in-trays of senior managers in STC, with suitable amendments to maintain confidentiality and to fit into STC's Geo-Systems Division in which this and some of the other exercises take place. The participant is asked to stand in for the Division's General Manager and has two hours in which to deal with various memos, letters, reports and other documents as he sees fit. He is then asked to fill in an action sheet on which he summarizes how he dealt with each item. He is then interviewed by an assessor and asked to explain why he took the various actions, and encouraged to clear up any outstanding issues.

Committee exercise. Six participants form an appointments committee set up to fill a vacancy within Geo-Systems Division. They are each given written details of a candidate to propose for the job; they, as a group, are instructed to ensure that the best person is appointed to the job. However, each individual is told to try as hard as possible to get his own candidate selected. The candidates are allocated at random, and each has roughly the same number of strengths and weaknesses. The participants in turn present the case for their own candidate for up to four minutes. Then there is an unconstrained discussion for forty minutes before (usually though not always) deciding on an appointee.

Business decisions exercise. The participants form the executive boards of three companies, each competing with the others in the same mar-

McKeachie, 1986). This is particularly true among those whose intellectual levels are very low. With adults of average intelligence, increases tend to be quite modest; some people improve hardly at all. Perhaps if adults could devote the time to learning that children do, more impressive increases would be recorded; but this is rarely possible. Hence performance changes, in terms of both level and type of work done, are much more likely to result from changes in job placement than from efforts at intelligence development.

A related problem arises because people tend not to evaluate their own intellectual abilities very accurately (Mabe and West, 1982). In particular, studies have shown that individuals with limited abilities are more likely to overestimate their competence than are high-ability individuals. The upshot is that those who might benefit the most from efforts at intellectual development are unlikely to consider such measures necessary. Adults rarely avail themselves of remedial courses in English and mathematics, although

ket. The business environment and variables have been tailored to simulate a small division of STC operating in a competitive market. The "boards" run their companies over a simulated two-year period (eight decision periods of around thirty minutes each) during which time they have to decide on such factors as prices to be charged; promotion costs; production levels; capital investment; and loan levels. The decisions are fed into a computer and the effects of the decisions are quickly fed back. There are three phases of the exercise as far as the assessors are concerned: period 1, periods 2–5, and periods 6–8. This split spreads the assessors' workload, since it is impossible to rate four participants on twelve dimensions in any one phase.

Business plan presentation. One item in the intray exercise is the draft of a business plan for Geo-Systems Division. In this exercise the participants are asked to make a short presentation (ten to fifteen minutes) to two of the assessors on what they consider ought to be done to get the draft plan into an acceptable form.

Letter writing exercise. Each participant (in this capacity representing the division as a member of the appointments committee of the local technical college, which is well supported by the company) is required to write a firm but tactful letter. It is addressed to the chairman of the Board of Governors, urging that the present principal of the college should not have his appointment extended for another two years. The chairman has already suggested the extension and has no idea of the company's strong objections.

The assessors made eight different ratings based on their observations of performance on these managerial simulations using eight-point scales, as well as an overall evaluation using a three-point scale. In all categories, a positive correlation was found between verbal intelligence and the ability to understand and cope with the managerial situations. Intelligence of a verbal nature emerges as a very important contributor to managerial assessments at ITT.

SOURCE: Victor Dulewicz & Clive Fletcher (1982). The relationships between previous experience, intelligence, and background characteristics of participants and their performance in an assessment centre. *Journal of Occupational Psychology, 55,* 199–200.

some firms have had a degree of success with company-sponsored programs of this type.

■ INDIVIDUAL DECISION MAKING

Clearly, decision making is based on prior learning and involves problem solving and reasoning; thus, it is closely allied to learning and intelligence. Much decision making in organizations involves interaction between two or more individuals, and thus contains aspects of group process; decisions of this kind are treated in Chapter 8. Aspects of the decision-making process that relate specifically to individuals are what concern us here.

□ Approaches to Decision Making

Any decision—an individual deciding whether to pursue a certain career or a chief executive deciding whether to commit the company to a particular strategy—involves a gap between the current situation and some desired situation, a focusing of attention on this gap with the intent of reducing it, and a perception that the gap can be reduced and the problem solved. A series of three approaches to making decisions has been proposed. As the degrees of uncertainty and conflict surrounding a decision increase, first *maximizing*, then *satisficing*, and finally *incrementalizing* should be applied (Taylor, 1984; Grandori, 1984).

The idea of a scale of uncertainty that influences the approach that should be taken to decisions is reflected in the distinction between programmed and nonprogrammed decisions as set forth in Exhibit 2-6. Programmed decisions, which have right answers and involve minimal uncertainty, tend to be made by individuals below the top rungs of a hierarchic organization. Nonprogrammed decisions generally involve problems for which there are no obvious solutions and entail a great deal of uncertainty. Decisions of this type are usually faced by top-management personnel.

Maximizing. The **maximizing** approach to decision making involves maximizing the chances of achieving the desired objectives by considering all possible courses of action, exploring all conceivable consequences of taking these actions, and then making a choice. Pure maximizing involves considerable time and research and is therefore impractical, but close approximations do occur. Let us say that a young management trainee named Susan Sager has set her sights on a top-level position in her firm. Susan may accordingly gather a great deal of information about alternative career paths within the company and may develop well-informed projections of where each path will lead and when, including in her analysis substantial data on her own capabilities. This is rational career planning; it is also maximizing, or something very close to it.

Satisficing. Maximizing involves remembering and giving close attention to large amounts of data. With programmed decisions, using a computer or dividing parts of the problem among different individuals may be helpful, but these approaches are of little use in making nonprogrammed decisions. In such cases, a more appropriate strategy is *satisficing* (a term coined by administrative theorist Herbert Simon). **Satisficing** involves choosing a course of action that will result in reaching a desired goal without exploring all possibilities. Decision makers use highly simplified models of the problem and are guided by working hypotheses, rules of thumb, and heuristics. These decision makers are rational, but within narrow bounds—thus there is **bounded rationality.** People can, of course, choose to satisfice even when maximizing is still possible, but if sufficient uncertainty exists, satisficing is preferable to failed maximizing.

Susan Sager, our management trainee, might choose to look at career paths that involve rising through single functional areas of the business. After considering several options, she may decide to pursue marketing, the course followed by the current chief executive. This solution fits her view that "what worked for others should work for me." By narrowing her focus, however, Susan may fail to consider other specialties—or the possibility of pursuing multiple specialties—within the firm. She may also lose sight of changing times and corporate strategies and of her own special capabilities.

Incrementalizing. Incrementalizing—or, as it is sometimes called, muddling through—involves making a number of small choices rather than one large one; its goal is primarily to alleviate existing problems. A few short-term alternatives that should change the status quo are considered, as are the possible consequences of these choices. After the first decision the problem is redefined and one

Exhibit 2-6   Techniques of Decision Making Utilized in Programmed and Nonprogrammed Approaches

Types of Decisions	Techniques Available
1. Programmed Repetitive and routine A definite procedure has been worked out so that decisions do not have to be handled anew each time they occur	**Traditional** 1. Habit 2. Standard operating procedures 3. Organizational structure **Modern** 1. Operations research 2. Electronic data processing
2. Nonprogrammed Novel, unstructured, and unusually consequential No cut-and-dried method for handling the problem because it has not arisen before, or because its precise nature and structure are elusive and complex, or because it is so important that it deserves a custom-tailored treatment	**Traditional** 1. Judgment, intuition, and creativity 2. Selection and training of executives **Modern** 1. Heuristic problem solving applied to training humans 2. Constructing heuristic computer programs

Source: Adapted from Herbert A. Simon (1977). *The new science of management decision,* pp. 46 and 48. Englewood Cliffs, NJ: Prentice-Hall.

goes on from there. When incrementalizing, the decision maker's aspirations are not great, but given the many uncertainties involved they probably should not be. An application described by Charles Lindblom (1965), who originally developed the incrementalizing concept, is as follows:

> A city traffic engineer . . . might propose the allocation of certain streets to one-way traffic. In so doing, he might be quite unable to predict how many serious bottlenecks in traffic, if any, would develop and where they would arise. Nevertheless, he might confidently make his recommendations, assuming that if any bottlenecks arose, appropriate steps to solve the new problem could be taken at that time—new traffic lights, assignment of a traffic patrolman, or further revision of the one-way plan itself.

Susan Sager might seek an early initial placement in personnel, reasoning that this would be preferable to continued trainee status and that she could learn more about job opportunities in the company there. Once she had been in personnel for a while, she might reason, she would worry about what she should and could do next. Incrementalizing is the preferred approach under conditions of extreme uncertainty, but it can be used when it should not be—where satisficing or even maximizing is possible.

Using the Approaches.   Behavioral scientists have noticed certain predispositions that lead individuals to prefer one of the three decision-making approaches over the others, regardless of the amount of uncertainty present. Because of human cognitive limitations maximizing is not easily achieved, even on routine tasks, but there are individuals who will try very hard to approximate it and will continue to search out and study alternatives long after others have resorted to satisficing and incrementalizing (Gingrich & Soli, 1984; Klein, 1983). When rapid decisions are required or uncertainty levels are very high, those who seek to maximize may do less well than the others. But in situations where rational thought is needed—which includes much of business decision making—the person who tries to maximize would appear to be at a distinct advantage.

This advantage associated with the more rational, maximizing approach has been clearly demonstrated for career decisions such as that of Susan Sager (Blustein, 1987). Yet it is equally evident that many decisions in a variety of contexts relax the criteria of rationality to a point where they depart significantly from the maximizing approach (House & Singh, 1987). Box 2-3, dealing with a decision-making exercise carried out at MIT, shows how great the departure from maximizing typically is.

Studies of decision making reveal a good deal about how and when maximizing occurs (Steiner and Miner, 1986). A degree of stress in the situation can jolt people out of their complacency and contribute to a more extensive search for alternatives and thus a closer approximation to maximizing. Otherwise there is a tendency for many people to utilize only information sources that are readily available. Often the most readily available information is that which a person already has. As a result, people who know a lot about financial matters often propose financial solutions to business problems, those who are particularly knowledgeable in the marketing area advocate marketing solutions, and so on. Such tendencies have often been attributed to bias and strongly held values, and that may indeed be the case. But they can also result from preferences for satisficing and incrementalizing, rather than the extended search into new areas of knowledge that maximizing often entails.

It is important to recognize, however, that an extensive search for alternatives and analysis of their consequences is not always a sign that maximizing is in progress. It is quite possible to continue the search, not for the purpose of reaching a better decision, but to confirm or validate a decision already made in the satisficing or incrementalizing mode. The new information is put to a different use and acquired more selectively than in maximizing. We often do this "pseudo-maximizing" after making a major purchase somewhat impulsively. People may well continue to read ads and check other sources after buying a car, simply to prove to themselves that they made the right decision.

☐ Creativity

One factor that influences the way in which individuals make decisions is their creativity. Creative decisions are important to organizational effectiveness. They have been noted as a significant factor in productivity improvements, and they clearly make a contribution through their role in new product research and strategy formulation, among many other areas. From this standpoint, **creativity** is defined as

> socially recognized achievement in which there are novel products to which one can point as evidence such as inventions, theories, buildings, published writings, paintings and sculptures and films; laws; institutions; medical and surgical treatments, and so on (Barron & Harrington, 1981, p. 442).

Creative decisions are original and different, but they are not eccentric; they make a socially recognized contribution. Often they involve bringing together ideas and concepts from areas that have never been related to one another before, resulting in the creation of novel combinations.

The Creative Process. Intelligence plays an important role in creativity, and yet the two are not synonymous. To be creative one must first learn and develop a knowledge base in a particular field. Only then is it possible to go beyond what others have done and make a

BOX **2-3**   RESEARCH IN I/O PSYCHOLOGY

Departures from Maximizing in a Computer Simulation at MIT

A laboratory experiment was carried out at Massachusetts Institute of Technology (MIT) utilizing a computer simulation of the national economy. Subjects played the role of manager for the entire economy and made decisions accordingly; they had to invest sufficient capital plant and equipment to meet demand. Complete and perfect information were given regarding the structure of the simulated economy, the values of all relevant factors, and the past history of the system. The objective was to balance demand and supply. Perfect and complete information sufficient to reach a rational, maximizing solution were provided.

All aspects of the simulation were described to the subjects prior to play; questions regarding mechanics and rules were answered at any time, and there was no time limit. Subjects included MIT students from undergraduates to doctoral level, most with extensive exposure to economic concepts; scientists and economists from many countries of the world; and business executives, among them several chief executives. As a whole, the group was very economically sophisticated.

With perfect maximizing, something that was entirely possible given the information available, a score of 19 could be obtained; the mean score was in fact 591. The closest approximation to perfect rationality was more than four times greater than 19. In short, although the subjects had the wherewithal to make maximizing decisions, they did not do so. Typically they simplified the problem too much, and misperceived or ignored feedback on past decisions. Thus, they moved in the direction of both satisficing and incrementalizing to varying degrees depending on the individual. It was the subject's deficient mental models or modes of thought that hindered learning and decision processes. These models focused attention on inappropriate factors and relationships, thus distorting decision-making processes. The experimenter concluded that maximizing in decision making is very difficult to achieve in practice.

SOURCE: John D. Sterman (1989). Misperceptions of feedback in dynamic decision making. *Organizational Behavior and Human Decision Processes, 43,* 301–335.

creative contribution. Developing the knowledge base is in large part a function of intelligence and prior learning. But whether or not a person can then proceed into the unknown is a function of something else, and that something else is what we call creativity. A reasonably high level of intelligence, depending on how large the existing knowledge base is, is a necessary but not sufficient condition for creative achievement.

Creative problem solving is a cognitive process, but it appears to arise in the context of certain motivational patterns and personality characteristics. A review of research in this area notes the following (McCaskey, 1982, p. 116):

- Self-confidence and courage in resisting pressures to conform
- Humility in bowing to rules not of one's own making
- Ability to tolerate, and perhaps seek out, disorder and ambiguity
- Use of intuition
- Integration of opposites in the personality
- Willingness to work hard
- Disciplined impulse

Creative people are excited by the prospect of finding a way to impose their own new order on disorder and uncertainty. To do this may require resisting pressures toward conformity and retaining the status quo, but it also means remaining within the rules and values that define social recognition—a delicate and difficult balance that few are able to maintain.

Exhibit 2-7 sets forth the phases of the creative process. The primary flow is from unconscious scanning of the problem to a logical formulation of a solution, but a circling back to earlier phases is frequently required as obstacles are encountered; this is indicated by the arrows at the left.

Unconscious scanning requires immersing oneself in the problem materials—the knowledge base. It is here that problem finding and formulation occur. Short-circuiting this stage out of an impatience to act can easily abort the whole creative process. It is important to "stay and play." Gradually, however, the process moves into consciousness. There is an intuitive combining of contexts, even though they may seem contradictory, and a matching of these combinations against the demands of the problem to see if they might prove productive. Here a substantial tolerance for ambiguity, so that new and contradictory combinations and problem demands can be isolated and compared, is essential. Ultimately, if creative achievement is to result, there must be insight—the right combination or combinations must be found. In the last phase, what has been a largely unconscious and illogical process—one that the individual involved cannot fully explain—is wrapped in the trappings of rationality to gain acceptance and social recognition.

Encouraging Creativity.   When creativity is desired, and that certainly is not always the case in the organizational world, there are ways of encouraging it. Creativity needs freedom from constraints and, in particular, from time pressures. Unconscious scanning and intuitive combining must be allowed to run their course relatively unfettered. The atmosphere should foster, value, and reward creative endeavor. Often this means a setting somewhat removed from the day-to-day operating environments of organizations. Universities, research and development centers, and artist colonies have this quality. Ivory-tower detachment may mean being somewhat removed from the "real world," but it has its functions, nevertheless; it often permits creative problem solving to thrive. Creative people tend to do their best work in such free and supportive contexts.

A second factor encouraging creativity is training in creative problem solving. People can learn to be more creative, in part because the very fact that the organization is initiating such training signals a favorable climate shift toward creativity. Yet it also appears that training introduces various changes in cognitive modes of thought that facilitate creative endeavor. Through training, individuals can learn about defining problems, exploring the knowledge base for alternatives, combining elements, and evaluating ideas. Box 2-4 describes an approach to training that one company used to deal with a dearth of creative research ideas. Note that the company carried out a study to evaluate the impact of the training before investing in widespread application.

It has also been found that a creativity program of this kind works best when all participants are from the same work group (Basadur, Graen, & Scandura, 1986). Under these circumstances a new attitude toward creativity is introduced in the group as a whole; this attitude continues to operate uncontested back on the job. When the

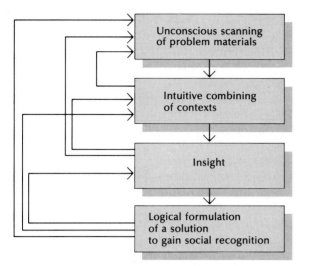

EXHIBIT 2-7 Phases in the Creative Process
In general, creative problem solving involves a movement from unconscious scanning of the situation, to intuitive combining of problem-related contexts, to insight, and finally to a solution. As the arrows at left indicate, however, obstacles frequently necessitate movement back and forth among the various phases.
SOURCE: Adapted from Michael B. McCaskey (1982). *The executive challenge: Managing change and ambiguity,* pp. 116 and 151. Boston: Pitman.

creativity training is applied to people from many different groups, these people return to work situations where they are in the minority. Here the climate does not change, and training effects are not reinforced; if anything, they are punished.

☐ Cognitive Style

Cognitive style refers to the characteristic ways in which people process and evaluate information. It is another factor that exerts an influence on decision making. As such the concept overlaps with certain of the approaches to making choices that we have considered, as well as with creativity. Unfortunately, research has not yet sorted out how various cognitive styles relate to other aspects of individual decision making. Furthermore, although a number of different models have been proposed and measures

developed, it is not clear how these relate to one another. In short, the area of cognitive style is much longer on theory and conceptualization at present than it is on research and application. Yet psychologists believe that increased understanding of the dynamics of cognitive style should lead to more effective decision making. The present discussion focuses on two of the better-known models of cognitive style.

The Slocum-Hellriegel Model. The Slocum-Hellriegel model classifies cognitive style on two dimensions: the ways in which information is gathered (sensation versus intuition) and the ways in which information is evaluated (thinking versus feeling). This is the model that underlies the questionnaire used to introduce this chapter. John Slocum and Don Hellriegel, the authors of that questionnaire, are at Southern Methodist and Texas A & M

BOX **2-4** RESEARCH IN I/O PSYCHOLOGY

Training in Creative Problem Solving

The management of a department engaged in applied engineering research within a large consumer-goods industrial company was concerned about the paucity of creative ideas emanating from its engineers. Consequently, a two-and-a-half-day training program was introduced on an experimental basis to see if it would kindle more creative achievements.

The training was devoted primarily to active practice and experiential learning. Various tasks were used to encourage participants to discover concepts related to creative problem solving not considered before. In one exercise the participants each formulated a definition of a problem from a case and then compared all the definitions, thus learning that the same problem could be viewed in several fruitful ways. At another point each person generated an individual work problem and then developed a solution and an implementation plan for that problem.

In order to evaluate the effectiveness of the training, three similar groups of employees were compared by means of what is referred to as an after-only design. One group received the creativity training, a second group viewed a film on

creativity and discussed it, and the third group received no special treatment at all. Various questionnaires and exercises intended to measure factors related to creativity were administered to all three groups immediately after the training, and in some cases two weeks later. If the training was to prove useful and thus suitable for all department members, those who received it should exhibit greater creativity after training than either of the other two groups.

The experiment was indeed a success. Those who had received the training exhibited evidence of improvements in their cognitive processes, attitudes toward creative endeavor, and creative problem-solving behavior. Furthermore, training effects transferred back to the job and were still evident some two weeks later; they may well have lasted much longer, but the experiment ended at that point.

SOURCE: Min Basadur, George B. Graen, & Stephen G. Green (1982). Training in creative problem solving: Effects on ideation and problem finding and solving in an industrial research organization. *Organizational Behavior and Human Performance, 30,* 41–70.

Universities respectively. A similar model but using a very different measure has been proposed by Rowe and Mason (1987).

The Driver Model. Michael Driver, at the University of Southern California, in conjunction with several colleagues, developed a two-dimensional classification of cognitive style. One dimension is the number of alternatives generated—single versus multiple—and the other is the amount of information used—moderately low (satisficing) versus high (maximizing). The resulting four basic cognitive styles are as follows (Driver &

Rowe, 1979; Driver, 1988; Driver, Brousseau, & Hunsaker, 1990):

Decisive (single alternative/low information). A small amount of information is used to generate a good enough decision. Once a decision is made, it is final. This style favors speed, efficiency, and achievement of results. It may be too rigid and simplistic, but it is dynamic, strong, and reliable.

Flexible (multiple alternatives/low information). Also employs a minimal amount of data to reach a decision. However, it continually absorbs new data and generates new solutions as needed. Adaptability as well as speed and efficiency is prized. It is strong in intuition, getting along well with others, and rolling with the punches; yet it can be shallow and indecisive as well.

Hierarchic (single alternative/high information). Shows a very high use of available information to meticulously generate one best solution. Then the solution is often implemented using an elaborate contingency plan. It utilizes rigor, precision, and long-range planning, but may also be dogmatic and over-controlling.

Integrative (multiple alternatives/high information). Uses a large amount of information, but simultaneously generates a number of possible solutions for implementation. There is a tendency to rely on creative synthesis rather than pure logic. It is highly inventive, empathic, and cooperative, yet it can be too complicated and wishy-washy.

Research has yielded some information on when each style works best. The decisive style was found to be superior in a structured government bureaucracy. The integrative style had advantages in a very unstable and complex aerospace firm. With greater stability but still considerable complexity (as in an airline), the hierarchic style proved preferable. Much more research is needed, but the general point is that different dominant styles are most appropriate in different contexts.

KEY TERMS

Cognitive processes
Learning
Intelligence
Individual decision making
Law of effect
Reinforcing (reinforcement)
Knowledge of results
Experiential learning
Active practice

Transfer of training
Single loop learning
Double loop learning
Maximizing
Satisficing
Bounded rationality
Incrementalizing
Creativity
Cognitive style

SUMMARY

Learning is a relatively permanent change, resulting from practice or experience, in the capability for responding. It operates primarily on knowledge-based skills and singular behaviors. Learning is fostered by strong motivation, perceived *reinforcement, knowledge of results, active practice,* and

transfer of training. It may be identified through the use of various approaches that contrast experimental and control conditions. In contrast, work within learning seminars to foster *double loop* approaches utilizes quite a different concept of learning.

Intelligence involves having a capacity for learning and using this capacity in problem solving, reasoning, and decision making. It and its various components play an important role in job performance. Verbal ability is particularly important in determining occupational level, while other abilities serve primarily to influence performance in specific jobs.

Decision making represents a moment at which a choice must be made in an ongoing process of evaluating alternatives for meeting an objective. The primary approaches involved, in order of priority, are *maximizing, satisficing,* and *incrementaliz-*

ing. The degree of uncertainty, as well as individual proclivities, determines which approach will be used. Decisions also vary in the extent to which *creativity* is called for. Creativity requires a combination of unconscious scanning, intuition, insight, and logical formulation. It may be encouraged through introducing a favorable climate and training. A closely related concept is that of *cognitive style.* Two well-known models of cognitive style, the Slocum-Hellriegel and the Driver models, indicate that various styles are effective, depending on the particular decision-making context.

QUESTIONS

1. How can creativity be encouraged? Is this appropriate in all circumstances?
2. What purposes do control groups and control conditions serve in evaluating learning and cognitive change?
3. How are single and double loop learning distinguished?
4. Under what conditions are the various approaches to choosing likely to occur? When should they occur?

5. Identify the roles played by the following in learning:
   (a) Law of effect
   (b) Identical elements
   (c) Relapse prevention model
   (d) Knowledge of results
6. How do intelligence and the various mental abilities relate to job performance?
7. What are some of the approaches used to differentiate cognitive styles?

CASE PROBLEM

ELIZABETH KASABIAN

Saleswoman

Beth Kasabian was one of the first women hired by a mechanical-parts manufacturing company for a sales position after the firm had come under considerable pressure from the Equal Employment Opportunity Commission. The EEOC had made it very clear that women would have to be hired for training to work in the company's previously all-male sales force and that they would have to be upgraded as rapidly as possible. The feeling in sales management was that it was much more important

to avoid any court action involving discriminatory employment practices than it was to continue the longstanding tradition of having only male sales personnel. Accordingly, an extensive recruiting effort to find women who wanted this type of work was initiated.

Beth was one of the initial group of sales trainees recruited. She was a particularly attractive candidate because she had had solid work experience, although in a different industry and in a different type of work. Since graduating from college with a degree in economics, she had worked for several years as a buyer and apparently had done well at it. However, her initial employer had experienced increased competition in the part of the country where she was located, and the resulting decline in business forced a layoff of a number of people with limited seniority. Thus Beth was looking for work at the same time the company was looking hard for saleswomen.

The company's regular sales training program consisted of six weeks of classroom learning followed by up to two years of on-the-job experience working with seasoned salesmen. The product line was quite diverse and there was in fact a lot to learn. By double teaming with experienced salesmen, the trainees learned to cope with unexpected situations, to keep the required records, and above all to present their various products to customers effectively. It was very important to understand fully the match between customer needs and product capabilities.

Beth handled the classroom training reasonably well. She had been at least an average student in college and apparently viewed the training as making similar demands. Her trainer evaluations contained statements such as the following:

> Beth has presented herself well for not having had any previous experience in this type of work. She appears to be extremely interested and cooperative at all times. However, she will have to learn a little more rapidly.

And later on:

> Her continued interest and cooperation have helped Beth develop into a fine student. She is learning somewhat more rapidly now and is good at retaining information once she understands things.

Similar statements continued to be made once Beth started her on-the-job training:

> Generally very good. Especially good at direct selling to customers in the retail setting. Has a large amount of enthusiasm and is very eager to learn.

> She works very hard and is not afraid to tackle any job. Beth is an exceptionally good employee and with proper development will benefit the company immensely.

> Performs all parts of the job well and is particularly good when it comes to techniques of selling. Beth has shown an unusual willingness to work and is constantly striving to learn more about the job.

It was clear that enthusiasm for Beth was snowballing. Far from discriminating against her and resenting her presence in a formerly all-male world, her superiors appeared to be unusually eager to help her. Everyone seemed to want very much for her to succeed. This attitude was fostered in part by continued governmental pressure to have more women placed in higher-level positions, but Beth's own eagerness and desire to learn contributed to it as well.

As a result of these factors, as well as several others, Beth was promoted to take over a sales territory on her own seven months after she joined the company. The opening in that particular territory had occurred rather suddenly when the salesman assigned to it developed health problems and had to leave the company. At least in part, the promotion decision was made then because the specific slot had become available at that time. The placement was viewed as an especially appropriate one for Beth because economic conditions in the territory were good and there was plenty of opportunity for market development. Furthermore, her new supervisor was of the same nationality and could be expected to be sympathetic, understanding, and a source of assistance when needed.

In actual fact the supervisor proved to be all these things. And initially he was just as enthusiastic about Beth as everyone else had been. Gradually, however, he began to have doubts, and by the time the year-end sales figures came in, he knew he had a serious problem.

Beth continued to be just as eager to learn as she had been the day she was hired, but to her boss, at least, this was not totally an asset. She did in fact have a great deal to learn. He would have preferred someone who knew more already and who felt less of a need to acquire new knowledge. Furthermore, under the pressures of day-to-day job responsibilities, with the need to call on customers on something approximating a regular schedule, Beth simply was not progressing very fast. She was no longer in a training position, and although she did receive assistance, this had to be secondary to getting the work done. Much of the time she was of necessity on her own, and any help had to be fitted in when both her supervisor's and her schedules permitted. Since both were often traveling, efforts to improve her understanding of the work tended to be intermittent. Under these circumstances Beth did not respond very well to training and in many respects did not really seem to comprehend her job.

Although she was showing slight gains in her sales of some products, her supervisor could see no reason why she should not be posting major gains in that area at that time, when economic conditions and competitive factors were all on her side. Furthermore, on a whole line of mechanical parts she was experiencing sizable losses quarter after quarter. This was a prime source of concern to her boss.

The training school did provide some instruction about these parts and their use. However, this instruction was male-oriented, assuming prior mechanical knowledge of the kind that most boys would have gained repairing a bicycle or working on a car. When the supervisor tried to teach Beth in this area, he found that he had to start from scratch. She could learn, all right, but it was a time-consuming process and often there was not sufficient time. As a result, she would go out and accept orders for the wrong parts, or not recognize when a particular part was what the customer needed. Many of the problem situations that developed would have seemed humorous in a different context. In any event, a number of customers were rapidly learning to take their business elsewhere.

At first the new saleswoman took her difficulties in stride, attributing them to her own greenness. After a while, however, her attitude began to change. She seemed to recognize that she should be doing better and that lack of experience was no longer an acceptable excuse. Her supervisor could see that the pressure was building and that she was getting rattled often. When he visited customers with her, she frequently made mistakes on calculations in filling out order forms and quoting costs to customers. Yet he had seen her make similar calculations back at the office with no difficulty, when she was not under time pressure and when no one was standing there waiting for the result. It was not uncommon for these situations to deteriorate to the point where the customer became irritated and the supervisor had to step in and bail Beth out.

It seemed almost certain that a number of equally bad situations must be developing in the supervisor's absence. In fact, eventually some feedback from customers began to come in, indicating that her mistakes and, with increasing frequency, her impatience were irritating customers. Yet attempts to discuss specific problem situations with Beth served only to arouse her defensiveness. On several occasions the supervisor strongly suspected that she was telling outright lies. At the least, what he had heard happened and what she said happened were many miles apart, though previously no one in the company, including her boss, would have believed she was capable of this kind of falsehood.

Questions

1. What factors related to learning and cognitive processes appear to contribute to Beth's difficulties?
2. To what extent may the fact that Beth is a woman be contributing to her problems?
3. If you were Beth, what would you do? Why?
4. If you were Beth's boss, what would you do? Why? Can you solve the problem in some creative way?

3

Motivation Theories and Their Applications

"Ann Mongio" worked as a librarian for the State of Washington, helping small city and county libraries with procedures and acquisitions. She was paid $19,500 a year. Comparing herself with other librarians she knew, she felt satisfied with her pay and did a good job. Her official job description read as follows (Remick, 1981):

> **Librarian 3—$1625 per month.** Represents the State Library to outside agencies. Provides consultative services to small city and county libraries (which serve populations up to 25,000) with respect to library development and operation. Or develops and maintains special library sections or collections in other state agencies or for legislative staff. Individuals in this classification are expected to use and interrelate both manual and computer resources to complete professional level work tasks such as entering and verifying holdings, cataloging, materials selection and acquiring new books. May serve as a team leader of two to four lower-level librarians and technicians. Lower levels work primarily within the State Library doing book and material selection, cataloging, and reference work. Our requirements: M.A. in Library Science from an accredited library school and two years professional librarian experience.

Ann had gotten to know several members of the State Women's Council and through them learned about certain studies that had been made of jobs in state government. She found out that librarians, 85 percent of whom were female, were paid less than maintenance carpenters and only about $1500 a year more than truck drivers, most of whom were men. But when she found the description of her brother's job as an automotive mechanic for the state, she really started thinking. He was paid $252 a year more than she was, and there were no female automotive mechanics at all. On the job-evaluation scale her brother's job was considered to be worth 175 points and hers 353—twice as much—yet his work actually paid better. His official job description was:

> **Automotive Mechanic—$1646 per month.** Performs journey-level automotive service and repair work on light, medium, and heavy equipment including diesel-powered units. Diagnoses mechanical problems, develops working plans and cost estimates for journey-level mechanical projects. Overhauls, rebuilds, or repairs drive-train components, frame, and chassis. Performs tune-ups. Operates a variety of mechanical test and measurement equipment common to the automotive trade.

What really bothered Ann was that she had put in years getting her education, while her brother had barely graduated from high school. The more she thought about her work situation in relation to her brother's, the angrier she got. There seemed to be no way of getting her pay up to what she felt it should be, and she certainly couldn't change the fact she had put all that time and money into her education. She almost regretted having obtained all that information about jobs, job-evaluation points, and pay levels. It was clear that the state was not giving equal pay for jobs of **comparable worth,** as indicated by the job-evaluation points assigned. Finally, she quit her job as a librarian and took a job with the telephone company learning to install and repair telephone lines and equipment. That job involved less responsibility, but at least she would be paid the same as the men.

Ann Mongio's experiences caused her to believe that she was being treated unfairly. Accordingly, she developed a desire (motivation) to do something about the situation. Eventually she left her job with the state and took a position where she would be treated more equitably. In this instance motivation resulted in turnover. This is only one of many types of motivation to be considered in this and the next chapter.

When we talk about **motivation** in the field of industrial-organizational psychology, we mean those processes within an individual that stimulate behavior and channel it in ways that should benefit the organization as a whole. An organization is activated by the motivation of its participants, just as a machine is activated by electricity. Internal, individual processes may set these motivating forces in motion and maintain them, or they may be activated by external influences such as a supervisor's warnings. Motivation theories are attempts to explain these processes that operate within the individual, whether they are induced internally or externally.

An abundance of theories about the nature of internal motivational processes has resulted in a number of differing definitions of work motivation (Mitchell, 1982b; Pinder, 1984; Steers & Porter, 1987). For the moment, let us not commit ourselves to any of these theoretical views. The general definition of motivation given above will suffice. It is important to emphasize, however, that our discussion of motivation in this chapter and the next starts from the assumption that what happens within a person significantly affects performance.

In the discussion of the various theories that follows, an attempt is made to answer certain key questions (Miner, 1980c; 1981):

1. What measurement methods are available to help identify the components of the theory?
2. Does the theory contribute to the prediction of performance levels?
3. In what specific arena does the theory operate most effectively?
4. What appears to be the exact nature of the theory's major components?
5. How and to what extent can the motivational processes specified by the theory be modified to improve performance?
6. How can the motivational processes described by the theory influence vocational choice?
7. In short, what is the scientific value of the theory, and what is its practical usefulness in the workplace?

The theories in this chapter are treated in an order running from what are usually described as *content theories,* in that they deal with specifically defined motives, through to *process theories,* which focus primarily on the steps occurring as the motivational process unfolds. We start with need theories of an essentially content nature.

■ NEED THEORIES

Need theories in organizational behavior owe a strong debt to Henry Murray (1938), who headed the psychological clinic at Harvard University for many years. However, Murray's was a general theory of human needs and the environmental pressures that affect them, and thus it had no specific application to industrial-organizational psychology. The two major theories that are built on Murray's ideas and that do apply specifically to industrial-organizational psychology are **need-hierarchy theory,** proposed by Abraham Maslow, and **achievement-motivation theory,** initiated by David McClelland.

□ NEED-HIERARCHY THEORY

Abraham Maslow developed his theory over the last twenty-five years of his life starting in the early 1940s, but it was only toward the end of this period that he began to write about its specific applications to organizations. Maslow's (1943, 1954) theory telescopes Murray's extensive list of human needs and ranks them in a hierarchy of importance. In this scheme, lower-level needs are the primary influences activating human behavior, but as these needs are satisfied, higher-level needs emerge as the prevalent motivators. For example, the most basic (lowest-level) needs are physiological—those for food, water, sex, and so on. Unless these needs are satisfied, one cannot consider higher needs, such as the need for personal security or for positive relationships with others. In addition, deprivation at lower levels can shift the focus of behavior downward. Thus, physiological needs are **prepotent** over all other needs—that is, when unmet, these needs take over and direct behavior. Need hierarchies—which, according to Maslow, are inherent in human biology—are the same for all humans, but different people may be operating at different levels within the hierarchies.

The Hierarchies.   The primary hierarchy of needs in Maslow's theory, and the one almost always mentioned in popular treatments, is as follows, from highest to lowest:

1. *Need for self-actualization*—to realize (or actualize) one's full potential, to become, in Maslow's words, "more and more what one is, to become everything that one is capable of." Unlike the other needs, self-actualization is manifested differently in different people. It may, but need not, involve creative output.
2. *Esteem needs*—to feel adequacy, strength, achievement, confidence, independence, and freedom; also, to obtain attention, reputation, prestige, recognition, importance, and appreciation from others.
3. *Love* (social) *needs*—to affiliate with other people and to experience a sense of belongingness. Both giving and receiving are involved.
4. *Safety needs*—to be free of danger and thus secure. This involves avoidance of anxiety.
5. *Physiological needs*—to satisfy the basic needs of the body: food, water, sleep, sex, physical activity, and sensory satisfaction.

A second and entirely independent hierarchy contains only two types of needs:

1. *Needs for understanding and explanation*—to systematize, organize, and seek out relationships and meanings.

2. *Need for knowledge*—to be aware of reality, obtain facts, and satisfy curiosity.

These are cognitive needs, having to do with knowing, and they are usually discussed along with what are labeled *esthetic needs*—to crave beauty in one's surroundings and experience a sense of deprivation when ugliness prevails. Esthetic needs exist independently of the two hierarchies, and Maslow does not specify the conditions for their activation in human beings.

Box 3-1, which sets forth some of Maslow's views as they developed during his visit to an electronics firm called Non-Linear Systems, makes the point that management should recognize the need levels at which organization members are operating, and should adjust management principles accordingly. Position in the hierarchies can vary with the culture, but Maslow seems to be convinced that in the United States management must now focus on providing for higher-order needs such as self-actualization, esteem, and understanding. This in turn necessitates a management style that is neither authoritarian nor demeaning to subordinates.

Scientific Value and Practical Usefulness. Maslow's theory leaves much to be desired. Conflicting statements and ambiguities abound in his writings. At times, especially in his discussions of self-actualization, he borders on mysticism. A major problem is his constant need to adjust what was intended to be a comprehensive scientific theory, in order to deal with individual variations found in his clinical practice. Yet, because of its intuitive appeal and because no measuring instruments existed adequate to test and challenge it, the theory enjoyed uncritical acceptance for many years. Actually, Maslow's writings are more philosophical than scientific, and it is as philosophy that they have had the greatest usefulness (Huizinga, 1970).

BOX 3-1 I/O PSYCHOLOGY IN PRACTICE

Abraham Maslow on Different Management Principles at Different Levels in the Motivation Hierarchy

Abraham Maslow spent the summer of 1962 visiting a small (225 employees) southern California electronics firm called Non-Linear Systems. He was there at the invitation of the firm's president, Andrew Kay, to study a then two-year-old experiment intended to provide production employees with greater responsibility and challenge, thereby satisfying higher-order needs within Maslow's schema. During his visit Maslow kept a journal of ideas stimulated by exposure to this field application of his theory. Although the experiment had to be abandoned after five years because of financial pressures on the company, Maslow's comments provide a good picture of how his theory applies in practice.

> Where we have fairly evolved human beings able to grow, eager to grow, then [the well-known writer and consultant Peter] Drucker's management principles seem to be fine. They will work, but only at the top of the hierarchy of human development. They assume ideally a person who has been satisfied in his basic needs in the past, while he was growing up, and who is now being satisfied in his life situation. He was and now is safety-need gratified (not anxious, not fearful). He was and is belongingness-need satisfied (he does not feel alienated, ostracized, orphaned, outside the group; he fits into the family, the team, the society; he is not an unwelcome intruder). He was and is love-need gratified (he has enough friends and enough good ones, a reasonable family life; he feels worthy of being loved and wanted and able to give love—this means much more than romantic love, especially in the industrial situation). He was and is respect-need gratified (he feels respect-worthy, needed, impor-

tant, etc.; he feels he gets enough praise and expects to get whatever praise and reward he deserves). He was and is self-esteem-need satisfied. (As a matter of fact this doesn't happen often enough in our society; most people on unconscious levels do not have enough feelings of self-love, self-respect. But in any case, the American citizen is far better off here let's say than the Mexican citizen is.)

> In addition, the American citizen can feel that his curiosities, his needs for information, for knowledge, were and are satisfied or at least are capable of being satisfied, if he wants them to be. That is, he has had education, etc.

> But now we can also ask what would be the proper principles of management for a person who is *not* satisfied in these various ways? How about the people who are fixated at the safety-need level, who feel perpetually afraid, who feel the possibilities of catastrophe, for instance, of unemployment, etc.? What would management be like with people who could not identify with each other, who were suspicious of each other, who hated each other—let's say as seems to be the case among the different classes in France, Germany, Italy, etc., at least much more so than in the United States?

> Clearly, different principles of management would apply to these different kinds of motivational levels. We don't have any great need to work out management principles for the lower levels in the motivation hierarchy. My main purpose here is to keep on making more explicit the high level of personal development that is unconsciously being assumed.

SOURCE: Abraham H. Maslow (1965). *Eupsychian management: A journal*, pp. 15–16. Homewood, IL: Irwin.

Gradually, improved methods have been developed to measure needs within the basic hierarchy, although the cognitive and esthetic needs remain unmeasured even today. As a result, some tests of Maslow's theory have been conducted. These tests have provided little support for the claim that lower needs are prepotent over higher, and they have never provided evidence that the theory predicts performance. Exhibit 3-1 presents a typi-

EXHIBIT 3-1   **Ranking of Various Types of Needs by Women Professionals and Managers and by Homemakers**

Ranking	Professional and Managerial Women	Women in the Homemaker Role
1	Self-actualization	Self-actualization
2	Autonomy	Social†
3	Esteem*	Autonomy
4	Security-safety	Security-safety†
5	Social	Esteem

*Found to be more important among professional and managerial women.
†Found to be more important among homemakers.
SOURCE: Adapted from Ellen L. Betz (1982). Need fulfillment in the career development of women. *Journal of Vocational Behavior, 20,* 60–61.

cal finding. The researcher thought that female homemakers, most of whom were dependent on others for their support, would focus on lower-level needs to a greater degree than would women working in professional and managerial positions. In this study, the esteem needs were split into autonomy and esteem aspects. The researcher found that in neither group of women did the needs rank in accordance with Maslow's hierarchy. Although safety and social needs emerge as more important among the homemakers, and, as expected, esteem needs are not considered important at all, the autonomy aspect of esteem does not differ markedly between the two groups, and self-actualization is of highest importance in both instances. All in all, the patterns do not fit the expectations created by the need-hierarchy theory.

Maslow's theory applies broadly to industrial-organizational psychology, but there is no evidence that it works particularly well in any specific area. Most of the need categories appear meaningful and useful, but self-actualization is a major exception. It is almost impossible to know whether self-actualization for a given individual has been measured correctly; and the ambiguous nature of Maslow's definition compounds the problem. Maslow formulated the need for self-actual-

ization in terms too vague to be meaningful, and existing tests probably are measuring something other than what he intended. There is no research indicating how the specific variables of need-hierarchy theory can be influenced to improve work performance. Although certain needs do show strong relationships to vocational choices, little has been done to actually put this information to use.

Several researchers have attempted to simplify the need-hierarchy theory by combining need categories. The best-known simplification, called *ERG theory*, telescopes the needs into three groups—existence (physiological and material-safety needs), relatedness (interpersonal safety, love, and interpersonal esteem needs), and growth (self-confirmed esteem and self-actualization needs) (Alderfer, 1972). Like the need-hierarchy theory, this model has not fared well in comprehensive tests (Rauschenberger, Schmitt, & Hunter, 1980). However, the growth-need concept has been used widely, especially in conjunction with work redesign efforts of the kind to be considered in the next chapter.

Given the difficulty of verifying the need-hierarchy theory in any form, why bother to consider it? The answer is that the needs themselves, independent of prepotency relationships and excluding self-actualization as

Maslow originally defined it, do seem to be important influences on performance in certain jobs. Furthermore, there is reason to believe that when physiological and, to some degree, safety needs are not satisfied, these low-level needs do tend to dominate an individual's motivational processes. Above this very basic level other needs become important, but which ones they are depends on the developmental experiences of each person. The simple regularities that Maslow envisaged do not adequately reflect the complexities of human motivation.

☐ Achievement-Motivation Theory

David McClelland's (1961, 1975) theory, like Maslow's, has its origins in the work of Henry Murray. Yet McClelland's views differ in a number of respects from those of Maslow. McClelland claimed that needs are learned, and that they are arranged in a hierarchy of potential for influencing behavior that varies from one person to another, not a hierarchy that is the same for everyone. As people mature, they learn to associate positive and negative feelings with things that happen to them and around them. Achievement situations, for instance, may come to produce feelings of pleasure, and as a result achievement motivation may establish itself toward the top of an individual's hierarchy. Then, when there is the slightest indication that achievement striving might be called for, that individual makes strong efforts to meet the challenge and relegates less intense needs to a subsidiary role.

Achievement, Power, and Affiliation Needs. The key construct of McClelland's theory is the achievement need, although he considers power needs and in certain respects affiliation needs as well. **Achievement motivation** is the desire to achieve success through one's own efforts and to take personal responsibility and credit for outcomes. It plays an impor-

tant role in the performance of **entrepreneurs**—those who start and develop their own companies. Because of its impact on entrepreneurial success, the achievement need is seen as a crucial factor in economic development. Countries whose cultures value and foster achievement motivation are expected to experience much faster economic growth than those that do not.

Within the management of large, established firms, however, especially at the higher levels, *power needs,* not achievement needs, play the predominant role in success. As currently formulated, McClelland's theory views a type of socialized, controlled, or somewhat inhibited power need as the crucial factor. A degree of altruism and pragmatism combines with the power need, diluting the pure need for self-aggrandizement. When this mix of strong power need and self-control is joined by a low need for affiliation, the result is the mature leadership-motive pattern—the key to managerial success. Thus a good manager thrives on socialized rather than personal power.

If the *affiliation,* or *social, motivation* is too strong, it may undermine managerial performance. Consider the following circumstances:

> For a bureaucracy to function effectively, those who manage it must be universalistic in applying rules. That is, if they make exceptions for the particular needs of individuals, the whole system will break down. The manager with a high need for being liked is precisely the one who wants to stay on good terms with everybody, and, therefore, is the one most likely to make exceptions in terms of particular needs (McClelland & Burnham, 1976, p. 103).

In this way strong affiliation motivation undermines effective managerial performance.

Scientific Value and Practical Usefulness. McClelland used the **Thematic Apperception Test** (TAT) as the primary means of measuring the motives for achievement, power, and affiliation (although most of the work done has been with achievement). Subjects tell stories in response to pictures selected to elicit the particular motive being studied, and the stories are then analyzed. The procedure has produced close agreement among different scorers in analyses of the same story, but less close agreement in analyses of stories produced at different times by the same subjects. To deal with these discrepancies, a wide range of strategies to measure diverse motives has been developed, but most of them do not have a clear relationship to the basic story-telling approach, and researchers have had difficulty sorting out the results. This is one of the few instances in which we appear to have too much measurement rather than too little. Yet some important findings have emerged from the efforts to test McClelland's formulations.

There can be no doubt that achievement motivation is an important factor in entrepreneurial success, and there is good reason to believe that achievement needs contribute to the choice of an entrepreneurial career. This is

the arena in which McClelland's theory is most valid. In addition, his ideas regarding achievement needs and their effects on economic development have proved useful. In the managerial arena, however, the results have been inconclusive: Sometimes achievement motivation has been shown to contribute to effective managerial performance, but more often it has not. The results obtained from the study of power motivation are more impressive, particularly with regard to the effect of high power need and low affiliation need on the leadership-motive pattern. Exhibit 3-2 demonstrates how this pattern influenced the rate of promotion at AT&T. The evidence there suggests that, in addition to achievement and power, affiliation needs also are important factors in organizational performance. Note in Exhibit 3-2 that managers with the leadership-motive pattern are more likely to rise to middle management; those without it more frequently stay at the lowest levels.

Techniques have been developed to increase the strength of achievement motiva-

EXHIBIT 3-2   Relationship between Leadership-Motive Pattern (High Need for Power, Low Need for Affiliation, and High Self-Control) and Promotion among Nontechnical Managers at AT&T

Level of Management Achieved Eight Years after Motives Were Measured	Managers Not Having Leadership Motive Pattern	Managers Having Leadership Motive Pattern
Lower management only (56% of group)	64%	34%
Middle management (44% of group)	36%	66%
Level of Management Achieved Sixteen Years after Motives Were Measured		
Lower management only (37% of group)	43%	21%
Middle management (63% of group)	57%	79%

SOURCE: Adapted from David C. McClelland & Richard E. Boyatzis (1982). Leadership motive pattern and long-term success in management. *Journal of Applied Psychology, 67,* 739.

tion. These techniques have been used primarily for two purposes: to foster minority entrepreneurship within the United States and to contribute to entrepreneurial growth in less developed countries. Box 3-2 provides an example of the former type of effort, and Exhibit 3-3 illustrates the latter type. Note in Exhibit 3-3 that the figures for both trained and untrained groups prior to training and for the untrained group afterward are essentially the same; the big difference is that after achievement-motivation training the trained

group has become much more entrepreneurial. Efforts have also been made to design power-motivation training programs for managers, but evidence on their effectiveness is inconclusive.

Atkinson's Views on Achievement. A number of attempts have been made to elaborate on or reinterpret McClelland's basic theory—too many, in fact, to discuss here. The work of John W. Atkinson, however, merits some attention. Atkinson collaborated with McClel-

---

BOX 3-2 I/O PSYCHOLOGY IN PRACTICE

Achievement-Motivation Training at Metropolitan Economic Development Association

The Metropolitan Economic Development Association, located in the Minneapolis–St. Paul area of Minnesota, is funded by the local business community and the Office of Minority Business Enterprise of the U.S. Department of Commerce. One weekend a month—from noon Friday to noon Sunday over a four-month period—it conducts a program of achievement-motivation training under the title "Business Leadership Training." The participants are small-business owners and potential entrepreneurs—most of them members of minority groups.

The training enables participants to develop achievement-motivated behavior patterns—problem solving, goal setting, business planning, and risk taking—through specially designed business games. Participants experience both the anxieties and satisfactions of setting and achieving personal and business goals; and the experiences are conceptualized to real-life situations through practice. Considerable emphasis is placed on examining and testing goals for specificity, realism, challenge, time-phasing, and personal commitment. Any obstacle that may hinder attaining a goal is closely evaluated. Topics discussed during training include state-created opportunities

for small businesses owned by the socially or economically disadvantaged. Participants also complete the Thematic Apperception Test and learn to interpret it so as to understand their own motives.

An evaluation of the program revealed that after training the participants clearly felt they had changed. Follow-up data over a one- to two-year period seemed to indicate they were right:

Participants, especially business owners, showed personal income increases well above the national average.

Among business owners, gross sales increased at a rate well above the national average.

Over half the business owners expanded their business by adding a new product or service or by opening a new business.

Twelve percent of those participants who had not previously owned a business started one after training.

Source: Metropolitan Economic Development Association (1977). Business leadership training—What's happening. *MEDA Reports, 5* (1), 1–7.

EXHIBIT 3-3   **Results of Achievement-Motivation Training in India**

Entrepreneurial Growth Activities	Two Years before Course		Two Years after course	
	Trained Group	Untrained Control Group	Trained Group	Untrained Control Group
Active in business development	18%	22%	51%	25%
Increased hours worked	7	11	20	7
Started new businesses	4	7	22	8
Made specific fixed capital investment	32	29	74	40
Increased number of employees	35	31	59	33

SOURCE: Adapted from David C. McClelland & David G. Winter (1969). *Motivating economic achievement*, pp. 213–217, 221, and 226. New York: Free Press.

land in the very early studies of achievement motivation, and since then has focused his research on the need to achieve.

Atkinson's (1977, 1982) views are closely allied with expectancy theory, which we will consider later in this chapter. According to Atkinson, the tendency to achieve success is a result of:

1. An individual's motivation toward achievement
2. That individual's expectation of success
3. That individual's valuation of success—how attractive success is as an incentive

This theory adds two important ideas: that the fear of failure can act as a force leading to success, and that long-term, career-oriented striving is an important factor in success. People may be conservative in their short-term achievement efforts simply to preserve the possibility that they will be successful in the long run.

In a further modification of the concept of individual need hierarchies, Atkinson has hypothesized that certain motivations are extinguishable. A highly achievement-motivated person, for example, may strive hard

and well for some time to win a prospective promotion. But if this person's achievement need is not gratified, it ultimately will burn up, and needs lower in the personal hierarchy will begin to control behavior. Ideas like these have obtained considerable research support and represent important extensions of McClelland's views. Taken as a whole, achievement-motivation theory in its various forms is important because it takes certain of the needs considered by Murray and Maslow and specifies how they relate to work performance.

■ ROLE-MOTIVATION THEORIES

John Miner, the author of the present text, has developed four motivation theories, each of which applies to a very specific organizational and occupational context (Miner, 1980a, 1982). These theories deal with hierarchic or managerial motivation, task or entrepreneurial motivation, professional motivation, and group or sociotechnical motivation. The last theory has not as yet been validated by research, so only the first three are treated here. Although more clearly focused in their applications, these theories have something in common with need theories. They assume that internal forces energize and guide behavior, although the individual may not be fully aware of these forces. According to Miner, within each organization there exists a basic understanding of how certain kinds of work roles—managerial, entrepreneurial, and professional—can be performed well. The theories, like McClelland's need-for-achievement theory, are concerned with the motivational forces that combine to influence performance in certain types of jobs and organizational structures.

☐ Hierarchic (Managerial) Role-Motivation Theory

The **hierarchic role-motivation theory** was developed out of experience working with managers at Atlantic-Richfield during the 1950s (Miner, 1965, 1977). The theory suggests that certain strong motives contribute to being a better manager, being more satisfied with managerial work, and striving toward managerial positions.

Roles and Motives. The hierarchic role-motivation theory specifies six managerial roles and the motives that contribute to success in them. Role constellations of this sort are generally found in large, hierarchic business organizations. The roles and their motivational patterns are as follows.

1. Role: positive relations with authority figures; motivation: *a favorable attitude toward people in authority.* In a hierarchic system, there must be communication and interaction with superiors, and favorable attitudes toward authority figures facilitate this.
2. Role: competitive; motivation: *a desire to compete.* As one climbs toward the top of a hierarchic system, rewards such as promotions and high salaries become increasingly scarce, and it is necessary to compete with peers to attain these prizes.

3. Role: imposing wishes; motivation: *a desire to exercise power* over others. A hierarchic system requires managers to impose sanctions on and otherwise influence their subordinates. Those who derive satisfaction from these activities are more likely to perform them successfully.
4. Role: assertive parental; motivation: *a desire to assert oneself.* In a hierarchic system, the managerial role is often modeled on the parental role; accordingly, a take-charge attitude congruent with that role is required.
5. Role: standing out from the group; motivation: *a desire to assume a distinctive, differentiated status.* In a hierarchic system, managers must remain highly visible while at the same time remaining apart from the relative homogeneity of their subordinates. Thus a manager must want to assume a distinctive position.
6. Role: routine administrative; motivation: *a desire to perform routine managerial duties in a responsible manner.* In a hierarchic system, various routine decision-making and communications tasks must be carried out, so appropriate motivation and a sense of responsibility for such matters are required.

Scientific Value and Practical Usefulness. Considerable testing of the hierarchic role-motivation theory has been done. The resulting evidence indicates that the theory works well to predict performance effectiveness within the management ranks of medium-size and large hierarchic organizations. A measure also has been developed that serves to identify the appropriate area of application of the hierarchic theory, and of the three other role-motivation theories as well (Oliver, 1982).

A sizable body of evidence indicates that managerial motivation can be increased in some people through appropriate training. Box 3-3 describes a managerial role-motiva-

BOX 3-3 I/O PSYCHOLOGY IN PRACTICE

Managerial Role-Motivation Training at the University of Denver

A management development program sponsored by the University of Denver for managers in the area provides an example of how managerial role-motivation training works. The participants were seven men and three women in their thirties and forties who held positions in lower and middle management. Several worked for the Adolph Coors Company and the rest were with different firms.

The training was conducted over three days, during which the participants resided at a mansion owned by the university. Lectures and discussion focused on the nature and significance of ineffective performance in a subordinate. The managers were asked to consider various types of performance problems, figure out what might have caused the problems, and determine what could be done to overcome them. The participants also introduced managerial experiences of their own that had presented them with particular difficulties.

In order to determine the effects of training, the managers were tested for managerial motivation when the program began and again when it ended. Five of the managers changed very little over the three days; the other five, however,

exhibited substantial motivational increases. Some examples are as follows.

· A personnel manager for a large firm had below-average managerial motivation at the beginning of the program, but experienced change sufficient to place her above the norm for personnel managers. The improvement was roughly equal across the various aspects of managerial motivation.

· A first-line manufacturing supervisor evinced about average overall managerial motivation for a person in that type of position, with particular strength in his attitude toward authority. Over the period of the course there was a major increase in motivation, especially in his desire to compete and his desire to assert himself.

· A plant purchasing manager who reported to a vice president initially scored well below what would be expected, considering his relatively high position in his company's hierarchy. During the course he showed considerable improvement, although he did not reach a point consonant with his position. Increases were most pronounced in feelings toward authority figures and competitiveness.

tion training program held over a three-day period. The more usual procedure, however, has been to conduct training sessions once or twice a week over several months. Research also reveals that managerial motivation measures can be used effectively to identify people who will perform well in managerial careers.

It is interesting to note that while managerial role-motivation training can yield a change in motivation over a relatively brief period, standard university course work has no such effect. Even exposure to the managerially oriented content of an MBA program in a business school brings about no change in managerial motivation (Bartol & Martin, 1987).

Although the McClelland and Miner theories appear to contain a number of overlapping constructs—need for power and a desire to exercise power, for example—the research on this subject suggests that each theory can stand on its own (Stahl, 1986).

☐ Professional Role-Motivation Theory

The **professional role-motivation theory** applies to professionals working in organizations such as law firms or in private practice, as well as to people such as research and development scientists employed in professional contexts within larger hierarchic organizations. According to the theory, to the extent that people possess professional role motives, they should perform well as professionals, enjoy professional work, and choose professional careers.

Roles and Motives. The professional role-motivation theory is concerned with five roles and their associated motivational forces:

1. Role: knowledge acquisition; motivation: *a desire to learn.* In a professional system, it is essential that technical knowledge and expertise be developed, transmitted, and used in the service of clients.
2. Role: independent action; motivation: *a desire to work independently.* Professionals have private and personally responsible relationships with clients that require independent action based on an individual's best professional judgment.
3. Role: status acceptance; motivation: *a desire to acquire status.* In a professional system, the provision of services to clients is predicated on client recognition of the professional's expert status. Professionals who lack status often find that their services go unutilized.
4. Role: providing help; motivation: *a desire to help others.* In a professional system, the relationship between the professional and the client is central and involves the expectation that the professional will help the client as much as possible.
5. Role: professional commitment; motivation: *a value-based identification with the profession.* Professionals should feel strongly committed to their profession and to its ethical norms.

Scientific Value and Practical Usefulness. The professional role-motivation theory was developed and tested using professors who taught management courses at colleges and universities (Miner, 1980b). As expected, pro-

fessional motives were found to be much stronger among those who had successful careers. Managerial motivation, in contrast, was unrelated to performance as a professor. Exhibit 3-4 shows the results of a study conducted among labor arbitrators (most of them lawyers), who render judgments in disputes between unions and management. When management representatives evaluated the arbitrators' performances, a positive correlation was found between high ratings and high professional motivation. Those arbitrators who were not highly motivated were judged to be less competent. It appears that the professional role-motivation theory is a good predictor of professional performance in this context.

☐ Task Role-Motivation Theory

In the preceding two role-motivation theories, success is measured in accordance with the expectations of superiors or professional norms. The **task role-motivation theory,** in contrast, deals with organizational situations where definitions of success and failure are inherent in the demands of the task itself. An entrepreneur, for example, can either make a fortune or go bankrupt, depending on the extent to which the impersonal task criteria of the marketplace are met. The theory developed to deal with this kind of situation has much in common with McClelland's achievement-motivation theory. People who possess strong task role motives would be expected to be successful entrepreneurs, to enjoy being entrepreneurs, and to want to start their own companies.

Roles and Motives. The task role-motivation theory deals with the following five roles and their associated motives:

1. Role: individual achievement; motivation: *a desire to achieve through one's own efforts and to be able to accept the credit for one's*

Exhibit 3-4   Professional Motivation of Labor Arbitrators Who Are Rated as Low and High Performers

Professional Motivation Measures	Percentage of Arbitrators Rated Low or High in Performance with Various Professional Motivation Scores	
	Percentage Rated Low	Percentage Rated High
Overall professional motivation:		
High	22	54
Medium	39	26
Low	39	20
Desire to acquire knowledge:		
High	26	50
Medium	29	35
Low	45	15
Desire to act independently:		
High	26	45
Medium	48	35
Low	26	20
Desire to acquire status:		
High	22	45
Medium	26	35
Low	52	20
Desire to help others:		
High	26	41
Medium	39	46
Low	35	13
Value-based professional commitment:		
High	32	54
Medium	10	28
Low	58	18

own success. In a task system, it is important that people be drawn toward task performance rather than seek means of avoiding it, and a major incentive is an intrinsic desire to achieve.

2. Role: risk avoidance; motivation: *a desire to avoid risk,* to leave as little as possible to chance. In a task system, continued performance depends on the capacity to maintain personal control over outcomes so that

some unexpected event does not undermine the whole effort. Too much risk can mean organizational failure that forces the entrepreneur out of the role he or she likes best. This emphasis on avoiding risk is at variance with common conceptions of the entrepreneurial role.

3. Role: seeking results of behavior; motivation: *a desire for feedback.* In a task system, feedback on the level and results of one's

performance is necessary so that one can attribute success to one's own efforts. For many entrepreneurs, profit measures are a primary source of feedback.

4. Role: personal innovation; motivation: *a desire to introduce innovative solutions.* Innovations, because they can easily be identified as one's own, have been found to strengthen the desire to achieve in a task system.

5. Role: planning and goal setting; motivation: *a desire to plan*—to think about the future and anticipate future possibilities. Individuals who enjoy setting and then working toward future rewards are more likely to succeed in a task system.

Scientific Value and Practical Usefulness. Much of the support for task role-motivation theory derives from the work already reviewed dealing with achievement-motivation theory. That theory has demonstrated considerable value and usefulness in the limited domain of entrepreneurship. Because of the similarity in the two theories, one would expect that achievement-motivation training, as described in Box 3-2, would serve to increase task as well as achievement motivation, and that achievement-motivation measures would be applicable within the task domain.

Exhibit 3-5 summarizes results of a direct test of task motivation theory in a number of small high-tech firms. Note that, in general, task motivation levels are consistently higher among the entrepreneurs who started their own firms than among managers and scientists who did not. A closer look reveals that the entrepreneurs whose firms have grown more rapidly are characterized by higher task motivation than either the nonentrepreneurial managers and scientists or the entrepreneurs of slower-growing firms. As with the managerial and professional theories, the task theory appears to provide valuable information on the motive pattern that makes for good performance in a major work arena (Miner, Smith, & Bracker, 1989).

■ EQUITY THEORY

A number of different theories involving concepts of deprivation, justice, fairness, and equity have been developed in the social sciences to explain aspects of motivation (Cook & Hegtvedt, 1983). Among these, the **equity theory** of J. Stacy Adams is most relevant for our purposes, in part because it is spelled out in detail and in part because it focuses directly on organizational behavior and performance (Adams, 1963, 1965). Adams devel-

Exhibit 3-5   Average Task Motivation Scores of High-Tech Entrepreneurs and Nonentrepreneurial Manager/Scientists in Similar Firms (Expressed as a Percentage of the Range of Scores)

Task Motivation Measures	Managers/Scientists	Entrepreneurs		
		Total Group	Owners of Firms with:	
			Little Growth	Faster Growth
Overall task motivation	57%	70%	53%	87%
Desire to achieve through one's own efforts	56	67	52	81
Desire to avoid risks	50	58	50	66
Desire for an index of performance level	34	45	35	54
Desire to introduce innovations	74	79	68	90
Desire to think about the future and plan	56	62	54	69

oped his views in the 1960s while employed as a personnel research psychologist with the General Electric Company.

☐ Formulas and Propositions

Adam's theory is rooted in the traditional employee–employer exchange whereby the employee gives something (inputs) and then gets something in exchange (outcomes) from the employer. To elicit rewards, inputs, such as some kind of work effort, must be relevant to the employment relationship. Similarly, outcomes, such as pay, will not be effective unless they are seen as meaningful compensation. Exhibit 3-6 lists inputs and outcomes considered important by clerical and production workers. Note that the two groups do not necessarily think alike, especially in the case of inputs.

The balance in the employment exchange can be calculated by dividing a person's outcomes by inputs. If the outcomes are greater, the person is being overrewarded; if the inputs are greater, the person is being underrewarded. But whether either of these imbalances contributes to feelings of inequity depends on how the person involved perceives the inputs and outcomes of his or her **reference group,** such as coworkers, relatives, or fellow professionals. The exchange does not occur in a vacuum; it must be evaluated against some norm. If one sees oneself as being treated in the same way as one's chosen reference group, a feeling of **equity** results. The following formula applies:

$$\frac{\text{Person's Outcomes}}{\text{Person's Inputs}} = \frac{\text{Reference Group's Outcomes}}{\text{Reference Group's Inputs}}$$

Ideally, in this calculation, outcomes and inputs should be weighted so as to reflect their relevance to the situation (Vecchio, 1984). Thus outcomes such as pay or job security are generally given greater weight than, say, interpersonal relations with peers.

Inequity motivation, which develops when the two ratios depart from each other in either direction, induces a person to act to restore equity. If someone experiences overreward (relative to the reference source), there may be a feeling of guilt; if there is underreward, anger is often aroused. (As might be expected, the anger response is set off much more easily than the guilt reaction.) Strong inequity motivation commonly results in situations where workers feel they are putting in long hours and working very hard for little pay, while management is taking long lunches and collecting huge bonuses.

Adam's formula for calculating equity and inequity can be supplemented with the following propositions, which Adams incorporated into his theory:

1. Individuals will try to maximize their overall outcomes (rewards minus punishments).
2. Groups and organizations can maximize their collective reward by developing systems for equitably apportioning resources among members and then encouraging members to accept and adhere to those systems.
3. In general, groups and organizations will reward members who treat others equitably and punish members who treat others inequitably.
4. Individuals who believe that they are in inequitable job relationships will become distressed and will attempt to eliminate their distress by restoring equity. The greater the inequity, the greater the distress, and the more intense the effort to restore equity (Hatfield & Sprecher, 1984, p. 96).

A good example of an organizational equity system is job evaluation, which serves to analyze jobs so that greater outcomes (usually

EXHIBIT 3-6 **Rankings of Various Employment Inputs and Outcomes by Clerical Workers and Production Workers**

Inputs	Rankings	
	Clerical Workers	*Production Workers*
Quality of work performed	1	*
Reliability	2.5	2
Acceptance of responsibility	2.5	8
Job knowledge	4	*
Cooperation with others	5.5	*
Self-improvement	5.5	*
Attitude	8	8
Quantity of work performed	8	4.5
Initiative	8	*
Intelligence	*	2
Personal involvement with task accomplishment	*	2
Experience	*	4.5
Adaptability-versatility	*	6
Written communication skill	*	8

Outcomes	Rankings	
	Clerical Workers	*Production Workers*
Job security	1	4.5
Pay	2.5	1
Competent supervisor	2.5	4.5
Possibility of growth	4.5	2.5
Fair supervisor	4.5	6.5
Recognition	7	8
Adequate working conditions	7	*
Interpersonal relations with supervisor	7	*
Achievement	10	9
Interpersonal relations with peers	10	*
Adequate planning and management	10	6.5
Advancement	*	2.5

*Ranked eleventh or above.

SOURCE: Adapted from Thomas J. Atchison & David W. Belcher (1971), Equity, rewards, and compensation administration. *Personnel Administration, 34* (2), 34. David W. Belcher & Thomas J. Atchison (1970). Equity theory and compensation policy. *Personnel Administration, 33* (3), 28.

pay raises) are provided in direct proportion to the increased work inputs required.

☐ Reactions to Inequity

A number of approaches may be taken to reduce inequity tension and restore equity. Probably most common are attempts to alter inputs and outcomes. A person who feels underpaid may contribute less time and effort to the job, thus reducing inputs. A person who feels overpaid might recommend a job restudy in an effort to bring the pay level down, thus reducing outcomes. Or the individual might donate a portion of his or her income to charity, thus reducing available cash and avoiding guilt.

It is also possible, at least for some people, to distort the level or importance of inputs and outcomes. People can and do find ways to perceive the level of their pay as different from what it really is; a person may remember last year's bonus as having been much larger than it actually was, for example. People can also justify disproportionately high outcomes by convincing themselves that they possess more job knowledge or intelligence than they actually do. Those who can find no way to restore equity may opt to escape the job situation by failing to report to work, requesting a transfer, or resigning. When this is not feasible, some people attempt to influence their reference group. The reference group's inputs and outcomes may come to be viewed in a different light, or a coworker may be pressured into leaving. Sometimes pressures from the reference group are encouraged, forcing workers to reduce their inputs. On occasion, the person switches his or her reference group in order to achieve the perception of greater equity. For instance, a very ambitious manager, who has been comparing himself to the company's top management, may decide instead to use his peers in the same department as a reference group.

The Ann Mongio example at the beginning of this chapter provides an instance of what can happen when a change in reference group produces a feeling of inequity.

☐ Scientific Value and Practical Usefulness

Research on equity theory often has been of the laboratory type, rather than field research, and has typically focused on the pay outcome. Conditions of overreward and/or underreward have been created experimentally, and the effects on performance have been observed. Box 3-4 provides an example of this type of research. Researchers have not yet developed measures of tension, guilt, and anger generated by inequity, inequity thresholds, and the like. Such measures are needed to move the theory forward, but even without them it is apparent that equity theory possesses considerable validity; it can predict both in its overreward and underreward aspects, although behavioral scientists believe that many overreward inequities are soon corrected through distortion and do not have long-term effects on performance. In contrast, research has shown, underreward inequity causes both absenteeism and turnover.

It is often difficult to apply equity theory in practice, as distinct from the more controlled laboratory settings where it has been tested, because of its lack of precision. What reference group will a given person use, and when? What reactions to inequity can be anticipated with a particular person in a particular situation? How do various individuals come to view certain factors as inputs and outcomes?

These practical problems are compounded by some uncertainty regarding when, where, and how inequity motivation operates. Researchers believe that two basic motives are involved and that each operates somewhat differently. One is a need to reduce guilt

BOX **3-4** RESEARCH IN I/O PSYCHOLOGY

The Initial Research on Equity Theory at New York University

A study was conducted at New York University in which students referred by the university placement office were hired to conduct market research interviews. The advertised rate for the work was $3.50 per hour, and the initial implication was that the work would continue for several months.

The twenty-two students who were hired were split into two equal groups, and all were actually paid at the rate of $3.50 per hour. At the time of hiring the experimental subjects were exposed to treatment intended to make them feel inequitably overcompensated for their work. They were told, "You don't have nearly enough experience in interviewing or survey work of the kind we're engaged in," but nevertheless, after some agonizing, they were hired. The control subjects, in contrast, were led to believe that their inputs were entirely appropriate to the pay and that they met all the qualifications. Thus, a condition of equity was established vis-à-vis "interviewers in general" as a reference source.

The interviewing job was terminated after roughly 2½ hours. Productivity in the experimental group, where presumably guilt had been induced, was significantly higher than among the controls. This is what equity theory predicts—in order to justify their inequitably high outcomes (pay), the experimental subjects should exert more effort to compensate for their lack of experience as an input, thus conducting more interviews in the allotted time.

Subsequent research was able to demonstrate that the greater output of the overreward inequity subjects was not caused by insecurity over the possibility of losing their jobs (Adams & Jacobsen, 1964).

SOURCE: J. Stacy Adams & William B. Rosenbaum (1962). The relationship of worker productivity to cognitive dissonance about wage inequities. *Journal of Applied Psychology, 46,* 161–164.

---

or shame; the other is a need to reduce anger or hatred. In the former instance, sizable differences between individuals play an important role. The theory of overreward inequity appears to work best with those who have a strong conscience and a sense of what is ethically appropriate (Vecchio, 1981). Such people may well mobilize guilt more readily. Similar processes probably operate with regard to anger reduction; thus, inequity reduction is generally less pronounced in certain cultural contexts and among gamblers, who presumably are used to inequities at the hands of chance. We have noted that the relative importance of certain inputs and outcomes varies, as can be seen in the comparison of clerical and production employees in Exhibit 3-6. The point is that the theory works differently with one person than another, and that it may not work with some people at all (Griffeth, Vecchio, & Logan, 1989). It obviously has its appropriate domain, but the exact nature of that domain is not clear.

Because of the emphasis on laboratory studies, little is known about how various types of inequity motivation can be influenced in practice. Certainly, matters of inequity have been of concern to compensation specialists for many years, but they appear to have utilized the specific tenets of equity theory very little in their work; the same can be said of vocational-guidance counselors. Overall, the major practical significance of equity theory is in its delineation of some very important motives that operate in the workplace. Beyond that it has much potential, but that potential has not been fully realized as yet (Scholl, Cooper, & McKenna, 1987). In any event, it is clear that equity theory is a quite different type of motivation theory than the need theories and role-motivation theories we have considered previously. Furthermore, it is not merely a theory of monetary compensation: It extends to nonmonetary factors such as status rewards as well (Greenberg, 1988).

■ EXPECTANCY THEORIES

Since they were first formulated in terms having relevance for industrial-organizational psychology, **expectancy theories** have been proposed in a number of forms. All, however, are based on the idea that behavior and performance are a result of conscious choice and that people will choose to do whatever they believe will result in the highest payoffs for them personally (Mitchell, 1982a; Landy & Becker, 1987). The earliest comprehensive theoretical presentations were those of Victor Vroom (1964) and Lyman Porter and Edward Lawler (1968). Lawler has continued to conduct research, write, and develop applications related to the theory. Since his views are the most current, the discussion of expectancy theory here is centered on them. Again, it should be recognized that expectancy theory, in any form, represents an approach to motivation different from any we have previously considered. There are some similarities, however, as we will see later.

□ The Model

Exhibit 3-7 provides a comprehensive picture of the expectancy model as it applies to motivation. In this model, **effort-to-performance** expectancy refers to the expectation (that is, the assessed probability) that if effort is exerted, the result will be successful performance (though successful performance may *not* result because the job is too difficult, the evaluation process is deficient, or the individual lacks the needed skills). **Performance-to-outcome expectancy** refers to the expectation (assessed probability) that should effort be successfully exerted, something that is desired will result, such as a financial reward. An incentive system may be in effect that specifies a certain pay level for so many units produced. The person believes this, and expects to be paid the designated amount upon completing the specified number of units. This is a performance-to-outcome expectancy. But it makes a difference only if the outcome, such as pay, has **valence**—that is, value or attractiveness. If the person has just inherited a fortune and does not care about the relatively small amount of pay involved, then additional pay as an outcome will not work as well in the motivational calculus as, say, an improvement in working conditions.

The distinction between first- and second-level outcomes in Exhibit 3-7 is important. A person may value pay in its own right, as for instance an entrepreneur who views the business's earnings and her own as feedback on how well she has achieved through her own efforts—an index of performance. But pay may also be a means to second-level outcomes. A person may want the money in order to achieve an affluent lifestyle and impress others who are viewed as important. Then pay must be considered in terms of its **instrumentality** for gaining the second-level outcome of a more affluent lifestyle. If the pay involved is not enough to gain what is desired, then it lacks instrumentality—and motivational impact. **Intrinsic outcomes** are those that come from within a person—feelings of accomplishment, of doing important work, of freedom. **Extrinsic outcomes** are provided or mediated by external

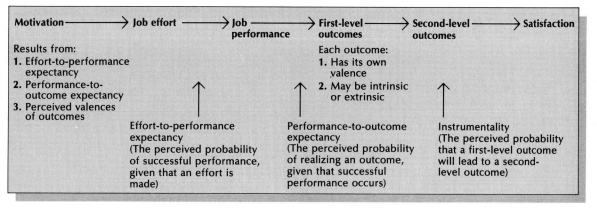

EXHIBIT 3-7   The Expectancy Theory Model
Expectancy theory posits that expectancies—perceptions of various cause-and-effect relationships—exert influence at different points on the continuum from motivation through job performance to satisfaction.
SOURCE: Adapted from Edward E. Lawler (1981). *Pay and organization development,* pp. 21, 231, and 234. Reading, MA: Addison-Wesley.

forces—a superior, the organization, other work-group members. This too is an important distinction.

The level of motivation in a given job situation is expressed in expectancy-theory terms by a formula. Questionnaires are used to measure the components of this formula, and the scores obtained are inserted in it. The formula is:

Motivation = Effort-to-Performance Expectancy × Sum of All Operating Factors (Performance-to-Outcome Expectancies × Their Valences)

Inherent in this formula are the following ideas:

1. A person's motivation to perform is determined by the performance-to-outcome expectancy multiplied by the valence of the outcome. The valence of the first-level outcome subsumes the instrumentalities and valences of the related second-level outcomes. The relationship is multiplicative: No motivation exists when either performance-to-outcome expectancy or valence is 0.

2. Since a level of performance has multiple outcomes associated with it, the products of all performance-to-outcome expectancies × valence combinations are added together for all the outcomes seen as relevant to the specific performance.

3. The summed performance-to-outcome expectancies × valences is then multiplied by the effort-to-performance expectancy. Again, the multiplicative relationship indicates that if either effort-to-performance expectancy or the summed performance-to-outcome expectancies times their valences is 0, motivation is 0.

4. Summarizing, the strength of a person's motivation to perform effectively is influenced by:
   (a) The person's belief that effort can be converted into performance; and
   (b) The net attractiveness of the events that are perceived to stem from good performance (Lawler, 1981, pp. 232–233).

These ideas are very similar to the precepts of behavioral decision theory (Naylor, Pritchard, & Ilgen, 1980) which involves conscious choices just as expectancy theories do, but tends to break down the process of choice into a greater number of components and thus achieves considerably greater complexity. Since they have not been adequately researched, however, the discussion here will not dwell on behavioral-decision-theory approaches to motivation beyond what is inherent in the expectancy-theory formulations.

☐ Scientific Value and Practical Usefulness

The components of expectancy theory have been measured, and as a consequence research related to the theory has been abundant. The measures, however, have been almost entirely of a conscious, self-report nature, where subjects attribute probabilities, make choices, and indicate importance; often the measures have been very short, containing very few questions. In the early years the measures used were not very good, and tests of the theory were often disappointing. More recently there have been major improvements in measures (Ilgen, Nebeker, & Pritchard, 1981). It is now apparent that expectancy theory can accurately predict a person's work effort, satisfaction level, and performance. People may not actually go through the whole complex process, but expectancy theory provides a good approximation of what they do go through (Ilgen & Klein, 1989).

It is also apparent that the theory works in certain contexts but not in others. There must be clearly established performance-to-outcome expectancies (that is, contingent rewards). The person must believe that performing well will bring desired results. The theory assumes conscious choice and maximizing, highly rational thought processes. Expectancy theory appears to work best with people who have an *internal* locus of con-

trol—who truly believe that what they do is their own decision and that they can control their own destiny. Expectancy theory does not work well with people who have an *external* locus of control—who believe that they are at the mercy of fate, luck, or other powerful outside forces. Given the appropriate kind of people, expectancy theory can yield reliable predictions of performance in companies where:

- People are recognized and rewarded in proportion to the excellence of their performance.
- Merit salary increase percentages are an accurate reflection of relative performance.
- The promotion system helps the best person get to the top, so that people with ability have a promising future.

That expectancy theory appears to work so well in the appropriate context, and yet has not developed much in the way of actual applications, is a major problem. Changing expectancies, deliberately creating an appropriate organizational context, purposely selecting people who will perform best under expectancy-theory conditions, and other strategies simply have not been tried. The theory seems to work particularly well in predicting the occupations and work organizations that students will choose upon leaving their studies (Ilgen & Klein, 1988; Wanous, Keon, & Latack, 1983). Yet specific methods of using the theory in vocational-guidance practice have not been developed. The major area in which expectancy theory has been applied is that of "cafeteria compensation"—programs that allow employees to select from among alternative outcomes those that have the highest valence for them, thus enabling the company to spend its compensation dollars in ways most likely to have a motivating effect. One such individualized approach to compensation is described in Box 3-5. This

BOX 3-5   I/O PSYCHOLOGY IN PRACTICE

"Cafeteria Compensation" at TRW

TRW, in its Defense and Space Systems Group, headquartered in Redondo Beach, California, was the first major U.S. company to institute a "cafeteria compensation" program that permits employees to make choices involving pay and various benefits. Prior to initiating its program, TRW conducted extensive surveys of employees on the subject. It was clear that individual preferences did exist and that employees would welcome the opportunity to align outcomes with individual valences. The actual choices that employees made mirrored the findings of the preliminary surveys.

The starting point for "cafeteria compensation" was the amount of medical and life insurance the company already paid for. Employees are required to keep a certain minimum of these two types of insurance, but beyond that minimum, they can choose to take their share of the surplus funds in cash or apply it to the purchase of additional benefits such as accidental death and dismemberment insurance or life insurance for their dependents. Employees can and do make changes in their choices as their circumstances and valences change. The employee information needed to administer the plan is maintained in a computerized system.

SOURCE: Shirley A. Curry (1982). A corporate response: The TRW experience. In Dallas L. Salisbury (Ed.), *America in transition: Implications for employee benefits*, pp. 55–71. Washington, DC: Employee Benefits Research Institute.

particular plan was developed at TRW, which, along with Educational Testing Service and American Can Company, was among the first firms to use the approach. Other plans now offer employees choices in reimbursement for child-care expense, additional paid vacation, more holidays, and other benefits.

KEY TERMS

Comparable worth

Motivation

Need-hierarchy theory

Achievement-motivation theory

Prepotent (prepotency)

Achievement motivation

Entrepreneurs (entrepreneurship)

Thematic Apperception Test (TAT)

Hierarchic role-motivation theory

Professional role-motivation theory

Task role-motivation theory

Equity theory

Reference group

Equity

Inequity motivation

Expectancy theories

Effort-to-performance expectancy

Performance-to-outcome expectancy

Valence

Instrumentality

Intrinsic outcomes

Extrinsic outcomes

EXHIBIT 3-8   **Ratings of the Scientific Validity and Practical Usefulness of Theories Considered in This Chapter**

	Scientific Validity		Practical Usefulness
Motivation Theory	*Locke & Henne* *(1 = none, 5 = very high)*	*Miner* *(1 = low, 3 = high)*	*Miner* *(1 = low, 3 = high)*
Need hierarchy	1.5	1	1
Achievement motivation	2.5	3	3
Role motivation	4.0	3	3
Equity	2.5	3	1
Expectancy	3.5	3	2

SOURCE: Adapted from Edwin A. Locke and Douglas Henne (1986). Work motivation. In Cary L. Cooper & I. Robertson (Eds.), *Review of industrial and organizational psychology*. Chichester, England: Wiley. John B. Miner (1984). The validity and usefulness of theories in an emerging organizational science. *Academy of Management Review, 9,* 296–306.

SUMMARY

We have considered four basic types of motivational theories that are important to organizational psychology: need, role motivation, equity, and expectancy. *Need-hierarchy theory* appears to be important because it asserts the *prepotency* of lower-level physiological and safety needs, and because it notes many other needs important in organizational psychology. *Achievement-motivation theory* serves the useful purpose of relating *achievement motivation* to *entrepreneurship* and emphasizing the importance of power and affiliation motivation in management.

The various *role-motivation theories* point up key motivational processes within strategic jobs in various organizational contexts—*hierarchic, professional, task,* and group. They then establish pivotal roles and the motives to meet them within each context. *Equity theory* explains why *motivation from inequity,* especially underreward inequity, is important and how it operates. *Expectancy theories* facilitate understanding of conscious, rational, maximizing motivation under circumstances that are congruent with this type of motivation.

Exhibit 3-8 provides information on the value and usefulness of the theories considered in this chapter, as rated in two independent assessments. Note that there is considerable agreement with regard to scientific validity—how well the theories held up under the close scrutiny of research investigation. Note also that although practical usefulness requires scientific validity, the latter does not guarantee usefulness; expectancy and, in particular, equity theories have not exhibited the usefulness that their ratings of scientific validity might suggest.

QUESTIONS

1. How do inputs, outcomes, and reference sources operate in equity theory, and what problems does the theory have in dealing with these concepts?

2. With what kinds of people and under what organizational circumstances does expectancy theory work best? Why do you believe this is so?

3. How does the hierarchic (managerial) role-motivation theory operate, and what evidence is there of its value?

4. What are the types of needs included in need-hierarchy theory, and how do they relate to one another—in theory and in fact?

5. What are the key factors in expectancy theory, and how do they relate to one another?

6. How are Murray's need theory, Maslow's need-hierarchy theory, and McClelland's achievement-motivation theory related?

7. In what ways are the other role-motivation theories similar to and different from the hierarchic theory? How valid and useful are these other theories?

8. To what extent, how, and under what circumstances can the motives of McClelland's theory be influenced and developed?

9. In what respects does a perception of inequity serve to influence performance? Give examples.

10. How do achievement, power, and affiliation needs relate to performance in different contexts?

CASE PROBLEM

ADELE JONES
Publishing Executive

Adele Jones grew up in a middle-class family in the suburbs of Chicago. She did well in school, being something of a leader in various activities, and attended a small but prestigious liberal-arts college. There she worked on the school newspaper and eventually became managing editor, a job she thoroughly enjoyed—so thoroughly, in fact, that there was some question for a while as to whether she would devote enough effort to her studies to graduate.

One of Adele's most difficult decisions in college was the choice of a major. She probably would have selected business management if that had been available, but the college did not offer business courses and her family felt strongly that a liberal arts college was best for her. Finally her choice came down to English or political science. English was attractive because she had always done well in it and liked to write; she felt secure in it, and many of the people she knew on the paper were English majors. Political science was new to her, but she was attracted by the opportunity to learn about how people gained and retained power and influence. Finally she decided upon English, in large part because her father thought that would be better for her. She was never sure all through college whether she had made the right choice.

Adele's roommate in college was a psychology major named Shirley. Shirley found Adele fascinating, but never felt that she understood her. In a way the indecision over a major seemed to sum up the two sides of Adele, and it was almost impossible at any time to tell which side would win out. One side was very conventional; Adele wanted to do the right and expected thing and was very responsive to influence from her peers and her professors. It was not that she had any great need to be with people or to join groups. In fact, in many ways she was something of a loner. But when she was with people, she seemed to have a strong need to go along and not rock the boat—to conform to what she thought was expected of her, to play the role that others assigned to her.

The other side of Adele that Shirley saw was a woman who enjoyed getting others to do things for her. Adele was not really a very active person, but because she surrounded herself with people who were, she was able to get a lot done. Shirley herself sometimes felt manipulated and used; she was always running errands for Adele in situations that made it seem impossible to say no. Furthermore, underneath Adele's inclination to be a "nice person" and to do the "right thing" was a very strong desire to get what she wanted. Adele could be very patient, but in the end she did not like to lose—a fact that came out on the golf course very clearly. She had run a real campaign for the managing editor's job at the newspaper, and that campaign had started the day she joined the paper as a freshman. Adele seemed to want to position herself at the center of the action, but she also wanted to be in control of every situation so that nothing unexpected would happen. She was willing to work very hard and long to structure things the way she wanted them.

When the two young women graduated, Shirley still was not sure she understood Adele, nor was she sure that Adele understood herself. Adele had had some thoughts of going on to graduate school, perhaps to get an MBA, as Shirley was going to do. Yet because her college grades were not very good, she figured she could not get into one of the better programs and decided against it. She went home to the Chicago suburbs, married Peter, a young man she had known since childhood, and ultimately became a full-time housewife with several children to raise.

Peter took a job with a publishing house in the Chicago area and began to do some writing on the side. He sold a few articles, but that did not pay much, and finally he started writing books. He got to be quite good at it, and in many ways enjoyed the writing more than his work with the publishing firm.

Gradually, as the children entered school, Adele began working with Peter on his writing. She kept his files, did library research, wrote letters, and eventually even wrote first drafts for some of his chapters. She seemed to want to learn everything she could, and Peter was glad to teach her. He appreciated her help and told her so. At the same time, however, he felt that Adele's efforts were increasingly devoted less to helping him than to helping herself by learning the publishing business. There were times when she got involved with aspects of his work at the publishing company as well as his writing. She knew most of the people there and took pains to stay on good terms with them. Sometimes Peter felt that he was working for her, rather than vice versa. She knew about and expressed her opinion on almost everything he did. As a result, their relationship became somewhat strained.

Then one day Adele informed Peter that she had taken a job at the same publishing house where he worked. She felt that her absence from their home would not represent a problem because her salary would easily cover the expense of hiring a housekeeper. Over the next few years Adele did very well, and before long was moved into management. She was completely involved in her own work and no longer concerned herself with Peter's activities. In a way that was a relief to him, but it was also disconcerting; maybe, he thought, she had been using him all along, rather than trying to help him. Another irritant was Adele's habit of pointing out how well she was doing in *his* company while he was not moving up at all (although his writing was going very well).

Eventually the couple separated and divorce proceedings were initiated. Adele hired an expensive and high-powered lawyer who got her a handsome settlement as well as custody of the children. Not long after the divorce became final, Adele was placed in charge of a major division in her company; the job was well above Peter's, and so was the pay.

Questions

1. What kinds of motives appear to be at the top of Adele's motivational hierarchy? Can you see any changes in the patterns that dominate her behavior over time?

2. Which among the motivation theories discussed in this chapter help most to explain Adele's behavior? Document your answer with reference to specific points in the case.

3. How do you personally feel about Adele and the course of her career?

4

Motivational Practices and Their Theories

When management by objectives (MBO) was introduced at Honeywell, Inc., the Minneapolis-based electronics firm, it assumed a central role in the company's management. It was the means by which decentralized decision making, where decisions were moved down in the organization as far as possible, was carried out. All supervisors throughout the company set objectives for themselves and the units they supervised. Some divisions went even further, expecting *all* employees to set objectives and to use them in managing their job responsibilities.

In general, each person set approximately ten key goals. If properly formulated, these ten key goals covered the full range of the person's job responsibilities. Part of the goal-setting process required managers and their superiors to agree on a ranking and weighting for the set of objectives. Several times during the year the company reviewed progress toward goals. Goals could be changed, but such changes were generally discouraged.

The first unit of Honeywell's basic management course discussed the concepts of management by objectives, and that theme ran through all the subsequent units. The company ran workshops, training institutes, and divisional courses on management by objectives. The training department issued written materials and sent individual memos. The manager of training made countless telephone calls and personal visits, counseling managers on how to set goals, how to develop measures of progress, how to manage by objectives. After setting goals and then measuring the outcome, the company used the resulting data as the basis for appraisal of managerial performance. Levels of compensation also were substantially affected by the MBO system.

It was recognized that this system could be subverted for salary-change purposes. For instance, a boss could approve easy goals so that a person could build an inflated record of "achievement" that would justify a salary increase which the boss wished to grant for other reasons. Yet it was believed that subverting the system in this way would be difficult, because all individual goals had to fit into the organization's overall network of goals, and too-easy goals would conspicuously fail to do so.

SOURCE: Walter S. Wikstrom (1968). *Managing by—and with—objectives,* pp. 21–26. New York: The Conference Board.

Many companies, like Honeywell, introduced MBO on a major scale during the late 1950s and 1960s as a means of motivating primarily managerial job performance. The practice began at General Electric without reference to any particular theory and without having accrued any research. Only later did research and theory, in this case emanating from the laboratory, begin to attach itself to developing practice. This is characteristic of several of the motivational approaches considered in this chapter. Also considered are certain practices that began as applications of a particular theory but that moved rapidly, as a result of practical experience, to a position quite distant from the original theoretical base; the practices have now evolved to a point where they are really not applications of the original theories at all.

Yet all of these practices implicitly or explicitly presuppose an internal motivational process. They are used to arouse, direct, and maintain motivation at work, just as MBO is. Some now have a good theoretical base, while in other cases relevant theory is fragmentary at best; all, however, have been the subject of considerable research. We begin with the subject of goal setting generally, and then relate this to MBO practice.

■ GOAL SETTING

Although goal setting in industry is not new, only recently have we begun to learn how goal setting relates to performance and how it works best. This increase in understanding and use stems from the work of Edwin Locke.

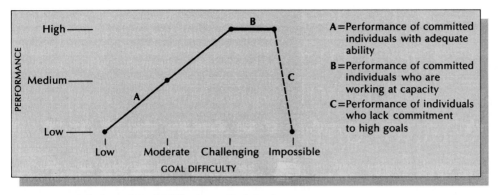

EXHIBIT 4-1   Relation of Goal Difficulty to Task Performance
The highest performance level is that of individuals committed to achieving difficult goals, who are thus stimulated to work at capacity.
SOURCE: Edwin A. Locke & Gary P. Latham (1984). *Goal setting: A motivational technique that works,* p. 22. Englewood Cliffs, NJ: Prentice-Hall.

Locke originally viewed his formulations, not as a theory, but as a technique to be applied in practice; he has, however, increasingly added theoretical concepts (Locke & Latham, 1990).

☐ Locke's Concept of Goal Setting

Locke's propositions regarding **goal setting** are as follows (Locke & Henne, 1986):

1. Difficult goals lead to higher task performance than easy goals, with performance levels on moderate goals falling between the two.
2. Specific, difficult goals lead to higher performance than no goals or vague goals such as "do your best."
3. The mechanisms by which goals affect performance are
   Directing attention and action
   Mobilizing effort
   Increasing persistence
   Motivating a search for appropriate performance strategies.
4. Feedback appears necessary for goal setting to work, because it allows people to compare their performance against their goals.
5. Goal commitment is necessary if goals are to affect performance.
6. Goal commitment is generally unaffected by the degree to which people participate in setting their own goals, but it is affected by expectations of success and degree of success.
7. Money rewards may encourage spontaneous goal setting, may lead to higher goals being set, and may lead to higher goal commitment.
8. Individual differences in factors such as personality and education are not generally related to goal-setting effectiveness.

Locke's first two propositions, emphasizing the important role of difficulty and specificity in goal setting, are central to the technique. Exhibit 4-1 documents how goal difficulty relates to performance.

The process by which goal setting operates is demonstrated in Exhibit 4-2. An important aspect of this model is the fact that goal setting itself is the factor closest to action, or performance. Because it is so close, it is

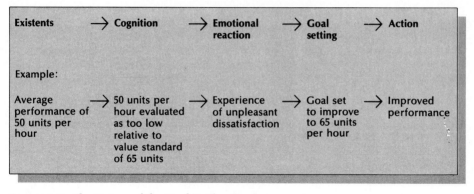

EXHIBIT 4-2   The Nature of the Goal-Setting Process
An individual's reactions to existing performance may lead to new goal setting, and thus to improved performance.

expected to be the best predictor of performance.

Scientific Value and Practical Usefulness of Locke's Formulations. There is ample evidence that goal setting carried out as Locke suggests does improve performance about 90 percent of the time (Locke, Shaw, Saari, & Latham, 1981; Mento, Steel, & Karren, 1987; Tubbs, 1986). The earliest such evidence came primarily from laboratory studies in which college students were assigned goals of varying difficulty and type, and their performance on inconsequential tasks observed. Through the efforts of Gary Latham, this work was extended to the organizational context. There is now considerable evidence that goal setting works in the real world just as it does in the laboratory. A good example of how this occurs appears in Box 4-1, about goal setting by logging crews supplying timber to Georgia Kraft Company.

An important, and still not fully answered, question is whether goal setting works best with certain kinds of people. Are some people more likely than others to set goals, set difficult goals, define specific goals, or seek out the necessary feedback information? Here McClelland's theory of achievement motivation appears to be relevant (Hollenbeck,

Williams, & Klein, 1989; Matsui, Okada, & Kakuyama, 1982). Individuals with strong achievement motives seem to be more responsive to goal setting in certain of its performance-related aspects. This came out clearly in a study conducted in Japan, in which college students set their own goals. A reasonable conclusion is that goal setting should be both prevalent and highly effective among entrepreneurs.

Research also indicates that goal setting is particularly effective among those who are characterized by high levels of self-esteem (Hollenbeck & Brief, 1987). Apparently, what happens in goal setting is that individuals come to exert more effort on the task and also do more planning and organizing to carry out the task; the way in which performance is influenced is very similar to the way job knowledge affects performance (Earley, Wojnaroski, & Prest, 1987). It is not surprising that self-esteem, especially self-esteem related to the specific task at hand, creates a highly favorable context for goal setting. Another finding may also be tied to self-esteem. In general it appears that setting difficult and specific goals works better to improve performance when the task to be accomplished is not very complex. Goal setting works with very complex tasks, but not as well (Wood,

BOX 4-1 RESEARCH IN I/O PSYCHOLOGY

Goal Setting by Logging Crews Supplying Timber to Georgia Kraft Company

Much of the logging in the southern United States is done by independent operators who hire their own crews and sell cut timber to large wood-products firms. The low productivity of these independent operators has been a major concern of their customers. Accordingly, Georgia Kraft Company undertook an experiment with some of its suppliers to see if goal setting could help to increase productivity.

Ten pairs of logging crews were identified, each similar in size, mechanization of equipment, type of terrain worked, prior productivity, and employee attendance. Within each pair one crew was trained in goal setting and the other was not. Appropriate specific production goals, expressed in terms of cords of wood to be cut each week, were established for all crews but were communicated only to the crews with training in goal setting. Furthermore, only the trained

crews were provided with tally meters that sawyers could use to count the number of trees felled, which gave them feedback on results.

Over a twelve-week period, results obtained by the crews trained in goal setting were well above those for the crews without specific goals. In seven of the ten pairs of crews the goal setters had cut more cords per labor hour—often substantially more. In the three remaining sets of crews the performance results were much the same whether or not goal setting occurred. The goal-setting crews had better attendance records and achieved their higher output without detrimental consequences, such as increased injuries or turnover.

SOURCE: Edwin A. Locke & Gary P. Latham (1984). *Goal setting: A motivational technique that works.* Englewood Cliffs, NJ: Prentice-Hall.

Mento, & Locke, 1987). Perhaps highly complex tasks serve to erode the confidence of individuals with even the highest self-esteem, at least to some degree. Actually, there is evidence that there are tasks where setting difficult goals can prove to be a detriment. The extent of this phenomenon is not as yet clear, however (Earley, Connolly, & Ekegren, 1989).

An important issue is whether the challenging and specific goals that make a difference in performance are assigned, usually by a superior, or are developed by the person doing the work. There is no question that people typically accept assigned goals (unless they are totally impossible) and that assigned goals do improve performance. But setting one's own goals can also work (Latham, Erez, & Locke, 1988). If people set hard goals for themselves, their performance improves accordingly. The major advantage of setting

one's own goals comes from goal acceptance: A goal that one establishes for oneself—a career objective, for instance—is more likely to become part of oneself. That means that a person with self-set goals is most likely to realize the full advantage of goal setting. Yet many assigned goals in the business world are just as well accepted. Thus the goal setting must be done by the individual only when acceptance is likely to be a problem.

☐ Management by Objectives

Management by objectives (MBO) involves a programmatic use of goal setting throughout an organization or major segments of it, as was the case at Honeywell. Although MBO programs vary widely, all involve setting and recording objectives, working toward them, and subsequently reviewing how well they

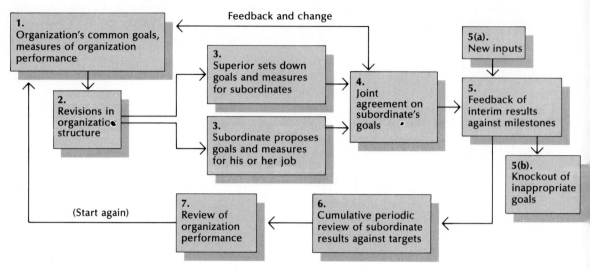

EXHIBIT 4-3   The MBO Process
Superior and subordinate together work out objectives for the subordinate; periodic review of results may lead to changes in the organization's goals and structures or in the subordinate's status or salary.
SOURCE: George S. Odiorne (1979). *MBO II: A system of managerial leadership for the 80s,* p. 75. Belmont, CA: Fearon Pitman.

were met. The process, which starts at the top, is an important part of the firm's strategic planning process. Considerable paperwork is usually involved as goals are recorded, progress is reported, and evaluations are carried out. Exhibit 4-3 depicts the cycle of goal setting and evaluation, showing how organizational goals and individual goals interact within the MBO context.

Scientific Value and Practical Usefulness of MBO.   Because MBO has been around for some time and many companies have tried it, there has been ample opportunity to study its effects. Many MBO programs have been extensively analyzed, including those at Purex Corporation and at the Black and Decker Company (Carroll & Tosi, 1973; Raia, 1974). One reaction to this research points out:

The less sophisticated the research approach, the more likely the study is to show MBO as effective. There are also tendencies for MBO

to be more effective in the short term (less than two years), in the private sector, and in organizations removed from direct contact with the customer. . . . MBO can be effective, but questions remain about the circumstances under which it is effective (Kondrasuk, 1981, p. 425).

Several types of problems emerge from MBO techniques. Many programs require time-consuming reports to higher management. If this paperwork is short-circuited or gets behind schedule, the whole program can lose credibility. The MBO process tends to emphasize short-term goals at the expense of more significant long-term goals. Coordination can prove difficult when individuals exert strong influence on their own goals. In many respects MBO depends on precise job analysis. Thus two managers may define their jobs to include the same activities and set overlapping objectives, especially if the activities are attractive ones; other, unattractive activities may be left out completely. In one company, responsibility for hiring new salespeople was claimed by managers in both human resources and marketing; both set objectives as to the number and quality of people to be hired, and both specified methods of recruiting and selection to meet their objectives, though the methods were substantially different. Yet neither department offered a plan for the improvement or firing of ineffective salespeople, and thus one important aspect of the job was totally neglected.

In MBO programs such as that at Honeywell, where performance appraisals and compensation are tied to goal attainment, some individuals show positive initial performance results, but these results erode rapidly from the third year on. Often, managers are able to get relatively easy or vague goals accepted for themselves, thus assuring themselves of sizable compensation increases when they meet those goals. In such cases the motivational benefits of difficult and clearly specified goals are lost. Others become angry and disillusioned when they cannot meet the hard goals they set the first year and are later denied compensation as a result of this "failure." Next time around, they know better than to get caught in the same trap: They too set easy or ambiguous goals. In some cases MBO seems to just fade away as managers lose interest and fail to keep up with the demands of the program. This appears particularly likely where large numbers of new people are moved into management positions; they do not view the existing MBO program as their own and thus feel no commitment to making it a success.

☐ Goal Setting in Perspective

Setting hard and specific goals can contribute to performance and productivity. To the extent that this kind of goal setting is incorporated into it, MBO can make a useful contribution. The problem is that it is difficult to implement this process and maintain it over time in a formal MBO program. The use of assigned goals may help overcome problems of poor coordination, eroded difficulty levels, and creeping ambiguity; but then goal acceptance by managers and employees may suffer. The net result is that most companies cannot make MBO work to anywhere near its full potential. The typical disparity between MBO in practice and in theory seems to be sizable. It is not clear why, but MBO in practice has not proved to be what its creators anticipated.

An alternative, and perhaps the best, approach is to place the greatest emphasis on assisting people at all levels to set goals for themselves, but not within a formal system. People may record their informal goals, but they need not show them to others or discuss them. Supervisors may assign goals to subordinates simply for the purpose of motivating themselves to achieve their own goals. Goal setting can be fostered in training programs. The point is to create a culture in which goal setting is valued. If stories begin to spread within a company describing how goal setting has led to major successes, then goal setting has clearly achieved a valued status. Even when it has not, individuals may improve their performance and advance their careers by using it.

■ WORK REDESIGN

Work redesign as a method of increasing motivation has been the subject of a great deal of writing and research over the years (Aldag & Brief, 1979; Griffin, 1982). Like goal setting, the work-redesign approach was originally proposed to increase the energy a person commits to the job. Work redesign involves rewriting job descriptions and changing the nature of the work so as to engage higher levels of motivation. It is possible that in this process more difficult and more specific goals are set and that this is the reason for any positive results. However, work-redesign theories and programs emerged from a different background than goal setting, and there has been little overlap between the two techniques to date.

☐ Herzberg's Approach

One of the earliest approaches to work redesign was that of Frederick Herzberg, who labeled his technique **orthodox job enrichment.** The initial wide-scale application of this technique was undertaken by AT&T during the 1960s (Ford, 1969). Herzberg himself ties his job-enrichment approach to the theory of work satisfaction and motivation that he devised, called **motivation-hygiene theory** (sometimes referred to as "two-factor theory"). However, it is not at all clear that orthodox job enrichment really owes much to motivation-hygiene theory. Furthermore, motivation-hygiene theory has not held up well under the scrutiny of research, and must now be regarded as of mainly historical interest (Miner, 1980; Pinder, 1984). Orthodox job enrichment itself, in contrast, has fared well in the hands of researchers and is still very much a viable concept.

Motivation-Hygiene Theory. Motivation-hygiene theory is related to orthodox job enrichment primarily insofar as the two incorporate certain overlapping concepts (Herzberg, Mausner, & Snyderman, 1959). According to the theory, job satisfaction is an outgrowth of five intrinsic aspects of the work—the **motivators.** They are:

· Achievement
· Verbal recognition
· The challenge of the work itself
· Responsibility
· Opportunity for advancement, promotion

These five factors are considered to be closely connected. When they are present in a job, a person's basic needs for personal growth and self-actualization will be satisfied; positive feelings and improved performance will result. Opportunity for growth is also treated as a motivator, although this category lacks support in the original theoretical research.

Job dissatisfaction is said to result from a completely different set of factors, which characterize the context in which work is performed. Primary among these factors, which are called **hygienes,** are:

· Company policy and administrative practices
· Technical quality of supervision
· Interpersonal relations, especially with supervisors
· Physical working conditions
· Job security
· Benefits
· Salary

Hygienes can serve to remove dissatisfaction and improve performance to a point, but beyond that, improving them does nothing. Instead, to elicit strongly positive feelings and high levels of performance, it is necessary to concentrate on motivators.

Orthodox Job Enrichment. Orthodox job enrichment is a method of increasing the motivators of a job; so far, the application seems to follow from the theory. But the hygiene part of Herzberg's theory is nowhere to be found in orthodox job enrichment. Furthermore, job enrichment stresses only three of the motivators, those called generators: the work itself, responsibility, and opportunity for advancement. The other two motivators, achievement and recognition, are cast as bit players at best. Yet in motivation-hygiene theory, achievement and recognition are the primary motivators. Contradictions such as these make it hard to understand how orthodox job enrichment can be viewed as a natural outgrowth of motivation-hygiene theory.

A key consideration in orthodox job enrichment is **vertical loading** (as contrasted with horizontal loading, in which nonchallenging tasks are added, creating only a greater quantity of the same work.) Vertical loading often introduces tasks previously carried out by a superior; it is a qualitative change, inherent in many aspects of the enrichment process (Herzberg, 1976; pp. 114–118, 131). Vertical loading may be achieved by removing certain controls, giving people a complete unit of work, granting additional authority, increasing individual accountability, making reports available directly to the worker, introducing new and more difficult tasks, and making individuals experts in specific areas.

There appear to be at least eight key aspects of the enrichment process:

1. *Direct feedback.* Performance results go to the employee directly and in a nonevaluative manner, rather than through a superior. Example: Targets on a rifle range fall down when hit, as a direct result.
2. *Client relationships.* There is a particular customer or client either inside or outside the organization for whom the work is performed. Example: Unit assemblers are the "customers" for the components produced by the company's various manufacturing processes.
3. *New learning.* Opportunity exists for individuals to experience psychological growth through new and meaningful learning. Example: A laboratory technician is given a chance to learn certain skills utilized by the research scientists.
4. *Scheduling.* People can schedule their own work within the limits dictated by realistic deadlines. Example: Work breaks can be taken at the individual's discretion rather than at times set by management.

5. *Unique expertise.* Individuals can apply their special skills to perform the task at hand in their own way. Example: A secretary who knows how to use a word processor can produce multiple copies of a form letter much faster on that machine than on a typewriter (and is then free to use the time saved to perform other tasks).
6. *Control over resources.* Employees are provided with individual budgets that make them directly accountable for costs. Example: Cost-accounting procedures are moved below the management level to the individual or work team.
7. *Direct communications authority.* Individuals can communicate with others as needed to get the job done. Example: An employee communicates directly with the supervisor of an outside department, without going through her boss.
8. *Personal accountability.* The person doing the work is directly accountable for results. Example: Quality control is the responsibility of the individual rather than of a supervisor or external unit.

Box 4-2, which deals with orthodox job enrichment as introduced at Hill Air Force Base, illustrates how these concepts can be employed.

Scientific Value and Practical Usefulness. Job enrichment along the lines described does not always work to reduce costs and improve performance. This was evident at Hill Air Force Base, for instance, in several of the job areas mentioned in Box 4-2. In the initial work at AT&T, the results were very impressive among clerical personnel who answered shareholder inquiries related to company stock, but some blue-collar workers actively resisted job enrichment.

Even under ideal circumstances, as at AT&T, some 10 to 15 percent of those whose jobs are enriched do not respond positively.

BOX 4-2   RESEARCH IN I/O PSYCHOLOGY

Orthodox Job Enrichment at Hill Air Force Base

Orthodox job enrichment was introduced at Hill Air Force Base in Utah by a project team headed by Frederick Herzberg. The approach used was to give key people in various areas of operation extensive training in job enrichment procedures, and then guide them to be sure that job changes emphasized motivators (not hygienes) and vertical rather than horizontal loading. The project team also helped develop measures of the job enrichment program's effectiveness.

Initially 11 pilot projects were undertaken involving jobs in distribution, material management, personnel, civil engineering, transportation, data automation, procurement, and maintenance. Over a ten-month period, the changes obtained a saving of $250,000, attributable to reduced costs for materials, fuel, and personnel and to increased units of production. The largest part of the savings occurred in two aircraft maintenance activities, while several of the projects failed to yield any tangible benefits at all.

Subsequently the number of projects was increased to 29, concentrating on the same general areas. This effort saved an estimated $1.75 million in two years. The saving resulted from reduced sick leave, lower turnover, less overtime and rework, reduced labor, and material savings.

Measures of job satisfaction, obtained over twelve months prior to the job enrichment pro-gram and during the program itself, indicate markedly accelerated satisfaction levels during the period of job enrichment. The proportion of employees studied who showed increased satisfaction in the two periods was as follows:

	Before Job Enrichment	During Job Enrichment
Overall satisfaction	33%	76%
Satisfaction in various motivator areas		
Achievement	28	67
Recognition for achievement	15	20
Work itself	10	70
Responsibility	15	80
Advancement	23	62
Growth	30	72

Satisfaction with recognition for achievement was the only category that failed to improve considerably over the preceding period.

SOURCE: Frederick I. Herzberg (April 1977). Orthodox job enrichment: A common sense approach to people at work. *Defense Management Journal*, 21–27.

In other instances a whole program may fail to yield the desired results. Unfortunately, orthodox job enrichment has little to say about when and why these failures can be expected to occur; that is probably its major shortcoming. It also gives little attention to the idea that people might enrich their own jobs, instead describing only processes that management should carry out in order to enrich the work of those at lower levels.

☐ The Hackman-Oldham Approach

The approach to job enrichment proposed by Richard Hackman and Greg Oldham has a major advantage in that it does try to explain when the technique will and will not achieve its objectives. This approach, which focuses on job characteristics, has gone through a number of versions. In its original form the underlying theoretical base was expectancy

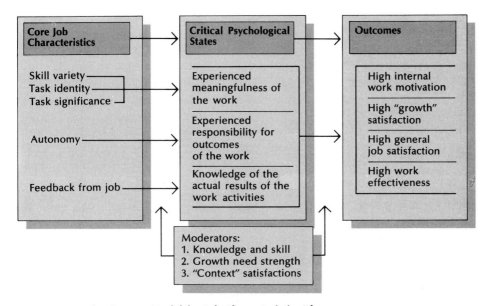

EXHIBIT 4-4   The Current Model for Job Characteristics Theory
The Hackman-Oldham theory describes positive job characteristics that produce psycho-
logical states that lead to job satisfaction and effectiveness.
SOURCE: Richard Hackman & Greg C. Oldham (1980). *Work redesign,* p. 90. Reading, MA: Addison-
Wesley.

theory, as discussed in Chapter 3, and
Edward Lawler was a major contributor. Both
Lawler and the expectancy theory formulations have now disappeared from this
approach. The common ground between the
recent formulations of **job characteristics theory** and orthodox job enrichment is that both
offer approaches to job enrichment. Their theoretical backgrounds are quite different.
Actually, the Hackman-Oldham approach can
be traced back to practices originally recommended by Turner and Lawrence (1965).

Job Characteristics Theory. The current
model for the theory, disgramed in Exhibit 4-
4, requires some basic definitions, many of
which overlap with those used by Herzberg
in his orthodox job enrichment theory.

Skill variety is the degree to which a job requires a variety of activities, skills, and talents.

Task identity is the degree to which a job
requires completion of a whole and identifi-
able piece of work from beginning to end and
has a visible outcome.

Task significance is the degree to which the job
has a substantial impact on the lives of other
people, whether inside the organization or in
the world at large.

Autonomy is the degree to which the job provides the individual with substantial independence and discretion in scheduling the work
and in deciding on procedures to be used.

Feedback from job is the degree to which the
required work activities provide the individual with direct and clear information on the
effectiveness of performance.

These five characteristics are measured
with a standardized questionnaire and the

resulting scores inserted in a formula to calculate the motivating potential of the job.

These core job characteristics produce certain critical psychological states in certain people under certain circumstances:

Experienced meaningfulness is the degree to which the individual experiences the job as one that is generally valuable and worthwhile.

Experienced responsibility is the degree to which the individual feels personally accountable for the results of the work done.

Knowledge of results is the degree to which the individual understands how effectively he or she is performing the job.

The core job characteristics combine according to the following formula:

$$\begin{matrix} \text{Motivating} \\ \text{Potential} \\ \text{of the Job} \end{matrix} = \left(\dfrac{\begin{matrix}\text{Skill} \\ \text{Variety}\end{matrix} + \begin{matrix}\text{Task} \\ \text{Identity}\end{matrix} + \begin{matrix}\text{Task} \\ \text{Significance}\end{matrix}}{3} \right)$$

$$\times \text{Autonomy} \times \text{Feedback from Job}$$

This **motivating potential** in turn leads to the desired outcomes. These naturally include internal work motivation, along with satisfaction of the need for growth. Overall job satisfaction is another important outcome, though not necessarily including satisfaction with specific job aspects such as pay and supervision. High work effectiveness refers to both the quality and quantity of goods and services produced. The current model of job characteristics theory does not anticipate reduced absenteeism and turnover as outcomes, although earlier versions of the theory did include them (and failed to include quantity of output as well).

For this whole process to work as anticipated—from core job characteristics through to outcomes—the presence of certain moderators is required. A moderator variable serves to specify when another variable will predict

success and when it will not. This theory considers the moderators responsible for the successes and failures of job enrichment. Initially, only one moderator was discussed, the strength of **growth needs.** People with strong needs for growth responded to enriched jobs with more positive outcomes, and people with weak growth needs did not, or even responded negatively. The concept of growth need is taken from ERG theory, as discussed in Chapter 3.

For job enrichment to work, in addition to growth needs, a person must possess the knowledge and skill required to do the work well. Otherwise, as inadequate work causes negative consequences, there will be disillusionment with the enriched job and ultimately a tendency to avoid it. Finally, for enrichment to work, there must be a degree of overall satisfaction with the job context. If a person worries about job security, feels unfairly compensated, and encounters problems with coworkers and the boss, that person cannot give much attention to the challenge of job enrichment.

These moderator relationships have been summarized as follows:

The worst possible circumstance for a job that is high in motivating potential would be when the job incumbent is only marginally competent to perform the work *and* has low needs for personal growth at work *and* is highly dissatisfied with one or more aspects of the work context. The job clearly would be too much for that individual, and negative personal and work outcomes would be predicted. It would be better, for the person as well as for the organization, for the individual to perform relatively more simple and routine work. On the other hand, if an individual is fully competent to carry out the work required by a complex, challenging task *and* has strong needs for personal growth *and* is well satisfied with the work context, then we would expect both high personal satisfaction and high work motivation and performance (Hackman & Oldham, 1980, p. 88).

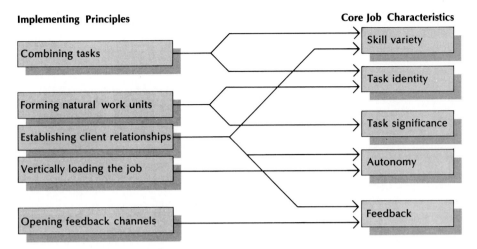

Implementing Principles

Combining tasks

Forming natural work units

Establishing client relationships

Vertically loading the job

Opening feedback channels

Core Job Characteristics

Skill variety

Task identity

Task significance

Autonomy

Feedback

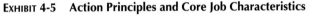

EXHIBIT 4-5   Action Principles and Core Job Characteristics
In the Hackman-Oldham theory, five action principles can affect the core job characteristics, which in turn lead to the four areas of outcome (see also Exhibit 4-4).
SOURCE: Richard Hackman & Greg R. Oldham (1980). *Work redesign*, p. 135. Reading, MA: Addison-Wesley.

Action Principles. At the level of theory, orthodox job enrichment and the job characteristics approach differ in many respects; at the level of practice, however, they are similar. Exhibit 4-5 lists the five action principles of job characteristics theory and shows how they help to enrich jobs by affecting the core job characteristics. Box 4-3 describes the application of these principles in a program to enrich certain jobs at Bankers Trust Company in New York City.

What is different about the job characteristics approach is that it says job enrichment should not be attempted everywhere, with everyone. It is simply not appropriate in some work contexts and for some types of people. Thus, individual and organizational diagnosis should precede any attempt to enrich jobs. Person–environment fit is important (Kulik, Oldham, & Hackman, 1987).

Scientific Value and Practical Usefulness. Job characteristics theory has been the subject of considerable criticism, at least some of which has turned out to be misdirected

(Berlinger, Glick, & Rogers, 1988; Roberts & Glick, 1981). Techniques to measure the theory's constructs have been developed and have proved useful in research as in practical applications. The theory appears to be accurate in describing how core job characteristics operate generally. Research, however, has questioned the independent contribution of the autonomy factor and the importance of task identity in achieving job enrichment. Yet the inclusion of these factors in the model probably does little harm. As for the formula determining motivation potential, it appears that in most cases simply adding the five core dimensions together would be better than applying the more complex formula.

Job characteristics theory has come in for some of its strongest criticism with respect to the moderators. Yet recent comprehensive reviews indicate that the growth-need moderator does in fact operate as the theory hypothesizes (Fried & Ferris, 1987; Loher, Noe, Moeller, & Fitzgerald, 1985; Spector, 1985). People with strong growth needs are more likely to benefit from job enrichment.

BOX 4-3 I/O PSYCHOLOGY IN PRACTICE

Job Enrichment at Bankers Trust Company

The Bankers Trust Company undertook a job enrichment program in its regular and special accounts section, which handles deposits to customer checking accounts, because the section suffered from low productivity, high error rates, high turnover, and substantial dissatisfaction with pay. The program began with a training program for supervisors in which a long list of possible job changes was developed and then pruned back to a workable set of plans. These plans called for the consolidation of three jobs. The idea was to put back together a natural unit of work that had previously been divided. Jobs involved in this reorganization were concerned with comparing checks with signature cards, noticing dates and endorsements, and pulling mutilated checks. In addition, the clerks were given more responsibility for paying problem checks on their own, including some checks of substantial value. In connection with this process, the clerks were put in direct contact with branches and other contact sources, thus taking over communications previously handled only by their supervisors. Feedback on performance was provided through a management-by-objectives type of appraisal system.

The reported results were as follows:

Forgeries paid dropped 56 percent.

Items misfiled dropped 19 percent.

Complaints from branches dropped 25 percent.

Staffing level was reduced 16 percent in spite of a somewhat increased volume of work.

A productivity level of 110 was attained, exceeding the target figure of 98.

SOURCE: W. Philip Kraft & Kathleen L. Williams (1975). Job design improves productivity. *Personnel Journal, 54,* 393–397.

However, from a practical viewpoint, it appears most fruitful simply to ask people whether they want enriched work. It turns out that answers to the question "Do you want an enriched job, and if so, what would you like to see changed?" can be very useful as moderators (Cherrington & England, 1980). Additional questions might deal with the other two moderators as well—knowledge and skill, and job context satisfaction. These latter have been studied relatively little to date, although they are supported by some evidence.

The key question remains: Can implementing the job characteristics theory lead to improved performance and productivity? The answer is somewhat disappointing: Maybe.

Outcomes such as high internal work motivation, high growth satisfaction, and high general job satisfaction are likely to be achieved. But high work effectiveness is another matter. This kind of job enrichment has sometimes achieved positive results for both quantity and quality of output, but not always. There is reason to believe that performance effects that are initially positive may dissipate over a year or so. The theory is by no means invalid, and following it can help bring about certain results that many individual organization members want, including a more pleasant work experience. But to date, job characteristics theory and job enrichment generally have fallen somewhat short of their hoped-for potential. In the overall context of job enrichment, the successes achieved at Hill Air Force Base and Bankers Trust Company (see Boxes 4-2 and 4-3) must be considered better than average in terms of results achieved. However, they are not alone in reporting positive outcomes. A recent study carried out in a government office provided clear evidence of productivity gains when growth need strength was taken into consideration (Graen, Scandura, & Graen, 1986). There is also evidence that adding other job characteristics, such as freedom from danger and the intellectual demand of the work, to the motivating potential of the job can improve prediction of outcomes (Zaccaro & Stone, 1988).

☐ Alternative Work Schedules

Alternative work schedules include *compressed work weeks, flexible working hours, part-time employment,* and *job sharing.* Only the first two approaches have been advocated as techniques intended to improve productivity, so this discussion will focus on them. Both have received strong policy support from government (Rosow & Zager, 1981). Both involve changes in job requirements (although primarily in scheduling rather than in job content), and both have been studied extensively (Ronen, 1984). Like job enrichment in the early period, these practices are practically devoid of theory.

The Compressed Work Week. A **compressed work week** is one in which the standard number of working hours remains the same, but employees work longer hours per day and fewer days per week. The most common compressed schedule is a four-day week of roughly ten hours per day. A twelve-hour day with varying work weeks of three and four days is also frequently used. Box 4-4 which deals with the introduction of twelve-hour shifts at Temple-Eastex, describes an example of the latter.

The compressed work week has met with mixed results. The general finding is that employees like the new schedules, which sometimes—but not always—means an overall increase in job satisfaction. Absenteeism tends to decrease, simply because the days are longer and thus more pay is lost for each day of absence. Performance improves under certain circumstances, but usually does not. The fact that employees, having already put in a ten- or twelve-hour day, are often less willing to work overtime can be a drawback.

Compressed work weeks have been widely used in computer operations. In one study of this type of application, it was found that those employees who participated in the decision to implement a compressed work schedule were subsequently most pleased with it. In this case there were clear reductions in overtime and sick time. Fatigue did not appear to be a problem (Latack & Foster, 1985).

Flexible Working Hours. **Flexible working hours** (often called **flextime**) are systems in which the individual employee is given some choice about when he or she will put in the required number of working hours; the employee typically has discretion regarding starting time, lunch-hour scheduling, and leaving time, but is required to be present during specified "core hours" in the late morning and early afternoon. Sometimes a set number of hours must be worked each day; in other instances employees can accumulate credits and debits over a period of time, such as a month. Sometimes employees are required to submit schedules for discretionary hours in advance. Exhibit 4-6 provides two examples of flextime arrangements.

Employees tend to react to flexible hours much as they do to compressed work weeks. But in other respects—quantity and quality of output, absenteeism, accident rates, and the like—the flexible hours technique is more

BOX 4-4   I/O PSYCHOLOGY IN PRACTICE

The Compressed Work Week at Temple-Eastex

A compressed work week involving a change to twelve-hour shifts was introduced in the pulp and paperboard division of Temple-Eastex, largely because of pressure from the employees and their union. The company surveyed other firms in the paper industry and found none that had experience with compressed work weeks. Implementing the proposal required substantial revisions in the union contract because the company wanted to be sure that the change in work schedules did not result in a de facto wage increase, did not have a negative impact on safety or productivity, and did in fact have general employee approval. Analyses suggested that the company had no cause for concern about these matters. The change from eight-hour to twelve-hour shifts is summarized in the accompanying schedules. The actual number of days off for four weeks, totaling all shifts, increased from 29 to 55; the actual number of hours worked stayed exactly the same.

The Eight-Hour Schedule

	Week 1							Week 2							Week 3							Week 4						
	S	M	T	W	Th	F	S	S	M	T	W	Th	F	S	S	M	T	W	Th	F	S	S	M	T	W	Th	F	S
Shift A	E	E	E	E	—	D	—	D	D	D	D	D	—	—	—	—	G	G	G	G	G	G	G	—	—	E	E	E
Shift B	G	G	—	—	E	E	E	E	E	E	E	—	D	D	D	D	D	D	D	—	—	—	—	G	G	G	G	G
Shift C	—	—	G	G	G	G	G	G	G	—	—	E	E	E	E	E	E	E	—	D	D	D	D	D	D	D	—	—
Shift D	D	D	D	D	D	—	—	—	—	G	G	G	G	G	G	G	—	—	E	E	E	E	E	E	E	—	D	D

D = 7:00 a.m. to 3:00 p.m.; E = 3:00 p.m. to 11 p.m.; G = 11:00 p.m. to 7:00 a.m.; — = off day.

The Twelve-Hour Schedule

	Week 1							Week 2							Week 3							Week 4						
	S	M	T	W	Th	F	S	S	M	T	W	Th	F	S	S	M	T	W	Th	F	S	S	M	T	W	Th	F	S
Shift A	D	D	D	D	—	—	—	—	—	—	—	—	N	N	N	N	—	—	—	D	D	D	—	N	N	N	—	—
Shift B	N	—	—	—	D	D	D	—	N	N	N	—	—	—	D	D	D	D	—	—	—	—	—	—	—	N	N	N
Shift C	—	—	—	—	N	N	N	N	—	—	—	D	D	D	—	N	N	N	—	—	—	D	D	D	D	—	—	—
Shift D	N	N	N	N	—	—	—	D	D	D	D	—	—	—	—	—	—	—	N	N	N	N	—	—	—	D	D	D

D = 6:00 a.m. to 6:00 p.m.; N = 6:00 p.m. to 6:00 a.m.; — = off day.

SOURCE: Robert D. Brinton (1983). Effectiveness of the twelve-hour shift. *Personnel Journal, 62,* 394.

likely to yield positive results (Greene, 1984). In general, however, complete flexibility in scheduling, as contrasted with the limited approaches noted in Exhibit 4-6, does not yield any additional advantage.

Exhibit 4-7 portrays the effect of flextime on productivity in certain programming units of Florida state government. Experimental units with flextime were compared to control units without it. The pretest measures are

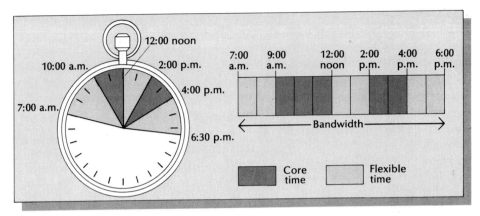

EXHIBIT 4-6   Two Examples of Flextime Schedules
Flextime employees must work during the stipulated "core time" hours, but can choose their remaining work hours from those labeled "flexible time." In both of these examples employees are expected to schedule their lunch hours for any time between 12:00 noon and 2:00 p.m.
SOURCE: Simcha Ronen (1984). *Alternative work schedules: Selecting, implementing, and evaluating,* p. 75. Homewood, IL: Dow Jones-Irwin.

EXHIBIT 4-7   Effect of Flextime on Productivity in Programming Units of Florida's State Government
Comparing an experimental group using flextime with a control group, the Florida state government found that flextime considerably improved productivity.
SOURCE: David A. Ralston, William P. Anthony, & David J. Gustafson (1985). Employees may love flextime, but what does it do to the organization's productivity? *Journal of Applied Psychology, 70,* 278.

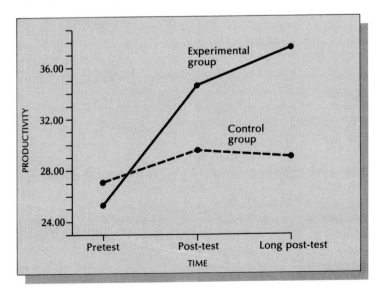

averages over a six-month period before flex-time was introduced; the posttest measures are averages for the six months following the introduction of flextime in the experimental units; and the long posttest measures are averages for the second six-month period after the posttest. Thus, the data cover two years including the test period itself. Overall, flextime appears to account for a 36 percent improvement in production output. One major factor was that with flextime programmers spent less time waiting for access to the computer.

Generally, compressed work weeks and flexible working hours can be expected to do some good and little harm (Dunham, Pierce, & Castañeda, 1987). These alternative work schedules may prove very beneficial, as in the Florida state government case. Unfortunately, at present these are techniques in search of theories, and it is impossible to say when they will work and when they won't. It is clear, however, that they can have motivational effects, probably more on how people do their work than on how much effort they put into the job. In some instances, a degree of job enrichment seems to occur simply because of the nature of the scheduling changes. However, managers may well oppose flextime because of the difficulties it creates; for managers, supervision of employees outside the core hours can present a major problem.

■ ORGANIZATIONAL BEHAVIOR MODIFICATION

The motivational practice known as organizational behavior modification clearly arose as an application of the theories of B. F. Skinner (1953, 1971, 1974). However, as experience with the practice developed, it in essence outgrew the theory. At this point organizational behavior modification became attached to another, related theory, the social learning theory of Albert Bandura (1977). The following discussion traces these developments and

in the process provides an understanding of the nature of organizational behavior modification.

□ The Nature of Operant Learning

Skinner's behaviorism is a theory of learning, not motivation per se, and accordingly its terminology is that of the learning field. Yet the consequences of applying the theory are much the same as those of motivational theories such as expectancy theory (see Chapter 3). Furthermore, as noted in Chapter 2, motivation and learning are closely related concepts, and the discussion of reward systems in the final part of this chapter relies in a number of respects on concepts inherent in organizational behavior modification. For these reasons we take the liberty of treating organizational behavior modification as a motivational practice.

One of Skinner's key concepts is *operant learning*. Behavior may represent a reflex response to environmental changes or a learned reaction that affects the environment; the former is considered relatively unimportant, while the latter—known as *operant learning*—is theoretically central. In **operant learning,** certain initially randomly produced behaviors are strengthened through reinforcement and thus come to occur more frequently.

□ Contingencies of Reinforcement

Four types of reinforcements may be used in strengthening certain behaviors and weakening others. They are called **contingencies of reinforcement.**

Positive reinforcement involves providing some reward contingent upon the subject's performing the desired behavior. This reward can be of a physiological nature, such as food, water, or sex, but in the organizational context we are typically talking about such things as promotion, increased compensation, praise, or more desirable working conditions. What is a reward for one person may not be for another; it all depends on past experiences.

Avoidance learning involves the withdrawal or prevention of an unpleasant condition contingent upon the appearance of the desired behavior. For instance, suppose that a person whose performance has been unsatisfactory has been constantly watched, prodded, and criticized by superiors. When the person begins to do the job right, the constant surveillance stops and the individual is freed of the unpleasantness.

Extinction involves the withdrawal of a positive reinforcer so that undesired behavior gets weaker and eventually disappears. For instance, an individual who has frequently argued with his supervisor, urged on by the approval of his fellow workers, may be shifted to a work group where his undesirable behavior is ignored or to an isolated work station.

Punishment involves providing negative consequences after an undesired behavior, with the intent of decreasing the frequency of the behavior. Many behaviorists believe that punishment frequently fails because:

1. It serves only to suppress behavior temporarily rather than change it permanently.
2. It generates emotional behavior, often directed against the person who administers the punishment.
3. It can bring about a generalization to unintended circumstances so that the person does not exhibit the behavior in question even when it is appropriate.
4. It can turn the person doing the punishing into an "aversive stimulus" so that that person cannot take any action that will be perceived as positive reinforcement.

Studies of if, how, and when punishment should be used in operant learning have yielded no definitive answers. It is apparent, however, that companies quite frequently use discipline in the form of oral and written warnings, suspensions without pay, and discharges in dealing with difficult employees. Research data indicate that moderate forms of punishment such as informal discussions oriented toward problem resolution and brief suspensions can defuse tense situations and boost performance. More severe punishments, in contrast, adversely affect performance, possibly because of the factors mentioned above (Beyer & Trice, 1984).

☐ Reinforcement Schedules

Reinforcement may be continuous in that every instance of a desired behavior is followed by, say, a word of praise from a supervisor. Obviously, this is not practical in many work situations, especially those in which numerous people report to the same superior. Furthermore, continuous reinforcement learning is subject to rapid extinction if the reinforcer is removed. Accordingly, behaviorists advocate some kind of **partial reinforcement,** in which reinforcers are given after only some, not all, instances of the desired behavior. Learning is slower this way, but it is more likely to be permanent. Four different schedules of partial reinforcement, moving from the most to the least preferred, are usually considered.

Variable ratio reinforcement occurs after some set number of desired behaviors, with this number changing continually but varying around a preestablished average.

Fixed ratio reinforcement always occurs after the same fixed number of desired behaviors have been exhibited.

Variable interval reinforcement occurs after a desired behavior at some varying interval of time, but with the intervals distributed around a preestablished average.

Fixed interval reinforcement occurs when the desired behavior appears after a fixed amount of time has passed since the preceding reinforcement.

BOX 4-5 RESEARCH IN I/O PSYCHOLOGY

Reinforcement Schedules at Weyerhaeuser

The Weyerhaeuser Company, and the wood products industry in the Northwest generally, had been plagued by mountain beavers that eat newly planted tree seedlings. To limit the resulting losses, the company hired trappers to catch the beavers. These trappers were paid a base rate of $7 per hour.

For the purpose of comparing reinforcement schedules, baseline measures of the number of beavers caught were maintained over a four-week period. For the remainder of the trapping season two different schedules were used in applying an incentive bonus to different groups of trappers:

- On the continuous reinforcement schedule, the trappers received $1 per beaver caught for all beavers.
- On the variable ratio schedule, the trappers received $4 contingent upon presenting the

beaver and *also* predicting twice whether the role of a die would yield an even or odd number—a one in four chance.

On the continuous schedule the trappers increased their output by 50 percent over the baseline period. On the variable ratio schedule they increased the number of beavers caught by 108 percent. Both of these increases were of significant magnitude, but the variable ratio results were distinctly more so. It appeared that the variable ratio schedule made the job seem more rewarding and challenging.

SOURCE: Lise M. Saari & Gary P. Latham (1982). Employee reactions to continuous and variable ratio reinforcement schedules involving a monetary incentive. *Journal of Applied Psychology, 67*, 506–508.

Box 4-5, drawn from a study conducted at Weyerhaeuser, a wood products company, shows how reinforcement schedules can work. In this particular example experienced trappers were involved. Other data indicate that among novice trappers a continuous reinforcement schedule works better.

☐ The Process of Organizational Behavior Modification

Organizational behavior modification (sometimes referred to as *O.B. Mod.*) is a means of putting the learning concepts we have been considering into practice. Exhibit 4-8 lists five steps for using organizational behavior modification to change behavior patterns. An important aspect of the approach set forth in Exhibit 4-8 is that some attempt is made to measure the impact of the learning intervention and identify learning effects.

However, because there is no control condition, the possibility exists that any change noted has resulted from some external factor, such as the announcement of a wage increase. The approach used in Exhibit 4-8 would not serve to pinpoint the cause in such cases.

To deal with this problem, and more clearly identify the factors that promote learning, what is called an ABAB design is recommended (Luthans & Davis, 1982). Exhibit 4-9 describes such a study conducted in a large manufacturing firm. The steps are as follows:

A. *The baseline period:* Establish a baseline measure of behavior prior to learning.

B. *The period of intervention:* Introduce the learning intervention while continuing to measure.

A. *The period of no intervention:* When the behavior has stabilized at a new level, withdraw the learning intervention and

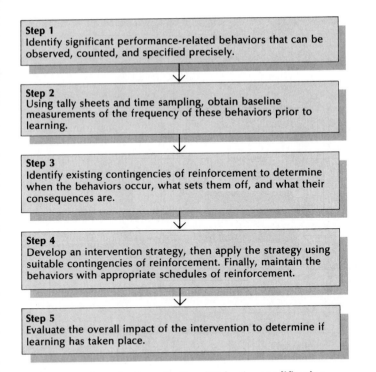

Step 1
Identify significant performance-related behaviors that can be observed, counted, and specified precisely.

Step 2
Using tally sheets and time sampling, obtain baseline measurements of the frequency of these behaviors prior to learning.

Step 3
Identify existing contingencies of reinforcement to determine when the behaviors occur, what sets them off, and what their consequences are.

Step 4
Develop an intervention strategy, then apply the strategy using suitable contingencies of reinforcement. Finally, maintain the behaviors with appropriate schedules of reinforcement.

Step 5
Evaluate the overall impact of the intervention to determine if learning has taken place.

EXHIBIT 4-8   **Steps in Organizational Behavior Modification**
These are the five basic steps by which organizational behavior modification is achieved. If at step 5 it becomes apparent that the intervention developed in step 4 has not had the desired impact, the process starts over again with step 1.
SOURCE: Adapted from Fred Luthans & Robert Kreitner (1985). *Organizational behavior modification and beyond: An operant and social learning approach,* pp. 76–92. Glenview, IL: Scott, Foresman.

reestablish baseline conditions. This reversal should cause the behavior to revert to the baseline level.

B. *The period when intervention was reintroduced:* When the behavior has stabilized back at the baseline level, reintroduce the same learning intervention and see if the behavior frequency changes once again.

If withdrawing the intervention (the second A step) does not cause the behavior to shift back toward the baseline level (as it does in Exhibit 4-9), it is possible that some external factor, such as a pay raise, produced the initial results.

Exhibits 4-8 and 4-9 represent only two of many approaches to organizational behavior modification. The following list specifies the many steps actually involved in putting organizational behavior modification into practice. It should be evident that a substantial effect on employee performance is not obtained without considerable attention to details.

1. Select rewards that are in fact reinforcing for an individual employee.

2. Wherever possible, identify and use new types of rewards.

3. Look for rewards that are naturally occurring, such as praise and profit sharing.

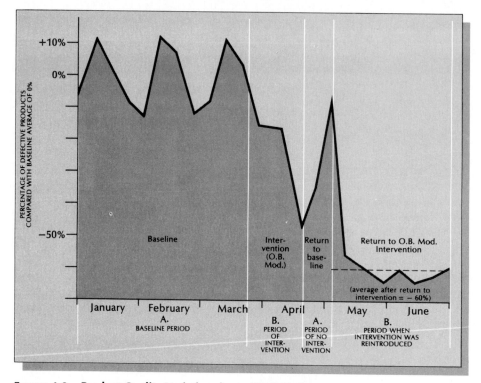

EXHIBIT 4-9   Product-Quality Variations in an ABAB Design
In a study of organizational behavior modification, the intervention was introduced, withdrawn, and then reintroduced. The fact that the percentage of defective products rebounded toward the baseline level when the intervention was withdrawn indicates that the intervention, not some external factor, was causing the change.
SOURCE: Fred Luthans, Walter S. Maciag, & Stuart A. Rosenkrantz (1983). O.B. Mod.: Meeting the productivity challenge with human resources management. *Personnel, 60*, 35.

4. Give out enough of the reward so that it is worthwhile for the employee to respond.

5. Provide rewards contingent upon performance of appropriate work behavior.

6. Set up reinforcers so that they follow desired behaviors as quickly as is practical.

7. Make sure that rewards follow rather than precede the desired behavior.

8. Make sure that rewards are contingent on specific behaviors rather than broad outcomes, such as an overall increase in sales.

9. Start out by rewarding behavior that is close to the employee's current level.

10. Reward small steps of improvement toward a final goal.

11. Establish a system that will overreward rather than underreward desired behaviors.

12. State objectives in positive terms. (This reflects the common behaviorist tendency to deemphasize punishment.) (O'Brien, Dickenson, & Rosow, 1982, pp. 23–28).

When rules such as these are followed, organizational behavior modification can produce striking results. Successful applications have been reported in a number of organiza-

BOX 4-6   I/O PSYCHOLOGY IN PRACTICE

Effects of Removing Contingent Reinforcement on Major League Baseball Pitchers

Prior to 1977 major league baseball players renegotiated their contracts every year with the results contingent in large part on the previous year's performance; as a result, there was contingent reinforcement of performance. Beginning in 1977, however, a number of players negotiated guaranteed three- to ten-year contracts for very sizable sums. This represented a removal of contingent reinforcement, since the payments were assured irrespective of the individual's performance level. It is instructive to look at performance levels, in this case of pitchers, before and after the introduction of their long-term contracts.

- The average number of earned runs given up by a pitcher per nine innings increased.
- The number of winning games pitched per season decreased.
- The number of innings pitched per season declined.
- The number of games in which a pitcher appeared during a season declined.

The pitchers' performance in regard to number of games lost, strikeouts, hits, and walks also deteriorated subsequent to the signing of the long-term contract. What had been a pattern of steadily improving performance up to that time shifted sharply to one of steady decline. Furthermore, comparisons with other pitchers not on long-term contract indicated that the performance changes were almost certainly related to the change in methods of reward; the pitchers serving as controls did not exhibit the same pattern of decline in performance.

To the extent that major league baseball has shifted from contingent to noncontingent rewards, it seems that it has done itself—and the fans—a disservice.

SOURCE: Richard M. O'Brien, Alyce M. Dickenson, & Michael P. Rosow (1982). *Industrial behavior modification: A management handbook*, pp. 91–114. Elmsford, NY: Pergamon Press.

---

tions, including many *Fortune* 500 companies. Examples of improved performance include increased flight bookings by reservation personnel at Scandinavian Airlines, increased sales to grocery stores by sales personnel at General Mills, improved preventive maintenance of motor vehicles in the U.S. Marine Corps, improved processing of paperwork at the U.S. Department of Housing and Urban Development, increased output in various units of the Virginia National Bank, and reduced accident rates among Kansas City, Kansas, bus drivers (Haynes, Pine, & Fitch, 1982; O'Brien et al., 1982). In contrast, Box 4-6 provides a striking example of how performance can decline in the absence of appropriate reinforcement.

☐ From Radical Behaviorism to Social Learning Theory

In the view of so-called radical behaviorists, operant behavior (learning) is basically a consequence of stimulus and reinforced response. According to B. F. Skinner, who pioneered the radical behaviorist view, individual attitudes, motives, expectations, memories, and other internal states may exist, but they are merely by-products; they do not cause behavior.

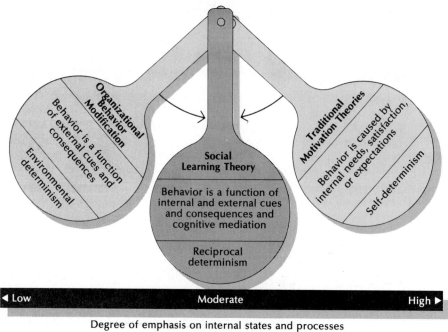

**Degree of emphasis on internal states and processes
when explaining job behavior**

EXHIBIT 4-10   The Pendulum Swing toward Social Learning Theory

A strict view of organizational behavior modification stresses external influences on
behavior, while traditional motivation theories emphasize internal processes. Recently,
these extreme views have both begun to shift toward a more moderate social learning
approach, which maintains that both internal and external factors, mediated by learning,
determine behavior.

SOURCE: Robert Kreitner & Fred Luthans (1984). A social learning approach to behavioral management: Radical behaviorists "mellowing out." *Organizational Dynamics, 13,* 50.

Organizational behavior modification theorists originally espoused such a view.
However, it became increasingly apparent
that this approach cannot effectively account
for the complexities of work behavior in organizations. In the past few years there has been
a theoretical shift toward the assumption that
various internal factors and cognitive processes have a causal effect on learning
(Kreitner & Luthans, 1984; Luthans &
Kreitner, 1985). At the same time, O.B. Mod.
theory has incorporated aspects of **social
learning theory** (Bandura, 1977). Exhibit 4-10
illustrates the pendulum swing involved in
this change.

Social learning theory says that much
learning occurs through modeling one's
behavior on the actions of others. People
select, organize, and change stimuli around
them as they learn new behaviors; they also
anticipate consequences of their acts—
rewards and punishments, for instance—and
their behaviors are motivated accordingly. In
contrast to radical behaviorists, social learning theorists believe that cognitive processes
play an important role in learning.

With the incorporation of social learning
concepts, organizational behavior modification can deal with approaches such as **self-
management,** whereby people regulate their

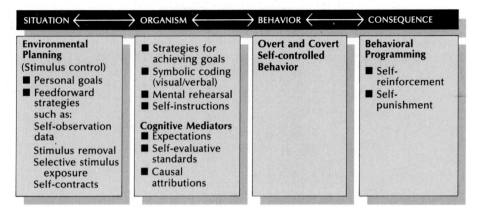

SITUATION ⟷	ORGANISM ⟷	BEHAVIOR ⟷	CONSEQUENCE
Environmental Planning (Stimulus control) ■ Personal goals ■ Feedforward strategies such as: Self-observation data Stimulus removal Selective stimulus exposure Self-contracts	■ Strategies for achieving goals ■ Symbolic coding (visual/verbal) ■ Mental rehearsal ■ Self-instructions **Cognitive Mediators** ■ Expectations ■ Self-evaluative standards ■ Causal attributions	**Overt and Covert Self-controlled Behavior**	**Behavioral Programming** ■ Self-reinforcement ■ Self-punishment

EXHIBIT 4-11   **The Nature of Self-Management**
The many reciprocal processes involved in self-management listed here indicate how important internal factors are in generating behavior—a fact that organizational behavior modification theory has only recently begun to take into account as it incorporates social learning concepts.
SOURCE: Fred Luthans & Robert Kreitner (1985). *Organizational behavior modification and beyond: An operant and social learning approach,* p. 163. Glenview, IL: Scott, Foresman.

own actions. Self-management requires the deliberate manipulation of stimuli, internal processes, and responses to achieve personally identified behavioral outcomes. Exhibit 4-11 outlines the process. Note the frequent reference to internal thought processes—planning, personal goals, self-contracts, mental rehearsal, expectations, and the like—and the important causal role given these processes in the creation of self-controlled behavior. There is evidence that employees trained in self-management significantly reduced their absenteeism as a result (Latham & Frayne, 1989).

Self-management is much more important in organizations than has generally been recognized, although it is not sufficient in and of itself to produce a coordinated organizational effort. Self-management has the advantage that it removes any chance of criticism on grounds of unethical manipulation of others for one's own benefit, as when a manager "uses" a subordinate. Self-management is the essence of self-determination and self-control, as opposed to being controlled by others.

☐ Behavior Modeling

Other than in the area of self-management, organizational behavior modification has been used primarily in dealing with nonmanagers in hierarchical organizations. Below the managerial level, it is much easier to prevent unintended environmental factors from intervening and disrupting the learning process. In contrast, **behavior modeling,** which like self-management is closely allied to social learning theory, has been used primarily, although certainly not exclusively, at the management level. The following excerpt describes a behavior modeling program prepared by Mandev Training Corporation for retail-store personnel selling large appliances, radios, and televisions.

The program focused on specific aspects of sales situations, such as "approaching the customer," "explaining features, advantages, and benefits," "closing the sale," and the like. The usual behavior modeling procedure was followed of presenting guidelines or "learning points" for handling each aspect of a sales inter-

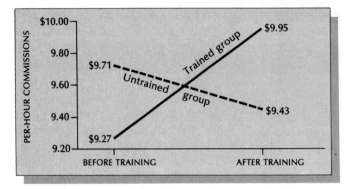

EXHIBIT 4-12 **Effects of Behavior Modeling on Retail Sales Performance**

Sales, as reflected in per-hour commissions, increased significantly among appliance store personnel who had received behavior modeling training. In the training, the employees learned guidelines for appropriate behavior in each stage of a sales transaction, watched a videotape in which a model demonstrated these behaviors, and then role-played the behaviors themselves.

SOURCE: Herbert H. Meyer & Michael S. Raich (1983). An objective evaluation of a behavior modeling training program. *Personnel Psychology, 36*, 759.

action, followed by the presentation of a videotaped situation where a "model" sales associate followed the guidelines in carrying out that aspect of the sales interaction with a customer. The trainees then practiced the same situation in role playing rehearsals. Their performance was reinforced and shaped by their supervisors, who had been trained as instructors (Meyer & Raich, 1983, p. 756).

The results obtained in stores where the behavior modeling training was applied and in comparable stores where more traditional sales training was used are presented in Exhibit 4-12. Not only was behavior modeling shown to be more effective in increasing sales, but also there was reason to believe that it decreased turnover (not shown in Exhibit 4-12).

Similarly positive results were obtained in initial evaluations of the behavior modeling approach at General Electric during the early 1970s and somewhat later at AT&T

(Goldstein & Sorcher, 1974; Moses & Ritchie, 1976). But behavior modeling is not foolproof. A study conducted in a large manufacturing plant dealt with a behavior modeling program designed to help managers motivate employees to solve problems, handle complaining employees, discuss poor work habits and potential disciplinary action, recognize poor employee performance, and overcome resistance to change (Russell, Wexley, & Hunter, 1984). The study indicated that the managers clearly did learn from the program. But they did not incorporate the learning into their job performance; presumably, transfer of training was lacking because the needed reinforcements did not occur back on the job.

This does not mean that behavior modeling is inherently deficient. It does mean that steps need to be taken to reinforce the learning process after training has terminated. Only then can transfer of training and continuing performance effects be anticipated (Fox, 1988).

■ REWARD SYSTEMS

Companies have devised various methods of rewarding employees so that they will contribute as much as possible. Many of the techniques we have been considering involve rewards (and perhaps punishments) which are contingent on the employee's behavior. The law of effect (which we considered in Chapter 2), expectancy theory (which we considered in Chapter 3), and organizational behavior modification provide particularly strong examples. Yet reward systems focused on arousing strong motives antedate these theories by many years. Various incentive systems permitting employees to earn more when they produce more have existed for a long time; they received a strong impetus from the writings of Frederick Taylor in the early 1900s. Learning and motivation theories provide some guidelines as to the effective use of rewards, as we have noted; but practice has produced a wide range of alternative systems, and the theories say little about their relative advantages and disadvantages.

□ The Role of Rewards in Organizations

The role of reward systems in organizations is best understood as an **inducements—contributions balance** (Knoke & Wright-Isak, 1982). A young woman is induced to start work for the local McDonald's franchise partly by the pay and partly by the opportunity to work with some of her friends. She continues her employment and does the things expected of her, thus contributing to the franchise's goals, because she continues to receive the pay she was promised and because her friends continue to work there. So she contributes her presence and her willingness to do what the firm desires in return for the extrinsic rewards of pay and interaction with friends. It is entirely possible that she will stay longer, be absent

less, and work harder if she is promised increased levels of these rewards—more pay and more friends hired—for doing so. This concept of contingent reward, in conjunction with the inducements-contributions concept, provides a theoretical underpinning for the use of reward systems in organizations.

There is considerable evidence that positive rewards and occasional punishments, appropriately administered, can have positive effects on performance (Podsakoff & Todor, 1985; Szilagyi, 1980). Rewards may be extrinsic or intrinsic. However, practice has concentrated heavily on extrinsic rewards involving pay, so our discussion will likewise stress this area.

□ Monetary Reward Systems

Pay is given both to get people to work for a particular organization and to get them to perform as well as possible once they are hired. These two objectives necessitate a balancing act in the administration of compensation plans. The company must try to maintain salary levels that are competitive within the industry, while trying to give itself enough leeway to maintain an equitable internal wage structure.

Administering Compensation. Companies first need information on wage levels in the various labor markets in which they compete for employees. What are other employers paying? Normally they will have to meet or exceed the going market rate if they are to attract the best people and retain them after they are hired and trained. In order to obtain the needed information and establish wage levels, companies typically utilize **wage survey** data. Exhibit 4-13 provides information on the sources of such data; many firms use multiple sources.

Second, companies must establish an internal wage structure through some type of **job evaluation.** Which jobs should pay more and which should pay less? Administrators must

EXHIBIT 4-13   Sources of Wage Survey Information Used by Manufacturing Firms

Source of Survey Data	Percentage of Firms Using Source
Company does its own survey	Over 50%
A local area association of employers	Over 50%
Another employer in the local area	25–50%
Another employer in the industry	25–50%
An association of employers in the industry	25–50%
An outside consulting firm	25–50%
The U.S. Bureau of Labor Statistics	25–50%
A state or local government agency	Under 25%
Other managerial or professional associations	Under 25%

SOURCE: Adapted from Bureau of National Affairs (1981). *Wage and salary administration: Personnel policies survey no. 131,* pp. 3–4. Washington, DC: Bureau of National Affairs.

establish an equitable classification of jobs, but they must also keep an eye on what the wage surveys say about rates for different jobs in the marketplace. The usual practice is to establish the position of the various jobs in the overall structure, working from job analysis information. Once the jobs are positioned, they are priced on the basis of wage survey data and company compensation policies.

As a result of these processes intended to attract and retain employees, many companies find themselves with a payroll budget that represents the most they can or wish to pay. Adding funds beyond this so that truly outstanding employees are paid at a much higher level does not seem attractive, even though in the long run the company might reap a solid return on the investment. But the firm that does wish to pay according to performance, in some or all of its jobs, can use various plans involving merit, commission, bonus, or piece-rate payments.

Types of Incentive Systems. Exhibit 4-14 notes two basic types of **incentive systems** and describes some consequences of using each type. Merit-pay systems provide greater wage or salary increases to those who perform better, while bonus systems provide for a lump-sum payment each time performance

is rated good. Within each of these types of systems, the monetary incentive may be given to individuals based on their performance or to all members of a group based on the group performance or to all or some employees based on organizational performance. Clearly, the individual plans do a better job of tying pay to performance and thus providing contingent rewards, but they may do so at the cost of producing negative side effects and discouraging cooperation. Employee acceptance may be low, especially with bonus systems. Whether these considerations should outweigh the potential usefulness of individual incentives depends on the nature of the job.

For an incentive plan to work, certain conditions must be met (Locke & Latham, 1984, pp. 117–120):

1. The employees must value the extra money they will make under the plan.
2. The employees must not lose important values (health, job security, and the like) as a result of high performance.
3. The employees must be able to control their own performance so that they have a chance to strive for the rewards.
4. The employees must clearly understand how the plan works.

EXHIBIT 4-14   Effectiveness of Merit-Pay and Bonus Incentive Systems in Achieving Various Desired Effects

Type of Compensation Plan	Performance Measure Used	Desired Effects			
		Tying Pay to Performance	Minimizing Negative Side Effects	Encouraging Cooperation	Gaining Acceptance
Merit-Pay Systems					
For individuals	Productivity	Good	Very good	Very poor	Good
	Cost effectiveness	Fair	Very good	Very poor	Good
	Ratings by superiors	Fair	Very good	Very poor	Fair
For groups	Productivity	Fair	Very good	Poor	Good
	Cost effectiveness	Fair	Very good	Poor	Good
	Ratings by superiors	Poor	Very good	Poor	Fair
For organization as a whole	Productivity	Poor	Very good	Fair	Good
	Cost effectiveness	Poor	Very good	Poor	Good
Bonus Systems					
For individuals	Productivity	Very good	Fair	Very poor	Poor
	Cost effectiveness	Good	Good	Very poor	Poor
	Ratings by superiors	Good	Good	Very poor	Poor
For groups	Productivity	Good	Very good	Fair	Fair
	Cost effectiveness	Fair	Very good	Fair	Fair
	Ratings by superiors	Fair	Very good	Fair	Fair
For organization as a whole	Productivity	Fair	Very good	Fair	Good
	Cost effectiveness	Fair	Very good	Fair	Good
	Profit	Poor	Very good	Fair	Fair

SOURCE: Adapted from Edward E. Lawler (1981). *Pay and organization development*, p. 94. Reading, MA: Addison-Wesley.

5. It must be possible to measure performance accurately (using indexes of productivity, cost effectiveness, or ratings as in Exhibit 4-14).

Box 4-7 describes the monetary incentives used at Lincoln Electric Company, an example of a monetary incentive plan that has been operating for many years and has apparently had very good results.

Scientific Value and Practical Usefulness. Monetary incentives can exert a sizable impact on performance, especially incentives for the individual. Exhibit 4-15 compares research results in this area with findings about motivational techniques considered in this chapter. Monetary reward techniques are clearly the most effective. Furthermore, there is now reason to believe that the long-term motivational effects of monetary incentives are even greater than those noted in Exhibit 4-15 (Wagner, Rubin, & Callahan, 1988).

EXHIBIT 4-15   Performance Improvements Associated with Various Motivational Techniques

Motivational Technique	Average Percent Improvement in Performance
Monetary rewards	
Individual	30
Group	20
Goal setting	16
Job enrichment	9

SOURCE: Adapted from Edwin A. Locke & Gary P. Latham (1984). *Goal setting: A motivational technique that works,* p. 117. Englewood Cliffs, NJ: Prentice-Hall.

BOX 4-7   I/O PSYCHOLOGY IN PRACTICE

Monetary Incentives at Lincoln Electric Company

The Lincoln Electric Company of Cleveland, Ohio, manufactures arc-welding equipment and electric motors. It has been experimenting with various types of incentive pay plans throughout most of its ninety years of existence.

This nonunion company uses a piece-rate pay system for as many jobs as possible, based usually on individual but occasionally on group output. However, a guaranteed daily minimum is paid for each job, determined through regular job evaluation procedures. In addition, a sizable proportion of year-end profits is placed in an employee bonus pool. This pool is allocated among units, and within units it is allocated to individuals according to their performance ratings. Thus, a person rated low within a unit loses out to those rated higher. It is not at all unusual for employees to double their yearly compensation as a result of bonus earnings. Jobs guarantee at least thirty hours of work a week.

Even without the monetary incentives, the company's compensation levels are high enough that most employees make a very good living. Turnover is low, and there are long waiting lists for employment. Productivity is sufficiently high that the company is able to remain competitive in its industry even with its high compensation costs per employee.

Yet positive results require a lot of thought, both for the company using the plan and for the employee who may be compensated by it. Such a plan may have negative consequences as well as positive: Jealousy is common; many individuals simply do not want to work under this much pressure, even though they might benefit financially if they did; and distrust and friction can run high, especially when a plan is first introduced. Yet as Lincoln Electric's experience indicates, the problems can be overcome or at least minimized. In many cases monetary incentives are effective for the company and rewarding for the individual.

■ REWARDS AND PUNISHMENTS

As we noted in the discussion of behavior modification, punishments can also have a favorable impact on performance, although not as frequently as rewards. The following guidelines, based on what is known to date, explain the appropriate use of punishment in organizations (Arvey & Ivancevich, 1980, pp. 126–129):

1. Punishment is more effective if it is applied immediately after the undesirable behavior occurs.

2. Moderate levels of punishment are more effective than low or high intensity levels.

3. Punishment procedures are more effective when the person doing the punishing has a relatively close and friendly relationship with the employee being punished.

4. Punishment of undesired behavior is more effective when it follows every instance of the behavior, when it is administered consistently to different employees by the same manager, and when different managers are consistent in their punishment for the same undesired behavior.

5. Punishment is more effective when clear explanations are given as to why it is needed, how it can be avoided, and what will happen if the undesired behavior is repeated.

6. Punishment is more effective when alternative desirable behaviors are available and can be rewarded.

In practice, the use of punishment in an organization tends to be severely constrained by formal disciplinary procedures. Often these procedures are stipulated in a union contract, although companies without unions may well have formal systems as well. Frequently there are stated procedures for appeal and arbitration in case of an impasse. Consequently, punishment and discipline in the workplace have largely become the province of lawyers. Disciplinary action may be more closely related to legal considerations than to performance and productivity.

A lawyer with much experience in these matters (Redeker, 1983, p. 21) explains the steps that are taken in most **formal disciplinary systems:**

1. An employee who has committed an infraction is warned orally and told that if the same infraction recurs within some specified period, disciplinary action will follow.
2. If the employee again commits the same or a similar violation within the specified period, the employee will be given a written warning that will be placed in his or her personnel file. The employee will be told that, if the infraction is repeated within a specified period, he or she will be disciplined more severely.
3. If the employee again transgresses in the same manner and within the specified period, he or she will be suspended without pay for a period and will be given a final warning. This final warning will clearly specify discharge as the result of another such infraction within a stated time.
4. If the employee again violates the same rule within the specified time, the employee will be discharged.

Formal systems of this kind can prove quite effective in dealing with performance problems. In certain respects they closely parallel the research-derived guidelines for the use of punishment. But they do severely constrain what an individual manager can do; it is not easy to work within this kind of formal system and still consider individual differences in the motivational hierarchies of various people.

A final point relates to the motivational impact of punishment and formal discipline on others who are in a position to observe what has happened. Much business practice assumes that observing punishment that has happened to others represents a learning experience and that coworkers will put this information to good use, thus avoiding the behaviors they have seen punished and improving their own performance. Surprisingly little research has been done on this topic. But what has been done supports existing practice unequivocably; punishment can act in an indirect, or vicarious, manner to yield informational value to others, and contribute to their improved performance (O'Reilly and Puffer, 1989; Schnake, 1986).

KEY TERMS

Goal setting
Management by objectives (MBO)
Work redesign

Orthodox job enrichment
Motivation-hygiene theory
Motivators

Hygienes

Vertical loading

Job characteristics theory

Motivating potential

Growth needs

Compressed work week

Flexible working hours (flextime)

Operant learning

Contingencies of reinforcement

Positive reinforcement

Avoidance learning

Extinction

Punishment

Partial reinforcement

Variable ratio reinforcement

Fixed ratio reinforcement

Variable interval reinforcement

Fixed interval reinforcement

Organizational behavior modification

Social learning theory

Self-management

Behavior modeling

Inducements-contributions balance

Wage survey

Job evaluation

Incentive systems

Formal disciplinary systems

SUMMARY

This chapter has considered a variety of motivational techniques used in organizations: *goal setting*, including *management by objectives; work redesign* and *job enrichment*, including alternative work schedules; *organizational behavior modification*, including *self-management* and *behavior modeling; reward systems*, especially monetary *incentives;* and *punishment* and *disciplinary procedures*. All seem to have value in increasing performance and productivity, at least when used appropriately.

Goal setting can be a very effective procedure for improving performance. Positive results have been obtained 90 percent of the time, and the average improvement has been 16 percent. Positive results are more likely to be achieved from individual goal-setting plans, however, than from formal management-by-objectives programs. The many difficulties inherent in MBO make it unlikely that these programs will have continuing positive motivational effects.

Job enrichment appears to work less frequently than goal setting, although it still can be effective if applied with appropriate people under the right circumstances. *Job characteristics theory* is useful for identifying the circumstances under which job enrichment will prove most effective. Improvements from job enrichment average 9 percent, well

below the results of goal setting and of monetary incentives. Work redesign, involving alternative work schedules such as *compressed work weeks* and *flextime*, may also have positive effects on productivity, but the most consistent finding is that employees like these schedules.

Organizational behavior modification uses various *contingencies of reinforcement* and reinforcement schedules to bring about behavior change. It has proved quite effective in improving performance. With the addition of *social learning theory* concepts, it has been extended to self-management and behavior modeling.

Reward systems, and in particular monetary reward systems, are widely used in the business world. Nevertheless, companies often lose the incentive value of money for improving performance. Sometimes this happens because the reward programs have unanticipated negative side effects, and sometimes companies fail to establish such programs because the normal payroll costs of attraction and retention are all they feel they can afford. On the average, individual *monetary incentives* yield a 30 percent performance improvement and *group incentives* yield a 20 percent improvement. The use of punishment appears to be somewhat less effective but when it is applied appropriately, it can lead to improved performance.

QUESTIONS

1. Why do individual monetary incentive systems tend to have greater motivational effects than group incentive systems?
2. What are the different types of alternative work schedules? What do they accomplish?
3. How do orthodox job enrichment and the job characteristics approach differ? How are they similar?
4. Why do MBO programs often run into difficulty after a couple of years?
5. How do formal systems of discipline operate? What are their advantages and disadvantages?
6. What are the various contingencies of reinforcement, and how useful are they?
7. What are the various constructs included in job characteristics theory, and what evidence exists regarding their importance to the theory?
8. How does goal setting operate, and what factors do and do not influence its success?
9. What is motivation-hygiene theory? How does it relate to orthodox job enrichment?
10. Why is social learning theory necessary to organizational behavior modification?

CASE PROBLEM

WILLARD DAVISON
Industrial Salesman

Willard Davison entered the company's employ in an unusual manner. The process started when his father-in-law called the president and asked if there was a position available that Will might be able to handle. A note subsequently traveled down through channels and landed on the desk of the man in charge of sales recruiting. The note indicated only that this was a young man whom the president felt might be useful to the organization and that the young man's father-in-law owned a firm which for many years had been a major purchaser of the company's products. Shortly thereafter, Will was asked to come into the personnel office. He was interviewed and hired. Having had prior work experience, including some selling, he was placed directly as a salesman. He would attend the sales training school and then double up for about two months with the man currently in his territory. Subsequently that man would be transferred and Will would take over.

From the beginning it was apparent that the company had not gained a particularly effective salesman. During the two-month field training period, the two men traveled together, but the other man did all the work. Frequently Will stayed in the car or in a nearby bar, if he could find one, while their business was being transacted. The old-timer, who was considered one of the top salesmen in the company, was very happy to be out of the situation when the two months were over. Besides having received practically no assistance from Will in performing his job, he had had to find Will when he wandered off, get him up in the morning, and somehow find a way to force him to learn something about the territory and the products he was supposedly selling. It had not been easy.

Will remained in the territory for four years. During that time it slumped from its previous high position to one somewhat below the company average. Most of the drop occurred within the first year. The thing that disturbed the sales manager most, however, was that sales continued at the same relatively low level in spite of a large amount of new industrial construction in the area, which should have produced a lot of new business. As far as could be determined, Will seldom, if ever, called on these new plants. It was not surprising that competitors got their business. As time went on, it became increasingly clear that the job was being handled poorly in other respects. Customers became angry because the salesman failed to keep many of his appointments. Orders were often delivered late because Will had delayed several days before putting them through to the regional office. Will didn't know anything about several new products that customers had asked about after seeing advertising material on them. On occasion he had gone to sleep in the reception room while waiting to see a purchasing agent. He spent a considerable part of his time playing golf instead of making sales calls. The only reason Will was retained in a sales capacity was that no one knew what else to do with him. He had been repeatedly informed of the unsatisfactory nature of his performance, but with no effect.

Finally, after a change of regional managers, Will was brought into the office and put to work in a job involving primarily clerical duties connected with product distribution. It was hoped that the increased surveillance possible in the office might permit greater control over his activities. He was told at the time of transfer that he was considered only barely satisfactory as a salesman, if that, and that a considerable improvement in performance would be expected. Will agreed that he had not done a very good job in the field, but he felt he could do better.

During his 2 1/2 years in the office, his superiors became increasingly dissatisfied. He was almost invariably late arriving in the morning, and his attendance record was unusually poor. He showed almost no enthusiasm for his work, although he was greatly interested in a wide range of outside activities: golf, sailing, hunting, horseback riding, bridge, football, sports cars. He and his wife were very active in the social life of the community, spending considerable time at the country club and entertaining frequently.

When Will's failures were called to his attention or when he was pushed to complete work for which others were waiting, he often became resistant and stubborn. Pressure and criticism had only a minimal effect. He seemed to take the attitude that nobody had a right to tell him what to do, that if they didn't like his work they could find someone else to do it. On other occasions, when discussing these problems with his boss, he would admit frankly that he was not performing at the level generally expected, but he conveyed the impression that he didn't care much. When he did work he was quite capable of

doing a satisfactory job, although he showed little initiative in going beyond what was expected. Errors in his reports were not especially frequent, although it should have been possible for him to eliminate them entirely if he had been willing to take the time to check his work.

The culmination was a decision to put Will on probation for two months. If there was no improvement during that time the company would have to seriously consider asking him to find a job elsewhere. This decision was reached only after consultation at rather high levels in the company. To lose the business provided by Will's father-in-law would certainly represent a most unfortunate consequence. Therefore every effort would be made to keep him if he could perform at an even minimally effective level.

At the end of the two months, it was evident that Will's performance could not be called satisfactory. The pile of uncompleted work on his desk was as high as it had ever been, and he had missed several days from work which just happened to coincide with the beginning of the hunting season. The question of what to do now was passed rapidly up through channels until it settled on the desk of the vice president for industrial relations. The latter assembled all the information available, utilizing both personnel records and data provided by some of his friends who were familiar with Will's family, and came up with the following picture.

Young Will had been a problem to his family for many years. He had been sent to a military prep school which was strong on discipline but not very demanding scholastically. There he had maintained a barely satisfactory record in his course work while participating in one escapade after another. He probably would have been thrown out of school long before graduation had it not been for two factors. His family was a major contributor to the various fund-raising campaigns that were conducted each year, and the headmaster had interpreted Will's behavior as a personal challenge to his ingenuity. Somehow the boy not only graduated but, as a result of a surprisingly good performance on his college entrance examinations, gained admission to a small but well-regarded college.

Free of military school discipline, however, Will devoted his efforts to having a good time, and flunked out at the end of the first year. He then entered a college in the South which was particularly desirous of attracting northern students, and eventually graduated. Shortly thereafter he married and entered the employ of his father-in-law's firm, with the objective of learning the various aspects of the business and perhaps eventually rising to a policy-making position.

After about three years, however, there had apparently been a change of plan, and it was then that the father-in-law had assisted Will in obtaining the sales position with his present employer. The official explanation was that he was expected to gain broadening experience through exposure to the policies and procedures of another company. There were persistent rumors, however, that family relationships had been badly strained as a result of the young man's poor showing on the job and his frequent vacations. The father-in-law had apparently proposed, and perhaps forced, the job change as a solution to an intolerable situation.

The vice president's study of the problem produced some additional information. Will and his wife both came from families with considerable money. Both families had been generous in their financial gifts to their children, with the result that the young Davisons were very well off. In addition, family pressures were such that Will would almost certainly be reemployed by his father-in-law's firm if he should lose his present position. Will had apparently been aware of this fact for some time.

Questions

1. How and how effectively might goal setting be used to solve Willard Davison's motivational problems? Document your position from the information given.
2. How and how effectively might job enrichment be used to solve Will's motivational problems? Document your position from the information given.
3. How and how effectively might organizational behavior modification be used to solve Will's motivational problems? Document your position from the information given.

4. How and how effectively might monetary incentives be used to solve Will's motivational problems? Document your position from the information given.
5. How and how effectively might discipline be used to solve Will's motivational problems? Document your position from the information given.
6. How would you deal with this situation if you were the industrial relations vice president? Why?

5

Attitudes, Commitments, and Values

Sears, Roebuck has conducted periodic attitude surveys among its employees for many years to evaluate managers, to predict aspects of performance, and to warn of problems that might lead to union representation of employees in a given location. The company has good evidence that this early warning system works.

In one instance attitude-survey scores were compared with the degree of union activity during the months following the survey in 250 work units located all over the United States. Level of union activity was scored numerically as follows:

0. No union activity.
1. Handbilling of the unit by outside union representatives only.
2. Some employees signed cards endorsing a union.
3. Enough of these authorization cards were signed to justify unionization meetings.
4. A union filed a representation petition with the National Labor Relations Board (at least 30 percent of employees must sign authorization cards).

5. Union election held and won by company.
6. Union election held and won by union.

Dissatisfaction with supervision was the greatest contributor to high levels of union activity. However, dissatisfaction with coworkers, with career opportunities, with the company as a whole, with the amount of work expected, with the physical surroundings, and with the kind of work done all contributed as well. There was no question that higher levels of dissatisfaction in a unit meant that a union subsequently would come closer to the goal of organizing the unit and representing its employees.

With advance information on potential trouble spots, Sears, Roebuck could take steps to reduce job dissatisfaction long before any union organizers appeared on the scene.

SOURCE: W. Clay Hamner and Frank J. Smith (1978). Work attitudes as predictors of unionization activity. *Journal of Applied Psychology, 63,* 415–421.

There are other reasons why attitudes and attitude surveys are important to organizations, but this is a good example. Employee attitudes do relate to union activity. As we will see, there are many other significant roles they play as well.

Attitudes, commitments, and values all involve emotional reactions to people and things. We will differentiate among them as we proceed, but the important point to keep in mind throughout this chapter is that we are dealing with feelings. It is also important to be aware that a much larger body of knowledge about attitudes, commitments, and values exists, extending well beyond the bounds of industrial-organizational psychology into social psychology, sociology, and anthropology. This discussion, however, will limit itself to what is directly relevant for present purposes. The discussion begins with a simple precept: Attitudes can cause a person to act in

certain ways and not to act in others (Chaiken & Stangor, 1987).

■ WORK ATTITUDES AND JOB SATISFACTION

In the work situation, attitudes are a major potential source of performance differences—of variations in quantity and quality of output, absenteeism, turnover, and other aspects of performance. Whether attitudes actually produce behaviors, however, depends on a host of other factors. An employee who hates her job may not leave because there is nothing else available that pays as well. A worker who loves his job may not produce very much because there are no salient rewards for doing so.

An **attitude** can be defined as the degree of positive or negative feeling a person has toward a

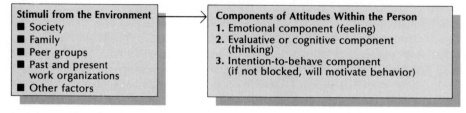

EXHIBIT 5-1   The Nature of Attitudes
Attitudes have their source in environmental stimuli, and the various components of these attitudes result.

particular attitude object, such as a place, thing, or other person. . . . When we speak of positive **job attitudes** we mean that the people involved tend to have pleasant internal feelings when they think about their jobs, although different aspects of one's job are bound to bring about different sorts of feelings (Pinder, 1984, p. 82).

Exhibit 5-1 outlines how attitudes are created by environmental stimuli and identifies the three components of attitudinal structure.

☐ The Nature of Job Satisfaction

Job satisfaction is often thought to be synonymous with job attitudes, but it is important to recognize that those with different theoretical orientations may use the term somewhat differently. Some measure job satisfaction in terms of the gratification of strong needs in the workplace. Others see it as the degree of discrepancy between what a person expects to receive from work and what that person perceives is actually received. It can also be defined as the extent to which work is seen as providing those things that one considers conducive to one's welfare. In yet another view, job satisfaction is considered a purely emotional response to a job situation (as opposed to the combination of emotional, mental, and behavioral components indicated in Exhibit 5-1). There are additional views as well. For our purposes, however, it seems desirable to maintain a broad perspective and

treat job satisfaction as generally equivalent in meaning to job attitudes. However, it does appear that job satisfaction in its various aspects is a function of the discrepancy between what is experienced in a job and what is wanted, as a standard of comparison (Rice, McFarlin, & Bennett, 1989).

Those who study job attitudes have been divided on the question of whether attitudes are determined by internal factors (the characteristics or traits of the individual) or external factors (the environmental forces that affect a person). For many years the assumption was that the work situation alone made for satisfied or dissatisfied workers. Hence, an individual whose job responsibilities were adjusted or who moved to a different job was expected to experience a concomitant shift in job satisfaction level.

During the 1980s, however, it became apparent that, although one's job situation is important to one's job satisfaction level, people who exhibit considerable job satisfaction at one time are likely to be happy with their job several years later—even if they have changed occupation or employer or both. Others apparently remain dissatisfied in numerous work situations (Gerhart, 1987; Staw & Ross, 1985). It may be that some people continue to seek out situations where they will be satisfied, while others are drawn toward situations where they will not. Or people's attitudes about facets of their environment unrelated to their work situation

BOX 5-1   RESEARCH IN I/O PSYCHOLOGY

Is Job Satisfaction Inherited?

A study conducted at the University of Minnesota dealt with the job satisfaction levels of twins formed from a single egg, and thus identical in heredity, who were raised apart in different environments from an early age. The question was whether these twins with different experiences but identical heredities had similar levels of job satisfaction.

Thirty-four pairs of twins completed items from the Minnesota Job Satisfaction Questionnaire at an average age of almost 42 years. Satisfaction levels were indicated for what the respondents felt was their major job, which in roughly two-thirds of the cases was the present job. If heredity were not a factor in job satisfaction, no correlation between the scores of the twins would be expected.

There was a significant relationship, with twins more likely to have similar job satisfaction levels than others who were not related. The findings did not indicate a large genetic component in job satisfaction, but they did clearly establish its existence. Furthermore, there was a tendency for twins to hold very similar jobs. However, when this tendency was removed from the analysis statistically, the association between heredity and job satisfaction remained equally strong.

The findings are interpreted to mean that organizations may have less influence over job satisfaction than has been commonly believed.

SOURCE: Richard D. Arvey, Thomas J. Bouchard, Nancy L. Segal, and Lauren M. Abraham (1989). Job satisfaction: Environmental and genetic components. *Journal of Applied Psychology, 74,* 187–192.

may be manifested in ways that affect job satisfaction. The point is that both forces internal to the person and external forces do operate. Furthermore, very recent findings support the view that genetic forces are involved in job satisfaction. As Box 5-1 demonstrates, there is a tendency for individuals to bring satisfaction or dissatisfaction to the employment context as a function of their hereditary makeup, not just as a consequence of the personalities they have developed during their formative years.

The National Picture. As indicated in Exhibit 5-2, which is based on a nationwide sample of 10,000 hourly employees at thirty-seven firms throughout the United States, overall job satisfaction depends on a number of interacting variables. The respondents, all of whom presented a consistent picture of sat-

isfaction or dissatisfaction (those whose answers were vague were excluded from the sample) answered questions on eighteen aspects of job satisfaction.

Most respondents expressed positive feelings toward the company and its work, and 64 percent believed that their company was concerned with producing a quality product. On more basic issues, however, the respondents indicated considerable dissatisfaction. Many complained about lack of opportunities for advancement, inappropriate job demands, failures in worker–management communication, and their employer's unresponsiveness to needs for change. Immediate, first-level supervision was viewed more favorably than management at higher levels. Other surveys asking somewhat different questions indicate that safety and health hazards, inflexible work hours, insufficient fringe benefits, and

Exhibit 5-2 Job Satisfaction Levels among Hourly Employees

Aspect of Job Satisfaction	Percent Consistently		Net Effect
	Satisfied	Dissatisfied	
Rewards			
Pay and benefits	39%	45%	−6%
Opportunities for advancement	30	52	−22
Job situation			
Job demands	29	58	−29
Work group atmosphere	49	39	+10
Supervision and management			
Skill of immediate supervisor	53	34	+19
Skill of middle and upper managers	35	41	−6
Communication			
Upward communication	32	51	−19
Downward communication	34	50	−16
Clear specification of goals	32	49	−17
Employee input to decisions	28	49	−21
Corporate philosophy and policy			
Concern for employees	43	42	+1
Dealing with problems	36	44	−8
Responding to need for change	31	47	−16
Concern for productivity	44	42	+2
Concern for quality	64	23	+41
The company and its work			
Identification with company	54	26	+28
Contribution to society	67	17	+50
Intrinsic value of the work	83	11	+72

Source: Adapted from William Rabinowitz, Kenneth Falkenbach, Jeffrey R. Travers, C. Glenn Valentine, & Paul Weener (1983). Worker motivation: Unsolved problem or untapped resource? *California Management Review, 25* (2), 48–53.

monotony of tasks also contribute significantly to dissatisfaction (Staines & Quinn, 1979).

Individual Significance. As noted earlier in this chapter, job dissatisfaction stems in part from actual workplace conditions and in part from an individual's attitude toward work in general. Since most people want to feel good about their lives, and since work generally takes up half of an individual's waking hours, job satisfaction must be considered important in its own right, not just as a means to an end. It has individual significance independent of its contribution to organizational goals, such as productivity.

The question remains: How does one obtain satisfaction from a job? A clue comes from research findings indicating that managers at higher levels tend to feel more satisfied. Older people, too, at least those up to the age of 69, evince greater job satisfaction (Bergmann, 1981; Rhodes, 1983). To the extent that job satisfaction is viewed as deriving from some type of compatibility between the job and the person, these findings are only logical (Pulakos & Schmitt, 1983; Swaney & Prediger, 1985). Upper-level managers are often able to write their own job descriptions, thus shaping their work responsibilities and schedules according to their personal preferences. Similarly, older people have had more time to try different types of work and to learn about themselves, so they are more likely to have found a satisfying job fit.

Job satisfaction, in short, comes either to those who enter a line of work where they can make over the job in their own image or to those who find a job that fits them. Either course takes time, as well as the foresight to think through career considerations and make personal job satisfaction a major goal. In any event, a person who is first entering the work force should not expect to find immediate job satisfaction. A degree of dissatisfaction may be necessary to gain satisfaction at some future point, as when college students spend many hours studying, writing papers, and attending classes in the hope of preparing themselves for a rewarding career. Yet individuals vary in their potential for contentment. Some may never find job satisfaction; some may not even seek it. There is evidence that job satisfaction is more likely to accrue to those who experience a generalized life satisfaction (Tait, Padgett, & Baldwin, 1989).

☐ Consequences of Job Satisfaction

People react to job satisfaction or dissatisfaction in a number of ways. These reactions, in turn, can have important implications for job performance. Employees who think that they have been treated badly may feel justified in stealing from an employer, thereby helping themselves to what they see as a morally justifiable supplement to their wages (Hollinger & Clark, 1983). For instance, a household worker who feels underpaid and mistreated may resort to "toting"—taking home food and various small articles belonging to .the employer—as recompense. It makes no difference whether theft is a response to true or imagined mistreatment; the larcenous employee genuinely feels dissatisfied with his or her job.

Similarly, job dissatisfaction appears to be associated with emotional illness and symptoms of emotional disorder (Kavanagh, Hurst, & Rose, 1981; Wiener, Vardi, & Muczyk, 1981), such as loss of appetite, difficulty in sleeping, or, in extreme situations, emotional breakdown. Or other sources of stress in an individual's life, such as a troubled marriage, may combine with job dissatisfaction to push the person over the edge. Sometimes a vicious cycle develops in which job dissatisfaction causes an emotional symptom (say, tension headaches), and the symptom then feeds back and contributes to even greater job dissatisfaction.

Theft and emotional illness are extreme reactions to job dissatisfaction. More often, dissatisfaction is manifested in the form of increased union activity, decreased output, absenteeism, and employee turnover. It is to these areas that we now turn.

Union Activity. Historically, for many companies the primary reason for identifying job satisfaction levels was to prevent unions from organizing workers. If sources of dissatisfaction could be pinpointed in advance, appropriate action could be taken and union organizing attempts thwarted. Data clearly indicate that dissatisfied employees are more likely to vote for a union, and employee groups in which dissatisfaction is pronounced are more likely to become unionized (Gilmore, Fried, & Ferris, 1989; Premack, 1984). The discussion that began this chapter, which describes attitude surveys conducted among employees of Sears, Roebuck, shows how this process may operate.

Quantity and Quality of Output. Organizational scientists have had difficulty determining the relationships between job satisfaction and performance outputs. Until the early 1950s, most assumed that a satisfied employee was a productive employee; thus whatever made for employee satisfaction helped the

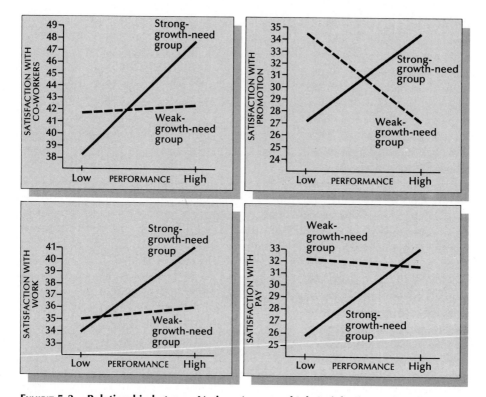

EXHIBIT 5-3   Relationship between Various Aspects of Job Satisfaction and Performance Levels among Employees with Strong and Weak Growth Needs

Satisfaction with coworkers, promotion opportunities, the nature of the work, and pay goes with high performance among those with strong growth needs. Among those with weak growth needs, no such relationship is present—and, in fact, satisfaction with promotion opportunities goes with low performance.

SOURCE: Adapted from Ahmed A. Abdel-Halim (1980). Effects of higher order need strength on the job performance–job satisfaction relationship. *Personnel Psychology, 33,* 341.

company as well. By the mid-1950s, however, a number of research studies had failed to establish a clear link between satisfaction and productivity. In the ensuing years, with more studies and better analyses, researchers have crept back toward—but have not yet actually reached—the original view.

In essence, when we consider an average situation, based on all the recent studies of the relationship of job satisfaction to performance, we find that a positive correlation does exist (Iaffaldano & Muchinsky, 1985; Petty, McGee, & Cavender, 1984). The rela-

tionship is not very strong, and there are numerous specific instances where satisfied employees have produced less than dissatisfied employees, but the overall positive association is there.

This tendency becomes much more pronounced under certain circumstances, both within the individual and in the work environment. Exhibit 5-3, which illustrates the relationship of job satisfaction to performance among the employees of a large drugstore chain, reveals a strong positive relationship when only the people with strong growth needs (see Chapters 3 and 4) are considered. Among those without such needs, no positive relationship between satisfaction and performance is evident, and indeed high satisfaction with promotional opportunities goes with low performance.

Aspects of the work environment can also influence the performance–satisfaction relationship. One study showed that within a department store chain, intense time and performance pressures produced a situation where performance and job satisfaction were essentially unrelated. But in the absence of these pressures, a strong positive relationship developed between performance and job satisfaction (Bhagat, 1982). It appears that the natural tendency is for employees to be either satisfied and productive or dissatisfied and less productive. However, aspects of the individual, such as the absence of strong relevant motives, and of the situation, such as strong performance pressures, can interfere with this natural tendency and negate it.

When performance and satisfaction are positively related, it is often difficult to discern which variable is affecting the other. People may feel happy because they are doing well at work, or unhappy because they are performing poorly. Conversely, satisfied employees who are free of stress may therefore be more productive, and certainly dissatisfied workers may take their displeasure out on the company and produce less. The arrow can point in either direction, or both at the same time (that is, satisfaction causes good performance and the latter in turn adds to the feeling of satisfaction).

Absenteeism. It has long been posited that dissatisfied employees are more likely than satisfied employees to be absent from the workplace. Many recent studies support this conclusion, but not strongly (Hackett, 1989). All that can be said with certainty is that job satisfaction tends to be associated with less absenteeism, especially when frequency-of-absences rather than total-time-lost measures are used and when the analysis is restricted to absences over which an employee has some control. This is evident in the situation described in Box 5-2, which discusses how the Sears, Roebuck attitude surveys serve as predictors of absenteeism. Often, however, company rules regarding what is and is not acceptable absenteeism and pressures enforcing them intervene. Unexcused absences differ considerably from excused absences, and when the two are grouped together, the tendency for absenteeism to follow dissatisfaction often disappears (Blau, 1985).

Employee Turnover. Virtually every model of the turnover process that has been proposed gives a central role to job satisfaction. Note the position of satisfaction in Exhibit 5-4, which represents the most complex and advanced of these models. Although many other factors are involved in the decision to leave a job, dissatisfaction is the central impetus. Major studies carried out in organizations as diverse as the Hillsborough Community Mental Health Center in Tampa, Florida, and the U.S. Marine Corps have supported the model presented in Exhibit 5-4 in many of its aspects (Michaels & Spector, 1982; Youngblood, Mobley, & Meglino, 1983). In these and other investigations, job satisfaction has been found to play a significant role in turnover.

Yet there clearly are conditions under which dissatisfied employees do not leave. When, for instance, labor-market conditions are such that jobs are hard to find, the normal relationship between satisfaction and turnover is disrupted. Another important variable is depicted in Exhibit 5-5. In this instance turnover was measured in terms of voluntary departures only; it did not include firings, and performance was determined from supervisors' ratings. Note that there is a strong job satisfaction–turnover relationship among the low-rated performers. A person who is dissatisfied and viewed as a poor

BOX 5-2 RESEARCH IN I/O PSYCHOLOGY

The Sears, Roebuck Attitude Surveys as Predictors of Absenteeism

Sears, Roebuck relies on periodic employee-attitude surveys to point up potential absenteeism problems in specific units. An indication of the effectiveness of this approach was provided when a severe snowstorm hit the Chicago area, where Sears, Roebuck has its headquarters. At such times it is unreasonable to expect employees to show up for work. Those who do make it to work must put out an unusual effort, and those who do not certainly cannot be reprimanded or punished.

Comparisons were made between levels of job satisfaction identified several months before the storm and absenteeism levels on the day of the storm for twenty-seven work units in the Chicago headquarters. Where there was dissatisfaction, there also was absenteeism; the more satisfied employees were the ones who made the extra effort to come in. Dissatisfaction with career futures and supervision had a particularly strong tendency to keep employees away from work. But dissatisfaction with financial rewards, the company, the kind of work performed, and the amount of work were also important. It appeared that those who were more dissatisfied simply felt no need to struggle through the blizzard to go in to work; those who were more satisfied apparently enjoyed their work and wanted to be present if they possibly could.

On the same day as the storm in Chicago, the company conducted a comparison analysis with its office in New York City, where weather was no problem. In Chicago absenteeism averaged 30 percent; in New York it was 4 percent. Job satisfaction levels showed minimal relationships to absenteeism in New York that day.

It was apparent that absenteeism is most strongly affected by job dissatisfaction under special circumstances, when employees are free to come to work or not at their own discretion, and few if any sanctions are operating.

SOURCE: Frank J. Smith (1977). Work attitudes as predictors of attendance on a specific day. *Journal of Applied Psychology, 62,* 16–19.

worker is particularly likely to leave. In contrast, good performers—both those who are satisfied and those who are not—are unlikely to leave their jobs, apparently because they are offered strong inducements to stay, such as raises and promotions. These inducements seem to override dissatisfaction.

☐ The Importance of Job Satisfaction

When allowed to operate freely, job satisfaction can contribute substantially to organizational effectiveness. It can contribute to productive output in the form of high quantity and quality of products or services, as well as to organizational maintenance objectives as represented by low absenteeism and turnover. Yet in a great many instances aspects of the individual, the organization, or the environment constrain the satisfaction–productivity relationship to the point where its practical importance is minimal. A very dissatisfied employee may work hard, produce, be present every day, and stay with the company for many years if there is no place else to go, the person desperately needs a job, and there is a real prospect of being fired should good performance not be maintained. Ultimately, stress may catch up with such a person and signs of poor corporate citizenship may

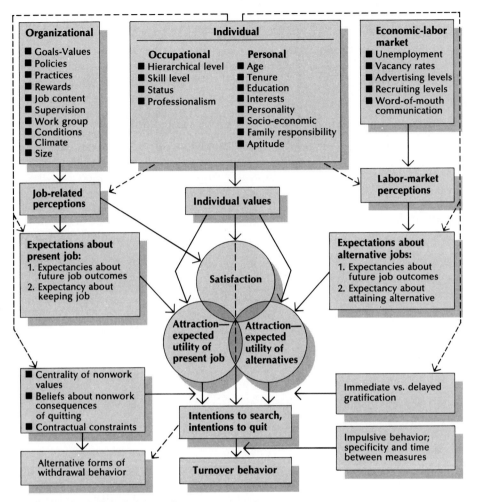

EXHIBIT 5-4   Model of the Employee Turnover Process
Note that among the many factors that contribute to turnover behavior, satisfaction holds
a central position.
SOURCE: William H. Mobley, Rodger W. Griffeth, Herbert H. Hand, & Bruce M. Meglino (1979).
Review and conceptual analysis of the employee turnover process. *Psychological Bulletin, 86,* 517.
See also William H. Mobley (1982). *Employee turnover: Causes, consequences and control,* p. 126.
Reading, MA: Addison-Wesley.

appear, but such denials of natural satisfaction–output patterns can maintain themselves
for long periods.

Hence job satisfaction may well be more
important to the individual than to the
employing organization. In American society,

responsibility for attaining job satisfaction is
usually assigned to the individual rather than
to the organization. Individuals can change
jobs, thereby obtaining more satisfying work.
Organizations can shift people from job to job
within the firm, but their capacity to move

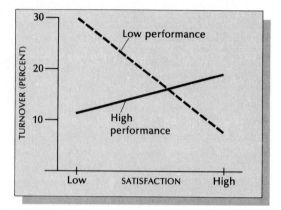

Exhibit 5-5   Relationships between Employee Turnover Rates and Satisfaction Levels for Low and High Performers
Among low performers, dissatisfaction goes with high turnover, as expected; but this is not true among high performers.
Source: Daniel G. Spencer & Richard M. Steers (1981). Performance as a moderator of the job satisfaction–turnover relationship. *Journal of Applied Psychology, 66,* 513.

people from organization to organization is very limited. The only obvious exception is when a firm provides outplacement assistance to its laid-off workers.

■ TYPES OF WORK-RELATED COMMITMENTS

Work-related commitments have been proposed in a variety of forms—job, career, professional, organizational, and others. Of these, *organizational commitment* has received the most attention within the field of organizational behavior. A distinction may also be made between *attitudinal commitment* and *behavioral commitment,* reflecting two different ways in which individuals may attach themselves to job, career, profession, organization, and so on. Of these two, attitudinal commitment has received more attention within the field of organizational behavior.

□ The Nature of Organizational Commitment

Given the current thrust of theory, research, and application, it is appropriate to focus initially on organizational commitment defined from the attitudinal standpoint. This is particularly appropriate because organizational commitment defined as a work attitude has much in common with job satisfaction, although the two are distinct constructs (Brooke, Russell, & Price, 1988). **Attitudinal commitment** to an organization may be defined as

> . . . the relative strength of an individual's identification with and involvement in a particular organization. Conceptually, it can be characterized by at least three factors:
> a) a strong belief in and acceptance of the organization's goals and values;
> b) a willingness to exert considerable effort on behalf of the organization;
> c) a strong desire to maintain membership in the organization (Mowday, Porter, & Steers, 1982, p. 27).

Inherent in this definition is the idea of organizational or company loyalty, but commitment goes beyond loyalty to a more active contribution. As an attitude, organizational commitment is more global than job satisfaction because it applies to the organization as a whole, not just to the job; and it is more stable, because day-to-day events at work are unlikely to shift it. It is also important to note that the definition of attitudinal commitment incorporates the presence (or absence) of a desire to maintain membership in the organization. In Exhibit 5-4, organizational commitment is inherent in the intentions to search and to quit. Thus it is closer to turnover behavior than job satisfaction is.

The Commitment Process. Exhibit 5-6 presents a three-stage view of the commitment process. It is evident that commitment can

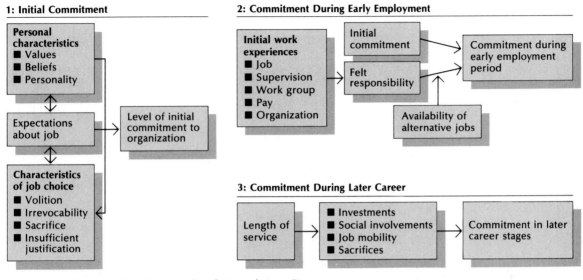

1: Initial Commitment

2: Commitment During Early Employment

3: Commitment During Later Career

EXHIBIT 5-6   Stages of the Organizational Commitment Process
Commitments during the initial period, during early employment, and during the later career period tend to be fueled by different factors.
SOURCE: Richard T. Mowday, Lyman W. Porter, & Richard M. Steers (1982). *Employee–organization linkages: The psychology of commitment, absenteeism and turnover*, pp. 49, 56, and 65. New York: Academic Press.

emerge very early in employment. Certain individuals have a strong built-in potential for commitment to an organization and rapidly attach these feelings to the firm that hires them. In fact, one way a company can foster organizational commitment is to hire people with considerable commitment potential.

Yet as Exhibit 5-6 shows, factors in the early employment situation can influence commitment levels. Amplifying what is shown, overstaffing to the extent that new employees do not have enough work to do that is meaningfully related to organizational effectiveness can contribute to a rapid erosion of initial commitment. So too can behavior at the helm of the organization indicating that top-level managers are using their positions for personal purposes, such as making political connections, rather than contributing to organizational objectives. At later career stages organizational commitment tends to

accelerate because over time a variety of ties to the employing organization and its people have developed. Seniority often confers advantages, and opportunities in the job market often decrease with age, prompting many people to strengthen their company ties in the later stages of their careers.

Contributors to Organizational Commitment. Box 5-3 describes a study of the U.S. Army Reserve, which found a number of related factors—including overall job satisfaction, intention to stay, and group cohesion—that do contribute to organizational commitment, and a number of other factors that do not.

In addition to the factors cited in the box, trust and confidence in management appear to play a very significant role in commitment. If employees do not believe that they can rely on a company's management, they are much less likely to commit themselves to that company. Cultural differences in organizational

BOX 5-3 RESEARCH IN I/O PSYCHOLOGY

Organizational Commitment in the U.S. Army Reserve

The U.S. Army Reserve has as one of its major concerns the retention of its personnel. Given the investment made in training and the need to maintain a large standby force in case of war, everything possible must be done to keep turnover low. Doing so is not easy under the conditions of the all-volunteer policy that has been in effect since 1973. In view of the facts that organizational commitment is closely connected to turnover, and that competing commitments to civilian jobs, home, and family can easily pull reservists away, it is not surprising that the U.S. Army Reserve has a considerable interest in organizational commitment.

In order to learn more about how commitment works in the military reserve, attitude surveys were conducted among members of two battalions—one consisting of combat engineers and the other of noncombatant medical and support personnel. The idea was to determine how various job factors contributed to organizational commitment. Typical items (to be rated on a five-point scale) for each job factor were:

Organizational commitment: I talk up this unit as a great place to work for.

Job variety: I do the same job in the same way at every meeting.

Communication: How well are you informed about what is to be done?

Promotion: I have a dead-end job.

Compensation: I am very much underpaid for my work.

Group cohesion: I am part of a close-knit group.

Job satisfaction: I find real enjoyment with my military work.

Discipline: Discipline is too lax.

Training: The training we receive is poor.

Time management: Too much time is spent waiting around.

Spouse nonconflict: How does your spouse feel about your military schedule?

Civilian career nonconflict: My reserve duty is causing problems with my civilian work.

Intent to stay: Which most clearly reflects your feelings about your future in the military within the next year (leave or stay)?

Of these factors, job satisfaction was most closely related to organizational commitment; intent to stay came next. Among the remaining factors, only group cohesion showed a consistently positive relationship. For the purposes of the military, the low impact that factors such as compensation and spouse nonconflict have on turnover is particularly important. However, the lack of clear-cut relationships between turnover and the remaining factors severely restricts the steps that can be taken to foster organizational commitment among reservists.

SOURCE: Thomas N. Martin & M. Shawn O'Laughlin (1984). Predictors of organizational commitment: The study of part-time Army Reservists, *Journal of Vocational Behavior, 25,* 273–279.

commitment have also been found—and they contradict what many observers had hypothesized. Organizational commitment in the United States turns out to be stronger than in either Japan or Korea, both of which are at essentially the same level in this regard. In all three countries age and tenure with the firm were found to be positively related to commitment; but in the United States, existing organizational practices, or perhaps the nature of the people themselves, seem to make for stronger emotional ties to the company (Cook & Wall, 1980; Luthans, McCaul, & Dodd, 1985).

☐ Consequences of Organizational Commitment

Given the nature of organizational commitment and the factors that contribute to it, what can be said about its relationships to the various dimensions of performance? How closely do the findings on commitment duplicate those for job satisfaction?

Organizational Outcomes. Among the most stable findings regarding organizational commitment is the consistent and strong relationship to turnover—a relationship that appears to be even more pronounced than that for job satisfaction (Parasuraman & Alutto, 1984; Reichers, 1985). This is not entirely a matter of the inclusion of maintaining membership in the organization in the definition of organizational commitment. Even without this aspect, higher organizational commitment contributes to reduced turnover.

Relationships to absenteeism and quantity and quality of output are less pronounced, but they are found on occasion. As with job satisfaction, in the absence of other variables high commitment is positively related to low absenteeism and high productivity. As with job satisfaction, however, numerous other factors operate in practice to cloud the impact of organizational commitment on performance. In general, organizational commitment lessens the chances of turnover while at the same time providing a reservoir of potential energy on which the organization can draw in times of crisis and need. At such times commitment should yield both better attendance and improved output.

Individual Significance. From the viewpoint of an individual employee, organizational commitment can have both positive and negative aspects. Just as companies may find it difficult to get rid of highly committed employees who probably should be let go for other reasons, highly committed employees may find it difficult to let go of companies that in other respects they might be better off leaving. People can hamper their careers and their development by becoming so committed to a company that they pass up attractive opportunities elsewhere.

Commitment certainly can bring rewards and satisfactions too. Many of the people who rise to the top of large corporations are strongly committed individuals who stay with that company throughout their careers (Miner, 1985a). For those individuals who are prone to establishing strong commitments to organizations, failure to do so can be a source of considerable discomfort and stress. In short, from an individual viewpoint whether organizational commitment is a plus or minus depends first on the nature of the individual and second on characteristics of the employing organization. It takes a good fit between the two for commitment to work.

☐ Union Commitment

A question arises as to what happens to the commitment process when the individual is a union member. Does union membership damage company commitment? How are organizational outcomes affected by **union commitment?** Although results vary from study to study, the most general finding is that the two types of commitments are positively related, but not to any marked degree (Conlon & Gallagher, 1985). That is, there is a slight tendency for those who are more committed to the company to be more committed to the union as well, and the level of commitment to each is likely to be much the same. There is no reason to believe that union com-

Exhibit 5-7   **Relationships between Company and Union Commitments and Various Measures of Job Performance**

Measures of Job Performance	Company Commitment	Union Commitment
Supervisory ratings of performance	+ +	+
Infrequent absenteeism	+	0
Short duration of absenteeism	0	0
Stayed rather than engaged in voluntary turnover	+ +	0
Stayed rather than engaged in involuntary turnover	+ +	+

+ + Strong positive relationship.
 + Some positive relationship.
 0 No relationship.

Source: Adapted from Erik W. Larson & Cynthia V. Fukami (1984). Relationships between worker behavior and commitment to the organization and union. *Academy of Management Proceedings, 44,* 225.

mitment interferes with company commitment; if anything, it tends to enhance positive feelings about the company.

Exhibit 5-7 presents data on performance relationships among unionized truck drivers working for a large metropolitan newspaper. The general pattern found for company commitment parallels the results of other studies. Union commitment, where it is related to the measures of job performance at all, shows somewhat weaker relationships. This is not surprising in view of the fact that performance is defined in terms of company goals; company commitment should be a better predictor. If measures incorporating union goals were used instead, the pattern might well be reversed. These and other data indicate that people may have multiple commitments to organizations, professions, jobs, and so forth, without adverse effects on performance.

Research on union commitment has now established itself as a major component of industrial-organizational psychology (Friedman & Harvey, 1986). In doing so it has given considerable support to an earlier, and somewhat less convincingly validated concept, that of **dual allegiance**—the idea that many employees are favorably disposed to both the company and the union (Purcell, 1960).

☐ Behavioral Commitment

Until this point our discussion has focused entirely on attitudinal commitment. **Behavioral commitment** is closely related to attitudinal commitment and yields similar results, at least insofar as turnover is concerned, but is different in a number of respects (O'Reilley & Caldwell, 1981). Box 5-4 provides examples of behavioral commitment. Each vignette presented in the box involves an **escalation of commitment** and an increasing allocation of resources to a decision that gives every indication of being wrong. The tendency is to escalate commitment above and beyond what is warranted, in an effort to somehow justify the original decision. This is the defining characteristic of behavioral commitment. In the organizational context, a person may become increasingly committed to a job simply to justify the decision to take the position in the first place; behavioral commitment and low turnover thus go hand in hand. The relation of behavioral commitment to quantity and quality of outputs, in contrast, is somewhat tenuous. A person may devote increasing time and effort to attaining a performance goal that may be unreachable. In such cases behavioral commitment is often associated

BOX 5-4 I/O PSYCHOLOGY IN PRACTICE

Examples of Behavioral Commitment

1. An individual has spent three years working on an advanced degree in a field with minimal job prospects (e.g., in the humanities or social sciences). The individual chooses to invest more time and effort to finish the degree rather than switching to an entirely new field of study. Having obtained the degree, the individual is faced with the options of unemployment, working under dissatisfying conditions such as part-time or temporary status, or starting anew in a completely unrelated field.

2. An individual purchased a stock at $50 a share, but the price has gone down to $20. Still convinced about the merit of the stock, he buys more shares at this lower price. Soon the price declines further and the individual is again faced with the decision to buy more, hold what he already has, or sell out entirely.

3. A city spends a large amount of money to improve its sewer and drainage system. The project is the largest public works project in the nation and involves digging 131 miles of tunnel shafts, reservoirs, and pumping stations. The excavation is only 10 percent completed and is useless until it is totally finished. The project will take the next twenty years to complete and will cost $11 billion. Unfortunately, the deeper the tunnels go, the more money they cost, and the greater are the questions about the wisdom of the entire venture.

4. A company overestimates its capability to build an airplane brake that will meet certain technical specifications at a given cost. Because it wins the government contract, the company is forced to invest greater and greater effort into meeting the contract terms. As a result of increasing pressure to meet specifications and deadlines, records and tests of the brake are misrepresented to government officials. Corporate careers and company credibility are increasingly staked to the airbrake contract, although many in the firm know the brake will not work effectively. At the conclusion of the construction period, the government test pilot flies the plane; it skids off the runway and narrowly misses injuring the pilot.

5. At an early stage [July 1965] of the U.S. involvement in the Vietnam War, George Ball, then Undersecretary of State, wrote the following in a memo to President Johnson: "The decision you face now is crucial. Once large numbers of U.S. troops are committed to direct combat, they will begin to take heavy casualties in a war they are ill equipped to fight in a noncooperative if not downright hostile countryside. Once we suffer large casualties, we will have started a well-nigh irreversible process. Our involvement will be so great that we cannot—without national humiliation—stop short of achieving our complete objectives. Of the two possibilities, I think humiliation would be more likely than the achievement of our objectives—even after we have paid terrible costs."

SOURCE: Reprinted from Barry M. Staw (1981). The escalation of commitment to a course of action. *Academy of Management Review, 6,* 577–578.

with reduced absenteeism and even considerable overtime, as well as increased job effort. However, considerable stress may be mobilized, especially if the all-out effort does not yield results.

Although most of the research on organizational commitment has focused on attitudinal commitment, certain things are known about behavioral commitment, (Bazerman, Giuliano, & Appelman, 1984; Northcraft &

Wolf, 1984). The person who is originally responsible for a decision is the one who can be expected to escalate commitments to it. If someone else takes over, behavioral commitment does not represent a problem; that person has nothing to justify. Also, groups tend to engage in the escalation process in much the same way as individuals do. Thus a bank loan officer who first approved lending money to a firm might continue to authorize loans even after the firm shows a long string of losses. The situation would be much the same if the initial loan had been decided upon by a committee of bank officers; "throwing good money after bad" would still be the typical response.

Although recent research suggests that behavioral commitment may not be as widespread as originally suggested, it remains an important organizational phenomenon (Davis & Bobko, 1986). It is a process that decision makers need to be aware of.

■ VALUES AND ETHICS

Values are the explicit or implicit conceptions of the desirable held by an individual or a group; they influence selections from available modes, means, and ends of action. Whereas values are generalized conceptions, attitudes are organizations of several beliefs around specific objects or situations. Values uphold standards, while attitudes reflect multiple, often changing opinions (Spates, 1983). Values concern what *should be*; they are the normative standards by which human beings are influenced in their choices among alternative courses of action.

A **value judgment** involves an interplay between cognitive and emotional elements of an individual's value system. Exhibit 5-8 shows how cultures, societies, organizations, and role sets operate through values to yield decisions and behavior in organizations. Because values are ultimately rooted in cul-

ture and thus have strong support, they are extremely resistant to change.

□ Values in International Perspective

Because values are so closely related to culture, they have been studied extensively in an international context. The objective has been to identify differences in values from one country to another and to determine whether countries can be grouped according to similar values.

Cultural Differences. One of the most comprehensive comparisons of cultural values around the world has been conducted within the IBM Corporation (see Box 5-5). Even though the study focused on a single company, within which the organization's own culture would be expected to exert a homogenizing effect, substantial value differences were found among IBM's facilities in various countries. In view of findings regarding perceptions of the effects of different factors on productivity (McInnes, 1984), it is interesting to compare the values of IBM employees in the United States, Great Britain, and Japan. Perceptions of productivity appear to be very similar in the United States and Great Britain (as are the value patterns), whereas Japanese employees have rather different views of productivity—and different values—from those of IBM employees in the other two countries.

This concept is pursued further in a study comparing the values of American managers employed by AT&T and Japanese managers employed by various companies. Exhibit 5-9, which lists a comprehensive set of values developed by Milton Rokeach (1973), confirms that sizable value differences exist between the two countries, many of which parallel the IBM findings.

Values and Managerial Success. In contrast to the sharp differences in values often found when countries are compared, data on the

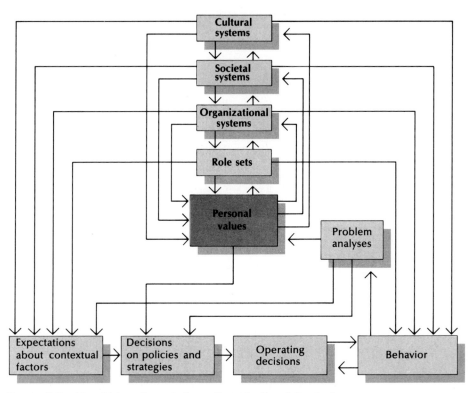

EXHIBIT 5-8   How Values Operate in an Organizational Context
The cultural systems, societal systems, organizational systems, and role sets impinging directly on a person interact with personal values. These values, expectations about the environmental context, and analyses of the problem at hand then set the decision process in motion.
SOURCE: Janice M. Beyer (1981). Ideologies, values, and decision making in organizations. In Paul C. Nystrom and William H. Starbuck (Eds.), *Handbook of organizational design,* vol. 2, p. 169. Oxford, England: Oxford University Press.

relationships between values and *managerial success* exhibit much more homogeneity (Bass & Burger, 1979; England, 1975). Contrast the following lists:

pragmatism	passivity
dynamic action	security
achievement	status quo
influential leadership	affection
expertise	self-actualization
prestige	pleasure
duty	

Across a wide range of industrialized cultures, successful managers—those who earn high salaries and have risen through the ranks quickly—espouse the values listed on the left. The list on the right reflects the values of the less successful managers. This *convergence* of values across cultural lines no doubt facilitates business transactions around the world. It also makes for more effective transfers of individuals from country to country within the multinational operations of a single company. Since values tend to influence

---

BOX 5-5 RESEARCH IN I/O PSYCHOLOGY

Values in the Multinational Operations of IBM

IBM administered an extensive questionnaire to 116,000 of its employees in sixty-seven countries. The questionnaire was translated into eighteen languages. Analyses identified four principal value dimensions that could be derived from the questionnaire:

Power distance—the extent to which there is acceptance of the view that power in organizations is distributed unequally; hierarchy is valued.

Uncertainty avoidance—the degree to which there is a feeling of discomfort associated with uncertainty and ambiguity, so that there is support for any measure that promises certainty and protects conformity; risk avoidance is valued.

Individualism—a preference for a social framework in which people are supposed to take care of themselves and their immediate families only, as opposed to collectivism, where people can expect relatives, clans, or other such groups to look after them; individual responsibility is valued.

Masculinity—a preference for achievement, heroism, assertiveness, and material success (as opposed to "femininity," which stresses relationship, modesty, caring for the weak, and the quality of life); assertiveness is valued (by both men and women).

In the initial analyses the four values were measured in the forty countries where the largest numbers of employees worked. The rankings (from a high of 1 to a low of 40) for seven highly industrialized countries on the four values were as shown in the table below.

While the United States, Canada, and Great Britain show strong value similarities, this is not true of the other countries. France and Japan are quite different from the other five countries and from each other. Note, for example, that the masculinity value received a ranking of 1 (out of 40) from Japanese respondents, while the French ranked it at only 29. The data clearly indicate that in doing business in all these countries, IBM faces very different value patterns and can expect to encounter major differences in what its employees in the various countries consider important.

Source: Geert Hofstede (1980). *Culture's consequences—International differences in work-related values.* Beverly Hills, CA: Sage. Geert Hofstede (1985). The interaction between national and organizational value systems. *Journal of Management Studies, 22,* 347–357.

	Power Distance	Uncertainty Avoidance	Individualism	Masculinity
United States	26	32	1	13
Canada	27	31	4	21
Great Britain	31	36	3	8
France	8	8	10	29
West Germany	31	18	15	9
Italy	23	14	7	4
Japan	22	4	23	1

EXHIBIT 5-9   Strongly Held Values of American and Japanese Managers

Distinctly Stronger in United States	Distinctly Stronger in Japan	No Difference
Family security (taking care of loved ones)	A comfortable life (a prosperous life)	Responsible (dependable, reliable)
Inner harmony (freedom from inner conflict)	An exciting life (a stimulating, active life)	Freedom (independence, free choice)
Mature love (sexual and spiritual intimacy)	A sense of accomplishment (lasting contribution)	Happiness (contentedness)
Self-respect (self-esteem)	A world at peace (free of war and conflict)	Wisdom (a mature understanding of life)
Ambitious (hard-working, aspiring)	Self-recognition (respect, admiration)	Broad-minded (open-minded)
Capable (competent, effective)	Helpful (working for the welfare of others)	Intellectual (intelligent, reflective)
Honest (sincere, truthful)	Cheerful (lighthearted, joyful)	
Independent (self-reliant, self-sufficient)	Courageous (standing up for your beliefs)	
Logical (consistent, rational)	Forgiving (willing to pardon others)	
Loving (affectionate, tender)		

SOURCE: Adapted from Ann Howard, Keitaro Shudo, & Miyo Umeshima (1983). Motivation and values among Japanese and American managers. *Personnel Psychology, 36,* 888–889.

decisions considerably (see Exhibit 5-8), the relative homogeneity of the values of successful managers produces a much-needed consistency and stability in operations.

☐ The Mesh of Values and Jobs

Values clearly can contribute to success and high levels of performance when an individual's values mesh with the requirements of his or her job. Yet people can hold values that conflict with specific job requirements or with the values inherent in the organization's overall culture.

Values that May Conflict. In the business world, as in other arenas, certain values seem more likely than others to create problems (Miner, 1985b). The problems caused by clashing values tend to be long-lasting, simply because values are unlikely to change. Conflicts often arise because people with strong equity values and feelings regarding fairness believe their values have been violated by a superior or by the company as a whole. Similarly, strong *freedom values* can run afoul of bureaucratic rules and regulations, especially among creative scientists. *Moral values,* which are often supported by strong religious convictions, can clash so severely with job demands that the person experiences difficulty in doing his or her work. Sales jobs in particular often require people to do and say things that may violate strongly held *honesty values.*

Exhibit 5-10   Anti-Business Values Related to College Major and Career Choices

College Major	Mean Anti-Business Value Scores*	
	Choosing a Business Career	Choosing a Nonbusiness Career
Social Science	56	65
Economics	49	62
Engineering	50	Insufficient cases
Management	48	Insufficient cases
Total	50	64

*Possible scores range from 14 to 98, with higher scores representing more intense anti-business values.

SOURCE: Adapted from Andrew Duff & Stephen Cotgrove (1982). Social values and the choice of careers in industry. *Journal of Occupational Psychology, 55,* 100.

A value problem that younger employees often experience in the business world is depicted in Exhibit 5-10. In this instance, *anti-business values* associated with left-of-center political views were studied in relation to career choices. There was a strong tendency for those with more intense anti-business values to choose nonbusiness careers, thus avoiding conflict. But some who were anti-business—particularly social science majors—did seek careers in business nevertheless, presumably out of a desire to earn more money. Where personal values are in such direct conflict with the values that underlie the business system, problems seem almost inevitable.

Personal–Organizational Value Fit.   A recent national survey of managers sought to determine the extent to which individual managers shared values with their organizations (Posner, Kouzes, & Schmidt, 1985). One key finding was that managers who experienced a good mesh were more successful and were more likely to believe that they would fulfill their career ambitions. They were also more confident that they would stay with their present firm and more willing to work long hours. They viewed their firm and the people who worked around them as more ethical overall, and they experienced less stress in

the relationship between their family and work lives.

This and other studies provide strong support for the view that a congruence of values between individuals and their employing organizations substantially benefits both parties. Where such congruence is lacking, the individual can be expected to suffer; and if many such individuals are involved, the organization will suffer as well.

☐ The Work Ethic

The much-discussed **work ethic** is a value that defines work as important, virtuous, and a source of dignity. Work, as contrasted with leisure, is inherently good, and people should work even if their financial situation does not require it. Thus defined, a work ethic is part of overall work motivation, but far from all of it. Indeed, most of the motivational processes we have been discussing have little to do with the work ethic per se (Nord, Brief, Atieh, & Doherty, 1988).

Two questions have been the subject of considerable debate (Barbash, Lampman, Levitan, & Tyler, 1983; Vecchio, 1980): What changes have been evident in the work ethic in the United States in recent years? And have these changes had any significant effects on performance and productivity? Definitive answers have not yet emerged, but researchers have detected some decline in the prevalence of the work ethic in the United States over the past twenty years or so, at least in the male population. Among employed females the work ethic often conflicts with a homemaker ethic or a mothering ethic among those with young children at home (Walker, Tausky, & Oliver, 1982). Torn between strong values, women in this situation may experience some weakening of their work ethic. This is not surprising, but it does mean that females entering the labor force are not entirely able to compensate for the declining work values found among males. In any event, a great majority of American workers continue to espouse strong work values. More significantly, there is reason to believe that the work ethic is not the most important factor in productivity. Certainly considerations of an intellectual, emotional, motivational, and physical nature can compensate for those of an ethical nature. In sum, a declining work ethic is apparently not the key factor in America's productivity problems. There is more to these problems than this.

☐ Ethical Systems

Organizational ethics can strongly influence the evaluation of individual behavior and performance. It also directly affects the behavior of employees, who are rewarded or punished in accordance with the ethics of their company.

People believe differently and are viewed differently in one ethical system as opposed to another. The general public tends to see organizations with a strong sales, marketing, and advertising emphasis as having low ethical standards (political organizations and unions are viewed in a similar light). In contrast, professional organizations, other than those of a legal nature, are seen as quite ethical.

Corporate Codes. A major business-world reaction to pressures for more ethical behavior has been the issuance of **corporate codes of conduct.** These codes represent an effort to specify behavior that the company does or does not sanction across the myriad value systems and legal frameworks within which a company, particularly a multinational company, operates. Box 5-6 reprints a description of the approach to this dilemma taken by Norton Company, an approach generally considered to be both thoughtful and highly principled. Note the difficulties that emerge when local laws and local ethics of morality are at variance.

Exhibit 5-11 indicates the types of behaviors that are most frequently covered by codes of ethics. Clarification of the two ethical dimensions cited most often—"employee's relation to firm" and "firm's relation to government"—is the primary reason that most corporate conduct codes exist.

Individual Responses. Corporate codes, provided that they are widely understood and enforced, are likely to make people more ethical and more sensitive to ethical issues—although there is always the chance that they will merely drive unethical behavior deeper underground. Enforcement procedures, which are sometimes stated in the codes, often require surveillance by superiors, reporting the misconduct of oneself or others, internal audits, and affidavits indicating a knowledge of and compliance with the firm's ethical code. How well such procedures work depends on how a given firm administers them. Simply stating them in a conduct code probably does little by itself to ensure compliance.

A number of chief executives, including the heads of IBM, Bethlehem Steel, and Sperry and Hutchinson, have emphasized that top management must provide impeccable role models if ethical systems are to operate effectively (Cressey & Moore, 1983).

BOX 5-6 I/O PSYCHOLOGY IN PRACTICE

Morality and Ethics at Norton Company

[Norton Company is a diversified manufacturer that continues to concentrate much of its output in its original line of business—abrasives and grinding wheels.]

According to Norton's *Policy on Business Ethics:*

While moral standards are absolute, ethical behavior is a matter of spirit and intent as well as a matter of law. . . . [Thus] honesty and integrity are characterized by truthfulness and freedom from deception and fraud. These qualities are unchanging, not relative, and should vary neither by country nor by culture. They dictate one standard of conduct worldwide. If we are steadfast in this belief, ethical behavioral questions are easily answered in most situations. . . . [But] ethics is by definition a philosophy of human conduct, and it is axiomatic that all things human change. This means that our view of ethical behavior must be dynamic—sensitive to changes in values and customs that are certain to take place over time and between cultures.

Amplifying this, former General Counsel [Fairman] Cowan adds:

The word "morals" is used in the sense of standards which are absolute throughout the world: "Thou shalt not commit murder, bear false witness," etc. "Ethics," on the other hand, reflects philosophies of human conduct, established customs, and mores which may vary throughout the world and which are subject to change from time to time. It is in this nonabsolute area of ethics where difficulties are encountered in writing a worldwide code of business conduct that cannot possibly answer all the questions which will inevitably arise concerning its application to a particular set of circumstances in a particular country at a particular point in time. It is for this reason that the Norton board of directors, when it approved the code, at the same time appointed a Corporate Ethics Committee.

Two major sections of Norton's *Policy on Business Ethics* merit detailed study at this point—"Norton and the Law" and "Norton and Its Publics."

The "Norton and the Law" section deals with entertainment, gifts, favors and gratuities, political contributions, financial integrity, antitrust laws, conflict of interest, and use of confidential information. One of the most important aspects of this section is the requirement that every com-

---

Individual employees may not behave ethically just because top management does, but the rank and file is certainly more likely to behave unethically if they see corporate heads plundering the organization, violating laws, and otherwise behaving contrary to their own code of conduct.

Beyond this, the best way to ensure ethical on-the-job behavior is to select and retain honest and ethical people as employees. Corporate codes are more likely to receive the intended responses if the people to whom they are directed are scrupulous and truly want to do what is right.

KEY TERMS

Attitude

Job attitudes

Job satisfaction

Attitudinal commitment

Union commitment

Dual allegiance

pany transaction be correctly recorded, so that *no* scrutiny of records could prove embarrassing. In Fairman Cowan's words, "Observance of this policy [of recording] will go a long way to minimize the likelihood of company funds being used for an improper purpose."

In setting policy, Norton decided against strict compliance with all laws because it operates in parts of the world where petty officials not only expect but are openly permitted to receive small gratuities for performing their regular duties, despite local laws and regulations to the contrary. Accordingly, Norton specifies that gifts or gratuities may be given "to minor public employees for the performance of their public duty, where it is customary to do so, and where a normal and legitimate transaction might otherwise be impeded, *provided that the gifts or tips are recorded on the financial records of the company.*"

Such a situation occurred in Mexico. Norton has a manufacturing operation in the city of Puebla, 85 miles southeast of Mexico City, with its major market in Mexico City

itself. Midway between the two cities, there is a truck weight checkpoint at which all commercial vehicles must stop. To clear this point, one must pay a nominal tip to the inspector, whether the vehicle is within the load limits or not. Failing such payment, the shipment is certain to be delayed; in fact, the inspector might even require the driver to unload the truck for further inspection. Norton, which ships daily on this route, makes the requested payment.

Citing this as an instance where an official must be paid to have him perform his required duties, Norton notes that this is part of the practice and culture of the country. Norton honors this particular practice because it does not involve bribing an individual to do what he should not be doing. The driver is asked to enter payment to the inspector on his expense report and so identify it.

Source: Reprinted from Theodore V. Purcell & James Weber (1979). *Institutionalizing corporate ethics: A case history*, pp. 14–16. New York: The Presidents Association.

Behavioral commitment
Escalation of commitment
Values
Value judgment

Work ethic
Organizational ethics
Corporate codes of conduct

SUMMARY

Job satisfaction has been one of the most widely studied subjects in organizational behavior. It appears to stem both from aspects of the work situation and from individual characteristics. In general, dissatisfaction tends to be most pronounced when a company is viewed as unresponsive to an individual's needs. Hence, satisfaction tends to be higher when the individual can adjust the job to these needs or has had an opportunity to try a number of jobs and find one that fits best.

Exhibit 5-11   Employee Behaviors Most Frequently Covered by Corporate Codes of Ethics

Prohibited Behavior Variable	Ethical Dimension	Percentage of Firms Mentioning Variable within Ethical Dimension	Typical Treatment in Ethics Statements
1. *Extortion, gifts, kickbacks*	Employee's relation to firm	67%	
	Firm's relation to suppliers	18	
(a) Extortion			Explicitly prohibited
(b) Gifts			Generally prohibited with minor exceptions
(c) Kickbacks			Explicitly prohibited
2. Conflict of interest	Employee's relation to firm	65	Generally prohibited with minor exceptions
3. Illegal political payments	Firm's relation to government	59	Explicitly prohibited
4. Violation of laws in general	Firm's relation to government	57	Explicitly prohibited
5. Use of insider information	Employee's relation to firm	43	Explicitly prohibited
	Firm's relation to shareholders	8	
6. Bribery	Firm's relation to government	37	Explicitly prohibited
	Employee's relation to firm	34	
7. Falsification of corporate accounts	Firm's relation to shareholders (both variables)	28	Explicitly prohibited
Reporting full disclosure		34	
8. Violation of antitrust laws	Firm's relation to government	25	Explicitly prohibited
9. Moonlighting	Employee's relation to firm	25	Judgmental—usually tolerated if no conflict of interest
10. Legal payments abroad	Miscellaneous concerns	23	Some judgment
11. Violation of secrecy agreement	Employee's relation to firm	22	Explicitly prohibited
12. Ignorance of work-related laws	Firm's relation to government	22	Prohibited—employees to seek legal advice if in doubt
13. Fraud, deception	Firm's relation to customers	11	Explicitly prohibited
14. To justify means by goals	Miscellaneous concerns	10	Explicitly prohibited

SOURCE: Robert Chatov (1980). What corporate ethics statements say. *California Management Review, 22* (4), 22.

Other things being equal, job dissatisfaction is associated with dishonest behavior, stress, union activity, reduced quality and quantity of output, absenteeism, and turnover. The problem is that in practice other things seldom *are* equal, so the relationship of dissatisfaction to these factors is often much less pronounced than might be expected. Yet *job satisfaction* is extremely important to the individual. Even though an organization may have little need to provide it, people should seek job satisfaction for themselves.

Among the various types of commitments, *attitudinal commitment* to the organization has been most widely studied. It appears to operate in a manner similar to job satisfaction, to which it is closely related, but is more stable and is a better predictor of employee turnover. From an individual viewpoint, commitment to an employing organization can hamper or foster career progress, depending on how well the individual and the organization fit together. *Commitment to a union* appears not to dampen company commitment and in fact may enhance it. *Behavioral commitment* is quite different from attitudinal commitment, but it too can reduce turnover.

Values are concerned primarily with what should be, and are strongly rooted in culture. They vary substantially from one country to another, although the values that make for a successful managerial career tend to be very similar among industrialized nations. Where an individual's values conflict with requirements of the job or the values of the organization, major problems often result; anti-business values that are antithetical to the free-enterprise system represent a case in point. A value that has received considerable attention is the *work ethic,* which defines work as good in and of itself. In the United States, the apparent decline in the work ethic has been blamed for the productivity problems of the 1970s and 1980s. However, intellectual, emotional, and other factors can offset this impact.

Ethical systems reflect prevailing *values,* especially those of a moral nature. *Corporate codes of conduct* have been established as a method of fostering ethical behavior among employees. To the extent that codes are given visibility and compliance provisions are administered effectively, they can have a positive impact. Ethical standards are generally highest in companies where the top managers serve as ethical role models and where inherently honest people are hired and retained.

QUESTIONS

1. How do attitudinal commitment and behavioral commitment differ in both their nature and their consequences?

2. What appear to be the natural relationships between job satisfaction and both absenteeism and turnover? Why are these relationships not found more often?

3. How can companies foster ethical behavior among those working for them?

4. What are some of the major sources of job dissatisfaction among American workers?

5. What is known about cultural differences and similarities in values and their operation?

6. How and when does job satisfaction relate to productive output?

7. In what ways may organizational commitment have both positive and negative consequences for individual employees?

8. Why are concepts such as individual value–job fit, individual value–organization congruence, and the work ethic important?

9. How can job satisfaction be improved in an organization?

10. What is the nature of the organizational commitment process, and what factors influence it at different points in time?

CASE PROBLEM

CHUCK HOLEMAN
Retail Sales Representative

When he joined the company, Chuck Holeman gave every indication of becoming an outstanding employee. As a sales trainee he was consistently at the top of his group on the written examinations covering such matters as the characteristics of the company's products, policies of the company, and various sales techniques. In his field training he also demonstrated a high level of proficiency. The people he traveled with and worked with reported that he was a rapid learner who was, in contrast to many of the trainees, a real help. He did what he was told and did it right. The owners of the various retail outlets through which the company sold its products seemed to like him. Everyone commented on the time and effort he devoted to his job. The company had not had a young trainee who worked as hard in years. He wanted to learn everything about sales work that there was to be learned. Probably this constant search for new knowledge and the rapidity with which he absorbed it was a major factor in his popularity; another was his complete openness and honesty. Also, people seemed to enjoy answering the young man's questions. It gave them a feeling of importance, and Chuck clearly appreciated and remembered their replies. When he was promoted and given his own territory, most of the company's sales managers who knew him considered this promotion as merely the first step in a succession of moves that would take him to a high-level position in a few years.

However, the first figures that came in from the new sales representative's territory were very disappointing. There were losses on nearly all products—in some cases, very sizable losses. The supervisor was disturbed. This was not what he had expected. Nevertheless, the territory was known to be in bad shape, and any new person would inevitably have trouble there at first. The man who had been in it previously drank rather heavily, and partly because of this and partly because of a flippant attitude, he had lost a number of customers. They had apparently come to believe that the quality of the company's products was not sufficiently superior to that of

competing brands to compensate them for putting up with the company's representative. In large part the choice of Chuck Holeman for this territory had been dictated by this state of affairs. He appeared to be the kind of young man who could convey a more favorable image of the company and thus gain back the lost business. He was obviously an honest, sincere, and responsible person who wanted very much for people to like him.

When the figures for the second period came in, however, they were no better. In fact, they were slightly worse. The supervisor was sure he would be called on the carpet himself very shortly if this poor showing continued. He began to check into Chuck's background to see if there was anything that would explain his difficulties. The young man had graduated from high school and immediately signed up for a four-year hitch in the Navy. After an uneventful career in the service, he had entered college. The records indicated that he had stayed only two years, however, and further checking with Personnel revealed the reason: he had flunked out. Because of his experience in the Navy he had decided to work toward a degree in engineering. This soon proved to be an unfortunate choice, but Chuck apparently kept plugging away until his average finally dropped below an acceptable level. He seemed to believe that he had an obligation to stick with his original choice, no matter what happened. Actually, his only failures had been in mathematics courses, and he did have a few very good grades. All this information had been volunteered during the interviews. The personnel interviewer had been rather surprised at the time. Few candidates for jobs admitted to having flunked out of college, although occasionally the fact would come out later. In fact, some of the company's best salespeople had proved to have been college failures. Chuck, however, seemed to feel that he should not misrepresent himself in any way to a prospective employer.

Several other facts were unearthed as a result of further conversations with people in the company. Although Chuck had done extremely well as a trainee, there was some question as to whether he had really mastered the work on financial management, bookkeeping, and pricing. This was not a major aspect of the training program, but the company liked to have representatives who were competent to discuss such matters and who could even perhaps advise on accounting procedures occasionally. Often this proved an effective method of gaining a customer's confidence and appreciation, and paved the way for the establishment of new retail outlets. Also, the sales representatives did have to keep certain records themselves. One of the people with whom Chuck had worked in the field had noted some difficulty in this bookkeeping area and also felt that the young man was lacking in aggressiveness and vitality. Chuck worked hard, but he never got very enthusiastic about anything. He rarely seemed to get any enjoyment out of doing something well. This particular sales representative, who was very experienced, had not said much about these things at the time because he liked the young trainee and did not want to hurt his chances.

The supervisor decided that it was time to go out and talk with the people who worked in various retail establishments in the territory. The picture he got was not entirely what he had expected, but it did fit a pattern he had seen several times before. Chuck was generally liked or, rather, had no enemies. People considered him to be honest and reliable. He was, as management had hoped, a welcome relief after his predecessor. Many commented that he seemed worn out and solemn; at the same time, he clearly seemed to work hard. He would come in and get right down to business, often without even saying hello. He would run down the order sheet in a mechanical manner, ask if he could help with anything, and then hurry out. No one really felt he knew Chuck well. Several people who had dropped the company's products in favor of those put out by competitors since Chuck had become the sales representative said they had come to feel that they were totally uninformed about what the company was selling. They hardly knew enough to answer their customers' questions. Chuck never did anything more than take orders. He always seemed in a hurry to leave, and he was so unenthusiastic about everything, including his job and the products on his list, that it was somewhat depressing to have him around. He was a nice young man, though. No, he had never offered to help out with any book-

keeping and pricing problems related to his products. He acted as if he knew very little about such things. A check on several outlets that had dropped the company's products while the former sales representative was still in the territory revealed that, as far as anyone could remember, the new man had never called on them. One woman was clearly ready to change back and had been considering calling the office for several days. The supervisor himself signed her on the spot.

There were a number of other problems that were less evident at the retail level. Chuck was clearly not making use of the promotional material he received, and he was not pushing the high-profit items, as he had been instructed to do. In fact, he was deviating from company policy in so many ways that the supervisor clearly had to have a talk with him. In most such instances such a talk did very little good, but at least it protected the supervisor against criticism for not having issued a warning should more drastic action be required later on. Before talking to Chuck, however, the supervisor decided to check with Jim, the sales representative who had the adjacent territory and who was a friend of Chuck's. The two worked on their reports together. The information the supervisor got was at least consistent. According to Jim, Chuck was pretty upset. He knew he was in trouble, but apparently could not bring himself to do anything about it. At times he sounded as if he hated the job, but he was not one to quit. That Chuck and Jim did their reports together appeared to account for the fact that the problems with the bookkeeping and accounting aspects of the work had not become apparent at higher levels. Jim had taken accounting courses in college and was very conversant with that aspect of the business. There was no question about Chuck's difficulty in handling such matters. He rarely worked up a report that did not contain at least a few arithmetic errors. However, Jim thought Chuck would catch on eventually. He had in fact improved considerably during the past month.

As expected, the supervisor's talk with Chuck did not go very well. When faced with the facts, Chuck did not deny them. He wanted to do well and to follow company policy. He understood what he was supposed to do, but he could not help seeing things from the point of view of the customers too. They were human beings and it was not fair to take advantage of them. He pointed out that the high-priced items were almost identical with the less expensive ones and that some of the promotional material was, to say the least, questionable. It was hard to sell when you yourself did not believe the prescribed sales pitch. He felt the company was not being entirely socially responsible in what it was doing. As it turned out, Chuck had visited several of the establishments that had switched to competitive products as a result of the incompetence of the former sales representative in the territory, but he had never said anything to the people there. They seemed satisfied with what they had, and somehow he could not force himself to ask them to change, even though he knew he should. He admitted that sometimes the territory seemed to be more than he could handle, but said that he would lick it somehow. He was upset now, but things would get better. The supervisor did not think so, but decided to wait a little longer and see.

Not unexpectedly, the losses continued. Obviously, putting pressure on Chuck had done no good. The young man got more upset as a result, but otherwise there was little change in his behavior. Evidently things were not getting better and Chuck was not finding a way to solve his problems with the territory. Some other solution was required before sales disappeared entirely.

Questions

1. What specific kinds of attitudes and values caused Chuck Holeman's problems on the job? How did these manifest themselves?
2. Would you yourself find it difficult to follow the prescribed practices and policies in this kind of situation? What would you actually do in this regard if you were a salesperson in this company?
3. What would you do if you were Chuck's supervisor? Would you fire him?
4. Do you feel the supervisor waited too long before acting? If so, why?

6

Personality Processes Including Emotional Stress

Charles D., a 34-year-old airline copilot, was referred for a psychological evaluation following hospitalization resulting from symptoms similar to those of a heart attack. Medical tests proved negative, and Mr. D. was referred for evaluation of his "hyperventilation and anxiety as a result of fatigue and stress."

Mr. D. was seen for an extensive psychological evaluation. He was interviewed on two occasions and given a battery of psychological tests, including the MMPI (Minnesota Multiphasic Personality Inventory, a test that reveals personality traits) and the Rorschach (Inkblot Test, a projective test of personality characteristics). Results of the evaluation were communicated over two feedback sessions.

Mr. D. was quite outgoing and friendly in the sessions. He was very talkative and seemingly open. . . . Throughout the sessions he was outwardly compliant. He talked freely about his life and his problems as he viewed them. He expressed a desire to learn why he had experienced the physical problems. Mr. D. appeared to be an intelligent individual with a broad range of interests and a high mechanical aptitude. However, he was not reflective about psychological matters and had little insight into how his behavior affected other people.

The symptoms Mr. D. experienced reportedly occurred after a period of intense stress. Mr. D. had been flying a lot recently. In addition to the flying hours on his regular job, he had reportedly spent two weeks with his National Guard unit. . . . His "stressful situation" also involved a great deal of travel. The hospitalization occurred at the end of a three-day celebration that capped off a friend's wedding. The lengthy wedding party conflicted with a family responsibility—he was supposed to have taken his two sons to summer camp.

Mr. D. lived with his wife and two children but didn't spend much time at home. When he was not flying, he spent a lot of time with a girl friend who lived in another city. He reported that his wife was aware of his relationships with other women but did not want a divorce. He said that he did not want to get involved in a permanent relationship but liked to have affairs. He had, however, been with his present friend for three years.

The psychological tests indicated that Mr. D. appeared to be an individual who was experiencing a great deal of interpersonal conflict. He seemed to be an active and energetic person who tended to use poor social judgment at times. At the time of testing, he may have been experiencing some remorse about his behavior and his neglect of family responsibilities. He appeared to be an immature individual who was having some problems with alcohol abuse when tested. His hedonistic lifestyle, acting-out behavior, and alcohol abuse may have resulted in family and relationship problems that were placing great strains on him. His behavior at the time he was tested appeared to be generally sociopathic. He seemed to use denial to a great extent to deal with problems in his disruptive social life. He did not like to discuss problems or face interpersonal conflicts. When problems became intense, he was remorseful or felt the conflict in the form of physical distress.

There was a clear element of secondary gain in Mr. D.'s health episode. His physical "fatigue" provided excuses for his disruptive behavior, and he did not have to face the consequences of his actions. Mr. D. reacted to stress through denial and "escapist" tactics (such as running away and using alcohol). These defenses may work well enough for him much of the time, but under periods of intense stress, he appears to consume more alcohol and commit himself to things that produce further difficulties for him.

There is strong evidence in the testing that Mr. D. may be developing an alcohol addiction pattern. His alcohol abuse may be resulting in other lifestyle problems that are presently contributing to his high level of stress. His use of denial may prevent him from accepting his substance abuse problems at this time. Although Mr. D.'s problems are severe enough to warrant psychological treatment for alcohol abuse, he has not reached the point where he can accept treatment.

Further evaluation and treatment for alcohol abuse were recommended. Mr. D. agreed to accept a referral for treatment but failed to follow up on the recommendations. His FAA airman's medical certification was not renewed pending further information about his lifestyle problems.

SOURCE: Reprinted from James N. Butcher (1985). Personality assessment in industry: Theoretical issues and illustrations. In H. John Bernardin & David A. Bownas (Eds.), *Personality assessment in organizations*, pp. 302–305. New York: Praeger.

Charles D. underwent psychological evaluation for purposes of medical certification by the Federal Aviation Administration. Although physically healthy, his personality problems were sufficiently pronounced to result in his being grounded temporarily. The risks involved in permitting him to continue flying were too great.

Personality processes of this kind are the subject of this chapter. The topic of personality has its origins in areas other than industrial-organizational psychology. For this reason, much of the theory and research in the area is only peripherally related to the concerns of this book. Yet personality is a very important factor. People often succeed or fail because they have personality characteristics that make them do so. They may experience severe stress at work, become emotionally disturbed, and be unable to function effectively. This chapter will deal directly with those aspects of personality that relate closely to industrial-organizational psychology. A broader treatment of the area, including various theories that have evolved, is best left to other subfields within psychology.

■ PERSONALITY CONSTRUCTS AND PERFORMANCE

Box 6-1, describing the personality profile of effective managers of Sears, Roebuck stores, illustrates how personality factors can contribute to performance. Since the early 1940s, Sears has had a testing program for the selection of people to fill management positions that places strong emphasis on personality factors. Numerous studies have been conducted relating test scores to indexes of managerial job performance. Carrying out **validation** studies of this kind is one of the major functions of the company's personnel research. Throughout the long history of this testing program, personality measures have been consistently good predictors of managerial performance.

Box 6-2 shows a different version of the role of personality in performance. Gerstein, Reisman & Associates, like some other management consulting firms, emphasizes the different personality constellations required to implement different corporate strategies. It has become big business in the consulting industry to help companies put together the right management teams for their needs. Personality is a major consideration in planning these management teams.

□ The Meaning of Personality

Definitions of "personality" tend to be colored by the theoretical perspective of the person proposing the definition. In general, however, **personality** is a relatively stable set of characteristics that serve to determine how a particular individual behaves in various situations.

Personality is a very broad concept, and somewhat less useful for its breadth. Nevertheless, there are a number of constructs, not directly related to learning, cognitive processes, motivation, or any other topic discussed in Chapters 2–5, that need to be treated. Closely related to internal emotional states, they are probably best described as **personality traits.**

Traits and Situations. For a number of years, the field of personality theory has debated whether behavior is best predicted and understood by studying personality traits within the individual or by analyzing the specific situations in which behavior occurs (Pervin, 1985). This debate is now spilling over into the field of industrial-organizational psychology. In its extreme form, the **trait position** views a person as having built-in predispositions which, because of their rigid, compulsive nature, result in the same kind of action, regardless of the situation. Thus, an authoritarian boss would be domineering and punitive, whether working in a military con-

BOX 6-1 RESEARCH IN I/O PSYCHOLOGY

Personality Profile of Effective Sears, Roebuck Store Managers

As part of a continuing personnel research effort to be sure that Sears' testing program was working as it should, test data obtained seventeen years earlier were related to data on the performance of seventy-six current store managers. Two of the performance factors considered were merchandising ability and people-related ability. The rating form for these factors read as follows:

Rate all managers on the attached sheet (by ascribing a number between 1 and 99) on each of the following characteristics.

1. General skill and ability in performing the *merchandising* duties of a store manager's job.

1	10	20	30	40	50	60	70	80	90	99

Not good at merchandising but not sufficiently poor to be removed from the assignment

Solid, acceptable performance in the merchandising area of store management

A great merchandiser: in merchandising ability compares with the best the company has ever produced

2. General skill and ability in dealing with, *handling, and relating to all the people* who work in the store.

1	10	20	30	40	50	60	70	80	90	99

Not good at working with people but not sufficiently poor to be removed from the assignment

Solid, acceptable managerial performance in dealing with, handling, and relating to all people in the store

Great ability to work with, handle, and relate to people. Compares with the best the company has ever had

Personality characteristics common among store managers with higher scores were reflectiveness, dominance, self-confidence, optimism, and objectivity. These traits accompanied both high merchandising and high people-related ability. Additional traits associated with high merchandising ability were sociability, impulsivity, general activity, and social leadership. The one additional trait particularly associated with high people-related ability was composure.

A profile of a store manager who handles merchandising activities particularly well would read as follows:

This store manager is friendly, socially outgoing, and at ease in most situations. Naturally assertive, he readily takes over the leadership of any group of which he is a part and functions with assured self-confidence. He also has a kind of fast-moving, enthusiastic exuberance that allows him to express himself readily and carry others along with him. He likes excitement and change, and may be somewhat impatient with those who do not function as quickly or as enthusiastically as he does. Sensitive to the subtleties and nuances of situations, his thinking is also closely tied to reality. His high objectivity is unlikely to let personal feelings or emotions color his evaluation of situations or ideas. Cheerful and optimistic, he has the kind of emotionally robust outlook that allows him to encounter a wide range of situations without being personally bothered.

SOURCE: Jon V. Bentz (1985). Research findings from personality assessment of executives. In H. John Bernardin & David A. Bownas (Eds). *Personality assessment in organizations,* pp. 125–128. New York: Praeger.

BOX 6-2 I/O PSYCHOLOGY IN PRACTICE

Personality Characteristics Required in Various Strategic Situations

Gerstein, Reisman & Associates of Toronto is a consulting firm with a considerable practice in matching individuals to the strategic requirements of certain corporate situations. The rationale of this business is that when a product or closely related group of products reaches a point that calls for a specific strategy, this strategy can best be implemented by managers who have personality characteristics that mesh with the strategy. The firm determines the personality characteristics of candidates through lengthy, often day-long, interviews and assessment centers (an evaluation technique that uses situational exercises and sometimes psychological tests to identify job-related characteristics), and then relates the resulting personality profiles to strategic requirements specified by the company. The requirements might include the start-up of a new line of business, turnaround of an existing business, development of dynamic growth in an existing business, redeployment of efforts in an existing business, liquidation or divestiture of a poorly performing business, and management of a new acquisition for the firm.

At one extreme is the start-up situation, where the managers involved must create a vision of the new business, establish a core of technical and marketing expertise, and build a management team from scratch. Here Gerstein, Reisman looks for the following personality requirements:

Vision of the finished business

Hands-on orientation—a "doer"

In-depth knowledge in critical technical areas

Organizing ability

Staffing skills

Team-building capabilities

High energy level and stamina

Personal magnetism (charisma)

Broad knowledge of all key functions

At the other extreme is the situation that requires either selling a line of business that is doing poorly or shutting it down. In this situation the needs are to cut losses, make tough decisions, and arrange the best deal possible. Accordingly, Gerstein, Reisman & Associates seeks people who are:

Callous, tough-minded, determined, willing to be the bad guy

Highly analytical regarding costs and benefits, skeptical about current way of doing things

Not interested in glory, willing to do dirty jobs, not eager for glamor

Concerned about being respected, but not afraid to be disliked

Clearly, personality plays an important role in Gerstein, Reisman's staffing recommendations.

SOURCE: Marc Gerstein and Heather Reisman (1983). Strategic selection: Matching executives to business conditions. *Sloan Management Review, 24* (2), 36–39.

text where this type of behavior was supported or in a group of social service volunteers where it was not.

At the other extreme, the **situationist view** holds that behavior is entirely a function of the situation: People—all people—will be-

have in the same way in situations they perceive to be the same. The environment provides stimuli that totally control behavior. Thus, everyone would be authoritarian in the military context, and everyone would be nonauthoritarian with the volunteer helpers.

The Interactional Perspective. The extreme trait and situationist positions probably have few adherents, although many psychologists lean one way or the other. The position that underlies the following discussion of personality, one that has proved attractive within industrial-organizational psychology, is the **interactional view** (Schneider, 1983, 1987; Terborg, 1981). This view includes the following tenets:

1. Actual behavior results from a continuous process of interaction or feedback between the individual and the situation encountered.
2. The individual—an intentional, active contributor to this interaction—is changed by a situation and also changes it.
3. On the person side of the interaction, cognitive, emotional, and motivational factors and individual ability are essential causes of behavior.
4. On the situation side, the situation's psychological meaning and behavior potential for the individual are essential causes of behavior.

While this approach acknowledges the importance of processes within a person (the operation of traits), it also allows for the fact that people select, influence, and respond to situations. This type of interactional perspective on personality is most consistent with the results of research, and at the same time best fits the needs of industrial-organizational psychology.

☐ Assessment Centers

For a number of reasons, personality constructs and their measures have suffered historically from a certain amount of neglect and negativity in industrial-organizational psychology. Recently, however, a substantial body of research has developed indicating that personality constructs can play a very important role in explaining why people act as they do within organizations (Adler & Weiss, 1988; Day & Silverman, 1989). Although personality measurement generally will be considered along with other types of tests in Chapter 18, one approach needs to be noted here simply because it has made such a major contribution to our understanding of the role that personality processes can play in organizations (Howard & Bray, 1988). This is the assessment center method.

As noted in Box 6-2, Gerstein, Reisman & Associates utilizes the evaluation technique known as **assessment centers** to identify personality characteristics needed for different strategic contexts. At ITT (see Box 2-2), the center includes an in-tray exercise, a committee exercise, a business decisions exercise, a business plan presentation, and a letter writing exercise. Assessors observe the behavior and output of participants, and give them ratings on certain predetermined dimensions considered to be important in their work.

The dimensions rated are often personality characteristics, such as:

Sensitivity—consideration for the feelings and needs of others

Decisiveness—readiness to make decisions, render judgments, take action, or commit oneself

Career ambition—the expressed desire to advance to higher job levels, with active efforts toward self-development

Integrity—observance of social, ethical, and organizational norms in job-related activities

Independence—tendency to let one's own convictions determine action, rather than the opinions of others

Job motivation—capacity for gaining personal satisfaction from the activities and responsibilities available in the job

Work standards—desire to do a good job for its own sake

Initiative—efforts to achieve goals by influencing events and originating action; attempts to achieve goals beyond those called for; tendency to self-starting rather than passive behavior

Energy—evidence of a high activity level

Impact—ability to create a good first impression, command attention and respect, show confidence

There is ample evidence that assessments on dimensions such as these can accurately predict job performance and success, especially within the ranks of management (Gaugler, Rosenthal, Thornton, & Bentson, 1987; Klimoski & Brickner, 1987; Thornton & Byham, 1982). There is also evidence that self-assessments, where people identify their own personality characteristics, do not accomplish the same results.

This discrepancy is illustrated in Exhibit 6-1. For this study, college students assessed themselves on various personality characteristics, and an assessment center also measured them for the same characteristics. The assessment center's procedure involved:

A leaderless group exercise: Groups of six were to reach consensus on how to solve three hypothetical management problems.

An in-basket: Participants were to take appropriate action in response to fourteen written items concerning a particular job.

An oral presentation: Participants were to summarize and critique articles dealing with career development.

An in-depth interview: Participants were questioned for an hour about career-related matters.

Note in Exhibit 6-1 that the personality self-assessments are consistently higher (more

favorable) than the assessment center results. There clearly appears to be a bias toward overevaluation operating here. Uncorrected self-assessments do not provide a valid index of personality. If one really wants to know about oneself, other, more objective measures should be considered.

☐ Personality Characteristics Important to Performance

All these personality traits can play an important role in performance. In addition, several other characteristics have been studied in considerable detail.

Honesty and Dishonesty. Employee theft in many forms is a major problem for organizations. Theft is one component of ineffective performance, although it tends to receive less attention than aspects such as the quantity and quality of output. Theft is a function of such conditions as opportunity, perceived probability of detection and punishment, and existing group norms related to this kind of activity. But it can be reduced by initial selection of employees who are predisposed toward honesty (Hollinger & Clark, 1983). There does appear to be some kind of honesty–dishonesty dimension within people, even though its exact nature remains poorly understood.

The research in this area generally involves the use of polygraphs (lie detectors) and paper-and-pencil tests that question attitudes and behavior related to theft, drug and alcohol use, sabotage, and other aspects of honesty in job performance (McDaniel & Jones, 1988; Sackett, Burris, & Callahan, 1989). These **honesty tests** are used by many companies, especially in retailing, to screen out employees who might steal from an employer. To a great extent, both written tests and polygraphs achieve their purpose. In fact, both tend to elicit a surprising number of admissions of past dishonesty. However, it is also

EXHIBIT 6-1 Comparison of Assessment Center Findings and Student Self-Assessments Regarding Personality Characteristics

Personality Characteristic	Assessments		
	Low	Medium	High
Career ambition			
Self score	0%	12%	88%
Assessment center score	6	32	62
Impact on others			
Self score	0%	34%	66%
Assessment center score	10	39	51
Initiative			
Self score	11%	41%	58%
Assessment center score	34	32	34
Job motivation			
Self score	3%	15%	82%
Assessment center score	14	35	51
Sensitivity to others			
Self score	0%	19%	81%
Assessment center score	17	48	35
Work standards			
Self score	0%	9%	91%
Assessment center score	24	47	29
Overall potential			
Self score	0%	25%	75%
Assessment center score	14	48	38

SOURCE: Adapted from William L. Mihal & Janet L. Graumenz (1984). An assessment of the accuracy of self-assessment for career decision making. *Journal of Vocational Behavior, 25,* 245–253.

true that these measures, especially the polygraph, have been the subject of considerable controversy regarding the extent to which individual privacy is invaded. Recent legislation has severely limited the use of the polygraph by private employers.

Clearly, many people will behave dishonestly in some situations and not in others: A strong situational factor operates. But then there are those who are quite consistently honest or dishonest. Knowledge regarding these traits has been hampered by the great variation in social and cultural norms defining dishonest behavior. In some parts of the world, and within some groups in the United States, bribery and kickbacks are normal aspects of business transactions; elsewhere

they are considered dishonest and unacceptable. It is difficult to study honesty and dishonesty within the context of this relativism, yet the need to do so is great.

Locus of Control. In contrast to honesty, **locus of control** has yielded to research; a great deal has been learned about it (Spector, 1982, 1988). It is useful to see the various attitudes toward control as positions on a continuum. At one end of the continuum are people with an internal locus of control, who believe that their internal traits determine what happens in a given situation. At the other end of the continuum are people with an external locus of control, who feel that they are at the mercy of chance, fate, other people, and out-

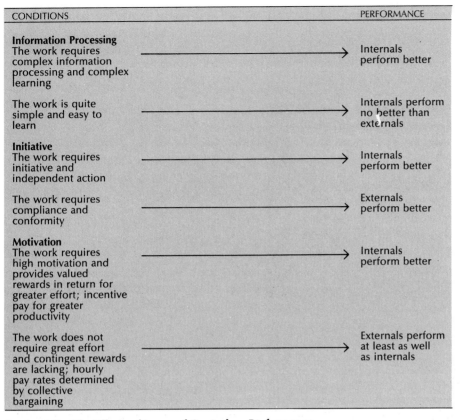

CONDITIONS	PERFORMANCE
Information Processing The work requires complex information processing and complex learning	Internals perform better
The work is quite simple and easy to learn	Internals perform no better than externals
Initiative The work requires initiative and independent action	Internals perform better
The work requires compliance and conformity	Externals perform better
Motivation The work requires high motivation and provides valued rewards in return for greater effort; incentive pay for greater productivity	Internals perform better
The work does not require great effort and contingent rewards are lacking; hourly pay rates determined by collective bargaining	Externals perform at least as well as internals

EXHIBIT 6-2   The Effects of Locus of Control on Performance

side events. "Internals" not only perceive themselves as having greater control over events in their lives but also seek out situations where they are likely to do so—by starting their own companies, for instance. "Externals" tend to be more conforming, more anxious, and less satisfied with their jobs.

Exhibit 6-2 summarizes much of what is known about performance and locus of control. There are jobs—usually of a professional, skilled, or managerial nature—where internals perform much better. A number of the motivational theories and practices considered in Chapters 3 and 4 are clearly applicable to internals. But so far theory has been less helpful in telling us what will produce high

performance levels among externals. There is evidence, however, that in one respect externals are particularly prone to performance difficulties. It appears that when they become frustrated at work they are very likely to engage in sabotage against an employer, purposely damaging valuable property or equipment (Storms & Spector, 1987).

Further insight into the nature of locus of control emerged from a very interesting study carried out among top executives of Canadian firms (Miller, Kets de Vries, & Toulouse, 1982). Most of these executives tended to be internals, but the group included a range of control types. The firms with more internal top executives pursued more innovative strategies—there were more industry leadership in research and development, more innovation in products and services, more frequent introduction of new products, and more drastic changes in product lines. Also, firms led by internals pursued more risky and aggressive strategies and extended their planning further into the future. The study demonstrated that the firms differed in many respects because of the personalities of their leaders.

Self-Esteem and Self-Efficacy. These two personality concepts come to industrial-organizational psychology from different sources, yet they are closely related and often overlapping (Brockner, 1988). Work on **self-esteem** has as its basic hypothesis the following view:

> People of high self-perceived competence and self-image should be more likely to achieve on task performance than those who have low self-perceived competence, low success expectancy, and low self-image concerning the task or job at hand, since such differential task achievement would be consistent with their self-cognitions. This assumes that task performance is seen as valued (Korman, 1974, p. 227).

Research supports this formulation, that performance has a consistent relation to level of self-esteem (Somers & Lefkowitz, 1983). In many respects, people with low self-esteem perform less well than those with higher levels of self-esteem. The process tends to be cyclical, with low self-esteem contributing to poorer performance, which in turn reinforces the low esteem.

Self-efficacy is concerned with self-perceptions of how well a person can cope with situations as they arise (Bandura, 1982). If people believe that they are capable of performing well in a situation, they are more likely to enter the situation, persevere in it, and end up doing a good job. Self-esteem may be a generalized trait; self-efficacy is always situation-specific, and it immediately precedes action. Measures of self-efficacy are

good predictors of occupational choice, and of future work performance as well (Lent & Hackett, 1987; Locke, Frederick, Lee, & Bobko, 1984). Box 6-3 describes a study that provides insight into how low self-efficacy may come about.

■ WORK, STRESS, AND EMOTION

The one aspect of personality that has been studied most in relation to industrial-organizational psychology is stress. The early work on stress was derived from the medical study of physiological responses to threats against the body (Selye, 1976). Much of this work concerned emotions such as anxiety and their manifested effects on bodily functioning. But with the introduction of the stress concept into the study of organizations, the study of stress has expanded considerably: It has focused on stress in relation to work and employment but has also moved into other areas. Stress, an aspect of personality like honesty, locus of control, and self-esteem, has an even greater impact on performance than these other characteristics.

☐ The Nature of Stress

Although **stress** has been defined in a number of ways, two definitions appear to be most apt:

> Stress is an adaptive response, mediated by individual characteristics and/or psychological processes, that is a consequence of any external action, situation or event that places special physical and/or psychological demands upon a person (Ivancevich & Matteson, 1980, pp. 8–9).
>
> Stress refers to an internal state of the individual who perceives threats to physical and/or psychic well-being. The term emphasizes a person's perception and evaluation of potentially harmful stimuli, and considers the perception of threat to arise from a comparison between the demands imposed upon the individual and

BOX 6-3 RESEARCH IN I/O PSYCHOLOGY

A Laboratory Investigation of the Sources of Low Self-Efficacy

Undergraduate psychology students were randomly assigned to one of six conditions:

	Proof-reading	Pricing Product Orders
Constructive criticism	1	4
Destructive criticism	2	5
No feedback	3	6

The first phase of the research involved exposing the students to either the constructive criticism, destructive criticism, or no-feedback conditions. The task here was to plan an advertising campaign for a new product. All students wrote out their proposals, which were given to an accomplice of the experimenter for evaluation under both criticism conditions. The evaluations were preestablished and had no necessary relation to the actual quality of the plan. The criticisms were provided in writing and included such comments as the following.

Constructive: Needed to give more attention to the slogans and packaging.

> I think there's a lot of room for improvement. He/she seemed unwilling to come up with new ideas.

Destructive: Didn't even try; can't seem to do anything right.

> I wasn't impressed at all. The whole thing needs to be fixed. I had the impression that he/she didn't try much at all (or maybe it's just a lack of talent). If

his/her work doesn't improve, I'd try to get someone else to do it.

In the no-feedback condition, the students did not receive an evaluation.

Before proceeding to either the proofreading or pricing product orders tasks, but after the task had been described to them, the students completed a brief form on which they rated their ability to perform the upcoming task on a seven-point scale (measure of self-efficacy level). The mean ratings for the students in each of the six conditions were:

	Proof-reading	Pricing Product Orders
Constructive criticism	5.3	5.5
Destructive criticism	4.9	5.1
No feedback	4.9	5.4

In the proofreading groups, self-efficacy was higher by a statistically significant degree when constructive criticism had been received than under either of the other two conditions. In the pricing product orders groups, it was the students who had received destructive criticism who differed from the others. Overall the study demonstrates that it is not criticism per se that causes low self-efficacy, but destructive criticism that is general, inconsiderate in tone, contains threats, or attributes poor performance to factors within the individual.

SOURCE: Robert A. Baron (1988). Negative effects of destructive criticism: Impact on conflict, self-efficacy, and task performance. *Journal of Applied Psychology, 73,* 199–207.

the individual's ability to cope with these demands. A perceived imbalance in this mechanism gives rise to the stress response, which may be physiological and/or behavioral (Krantz, Grunberg, & Baum, 1985, p. 354).

If one equates "stress" in the first definition with "stress response" in the second, the two definitions become comparable. It does seem useful to utilize the term "stress" to refer to an internal state and its immediate physiological concomitants, but the literature is by no means consistent in this usage, sometimes referring instead to the external stimuli. In any event, stress involves the arousal of negative or unpleasant emotional states, particularly anxiety.

The process of stress at work is described in Exhibit 6-3. The specific factors and characteristics noted under the major heads are important, but the list is not exhaustive. The key ingredients are (Krinsky, Kieffer, Carone, & Yolles, 1984):

1. Stressors, or sources of stress—stimuli that are perceived as threatening and that arouse negative feelings. The more stressors there are, the greater the likelihood of continued stress.
2. The frequency and duration of exposure to stressors. Anticipation of exposure can also set off stress reactions.
3. The intensity of physical and emotional reactions caused by stressors.

One's personal characteristics affect one's perception of stressors, the amount of exposure one permits oneself, and the intensity of one's reaction. There are sizable individual variations. Box 6-4, about air traffic controllers at O'Hare Airport, presents a good example of how the stress process works in a job that forces people to face their stressors over long periods.

Measuring Stress. The various factors and characteristics involved in the stress process,

as set forth in Exhibit 6-3, have been measured in a variety of ways. Physiological indexes may be used; for instance, the stress may affect serum cholesterol level of the blood. Other tests measure physiological changes associated with emotional arousal. One way to diagnose external sources of stress is to have the individual fill out a checklist of life events, noting crises and changes in the status quo. Recent and profound changes, such as the death of a spouse, a change in residence, trouble with in-laws, and pregnancy, produce the most stress. In most cases the events considered focus on life outside the organization, but changes and crises at work may be relevant as well.

Stress researchers have developed a variety of questionnaires asking people to describe themselves in certain ways. The questions may cover organizational stressors, work group stressors, job and career stressors, stress-prone personality characteristics, and other similar factors, as listed in Exhibit 6-3. Exhibit 6-4 shows items from a scale for measuring stress. This one deals with the tendency to continue high stress levels after external work stressors have been removed, and thus experience chronic states of stress. People with total scores of 24 or higher have been found to report more health problems, miss more days from work for health reasons, visit physicians more often, take more pain relievers and tranquilizers, and believe they perform less effectively because of not feeling well.

Stress and Performance. Exhibit 6-3 lists a number of potential outcomes from stress. In most cases these outcomes are clearly indicated by research: Job dissatisfaction does tend to result from stress, for instance, and so does a higher absenteeism rate. But low performance as one result of stress is a more complex issue.

For a number of years the inverted-U hypothesis has been accepted as describing the relationship between stress and perfor-

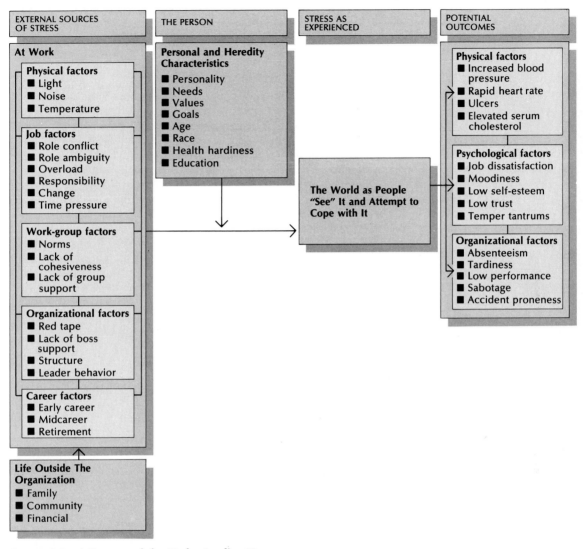

EXTERNAL SOURCES OF STRESS	THE PERSON	STRESS AS EXPERIENCED	POTENTIAL OUTCOMES

At Work

Physical factors
- Light
- Noise
- Temperature

Job factors
- Role conflict
- Role ambiguity
- Overload
- Responsibility
- Change
- Time pressure

Work-group factors
- Norms
- Lack of cohesiveness
- Lack of group support

Organizational factors
- Red tape
- Lack of boss support
- Structure
- Leader behavior

Career factors
- Early career
- Midcareer
- Retirement

Life Outside The Organization
- Family
- Community
- Financial

Personal and Heredity Characteristics
- Personality
- Needs
- Values
- Goals
- Age
- Race
- Health hardiness
- Education

The World as People "See" It and Attempt to Cope with It

Physical factors
- Increased blood pressure
- Rapid heart rate
- Ulcers
- Elevated serum cholesterol

Psychological factors
- Job dissatisfaction
- Moodiness
- Low self-esteem
- Low trust
- Temper tantrums

Organizational factors
- Absenteeism
- Tardiness
- Low performance
- Sabotage
- Accident proneness

EXHIBIT 6-3   A Framework for Understanding Stress
External stressors assail a person, who then experiences the stress in certain characteristic ways and experiences certain behavioral reactions.
SOURCE: Adapted from Michael T. Matteson and John M. Ivancevich (1982). *Managing job stress and health,* p. 53. New York: The Free Press.

mance (Exhibit 6-5). This hypothesis claims that, up to a point, stress serves to arouse a person and increase attention to the job, thus improving performance. Beyond that optimum level of stress, however, performance falls off (Ivancevich & Matteson, 1980). A diagram of this stress-response pattern takes the form of an upside-down U (see Exhibit 6-5). A good deal of laboratory research focused on decision making seems to confirm this view,

BOX 6-4 I/O PSYCHOLOGY IN PRACTICE

A Frequently Stressful Job: Air Traffic Controller at O'Hare

The air traffic controllers at O'Hare Airport in the suburbs of Chicago have to be ready, alert, and the best in the world. The pace is go-go, hectic, and unending. On a typical day, one out of every five persons who flies in the United States goes through O'Hare. Over 40 million passengers pass through annually; that is about 110,000 a day. During peak hours, O'Hare logs a takeoff or landing every twenty seconds.

By their own estimates, there are two or three midair-collision near misses every day with which controllers are involved. The controllers know that any let-up from constant vigilance, a slight error in instructions, or pushing the wrong button can mean the death of passengers. This intense struggle with responsibility for people is comparable to combat battle stress and has been labeled "collisionitis."

Most of the controllers at O'Hare are young, in their late 20s and early 30s. Nearly all are male. Although controllers are above average in intelligence, few have been to college. Of the ninety-four controllers and trainees working at O'Hare, only a few have been there more than ten years. Most don't last five years. The grinding pace, split-second decisions, the constant responsibility for people, and the fear of midair collisions all take their toll.

Richard Grayson, a former president of the American Academy of Stress Disorders, has examined many of the controllers in the Chicago area and found remarkably similar symptoms: insomnia, loss of appetite, anxiety, irritability, and sexual dysfunction. Railroad dispatchers and sonar operators on nuclear submarines undergo similar stress, but their symptoms are seldom as severe. One air traffic controller, who had his third near miss in a year, turned into what his friends described as "a vegetable." He finally quit, stating that he never wanted to see another airplane as long as he lived.

SOURCE: Reprinted from Michael T. Matteson & John M. Ivancevich (1982). *Managing job stress and health*, p. 90. New York: The Free Press.

and there are other supporting studies as well. An example of how stress may help to improve performance comes from a study in which participants in a management-development program filled out a personal life-events checklist and an index of their information-search activities. The checklist measured stressors experienced by the participants, while the information-search index reported efforts to perform rationally in the decision-making process. Results showed that the more stress participants experienced, the more extensive was their information search, presumably as a way of finding help in coping with a changed environment (Weiss, Ilgen, & Sharbaugh, 1982).

Yet research on the quality and quantity of work output in relation to stress levels has not typically indicated this kind of positive result from stress, nor has it supported the inverted-U hypothesis that some amount of stress is useful. Performance—whether measured by supervisor ratings, organizational perceptions of effectiveness, or job performance on job-related examinations—has repeatedly been found to decrease with increasing levels of stress (Jamal, 1984; Motowidlo, Packard, & Manning, 1986). In special situations this may not be true, but in general low performance can be anticipated where stress is high. A likely contributing factor is the physical symptoms often produced

Exhibit 6-4   Scale for Measuring an Individual's Job Stress

Scale values: After each of the six statements, record the number of the appropriate answer.

1. The statement is never true.
2. The statement is rarely true.
3. The statement is occasionally true.
4. The statement is sometimes true.

5. The statement is often true.
6. The statement is usually true.
7. The statement is always true.

After I leave work for the day, I continue thinking about all the problems and go through them again in my mind.   _____

I stay in "high gear" and have trouble relaxing once I leave work.   _____

Over the past few months, I find it is becoming increasingly difficult to unwind at the end of my work day.   _____

When I get home after work, I am so preoccupied with what happened on the job that I can't talk with my spouse or friends.   _____

Even when I'm away from the job, I spend much of my time thinking about my work.   _____

In describing me, my friends would say that I eat, drink, and think my job.   _____

Total score   _____

Source: Adapted from Michael T. Matteson & John M. Ivancevich (1983). Note on tension discharge rate as an employee health status predictor. *Academy of Management Journal, 26,* p. 541.

Exhibit 6-5   The Inverted-U Relationship between Stress and Performance
Some stress raises level of performance, but too much stress lowers it.

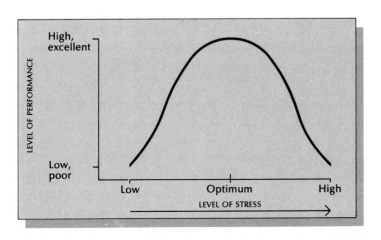

EXHIBIT 6-6   Primary Causes of Stress Cited by Women Managers

Stress Situation	Frequency of Mention
Work overload	Very high
Deadlines and time pressures	Very high
Conflict between work and off-work life	High
Poor interpersonal relationships at work	High
Situations over which control is lacking	High
Staff problems—unreliable staff	Above average
Staff shortages	Above average
Inadequate support from above	Above average
Role conflicts	Above average
Work underload	About average
Disciplining	About average
Feeling undervalued	About average
Discrimination and prejudice	About average
Keeping up with technological change	About average

SOURCE: Adapted from Marilyn Davidson & Cary Cooper (1983). *Stress and the woman manager,* p. 63. Oxford, England: Martin Robertson.

by stress, such as headaches, stomach aches, and other psychosomatic reactions (Frese, 1985). These would interfere with concentration on one's work.

☐ External Sources of Stress

Exhibit 6-3 lists a number of external sources of stress. More specifically, Exhibit 6-6 describes how female managers assess the various sources of stress. Clearly, their greatest problem is having too much work and not enough time to meet deadlines. Although we cannot discuss all the external sources of stress that various people experience, we can understand the ways in which these stressors operate by examining a few of the most common ones: role conflict and ambiguity, rotating shifts, and "sick organizations."

Role Conflict and Ambiguity.   People occupying positions face a range of expectations about their behavior. These expectations flow from a variety of sources, which are called a *role set.* Within this process are embedded two major sources of stress: role conflict and role ambiguity. **Role conflict** occurs when compliance with one type of perceived role expectations would make it difficult or impossible to comply with another type: the person is pulled at least two ways, perhaps more. **Role ambiguity** occurs when role-related information is lacking or not clearly communicated: The person simply does not have much to go on by way of clear job-performance guidelines. This process is summarized in Exhibit 6-7.

Role conflict is typically high in **boundary-spanning** positions that extend both inside and outside the organization (as with people in sales) or its departments (as with project managers); it is also high in innovative problem-solving positions and in management generally, especially at the upper levels. Role ambiguity is often high where there are no organization charts and no job descriptions developed from job analyses. Both factors produce tension and anxiety in many people, but in rather different ways (Jackson & Schuler, 1985; Newton & Keenan, 1987). Of

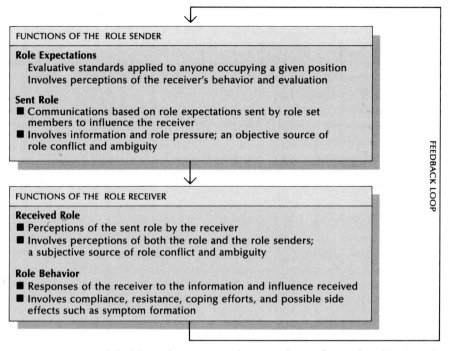

Exhibit 6-7   A Model of the Role Process and How Role Conflict and Ambiguity Relate to It
The role sender communicates expectations for the receiver to translate into behavior;
but sometimes inadequate role communication creates role conflict or ambiguity.
Source: Adapted from Robert L. Kahn, Donald M. Wolfe, Robert B. Quinn, J. Diedrick Snoek, &
Robert A. Rosenthal (1964). *Organizational stress: Studies in role conflict and ambiguity,* p. 26.
New York: Wiley.

the two, role ambiguity is more likely to have direct effects on absenteeism and other aspects of performance.

Rotating Shifts. Roughly a quarter of the working population is involved in some kind of shift work. Shifts may be permanent, so that the same individuals remain on day, evening, or night shifts over long periods of time; they can also be rotating, with people changing from one shift to another at intervals that are usually rather short. Studies indicate that **rotating shifts** are much more stressful for many people (Jamal, 1981). Emotional symptoms tend to be more prevalent among those on rotating shifts, social participation is less, absenteeism is more fre-

quent, and lateness for work is more of a problem. As noted previously, adapting to change appears to be stressful for many, and shift assignments that change frequently seem likely to increase this problem.

"Sick Organizations." In recent years a number of instances have been reported in which a set of very similar physical symptoms suddenly breaks out among workers at a given location. At first a single individual reports nausea, headaches, or faintness, usually in response to something like a strange odor; the same illness then spreads to others who work nearby. Investigation yields no evidence of any chemical or organic cause that might account for the symptoms, but always reveals the presence of numerous external sources of stress—in particular, work overload, role ambiguity, and role conflict. The stressors can consistently be traced to the actions—or inaction—of management. In such cases, "the concept of a **sick organization** is a valid one" (Schmitt, Colligan, & Fitzgerald, 1980).

High-stress, sick organizations need not always produce sudden symptom outbreaks of this kind; in fact, most do not. Nevertheless, it is true that many organizations with certain patterns of emotional pathology concentrated in their upper echelons tend to perpetuate stress-producing behavior down through their ranks. Ultimately the stress effects produce business problems and the organization becomes ineffective. Five neurotic management styles that can lead to sick organizations are described in Exhibit 6-8. For individual employees at lower levels the best solution in such instances is to seek work elsewhere, and many do just that. Unfortunately, however, many workers do not have that option, and for these people the stress produced by sick organizations can become far-reaching indeed.

□ The Person in Stress Reactions

The problems that stress generates depend on the type of person involved. Different people react strongly to different stressors; some are relatively immune to stresses of almost any kind. The description of a psychologist's report about an airline pilot at the beginning of this chapter shows how someone's personality problems can condition his or her stress reactions. The Federal Aviation Administration sought this report because of the pilot's stress-related difficulties.

Type A Personality. One stress-response pattern that has achieved much attention recently is known as the **Type A personality.** People with a Type A behavior pattern tend to react to stress by developing problems and

diseases of the heart (Booth-Kewley & Friedman, 1987; Friedman & Rosenman, 1974).

> [The Type A pattern] can be observed in any person who is aggressively involved in a chronic, incessant struggle to achieve more and more in less and less time, and if required to do so, against the opposing efforts of other things or other persons. The overt manifestations of this struggle include explosive, accelerated speech; a heightened pace of living; impatience with slowness; concentrating on more than one activity at a time; self-preoccupation; dissatisfaction with life; evaluation of the worthiness of one's activities in terms of numbers; a tendency to challenge and compete with others even in noncompetitive situations; and a free-floating hostility. The major facets or "core" elements of the behavior pattern are extremes of aggressiveness, easily aroused hostility, a sense of time urgency, and competitive achievement striving (Mathews, 1982, p. 293).

The **Type B personality,** in contrast, lacks these characteristics and is not prone to coronary problems. Type B people may well work hard and have considerable drive, but they feel no pressing conflict with people or time.

Emotions of anger and hostility play an important role in the Type A pattern. Such people experience strong stress reactions in the high-pressure environments in which they operate, but they also seek out these environments; indeed, it is almost as if they are addicted to them. The Type A pattern can be a two-edged sword: While placing people at high risk of heart-related illness and death, it also gives them the drive to do particularly well in certain kinds of work (Boyd, 1984; Taylor, Locke, Lee, & Gist, 1984). The Type A pattern is particularly common among small-business owners and entrepreneurs, and they are likely to head rapidly growing and profitable firms. Type A people are also likely to be productive and effective researchers when employed on university faculties. The Type A personality pattern can produce an exception

Exhibit 6-8 Neurotic Styles of Top Executives that Produce Sick Organizations

Key Factor	Neurotic Style				
	Paranoid	*Compulsive*	*Dramatic*	*Depressive*	*Schizoid*
Characteristics	Suspiciousness and mistrust of others; hypersensitivity and hyperalertness; readiness to counter perceived threats; overconcern with hidden motives and special meanings; intense attention span; cold, rational, unemotional	Perfectionism; preoccupation with trivial details; insistence that others submit to own way of doing things; relationships seen in terms of dominance and submission; lack of spontaneity; inability to relax; meticulousness, dogmatism, obstinacy	Self-dramatization, excessive expression of emotions; incessant drawing of attention to self; narcissistic preoccupation; a craving for activity and excitement; alternating between idealization and devaluation of others; exploitativeness; incapacity for concentration or sharply focused attention	Feelings of guilt, worthlessness, self-reproach, inadequacy; sense of helplessness and hopelessness—of being at the mercy of events; diminished ability to think clearly; loss of interest and motivation; inability to experience pleasure	Detachment, noninvolvement, withdrawnness; sense of estrangement; lack of excitement or enthusiasm; indifference to praise or criticism; lack of interest in present or future; appearance cold, unemotional
Fantasy	I cannot really trust anybody; a menacing superior force exists that is out to get me; I had better be on my guard.	I don't want to be at the mercy of events; I have to master and control all the things affecting me.	I want to get attention from and impress the people who count in my life.	It is hopeless to change the course of events in my life; I am just not good enough.	The world of reality does not offer any satisfaction to me; my interactions with others will eventually fail and cause harm, so it is safer to remain distant.
Dangers	Distortion of reality due to a preoccupation with confirmation of suspicions; loss of capacity for spontaneous action because of defensive attitudes	Inward orientation; indecisiveness and postponement; avoidance due to the fear of making mistakes; inability to deviate from planned activity; excessive reliance on rules and regulations; difficulties in seeing "the big picture"	Superficiality, suggestibility; the risk of operating in a nonfactual world—action based on "hunches"; overreaction to minor events; others may feel used and abused	Overly pessimistic outlook; difficulties in concentration and performance; inhibition of action, indecisiveness	Emotional isolation causes frustration of dependency needs of others; bewilderment and aggressiveness may result

Source: Manfred F. R. Kets de Vries and Danny Miller (1984). *The neurotic organization*, pp. 24–25. San Francisco: Jossey-Bass.

to the theory that stress yields poor work performance. In part at least, the superior performance of Type A people appears to be due to their devoting more time to their work (Byrne & Reinhart, 1989).

Some recent research suggests an explanation for the high performance levels that Type A people often achieve. There is reason to believe that there are two major components bound together within the Type A behavior pattern. One is an achievement-striving component that involves highly competitive, hard-driving behavior; this component is associated with improved performance but is unrelated to health considerations. The other component of Type A is an impatience and irritability factor that shows no relationship to performance, but is consistently associated with health problems. It seems that a free-floating anger, ready to be aroused at a minute's notice, is the source of the health-related problems that Type A's experience; this is the area in which stress manifests itself, not in achievement striving and competitiveness per se (Spence, Helmreich, & Pred, 1987; Spence, Pred, & Helmreich, 1989).

Negative Emotionality and Burnout. Burnout is a phenomenon first identified in the helping professions, such as medicine and social work. Practitioners who "burn out" experience a significant decline in their effectiveness in dealing with patients or clients. Definitions of this process vary, but certain common elements can be identified (Jackson, Schwab, & Schuler, 1986; Maslach, 1982). Burnout is an individual phenomenon, it is an internal state involving feelings and motives, and it is a negative experience for a person. This negative aspect includes a degree of emotional exhaustion, with loss of feeling and concern, loss of trust, loss of interest, and loss of spirit. There is a negative reaction to others, including aversion to clients, reduced idealism, and irritability. There is also a negative reaction to oneself and one's accomplishments, involving feelings of helplessness, depression, withdrawal, and inability to cope. It is now evident that burnout is not limited to the helping professions, although it may be more frequent there because of their emphasis on contact with people (Meier, 1984; Pines & Aronson, 1988).

An important factor in the development of burnout appears to be a generalized personality predisposition, in which the presence of particular stressors produces a stress reaction. It is known that different people tend to experience different levels of negative emotionality and distress whether stress is present or not (Watson & Clark, 1984). Thus, certain people seem to focus on the negative side of things. They are more introspective, tending to dwell on their failures and shortcomings; they are more likely to report dissatisfaction in almost any sphere. When this disposition toward negative emotionality is combined with continuing stress, the person becomes a candidate for burnout and for decreased effectiveness in work.

☐ Dealing with Stress

Dealing with stress is a concern both for the individual and for the employing organization. For individuals it is important because life, health, productivity, and income can be affected. For organizations it is important not only for humanitarian reasons but also because performance in all its facets, and thus organizational effectiveness, can be affected. And it is obvious that any benefits accruing from the work of stress-prone people, such as Type A's, are sharply reduced if the duration of these people's contributions is curtailed by stress-induced disability or death.

Exhibit 6-9 lists some approaches that have been proposed for dealing with stress. The distinctions between individual- and organizational-level approaches are not clear-cut, and stress can be reduced by making changes in either the individual or the organization or

Exhibit 6-9   Individual and Organizational Approaches for Dealing with Stress

Individual Level	Organizational Level
Meditation and prayer	Exercise facilities
Psychological withdrawal	Changing the physical environment
Planning ahead	Management by objectives
An appropriate philosophy of life	Changing the organizational climate
Diet and nutrition	Health profiling
Exercise and physical activity	Selection and placement
Behavior modification	Job analysis and clarification
Social support from peers, family, et al.	Stress inoculation training
Actual withdrawal from the job	Changing organizational structures and processes
Assertiveness training	Increasing participation in decision making
Biofeedback	Increasing performance feedback
Progressive relaxation	Creative problem solving
Autogenic training	Delegation
Transactional analysis	Job restructuring
Anticipatory socialization programs	Conflict management
Time management	
Psychotherapy and counseling	
Self-assessment	
Systematic desensitization	

both. One approach involves a change in the person, so that either stress reactivity is reduced or strategies for coping with sources of stress in the environment are developed. The other approach involves a direct organizational attack on the stressors themselves. Thus, for example, role ambiguity might be reduced if an individual worker queried superiors at length as to what was expected; it might also be reduced if the company conducted a job analysis and developed a comprehensive job description.

There has been very little research about many of the approaches noted in Exhibit 6-9, at least with regard to their stress-reducing potential. They seem to make sense, given what is known about sources of stress and the human experience of stress, but they have not been systematically tested. Other approaches, however, have been studied more thoroughly. Two of these—social support and stress-management programs—deserve special attention.

Social Support.   There is ample evidence that **social support** from family, coworkers, superiors, and other people can minimize stress, so that its effects are less pronounced (Cohen & Wills, 1985; Kessler, Price, & Wortman, 1985). Negative effects of stress, including emotional illness, are much more frequent among those who are socially isolated, such as divorced people living alone, than among those who have many contacts with others. Emotional support—someone to talk to about problems, a source of encouragement, a shoulder to lean on—is important; so is informational support, where others can provide the knowledge needed to cope with stress or simply the understanding that reduces uncertainty. The very fact that one has friends and close relationships can bolster self-esteem and make one less vulnerable to stresses.

Exhibit 6-10 illustrates two ways in which social support can buffer stress. First, social support may prevent what would otherwise be viewed as a stressor from actually being

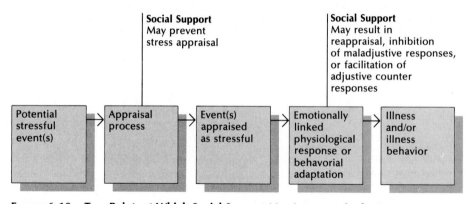

Exhibit 6-10   Two Points at Which Social Support May Intervene in the Stress Process
Sometimes social support can enable a person to avoid perceiving an event as stressful or
to adjust to a stressful event with no negative effects.
Source: Sheldon Cohen and Thomas A. Wills (1985). Stress, social support, and the buffering hypothesis. *Psychological Bulletin, 98,* p. 313.

perceived that way. For example, role conflict may be rampant in a given situation—as when a salesperson is faced with competing demands from customers, sources of supply, and legal requirements—but support from superiors may make this situation an exhilarating challenge rather than a source of severe stress. Second, social support may provide a person with the means to cope with stress when it does occur, so that the stress experience is minimal or short-lived. Thus, an effective trainer may provide the salesperson with the confidence, understanding, and skill to analyze the various demands and deal with each effectively, so that the stress is largely controlled.

Box 6-5 describes the stress at the Three Mile Island nuclear plant when one of the reactors malfunctioned. Studies of this crisis produced the major finding that stress levels varied considerably from one person to another and that social support played an important role in reducing the stress experienced by certain workers. This same type of finding, regarding the stress-reducing value of social support, has been obtained across a wide range of situations and occupations extending from veterinary medicine to construction work to police radio dispatchers (Osipow & Davis, 1988; Ganster, Fusilier, & Mayes, 1986; Kirmeyer & Dougherty, 1988).

Stress-Management Programs. Exhibit 6-9 notes a number of programs that may reduce the stress reactions of individuals. Although such programs are not widespread in the business world, a number of the larger firms have sponsored them. Consulting firms frequently make training of this kind available to clients. In many cases stress-management efforts are incorporated into health-promotion and physical-fitness programs.

The programs differ in a number of respects, but often include muscle-relaxation techniques, recognition of anxiety cues and training in how to deal with them, feedback of physiological measurements in order to control them, meditation, time management, and so on. The overall objective appears to be to help people become aware of sources of stress so that they can bring stress under conscious control and minimize its effects. Relatively little has been done to teach ways of going out into the environment and actual-

BOX 6-5   RESEARCH IN I/O PSYCHOLOGY

Stress Effects of the Accident at Metropolitan Edison Company's Three Mile Island Nuclear Power Plant

On March 28, 1979, a serious accident occurred at the Three Mile Island nuclear power plant near Harrisburg, Pennsylvania, threatening workers and nearby residents with severe radiation exposure. Sixty percent of the people living within five miles of the plant evacuated the area. Under these crisis conditions employees worked to deal with the threat. Subsequent studies provide a picture of the stresses experienced by these employees at that time.

The sheer amount of work to be done was a major source of increased tension. In addition, stress arose from conflicting demands on the employees' time and the need to perform tasks they did not feel qualified to do. The hazards inherent in the plant itself were a major source of stress, and so was the felt need to be in two places at once—at work and at home to deal with problems there. Anxiety levels ran very high, and many employees experienced symptoms of illness.

Studies show that there were substantial differences in the tension experienced by different individuals. Living closer to the plant seems to have helped in certain respects, because the demands of work and home could be coordinated more easily. Working closer to the damaged reactor also helped, presumably because these people were better informed and felt more able to do something about the situation. Finally, a feeling of strong social support from superiors and coworkers played an important role: It reduced stress, increased optimism, and decreased the incidence of symptoms.

SOURCES: Rupert F. Chisholm, Stanislav V. Kasl, & Brenda Eskenazi (1983). The nature and predictors of job-related tension in a crisis situation: Reactions of nuclear workers to the Three Mile Island accident. *Academy of Management Journal, 26,* 385–405. Rupert F. Chisholm, Stanislav V. Kasl, & Lloyd Mueller (1985). The role of social support during an organizational crisis: Stress reactions of nuclear workers to the Three Mile Island accident. *Academy of Management Proceedings, 45,* 197–200.

ly attacking sources of stress; instead, the goal has been to teach people how to respond to stressors with less stress. A typical **stress-management program** might include the following steps:

1. A definition of the program's objectives, and assessments of individual stress levels via questionnaires and physiological measures

2. Individual assessments of sources of stress, in the various areas noted in Exhibit 6-3

3. Analyses of individual differences in stress reactions, considering such factors as Type A personality and propensity for burnout

4. Introduction of stress-reduction techniques, such as relaxation, meditation, exercises, nutrition, and time management

5. Goal setting for future stress reduction

It appears that comprehensive approaches of this kind can reduce immediate stress levels (Murphy, 1984). There is no guarantee that many of the more abbreviated commercially available approaches actually do so, however, and even the comprehensive programs tend to have rather limited effects. Whether the stress reduction that does occur is sufficient to have a real impact on performance levels, emotional health, and the like is an open question at the present time. The evidence available suggests that major organizational changes—the kind that might drastically improve sick organizations, for instance—can yield much more far-reaching consequences. Nevertheless, the finding that both physiological and perceptual measures of stress are influenced by stress-management programs is an important result (Bruning & Frew, 1987; Higgins, 1986).

It is not clear whether the typical stress-management effort can have a meaningful impact on more severe occupational stress reactions that extend into the realm of clinical emotional disorder. What is evident is that these latter reactions can be alleviated to a substantial degree by various types of psychotherapy, even when the treatment is applied on a relatively short-term basis (Firth & Shapiro, 1986). The next question, of course, is whether psychotherapy might not be the method of choice for all stress-reduction purposes, regardless of the level of severity. That question remains unanswered at the present time.

KEY TERMS

Validation	Stress
Personality	Role conflict
Personality traits	Role ambiguity
Trait position	Boundary-spanning
Situationist view	Rotating shifts
Interactional view	Sick organization
Assessment centers	Type A personality
Honesty tests	Type B personality
Locus of control	Burnout
Self-esteem	Social support
Self-efficacy	Stress-management program

SUMMARY

Personality has its primary roots in psychology, but has significant implications for other areas of industrial-organizational psychology as well. In many respects personality is the subject matter of Chapters 2 through 5, but this chapter considers some aspects that are not discussed elsewhere. Among these are *honesty* levels, *locus of control, self-esteem,* and *self-efficacy.* In understanding personality, it is important to comprehend the roles played by *traits* and situational factors, and to know about the relations among them.

One personality factor that has been given much attention recently is reaction to *stress.* In general, stress appears to have a negative impact on performance, although in some instances this is not the case. Among the important sources of stress on individuals are *role conflict* and *ambiguity, rotating shifts,* and *sick organizations.* Individual characteristics affecting stress responsiveness are *Type A personality* and *burnout*. External sources and personal traits interact to produce stress reactions in individuals, including emotional and physical symptoms and performance deficits.

Social support from family members and coworkers has been found to be a major factor mit-

igating stress reactions. In addition, various types of *stress-management programs* appear promising. Yet the most effective method of reducing stress remains the avoidance or removal of external stress sources—*role ambiguity, sick organizations,* and the like.

QUESTIONS

1. What do the following terms mean, and why are they important for organizational behavior?
   (a) Locus of control
   (b) Self-efficacy
   (c) Honesty tests
   (d) Self-esteem

2. How may stress be reduced? What evidence is available regarding the effectiveness of the various procedures?

3. What is the inverted-U hypothesis, and what is its current status? How have alternative views fared?

4. What is the significance of the following for understanding stress in organizations?

   (a) Type A and Type B personalities
   (b) Role conflict
   (c) Neurotic behavior in top executives
   (d) Burnout
   (e) Role ambiguity

5. What is the trait-versus-situation controversy, and how does it relate to industrial-organizational psychology?

6. In what ways may stress be measured? Are there any apparent advantages of one measure over another?

CASE PROBLEM

Marcia White
Utility Machine Operator

Marcia White was 32 years old when she started working in the plant. She had held several positions previously, after graduating from high school, but she had not worked for over five years. A recent divorce necessitated her return to work. She apparently had considered going back to the store where she had been employed as a sales clerk before her marriage; in the end she decided on the factory job because it paid more. She also had worked for several years as a file clerk for an insurance company, but did not seem interested in returning to a clerical position.

The first few months on the job proved to be a very rocky time for Marcia White. Her performance reports were studded with comments such as "poor quality of work," "very slow to learn," and "fails to remember things after they are explained." Yet there were some positive notes also: She was viewed as outstanding in her willingness to work and in her cooperativeness. On the more repetitive kinds of jobs she really did quite well, once she got over the uncertainties of the initial learning situation. Although her foreman at one point decided to terminate her employment within the probationary period, he gradually came to the conclusion that her work was improving sufficiently so that he could not justify such action. By the time she had been employed a year, he considered her "a reliable, steady worker, doing a good job."

In fact, the foreman had overcome his initial doubts to such a degree that he recommended Marcia for training as a relief machine operator. Initially this meant learning to operate the various types of machines in his department so that she could fill in when others were absent due to illness, vacations, and the like. Further down the road, however, was the prospect that she would be taught to do the work in other departments as well, and rotate from one group to another as needed to fill in the key positions as vacancies occurred. The training was entirely on-the-job. The personnel department accepted the foreman's recommendation, in spite of some reservations, because Marcia had good test scores in the verbal as well as numerical and mechanical areas, and thus seemed to have considerable potential for learning a diverse range of jobs. Marcia agreed to accept the utility operator position, also in spite of some reservations, because, as she said, "I'm here to make some money, and the relief job pays."

Actually, the initial training on the various machines in the department went well. The foreman was quite pleased. Marcia's own lack of enthusiasm was a little disconcerting, but then she never had been one to express her emotions. She just plugged away doing whatever anyone told her to do. She clearly did not want to antagonize anybody, and in fact she worked quite hard in an effort to make the other workers like her. In this she was only partially successful. Because she lacked spontaneity and drive, some of her coworkers considered her a rather dull person, but over time she was successful in gaining a certain amount of acceptance from the others.

Clearly this sense of belonging to the group was very important to her. The foreman noticed that every time something happened to upset her, she was likely to spend a considerable amount of time talking about it to the people in the department whom she considered her closest friends. At such times she would typically ask the others, one after another, what she should do; she seemed to lack a capacity to handle problems on her own, but getting the advice of others did appear to reassure her, at

least temporarily. The foreman found himself caught up in this process, too. She was particularly worried about her financial affairs, and often asked him for help in this area. It was rather disturbing, however, to have her ask the same questions time after time. He knew she heard what he said, but he never was certain whether she actually followed his advice. If she did, it didn't seem to stop her from continuing to worry the problem to death, often over a period of several weeks.

Marcia's period of utility work within the department elicited the following evaluation of her performance:

> Effectively supplies utility relief on the various positions. Maintains reliable reporting, applies self, and maintains normal volume of work, meeting schedules within regularly scheduled hours for the job.

In contrast, as Marcia began to move out into other departments to learn new duties and undertake new kinds of machine work, the evaluations from the supervisors involved included the following:

> Mrs. White has had to acquire a working knowledge of a variety of jobs for which utility relief had previously been supplied by other personnel. Her progress in acquiring training and providing utility relief has been satisfactory, but she requires further development.

Another foreman said:

> Her rate of learning the assignments was slower than other incumbents'.

And another:

> She is apparently unable to grasp the various machine operations and will never make an effective utility operator.

And another:

> She keeps asking questions and wants help. It is impossible to get through to her.

By now Marcia was rotating among eight different positions in perhaps twice as many departments. Although in one sense she had a great many foremen in charge of her work, in another sense she was entirely on her own. None of the foremen saw her long enough to make a truly comprehensive evaluation or really get to know her. Furthermore, she was expected increasingly to come in and perform whatever work was required without guidance and with very little supervision.

On one particular day Marcia arrived for work in a new department, where she was expected to work completely on her own, and very shortly began to complain that her eyes were bothering her. She could not see very well and felt both nervous and nauseated. Her foreman sent her to the dispensary, where all the tests that could be performed revealed no plausible physical cause for her problem. At 11:00 A.M. she was sent home for a rest.

The next day Marcia said she was feeling better, but the foreman noted that she was visibly nervous and upset. The following day she was scheduled to move to another new department; she felt she needed help, in spite of the fact that she had done exactly the same work back in the old department for weeks on end. By the end of the next day she was in fact running several hours late.

The problem was referred to the personnel department, and Marcia was called in. She said she thought her training had been adequate, but agreed that under pressure she became very nervous. The personnel woman made a notation in Marcia's file that "Mrs. White is rather difficult to fathom. From conversation you cannot tell whether she is being impressed or not. It would appear that she is extremely nervous. Furthermore, she has some difficulty with her eyes, which clearly interferes with her work."

As time went on, this "difficulty with her eyes" became more acute. On one occasion a forewoman telephoned the dispensary to say that Marcia was having some kind of attack, in which she could not see. She was also chilled and suffering pain in her stomach. The forewoman also raised a question as to whether Marcia might have hearing difficulties because of the need to repeat instructions to her.

The medical people could not pinpoint a real problem.

Somewhat later another supervisor indicated that Marcia would not be a satisfactory replacement for a worker going on vacation. She did not appear to have what it took to do the job. Marcia said that she would be willing to forgo her own vacation to undergo any training that might be required. She added, however, that she was having trouble with her eyes and that this had been affecting her work recently. She could see light but could not see objects clearly. The problem seemed to come and go. She could not remember ever experiencing anything like this before, and it bothered her considerably. The plant physician did not seem to know what the cause was and was no help at all. Questioned as to whether she thought this might be something that happened when she was under pressure, Marcia rejected this possibility on the grounds that she had had attacks when she felt perfectly relaxed.

She said that her reason for discussing her disability was that the attacks came on suddenly and she was afraid she might injure herself if she was operating certain machines. Also, while the attacks lasted it was almost impossible for her to work. It was because of the trouble with her eyes that she continually got behind schedule these days.

Yet, when asked what could be done to help her improve her work, Marcia now suggested she be given a refresher course on the various machines. She felt that she needed more help and guidance. It was pointed out to her that she had already had a great deal more on-the-job training than any of her predecessors, and that she herself had previously considered her training adequate. She still felt she needed more training; that several of the supervisors in departments where she had to work didn't like her and had not given her the amount of attention she needed. These same supervisors were of the unanimous opinion that Marcia White needed far too much supervision.

Questions

1. How does Marcia White's eye problem interfere with her performance, and what appears to be the cause of this physical difficulty?

2. Do you see any evidence that Marcia is using her physical problem, either consciously or unconsciously, to get what she wants?

3. Would you accept Marcia's own analysis of what should be done in her case? Can you explain her solution on grounds other than rational problem solving?

4. Are any other factors of the kinds discussed in this chapter involved here? If so, which ones are they, and how do they contribute to Marcia's difficulties?

5. If you were faced with the problem of doing something about Marcia, what would you do? Why? What do you think your chances of working out a successful solution are?

7

Groups in Organizations

Musashi Semiconductor Works, located in the suburbs of Tokyo, employs 2700 people. The plant manufactures semiconductor memory and logic devices, microcomputers, and computer boards. After the decision was made to emphasize small-group activity at Musashi, training programs to this end were implemented at all levels of management. At all but the very lowest levels, these programs were conducted either outside the company or at parent-company headquarters. This training phase lasted four years.

The workers at Musashi are organized into 360 groups, each with from eight to ten people. Membership is determined primarily by work station, although there is some self-selection. Group members typically hold the same rank or position, but are of mixed sex and age. Small-group systems are highly democratic at the worker level; each group elects its own leader from among its members. Above the worker small-group level is a hierar-chy of councils and committees, with levels that parallel the formal structure of the plant. At all levels, the group system generates and processes improvement proposals of numerous kinds. In addition, the small-group system has a number of functions related to implementation, housekeeping, and the like, which go beyond the improvement proposals. The complex group structure generated in the plant is illustrated in the accompanying diagram.

Experience at Musashi suggests that, with group systems of this kind, managerial support is crucial to success. Although the group system exists outside the formal hierarchy, linkages between the group system and the hierarchy are strong and sophisticated. In many respects the group system is driven by the hierarchy.

SOURCE: William H. Davidson (1982). Small group activity at Musashi Semiconductor Works. *Sloan Management Review, 23* (3), 3–14.

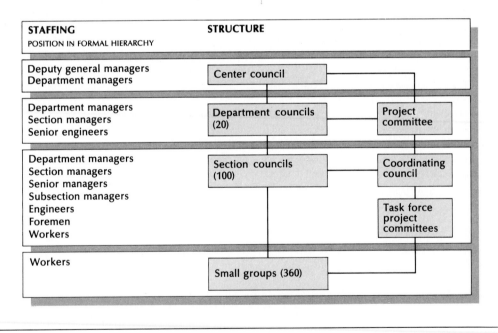

The Musashi plant is part of the Hitachi Corporation. That company emphasizes groups at all levels of its operations. In Japan, such an emphasis on groups is common. In the United States, fewer self-conscious attempts to build an organization of groups are made. A firm can actually operate through one-on-one, separate relationships between a superior and each subordinate. Unless we describe these superior–subordinate dyads as groups, such a firm has no formal group structure at all. Yet informal groups can be expected to form even in firms of this kind, without the assistance or even approval of management. Thus, groups represent a significant factor to consider in all organizations; their roles and importance can vary considerably, but their existence can be assumed. They can and often do play an important role in individual performance and organizational effectiveness. That is why we need to understand them.

An outline of the flow of group processes appears in Exhibit 7-1. These topics are discussed in this chapter and to varying degrees in the remaining chapters of Part Two.

EXHIBIT 7-1   The Flow of Group Process and Action
Various characteristics of supervisors, technologies, and groups interact to produce individual and collective outcomes, which in turn may modify the original characteristics.
SOURCE: Thomas G. Cummings (1981). Designing effective work groups. In Paul C. Nystrom and William H. Starbuck (Eds.), *Handbook of organizational design,* Vol. 2, p. 251. Oxford, England: Oxford University Press.

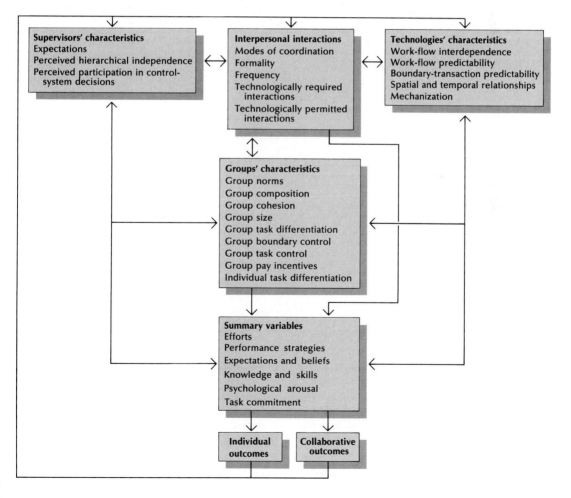

■ ROLES OF GROUPS IN ORGANIZATIONS

We tend to think of organizational groups as small combinations of workers such as those formed at Hitachi's Musashi plant. Yet groups operate in many ways and perform many roles. Before considering these types of groups, however, we need to define what a group is.

☐ The Nature of Organizational Groups: Definitions

A widely cited definition of a **group** was proposed some years ago by Dorwin Cartwright and Alvin Zander (1968, pp. 46, 48):

> A collection of individuals who have relations to one another that make them interdependent to some significant degree. . . . When a set of people constitutes a group, one or more of the following statements will characterize them:
>
> They engage in frequent interaction.
>
> They define themselves as members.
>
> They are defined by others as belonging to the group.
>
> They share norms concerning matters of common interest.
>
> They participate in a system of interlocking roles.
>
> They identify with one another.
>
> They feel the group to be rewarding.
>
> They pursue interdependent goals.
>
> They have a collective perception of their unity.
>
> They tend to act in a unitary manner toward the environment

What we really have here is a checklist. The more items in the checklist that apply, and the more strongly they apply, to an aggregate of people, the more "groupness" that aggregate possesses. Other researchers have proposed checklists similar to the Cartwright-Zander list; in the process they have added several statements that also help to define a group (Alderfer, 1977, p. 230; Luft, 1984, p. 7):

> Some differentiation of behavior or function must begin to emerge.
>
> There must be more worth or value in being within the group than in being outside of it.
>
> Group members, acting alone or in concert, have significantly interdependent relations with other groups

A number of characteristics emerge consistently in such lists. But groups are best defined in terms of a degree of groupness—a continuum. Some groups are very groupy; some are hardly groups at all.

Movement along this continuum can be encouraged: Companies can and often do foster groupness (Zander, 1982). One way is to place people in frequent proximity, thus encouraging social interaction. It also helps if these people are similar in beliefs, values, and other respects. It is often possible to distinguish a group by setting aside a location for it, naming it, perhaps even emphasizing common modes of dress within it. The point is that members and nonmembers alike can see that a group exists and can distinguish its members. Box 7-1 describes one observer's arguments in favor of an intensive pursuit of groupness within American organizations. This proposal is in one sense a fantasy, but it is a fantasy that might be worth living out. It certainly is possible to have much more groupness in organizations than we typically do today.

☐ Membership and Reference Groups

The groups discussed here and in Box 7-1 are **membership groups,** to which people actually belong: these are different from **reference groups,** against which a person weighs his or her attitudes and behavior, and which may or may not also be a membership group.

BOX 7-1   I/O PSYCHOLOGY IN PRACTICE

Suppose We Took Groups Seriously . . .

The famous Hawthorne studies of worker performance and productivity were conducted at a plant of the Western Electric Company near Chicago in the 1920s and 1930s. These studies were among the first to emphasize the role of group processes in organizational behavior and later became instrumental in the development of the human relations movement. In 1974 Western Electric sponsored a symposium in which a number of distinguished scholars met to present papers and discuss topics related to the original Hawthorne studies. One of these papers, by Harold Leavitt of Stanford University, provides a vivid picture—or "fantasy," to use Leavitt's word—of the role groups could play in organizations.

Leavitt's argument begins with a statement of why groups are worth considering as fundamental building blocks of organizations:

1. Small groups are good for people. They satisfy important membership needs. They provide support in times of stress and crisis.

2. Groups are good problem-finding tools. They may be useful in promoting innovation and creativity.

3. Often groups make better decisions than individuals.

4. Groups make great tools for implementation. They gain commitment from their members.

5. Groups can effectively control and discipline their members in ways that organizations otherwise find difficult.

6. Small groups provide useful mechanisms for fending off the negative effects of large organizational size.

7. Groups are natural phenomena and facts of organizational life. They will exist anyway; one might as well plan on them.

One could quarrel with a number of these points, and indeed many have, but they also contain considerable truth. Then the argument builds: What might a seriously groupy organization look like?

One approach is simply to take the things organizations do with individuals and try them out with groups. The idea is to raise the level from the atom to the molecule, and *select* groups rather than individuals, *train* groups rather than individuals, *pay* groups rather than individuals, *promote* groups rather than individuals, *design jobs* for groups rather than individuals, *fire* groups rather than individuals and so on. Leavitt develops these ideas further, discussing the pros and cons at some length. But he comes back to his major theme at the end of his presentation:

> Management should consider building organizations using a material now understood very well and with properties that look very promising, the small group. Until recently, at least, the human group has primarily been used for patching and mending organizations that were originally built of other materials. The major unanswered questions in my mind are not in the understanding of groups, nor in the utility of the group as a building block. The more difficult question is whether or not the approaching era is one in which Americans would willingly work in such apparently contra-individualistic units. I think we are.

SOURCE: Harold J. Leavitt (1975). Suppose we took groups seriously. . . . In Eugene L. Cass & Frederick G. Zimmer (Eds.), *Man and work in society*, pp. 69–70, 72, 77. New York: Van Nostrand/Reinhold.

A first-line production supervisor may identify strongly with management, may desire to remain a member of management throughout her career, and may adopt attitudes and behaviors that she believes to be characteristic of managers generally. She tries to become as much like other managers as possible. In doing so, she adds to her actual membership position as a manager the use of management as a reference group.

Another production supervisor may simply be using the position to make enough money to go to law school. For this person, lawyers, not managers, are her primary reference group. In this instance there is a distinct separation between membership and reference groups. Separations of this kind need not damage membership-group relationships. A problem arises, however, when status considerations become involved, as they often do, so that an individual tends to reject the membership group in favor of a reference group perceived to have higher status. Then, membership-group relationships can suffer severely. In cases like this, consideration of reference groups can be important to a company.

☐ Formal Work Groups

It is useful to distinguish a number of types of membership groups in organizations (Eddy, 1985). Much of the writing on group behavior emphasizes the formal work units at the base of the company pyramid. Typically, these are specified as separate units in an organization chart, and consist of a single superior and the workers reporting to him or her. Often, especially in production, these groups far exceed the limits of appropriate small-group size—usually considered to be something like twenty to twenty-five people. Where this is the case, some sort of informal division into smaller groupings is inevitable, with or without the organization's approval.

Although **formal work groups** usually work under a single supervisor, combining their efforts to get a particular job done, they may have two or more bosses, as in so-called **matrix structures.** Thus, a production group that makes several products may have the traditional boss who reports up the line in manufacturing; in addition they may have several bosses, one for each product, with entirely different reporting relationships. Each of these bosses is concerned with all aspects of that particular product, from basic conception through customer delivery. Having multiple bosses like this can be a source of considerable conflict.

Important distinctions among formal work groups involve the extent to which they actually operate as groups and how much influence they have over their own functioning. In some instances—a sales district with multiple territories, for example—members are not especially interdependent; each can function pretty much alone. Sales personnel within a district, for instance, may have no need to spend time with one another and in fact may not do so; their only contacts may be with their common district manager.

In production, by contrast, the work is usually split up, with different people doing different things; at some point the results of all their efforts come together in the form of a completed product or subassembly. There may be, and may need to be, much interaction in producing the output, with a much higher level of groupness as a result. Furthermore, such groups can become quite autonomous and self-managed, with the full approval and support of higher management. These group-based arrangements are considered in detail later in this chapter. Exhibit 7-2 diagrams the arrangement of formal work units with low and high groupness.

☐ Management Teams

A **management team** consists of a manager above the first level and that manager's immediate subordinates, who are also managers. Such a group may well consist of man-

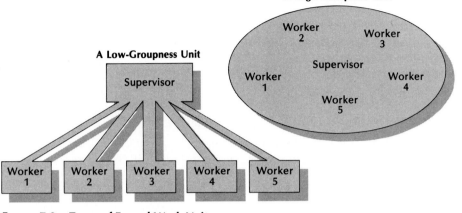

EXHIBIT 7-2   Types of Formal Work Units
Members of a work group may be only loosely connected, or may be highly interdependent.

agers who spend little time interacting with one another in the course of their daily work. It may contain a chief executive officer and the other company officers reporting at that level, or a general supervisor and the direct supervisors who report to him or her.

Of course, even these loose relationships can be broken up into superior–subordinate dyads, as in the low-groupness situation shown in Exhibit 7-2. And a significant level of groupness may be encouraged. This occurs when superior and subordinates communicate with one another often by telephone, memo, and personal visits; when meetings of the group are called periodically to discuss common problems; and when retreats are held occasionally to get group members away from the day-to-day work context so they can do some planning. These and other efforts at managerial team development have in fact become rather popular recently.

☐ Part-Time Groups

Committees, boards, councils, engagement teams, and the like characteristically operate on a part-time basis, in that the members usu-

ally devote most of their time to other positions, and thus are members of other groups. Such **part-time groups** may fail to develop high levels of groupness, especially if they are convened on a temporary basis to deal with a specific issue after which they disband, or if they have a frequently changing membership. Yet if a part-time group has stable membership and frequent meetings, as some corporate boards of directors have, considerable groupness can develop.

Groups of this kind frequently operate to bring about horizontal communication across major sectors of a firm; for example, a safety committee might contain management representatives from all line departments. On occasion part-time groups include members who come from outside the firm. Groups containing company lawyers along with lawyers from an outside law firm may well work together for years while a particular case winds its way through the courts. Outside consultants are often members of a company group convened to deal with some specific issue. A group may experience reduced groupness when outsiders are included, but their expertise may be essential.

☐ Temporary Groups

Part-time groups can of course have a rather short lifespan, and thus would be **temporary groups** as well. In addition, there are full-time groups such as project teams and task forces to which people are assigned for a temporary—and usually predetermined—period and which are disbanded once their mission is accomplished. This kind of situation is common in research and development, where a group of scientists is put together to develop a particular product idea. When the product is ready for marketing, the group disbands and the members are reassigned. In fact, much professional work is done in temporary groups: Lawyers work together on a case, consultants work together on an engagement, architects work together on a building project, and so on.

☐ Informal Groups

The groups we have been considering are formally constituted to help an organization reach its goals. But groups also emerge in organizations to serve the personal goals of the members. The membership of an **informal group** may or may not be identical with that of some formal group. For instance, some members of a formal work group may reject membership in the informal group, for some reason such as different reference-group ties, or they may be rejected by the informal group. The informal group may at the same time incorporate members of other formal groups, as where frequent interaction is fostered by carpooling, lunchtime arrangements, and recreational interests.

Informal groups at the worker level were first studied as part of the Western Electric Company research noted in Box 7-1. That study considered the possibility that informal groups might deliberately limit their output so as to protect less productive members or to prevent output goals established by management from being increased. More recent studies of other aspects of informal groups have revealed that they can differ considerably.

Differing Characteristics. The pioneering research into different types of informal work groups was conducted by Leonard Sayles, using data on some 300 unionized groups in the manufacturing operations of thirty companies. Some of the findings are noted in Exhibit 7-3. It is apparent that informal groups can achieve differing levels of groupness just as formally sanctioned groups do. They can place themselves in opposition to management to varying degrees, and they can pursue the self-interest of their members in different ways and to a varying extent.

The important conclusion to be reached from this line of research is that informal groups are not good or bad per se, from any particular perspective—management, the individual group member, the union, or whatever. For instance, some informal groups are harmful to management's interests and some are helpful. Some fifty years ago, when union organizing was at its peak, many managements made concerted efforts to eliminate or at least stifle informal groups of all kinds; but such efforts no longer seem warranted. However, management can be expected to try to influence informal groups in such matters as their degree of groupness, norms, membership, and leadership.

Coalitions. **Coalitions** are informal groups, usually composed of managers and professionals, who unite at least temporarily to pursue a particular objective. Coalitions are major instruments of organizational politics. A coalition has the following features (Stevenson, Pearce, & Porter, 1985, pp. 261–262):

It is an interacting group of individuals.

It is deliberately and self-consciously constructed by members.

It operates independently of the formal structure of work units.

Exhibit 7-3   **Characteristics of Four Types of Informal Work Groups**

Characteristics	Types of Groups			
	Apathetic (essentially passive with high activity only on occasion)	Erratic (unstable, highly demonstrative, volatile)	Strategic (persistent, calculated self-interest activity)	Conservative (restrained pursuit of self-interest)
Degree of groupness	Low	Medium	High	High
Management evaluation	Somewhat unfavorable	Distinctly unfavorable	Somewhat favorable	Distinctly favorable
Participation in union activities	Low	Above average	High	Below average
Level of grievance and pressure activity	Low	Above average	High	Below average
Frequency of unplanned, spontaneous outbursts	Below average	High	Below average	Low

SOURCE: Adapted from Leonard R. Sayles (1958). *Behavior of industrial work groups: Prediction and control,* pp. 39, 71. New York: Wiley.

It lacks a formal internal structure of its own.

It recognizes who is and is not a member.

It is formed around issues.

It focuses on a goal or goals external to the coalition.

It plans concerted action by members acting as a group.

Coalitions are more likely to form under certain circumstances: when the allocation of resources in an organization changes; when inequities are perceived; when opportunities for members to interact increase; when members have more discretion in carrying out their jobs, as in higher management; or when previous coalitions have existed but subsequently disbanded.

Exhibit 7-4 diagrams the process of coalition development. When coalitions perform a joint action, such as a petition or a memo, they typically elicit a response either from higher management or from other coalitions spawned in opposition or support. At this

point they may well become dormant; or else they may continue to press their point, ultimately achieving formal status. The informal group may become a standing committee or even a new department.

■ GROUP PROCESSES

The various types of groups within organizations differ substantially, as we have noted, but they also share certain underlying processes, or dynamics. Exhibit 7-1 illustrates how these group processes emerge and how they contribute to outcomes. In this section we focus on group characteristics, explaining how they generate individual and collaborative outcomes.

□ Group Maturity

An important consideration underlying all the group characteristics noted in Exhibit 7-1 is the maturity, or level of development, of the group. Newly formed groups are imma-

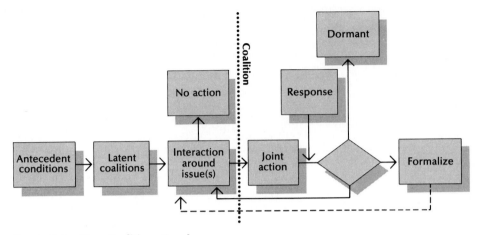

EXHIBIT 7-4   How Coalitions Develop
In responding to conditions and issues, coalitions produce action and then either become dormant or become formalized as an ongoing group.
SOURCE: William B. Stevenson, Jone L. Pearce, & Lyman W. Porter (1985). The concept of "coalition" in organization theory and research. *Academy of Management Review, 10,* 265.

ture. In many cases they are predominantly, or in some cases totally, made up of members who are new to the organization. In such instances group development and socialization into the organization go hand in hand; these two processes clearly have many similarities (Wanous, Reichers, & Malik, 1984).

Stages of Development. Exhibit 7-5 presents a model of **group development.** In the early stages problems need to be resolved relating to power and authority relationships within the group. Later on, there are problems involving interpersonal relationships among all members.

Initially group members engage in a good deal of questioning regarding why they are there, who is in charge, and what their goals are. As the group moves from the orientation stage to the conflict and challenge stage, members increasingly repudiate their initial reliance on the leader. There is frequent testing and questioning of the leader, even outright rebellion. Power and status distributions throughout the group are in flux, and a great

deal of time and energy is devoted to this issue. Some groups never move beyond this stage. If they do, an increasing degree of cohesion develops, members find their own niches, and internal group structures and procedures are established. As the members resolve their uncertainty over power and authority, they begin to achieve cohesion, viewing themselves as a group.

Next comes a stage of delusion, in which members convince themselves that all the group's problems have been resolved. They make every effort to maintain a feeling of harmony and to gloss over differences. Interaction among members is at a high level. But gradually it becomes apparent that this is not working well enough. Maintaining the façade of oneness takes a great deal of time and energy. Cliques and subgroups emerge. Members become disillusioned over unrealistic expectations for the group. To some degree cohesiveness is eroded. To resolve these interpersonal relations problems, members must come to understand the group (what it can and cannot be) and the individual mem-

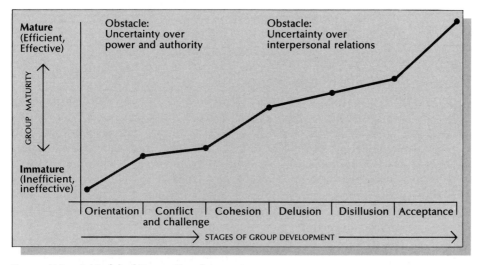

EXHIBIT 7-5   A Model of Group Development
As groups mature, they pass through various stages of conflict and harmony.
SOURCE: Linda N. Jewell & H. Joseph Reitz (1981). *Group effectiveness in organizations*, p. 20. Glenview, Ill.: Scott, Foresman.

bers (what they expect of the group). Then, a greater flexibility appears, and a capacity to adjust to the situation. Individuals and subgroups gain influence depending on the skills and abilities needed at the time. In short, a stage of acceptance of individual differences is reached.

Signs of Maturity. Not all groups get through all the stages to acceptance. When they do, the resulting mature group tends to have the following earmarks:

Members are aware of one another's assets and liabilities in regard to performing the group's task.

Members accept these individual differences as given; they do not label these differences good or bad.

Members recognize and accept patterns of authority, status, and interpersonal relationships.

Members make group decisions rationally, giving minority opinions an opportunity to be heard and considered.

Members engage in conflict over substantive issues involving task accomplishment, not over emotional issues and group process.

Members are aware of how the group works and how they fit in.

When maturity of this kind has been developed, a group can get on with its immediate task and be highly productive, without devoting excessive energy to its internal dynamics.

☐ Group Norms

Group norms are the informal rules or standards that groups adopt to regulate and regularize the behavior of group members (Feldman, 1984). They may or may not match the norms, values, and policies of the surrounding organization. Norms tend to become established during the process of group development, although mature groups may adjust their norms to deal with varying situations.

Norms develop only with regard to behaviors that are significant for the group. One important area is group survival: There are often strictures on behavior in relation to potentially competing groups or entities. Members should not discuss with outsiders the internal workings of the group or the activities of other members. Similarly, certain standards serve to protect the group from outside forces and interference—such as standards for dealing with acceptable productivity, rate busting, and restriction of output.

Other norms are intended to simplify or standardize the behavior expected of members, so that the group can function more smoothly and effectively. Often this involves establishing informal roles for different members—one is to monitor activities in the organization as a whole, one is to defuse conflicts within the group, one is to see that performance norms are maintained, and so on. Norms of this kind may also specify rotation of housekeeping duties, conduct during group meetings, and the like.

Group embarrassment can be a problem, and norms are often specified in order to avoid it. If possible, member behavior that would embarrass the group is hidden from public view and smoothed over. Some topics may be taboo, such as romantic involvements, especially within the group, and religious differences. The goal is to prevent the embarrassment to all the members that goes with individual or group failure.

In addition, there are almost always norms that express the central values of the group and that clarify what makes the group distinctive. Thus, a top-management group may have norms with regard to dress, club memberships, areas to live in, and the like, which serve to reinforce the high status of the group. Often the process of norm enforcement itself has the added purpose of demonstrating the

power of the group and its significance for individual members.

Box 7-2, dealing with conflict between group norms and organizational goals at Eastern Airlines, provides a vivid example of how groups may come into conflict with the organization in pursuing security and survival, avoidance of embarrassment, and strong values. But how are these norms enforced? How can they have such strong impact on members? The following description by Alvin Zander (1982, pp. 46–47) provides some insight into the process of norm enforcement:

> A member who does not behave according to a group's standard may be ignored at first because saying nothing is less embarrassing and more convenient than pressing for change. Groupmates more often avoid a deviant when the standard violated is not critical for the fate of the group. If participants do not turn away from a deviant, they may try to change him by some means that cause little strain for themselves. They may talk about his undesirable activities outside his range of hearing, assuming that rumors about the conversation may reach him. If this does not work, they may talk about him where he can overhear what is being said. If this ploy has no impact, a few members speak to him directly about his behavior. If none of these approaches is effective, they ask an official to meet with the misbehaving member. When a high-status person cannot make a member conform, unofficial, self-appointed enforcers may take over.

☐ Group Cohesion

Another characteristic of groups (noted in Exhibit 7-1 and touched upon in the discussion of stages of development) is the group's **cohesion.** Strongly enforced norms are a factor in group cohesion, but other factors also contribute to it.

The Nature of Cohesion. Cohesion levels reflect the extent to which members desire to

BOX 7-2 I/O PSYCHOLOGY IN PRACTICE

Conflict between Group Norms and Organizational Goals at Eastern Airlines

Like many other airlines, Eastern had a problem with employees who stole from passenger baggage and cargo shipments or transported drugs. These problems were most acute at the Miami and New York locations. Because they related to customer confidence and thus to sales, these problems threatened the airline's very existence.

Nevertheless, the airline's appeals for employee support in solving these problems met considerable resistance. In many cases the thefts and drug activities could not have occurred without the knowledge of other members of the perpetrators' work groups, yet norms in these groups consistently prevented honest employees from "ratting on" their coworkers.

In response, the company instituted a program to encourage anonymous tips. Employees were asked to report crimes that had occurred or crimes that they knew were being planned by calling Wackenhut Corporation, an independent security firm retained by Eastern. Rewards for information were to be paid, up to $10,000. The company acknowledged its discomfort at encouraging employees to turn each other in, but knew no other way to solve the problem. The union supported the company's efforts. The hope was that individual motivation could be strengthened enough to overcome group norms that tolerated these crimes.

---

remain in a group because they are attracted to it and to one another. Group cohesion and groupness per se are closely related, but groupness extends beyond the more limited concept of cohesion (see the discussion of groupness at the beginning of this chapter).

Cohesive groups tend to interact more, influence members more, and perceive more favorably their own products and activities than other, looser groups do. In such groups satisfaction with coworkers tends to be relatively high, although other aspects of job satisfaction are not influenced (O'Reilly & Caldwell, 1985). Also, the tasks performed by cohesive groups tend to be inflated in value, so that members perceive their work as more significant.

A number of factors contribute to group cohesion. Greater similarity among members is important, as is more opportunity to communicate and interact. High status, including an unusually successful record of performance, can contribute. Groups that make it hard for people to become new members, so

that they must make a substantial investment in the entry process, are likely to attain greater cohesion. The initiation rites of sororities and fraternities serve this function. Smaller group size tends to facilitate member interaction, and thus cohesion. Small groups maintain homogeneous memberships more easily. Payment systems that reward the output of the group rather than of individuals can also play an important role.

Group cohesion is especially likely to grow when the group feels threatened or attacked from the outside. While working in the Research and Development Department at Atlantic Refining Company, the author had the experience of watching a department where work groups pulled together and individual competition almost entirely disappeared, as persistent rumors circulated that the department would be reorganized and many activities shifted to manufacturing. (In the end, the increased cohesion failed to protect the groups; the reorganization did occur, and many people lost their jobs.)

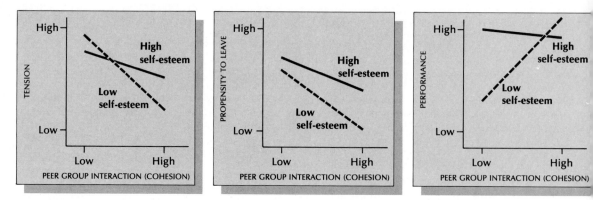

EXHIBIT 7-6 How Self-Esteem Level Influences the Relation of Group Cohesion to Stress, Propensity to Leave, and Performance
High cohesion is more important to low-self-esteem people: It helps their adjustment and performance substantially. High-self-esteem people show only slightly improved adjustment and slightly *lowered* performance.
SOURCE: Kevin W. Mossholder, Arthur G. Bedeian, & Achilles A. Armenakis (1982). Group process-work outcome relationships; A note on the moderating impact of self-esteem. *Academy of Management Journal, 25,* 581.

The Relationship between Cohesion and Performance. Since cohesion is defined in terms of attraction to a group, it is not surprising that high cohesion contributes to lower absenteeism and turnover. It is apparent that cohesion can also make for more effective group performance—and, in turn, performance can contribute to cohesion (Dorfman & Stephan, 1984).

Yet ample evidence indicates that the relationship is not always beneficial. A major factor is how group norms and standards relate to organizational objectives. If there is trust between group and organization, so that both are trying to accomplish the same thing, then cohesion enhances output because the group has developed enough maturity to be able to provide social support for members in dealing with stress and to mobilize a concerted effort in times of crisis.

However, when an informal group develops with self-protective objectives that differ from those of the company, cohesion can be a very effective weapon against the company and against the productivity it desires. The strategic type of group noted in Exhibit 7-3 is one example, and the erratic type of group can be another. Informal groups form in order to serve their members, and if doing so means thwarting company productivity goals, then the quantity and quality of output may well suffer.

Exhibit 7-6 demonstrates an important point about this process. In this study high-self-esteem individuals are relatively uninfluenced by the degree of cohesion in their groups. With greater group cohesion they do experience some desirable reduction in stress and in propensity to quit, and some undesirable reduction in performance level, but not very much reduction in any of these respects. Group cohesion has its greatest impact on low-self-esteem members. High cohesion produces a much greater drop in tension for them, as well as a greater reduction in propensity to leave and a substantial increase in performance, consistent with the greater stress reduction. Put simply, group cohesion means more to low-self-esteem people; high-self-esteem individuals do not need it.

Cohesive groups tend to support and protect their members as best they can. But, as so often happens with humanitarian efforts, such protectiveness may be misguided. A cohesive group may protect a thieving employee from being caught or an alcoholic employee from being identified, but the result may be only to encourage more stealing or more drinking. By the time the problem does come out into the open, it may be so advanced that simple solutions are no longer possible and only drastic actions will suffice to remedy the ineffective performance (Miner, 1985).

Another problem arises because informal groups tend to reject potential members who do not conform to group norms. Such ostracism can leave people with no group affiliation at all, and if they lack self-esteem, this isolation can seriously impair their performance. The rejected employee experiences stress and anxiety, and the results are negative for all concerned—except possibly the group. However, if the rejected person has other strong ties to membership or reference groups or is strong enough to handle the situation, performance may not suffer and may even improve.

☐ Factors in Effectiveness

Group maturity, norms, and cohesion can all have important implications for the performance levels of individuals and of the group, but additional factors must be taken into account.

Social Facilitation.   Studies conducted over a number of years have noted a tendency for output to improve when individuals work in the presence of others. This is, of course, not entirely a group phenomenon; people can work well in the presence of others and not be members of a group at all. Yet the group situation is more likely to provide the conditions for this **social facilitation** to occur.

As evidence has accumulated, it has become apparent that social facilitation does not necessarily lead to more effective perfor-

mance (Bond & Titus, 1983). On relatively simple, routine tasks, social facilitation does occur in the form of increased quantity of output, but quality is affected very little, if at all. The presence of others appears to make many people speed up their work, but they do not appear to increase their attention to errors. Where the work is more complex, requiring closer attention, the presence of others is likely to have negative effects on performance. Under these circumstances, speed or quantity of output suffers somewhat less than accuracy. However, in neither case is the impairment very pronounced.

Social Loafing and the Free Rider.   Another set of studies has dealt with the tendency of certain people to obtain benefits from group membership while not sharing proportionately in the cost of those benefits (Albanese & Van Fleet, 1985). This tendency to shirk and do less than one's share may be counteracted by norms of fairness in the group, but if the "free rider" can avoid enforcement of the group's fairness norms or if such norms are weak, **social loafing** can have a real impact on group effectiveness. However, when each member's contribution is highly visible, and especially when individual-performance controls or incentives are in operation, free-rider behavior tends to be limited (Matsui, Kakuyama, & Uy Onglatco, 1987; Price, 1987).

Social loafing seems most likely to occur in newly formed or temporary groups, where the level of groupness is not very high. Loafing can be noted, for instance, in student teams working on case analyses or playing business games to fulfill course requirements. In such instances, where the task is quite complex, social loafing and social performance impairment may combine to reduce overall performance levels substantially. In other, more routine, kinds of work, social loafing and social facilitation may cancel each other out, so that there is little overall effect one way or the other.

■ PARTICIPATIVE GROUPS AND GROUP-BASED SYSTEMS

A number of approaches have been developed in order to utilize the power of work-group processes. These approximate the kind of thing Harold Leavitt had in mind when he suggested much greater use of small groups (see Box 7-1). When these small-group approaches are applied to major components of organizations, or to organizations as a whole, they come under the heading of organization development (the subject of Chapter 11). However, we will restrict ourselves here to the internal functioning of the participative groups themselves.

☐ Laboratory, Sensitivity, or T-Group Training

It is important to understand the processes involved in laboratory training, sensitivity training, and T-groups. These three terms are often used interchangeably, although T-groups are actually components within the two other, broader programs. Generally, these are very short-lived, temporary training

systems, operating as part of management-development programs. Most companies do not use laboratory training extensively, although these techniques were once quite popular. Components of the T-group process have survived in team building and autonomous work groups.

What Is Involved?   Exhibit 7-7 outlines a typical schedule for a week-long **laboratory training** program. It includes lectures and experiential exercises, but the core of the training is the **T-group** (T stands for "training"). In these groups members learn about group processes, interpersonal relations, and group development. Although there is a trainer, or sometimes more than one, he or she does not impose a structure on the group. There is no specified task to be performed, so members often are initially frustrated and embarrassed. As the program goes on, however, it becomes apparent that the task is simply to learn about groups and one's own relationships in them. The trainer encourages openness in expressing feelings. The group discusses topics such as the effects of authority, the motives of members, and the need to be understood. Members gradually open up,

EXHIBIT 7-7   Schedule for a Week-Long Training Laboratory

	Sun.	Mon.	Tues.	Wed.	Thurs.	Fri.
9:00–11:00		T-group	T-group	T-group	T-group	T-group
11:00–11:30		Coffee break	Coffee break	Coffee break	Coffee break	Coffee break
11:30–12:30		General session	General session	General session	General session	General session
12:30–1:30		Lunch	Lunch	Lunch	Lunch	Lunch
1:30–3:30		T-group	T-group	Exercise	Exercise	Exercise
3:30–6:00	Opening session	Free time	Free time	Free time	Free time	Free time
6:00–7:30		Dinner	Dinner	Dinner	Dinner	Dinner
7:30–9:30	T-group	T-group	Tape-listening exercise	Free time	Exercise or training film	Free time

becoming more willing to reveal themselves and trust the others. The group moves at least partway toward maturity, and cohesiveness increases. This process of self-revelation can make some members uneasy; the less emotionally stable individuals may even become extremely anxious. Yet in the end the group typically does tend to develop some structure that may prove beneficial.

At least one objective in such training has been to make groups more central to the ongoing operations of organizations. One of the early advocates of this approach, Chris Argyris (1962, p. 26) stated the major training goals as follows:

Giving and receiving nonevaluative descriptive feedback

Owning and helping others to own their values, attitudes, and feelings, as well as helping others to develop their degree of openness

Experimenting (and helping others to do the same) with new values, attitudes, ideas, and feelings

Taking risks with new values, attitudes, ideas, and feelings.

The result should be that members develop interpersonal skills, so that the group can function more effectively.

Other early advocates, such as Edgar Schein and Warren Bennis (1965), stressed the values of science and of democracy, as these values can be embodied in the T-groups. The former included a spirit of inquiry, expanded consciousness and choice, and authenticity in interpersonal relations. The latter involved collaboration and conflict resolution through rational means. Box 7-3, describing laboratory training at TRW, shows how a comprehensive laboratory training program developed in one company and how it related to ongoing operations.

Consequences. As a result of the T-group experience, people do change—not all, but a goodly number. These changes tend to involve greater self-awareness, better understanding of others, increased competence in handling interpersonal conflicts, increased reliance on group processes in dealing with other people, and greater commitment to humanistic values. In short, members change as the objectives and values of the approach say they should change. No doubt this represents a positive result for companies, such as TRW, that are already highly group-based. Their groups may function more effectively.

In many cases, however, participants in laboratory training encounter difficulties when they return to their jobs. They often experience frustration, conflict, and a lack of integration between training ideals and job realities; the two sets of values do not mesh, and the interpersonal skills that the participants developed remain largely unused. Shortly, either the changes derived from the laboratory experience disappear, or the individual leaves the company. Actual performance improvements are rare. For these reasons, laboratory training as such has been abandoned by many firms.

☐ Team Building

In order to cope with these problems, companies have increasingly come to utilize a procedure known as **team building,** or *team development*, and have moved away from pure laboratory training per se. Actually, there was a transition phase in which T-group procedures were applied to groups composed of a manager and the people who reported to him or her—what were called **family groups.** This family analogy remains common in team building today (Ritvo & Sargent, 1983).

What Is Involved? Box 7-4, describing how Mead Corporation went about team building,

BOX 7-3 I/O PSYCHOLOGY IN PRACTICE

Laboratory Training at TRW

TRW is a research-based firm staffed with a high proportion of engineers. Much of the work is done in project teams, requiring that people work together to solve complex problems. It is not surprising that such a company was one of the first to adopt laboratory training on a widespread basis.

Initially a number of company executives attended sensitivity training programs held at UCLA and National Training Laboratories locations, where the groups contained people from a number of companies. It was not long, however, before the company began conducting in-house laboratories. The groups were composed of managers and professionals drawn from units throughout the organization. Participation was intended to be voluntary. Outside consultants were used as trainers along with company managers—personnel people and others. Initially there was a strong emphasis on using outside trainers, but later the pendulum swung in the other direction, and most trainers were company personnel.

The objective in introducing the laboratories was to change the culture of a company that was already heavily group-based in its structuring but wished to become more so. Laboratories were conducted frequently, and a great many individuals participated. At first the focus was on getting key people at the top involved, but before long the program had spread well beyond this nucleus. In order to bring the laboratory experience closer to the work itself, a number of features were added to the standard week-long laboratory.

These features included prework sessions, conducted before the training started, in which participants were told what the laboratory training entailed and why it was important to the company. After the laboratory program, on-site sessions were conducted at intervals to phase the training experience into the work situation. An opportunity to attend a micro-laboratory was also extended to employees' spouses, so that they might better understand what their husbands and wives were experiencing.

SOURCE: Sheldon A. Davis (1967). An organic problem-solving method of organizational change, *Journal of Applied Behavioral Science, 3,* (1), 3–21.

focuses on the top-management team. Although team building may be applied below the management level, management teams are the usual area of concern. The intent is to transform low-groupness units into high-groupness units, as indicated in Exhibit 7-2, and in the process enable the groups to manage their problems and accomplish their goals. Team building focuses more directly than T-groups do on the actual tasks of the group. Interpersonal issues and group process usually are involved in team building, but only as they relate directly to task considerations. In the process of team building, information is collected from inside, and sometimes from outside, the organization, and is used to plan changes in task-related behavior.

As at Mead, team building usually involves a trainer-facilitator, and these trainers may approach the process differently. One approach places a strong emphasis on setting group goals, identifying impediments to goal achievement, and planning action to achieve goals. Another approach stresses group development and interpersonal skills, viewing these as preludes to effective group action. The Mead experience appears to have been more of this latter kind; T-group procedures remain clearly in evidence. There is

BOX 7-4   I/O PSYCHOLOGY IN PRACTICE

Team Building at Mead Corporation

[The head of a division at Mead Corporation describes the division's team building in the following paraphrase.]

The first step is to build a cohesive management team at the top. Our team was built through sheer hard work, open and honest dialogue between members that led us to understand and accept differences. We found that working together as a team was critical to our success. We employed an outside facilitator to help us. Our first meetings were tough and full of game playing. We needed time to get to know one another well enough to understand each other's true motives. We simply needed to develop the trusting relationships found in mutual friendships.

In the process, we learned some new skills. We worked on effective two-way communications; we learned how to tap into feelings and nonverbal communications. We practiced group leadership skills and learned how to make decisions by consensus. We practiced group problem solving which included effective methods of brainstorming. This team-building effort took about a year of intensive effort. Once the man-

agement team was functioning, it was possible to begin moving down through the organization.

The second step is creating a strategic vision for the organization. Once the top management team has jelled, the determination of a sound business strategy takes at least six months of effort. The strategy is best developed through a participative process, using internal resources and task teams working from the bottom up.

Finally, to assure broad participation, coordinating committees, policy boards, and task teams should be established. These can range from daily get-togethers to address quality issues in production to monthly executive policy meetings. Task teams can be used to address issues ranging from redecorating the cafeteria to developing a business strategy for a new product line. These groups need to be formally structured. Structuring the time spent together facilitates the ongoing communications and consensus-building activities.

SOURCE: Charles W. Joiner (1985). Making the Z concept work. *Sloan Management Review, 26* (3), 59–60, 62.

---

also an approach that primarily considers the different roles group members play. The focus there is more on role learning and understanding than on interpersonal behavior.

Consequences.   How well does team building in its various forms work? Participants tend to like it and to believe that the process is effective in producing important changes in the organization. Yet evidence that team building actually makes for more effective group performance is mixed at best (Woodman & Sherwood, 1980). Two of the

best studies conducted on this question have found no meaningful average change across groups at all (Eden, 1985; Woodman & Sherwood, 1980).

The most plausible interpretation is that team building often increases group cohesion, and accordingly makes many people feel good about their group relationships. But the mere fact of increased cohesion is not sufficient to improve performance. It may or may not, depending on other factors. One might expect that the goal-setting type of team building would be more effective, simply because it develops positive performance

BOX 7-5 I/O PSYCHOLOGY IN PRACTICE

Autonomous Groups in a Favorable Context: Sweden's ALMEX Firm

Both the legal system and the cultural values of Sweden are very favorable to industrial democracy and group-based systems. ALMEX produces a portable mechanical ticket machine for use on public transportation; it exports its product to more than forty countries; it has been highly profitable; and it utilizes autonomous work groups. These groups operate in the assembly, service shop, inspection, tool shop, packing, planning, experimental shop, electronic parts, and electronic testing departments and in a subdepartment of the engineering shop.

Most of these autonomous work groups function in accordance with an agreement between the union and management. These agreements provide for autonomous work-group operations as follows:

1. The group, after internal discussion, makes all decisions within its area of competence that do not interfere with the decision making of other groups.

2. Each production group is collectively responsible for production assignments.

3. Supervisors appointed by the employer are replaced by a contact person, who is a member of the group elected by and responsible to the group.

4. The group decides on supervision and internal distribution of work.

5. The production group must cooperate in all directions; technical experts and sales personnel cannot give orders to the group but should reach joint agreements.

6. The group is responsible for training its members, for job rotation, and for development of production methods.

7. The group must consult the production manager if agreed-on production plans are jeopardized or if there are serious disturbances in production flow, supplies, and the like.

8. If the group cannot solve internal conflicts, any group member is free to bring the problem to the union or the production manager.

It is accepted that people are different and that some people produce more than others. No comparison is made between individuals, and wage differences are abolished. Every member is given the opportunity to learn all tasks within the group's working area. The group is not allowed to recruit new members or replace workers without the consent of the union. The group is encouraged to give support to members with social or other types of problems. The contact persons are rotated periodically and serve at the pleasure of the group.

SOURCE: Bertil Gardell (1983). Worker participation and autonomy: A multi-level approach to democracy at the work place. In Colin Crouch & Frank A. Heller (Eds.), *International yearbook of organizational democracy, volume 1. Organizational democracy and political processes,* pp. 364–365. Chichester, England: Wiley.

---

norms along with cohesion. There is some reason to believe this can be true. However, the goals set may not be very high, and the goal setting can be more of a social façade for the group than a firm commitment to action. Thus, even team building oriented toward goal setting is no guarantee of increased effectiveness.

□ Autonomous Work Groups

One of the most widely used approaches to harnessing group processes for productivity is the **autonomous work group,** sometimes called the *self-managing work group.* Numerous projects introducing autonomous groups have been undertaken throughout the world,

EXHIBIT 7-8   A Scale of Levels of Group Autonomy

Most autonomous	The group can influence the formulation of its qualitative goals.
	The group can influence the formulation of its quantitative goals.
	The group decides whether it wants a leader for the purpose of regulating boundary conditions, and if so, who.
	The group can govern its own performance above and beyond where and when to work.
	The group can decide when to work.
	The group makes decisions in connection with the choice of production methods.
	The group determines the internal distribution of tasks.
	The group decides on its own membership.
	The group decides whether it wants a leader with respect to internal questions, and if so, who.
Least autonomous	The group determines how work operations will be performed.

SOURCE: Adapted from Jon Gulowsen (1972). A measure of work group autonomy. In Louis E. Davis & James C. Taylor (Eds.), *Design of jobs*, pp. 376–378. Baltimore: Penguin.

all of which have much in common (Emery & Thorsrud, 1976; Herbst, 1976).

What Is Involved?   Box 7-5, dealing with the group-based system of ALMEX in Sweden, illustrates how autonomous groups fare in a favorable context. The ALMEX situation provides for a considerable degree of group autonomy. The firm contains both autonomous and traditional work groups. Each group decides which mode to use. Sweden's socialist form of government and the cultural values that support it appear to provide a very favorable climate for group-based systems, which are extensively and quite successfully used there.

Exhibit 7-8 presents a scale of increasing degrees of autonomy that may be given to groups. The main issue is how much authority should be shifted from management to the work group. In actual fact, no groups are completely autonomous, so perhaps the term "semiautonomous" would be more appropriate. Even the most autonomous groups are dependent on the company for resources, and the company remains responsible for legal compliance within the larger society. (For example, a group cannot bar individuals from membership on the basis of race or gender, because that would violate existing law.) And there is always a hierarchic system of management that operates above the work-group level; autonomous groups operate only at the bottom of the organizational pyramid.

Exhibit 7-9 shows the relation of autonomous work groups to a total organization structure—in this case, a Sherwin-Williams Company plant. These teams (work groups) are not at a high level of autonomy according to the criteria listed in Exhibit 7-8, because their team leaders are appointed by the company. However, there are fewer managers and levels of management in this organization than are typical for a unit of this size—160 employees. Furthermore, the managers have received extensive team-building training and are expected to operate as facilitators and consultants in dealing with the teams. It is apparent that Sherwin-Williams, in operating units of this kind, has shifted considerable authority down to the work-group level.

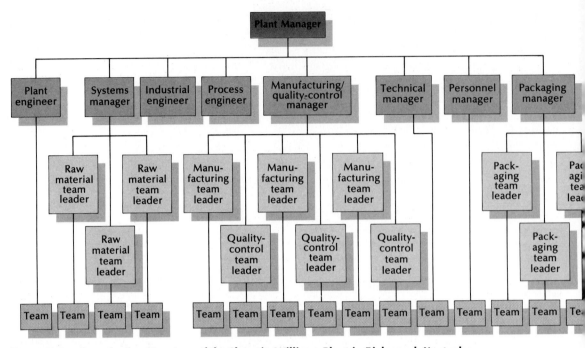

EXHIBIT 7-9   Organization Structure of the Sherwin-Williams Plant in Richmond, Kentucky
This facility uses a moderately autonomous team system: Team leaders are appointed by the company, but work teams are important and have substantial authority.
SOURCE: Ernesto J. Poza & M. Lynne Markus (1980). Success story: The team approach to work restructuring. *Organizational Dynamics, 8*(3), 16.

Consequences. Research dealing with the consequences of introducing autonomous work groups has been summarized as follows:

> The results often are positive. It is hard to predict whether the outcomes will be greater output, better quality, less absenteeism, reduced turnover, fewer accidents, greater job satisfaction, or what, but the introduction of autonomous work groups is often associated with improvements. It is difficult to understand why a particular outcome such as increased productivity occurs in one study and not another, and why on some occasions nothing improves. Furthermore, what actually causes the changes when they do occur is not known. The approach calls for making so many changes at once that it is almost impossible to judge the value of the individual variables. Increased pay,

self-selection of work situation, multiskilling with its resultant job enrichment, and decreased contact with authority almost invariably occur in autonomous work groups (Miner, 1982, pp. 110–111).

Thus it is not at all clear that the increased emphasis on group processes and industrial democracy is the cause of the positive results. From a management viewpoint, however, the group emphasis is appealing in several ways. In the United States, at least, autonomous work groups have proved effective in keeping unions out of some companies. Also, fewer employees, especially managers, are needed to staff a given operation when autonomous groups are involved, and thus costs are reduced. At the Sherwin-Williams plant the original staffing forecast was 200;

with the advent of autonomous groups the staffing actually required was only 160.

From an employee viewpoint, the success of autonomous work groups depends on the individual. For strong individualists the forced social interactions may be distasteful. Some rebel against the "tyranny" of group decision, just as others might rebel against the "tyranny" of managerial authority. Success with autonomous groups tends to come more easily in start-up situations, when prospective group members can decide on a purely voluntary basis whether this is what they want. Groups and group activities are very attractive to some people, but definitely not to all. Nevertheless, there are probably more people in the United States now who would like to work in these groups than there are autonomous work groups to absorb them. For this reason, among others, these groups are likely to appear with increasing frequency (Goodman, Devadas, & Hughson, 1988).

KEY TERMS

Group (groupness)
Membership groups
Reference groups
Formal work groups
Matrix structures
Management team
Part-time groups
Temporary groups
Informal group
Coalitions
Group development

Group norms
Group embarrassment
Cohesion
Social facilitation
Social loafing
Laboratory training
T-group
Team building
Family groups
Autonomous work group

SUMMARY

A *group* is a collection of individuals who are interdependent to some degree. In many respects it is more meaningful to speak of degrees of groupness rather than of group or nongroup. In any event, clear distinctions should be made between typical *membership groups* and *reference groups* against which people gauge their own attitudes and behavior.

Organizations contain a variety of membership groups. Among these are *formal work groups, management teams, part-time groups, temporary systems,* and *informal groups.* Organizations can do much to influence the degree of groupness in each of these contexts. Informal groups have been of particular interest to those with a human-relations or humanitarian perspective. Informal groups may take a variety of forms and may relate to productive output in different ways. Recently *coalitions,* formed at higher levels in the organization to pursue specific issues, have received special attention.

A major concern of researchers and practitioners over the years has been the nature of group processes. Group composition, *norms, cohesion,* size, tasks, and the like have been studied at some length. There is evidence that groups go through certain stages of *development* and ultimately reach a level of maturity where they are able to focus on task accomplishment rather than on their own internal processes. Two of the most important factors in group functioning are their level of *cohesion* and their *group norms.* Cohesion and norms combine to determine attitudes toward, and levels of, productivity. Cohesive groups can operate to protect members in ways that may not be in the best interest of either individual or organization. They can also ostracize individuals, with varying effects. The mere presence of others can have effects on performance, depending on the nature of the task. Also, under certain circumstances, groups appear to encourage *social loafing* and free riders.

Having obtained information about group processes, social scientists have proposed various ways to apply their knowledge to organizations. The earliest such approaches involved *laboratory* and sensitivity *training* through *T-groups.* But these approaches did not sufficiently mesh with hierarchic forms of organization, and they gradually gave way to *team building,* with a greater emphasis on accomplishing tasks. The most effective approach of this kind has proved to be the *autonomous work group;* yet even here there is a substantial need for increased understanding. Knowledge of how these group processes operate is clearly insufficient. But some additional information is available on group-based systems operating within the context of organizational development, and this information will be presented in Chapter 11.

QUESTIONS

1. Under what conditions is group cohesion likely to be at a high level? How does cohesion relate to performance?

2. What has been the history of T-groups, and why have they developed as they have?

3. What are the differences among reference groups, formal work groups, part-time groups, and temporary systems?

4. In what areas do group norms function? How are they maintained?

5. What is a group? How may we determine the degree of groupness?

6. How do social facilitation and social loafing operate? What factors influence them?

7. Why and how may autonomous work groups be effective? What makes them attractive and unattractive, to management and to the individual employee?

8. How do informal and formal groups differ? What are some types of informal groups? What distinguishes the type of informal group called a coalition?

9. What is meant by group maturity, and what stages must a group go through to achieve it?

10. How does team building differ from T-group programs?

CASE PROBLEM

JOE JOHNSON
Production Foreman

Joe Johnson started work at the plant right after leaving school. The town was small and did not offer much opportunity for employment to a young man 17 years of age seeking his first job. Furthermore, the economic picture in the country was poor, and it was no time to do anything but grasp whatever kind of work came along and hold on tight. What came along for Joe was a chance to join one of the loading crews at the factory. He quit school before graduation in order to be sure the opportunity did not slip through his fingers. His father, who had worked in the maintenance department at the plant practically since it started up, felt it would be best for Joe to take the job. Also, several of Joe's friends who were already employed on the same crew urged him to join them.

Although the loading-crew jobs were usually considered starting positions from which people moved into production as openings occurred, this particular crew remained almost intact for a number of years. Characteristically, when a promotion was offered to a young man in the crew, he would turn it down, indicating that he preferred to stay with his present group. Joe was no exception. He declined three offers of better-paying jobs before finally moving to a production unit, and even then he accepted the transfer only because his crew was being broken up. Unfortunately, he had hardly started his new work when orders arrived for him to report for military service.

Four years passed before Joe returned to his home town to stay. He turned up at the plant personnel office several days later. A few questions brought out the facts that he wanted to return to his old job, that he had married a local woman while home on leave, and that he was very glad to be home. Military service had been all right, but he preferred the friends he had grown up with to the hodgepodge of people from everywhere that he had been exposed to in the Army. His service record was satisfactory, although he had never risen above the rank of corporal. There was little question about his being given a job. Legal requirements regarding the reemployment of returning veterans were of course important, but in addition his previous employment record carried the notation, "A willing employee, completing all work promptly with a minimum of errors; has done a commendable job." Everyone was glad to have him back.

The years that followed were relatively uneventful. Several of the boys from the old loading crew went away to college on the GI bill. Some took higher-paying jobs in the city, although many of them eventually drifted back to the plant. Joe held on tight to what he had and stayed with the people who understood him. He was well thought of and well liked, and it was obvious that he enjoyed his friends at work and his family. There were occasional opportunities to work elsewhere—both outside the plant and with other groups within—but none were sufficiently attractive to Joe.

As time went by, Joe accumulated more and more seniority. With his service years added in, he began to develop a real stake in his job. He talked about this a lot: the fact that he was an old-timer, that he remembered how things used to be, and that he had stayed with the gang through thick and thin. Gradually, opportunities to take increased responsibility arose. The foreman was often away because of conferences, illness, or vacations. It was traditional that the senior person take over in his absence. Joe was that person. He was never formally selected, and in fact, the superintendent was not even consulted. It had just always been done that way.

However, when the foreman rather suddenly took a disability retirement, a more formal decision had to be made with regard to a replacement. Several candidates were considered, but Joe Johnson obviously had the inside track. It would be hard to turn him down. He knew the work, had had supervisory experience as an alternate to the foreman, and, perhaps most important, was popular throughout the plant. The combination of seniority, experience, and popularity was hard to argue against. If Joe was not selected, a number of people—especially the old-timers—might be rather unhappy. There was little point in running the risk of stirring them up. After all, Joe probably was the best person for the job. The appointment went through without a hitch.

The work continued much as before. The new foreman seemed to be doing all right; at least, there was no trouble from his group. Grievances and disciplinary actions were in fact at an all-time low. The unit was overstaffed according to company standards for the type of work done, but so were a number of other groups in the plant. Also, breakdowns seemed to be rather frequent. However, that could not be considered Joe's fault. The equipment was old and the maintenance department overworked. Nobody could break any production records with that kind of a situation. Yet it was because of the maintenance problem that the trouble started.

Late one afternoon a maintenance foreman, who had a reputation as a good "management man" and also as one of Joe Johnson's least ardent admirers, reported a strange situation to his boss. He and his crew had been working on the equipment again and finished up in Joe's area about midafternoon. But the operators were nowhere in sight. A check of the time cards indicated that the three men were in the plant, although nobody seemed to know where at the moment. Joe said he would take care of it and tell the men what the maintenance crew had done when they were located. When the maintenance foreman went through the area an hour later to get some parts, the three men were still not there, although they were still punched in.

An informal check was made just before five o'clock and the three men were clearly not in evidence. Yet their time cards were punched out as of quitting time. Joe was called on the carpet the next morning. He had very little to say. The men must have been around the plant somewhere. Things had been pretty hectic the preceding afternoon, and he had not had time to look for them. No, they had not checked with him before leaving the area, but he had to be off the floor several times early in the afternoon. No, he had not seen them check out at five.

One of the three workers, however, was less reticent. When the breakdown occurred and the maintenance people were called, he said, he and the other two workers had washed up, gone out the gate, and stopped at a bar down the street for a beer. They just had not made it back by quitting time. With this start the rest of the story could be pieced together rather easily. Apparently the foreman had not seen his three men leave, but when their absence became evident he had done nothing to find them. Presumably he knew from past experience where they were. He had asked the others to work a little harder so that the absences would not show up in the production figures. This had been done. At first it was not completely clear who had punched the men out at quitting time. However, by a process of elimination the field was narrowed down to two men, one of whom was Joe. A second period of questioning brought a confession. Yes, he had been the one.

Further investigation unearthed a number of similar instances. One man who had frequently arrived at work under the influence of alcohol on Monday mornings only to be sent home had never lost any pay because of these episodes, a fact which he himself found hard to understand. Apparently his time card had always been turned in to indicate a full day's work. Another man whose absenteeism was so excessive as to make continued employment questionable suddenly started working very steadily—at least, on the record. However, questioning indicated little change in his actual behavior. The company was obviously paying for a good deal of work that was not being performed. A decision was tentatively reached to discharge Joe Johnson for inability to fulfill the requirements of his job.

When this conclusion was told to Joe, he launched into a long and impassioned plea for "just one more chance." He was in debt, his youngest child was sick, and his father, who had retired from the company just over a year before, had been ill for several months. The effect of his discharge on the father's condition might be drastic. But there was more to be taken into account than just his personal problems. For one thing, he had not intended to do anything wrong, but only to protect the gang so they would not get in trouble. The gang was likely to be rather unhappy if he tried to take action in cases like this. It seemed best not to stir them up. In the end it was easier to punch the time cards for them and forget the whole thing. There was less trouble that way, and anyhow it was a good thing for a foreman to remain popular with his people. By the time he had finished, Joe had created the impression that he had not only exhibited admirable loyalty to his group but also had done the company a good turn by keeping the workers happy and morale at a high level. Even the superintendent felt a little sorry for him.

Questions

1. How do you feel about Joe Johnson and his behavior? Was what he did right? Was it in the company's interest? Was it the way a supervisor should behave?

2. What exactly are the group factors that produced Joe's performance problems? Do you think these are common sources of difficulty for managers?

3. Is there any evidence that the company might have been in part responsible for the situation that developed? If so, how?

4. What factors other than the direct group influences can you identify as contributing to Joe's difficulties? Were any individual factors operating, for instance?

5. If you were faced with making the decision in Joe's case, what would you do? Why?

6. It is clear that the superintendent felt sorry for Joe. Would you tend to feel the same way? If so, do you think this feeling might have influenced the decision you indicated in your response to Question 5?

8

Group Decision Making

BASF Corporation is a large German petrochemical company that embarked on a strategy of geographic expansion after facing mounting environmental problems and resource scarcity at home. After two successful ventures in the United States, BASF purchased a site at Victoria Bluffs, South Carolina, and proposed a project that would initially cost $125 million and eventually create 22,000 jobs.

Victoria Bluffs, an area of high unemployment, is located approximately eight miles from the resort community at Hilton Head. The South Carolina Development Board had actively campaigned to attract industry to the area. However, substantial controversy developed over the plant site, and court action was initiated to stop construction. Hilton Head developers, environmentalists, and conservationists opposed the project. BASF's top management had met with opponents and indicated a willingness to ensure environmental safety, but this did not satisfy the critics.

BASF had identified alternative sites that were economically feasible and unlikely to meet external resistance, but the costs were somewhat higher. BASF had to decide whether or not to pursue the Victoria Bluffs site, which now appeared certain to involve court action.

A group consisting of experts within the company, as well as several company managers, was convened to make the decision. This group reviewed all available information and reached a conclusion that the Victoria Bluffs site should not be pursued further. This decision was supported by BASF's top management. An alternative site near an existing petrochemical plant was selected, construction was started quickly, and the plant was on-line within four years.

SOURCE: Stephen A. Stumpf, Dale E. Zand, & Richard D. Freedman (1979). Designing groups for judgmental decisions. *Academy of Management Review, 4,* 597–598.

This decision on plant location represents one way that group decisions are often made in the business world. The following is an example of another group approach

---

After Delta Airlines founder C. E. Woolman suffered a serious heart attack, he encouraged his key executives to work as a group. The team approach was very effective, and after Woolman died in 1966 the group stayed together to run the airline.

At present, nine key executives, all of whom are long-time Delta employees, constitute the governing board. "We have taken the interchangeability-of-parts concept we have in our standardized fleet of airplanes and applied it to management," says chief executive officer David C. Garrett. "We have a group of senior officers who are almost interchangeable because lines of communication are so short you never need to worry about someone not knowing what is going on. It's not a committee structure. People have very clearly defined responsibilities to make decisions in their areas. But the way the interchangeability of it works is that at our meetings every Monday morning everybody is constantly being updated."

"We do respond very quickly to fires that develop," says Robert Oppenlander, the airline's senior vice president for finance. "We've all been working here together for a long time so we can work together very quickly. We try to keep each of us well enough informed every Monday morning about each other's division that we have the knowledge to make the right decision." Because all nine key executives are always fully informed about the workings of the company, if necessary a few or even one can make a decision for the group as a whole.

SOURCE: Stanley C. Vance (1983). *Corporate leadership: Boards, directors and strategy,* pp. 205–206. New York: McGraw-Hill.

Frequently in situations like that at BASF Corporation, **group decision making** involves having specialists prepare one or more staff reports on the pros and cons of various alternative courses of action. These are presented either orally or in writing to the group and form a basis for group discussion. The decision may be made by the individual in charge after listening to the discussion, by group consensus, or by some kind of voting procedure.

The group decision-making approach used by Delta Airlines typifies how many decisions are made at the top levels of large corporations (Vancil & Green, 1984). Here, because the group constantly shares and reviews information in areas where decisions are likely to be required, actual decisions may be made by a subset of the group, or even by a single member. These decisions are very likely to be identical with the ones the group as a whole would make. Exposure to a common organizational culture over a long period of time makes group members process information in similar ways. As a result, decisions that would appear to an outsider to be individual in nature are so conditioned by group processes that they are in fact group decisions.

Our discussion of individual decision making in Chapter 2 focused on the many ways that people make choices. We also looked at individual creativity and personal cognitive styles. In organizations, however, much decision making is done in groups using approaches similar to those described at BASF and Delta. Several questions immediately arise: Are groups more effective decision makers than individuals? Do groups add anything to the decision-making process beyond combining individual decisions? Are certain types of decisions best left to groups and others to individuals? These are the kinds of questions we will attempt to answer in this chapter.

CREATIVITY IN GROUPS

A major issue in the use of groups for decision making relates to the matter of creativity. The view has long predominated that creativity is an individual matter—that true creativity is achieved only by the lone scientist working late at night in the laboratory, the artist struggling with a painting in the studio, the writer slaving over a manuscript. How does group decision making fit into this concept of the creative process?

Ways to Foster Creativity

Because decision making in organizations is so frequently group-based and requires creativity as well, a variety of approaches have been developed to make group decisions as creative as possible. By looking at some of these approaches, we can get an idea of how group processes influence creativity.

Brainstorming.   **Brainstorming** is a technique for solving problems and developing new ideas through unrestrained, spontaneous discussion. It is widely used in the creative departments of advertising agencies, and in fact originally developed there. A number of brainstorming approaches have evolved, but most research focuses on the basic procedure, which follows certain guidelines (Taylor, 1984):

Group members suggest as many ideas as possible related to the idea of primary concern. The more ideas, the more likely some will be creative; poor ideas can be eliminated later on.

The more outlandish an idea, the better. Even ridiculous suggestions may point the way to a truly creative decision.

Members are expected not only to contribute their own ideas but also to build on the ideas of others. As a result, most of the ideas produced in the end belong to the group, not to a single individual.

Initially, criticism of either one's own or others' ideas is to be avoided at all costs. Evaluation comes later, and is not allowed to inhibit the creative process.

This kind of approach tends to produce more creative output than the usual give-and-take of group discussion. Socially skilled people who are highly motivated are often particularly good at brainstorming. The technique works even better if the group involved is a cohesive one that has been in existence for some time and has had a chance to develop mutual trust. Yet even under optimal conditions, brainstorming is not always successful in avoiding the inhibiting effects that anticipated social pressure from other participants can have on individuals.

Nominal Groups.   Various so-called nominal-group approaches have been developed to go beyond what appears to be possible with brainstorming. Strictly speaking, **nominal groups** are collections of individuals, each of whom independently develops a solution to a common problem. A hierarchic superior or another designated individual then reads or listens to the proposals of each person and selects the ideas to be implemented. Nominal groups may consist of people who have never met; in such cases they are not really groups at all.

A somewhat different approach that has attracted considerable attention involves a structured sequence of steps and usually requires the presence of a trained leader. To begin, each group member is given the basic problem in written form. This is followed by (Delbecq, Van de Ven, & Gustafson, 1975, p. 8):

1. Group members silently putting their ideas in writing

2. Round-robin feedback from group members to record each idea in a terse phrase on a flip chart

3. Discussion of each recorded idea for clarification and evaluation

4. Individual voting on priority ideas, with the group decision derived through rank-ordering or rating

Recent extensions of this approach have served to emphasize the importance of separating both idea generation and idea evaluation from specific individuals. It appears that nominal-group approaches work best when the initial recording of ideas is done anonymously and when secret ballots are used for voting (Fox, 1987).

Exhibit 8-1 summarizes the differences between the nominal-group approach and brainstorming; it also contrasts both of these with ordinary group decisions. In terms of idea generation, the nominal-group approaches often facilitate the process whereby a decision is actually implemented (White, Dittrich, & Lang, 1980). However, carrying out the four-step nominal-group approach is not always easy. Considerable preparation is required, and some participants may resist the restrictions imposed on their behavior. Box 8-1 describes some of the ways that nominal-group procedures have been used at ARA Services.

The Delphi Technique.   Exhibit 8-1 includes data on a third group method of fostering creativity, the **Delphi technique,** which is in fact a special type of nominal-group approach. First, a panel of knowledgeable individuals is selected. These individuals do not meet face to face at any point. They proceed as follows (Jewell & Reitz, 1981, p. 97):

1. Each group member independently and anonymously writes down comments, sug-

Exhibit 8-1   **Effectiveness of Various Characteristics of Creativity-Fostering Approaches as Contrasted with Ordinary Group Decision Making**

Characteristics	Ordinary Group Decisions	Approaches to Fostering Creativity		
		Brainstorming	Nominal Group	Delphi Technique
Number of ideas generated	Low	Moderate	High	High
Quality of ideas generated	Low	Moderate	High	High
Amount of actual social pressure	High	Low	Moderate	Low
Costs in time and money	Moderate	Low	Low	High
Degree of task orientation	Low	High	High	High
Potential for conflict among group members	High	Low	Moderate	Low
Members' feelings of accomplishment	Varies	High	High	Moderate
Members' commitment to the solution	High	Varies	Moderate	Low
Degree of group cohesiveness built	High	High	Moderate	Low

Source: Adapted from J. Keith Murnighan (1981). Group decision making: What strategies should you use? *Management Review,* Feb., 61.

gestions, and solutions to the problem confronting the group.

2. All comments are sent to a central location, where they are compiled and reproduced.

3. Each member is sent the written comments of all other members.

4. Each member provides feedback on the others' comments, writing down new ideas stimulated by their comments and returning them to the central location.

5. Steps 3 and 4 are repeated as often as necessary until consensus is reached or until some kind of voting procedure is imposed to reach a decision.

Originally, the Delphi technique was conducted by mail or through company inter-office communication channels. Today, computer conferencing speeds the process considerably, while maintaining both anonymity and the capacity to explore divergences of opinion. The approach has been used most often in areas where intuition and value judgments are important, such as human-resource utilization, social-policy formulation, and corporate environmental scanning to identify threats to and opportunities for a company. Delphi serves to generate many useful ideas, although the lack of social contact inherent in the approach tends to undermine both commitment to the decision-making process and group cohesiveness in implementing the decision. Frequently, although not universally, a group norm begins to emerge in the form of a preferred type of solution. This implicit group pressure produces a movement toward consensus.

☐ Group Processes and Creativity

In any discussion of group decision-making processes, it is important to understand the distinction between **idea generation** and **idea evaluation.** A basic aim of the various approaches fostering group creativity is to

BOX 8-1 I/O PSYCHOLOGY IN PRACTICE

Uses of Nominal-Group Procedures at ARA Services

ARA Services first used the nominal-group approach in connection with a reorganization of its Food Services division from a primarily product-based structure to a geographic one. The objective of conducting nominal-group procedures was to elicit concerns regarding organizational and personal problems from the managers who would be affected, and thus to determine the specific causes of their anxiety about the restructuring. The purpose of this initial use was strictly to identify problems. A more traditional problem-solving application followed, in which the nominal-group approach was used to identify solutions to the previously identified problems associated with restructuring. Many of these solutions were put into effect; their quality was judged to be very high. At least partly because of these ideas, the reorganization was carried out in a single year, rather than the projected two.

In this process the nominal-group approach was also used to establish leadership roles. The managers selected to head the subdivisions of the new structure were trained in nominal-group procedures and then conducted problem-solving meetings with their new subordinates. Thus the nominal-group procedure became a means of establishing the new management teams.

Subsequently, the approach was used by various area sales vice presidents to capture ideas of sales personnel while minimizing the rejection of ideas that had previously occurred in interacting sales meetings. The following is a description of one such use:

> During a very hectic meeting in which there appeared to be no attention to any task, the vice president wanted to solicit concerns of the individuals about changes in organization and economic pressures. He turned to the director of manpower and organization development and asked, "Should we try a nominal group?" The director's response was, "I don't think it will work, but try it anyway." He then gave the instructions for the technique (most of the sales group had already had prior experience with it) and started the quiet writing. Immediately, the group turned to the task and the round-robin elicitation produced 55 items to which he later responded.

SOURCE: Andre L. Delbecq, Andrew H. Van de Ven, & David H. Gustafson (1975). *Group techniques for program planning: A guide to nominal group and Delphi processes,* pp. xiii–xiv. Glenview, Ill.: Scott, Foresman.

reduce or eliminate the inhibiting effects of social interaction. Group norms and pressures, whether openly expressed or internalized by group members, can inhibit creativity so that good ideas either are not generated or are not presented to the group. Idea evaluation, in contrast, often benefits from collaborative efforts.

Idea Generation. The expression of strong emotions and opinions by group members tends to have a counterproductive effect on the generation of ideas (Guzzo & Waters,

1982). Therefore, decisions requiring creativity—such as those involving product development, a new advertising campaign, or top-level strategy formulation—should be made in an atmosphere that is free of group constraints. Group decision making in these situations can also foster social loafing, with some members "hiding" in the group and making no real contribution at all. Approaches such as nominal groups tend to prevent this.

Later, after a pool of good ideas has been generated and it is necessary to select among them, group interaction can be beneficial. Furthermore, some tasks require little if any idea generation and, hence, little creativity. For instance, a group of managers who are attempting to learn how to use a computer system can assist one another and correct one another's errors. In cases such as this, group interaction can serve a very useful purpose.

Idea Evaluation. When idea evaluation is involved—as when a choice must be made among alternative creative proposals or when the appropriate solution to a problem must be identified—group procedures offer some advantages:

> Group performance is generally qualitatively and quantitatively superior to the performance of the average individual. Group performance, however, is often inferior to that of the best individual in a statistical aggregate and often inferior to the potential suggested in a statistical pooling model. The performance of one exceptional individual can be superior to that of a committee, especially if the committee is trying to solve a complex problem (Hill, 1982, p. 535; see also Bass, 1983, p. 137).

In short, in most cases groups can do the job of idea evaluation better than individuals. But there is a possibility that individualized approaches to idea evaluation have been underestimated. Laboratory research on this issue is sketchy, and no sure-fire method is available for identifying individuals who can analyze ideas on their own. Some evidence exists that groups can identify individual expertise within their own ranks, but this is not always the case (Libby, Trotman, & Zimmer, 1987; Miner, 1984; Yetton and Bottger, 1982).

Groups that have been in existence for some time, such as the top-management group at Delta Airlines, may be better at identifying the member who is best suited to evaluate certain ideas. In organizations where promotions have been made carefully, the most able members are often in a position to take charge of decision processes. Yet there is now some evidence that on occasion, at least in newly formed groups, the group decisions can be superior to even the best individual decision (Sniezek & Henry, 1989). We clearly do not know all the answers at the present time.

At this point, group decision making is an appropriate conservative strategy. At least it eliminates the possibility of having a decision made by an ill-qualified individual. As the study with University of Illinois students described in Box 8-2 indicates, group memory performance is far superior. This may underlie the better idea evaluation in groups.

☐ The Phases of Group Decision Making

The six steps or phases of group decision making listed below do not apply in all instances, but adherence to those precepts will increase a group's chances of reaching sound, well-informed decisions. The various approaches to foster creativity are typically introduced at Step 2.

1. Explore, clarify, and define the problem fully so that everyone involved understands the nature of the problem.
2. Take time to generate ideas, look at as many alternatives as possible, and avoid premature decisions, so that as wide a range of good ideas as possible is considered.
3. In evaluating ideas, take time to combine parts of ideas, examine possible consequences, and compare them with desired outcomes.
4. Once a solution is found, plan an implementation procedure, establishing who should do what and when.
5. Devise an evaluation system so that the group can monitor the implementation of its decisions.

BOX 8-2   RESEARCH IN I/O PSYCHOLOGY

A Laboratory Study of Group and Individual Memory Performance at the University of Illinois

Psychology students at the University of Illinois listened to a tape-recorded mock trial involving an assault case. In the process the prosecuting attorney presented his case of twenty-five facts, followed by the defense attorney who presented his twenty-five facts. The students were presented with the task as one of reaching a verdict in the case, and in fact they were asked for a decision. However, the major objective was to study memory for the fifty facts.

Twenty minutes after the trial presentation the students were asked about their memory of the facts. In half of the experimental conditions individual subjects performed the memory tasks; in the other conditions, groups of four interacted to perform the tasks collectively and produce a collective result. First the students were asked to recall verbatim as many facts as possible. They were also asked to recall the order in which the facts were presented. Both the individuals and

the groups had twenty-five minutes in which to do this. Then the same individuals and groups were given thirty statements of facts to be judged as to their truth or falsity.

Groups recalled more facts correctly and made fewer major changes in facts than the individuals. Groups also did better in recalling the order of facts. On the recognition task, groups were superior in identifying those tasks that were true and those that were not. No matter what measure of memory one used, the four-person groups proved to be more effective than individuals working alone.

Source: David A. Vollrath, Blair H. Sheppard, Verlin B. Hinsz, & James H. Davis (1989). Memory performance by decision-making groups and individuals. *Organizational Behavior and Human Decision Processes, 43,* 289–300.

6. Assemble the evaluation data to analyze the effectiveness of steps 1 to 5. If necessary, go through steps 1 and 5 again. Also consider the maturity level the group has achieved (Morris & Sashkin, 1982).

■ WHERE GROUP DECISION MAKING CAN GO WRONG

Embedded in group processes are certain factors that may lead groups to go wrong—often seriously wrong—in their decision making. Perhaps with an awareness of these factors, erroneous decisions can be avoided. Group processes can negatively affect performance in a variety of ways (Swap, 1984).

□ Conformity

In the early 1950s, social psychologist Solomon Asch carried out a series of classic studies in which he demonstrated that group pressure can influence an individual member to agree with the majority's view even when it contradicts external reality. Thus, when seven members of a group (who in fact were Asch's confederates in the experiment) insisted that one of the three vertical lines on a card was the same length as the standard line on another card, many subjects wound up agreeing—even though a different line was obviously the correct match.

Distortions of this kind have since been studied widely, and among other findings there is evidence that Asch's initial results can be reversed, so that under appropriate circumstances minorities of two or more can influence the majority within a group to conform to their view (Asch, 1951; Tanford & Penrod, 1984). Such results can be achieved even among groups with a low level of groupness. The point is that social pressures can be very strong, inducing people to change their attitudes, perceptions, and behaviors. That even very diverse groups typically reach a consensus and endorse their decision unanimously is evidence of how strong a force **conformity** can be.

□ Groupthink

A phenomenon in which conformity clearly plays an important role has been labeled **groupthink** by Irving Janis, who developed his ideas from a study of policy fiascos at the national level—the attack on Pearl Harbor that precipitated U.S. involvement in World War II, the escalation of the Korean War under President Harry Truman, the Bay of Pigs invasion of Cuba during John Kennedy's administration, escalation of the Vietnam War under Lyndon Johnson, and somewhat later the Watergate coverup in Richard Nixon's administration.

The Nature of Groupthink.   The groupthink process is illustrated in Exhibit 8-2. Closely tied to high levels of group cohesion, groupthink is a way in which people think when deeply involved in a cohesive in-group, when the members' desire for consensus overrides their motivation to evaluate alternatives realistically. The symptoms of groupthink listed in part C of Exhibit 8-2 can be elaborated somewhat more fully as follows:

1. An *illusion of invulnerability*, shared by most or all of the members, which creates excessive optimism and encourages taking extreme risks

2. A *belief in the inherent morality of the group*, which inclines members to ignore the ethical or moral consequences of their decisions

3. *Collective rationalizations*, which lead members to discount warnings or other information that might cause them to reconsider their assumptions before they recommit themselves to past policy decisions

4. *Stereotypes of out-groups*, which induce members to view opposition leaders as too evil to warrant genuine attempts to negotiate or as too weak and stupid to counter the in-group's actions

5. *Self-censorship* of deviations from the apparent group consensus, reflecting each member's inclination to minimize the importance of his or her own doubts and counterarguments

6. A shared *illusion of unanimity*, which creates the complacent belief that all members' judgments conform to the majority view

7. *Direct pressure on dissenters*, in which any member who expresses strong arguments against any of the group's stereotypes, illusions, or commitments is informed that dissent is contrary to what is expected of all loyal members

8. The emergence of *self-appointed mindguards*—members who protect the group from contrary information that might shatter their shared complacency about the effectiveness and morality of their decisions

It is important to recognize that the evidence for groupthink as it has been described comes from American studies of policy decisions at the very highest levels. Attempts to replicate these results in a laboratory context have not been successful, but there is good reason to question whether even the best of these laboratory studies actually reproduced

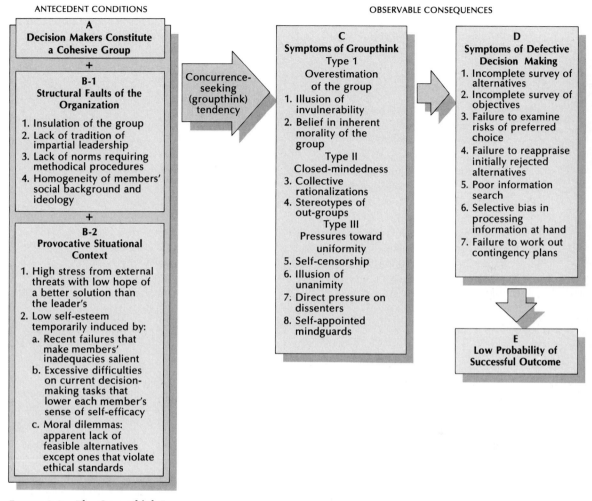

ANTECEDENT CONDITIONS   OBSERVABLE CONSEQUENCES

A
Decision Makers Constitute a Cohesive Group

+

B-1
Structural Faults of the Organization

1. Insulation of the group
2. Lack of tradition of impartial leadership
3. Lack of norms requiring methodical procedures
4. Homogeneity of members' social background and ideology

+

B-2
Provocative Situational Context

1. High stress from external threats with low hope of a better solution than the leader's
2. Low self-esteem temporarily induced by:
   a. Recent failures that make members' inadequacies salient
   b. Excessive difficulties on current decision-making tasks that lower each member's sense of self-efficacy
   c. Moral dilemmas: apparent lack of feasible alternatives except ones that violate ethical standards

Concurrence-seeking (groupthink) tendency

C
Symptoms of Groupthink
Type 1
Overestimation of the group
1. Illusion of invulnerability
2. Belief in inherent morality of the group
Type II
Closed-mindedness
3. Collective rationalizations
4. Stereotypes of out-groups
Type III
Pressures toward uniformity
5. Self-censorship
6. Illusion of unanimity
7. Direct pressure on dissenters
8. Self-appointed mindguards

D
Symptoms of Defective Decision Making
1. Incomplete survey of alternatives
2. Incomplete survey of objectives
3. Failure to examine risks of preferred choice
4. Failure to reappraise initially rejected alternatives
5. Poor information search
6. Selective bias in processing information at hand
7. Failure to work out contingency plans

E
Low Probability of Successful Outcome

Exhibit 8-2   The Groupthink Process
This diagram shows how a cohesive group plus structural faults of the organization plus a provocative situational context combine to produce concurrence seeking, then symptoms of groupthink, then defective decision making, and finally a low probability of success.
Source: Irving L. Janis (1982). *Groupthink: Psychological studies of policy decisions and fiascoes,* p. 244 (also pp. 174–175). Boston: Houghton Mifflin.

the kind of situation Janis was describing (Leana, 1985). The threat of groupthink seems greatest at very high levels of cohesion, where groups have been together for some time and where externally produced stress introduces a degree of isolation. This kind of situation is extraordinarily difficult—if not impossible—to generate in the laboratory.

Avoiding Groupthink.   Janis's suggestions for avoiding groupthink are outlined in Exhibit 8-3. In essence, the intention is to open up the

EXHIBIT 8-3   Suggested Antidotes for Groupthink

1. The leader of a policy-forming group should assign the role of critical evaluator to each member, encouraging the group to give high priority to airing objections and doubts.

2. The leaders in an organization's hierarchy, when assigning a policy-planning mission to a group, should be impartial instead of stating their preferences and expectations at the outset.

3. The organization should routinely follow the administrative practice of setting up several independent policy-planning and evaluation groups to work on the same policy question, each carrying out its deliberations under a different leader.

4. Through the period when the feasibility and effectiveness of policy alternatives are being surveyed, the policy-making group should from time to time divide into two or more subgroups to meet separately, under different chairpersons, and then come together to hammer out their differences.

5. Each member of the policy-making group should discuss periodically the group's deliberations with trusted associates in his or her own unit of the organization and report their reactions back to the group.

6. One or more outside experts or qualified colleagues within the organization who are not core members of the policy-making group should be invited to each meeting on a staggered basis and should be encouraged to challenge the views of the core members.

7. At each meeting devoted to evaluating policy alternatives, at least one member should be assigned the role of devil's advocate, expressing as many objections to each policy alternative as possible.

8. Whenever the policy issue involves relations with a rival organization, a sizable bloc of time should be spent surveying all warning signals from the rivals and constructing alternative scenarios of the rivals' intentions.

9. After reaching a preliminary consensus about what seems to be the best policy alternative, the policy-making group should hold a second-chance meeting at which the members are expected to express as vividly as they can all their residual doubts and to rethink the entire issue before making a definitive choice.

SOURCE: Adapted from Irving L. Janis (1982). *Groupthink: Psychological studies of policy decisions and fiascoes*, pp. 262–271. Boston: Houghton Mifflin.

decision-making process in various ways; one way is to have separate groups work on the same problem, in a manner reminiscent of the nominal-group approach. Groupthink is discouraged if the decision-making process is visible and if questioning both from inside and outside the group is encouraged. Decisions should not be rushed, because delay may give reservations a chance to surface. Vigilance needs to be encouraged (Janis, 1989).

That effective managers do in fact foster these kinds of approaches is illustrated by the following statement made by Alfred P. Sloan, chief executive officer of General Motors from 1928 to 1956, at the end of a lengthy meeting of his top-management group:

Gentlemen, I take it we are all in complete agreement on the decision here. Then I propose we postpone further discussion of this matter until our next meeting to give ourselves time to develop disagreements and perhaps gain some understanding of what the decision is all about.

☐ Group Polarization and the Risky Shift

After group discussion, group members tend to shift toward whichever end of the issue, more risky or more conservative, they already favored; the degree of this group-based shift tends to relate strongly to the degree of existing prior tendency in that direction (Bordley, 1983; McGrath & Kravitz, 1982). If the group was prone to risk originally, group discussion intensifies this inclination. If the group started out conservative, discussion only accentuates the tendency toward caution. This suggests that a leader's initial instructions to a group can exert a tremendous influence. Yet the initial research, and much that has emerged since, has documented a group tendency toward solutions that contain a degree of risk. **Group polarization**—toward caution or risk—is a reality, but the tendency toward **risky shift** seems more prevalent, and certainly more of a problem.

The fact of the matter is that after group discussion individuals often are more likely to accept high-risk decisions than they were initially. The process evolves as follows:

1. The average preferred decision within the group shifts in a risky direction.
2. Greater agreement emerges within the group, converging on this more risky position.
3. No individual moves to a decision more risky than that preferred by the riskiest group member before the discussion began; thus initial group composition is an important consideration.
4. Most of the comments in the discussion tend to favor risk.

Certainly all cautious decisions are not correct, just as all risky decisions are not wrong, but there is evidence that many companies that go into irreversible decline have become involved in risks of such magnitude that alternative strategies are precluded: They put all their eggs in one basket, gamble recklessly, believe in overoptimistic forecasts—and suffer the consequences (Richards, 1973). It appears that risky shift is a problem that can operate to the detriment of certain companies, particularly relatively small ones. Certainly it is an aspect of group decision making that is worth considering.

☐ Escalating Behavioral Commitments

Closely related to risky shift, and perhaps in some instances directly involved in it, is **behavioral commitment,** which was described in Chapter 5. This phenomenon occurs among groups at least as often as among individuals (Bazerman, Giuliano, & Appelman, 1984). Groups are inclined to invest more and more in their initial decisions, simply to justify having made them in the first place, even though it is clear to outside observers that the initial decisions were wrong. The solution to this type of group decision-making problem, as with its individual variant, is to have subsequent decisions made by a group or individual who was not involved in the initial one. In any event, it is important to recognize that decision-making groups are subject to the problems that individuals experience in making decisions.

■ THE EFFECT OF GROUP COMPOSITION ON DECISION MAKING

Within organizations, groups are constantly being created and reorganized. At such times questions always arise regarding how many people, what type of people, and which decision-making structure will be most effective. To what extent does the composition of a group influence its decision-making performance? These are the issues to which we now turn.

☐ How Large Should the Group Be?

Larger groups tend to contain a more diverse array of people unless steps are taken to select individuals who are alike. Thus larger groups are more likely both to have the resources to solve a problem well and to become embroiled in internal conflict. Larger groups also tend more often to include two or

EXHIBIT 8-4   Effectiveness of Groups of Various Sizes for Making Creative Decisions
This scale represents the relative effectiveness of various-sized groups.

Number of Group Members

1	2	3	4	5	6	7	8	9	10	11	12	13	14	15	16 plus

←— Clearly —→   ←— Optimal range —→   ←Increasingly too large →
too small   for face-to-face
discussion

more members who are very similar to one another and are thus likely to stick together. This, plus the fact that opportunities for each member to communicate with all the others are limited, fosters splintering and clique formation in larger groups.

Since **group size** clearly does affect performance, how large should the group be? It depends on the decision to be made. Where the decision is a complex one, groups of four or fewer members do poorly (Huber, 1980). Yet it is also true that as groups get very large, coordination of efforts becomes almost impossible, and members tend to become frustrated over the limitations on their ability to communicate and to exert influence. Generally, the best guideline for groups dealing with creative tasks is a minimum of seven or eight members and a maximum of ten to twelve (see Exhibit 8-4). However, where member interaction is restricted, as with nominal groups and the Delphi technique, considerably larger groups can be used.

In the case of a **programmable decision** (for which a definite pattern exists), where the task is to find the *right* answer rather than to create the *best possible* one, the key consideration is not group size, but expertise of members. Adding members tends to add to costs, because more person-hours are used to achieve a result that could have been achieved with fewer members. Groups with more than five members can add little to decision quality when the problem faced permits a reasonably certain answer (Ashton, 1986; Yetton & Bottger, 1983). The clear implication is that groups should be reconstituted, broken into subgroups, or enhanced in size in accordance with the nature of the problem at hand.

☐ **How Similar Should the Members Be?**

People differ in many ways—by demographic characteristics such as age, sex, geographic origin, and the like, as well as various individual characteristics of the kind considered in previous chapters. A question arises as to whether decision-making groups should be formed so as to contain as diverse—or as homogeneous—an array of individuals as possible. In other words, is **group similarity** important?

The answer, as with size, depends on the requirements of the decision. The more similar the members are, the easier it is for them to organize themselves and get down to work. Yet a homogeneous group often operates like a single individual, since one member's ideas are likely to be much the same as another's. Diversity almost invariably brings some conflict and difficulty in communicating, yet diversity makes it possible to apply varied abilities, viewpoints, and information to the problem. This is important when a decision must be creative. Where members have essentially the same backgrounds, values, and information, fewer alternative approaches tend to be generated. However, diversity should not range so far that individuals are included who have nothing to contribute at all.

BOX 8-3   RESEARCH IN I/O PSYCHOLOGY

An Aborted Attempt to Form Engagement Teams at McKinsey and Company

Several people working in the San Francisco office of McKinsey and Company, a management consulting firm, decided to form teams on the basis of what was known about the similarities and differences among staff consultants. These "engagement teams" consisted of as few as three and as many as fifteen consultants, each working on some problem for a single client. Most teams had from three to six members. The teams stayed together an average of something over six months, although some teams' engagements with a client lasted more than two years. In most cases consultants served on several teams at once in both part-time and temporary assignments.

The idea was to have consultants who differed from one another constitute the teams working on problems requiring a creative approach—such as those involving strategic planning, product marketing, and acquisitions, where unique solutions had to be worked out for each specific situation. Many problems, however, required routine applications of solutions that had been used many times before: setting up a compensation program or an inventory-control system, for example, or instituting cost-reduction procedures. Here, teams were to be set up so that the members were as similar as possible to one another.

To organize the various teams, data were collected on the consulting experience, educational background, and personality characteristics (measured by appropriate tests) of the thirty consultants in the office. People could then be placed on teams in accordance with either their similarities or their differences, depending on the nature of the problem to be dealt with. All that remained was to show the office's managing director, who actually assigned cases, how to use the approach.

At this point, the whole project came to an abrupt halt. The managing director pointed out that he already had too many considerations to take into account in making assignments. These included accommodating client preferences, matching consultant knowledge with problem requirements, minimizing travel time and costs, getting engagements started as soon as possible after client requests, and keeping consultants busy so that as much of their time as possible could be billed to clients. He simply did not have time left to consider consultant similarities and differences. He may or may not have been right in giving the homogeneity–heterogeneity issue such low priority. The reality is that no one ever found out.

On programmable decisions, in contrast, the reduced friction of homogeneous groups is likely to be a distinct plus. Similar people understand one another and can communicate readily; cohesion comes more easily. A homogeneous group is more likely to find the right answer and get it implemented. The distinction between such routine decision-making situations and those of a creative nature is demonstrated in Box 8-3, which describes an effort by McKinsey and Company to form engagement teams.

☐ Which Decision-Making Structure Should Be Used?

Historically, companies have made extensive use of groups consisting of internal staff experts, outside consultants, or both in making decisions about strategy formulation, market planning, and other matters that are important and require creative input. More recently, this traditional approach has been challenged, and new methods of forming and utilizing groups to make nonprogrammable

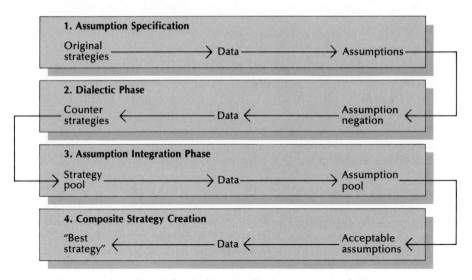

EXHIBIT 8-5 Steps in Using Dialectical Inquiry for Strategy Formulation
This diagram shows the flow from assumption specification to the dialectic phase to assumption integration, to composite strategy creation as dialectical inquiry progresses.
SOURCE: Ian I. Mitroff & James R. Emshoff (1979). On strategic assumption making: A dialectical approach to policy and planning. *Academy of Management Review, 4*, 5.

decisions have been proposed. These newer procedures fall into two categories: dialectical inquiry and devil's advocacy.

Dialectical Inquiry. **Dialectical inquiry** has its roots in philosophical debate and involves arguing logically about conflicting opinions regarding a problem in order to arrive at the best solution. Exhibit 8-5 outlines one approach of this kind. Within a company, two or more homogeneous groups are formed that reflect alternative viewpoints. Within each group, members have a similar personality makeup and share a desire to work together on the same kinds of tasks. An effort is made to maximize differences between the groups, especially in knowledge and perspectives on the problem. The groups then move through the steps shown in Exhibit 8-5. Each group's first goal is to come up with a strategy based on its assumptions about the problem in phase 1. Then, in phase 2, each group argues against the other's position. With this

information out on the table, the groups can move toward integration of ideas and a composite strategy. Note that this approach incorporates both member similarities and member differences in the decision-making process. Given the fact that dialectical inquiry is intended for use in creative problem solving, the inclusion of member differences appears to be an important consideration.

Box 8-4 describes Eastman Kodak's adaptation of dialectical inquiry. Although agreement on a marketing plan is a goal of this approach, a full consensus does not always occur. Even so, the procedure can produce useful indications of what the company's market information needs are.

Devil's Advocacy. An alternative to dialectical inquiry is the **devil's advocacy** procedure. We have already noted one application of this procedure in discussing groupthink (see point 7 in Exhibit 8-3). Devil's advocacy is often applied to strategies developed by a

BOX 8-4   I/O PSYCHOLOGY IN PRACTICE

Dialectical Inquiry Used for Market Information Purposes at Eastman Kodak

Eastman Kodak operates in many markets around the world. Its market planning involves determining information needs, gathering, storing, and analyzing market information, and evaluating the whole market-information-gathering system. Dialectical inquiry, which is called "strategic assumption surfacing and testing" at Eastman Kodak, is frequently used to identify market information needs related to a given strategy.

The process begins with group formation. Divergent groups—often more than two—are formed to represent the full range of views on a problem. These groups are made as internally homogeneous as possible; each consists of like-minded people. The groups, however, are as different from one another as possible, and taken together they cover all positions that might have an impact on the ultimate strategy.

In the first step of the dialectical process itself, each group, meeting separately, identifies the assumptions behind its position and rates them on both their importance and their plausibility. Each group then presents its most persuasive and its most damaging assumptions to the other groups. The idea here is to make sure that what one group takes for granted does not go unchallenged by another group and to ensure that important aspects of strategy are not neglected because of the desire for consensus that often develops within groups.

The second step is debate among the groups. Each group is given an opportunity to challenge the other groups' assumptions and defend its own. The goal is not so much to convince others as, again, to confirm that what each group takes as given is not necessarily accepted by others.

The third step is the analysis of information requirements to resolve the high levels of uncertainty in any of the important assumptions. In this way market information needs are identified, and guidelines for data collection (market research) are established.

The fourth step is synthesis, where an attempt is made to achieve consensus among the positions. What strategy will best meet the requirements of all positions that remain viable? This step permits further refinement of market information needs.

The feeling among Eastman Kodak managers who have used the process is that step four is the weakest link in dialectical inquiry. There is a concern that the planning process will not be converted to action. As one manager put it, "I'm not sure we came out with a commitment. Did the process in a sense artificially bring us to a consensus?" This uncertainty, however, can be a problem in any planning effort, no matter what decision-making process is used.

SOURCE: Vincent P. Barabba (1983). Making use of methodologies developed in academia: Lessons from one practitioner's experience. In Ralph H. Kilmann, Kenneth W. Thomas, Dennis P. Slevin, Raghu Nath, & S. Lee Jerrell (Eds.) *Producing useful knowledge for organizations,* pp. 147–166. New York: Praeger.

planning unit. After development, the plan is turned over to certain staff members whose job is to determine what is wrong with it—to identify assumptions and biases inherent in the plan that jeopardize its value. (The term "devil's advocate" originally referred to the Catholic Church official who is appointed to present reasons that a candidate for sainthood should *not* be canonized. It has been extended to apply to anyone who defends an opposing position for the sake of argument.) If the plan withstands the scrutiny of the devil's advocates, it can be presumed to be free of the effects of groupthink and premature confor-

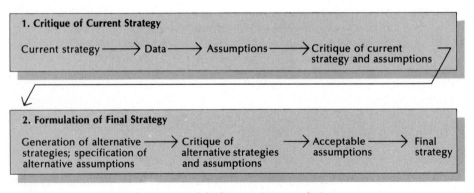

EXHIBIT 8-6   A Devil's Advocacy Model of Strategic Formulation
Critiques of current strategy form the basis for the formulation of final strategy.
SOURCE: Richard A. Cosier (1981). Dialectical inquiry in strategic planning: A case of premature
acceptance. *Academy of Management Review, 6,* 647.

mity to a norm, and thus viable. Although such an approach can be used with individuals, it is common to utilize groups in both the initial proposal and the critique of a decision (Schwenk, 1988).

Devil's advocacy can exert a very negative influence, leaving the company with no decision at all. Unlike dialectical inquiry, it does not attempt to develop a variety of alternative solutions. In some cases, however, devil's advocacy does go beyond the critique of *current* strategy, as outlined in Exhibit 8-6, to the formulation of a final strategy. This additional phase involves the generation of alternative strategies followed by critique of each plan until a solution is found that can withstand rational attack.

Considerable debate has arisen in the social science community as to which procedure is better: dialectical inquiry or devil's advocacy. Laboratory research has not, as yet, yielded results that are conclusive enough to settle the dispute (Cosier & Rechner, 1985; Schweiger & Finger, 1984). Not surprisingly, students do not approach complex business problems in the same way that experienced managers do; for one thing, the students are not nearly as conservative. Thus, studies using students cannot be generalized to the

type of situation depicted in Box 8-4. All in all, it seems likely that dialectical inquiry and devil's advocacy can be equally effective if applied with appropriate attention to rational outcomes. It may well be that the differences between the two are not as great as their respective proponents have imagined.

■ QUALITY CIRCLES

Quality circles are groups of employees, primarily from the lower levels of the organization, operating to yield what amounts to a group-based suggestion system. Quality circles are a recent phenomenon in the United States and are growing rapidly in popularity. Although they have quite different origins, quality circles can closely resemble team building (considered in Chapter 7).

Quality circles are defined specifically as five- to fifteen-member, same-site, voluntary work groups, which meet regularly during working hours and are specially trained to identify and solve task-related problems without the direct leadership of immediate supervisors.

The process consists of a continuous cycle of phases. Phase 1 consists of identifying, ranking-selecting, and solving a work-site problem; it is basically an exercise in goal setting and achievement. After a rigorous training programme, members gather data, often from outside the work-site area, and organize and analyze it using statistical and cause-effect techniques. During phase 2 the group formally presents its solution and rationale to middle and/or top management. In this phase the group actively tries to influence management several levels removed from the group, circumventing immediately positioned supervisors. Within a short predetermined time period, phase 3 begins. Management notifies the group as to whether it accepts or rejects the proposed solution. If management's response is negative, it provides reasons for its decision. The group then may adjust or reject the original solution, or possibly select a new problem for analysis and solution. If management's response is positive, the group proceeds to phase 4, where it helps to implement the solution, including monitoring its effectiveness through data collection and analysis. Thus the process is continuous, operating within a new structure nested within the original organization but not bound completely by traditional practices and procedures in areas such as decision making and communications (Wolff, 1987, p. 4).

☐ Japanese Origins

The quality-circle idea originated in Japan in the early 1960s and has remained strong there. It was fostered in part by American consultants who came to Japan after World War II to assist in reconstructing the Japanese economy, but the basic concept is Japanese. At the time, Japanese products that were sold in the world market were believed to be of very poor quality, and a major focus of post-war development was on changing that image. Extensive quality-control training was instituted throughout the country. Many

business managers who learned quality-control techniques thereupon enlisted the help of their workers in solving product-quality problems. Small groups of employees began to meet regularly to discuss and propose solutions to problems that occurred in their sector of the company. During these meetings, the workers typically sat around a table—hence the term "quality circle."

In the mid-1970s, groups of Japanese managers touring the United States introduced a number of West Coast companies to the quality-circle idea. The approach proved particularly attractive in the aerospace industry, which was then having considerable difficulty meeting government quality standards on its contracts. Lockheed Aircraft's space and missile unit at Sunnyvale, California, is often credited with being the first American plant to adopt a quality-circle system, although there apparently were earlier partial applications in the United States. Several of the people who set up the program at Lockheed subsequently founded their own consulting firms, which helped to spread the quality-circle concept throughout the United States.

☐ What Is Involved

Although our major concern is with quality circles as a group decision-making mechanism, it is important to understand that in most applications much more is involved than group-level decision-making processes. Typically a complex structure extending well up into the organizational hierarchy is also involved.

Problem-Solving Process.   Exhibit 8-7 depicts the technique for solving one problem in a single quality circle. Note that data are obtained from outside the circle, and the final decision on whether or not to implement the solution rests with management. The circle, which meets face to face at least once a month

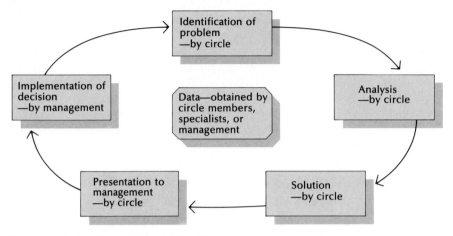

EXHIBIT 8-7 Problem Solving in Quality Circles
In the quality-circle problem-solving process, both the circles and management have distinct roles.
SOURCE: Naoto Sasaki & David Hutchins (1984). *The Japanese approach to product quality: Its applicability to the West,* p. 68. Oxford, England: Pergamon.

and usually more frequently, decides what it will recommend to management and how that recommendation will be presented. Brainstorming procedures are often used so as to maximize creativity, and the circles are trained in methods of identifying problems, tracking down cause-and-effect relationships, and formulating solutions. One common practice is to divide large circles into subcircles of perhaps five, or even just two or three, members, each with its own leader. In many cases, the quality circle assigns specific problems to a subcircle for solution.

Overall Organization. Exhibit 8-8 shows how a quality-circle organization fits into the

EXHIBIT 8-8 Structure of the Quality-Circle Program in Toyota Motor Company Plants
The plant hierarchy at the right parallels the quality-circle structure.
SOURCE: Philip C. Thompson (1982), *Quality circles: How to make them work in America,* p. 22. New York: AMACOM.

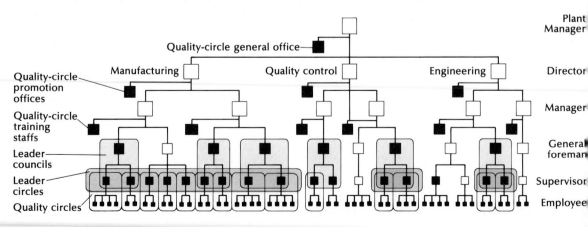

BOX 8-5   I/O PSYCHOLOGY IN PRACTICE

Quality Circles at Hughes Aircraft

Hughes Aircraft was one of the first American aerospace firms to adopt quality circles in the mid-1970s and has had a very good record of maintaining them. The program began with four pilot circles at the Carlsbad, California, plant of the Industrial Products Division. Within four years the company had 250 circles in its Arizona and California locations. The company attributes to quality circles numerous improvements in product quality, service, job performance, safety, working conditions, individual growth, company morale, and productivity. Specific examples include:

Simplified computer training program

Display of quality-control charts for circuit board with major problems

Readability of purchase order improved

Parts control improved

Sample boards redesigned for assembly

Ultrasonic cleaner used to clean parts

Simplified front-end assembly procedure

Instituted proper cleaning of welders' probe tips

Improved and controlled production micrometers

It has proven important to identify and train very good facilitators, who are a major key to the success of the quality circles. Both the facilitators (who operate in that role on a part-time basis) and circle leaders require up to twenty hours of initial training, and ongoing training after that. Without continuing attention in this area, problems inevitably arise. Support of the quality-circle program has been consistently strong at the top, but lapses have occurred at the middle-management level. Appropriate introduction of the program, training of middle managers, and reporting procedures can overcome this problem; however, continuing attention is required to keep it from cropping up again. Minutes of circle meetings and reports of results must be maintained on a continuing basis, and regular reports should be issued to keep everyone informed of progress and to make circle activities visible. This, in turn, prevents the program from losing momentum. In short, a quality-circle program that contributes to productivity will not run itself. It requires hard work and commitment from everyone involved.

SOURCE: Naoto Sasaki & David Hutchins (1984). *The Japanese approach to product quality: Its applicability to the West,* pp. 71–78. Oxford, England: Pergamon.

overall company structure in the Toyota Motor Company's plants. Not all quality-circle organizations are this extensive, but the existence of parallel hierarchies—quality circle and regular managerial—is typical. The structure of the quality-circle hierarchy is important because it has a lot to do with how the circles themselves are implemented, are trained, and go about identifying problems and proposing solutions.

Toyota plants usually have a steering committee of from five to fifteen members attached to the quality-circle general office to oversee and direct the program. A full-time program coordinator may also be in that office. At lower levels in the quality-circle structure are various facilitators who are involved in promoting the circle program, monitoring programs and reports, and above all training. At Toyota, as in most other Japanese companies, internal personnel are specially selected for this purpose. In the United States, external consultants are often used. As noted in Box 8-5 these facilitators are a major factor in the success of the quality-circle program at Hughes Aircraft, where the position of facilitator is used as a training ground for promotion into management.

As Exhibit 8-8 shows, the employee quality circles are attached to various leader circles made up of middle-level managers, who are expected to act as a bridge between employee groups and upper-level managers. In American companies, middle-level leader circles are not so common, and effective bridging to upper-level managers is less likely to occur.

Introducing the Program. As noted in Box 8-5, busy middle managers may resent having to do the extra work a quality-circle program requires. Others, including union leaders, may resist as well because they fear that the circles may undermine union influence with employees. Therefore, if the program is to be effective, it must be planned carefully and preceded by ample training of participants. This start-up phase, as depicted in Exhibit 8-9, can last as long as a year and a half. Many American companies have introduced quality circles much more rapidly than that. However, Japanese firms have typically moved even more slowly, and these firms have had the best record of maintaining continued momentum in their quality-circle programs. The ideal start-up duration depends on the particular company, but short-circuiting any of the steps in Exhibit 8-9 can result in a less than optimal program—or one that never gets off the ground.

☐ Effectiveness of Quality Circles

How well do quality circles work? Until recently, we have had to rely on testimonials, most of which came from consultants in the field or from company people who had been actively involved in promoting quality-circle programs within their companies. Now, however, a body of objective research evidence in the area is beginning to accumulate.

Testimonials. The improvements at Hughes Aircraft noted in Box 8-5 are based on **testimonials**—subjective statements of approval and recommendation. Nobody knows how many of the improvements would have happened anyway, without quality circles, or could have been achieved simply through good management. Some innovations may turn out not to be improvements after all, or savings attributed to them may be overestimated. It is also possible that improvements ascribed to quality circles actually originated elsewhere in the organization. Or perhaps the specified action did not occur at all, at least not in the stated form. The point is that the people giving testimonials have a vested interest in making quality circles look good. Various forces, including selective perception, may lead them to reach conclusions that in large part reflect their enthusiasm rather than objective information.

Despite their subjectivity, testimonials have been a major factor in the increased use of quality circles in the United States. Reports on programs at companies such as Lockheed, Hughes Aircraft, Martin Marietta, Motorola, Control Data, and Honeywell indicate substantial savings—often over $1 million a year. But these reports give rise to questions as to how the savings were calculated. Moreover, some quality-circle programs have been outright failures (Ledford, Lawler, & Mohrman, 1988; Meyer & Stott, 1985; Smeltzer & Kedia, 1985).

Maintaining a quality-circle structure like that described in Exhibit 8-8, and carrying out the extensive training—which in some cases has extended to teaching all employees the complex techniques of statistical quality control—can be very costly. When all expenses (including consultants' fees and an appropriate share of the time of company employees) are taken into account, what were first thought to be savings may turn out to be net losses. Furthermore, some circles produce nothing of value, and others yield only a few useful ideas in a period of initial enthusiasm. Rapid burnout of programs is a major problem, at least in the United States. Even in

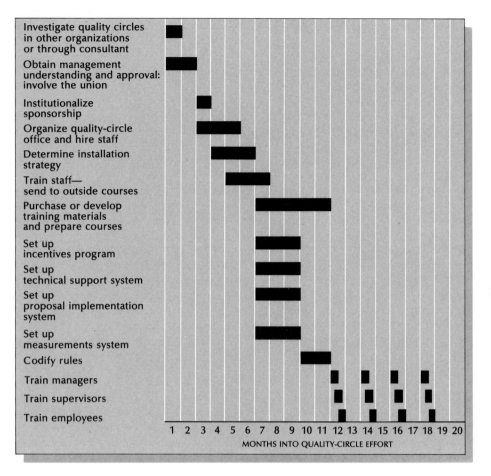

EXHIBIT 8-9   Timetable for Start-up of a Quality-Circle Program
The start-up of a quality-circle program is a lengthy process with many steps. It extends over at least eighteen months.
SOURCE: Philip C. Thompson (1982). *Quality circles: How to make them work in America,* p. 173. New York: AMACOM.

Japan, programs may require strong managerial pressure to survive. Overall, it appears that some quality circles do and some do not yield net benefits to productivity. We can be sure of very little on the basis of testimonials.

Research Evidence.   Solid research has begun to yield objective data on the effectiveness of quality circles. Research in an electronics firm indicated that quality circles gave their participants a perception of greater influence, but not necessarily an increase in job satisfaction;

there was also some evidence that the participants viewed their jobs as enriched (Rafaeli, 1985). In a study carried out within a county government, clear difficulties in maintaining momentum were observed, and attitude changes attributable to the quality circles were minimal at best. Yet some of these circles apparently did contribute to greater efficiency, reduced overtime, less absenteeism, and the like (Wolff, 1983).

Another study compared quality circles in a maintenance unit with those in a medical

Exhibit 8-10   Differences between More Effective and Less Effective Quality Circles

Variables	More Effective Circles	Less Effective Circles
Group cohesion	Higher	Lower
Group dedication to performance norms	Higher	Lower
Overall job satisfaction	Higher	Lower
Intrinsic work satisfaction	Higher	Lower
Satisfaction with coworkers in regular work group	Higher	Lower
Level of self-esteem	Higher	Lower
Perceived company commitment to the quality-circle program	Higher	Lower

Source: Adapted from Ricky W. Griffin & Sandy J. Wayne (1984). A field study of effective and less effective quality circles. *Academy of Management Proceedings, 44,* 220.

facility staffed by U.S. Army personnel, many of them civilians, on a single military base. Within the medical facility, the program deteriorated rapidly. However, the quality circles in the maintenance unit were shown to have had positive results, probably because, according to the researchers, "leaders were thoroughly trained, meticulous in training their own subordinates, and assisted by a competent full-time facilitator" (Steel, Mento, Dilla, Ovalle, & Lloyd, 1985).

Exhibit 8-10 compares more effective and less effective quality circles within a manufacturing firm. The more effective quality circles were defined as those whose members suggested more improvements, had more improvements adopted by management, and viewed the quality circles more favorably. Because this was a cross-sectional study, in which all data were collected at one time, it is impossible to say with certainty whether quality-circle effectiveness caused the results, or vice versa. Nevertheless, there is a close tie between effectiveness and many positive aspects of group processes. Given the findings from prior research in group dynamics, it seems likely that groups that are functioning smoothly in terms of cohesion, norms, coworker relationships, and support of mem-

bers would contribute in some degree to greater quality-circle effectiveness.

Studies extending over several years provide evidence that quality circles can act to improve not only the quality, but also the quantity of output and reduce absenteeism rates (Marks, Mirvis, Hackett & Grady, 1986; Tang, Tollison, & Whiteside, 1987). It seems clear that a causal impact on performance can occur. Yet a review of the research emphasizes the problems involved in securing a positive outcome. In this review there were sixteen studies in which the results were described as uniformly positive and only eight in which the results were said to be uniformly negative, but another nine studies produced results considered to be mixed or nonsignificant (Barrick & Alexander, 1987).

Theoretical Implications. The research findings indicate that quality circles can enhance performance, but not always. Sizable investments in training and support seem to be required for success, and the successes may not emerge for some time. In addition, some researchers have suggested that many existing quality-circle procedures could be improved (Goldstein, 1985).

For example, strictly voluntary involvement in quality circles may attract only the more ambitious employees, who probably would find other ways to contribute anyway; accordingly, every effort should be made to encourage wider employee involvement in quality circles. The mesh between what is known about effective creative decision making in groups and what makes for effective quality circles is not all that good. The brainstorming emphasis in quality circles should help, but nominal-group procedures and efforts to identify best members could help even more. There is a significant chance that conformity pressures, groupthink, polarization, and the like may emerge as circles develop cohesion. The result could be an initial burst of positive results followed by very little. One way to prevent this from happening is to rotate membership in the circles.

Quality circles are often structured in ways that serve to stifle individual creativity. After the start-up it may be best to reduce overhead, rotate leadership, and otherwise free up members. The results of research on group size and on similarities and differences probably could be utilized more effectively in forming groups. Formal work groups seem not to be the most effective units. Although money is used as an incentive in some traditional suggestion systems, financial rewards are rarely used with quality circles. Strategists have suggested that the establishment of such reward systems could revitalize some dormant quality circles. In short, improvements in quality circles could be made on the basis of what is now known about group dynamics and group decision making. In any event, evaluation research should be carried out to see if a quality-circle program is yielding sufficient benefits to warrant further investment (Greenbaum, Kaplan, & Metlay, 1988).

KEY TERMS

Group decision making

Brainstorming

Nominal groups

Delphi technique

Idea generation

Idea evaluation

Conformity

Groupthink

Group polarization

Risky shift

Behavioral commitment

Group size

Programmable decision

Group similarity

Dialectical inquiry

Devil's advocacy

Quality circles

Testimonials

SUMMARY

Group decision making is widely used in organizations, although not always in the most effective manner. A major problem arises in attempting to keep groups from stifling their members' creativity. Among the approaches proposed for this purpose are *brainstorming, nominal groups,* and the

Delphi technique. Each has its special characteristics, advantages, and disadvantages (see Exhibit 8-1). Such creativity-fostering approaches are particularly important in the *idea-generation* phase of decision making. Where idea generation is not important to a solution or where the objective is to evaluate and choose among ideas already generated, face-to-face discussion can be very effective. Also, most groups have members who are capable of substantially outperforming the group as a whole. The problem is to identify such individuals so that their capabilities can be put to good use.

Groups tend to induce *conformity* in their members. As a result, they can yield decisions that are less than optimal, and sometimes just plain bad. *Groupthink, group polarization* (including *risky shift*), and escalating group *behavioral commitment* are some of the ways groups can go wrong. A variety of procedures for coping with problems of this kind have been proposed, ranging from introducing greater rationality into group decision-making processes to taking the ultimate decision away from the group and placing it elsewhere. In any event, it is very important for those participating in group decisions to be aware of these potential problems.

On creative tasks, groups numbering between seven and twelve members perform best. On *programmable tasks* the upper limit appears to be five.

Having a very diverse membership helps with complex, creative decisions. Having very similar members is best if more routine, programmable decisions are called for. *Dialectical inquiry* and *devil's advocacy* are two ways of structuring creative group decision processes to bring out diverse assumptions and viewpoints. Both of these approaches appear to contribute to a more effective final decision, though the difference between the two may not be very great.

Quality circles represent a group decision-making approach that has been imported from Japan and is currently growing in popularity. The idea is to use existing employee knowledge and ideas to achieve improvements in product quality and other areas. Ideas are developed in the group and recommendations made to management, where the responsibility for acceptance and implementation resides. In many cases the quality-circle organization introduces a dual structure into the company (see Exhibit 8-8). Obtaining useful results appears to depend on thorough advance planning, effective training at all levels, and the employment of capable facilitators. Glowing *testimonials* have no doubt overstated the case for quality circles. Nevertheless, an emerging body of research and existing group theory appear to support the use of quality circles in some form.

QUESTIONS

1. What is groupthink?
2. Why have dialectical inquiry and devil's advocacy been proposed, and how do they compare in effectiveness?
3. How does brainstorming work? What are its positive and negative features?
4. What are quality circles and where did they originate? Why is their origin important?
5. Why and how has the Delphi technique been used? How effective is it in producing creative decisions?
6. In what ways are decisions that emanate from risky shift and from behavioral commitment similar?
7. What inherent advantages can make nominal-group procedures superior to brainstorming?
8. How well do quality circles work? What kinds of evidence have been used to answer this question, and how reliable is each kind?
9. In making creative decisions, why is it important to distinguish between idea generation and idea evaluation? How might each best be approached?
10. How do group size and the degree of similarity among members relate to decision making?

CASE PROBLEM

JOYCE GREENBERG
Lawyer

Joyce Greenberg filed a lawsuit charging discrimination under Title VII of the U.S. Civil Rights Act against her employer—and won. How and why Joyce did this is not only her story but also the story of decision-making processes in the law firm that had employed her.

The firm had been formed a number of years before by three men who left a leading law firm in the city to set up a practice initially to serve one corporate client—a company headquartered in the same city. The new law firm prospered and grew, providing services primarily to corporations and to high-level executives in client companies. Although other lawyers were admitted to partnership and shared in the firm's earnings, the three founders maintained primary control.

After a number of years two of the founders retired, and for a while the firm was essentially run by one person. Before the remaining founder retired, he initiated a triumvirate of three senior members, modeled after the founding three, to head the firm, because it seemed reasonable to perpetuate what had worked well before. The unwritten rule guiding the firm was that if at all possible the triumvirate should make decisions in the same manner—and of the same nature—as the founders had done. Although there were a number of decisions, including the election of new partners, that required a vote of all the partners, in actuality these decisions were made by the triumvirate. The usual procedure in such instances was for the three to reach a consensus. Then that decision was leaked, often by a secretary, so that it had spread throughout the firm by the time the partners took a vote. Given that compensation decisions resided with the triumvirate, the results of votes by the partners as a body seldom deviated from what the triumvirate expected.

Several additional facts about the firm should be known. Almost all of the partners, and all three in the top group, had graduated from a single local law school. All were males. All but a few attended Protestant churches in the suburbs. Partners were expected to join one of two prestigious luncheon clubs in the center city, and most belonged to one particular country club that also had many client executives as members. All this was considered just good business.

Joyce Greenberg's problem started when she came up for election to partnership. This normally happened when a lawyer had been with the firm from six to ten years, depending on the ups and downs of the firm's business. It was general practice to limit the number of partners by electing only half of those proposed each year. Those who were not elected were expected to leave the firm as soon as they found another position. The partners often helped with these relocations, and every rejected candidate left within a year or so.

Two other lawyers came up for election to partnership at the same time as Joyce. John Brewster was from a well-known family in the city, had graduated from the local law school, and had belonged to the appropriate clubs for many years. He had done a good job in bringing new clients to the firm. However, he was generally viewed as a mediocre lawyer. A number of his cases had not gone well, primarily because he had failed to do the necessary research on legal precedents. Robert Endler had worked primarily with client executives setting up wills, trusts, and the like. He appeared to be very knowledgeable in this area, but outside of a few probate court appearances he had had practically no courtroom experience. It was unclear what would happen if one of the wills he had drawn up was tested in court. His father had been with the firm for a number of years and was a partner.

Joyce had graduated with distinction from a major national law school outside the city. She had tried but failed to obtain membership in the appropriate clubs. Being Jewish, she attended synagogue. Her performance record with the firm was outstanding. She had not done very well, however, in bringing new clients to the firm, probably in large part because she had not lived in the city before joining the firm.

John and Robert were elected to partnership; Joyce was not. She resigned shortly afterward and filed her discrimination suit against the firm. The U.S. Equal Employment Opportunity Commission took the case.

When the case went to court, the law firm's sole defense was that Title VII did not apply to law firms such as theirs and that therefore a charge of discrimination could not be upheld. This defense was the one advocated by the members of the triumvirate. The law firm from which the three founders had come was engaged to assist in the case; they advised that the proposed defense might not be sufficient. Nevertheless, when the triumvirate decided to continue on its original course, the other firm agreed to remain on the case.

Several sections of Title VII are relevant to the decision. An employer covered by the act, a qualified defendant,

> means a person engaged in an industry affecting commerce who has fifteen or more employees. . . . Such term does not include

(1) the United States, a corporation wholly owned by the Government of the United States, an Indian tribe, or any department or agency of the District of Columbia. . . .
(2) a bona fide private membership club (other than a labor organization).

Unlawful discrimination means

(1) to fail or refuse to hire or to discharge any individual, or otherwise to discriminate against any individual with respect to his compensation, terms, conditions, or privileges of employment, because of such individual's race, color, religion, sex, or national origin; or
(2) to limit, segregate, or classify his employees or applicants for employment in any way which would deprive or tend to deprive any individual of employment opportunities or otherwise adversely affect his status as an employee, because of such individual's race, color, religion, sex, or national origin.

The law firm clung to its original defense. It lost the suit and all subsequent appeals. The courts held repeatedly that it was a covered employer under the conditions of the act and that it had discriminated against Joyce.

Joyce was awarded damages by the court, and the firm was required to pay all her legal fees. In addition, the firm accrued legal charges of its own and a great deal of lost time among its own partners attributable to the case. But the biggest cost came later. The case had received a great deal of publicity in the local press over several years. After all appeals had been exhausted, a number of clients and potential clients began to wonder whether it was wise to entrust their legal problems to a firm that so clearly had mishandled a legal problem of its own. The firm's business began to suffer severely.

Questions

1. What deficiencies in the law firm's decision-making processes led to its final predicament? Note all you can and indicate the evidence for each.
2. Did the firm do anything that might have counteracted the deficiencies in its decision-making processes? Why did it fail to prevent the ultimate debacle?
3. To prevent similar problems in the future, how should the firm organize and carry out its decision making? Would these approaches have prevented the firm's problem over Joyce Greenberg? Explain.
4. How exactly does this case relate to matters of individual and organizational performance and productivity?

9 Leadership Styles

John Hanley took over at Monsanto in the early 1970s after a long and successful career at Procter & Gamble. Monsanto was in trouble, and Hanley moved quickly to correct the situation. His take-charge attitude alienated many subordinates, but he got results. Abrupt and controlling, sometimes insensitive to his impact on others, he nevertheless was the kind of person who made a difference.

When a subordinate said that something would be ready at a given time, it had better *be* ready. Hanley moved fast and expected others to keep up with him. Yet for all the demands on his time, he went out of his way to teach people whom he thought would benefit. His basic mode was to criticize; he seldom used lavish praise. Yet he could sympathize with managers who made mistakes, in large part because he was well aware that he made them too. His style was to charge ahead like an elephant—not smooth, not congenial—but intent on a planned course of action. Inevitably he made mistakes and angered people.

The following comments by subordinates are indicative:

> He's got warts like everybody else. . . . One of them is the fact that his rhetoric tends to outdistance our ability to produce, so that can result in increasing the expectations of our people beyond our ability to answer them in the short term. Because he gets so enthused, and he's so confident, the logistics can get away from him.

> He doesn't let anybody bubble up to challenge him, but in the process, he doesn't let anybody bubble up to help him either. . . . When Jack was down the line at P&G, he was a guy that liked to relate to people, but being up in the top spot he doesn't do it as well.

> I have seen him, where people have made big mistakes, be more forgiving than I would have been. . . . The severity comes in terms of the anxiety, or the desire on the part of the people to look good in his eyes. . . . You can tell when they sense that they've let him down. . . . That's the way I see him having his greatest impact on a lot of people.

> Things that he thinks he knows—like people planning—he comes on loud and strong. . . . Anything where he can do it himself he's super. At anything where he depends on the input of others he's less good, because his style doesn't allow him to sit down and rap with a group of guys, and allow them to participate in the conclusion.

> One of the things I find most frustrating about his style is when he calls you and asks if you have four or five minutes to talk over something. You don't have any more idea as to the subject. . . . He's all organized. He comes on at you like gangbusters. Walking in, you didn't even know what the subject was. Now he's done that to just about everybody.

Arthur Ochs ("Punch") Sulzberger was placed in charge at *The New York Times* at the age of 36, upon the death of another member of the controlling family. That was in 1963; the company's record since has been impressive. Sulzberger's approach reflects modesty, almost self-deprecation. He does not like confrontations and prefers shaking hands to chopping heads, although when he knows a thing needs to be done, he does it. He tends to give his people considerable freedom to act on their own. Good at picking people with talent, he also devotes a great deal of time and effort to developing them. The people who work for him are his friends, so he is very close to what is happening at the paper. His overall approach is conservative, slow, deliberate, but persistent.

His subordinates describe his style as follows:

> He's conservative in action. He doesn't leap over the parapet and say, "Gung ho. Let's kill the enemy." You go very, very carefully, a step at a time. You fortify as many positions as you possibly can, and you only proceed from one fortified position to the next when the next one's ready.

> His method of operation would be to give people working for him plenty of leeway, plenty of authority. When he concluded that they were going in the wrong direction, . . . he would step in and make personnel changes . . . then through consultation and discussion he would make sure that new plans evolved. . . . Discussions were held about problems or what might be done. He encouraged people to . . . propose solutions. The way that he works it is almost impossible to decide where the contributions came from.

> There are no meetings, except on the gravest problems, in which he isn't relaxed, and he usually has a joke to break tension. It is a great asset. It has eased many situations. . . . I don't know anyone here who is mad at him.

> He has a very high sense of the right thing to do. Where it affects people and things and ideas and in this case, the newspaper he loves . . . there's practically no limit to his willingness to put himself out. . . . He will look after his friends in top and lowly positions . . . he will go to great, great lengths to protect them.

He's involved through encouraging, on a one-on-one basis, everyone's best energies and talents. He's involved in trying to put together the people who will not only develop but also implement the program without being the person on top who is forcing the issue.

Having given the instructions to go ahead, he lets people run very hard. But in himself he is terribly, terribly slow-moving, very deliberately deliberate, so that whatever enthusiasms are worked up by the people doing the work . . . are always counteracted by his deliberateness.

He likes to wander around. . . . He goes to the tenth floor and sees [managing editor Max] Frankel . . . to the third floor and talks to people in the News Department. . . . Almost all of Punch's friendships are with people in the paper.

SOURCE : Harry Levinson & Stuart Rosenthal (1984). *CEO: Corporate leadership in action,* pp. 226–249. New York: Basic Books.

John Hanley and Arthur Sulzberger both have had very successful careers as managers and have made major contributions to their firms. Yet their styles as chief executive officers could not be more different. One wonders what would have happened had their positions been reversed—if Hanley had gone from Procter & Gamble to *The New York Times* and Sulzberger had started out at a young age as CEO of Monsanto. We cannot know the answer to that with certainty, but this is the kind of issue with which leadership theory is concerned. Why do seemingly very different kinds of people make effective leaders? How much of what happens is a function of the person, and how much is attributable to the situation? How flexible are people in the leadership styles they adopt? These are the types of questions that need to be considered.

This chapter and the following chapter, on leadership frontiers, are closely related. Most of the approaches treated in this chapter had their origins in the 1950s and the early 1960s, a period when the greatest concern in leadership was getting subordinate group members to share in making and carrying out decisions. Leadership theories of this era tended to contrast leaders who were concerned about and oriented toward their subordinates with those who were not. To varying degrees, leaders were exhorted to behave consistently in a style that took into account employee interests.

Generally, these early theories of leadership style remain viable today. Some continue to provide important insights; some are sources of more recent theories that have been built upon their foundations. All are discussed frequently when people write and talk about leadership issues.

In contrast, Chapter 10 considers a diverse array of more recent approaches to leadership, developed during the 1970s and in some cases the 1980s. Some owe allegiance to the earlier ideas considered in the present chapter and some do not, but all have substantially new aspects. For example, the later theories show much less concern with leadership style.

■ LEADERSHIP ISSUES

Before we begin our discussion of leadership-style theories, we need to consider some basic issues about the nature and role of leadership.

☐ Defining Leadership

Like many other terms in industrial-organizational psychology, "leadership" came from the common vocabulary. Both everyday usage and technical usage thus infuse the term with meanings. This factor and others have caused much confusion in defining leadership. A major textbook in the field handles the problem as follows (Yukl, 1989, p. 5):

It is neither feasible nor desirable at this point in the development of the discipline to resolve the controversy over the appropriate definition of leadership. For the time being, it is better to use the various conceptions of leadership as a source of different perspectives on a complex, multifaceted phenomenon.

This approach is of little help to anyone trying to reach a basic understanding of the term, but the viewpoint is understandable. Leadership definitions appear to have moved along the following scale, with the more recent views at the bottom of the list often encompassing prior definitions:

- Leadership as a focus of group processes
- Leadership as personality and its effects
- Leadership as the art of inducing compliance
- Leadership as the exercise of influence
- Leadership as an act or behavior
- Leadership as a form of persuasion
- Leadership as a power relation
- Leadership as an instrument of goal achievement
- Leadership as an emerging effect of interaction
- Leadership as a differentiated role
- Leadership as the initiation of structure

The *Handbook of Leadership,* drawing upon this scale, defines **leadership** broadly, as follows (Bass, 1990, pp. 19–20):

Leadership is an interaction between two or more members of a group that often involves a structuring or restructuring of the situation and the perceptions and expectations of the members. Leaders are agents of change, persons whose acts affect other people more than other people's acts affect them. Leadership occurs when one group member modifies the motivation or competencies of others in the group.

Within this definition it is important to distinguish between leadership that emerges out of and is maintained by the group and leadership that is imposed on the group from outside. John Hanley and Arthur Sulzberger were externally imposed leaders—Hanley by the largely external board of directors at Monsanto and Sulzberger by the family (of which he was a member) that owned *The New York Times.* Yet each in his own way also acquired a great deal of support from top management. Both probably would have been elected by that group ultimately, if that were the normal procedure. Thus, group-based and externally based leadership can be combined, and this situation is probably the ideal for organizations.

Exhibit 9-1 provides an overview of the whole leadership process. In this and the following chapter, we will discuss many of its components. It is apparent from Exhibit 9-1 that many factors need to be measured in studying leadership (Clark & Clark, 1990).

☐ Does Leadership Make a Difference?

Exhibit 9-1 indicates that what a leader does, although mediated by a host of intervening variables, does have a causal impact on group performance. Thus, it seems apparent that Hanley and Sulzberger did have an effect on the performance of Monsanto and *The New York Times;* certainly they acted in ways that clearly indicated they *thought* their behavior made a difference. Yet an opposing view maintains that environmental forces and aspects of group (or organizational) functioning are so dominant that leadership style does not matter much—that the group will function much the same with one leader as with another.

Leadership Influence. Taken as a whole, research indicates that leadership can make a difference, though it does not always do so (House & Baetz, 1979; Weiner & Mahoney,

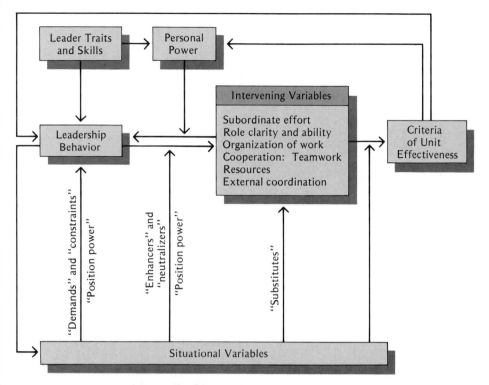

EXHIBIT 9-1   A View of the Leadership Process
A leader's traits and skills lead to certain kinds of power and behavior, which—interacting with variables in the situation—produce end results for the group and its members; these end results in turn affect the leader's power and behavior.
SOURCE: Gary A. Yukl (1989). *Leadership in organizations,* p. 269. Englewood Cliffs, NJ: Prentice-Hall.

1981). The behavior of leaders can have an impact on other group members that makes these members more or less productive. The effect on group performance appears to be most pronounced when it is positive. Really outstanding people in leadership roles tend to elicit highly effective performance from others. In any given organization, however, the number of leaders who really make a difference in this manner may not be very high; one study estimates the proportion at only about 15 percent (Smith, Carson, & Alexander, 1984).

Nonleadership Influences. The impact of leadership came to be questioned partly because research found that leadership behavior can be generated by the way subordinates act and by other aspects of the work situation (Sims & Manz, 1984). This research was interpreted to mean that when strong relationships existed between leader behavior and group performance, it was largely because differences in performance levels tend to cause different leader behavior, rather than the reverse (see Exhibit 9-2A). A very persistent finding was that poor subordinate performance made leaders act punitively. Therefore, the traditional causal impact from leader to subordinates (see Exhibit 9-2B) was thought to be weak or nonexistent. It now appears (in accordance with Exhibit 9-2C)

A. Performance Causes Behavior

| Leader behavior | ← | Causal influence | Group performance |

B. Behavior Causes Performance

| Leader behavior | | Causal influence | → | Group performance |

C. Reciprocal Influence

| Leader behavior | ← | Causal influence | → | Group performance |

EXHIBIT 9-2   **Causal Influences in Relationships between Leader Behavior and Group Performance**
In different situations, group performance may influence leader behavior, or the leader may affect group performance, or the influence may flow in both directions.

that the causal relationship is generally two-way. In any given situation, however, it could be primarily like either Exhibit 9-2A or 9-2B (group performance causes leader behavior, or vice versa). Some "leaders" are really passive responders to their subordinates; others exert proactive influence on their subordinates while remaining almost impervious to subordinate behaviors; and in still other cases the influence is reciprocal.

☐ Traits in Leadership

For many years it has been fashionable to conclude that different situations produce their own leaders and that leadership does not exist as a separate trait. This view has some relationship, of course, to the question of whether leadership makes a difference. As evidence has accumulated, however, it has become apparent that, within broad domains, leadership can be associated with a specified set of personality and motivational characteristics. Leaders apparently can adjust their behavior to meet the demands of a situation; thus a certain flexibility of style may be required. But in addition to this capability, certain other inherent traits can play an

important role. The point is that certain key traits of leadership may exist but be manifested differently according to the demands of a particular situation (Kenny & Zaccaro, 1983, p. 683):

> This can be harmonized with a leader-trait perspective by proposing that persons who are consistently cast in the leadership role possess the ability to perceive and predict variations in group situations and pattern their approaches accordingly. Such leaders may be highly competent in reading the needs of their constituencies and altering their behaviors to more effectively respond to these needs.

Clearly the pendulum is swinging back toward a leader-trait emphasis, but one that says certain behaviors do not guarantee leader success and that takes situational factors into account. There is now reason to believe that some of the early conclusions that seemed to support a strict situationist interpretation were erroneously derived (Lord, DeVader, & Alliger, 1986). Even the early studies appear now, with more advanced analyses, to support the role of factors such as intelligence, masculinity–femininity, and dominance in leadership.

BOX **9-1**   RESEARCH IN I /O PSYCHOLOGY

Male and Female Leaders at the U.S. Military Academy

Incoming plebes (freshmen) at the U.S. Military Academy at West Point undertake a six-week basic training in which they are instructed in military protocol, traditions, and skills such as marching, uniform care, and weapon use. This training is given primarily by junior and senior students who serve as squad leaders. There are ten to twelve plebes in each squad.

At the end of their first year, cadets also participate in a field training program. This training is combat-oriented and involves driving tanks, directing artillery fire, engaging in patrol and reconnaissance exercises, setting up communications networks, fabricating bridges, and the like. Here administrative coordination is provided by upperclass cadets who serve as platoon leaders, with forty cadets per platoon (actual training is done by regular army personnel).

Roughly 10 percent of the leaders in these two training programs are female cadets in their third and fourth years. The effectiveness and leadership styles of all leaders—male and female—were described by the plebe participants, using standardized questionnaires.

The questionnaires revealed that whether the leader was male or female mattered very little in these settings. There were few differences between males and females either in their success as leaders or in the nature of their leadership styles. Also, the relationship between leadership style and success was much the same for both groups. This has been the general finding at the Academy in analyses of real operational leadership roles.

SOURCE: Robert W. Rice, Debra Instone, & Jerome Adams, (1984). Leader sex, leader success, and leadership process: Two field studies. *Journal of Applied Psychology, 69,* 15–16, 26–27.

☐ Male and Female Leaders

As increasing numbers of women have moved into management positions, and even more are preparing to do so in the future, a question has arisen as to whether females lead in the same way as males, out of the same traits, and with the same effectiveness. The answer is not at all clear. What does seem to be true is that males and females who become leaders operate in their jobs in much the same manner. Box 9-1, describing male and female leaders at the U.S. Military Academy, provides an example. However, laboratory studies in which college students are randomly assigned to leadership positions, whether or not they aspire to these positions, do not always show similar results for females and males.

☐ Substitutes for Leadership

Leadership substitutes are characteristics—task, organizational, or subordinate—that make leadership both impossible and unnecessary. A closely related concept is that of a leadership neutralizer—something that makes it impossible for leadership to make a difference (Howell, Dorfman, & Kerr, 1986). In practice, substitutes and neutralizers can be difficult to differentiate, and the term **substitutes for leadership** is often used as a general label for both.

The Nature of Leadership Substitutes.   Some leadership substitutes reside in the individual subordinate or follower. The subordinate's knowledge, experience, skill, or professional training may make it unnecessary for a leader

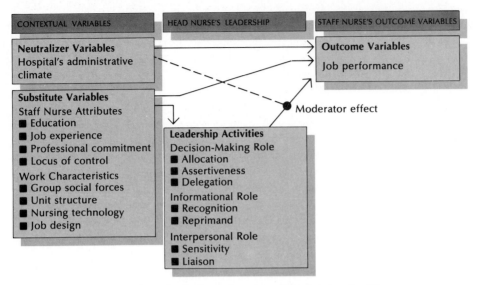

Exhibit 9-3   The Operation of Substitutes for a Head Nurse's Leadership
The hospital's administrative climate partly neutralized the head nurse's performance, while characteristics of the work and attributes of the staff nurses directly affected the work outcome, substituting for the head nurse's leadership.
Source: John E. Sheridan, Donald J. Vredenburgh, & Michael A. Abelson (1984). Contextual model of leadership influence in hospital units. *Academy of Management Journal, 27,* 60.

to lead; the subordinate may also refuse to be led. Similarly, certain types of work are structured with relatively little room for leadership. Activities often carried out by leaders are unnecessary when very routine tasks are machine paced (as on an assembly line), or when tasks are structured so as to provide automatic feedback on output (as with an automatic counter), or when work provides its own rewards (when it is intrinsically satisfying).

In addition, work groups themselves may take over activities normally allocated to supervision. This is particularly apparent in sociotechnical, autonomous, or leaderless work groups (discussed in Chapter 7). Organizational systems and procedures—such as rules, policies, standard operating procedures, and reward systems—may take decisions out of the hands of the leader. Sometimes a strong union has the same effect, if it has a contract that severely constrains man-

agement's rights (Hammer & Turk, 1987). Exhibit 9-3 shows how such factors may neutralize or moderate the impact of a head nurse's leadership on the performance of staff nurses.

Substitutes and Role-Motivation Theories. Leadership substitutes can also be understood in the context of the role-motivation theories considered in Chapter 3. Four such theories were noted there—hierarchic, professional, task, and group (Miner, 1982). If we consider leadership to be the role of a hierarchic manager, then professional, task, and group influences can be interpreted as substitutes for hierarchic influence. Professional motives, commitments, norms, and training make hierarchic supervision largely unnecessary. Similarly, commission salespeople, such as real estate agents, can operate with little or no supervision because the level of their earnings tells them whether or not they are performing adequately; the substitute for leadership is built directly into the task. In group systems, coworkers take over much of the leadership function by training one another, exerting pressure to perform, even allocating compensation; these are autonomous or self-managing groups. This view of the four role-motivation theories assumes that the hierarchic theory is the primary one, which may not always be true. However, it is a useful way of understanding what is meant by a leadership substitute.

■ PARTICIPATIVE LEADERSHIP THEORIES

Participation takes a variety of forms in organizations, ranging from employee ownership to a supervisor's request for the advice of a subordinate (Strauss, 1982). We have touched on many of these forms already—job enrichment, autonomous work groups, quality circles, and so on—and we will consider many more in subsequent chapters. Here, we are concerned with concepts of **participative leadership** in which managers are urged to share decisions and power with other members of their immediate group. This has been the major thrust of participation in the United States. In other parts of the world, particularly Europe, participation also means a legally mandated procedure whereby employees and employee representatives share in the top-level governance of the firm. This latter is called **codetermination.**

□ Theory X and Theory Y

Douglas McGregor formulated Theory X and Theory Y to characterize the two basic sets of assumptions that managers make about their subordinates (McGregor, 1960). According to McGregor, managers who adhere to **Theory X** have the following views:

1. Management is responsible for organizing money, materials, equipment, and people to achieve economic ends.
2. Insofar as people are concerned, this means directing their efforts, motivating them, controlling their actions, and modifying their behavior to fit organizational needs.
3. Without this kind of active intervention, work-group members would be passive and perhaps even resistant to organizational needs. They must therefore be persuaded, rewarded, punished, and controlled to obtain directed action.
4. The average person is indolent, lacks ambition, dislikes responsibility, prefers to be led, is inherently self-centered, resists change, and is gullible.

Theory Y starts out with the same first proposition as Theory X, but otherwise the two views are very different. Theory Y managers assume that:

1. Management is responsible for organizing money, materials, equipment, and people to achieve economic ends.
2. The job of management is to arrange organizational conditions and operations so that people can achieve their own goals best by directing their efforts toward organizational goals.
3. Work-group members are not by nature passive or resistant to organizational needs, although experience in organizations may make them so.
4. The motivation, potential for development, capacity for responsibility, and readiness to support organizational goals are all present in people; management does not put them there. It is management's job to make it possible for work-group members to recognize and develop these characteristics.

Using the Theories. McGregor considers Theory X to be the prevailing theory, but at the same time he views it as inconsistent with Maslow's need-hierarchy concepts (see Chapter 3); he accepts the latter without question. He espouses Theory Y in large part because it fits Maslow's views of the modern work force (see Box 3-1). Managing in the Theory Y mode includes:

1. Decentralization and delegation of decisions
2. Job enlargement
3. Participative and consultative management
4. Performance appraisal via self-imposed objectives and self-evaluation

Theory Y leadership is participative in style and probably creates a more effective organization. "Participative" for McGregor means that the leader is a teacher, professional helper, colleague, and consultant—rarely an authoritarian boss. The leader establishes relationships with other group members much like those of a professional with clients. Team building is a desirable embodiment of Theory Y assumptions.

Miles's Expanded Model. Exhibit 9-4 presents Raymond Miles's expanded concept of McGregor's Theory X–Theory Y formulation, utilizing three theories rather than two. In Miles's scheme, the **human resources model** is roughly equal to Theory Y. The human resources model is the preferred approach in theory, but in practice the other two are more prevalent—especially the human relations model, which to McGregor would represent only pseudo-participative leadership.

Stereotyping and Other Problems. A major problem with any type of leadership theory that uses a Theory X–Theory Y dichotomy is the resort to stereotyping (Miner, 1980, pp. 284–285):

Managers may indeed think in such terms, but there is a real question as to whether they should. In this view both theories are wrong, simply because people come in all varieties of individual differences and thus all stereotypes are wrong. There is ample evidence of the great range of human variation on a host of dimensions. The effective manager will recognize these variations and deal with each individual in terms of the kind of person he or she really is rather than placing all (or most) together in a single category, no matter how that category is defined. To do otherwise is to perceive almost every subordinate incorrectly to some degree, and at least some by a very large degree indeed.

Although this type of approach to participative leadership has not spawned a great deal of research, what has been done provides no real support for the view that Theory Y assumptions yield improved performance and productivity; they may, however, yield improved subordinate satisfaction. One apparent problem is the heavy reliance on need-hierarchy theory, which itself has not held up well under the close scrutiny of research. It is well to know about Theory X and Theory Y, and related propositions, because they are still part of many managers' vocabularies, but in fact the field has moved to more sophisticated views of participative leadership.

☐ The Theory of System 4 and 4T

The System 4 approach to participative leadership, which is the creation of Rensis Likert of the University of Michigan, is based on a large body of research and developing theory (Likert, 1979). Although derived from analyses of work groups and their leaders, some aspects of Likert's theory extend to the organization as a whole.

Systems 1 to 4. **System 4 theory** posits four primary systems of organization, with the participative-group system (system 4) coming

EXHIBIT 9-4   Miles's Expanded View of Theory X and Theory Y

<------------------------------------- *Theory X/Theory Y* ------------------------------------->

Traditional Model	*Human Relations Model*	*Human Resources Model*
Assumptions	**Assumptions**	**Assumptions**
1. Work is inherently distasteful to most people.	1. People want to feel useful and important.	1. Work is not inherently distasteful. People want to contribute to meaningful goals which they have helped establish.
2. What workers do is less important than what they earn for doing it.	2. People desire to belong and to be recognized as individuals.	
3. Few want or can handle work which requires creativity, self-direction, or self-control.	3. These needs are more important than money in motivating people to work.	2. Most people can exercise far more creative, responsible self-direction and self-control than their present jobs demand.
Policies	**Policies**	**Policies**
1. The manager's basic task is to closely supervise and control subordinates.	1. The manager's basic task is to make each worker feel useful and important.	1. The manager's basic task is to make use of "untapped" human resources.
2. The manager must break tasks down into simple, repetitive, easily learned operations.	2. The manager should keep subordinates informed and listen to their objections to his or her plans.	2. The manager must create an environment in which all members may contribute to the limits of their ability.
3. The manager must establish detailed work routines and procedures and enforce these firmly but fairly.	3. The manager should allow subordinates to exercise some self-direction and self-control on routine matters.	3. The manager must encourage full participation on important matters, continually broadening subordinate self-direction and control.
Expectations	**Expectations**	**Expectations**
1. People can tolerate work if the pay is decent and the boss is fair.	1. Sharing information with subordinates and involving them in routine decisions will satisfy their basic needs to belong and to feel important.	1. Expanding subordinate influence, self-direction, and self-control will lead to direct improvements in operating efficiency.
2. If tasks are simple enough and people are closely controlled, they will produce up to standard.	2. Satisfying these needs will improve morale and reduce resistance to formal authority—subordinates will "willingly cooperate."	2. Work satisfaction may improve as a "by-product" of subordinates making full use of their resources.

SOURCE: Raymond E. Miles (1975). *Theories of management: Implications for organizational behavior and development,* p. 35. New York: McGraw-Hill.

EXHIBIT 9-5   **Characteristics of Likert's Systems 1, 2, 3, and 4**

Areas of Differentiation	System 1: Exploitive Authoritative	System 2: Benevolent Authoritative
Motivational forces	Taps fear, need for money, and status. Ignores other motives, which cancel out those tapped. Attitudes are hostile, subservient upward, contemptuous downward. Mistrust prevalent. Little feeling of responsibility except at high levels. Dissatisfaction with job, peers, supervisor, and organization.	Taps need for money, ego motives such as desire for status and for power, sometimes fear. Untapped motives often cancel out those tapped, sometimes reinforce them. Attitudes are sometimes hostile, sometimes favorable toward organization, subservient upward, condescending downward, competitively hostile toward peers. Managers usually feel responsible for attaining goals, but rank and file do not. Dissatisfaction to moderate satisfaction with job, peers, supervisor, and organization.
Interaction-influence process	No cooperative teamwork, little mutual influence. Little upward influence. Only moderate downward influence, usually overestimated.	Very little cooperative teamwork, little upward influence except by informal means. Moderate downward influence.
Goal-setting process	Orders issued. Overt acceptance. Covert resistance.	Orders issued, perhaps with some chance to comment. Overt acceptance, but often covert resistance.
Communication pattern	Little upward communication. Little lateral communication. Some downward communication, viewed with suspicion by subordinates. Much distortion and deception.	Little upward communication. Little lateral communication. Great deal of downward communication, viewed with mixed feelings by subordinates. Some distortion and filtering.
Decision-making process	Decisions made at top, based upon partial and inaccurate information. Contributes little motivational value. Made on one-to-one basis, discouraging teamwork.	Policy decided at top, some implementation decisions made at lower levels, based on moderately accurate and adequate information. Contributes little motivational value. Made largely on one-to-one basis, discouraging teamwork.
Control process	Control at top only. Control data often distorted and falsified. Informal organization exists, which works counter to the formal, reducing real control.	Control largely at top. Control data often incomplete and inaccurate. Informal organization usually exists, working counter to the formal, partially reducing real control.

Areas of Differentiation	System 3: Consultative	System 4: Participative Group
Motivational forces	Taps need for money, ego motives, and other major motives within the individual. Motivational forces usually reinforce each other. Attitudes usually favorable. Most persons feel responsible. Moderately high satisfaction with job, peers, supervisor, and organization.	Taps all major motives except fear, including motivational forces coming from group processes. Motivational forces reinforce one another. Attitudes quite favorable. Trust prevalent. Persons at all levels feel quite responsible. Relatively high satisfaction throughout.
Interaction-influence process	Moderate amount of cooperative teamwork. Moderate upward influence. Moderate to substantial downward influence.	A great deal of cooperative teamwork. Substantial real influence upward, downward, and laterally.
Goal-setting process	Goals are set or orders issued after discussion with subordinates. Usually acceptance both overtly and covertly, but some occasional covert resistance.	Goals established by group participation, except in emergencies. Full goal acceptance, both overtly and covertly.
Communication pattern	Upward and downward communication is usually good. Lateral communication is fair to good. Slight tendency to filter or distort.	Information flows freely and accurately in all directions. Practically no forces to distort or filter.
Decision-making process	Broad policy decided at top, more specific decisions made at lower levels, based upon reasonably accurate and adequate information. Some contribution to motivation. Some group-based decision making.	Decision making done throughout the organization, linked by overlapping groups, and based upon full and accurate information. Made largely on group basis, encouraging teamwork.
Control process	Control primarily at top, but some delegation to lower levels. Informal organization may exist and partially resist formal organization, partially reducing real control.	Widespread real and felt responsibility for control function. Informal and formal organizations are identical, with no reduction in real control.

SOURCE: David G. Bowers (1977). *Systems of organization: Management of the human resource,* pp. 104–105. Ann Arbor: University of Michigan Press.

closest to the ideal. The other three systems come progressively closer to system 4. This means a shift in leader–subordinate relations from absence of mutual trust in system 1 to complete trust in system 4; from lack of subordinate freedom to discuss problems to complete freedom; from rare use of subordinate ideas to constant use; and from no subordinate involvement in decisions to full involvement. The full range of differences among the four systems is depicted in Exhibit 9-5. There is obviously a parallel here to the Theory X–Theory Y distinction, but with more categories and more detail. Systems 1 through 4 actually represent four different leadership styles.

Although they have received relatively little attention, two other systems within System 4 theory, also proposed by Likert, should be noted. In system 0, leadership tends to be highly permissive and laissez-faire, almost nonexistent. Job duties are not well established, so that there is considerable role ambiguity and role conflict. Supervisors may end up doing much of the work of their subordinates, rather than delegating and supervising. Such a system is unlikely to be effective. System 5, in contrast, could be expected to be very effective, even though no such organizations actually exist at present. System 5 organizations will be made up entirely of overlapping groups. The authority of hierarchy will disappear, and authority will accrue entirely from group relationships and linking-pin roles.

Key Propositions. The essence of System 4 theory is the **principle of supportive relationships** and certain related concepts concerning group processes. The idea is that if an organization is to be highly productive (Likert, 1961, pp. 103–105):

> The leadership and other processes of the organization must be such as to ensure a maximum probability that in all interactions and all relationships with the organization each member

will view the experience as supportive and one which builds and maintains a sense of personal worth and importance.

Management will make full use of the potential capacities of its human resources only when each person in an organization is a member of one or more effectively functioning work groups. . . . An organization will function best when its personnel function not as individuals but as members of highly effective work groups with high performance goals. Consequently management should deliberately endeavor to build these effective groups, linking them into an overall organization by means of people who hold overlapping group membership; the superior in one group is a subordinate in the next.

Effective leaders behave so as to foster perceptions of supportiveness and high performance goals; they are thus said to be **employee-centered.** They serve as **linking-pins**—superior to the group below and subordinate to the group above—thus tying together the myriad organizational groups.

Types of Variables. Exhibit 9-6 sets forth the major components of System 4 theory. Note that the causal variables include not only leader behaviors but also some factors which in other contexts are considered leadership substitutes. The time lag between changes in causal variables (a shift to participative leadership, for instance) and end-result changes can easily last for years. Accordingly, the intervening variables take on great importance. Measuring them can yield preliminary information about how well the long-range shift to participative leadership is working.

System 4T. In **System 4T** the T stands for "total"; what is distinctive is the addition of more factors contributing to an effective organization, beyond those which directly reflect participative leadership. These factors are:

1. The levels of performance goals desired by leaders and transmitted to subordinates

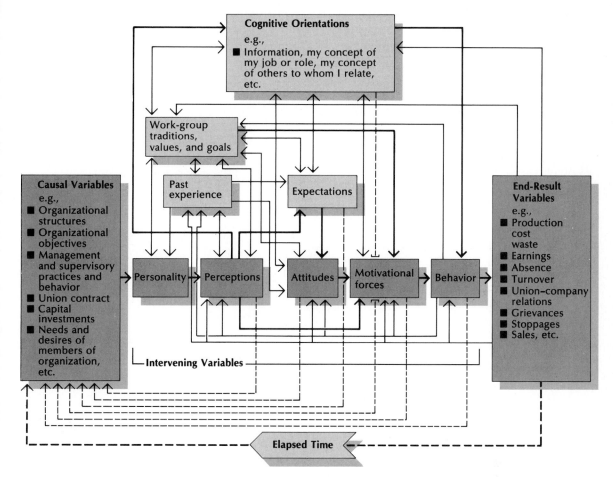

Exhibit 9-6   Pattern of Relationships among Causal, Intervening, and End-Result Variables for All Systems in System 4 Theory
Because a great deal of time can elapse between changes in causal variables and changes in end results, the intervening variables that operate in the meantime are very important as indicators of the success of the shift to participative leadership.
Source: Rensis Likert (1960). *New patterns of management,* p. 201. New York: McGraw-Hill.

2. The leader's levels of knowledge and skill

3. The extent to which the leader provides subordinates with planning resources, equipment, and training

4. The degree to which the organization's structure provides needed differentiation of groups and useful linkages among them

5. The extent to which working relationships within groups are stable

These most recent formulations actually give a substantially reduced role to participative leadership (Likert & Likert, 1976, p. 50):

If an organization, or a department, scores high on the system 1 to 4 scale and low on one or more of the other dimensions, such as technical competence or level of performance goals, the probabilities are great that it will not be highly effective.

BOX 9-2   RESEARCH IN I/O PSYCHOLOGY

System 4 at General Motors' Lakewood Plant

Before the attempt to move it toward System 4, General Motors' Lakewood plant in Atlanta was a disorganized and unproductive disaster area; it was also essentially a System 2, or benevolent authoritative, operation (see Exhibit 9-5). The plan to change began with training of both supervisors and hourly personnel. Among the hourly employees, this training dealt with such subjects as future products, organizational and facility changes, selected cost data, quality, and efficiency. For the supervisors, the training emphasized mutual understanding, trust, teamwork, communication skills, goal setting, and participation in decision making.

Hourly people were provided with regular information on how their labor costs compared to those in other GM plants. Work groups set goals for themselves in the areas of production, scrap, grievances, and the like, and they received direct feedback on the results. Supervisors were provided with a utility trainer to help them train new employees, solve problems of quality, rearrange operations, control salvage, get tools and supplies, check fixtures, and so on; the supervisor could concentrate on people problems. Hourly employees were encouraged to participate in planning model changes. In one instance, employees worked with engineers to redesign the work area where instrument panels were assembled in order to eliminate shadows. In another case, cushion-room employees set production goals that were higher than upper management would have dared to set for them. Within less than a year, work groups had clearly made a substantial shift toward System 4.

As the accompanying graph indicates, however, operating efficiency did not improve immediately; in fact, it dropped off for a time. Only after a lag of some three years did substantial increases in efficiency become apparent.

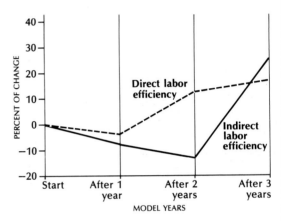

The changes in labor efficiency were paralleled by reductions in grievances, savings on tool breakage, lower scrap costs, and improved work quality. In moving toward the participative mode of System 4, Lakewood became one of General Motors' best-performing assembly plants.

SOURCE: William F. Dowling (1975). At General Motors: System 4 builds performance and profits. *Organizational Dynamics, 3* (3), 26–30.

Box 9-2 indicates how System 4 theory operates in the real world. It is clear that technical training, goal setting, feedback of results, and the like—in addition to participative leadership—were heavily involved in the General Motors program described in the box. Also, from a methodological viewpoint, this is clearly a demonstration, not a controlled study. No work groups that did not experience the changes were available to serve as controls. Thus, the improvements after three years might or might not have resulted from factors having nothing to do with System 4.

Participative Leadership in Perspective. Likert and his coworkers at the University of Michigan carried out many studies that appeared to support System 4 theory. Long-term research was conducted at the Harwood Company, a garment manufacturer headed by a social psychologist sympathetic to Likert's views. There have been many other studies using System 4 theory, at Detroit Edison, General Motors, and elsewhere. According to some arguments, participative leadership is an ethical imperative that should be followed no matter what the performance effects (Sashkin, 1984). Certainly the appeal to humanitarian values is a significant aspect of System 4 theory.

Likert's approach is an all-purpose theory, intended for every situation. As a theory of participative leadership, however, it has not been strongly supported by research. It does not always work, numerous cases disprove it, and even when it does appear to work, problems arise. Even the linking-pin aspect of the theory appears not to work in the manner anticipated (Ono, Tindale, Hulin, & Davis, 1988). Seemingly supportive research is typically difficult to interpret because of factors such as the following:

1. System 4 and especially System 4T include numerous factors such as goal setting, technical knowledge, and performance feedback which are known to affect performance positively. Almost all the research includes factors of this kind in addition to participative leadership. Thus, it is entirely possible that the results caused specifically by a participative leadership style are minimal or nonexistent. Other factors may account for any positive results.
2. Where participative managers evaluate their subordinates more favorably, their view may be distorted by "the use of democratic forms of influence tactics, which provide employees with some freedom to decide for themselves, and encourage the belief among managers that employees are self-motivated. Given average or better levels of performance, this belief leads to favorable evaluations" (Kipnis, Schmidt, Price, and Stitt, 1981, p. 327). In short, some evidence suggests that when studies use performance ratings by supervisors, which many do, the very nature of the participative leadership process can yield supportive results, regardless of actual performance levels.

Taking all factors into account, one must conclude that a participative leadership style alone is not sufficient to improve performance consistently. However, it may prove useful under certain circumstances, and it often does yield greater subordinate satisfaction. A recent review of experience with participative leadership theories, over the almost fifty years of their existence, came to the following conclusion (Locke, Schweiger, & Latham, 1986, p. 71):

> Both scientific literature and management experience have shown that, while participation *may* lead to greater involvement and better decisions, it does not necessarily do so. Participation is useful only under some circumstances.

■ CONTINGENCY THEORY OF LEADERSHIP

Like the participative approaches to leadership, **contingency theory** has had a long history. We will focus on the most recent of its several stages and on the management-training procedures that have emerged from it. The theory, and a great deal of the research related to it, are products of the work of Fred Fiedler of the Universities of Illinois and Washington. It applies to a wide range of work groups and their leaders, but not to groups that exist primarily for training purposes.

☐ The Least Preferred Coworker (LPC) Measure

The **least preferred coworker (LPC)** measure focuses on one leader characteristic; it is at the very core of contingency theory. Under certain circumstances (contingencies), leaders with low LPC scores seem to elicit effective group performance, but under other circumstances leaders with high scores produce the positive outcomes. LPC scores are obtained by asking leaders first to think of all the people with whom they have worked, and then to identify the one individual with whom "you worked least well." The leader then rates this least preferred coworker on a set of polar adjectives. The leader is free to select any least preferred coworker and does not identify who this person is. How the coworker is described says something about the person doing the describing. The scales look as follows.

◀ Quarrelsome   Harmonious ▶

| 1 | 2 | 3 | 4 | 5 | 6 | 7 | 8 |

◀ Untrustworthy   Trustworthy ▶

| 1 | 2 | 3 | 4 | 5 | 6 | 7 | 8 |

The present measure includes eighteen such scales. The person checks off the appropriate scale values, and then these values are totaled. Scores of 73 or above mean a high-LPC leader and scores of 64 or below mean low LPC.

The current interpretation is that high-LPC leaders are relationship-motivated; the fact that they cannot work well with a person does not mean that the two cannot be friends in other respects. Low-LPC leaders are task-motivated: Work is very important to these people, so work-related problems color perceptions of the other person in all areas. How to interpret LPC has been unclear since the very beginning; a number of interpretations have been proposed over the years. Even now there is reason to question the differentiation between relationship leaders and task leaders (Singh, 1983). Yet Fiedler's most recent view is based on that differentiation. He sees high-LPC leaders as exhibiting employee-oriented styles and low-LPC leaders as being much more performance-oriented in leadership style (Fiedler & Chemers, 1974).

The middle range of LPC scores, from 65 to 72, is not easily interpretable, and as a result the theory simply ignores these individuals. However, recent evidence indicates that these scores tend to be obtained by the leaders who actually perform best across a considerable range of situations (Kennedy, 1982). This evidence introduces a major new problem for contingency theory.

☐ Defining the Leadership Situation

We have noted that high LPC appears desirable in some situations and low LPC in others. How are these situations defined?

Leader–Member Relations. In classifying situations, the most important consideration is **leader–member relations.** To measure this factor, a leader is given these kinds of statements and asked to respond using a five-point scale from "strongly agree" to "strongly disagree":

There seems to be a friendly atmosphere among the people I supervise.

My subordinates give me a good deal of help and support in getting the job done.

On the basis of scores obtained from a number of statements like these, leader–member relations are defined as either good or poor.

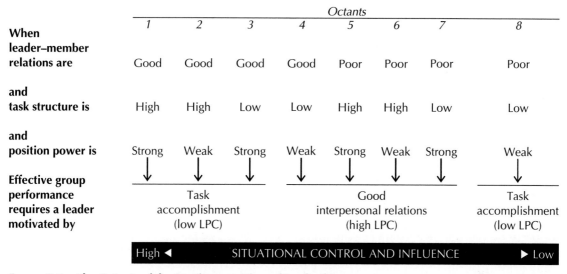

	Octants							
	1	2	3	4	5	6	7	8
When leader–member relations are	Good	Good	Good	Good	Poor	Poor	Poor	Poor
and task structure is	High	High	Low	Low	High	High	Low	Low
and position power is	Strong	Weak	Strong	Weak	Strong	Weak	Strong	Weak
Effective group performance requires a leader motivated by	↓ Task accomplishment (low LPC)			↓ Good interpersonal relations (high LPC)				↓ Task accomplishment (low LPC)

| High ◄ | SITUATIONAL CONTROL AND INFLUENCE | ► Low |

EXHIBIT 9-7   The Octants of the Contingency View of Leadership
When the eight combinations of situational variables (the octants) are arranged in order, from high situational control to low control, it can be seen that high and very low control situations require task-oriented leaders, while moderate control situations benefit from leaders oriented toward interpersonal relations.
SOURCE: Adapted from Fred E. Fiedler & Martin M. Chemers (1974). *Leadership and effective management,* p. 80. Glenview, IL: Scott, Foresman.

Task Structure.   The next most important factor in defining the nature of the situation is the amount of **task structure**—are roles clearly defined, are there specific goals, have formal procedures been established?

Leaders answer questions like the following, using a three-point scale from "usually true" to "seldom true":

Is it obvious when the task is finished and the correct solution has been found?

Is the evaluation of this task generally made on some quantitative basis?

Scores are analyzed to define the work as high or low in task structure.

Position Power.   Least important is the power inherent in the position. Line managers in manufacturing often have strong **position power,** while committee chairpersons have weak power. Typical questions are:

Can the leader directly or by recommendation affect the promotion, demotion, hiring or firing of subordinates? (Scored on a three-point scale from "can act directly" or "can recommend with high effectiveness" to "no.")

Does the leader have the knowledge necessary to assign tasks to subordinates and instruct them in task completion? (Scored on a three-point scale from "yes" to "no.")

Overall Situational Control.   As Exhibit 9-7 indicates, eight possible combinations, called "octants," result when each of these three situational variables is split into two categories at the middle of the range of scores. The ideal situation from the leader's standpoint—the one where the leader has the most control and influence—involves good leader–member relations, high task structure, and strong position power. As departures from this situation increase, the leader's situational control decreases. Reductions in control are greatest when leader–member relations become poor; they are next greatest when task structure becomes low. At the extreme of low situational control, all three aspects are negative and the job of the leader becomes very difficult indeed.

☐ The Octant Model

Exhibit 9-7 combines the various types of leader situations with LPC theory to specify which kind of leader is needed for effective group performance in which circumstances. In octants 1–3, the task-oriented, low-LPC leader achieves the best results because the situations make it relatively easy to exert influence. In the middle range, octants 4–7, control becomes more difficult and the relationship motivation of the high-LPC leader is required to get results. By octant 7, however, this relationship approach may not be working quite as well, and by octant 8 it will not work at all; once again, the most effective leader is the task-motivated, low-LPC individual.

☐ How Well Does Contingency Theory Work?

Contingency theory has been the subject of a great deal of research by Fiedler and others. The evidence from this research indicates that, as Exhibit 9-7 shows, LPC does indeed relate to performance in different ways, depending on the situation. However, the results in all octants do not consistently support the theory. Low LPC appears to be needed for effective group performance in octants 1 and 8, as predicted. Also, high LPC yields the expected results in octants 4 and 5. Support for the theory in the other four octants is very weak (Miner, 1980; Peters, Hartke, & Pohlman, 1985).

There is reason to believe that the LPC orientation of the leader can cause the positive outcomes. However, it is also true that high

levels of group performance can move the situation higher on the scale of situational control. Thus, leader–member relations may improve or position power may be increased, so that, with effective group performance, what was once an octant 6 situation becomes an octant 5 or even an octant 2 situation. This problem of instability in situation categories, coupled with the difficulties in defining LPC, makes the contingency theory of leadership very difficult to apply in practice. However, a major application of the theory has been proposed, and details on how to use it have been spelled out. This application has been developed by Fiedler and is called leader match.

☐ The Leader Match Concept

For some time, contingency theorists have advocated a type of situational engineering in which leaders are placed in situations appropriate to their LPC scores. The theory assumes that LPC itself is a stable characteristic that cannot be easily changed. Thus, people tend to be bound to a particular leadership style or pattern of styles. However, leadership situations can be changed either by reengineering the job itself or by moving a leader to a new position.

The Training. Leader match is a self-taught process utilizing a programmed learning text. The person first completes and scores the LPC scale, then fills out and scores measures of current leader–member relations, of task structure, and of position power. Next, the person is taught how to match LPC level with the leadership situation, and subsequently how to self-engineer that situation to mesh with his or her personality. This involves such approaches as influencing one's superior and even shifting to a new position. Another phase of the process deals with engineering the leadership situations of subordinate managers above the first level of supervision. The training is self-paced, with tests on the mate-

BOX 9-3   RESEARCH IN I/O PSYCHOLOGY

Leader Match at Sears, Roebuck

The Sears, Roebuck Company uses five of its department stores in the Midwest to prepare college graduates for careers at Sears. After nine months of training, the successful graduates are employed as division managers by various other stores throughout the chain. Sears randomly chose two of the five stores for eight hours of leader match training. In the other three stores, the same amount of time was devoted to training discussions. All five stores also provided the usual training, including lectures and on-the-job training.

Seven months after the conclusion of training, all former executive trainees (now division managers) were rated by their new store managers and staffs on eight performance scales developed by the company. All of those who had received leader match training were rated as superior on each of the eight scales.

SOURCE: Fred E. Fiedler & Martin M. Chemers (1984). *Improving leadership effectiveness: The leader match concept,* p. 10. New York: Wiley.

rial learned being incorporated as appropriate. It follows the contingency theory closely and introduces theoretical discussions, problems, questions, and statements of feedback. Sometimes the text is supplemented by lectures, discussions, and films.

Performance Consequences.   Box 9-3 illustrates the use of leader match and the results obtained at Sears, Roebuck. Evaluation of the overall results remains somewhat controversial. (Kabanoff, 1981; Wexley & Latham, 1981). Moreover, the fact that contingency theory itself works only part of the time provides further reason to question an approach such as leader match that assumes the theory always works. The studies of leader match do indicate that a change typically occurs because of training: Some performance improvement is likely. Yet the content of the training, and contingency theory itself, do not appear to be relevant factors in these studies. The change probably occurs because those involved are strongly stimulated to think about the leadership process and the leadership role, not because they learn more about contingency theory and how to use it. On the

evidence, leader match does appear to be a useful approach to improving performance, but not necessarily for the reasons that contingency theorists assume. Evidence to this effect continues to accrue, to the point where it hardly can be doubted. (Chemers & Fiedler, 1986; Jago & Ragan, 1986a, 1986b; Latham, 1988).

☐ Theoretical Extensions to Cognitive Resources

Very recently, Fiedler has proposed an extended theory which certainly does not repudiate the earlier contingency theory, but rather builds upon it and extends it into new domains. Variables such as leader stress, leader intelligence and thus cognitive abilities, member cognitive abilities, and leader experience are introduced. Key consideration is given to the extent to which the leader exhibits directive behavior. This cognitive resource theory is outlined in Exhibit 9-8. The primary assumptions and hypotheses of the theory relate to the decision tree set forth in Exhibit 9-8; these hypotheses continue to be stated in contingent form as in the octant

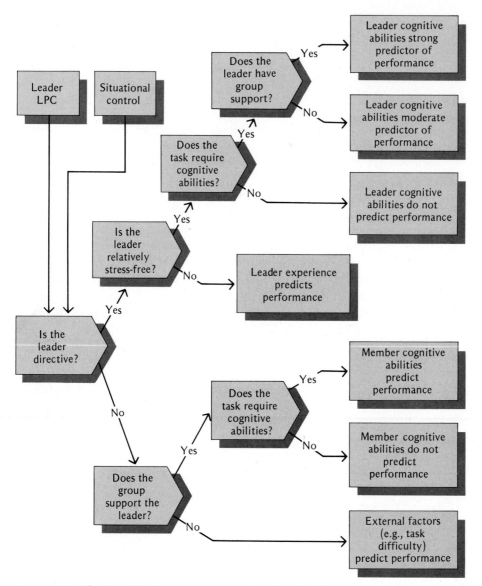

EXHIBIT 9-8   The Cognitive Resources Approach to Leadership
Leader LPC and the amount of situational control interact to determine whether the leader is directive. Then leader stress, task requirements, and the degree of group support serve to determine how well leader and group-member cognitive abilities and leader experience predict group performance.
SOURCE: Fred E. Fiedler & Joseph E. Garcia (1987). *New approaches to effective leadership: Cognitive resources and effective performance,* p. 9. New York: Wiley.

model. They are as follows (Fiedler & Garcia, 1987, p. 8):

Assumption 1. Intelligent and competent leaders make more effective plans, decisions, and action strategies than do leaders with less intelligence or competence.

Assumption 2. Leaders of task groups communicate their plans, decisions, and action strategies primarily in the form of directive behavior.

Hypothesis 1. If the leader is under stress, the leader's intellectual abilities will be diverted from the task, and the leader will focus on problems not directly related or counter to the performance of the group task. Hence, under stress, especially interpersonal stress, measures of leader intelligence and competence will not correlate with group performance.

Hypothesis 2. The intellectual abilities of directive leaders correlate more highly with group performance than do the intellectual abilities of nondirective leaders.

Hypothesis 3. Unless the group complies with the leader's directions, the leader's plans and decisions will not be implemented. Hence the correlation between leader intelligence and performance is higher when the group supports the leader than when the group does not support the leader.

Hypothesis 4. If the leader is nondirective and the group is supportive, the intellectual abilities of group members correlate with performance.

Hypothesis 5. The leader's intellectual abilities will contribute to group performance to the degree to which the task requires these particular abilities (that is, is intellectually demanding).

Hypothesis 6. Under conditions of high stress, especially interpersonal stress, the leader's job-relevant experience (rather than his or her intellectual abilities) will correlate with task performance.

Hypothesis 7. Directive behavior of the leader is in part determined by the contingency model elements, the leader's task motivation or relationship motivation (determined by the least preferred coworker scale), and situational control.

Although Fiedler and his associates have conducted considerable research on facets of the cognitive resources approach, much of this research was carried out before the theory was fully stated. Thus, this research contributed to the development of the theory rather than serving to test it. These ideas are intuitively appealing, and in most cases they square well with past research. However, it is still too early to come to any meaningful conclusions regarding their validity.

■ THEORIES OF CONSIDERATION AND INITIATING STRUCTURE, AND THEIR DERIVATIVES

Parallel with the development of System 4 and 4T theory by Rensis Likert and others and the development of contingency theory by Fred Fiedler has been a third major thrust in the leadership field: the development of the leader-consideration and initiating-structure constructs by Ralph Stogdill, Edwin Fleishman, and others at Ohio State University. These constructs have since been incorporated into several other theories, including the managerial grid and situational-leadership theory in this chapter and path-goal theory as described in Chapter 10.

□ The Consideration and Initiating-Structure Constructs

Initially, the efforts at Ohio State were strongly measurement-oriented. They focused on developing measures of the kinds of leader-

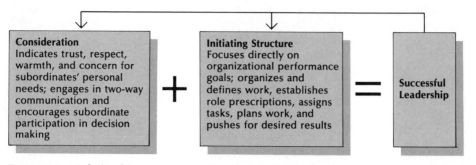

EXHIBIT 9-9   Relationships among Consideration, Initiating Structure, and Successful Leadership
The hi-hi hypothesis claims that successful leadership requires high levels of both consideration and initiating structure.
SOURCE: Based on Ralph M. Stogdill & Alvin E. Coons (1957). *Leader behavior: Its description and measurement,* pp. 153–162. Columbus: Bureau of Business Research, Ohio State University.

ship behaviors that leaders value and the kinds of behaviors their fellow work-group members perceive them as exhibiting. Many questionnaire items were tried out; what ultimately emerged were the two independent dimensions of leadership style noted in Exhibit 9-9: **consideration** and **initiating structure.** Box 9-4 describes an application of the theory at International Harvester. As this account indicates, some of the early thinking, in line with participative-leadership concepts, was that high consideration along with relatively low initiating structure would contribute most to leadership success.

The Hi-Hi Hypothesis.   Gradually, however, the view emerged that what was really most desirable in leaders was a high degree of both consideration and initiating structure. This is the view depicted in Exhibit 9-9; also depicted is a feedback loop, indicating that performance and leader behaviors such as consideration and initiating structure can have reciprocal influence.

However, research such as that noted in Box 9-4 has not always supported this so-called hi-hi hypothesis. Sometimes it is consideration that contributes to success, sometimes initiating structure, and sometimes both

or neither. What does appear to be consistently true, however, is that most people perceiving a highly productive work group *believe* that it must have a very active leader who is getting things done; so they assume that both high consideration and high initiating structure are present (Butterfield & Powell, 1981). The hi-hi hypothesis seems to have great intuitive appeal.

Furthermore, there is some reason to believe that the hi-hi hypothesis contains an element of truth. Among the aspects of consideration noted in Exhibit 9-9 are warmth and friendliness, and among the aspects of initiating structure is establishing role prescriptions. When these two limited aspects of the broader leadership styles are put together, there is a basis for concluding that effective performance will be fostered (Tjosvold, 1984). In contrast, a leader who is stiff and cold and who leaves subordinates alone to figure out what needs to be done tends to produce negative results.

Measurement Considerations.   Another factor to note is that there are different versions of the consideration and initiating-structure measures, and that at least in the case of the latter instrument, the version used makes a

BOX **9-4**   RESEARCH IN I/O PSYCHOLOGY

Consideration and Initiating Structure at International Harvester

For a number of years International Harvester Company conducted a central school for its first-line supervisors, in conjunction with the University of Chicago. The training involved a two-week course with a strong human-relations emphasis. Procedures employed included role-playing, discussions, and lectures as well as textbook readings. The topics covered were labor relations, planning and organization, logical thinking, economics, public speaking, human behavior, and team building. This training typically produced an immediate posttraining increase in consideration and a decrease in initiating structure.

Although these changes were consistent with the objectives of those conducting the training, they did not mesh as well with company practice on the plant floor. In production departments, supervisors high in consideration were rated as less effective by higher management, although they did have less absenteeism. Conversely, high initiating structure elicited very favorable ratings, even though these people had higher absenteeism and more grievances in their work groups.

Attempts to determine which emphasis prevailed—that of the training or that of the shop floor—clearly supported the latter. In one instance, comparisons were made among groups of supervisors who had attended the central school previously, at various times—2 to 10 months before, 11 to 19 months before, and 20 to 39 months before. There was also a control group that had not attended the school. All four groups had essentially the same average age, educational level, years of company seniority, and years in supervision. The trainers at the school hoped that at least the people who had attended the school most recently would show higher consideration and less initiating structure than the control group. This did not turn out to be the case, however. None of the trained groups had higher consideration scores or lower initiating-structure scores than those of the untrained control groups. The changes produced by the human relations training were clearly short-lived; they appeared to fade rapidly as the supervisors returned to their home plant locations.

SOURCE: Edwin A. Fleishman, Edwin F. Harris, & Harold E. Burtt (1955). *Leadership and supervision in industry*. Columbus: Bureau of Educational Research, Ohio State University.

great difference in the results obtained. For instance, when questionnaire items are included that deal with punitive methods, autocratic leadership, and a driving output orientation, leaders described by their subordinates as exhibiting high initiating structure tend to have subordinates who experience low job satisfaction; when these particular items are deleted, the subordinates of high-initiating-structure leaders experience high job satisfaction. There are other results that are equally unexpected.

The problem now appears to be that the original formulations regarding consideration and initiating structure were too comprehensive and global. The different factors do not necessarily go together, and may even cancel each other out. Within consideration, emotional warmth appears to be a plus for a leader, but allowing subordinates to participate in decision making may not be. Within initiating structure, structuring the work so that people know what to do is desirable, but pushing too hard for results, especially in cold and autocratic ways, may not be. The original hi-hi hypothesis now looks like a substantial oversimplification; leadership is much more complex than the hypothesis acknowledges.

Implicit Theories of Leader Behavior. The techniques developed to measure leader behavior ask group members to remember and evaluate what their leader has done over long periods of time. After considerable research, these memory demands now appear to be excessive. They tax human information-processing capabilities beyond their normal limits and thus may cause subordinates to resort to stereotypes and built-in **implicit theories** in rendering their descriptions of leaders. What subordinates use are not unlike the Theory X and Theory Y stereotypes described by McGregor as representing leader perceptions of subordinate behavior. Group members fill in forgotten details with assumptions about how a good leader ought to act. Often what we get is more a function of the thinking process of the person describing the leader than a description of that leader's actual behavior.

The questionnaire approach to studying leadership is thus brought into doubt. At least in part, the consideration and initiating-structure measures

> reflect a highly integrative process that may easily distort behavioral information as it is simplified and assimilated with other information. Such processes . . . complicate the development of behavioral theories of leadership in several ways:
>
> Measures may be far less accurate than researchers think they are.
>
> Important differences among similarly classified leaders are likely to be obscured by such assimilative processes.
>
> When raters know about a leader's performance, their ratings of his or her behavior may be substantially distorted. Hence, correlations between past performance and rated behavior may reflect performance-induced distortions in behavioral ratings as well as real causal effects of past behavior on performance (Lord, 1985).

What the recent data say is that if we truly want to understand leadership, not the peo-

ple describing it, either we should observe and describe specific leader behavior within a very short time perspective or we should use measures that permit some control over implicit theories.

☐ The Managerial Grid®

Another leadership theory which followed ideas about consideration and initiating structure, but which is distinct and independently conceived is the managerial grid (republished as the leadership grid in Blake & McCanse, 1991), originally formulated by Robert Blake and Jane Mouton. This approach had its origins in studies conducted for Exxon in an effort to improve leadership effectiveness within that company.

Basic Concepts. The essence of the grid approach is set forth in Exhibit 9-10. The two major dimensions of the theory are concern for people and concern for production. Concern for people is manifested by an emphasis on getting results through trust and respect, obedience, sympathy, or understanding and support; both the nature and intensity of concern for people are important. Concern for production is manifested by an emphasis on results, the bottom line, performance, profits, or mission; both quantity and quality of production are important. Note that in Exhibit 9-10 (unlike Exhibit 9-9) the two dimensions are not added together, but rather are seen as interdependent, combining to form a particular leadership style.

The five styles noted in Exhibit 9-10 are treated as benchmarks in the theory. Leaders are viewed as capable of freely selecting from among them.

At 9,1, characterized as the "Authority-Compliance" style, managers concentrate on maximizing production through the use of power, authority, and control.

At 1,9, "Country Club Management," managers concentrate on good feelings among

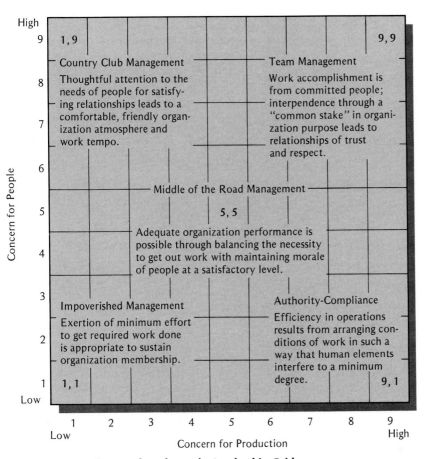

High

9 │ 1,9   9,9

Country Club Management ─── Team Management

8   Thoughtful attention to the   Work accomplishment is
    needs of people for satisfy-   from committed people;
    ing relationships leads to a   interdependence through a
    comfortable, friendly organ-   "common stake" in organi-
7   ization atmosphere and   zation purpose leads to
    work tempo.   relationships of trust
                                     and respect.

6

            ─── Middle of the Road Management ───

5   5,5

            Adequate organization performance is
            possible through balancing the necessity
4   to get out work with maintaining morale
            of people at a satisfactory level.

3

    Impoverished Management   Authority-Compliance

    Exertion of minimum effort   Efficiency in operations
2   to get required work done   results from arranging con-
    is appropriate to sustain   ditions of work in such a
    organization membership.   way that human elements
                                     interfere to a minimum
1   1,1   degree.   9,1

Low

    1   2   3   4   5   6   7   8   9
    Low   High
              Concern for Production

Concern for People

EXHIBIT 9-10   Major Benchmarks on the Leadership Grid
Managers can choose leadership styles from the various combinations of concern
for people and concern for production.
SOURCE: The Leadership Grid® Figure from Leadership Dilemmas-Grid Solutions, by Robert
R. Blake and Anne Adams McCanse, Houston: Gulf Publishing Company, p. 29. Copyright
© 1991, by Scientific Methods, Inc. Reproduced by permission of the owners.

colleagues and subordinates even if production suffers as a result.

At 1,1, "Impoverished Management," managers do the minimum required to remain
employed in fulfilling the leadership role.

At 5,5, "Middle-of-the-Road Management,"
managers concentrate on conforming to the
status quo and maintaining middle-of-the-
road positions.

At 9,9, "Team Management," managers use a
goal-centered approach that seeks results
through broad involvement of group members; participation, commitment, and conflict
resolution are emphasized.

This theory regards 9,9 as the preferred
style, the one managers *should* select regardless of the situation. Recently this grid
approach has been extended to groups using

much the same concepts as employed with individuals (Blake, Mouton, & Allen, 1987).

Evidence. No research has focused directly on the superiority of 9,9 leadership, as measured by managerial grid scales and by organizational indexes of performance effectiveness. However, there is evidence regarding the effectiveness of the 9,9 style as *judged* by groups of managers from various organizational contexts (Blake & Mouton, 1982). In most cases experienced managers clearly favor the 9,9 style. Yet this need not be an indication of the theory's worth. We have noted that people generally associate productive groups and high group output with very active leadership. The 9,9 style, like the hi-hi hypothesis, involves the combining of two types of activity at maximum levels. Thus the judged effectiveness of 9,9 leadership in all likelihood reflects the implicit theories of the judges much more than it proves the universal effectiveness of the approach. What is needed is solid performance-related research of the same kind that raised questions about the consideration and initiating-structure formulations. Such research is not available for the managerial grid itself, although many of the findings related to participative-leadership theories do appear applicable. (They yield little support for the grid perspective.)

☐ Situational-Leadership Theory

Situational-leadership theory is the creation of Paul Hersey and Kenneth Blanchard. Here the key leader behaviors are task behavior and relationship behavior. Task behavior consists of one-way communication, in which leaders explain what subordinates are to do and when, where, and how tasks are to be performed. Relationship behavior involves two-way communication, in which leaders provide emotional support and help (Guest, Hersey, & Blanchard, 1986). This theory's close ties to consideration and initiating-

structure theory are apparent; again we have the two distinct styles.

Which combination of the two leadership styles is appropriate depends on the task-relevant maturity of subordinates—the situation. One aspect of a person's maturity is ability to perform the job as influenced by education and experience. The other aspect is the person's level of motivation as reflected in achievement needs and willingness to accept responsibility. The two aspects combine to produce four levels of maturity, which create situations that call for four combinations of task and relationship behavior on the part of the leader, as diagrammed in Exhibit 9-11.

With low subordinate maturity (M1), leaders should define roles and direct the behavior of group members—the "telling" style (Q1). With low to moderate subordinate maturity (M2), leaders should still provide direction, but they can attempt to persuade subordinates to accept decisions and directions—the "selling" style (Q2). With moderate to high subordinate maturity (M3), initial direction is not needed, but group members should share in decision making to unleash blocked motivation—the "participative" style (Q3). Finally, with high subordinate maturity (M4), leaders should demonstrate their confidence in group members by letting them run the show themselves—the "delegating" style (Q4).

Situational-leadership theory is intuitively appealing and, like the managerial grid, it has been favorably received by practitioners. However, little research has been done on the accuracy of the theory. Also, there are problems with the measurement instrument used with the theory, and with logical inconsistencies and ambiguities in the theory itself. What research evidence there is appears to indicate that the use of a more directive, structuring style with low-maturity employees yields the expected superior performance outcomes (Vecchio, 1987). However, the theory did not work well at higher levels of subordinate

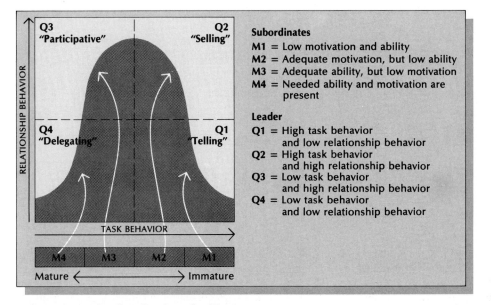

Subordinates
M1 = Low motivation and ability
M2 = Adequate motivation, but low ability
M3 = Adequate ability, but low motivation
M4 = Needed ability and motivation are present

Leader
Q1 = High task behavior and low relationship behavior
Q2 = High task behavior and high relationship behavior
Q3 = Low task behavior and high relationship behavior
Q4 = Low task behavior and low relationship behavior

Exhibit 9-11   The Situational-Leadership Concept
Subordinates may show any one of four different levels of maturity (ability plus motivation), causing a leader to choose the most appropriate leadership style from four possible combinations of task behavior and relationship behavior.
Source: Claude L. Graeff (1983). The situational leadership theory: A critical review. *Academy of Management Review, 8,* 286.

maturity. Claude L. Graeff (1983, p. 290) summarizes as follows:

> The theory makes minor contributions to the leadership literature. Perhaps most important is the focus on the truly situational nature of leadership and the recognition of the need for behavior flexibility on the part of the leader. In addition the recognition of the subordinate as the most important situational determinant of appropriate leader behavior is a perspective that seems justified and highly appropriate.

KEY TERMS

Leadership

Substitutes for leadership

Participative leadership

Codetermination

Theory X

Theory Y

Human resources model

System 4 theory

Principle of supportive relationships

Employee-centered

Linking pins

System 4T

Contingency theory
Least preferred coworker (LPC)
Leader–member relations
Task structure
Position power
Leader match

Consideration
Initiating structure
Implicit theories
Managerial grid
Situational-leadership theory

SUMMARY

Leadership has proved difficult to define, but essentially leaders are agents of change who modify the motivation or competencies of group members. If those in leadership positions behave primarily in response to the behaviors and performance of group members, then leadership does not really occur. Similarly, if other environmental forces such as professional norms, organizational practices, and built-in aspects of the task are the primary factors producing change, then these *substitutes for leadership* prevent leadership from occurring.

Generalized theories of *participative leadership* style are represented by McGregor's *Theory X* and *Theory Y* and by Likert's *System 4* and *System 4T*. Each urges leaders to share decisions and power with group members. Participative leadership of this kind is viewed as an active process of sharing, not a passive, laissez-faire process. Theories of this type have received uneven support from research. When positive results are obtained, they often appear to have been caused by factors other than participative leadership. The McGregor theory and those like it suffer from serious problems of stereotyping. There is also the difficulty, especially evident in research on the Likert theory, that involvement of average or better workers in participative management programs fosters a positive bias in the leader's ratings of subordinate performance.

Fiedler's *contingency theory* of leadership recognizes that participation as an aspect of relationship orientation will work in some situations, but not in others. Whether high or low *LPC* is desirable depends on the state of *leader–member relations, task*

structure, and *position power*. Using these three factors and two LPC levels, eight distinct situations are defined; however, research indicates that the theory's predictions are substantiated in only four of these situations. Furthermore, the *LPC* measure itself, as it is used in the theory, appears to be flawed in several respects. *Leader match* training, which is based on contingency theory, accordingly starts out with several strikes against it. Yet research suggests that leader match training does produce changes in people and that it can improve performance. The changes, however, may really be a consequence of factors not encompassed by contingency theory itself.

The initial formulations regarding *consideration* and *initiating structure*, which were developed at Ohio State University, have been extended to include the *managerial grid* and the *situational-leadership theory*. The original hi-hi hypothesis has not been supported overall, although there are situations in which it does appear to be valid. Research in the area of *consideration* and *initiating-structure* styles is clouded by problems with measurement techniques. In particular, perceptual biases and distortions caused by implicitly assumed leadership theories have plagued the research.

Both the *managerial grid* and the *situational-leadership theory* suffer from a lack of appropriate research tests. Accordingly, they appear more useful as ways of thinking about leadership factors than as clear-cut guides to actual practice. Both theories move only slightly beyond the original Ohio State formulations.

QUESTIONS

1. How have the consideration and initiating-structure constructs been affected by the ways in which they are measured? What problems are thus introduced?

2. What does the term "substitute for leadership" mean? What are some examples of the different types of substitutes?

3. Why is 9,9 management considered superior to 9,1; 1,9; 1,1; and 5,5? Why might experienced managers prefer it?

4. What do the following terms mean?
   (a) End-result variables and intervening variables
   (b) System 4 and System 4T
   (c) Linking pins and managerial hierarchy
   (d) System 0 and System 5

5. What is leader match, and how valid is it?

6. How does the maturity of subordinates operate within situational-leadership theory?

7. What problems are inherent in views such as McGregor's Theory X and Theory Y and Miles's expansion of McGregor's views?

8. Why is it important to consider the question, "Does leadership make a difference?" What is the evidence?

9. How does LPC operate within the contingency theory of leadership, and what problems are introduced as a result?

CASE PROBLEM

WAYNE TINDALL
Sales Manager

The most important thing in Wayne Tindall's early life was basketball. He was a star in high school and went on to a small college that was known outside the state primarily for its ability to develop top-ranking players in this sport. There he did well enough to attract the attention of one of the professional teams, and after graduation he received an offer that was sufficiently attractive to start him on a career in pro basketball. Although never an outstanding player, he managed to hold on for a number of years and in the process made a comfortable living. In fact, he was well into his thirties before he began to think seriously about what life might be like after his playing days were over. He and his wife had operated a fishing camp during the summer months ever since their college days, and both had always assumed, almost without thinking, that this would be their vocation after basketball ceased to provide an income. When, however, it came to the point that he could expect to play for only one or two more seasons, the need for somewhat more realistic planning forced Wayne to the conclusion that the fishing camp was no long-term solution. It had never been a particularly profitable venture, and there was little likelihood that it ever would be.

His thinking had progressed about this far when he got into a conversation with a businessman who was staying at the camp. This man urged him to try selling, pointing out that it required no special previous training. By the time they finished talking, Wayne had agreed to get in touch with the man at the end of the next season and to apply for a job with his company. The man was sure there would be a sales position available, and as it turned out, he was right.

It was company practice to break new people in by having them work under very close supervision at first. Then, as they learned, it was expected that they would require less and less direction until finally they could handle a territory almost entirely on their own. About three years of experience was characteristically required before a person was considered competent enough to work under minimal supervision. Wayne, almost from the beginning, was expected to complete his training in record time—perhaps as little as two years. He was older than many of the others, and his background as an athlete was widely respected in the company. Furthermore, he gave every indication of being a top-notch salesman. He learned quickly, he worked hard, and people liked him. He was one of those individuals who never see anything but the best in others and act accordingly. After a ten-minute conversation, people usually considered him a close and loyal friend. The progress reports sent in by his supervisor contained many glowing statements and emphasized his skill in handling people. There were several notations to the effect that he appeared to have considerable potential for supervisory work.

Largely because of these favorable reports, Wayne had a very brief career as a salesman. Eight months after he started, he was sent back to the home office to work in the advertising department, in part because the company wanted to provide him with a broader background of experience than was possible in sales work alone. The company tried to give people who showed some promise of rising into the ranks of management as much diverse training as possible. But it was also true that the advertising department badly needed another person. Had that not been the case, Wayne would have remained in sales much longer.

To an ex-basketball player who liked to spend his vacations out in the woods hunting and fishing, the world of advertising was less than appealing. Wayne stayed with it only because his job represented a road back to sales work, which he had enjoyed very much during his limited period of exposure. As it turned out, it was a rather long road. He spent over three years in the advertising department, devoting most of the time to seemingly interminable discussions with agency people. When he left, however, it was with a promotion and a solid record of accomplishment behind him. He was generally considered to have an unusually promising future in the company, although he himself had never indicated agreement with this opinion; nor did he appear terribly interested in achieving managerial success.

The new job placed him in charge of marketing a special line of products, which the company sold through a completely separate sales force assigned only to this work. The country as a whole was divided into two segments. Wayne was sales manager for the western area. It was a big jump for a man with no supervisory and very little sales experience. Management recognized this, but there was widespread confidence in the ex-basketball player. He would do all right.

It was impossible to evaluate Wayne's work adequately until about a year had passed. The sales figures were the crucial measure, and it always took a while for the impact of a new manager to show up in the figures. When sufficient time had passed for his leadership to be felt, however, the results, at least as indicated by the sales criterion, were not as good as had been expected. In fact, the western area had slipped behind the eastern in terms of percentage gain for the first time in many years.

The trouble seemed to be partly in Wayne's handling of sales personnel. Whenever one of his subordinates got into any trouble, no matter what the reason, Wayne was there to defend him or her. At times he came to the defense of his people unnecessarily, so eager was he to appear as their representative rather than as their leader. He would on occasion go to extraordinary lengths to do a favor for one of the salespeople or to help out when one was in a jam. As might have been expected under these circumstances, he rarely pushed anyone for more work or offered any criticism. Often, when he knew that something had to be done, he would do it himself rather than ask someone else to do the job. There were innumerable times when he made special trips hundreds of miles out of his way to see complaining customers. Normally the salesperson in the territory would have been notified of the complaint and told to handle it and to see that there were no further problems. Although they liked and respected Wayne for his honesty and sincerity, many of the salespeople, especially the newer ones, obviously had some feeling that they should be receiving more constructive coaching, which might help them to see what mistakes they had made and how they could improve. Their sales manager seemed to find it so hard to talk about the work at all that no one really knew where he stood.

This same reticence was not apparent in Wayne's dealings with people at higher levels. He usually checked on any proposed action that was not strictly routine, to get assurance from his supervisors that it was within company policy. On such occasions he frequently revealed a surprising failure to understand the situation facing him. Many of his questions indicated either that he lacked information regarding sales procedures or that he had not taken the time to think the problem through. In any event, he was obviously not considering many factors that he should have taken into account in making his decisions. For example, there were at least two occasions when he revealed that he did not know policy regarding acceptable charges on an expense account. In another instance he allowed a territory to remain unserviced for an excessive period of time because of a misunderstanding regarding company policy in this respect.

In addition, Wayne had not yet been able to organize his work well enough so that he could plan against future eventualities. He moved from one crisis to another, trying to do a great amount of work normally handled by the salespeople, trying to follow orders and policy to the letter, trying to keep up with his own workload. It was a difficult existence. At times there was some hope that he might break through and get on top of the situation. In recent months, however, this hope had become rather dim. Yet he maintained his air of outward calm, of sincerity and friendliness. He was without question trying to do the best job he could.

When these problems were discussed with him, Wayne exhibited the almost excessive deference that always characterized his relations with his superiors. He agreed entirely with the criticisms. He should set higher standards for his people and follow up to see that his orders were carried out. He should think things through before seeking help at higher levels. He should devote more thought to organizing his own work and let the salespeople do theirs. He should exhibit greater confidence in himself. One could not help feeling, however, that although Wayne agreed with every comment made, there was little likelihood that his behavior would actually change very much. If only he would argue a point, would give some indication that he cared about proving himself right. Without a strong wish to show that he could do the job and win out over adversity, he was not likely to change.

Time proved this prognosis to be largely correct. After three years the western area had definitely established its inferiority to the eastern. Sales were down, and the sales force was disorganized and inadequately trained. Wayne had not changed at all, in spite of repeated efforts on the part of the company to help him. It was clear that his time had run out and something would have to be done.

Questions

1. How would you characterize Wayne Tindall's leadership style? What aspects of his behavior contribute to this characterization?
2. Of all the theories and views treated in this chapter, which ones offer insight into Wayne Tindall's behavior as a manager, and exactly how do they do so?
3. Do you see any factors that contribute to Wayne's performance difficulties other than his leadership style? What are they, and what evidence leads you to your conclusion?
4. What would you do if you were in the position of Wayne's superiors? Why?
5. What would you do in this situation if you were Wayne Tindall?

10

Leadership Frontiers

The theories considered in Chapter 9 portray leadership with a broad brush. Some of those formulations apply the same leadership approaches to all leadership situations. Others divide up leadership according to different types of situations, and then specify appropriate approaches for each situation. What all have in common is that they attempt in one way or another to deal with leadership as a whole and to specify appropriate styles of leadership.

In contrast, the thrust of the more recent approaches considered in this chapter—including Vroom and Yetton's decision tree, the vertical-dyad linkage model, and attribution theory—has been to attempt to accomplish much less than the theories of Chapter 9, but with much more precision. For example, a theory might focus directly on the interaction between a leader and certain individual subordinates (not the group as a whole) and within this context examine the degree of influence exerted by the subordinate on decision making. The following instance described by Andrew Grove, a founder and president of Intel Corporation, is one where subordinate influence of this kind was very high (Grove, 1983, p. 73):

> When Intel was a young company, I realized that even though I was expected to supervise both engineering and manufacturing, I knew very little about the company's first product line, memory devices. I also didn't know much about manufacturing techniques, my background having been entirely in semiconductor research. So two of my associates, both of whom reported to me, agreed to give me private lessons on memory design and manufacturing. These took place by appointment, and involved a teacher/subordinate preparing for each; during the session the pupil/supervisor busily took notes, trying to learn.

Several of the theories that we will be considering deal with exactly this type of situation.

■ CHOICE APPROACHES TO PARTICIPATION

□ Vroom and Yetton's Decision Tree for Leadership

The Vroom and Yetton approach builds upon an approach developed earlier by Tannenbaum and Schmidt (1958), but provides much more specific guidelines for action. As Exhibit 10-1 shows, this approach utilizes various leadership behavior patterns, and the managerial choices among them. Certain of these behaviors are considered appropriate choices (within the feasible set) when a given group of factors is present, while these factors make other behaviors inappropriate. The combined factors present define the specific type of problem. The point is that a manager can do several things depending on what is appropriate in a given situation.

The Decision Process. The list of factors used in deciding which behaviors to employ varies depending on whether the problem is group or individual in nature. In either case, specific priorities are assigned, so that some factors are considered before others. The steps in deciding which behaviors are appropriate are as follows:

Step 1. Is there a quality requirement, so that one solution is likely to be more rational than another?

Step 2. Do I have sufficient information to make a high-quality decision?

Step 3. Is the problem structured?

Step 4. Is acceptance of the decision by subordinates critical to its implementation?

Step 5. If I were to make the decision myself, is it reasonably certain that it would be accepted by my subordinates?

Step 6. Do subordinates share the organizational goals to be attained in solving the problem?

EXHIBIT 10-1   The Vroom and Yetton Decision Methods

Types of Leadership	Managerial Decision-Making Behaviors	Used When Problem Involves	
		Entire Group	A Single Subordinate
Autocratic leadership ↕	The manager solves the problem or makes the decision using information available at the time.	✔	✔
	The manager obtains the necessary information at the subordinate level, then decides the solution independently.	✔	✔
Consultative leadership ↕	The manager shares the problem at the subordinate level, but only on an individual basis; the ideas and suggestions thus obtained may or may not influence the final decision, which is made by the manager.	✔	✔
	The manager shares the problem with the group as a whole; the ideas and suggestions thus obtained may or may not influence the final decision, which is made by the manager.	✔	
Group leadership ↕	The manager shares the problem with a single subordinate and together they arrive at a mutually agreeable solution.		✔
	The manager shares the problem with the group as a whole, and is willing to accept any solution that has the support of the entire group.	✔	
Delegated leadership	The manager delegates the problem to a single subordinate, providing relevant information but giving responsibility for solving the problem to the subordinate.		✔

SOURCE: Adapted from Victor H. Vroom & Philip W. Yetton (1973). *Leadership and decision-making,* pp. 13–14. Pittsburgh: University of Pittsburgh Press.

Step 7. Are the preferred solutions likely to cause conflict among subordinates? (Used only when problem involves the entire group.)

Step 8. Do subordinates have sufficient information to make a high-quality decision?

At each step in the **decision tree,** the manager makes a yes-or-no decision about that question and then goes on to the next question. When a single subordinate has the sole responsibility for making all the decisions about one type of problem, the chain of decisions looks as follows:

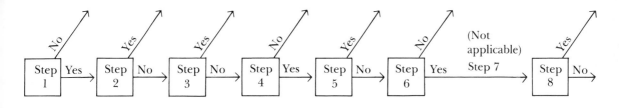

This combination of answers yields a choice of two appropriate behaviors from among those listed in Exhibit 10-1: group leadership, in which the manager shares the decision with a single subordinate rather than the whole group; and delegated leadership, in which the manager assigns the decision to a single subordinate. If time pressures are great, delegation is preferred. Where the pattern of yes-and-no answers is different, the theory might recommend autocratic or consultative leadership behaviors. When all these patterns of yes-and-no answers are put together, a decision tree with eighteen branches emerges. Thus the theory defines eighteen types of problems, each with its own set of appropriate behaviors.

Training in Making the Decisions. The idea of the Vroom and Yetton theory is that managers should ask themselves various questions when they face a problem, and should select an approach to solving the problem based on their answers to those questions. Yet the number of questions and the variations in leadership behavior combine to make this decision-making process quite complex. The conclusions endorsed by the theory are not intuitively obvious. Accordingly, Vroom has introduced a training program to help managers learn to follow more closely the dictates of the theory (Vroom, 1976). TELOS, a version of this training marketed by the Kepner Tregoe organization, is described in Box 10-1. This training is also referred to as managing involvement.

As proposed by Vroom, **TELOS training** explains the theory and gives trainees prac-

tice in using it to describe leader behavior. Managers use standardized cases to indicate what they would do in different situations. Next comes practice in simulated leadership situations, using the different leader behaviors, especially group leadership. A second set of standardized cases is then introduced, and the managers practice applying the theory to these cases. Since the cases are standardized, considerable information is available on how managers respond to them. Information on each manager's leadership approach is fed back to the manager via computer printout, along with information on how other managers act and what the theory prescribes. After this feedback, cases are reanalyzed and small-group discussions ensue. Members may feel considerable group pressure to shift their managerial behavior toward the theoretically prescribed norms. Presumably, this pressure causes the training participants to adopt new leadership patterns.

Revision of the Vroom-Yetton Theory. After more than ten years of application and study, Vroom and Yetton's theory was substantially revised to make it even more specific. The revisions described at that time are as follows (Jago, Ettling, & Vroom, 1985, p. 220):

The original problem attributes now assume 5-point scales to replace their previous Yes–No dichotomies. Furthermore, five attributes are added to the model:

1. Level of subordinate information
2. Time constraints
3. Geographical dispersion of subordinates

BOX **10-1** RESEARCH IN I/O PSYCHOLOGY

Kepner Tregoe's TELOS Program

The Kepner Tregoe organization, based in Princeton, New Jersey, has specialized for many years in providing corporate clients with training in managerial decision making. One of their programs is named TELOS. This is a two to two-and-a-half day program based directly on the Vroom-Yetton theory. The usual procedure is for Kepner Tregoe representatives to train managers from client firms in the methods of conducting TELOS training. These managers then carry out the actual training in their own companies.

The stated purposes of TELOS training are to:

1. Determine when and how to involve subordinates in resolving specific situations
2. Diagnose existing differences between a manager's intuitive approach and the Vroom-Yetton approach, using specific decision-making cases
3. Assist managers in formulating a personally effective leadership-choice model and in applying it to current job situations
4. Work out individual developmental plans in order to build desired changes into a manager's work behavior

Although Kepner Tregoe has conducted studies to determine how TELOS training changes participants and has found substantial change, its major concern from a marketing perspective is whether participants view the training favorably. Few programs of this kind can survive if they consistently elicit negative reactions from participants. When managers in thirteen companies were asked for their post-training reactions, 72 percent found that the program taught them some specific things they would do differently at work, 67 percent thought the program should help them generally in their current job, and 51 percent thought the course would help in their career development. No one reported the course was a waste of time. This is the kind of response to training programs that organizations such as Kepner Tregoe hope to receive.

SOURCE: Blanchard B. Smith (1979). The TELOS program and the Vroom-Yetton model. In James G. Hunt & Lars L. Larson (Eds.), *Crosscurrents in leadership* pp. 39–40. Carbondale, IL: Southern Illinois University Press.

4. Leader motivation to conserve time
5. Leader motivation to develop subordinates

. . . The concept of a feasible set, along with its attendant decision rules and decision tree, disappear from the model and are replaced with a set of seven equations that operate on the scaled problem attributes and a matrix of coefficients.

The five added attributes were in some cases considered in the earlier theory, but now they became specific factors dictating the use of one leadership behavior or another. Accordingly, the theory became more complex. However, it is now possible to specify not a set of feasible behaviors, any one of

which might be chosen, but a specific type of leadership behavior that is preferable. So the theory has been made much more precise. Adjustments continue to be made in the theory, but the major change which occurred with revision has been the introduction of specific equations (Vroom & Jago, 1988).

Is Performance Improved? Of the managerial-choice approaches to participation, only the Vroom and Yetton decision tree has received adequate research attention. Managers clearly do vary their approaches depending on the situation; sometimes the same manager will be autocratic and sometimes highly participative. This variation is not quite as great as the theory would project, but it is present.

In addition, and much more important, the more closely managers follow the recommendations of the theory, the more effective they will be (Field, 1982; Paul & Ebadi, 1989). Decisions that are made within the feasible set tend to be about 25 percent more effective than if they do not follow theoretical prescriptions (Vroom & Jago, 1988). This is not a large difference, but it is sufficiently significant to have practical impact.

Vroom and Yetton proposed their revisions largely in response to this lukewarm support for the decision-tree formulations. Initial results indicate that these revisions do provide greater precision, and managers who adhere more closely to the revised theory are likely to perform better. More work on the revised theory is needed, but if nothing else the managerial-choice approaches to participation clearly indicate that the across-the-board endorsement of participative leadership (inherent in certain theories discussed in Chapter 9) is inadequate.

A final point relates to the question of whether preferred solutions are likely to create conflict among subordinates—step 7 among the steps in deciding which behaviors are appropriate. If conflicts seem likely, the recommended solution is to share the problem with the group and thus defuse the conflict through participation. It turns out that this solution is not always correct. The appropriate approach depends on the manager's conflict-management skills; where these skills are limited, a resort to decision sharing with the group can make things worse, not better (Crouch & Yetton, 1987). Thus managers whose skills in this are limited should not resort to decision sharing.

☐ The Influence–Power Continuum

An approach similar to the managerial-choice theories is the **influence–power continuum,** set forth in Exhibit 10-2. Although its con-

cepts appear very similar to those of Exhibit 10-1, the historical development of views on the influence–power continuum has occurred independent of the approaches considered in the previous section. It is appropriate, therefore, to treat this theory separately. It is the original creation of Frank Heller (1971).

U.S. Research. A basic procedure employed in influence–power studies has been to consider vice presidents or major division heads and a single subordinate of each who was that superior's closest deputy. Fifteen large and successful companies were included in the U.S. research (Heller, 1971). Consultation (levels 3 and 4 in Exhibit 10-2) was the approach used most frequently by the superiors, although senior managers who had a large number of people reporting to them tended to use the time-saving approaches at the extremes (levels 1 and 6) more often. Low-influence and low-power patterns were more prevalent among personnel managers and general managers; also, managers with more experience used the low-influence, decision-sharing approaches more, primarily to improve the technical quality of the decision.

The studies found, as the managerial-choice research had also found, that managers varied their approaches to suit the demands of the situation. When the decision was of great importance to the company, requiring a clear commitment to company goals, the senior managers were particularly likely to use level 5 and 6 approaches. Also, if the senior manager perceived the subordinate as being less knowledgeable and experienced, then the high-influence and high-power patterns prevailed in the behavior of the superior.

Foreign Research. Subsequent research compared the U.S. data with findings from six European countries and Israel. The results on the influence–power continuum itself appear in Exhibit 10-3. Although some countries

Exhibit 10-2   The Influence–Power Continuum

Influence and Power of the Manager	Managerial Decision-Making Behaviors
High ↑	6. The manager makes the decision without discussion or explanation.
	5. The manager makes the decision but subsequently explains it in considerable detail.
	4. The manager makes the decision, but only after consulting subordinates and giving them an opportunity to offer advice.
	3. The manager consults subordinates and takes into consideration the advice received.
	2. The manager makes the decision jointly with subordinates, giving high priority to their views.
↓ **Low**	1. The manager delegates the decision, giving subordinates control over it.

report different influence styles for senior managers and for subordinate managers, especially in the United States, there is still a consistent pattern of differences between countries. Nations such as Sweden and France emphasize participative approaches; Israel does not. Thus national differences are important factors underlying the influence–power continuum.

There is also evidence that various factors have an impact on the use of participative approaches: the particular industry involved, the amount of uncertainty in the company's environment, the pressures present in the job situation, the personal characteristics of the decision maker, and the requirements of the task. Power sharing tends to produce greater skill utilization and more job satisfaction at the subordinate-manager level. Managers who utilize lower levels of influence and power so that greater participation is achieved are more likely to advance rapidly. However, it is not clear whether a participative approach facilitates success or whether success leads to the use of power sharing.

More recently, intensive studies have been carried out in Great Britain, the Netherlands, and Yugoslavia to examine the level of power

sharing at different stages of the decision-making process and the way this level relates to decision effectiveness. It is evident that participation may be desirable or not, depending on what one wishes to achieve and what kind of decision is involved (Drenth & Koopman, 1984; Heller, Drenth, Koopman, & Rus, 1988). With operational decisions involving a short time span and high frequency, and with decisions occurring in work groups low in the organization (much like the autonomous work groups considered in Chapter 7), participation was found to have generally positive consequences.

However, if one moves up the organization to complex decisions at higher levels, particularly strategic decisions, the pattern changes dramatically. The general pattern is for power sharing to yield negative results. Top management consistently views it unfavorably. Subordinate managers and professionals consider participation to be especially ineffective in the final phase of decision making when the actual commitment to action is made. This question of the level of decision making has not been considered previously. It appears that when matters of crucial import to the organization are at issue, top-level

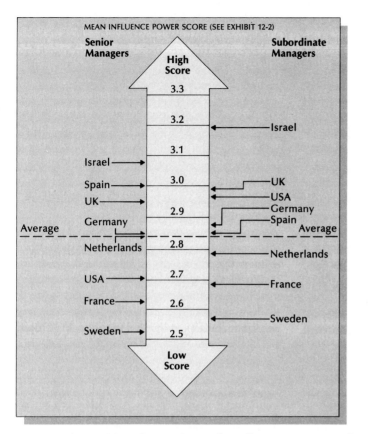

MEAN INFLUENCE POWER SCORE (SEE EXHIBIT 12-2)

EXHIBIT 10-3   Position of Countries on the Influence–Power Continuum
The self-descriptions of senior and subordinate managers from
each country indicate the level of influence that these managers
exert.
SOURCE: Frank A. Heller & Bernhard Wilpert (1981). *Competence and
power in managerial decision-making: A study of senior levels of organization in eight countries,* p. 99. New York: Wiley.

managers, who are paid to know about and
make these decisions, had better make them.

Participation and Delegation. Both the
Vroom and the Heller theories have in common that delegation is the most extreme step
in decision sharing. Recent evidence indicates
that delegation is in fact not just one more
step down on the decision-sharing ladder, but
qualitatively different as well (Leana, 1987). It
is something to which managers resort only
when the decision is of lesser importance,

more capable subordinates are involved, and
the superior is overloaded with work. At least
in some contexts, delegation can lead to
improved performance at the same time that
participative decision sharing makes for less
effective performance. It appears that theorists may have to take a closer look at the participation–delegation distinction in the future.
In the meantime, practitioners should consider carefully before resorting to delegation,
and should not view delegation as simply a
little more decision sharing.

■ THE VERTICAL-DYAD LINKAGE MODEL

Another approach that focuses on variations in leader participation with subordinates, but from a different perspective than the approaches we have been considering, is the vertical-dyad linkage model.

☐ In-group and Out-group Relationships

The essence of the vertical-dyad formulations is that the relationships between leaders and individual subordinates vary considerably and make a great deal of difference in leadership style. Leaders are not just naturally participative or autocratic to varying degrees. They tend to be more one or the other, depending on their relationships with different subordinates. A **vertical dyad** is a pair consisting of a leader and a single subordinate. The relationships within these pairings may be of a predominantly in-group or out-group nature.

> Based on the compatibility of some combination of leader's characteristics, a leader initiates either an in-group or an out-group exchange with a member early in the life of the dyadic relationship. . . . In-group exchanges will involve, first, the interlocking of more responsible tasks accepted by members and higher levels of assistance provided by leaders; and, second, working relationships will be characterized by greater support, sensitivity, and trust than occurs in out-group exchanges. . . . Once these structures emerge, they demonstrate high stability over time (Graen & Cashman, 1975, pp. 154–155).

In an **in-group relationship:**

> The superior can offer the outcomes of job latitude, influence in decision making, open and honest communications, support of the member's actions, and confidence in and consideration for the member, among others. The member can reciprocate with greater than required expenditures of time and energy, the assumption of greater responsibility, and commitment to the success of the entire unit or organization, among others (Dansereau, Graen, & Haga, 1975, p. 50).

When an in-group relationship develops, the behaviors exhibited by the manager and the subordinate depend on the interpersonal exchange, rather than the use of formal authority. There is more informality and more participation, although participation is not all that is involved. The leader extends greater negotiating latitude. The leader loses some control, but at the same time the in-group member cannot assume the equitable rewards that a more formal relationship would ensure; their relationship is more of a private bargain.

In contrast, where there is an **out-group relationship,** formal commitments do exist and the employment contract is in full effect, with its implicit acceptance of legitimate authority in exchange for pay and benefits. The subordinate does not have a close personal relationship with the superior, but enjoys the certainty and protection inherent in formal organizational commitments.

In-group, as opposed to out-group, relationships are expected to produce greater job satisfaction, less turnover, and fewer problems for subordinates. Ratings of subordinate performance by superiors are expected to be higher, at least partly because the in-group relationship may cause the superior to be favorably biased. But for the same reason the correlation of in-group or out-group status with independent performance criteria, such as number of units produced or number of errors, is less certain; the theory appears hopeful that these correlations do exist, but is not sure enough to make a definite assertion.

BOX 10-2 RESEARCH IN I/O PSYCHOLOGY

Effects of Vertical Dyads among Army National Guard Members

The U.S. Army has long been interested in the subject of leadership and has supported considerable research in that area. The Illinois National Guard was particularly interested to learn how vertical-dyad linkage concepts relate to various job attitudes, on the theory that this information might be useful with problems of retention and reenlistment.

In the study, the guardsmen completed measures of consideration and initiating structure to describe both their unit commanders and their first sergeants. They also completed measures of satisfaction with their coworkers, their unit commander, their first sergeant, and their unit as a whole; and they constructed indexes of the role ambiguity and role conflict inherent in their work.

When scored to reflect average group perceptions of the unit commanders and first sergeants,

the consideration and initiating-structure measures did show relationships to the satisfaction and role measures. However, when calculations were based on the consideration and initiating-structure scores provided by *individual* guardsmen, rather than on group average scores, the effects were much more pronounced. The individual scores, which included the effects of in-group and out-group relationships with a unit commander or first sergeant, were much better predictors of how the guardsmen felt about their military situation in general. This of course is exactly what vertical-dyad linkage theory would predict.

SOURCE: Ralph Katerberg & Peter W. Hom (1981). Effects of within-group and between-group variation in leadership. *Journal of Applied Psychology, 66,* 218–223.

☐ Consequences of Vertical-Dyad Relationships

Early studies of vertical-dyad linkages and their consequences were conducted almost entirely in universities. Gradually this arena has been extended, but even now relatively few analyses have been performed within private industry. Nevertheless, the theory has a solid grounding in research and appears to represent a natural extension of previous currents in leadership and organization theory (Graen & Scandura, 1987). The fact of in-group and out-group relationships has been demonstrated with sufficient frequency that there can be little doubt regarding the widespread existence of the basic phenomenom (Crouch & Yetton, 1988; Duchon, Green, & Taber, 1986).

Job Satisfaction and Related Concepts. Vertical-dyad linkage theory says that individual superior–subordinate relationships affect leadership style and have considerable impact on job satisfaction. This view is considered in Box 10-2, which describes a study carried out among Army National Guard members. The findings, as well as data from numerous other sources, indicate that it helps, in predicting outcomes, to consider the nature of relationships between a leader and a single subordinate. Furthermore, research in which some aspect of job satisfaction was the outcome has generally produced evidence that in-group status goes with greater satisfaction. Yet the hypothesis that in-group members are less likely to leave the organization than out-group members has produced mixed results; sometimes that happens, but by no means always.

BOX **10-3** RESEARCH IN I/O PSYCHOLOGY

Individual Effects among IBM Managers

As part of a comprehensive analysis of the roles of its managers, IBM's personnel research unit administered a questionnaire to a large number of first- and second-level managers. The dyads thus formed represented positions in field, plant, laboratory, and headquarters operations, and came from eight divisions of IBM's domestic operation. Although the survey was intended to serve a number of purposes, it was easily used to evaluate vertical-dyad linkage theory as it applied to this company.

Through survey responses it was possible to determine how much of an in-group nature each superior–subordinate manager dyad had. Results showed that in-group status was associated with greater job satisfaction on the part of the subordinate, and with fewer job problems generally. It was also found that in in-group relationships, the

superior tended to rate the subordinate manager as a more effective performer. Furthermore, there was some tendency for both superiors and subordinates in in-group dyads to rate their own performance more favorably than where the relationship was of an out-group nature.

Overall, the correlations involving performance measures were much less strong than those for job satisfaction and job problems. Since the IBM researchers were particularly concerned with predicting managerial performance, this result was not as helpful as they had hoped; they were not yet fully convinced of the value of vertical-dyad linkage theory at IBM.

SOURCE: Joseph G. Rosse & Allen I. Kraut (1983). Reconsidering the vertical dyad linkage model of leadership. *Journal of Occupational Psychology, 56,* 63–71.

Performance. Box 10-3 reports another instance where in-group/out-group status relates to job satisfaction, and also to rated job performance. The performance findings among these IBM managers were not very impressive, but they did exist. Similar results have been obtained in other studies. It is important to note that Box 10-3 describes a business application of the vertical-dyad linkage model. There had been some question as to whether the theory would work as well in this context; it is now apparent that it does.

Another recent application within the business world involved tellers in a medium-sized, multiple-branch bank. In this situation, too, job satisfaction—especially the tellers' satisfaction with a supervisor—was higher for in-group members, and performance ratings were also higher. However, when the quality of the tellers' work was measured, it had no relation to the in-group/out-group

categorization. In-group members did not make significantly fewer errors, nor was the dollar amount of their errors any less (Vecchio & Gobdel, 1984).

In spite of its many positive aspects, vertical-dyad linkage theory has not been very successful in predicting performance and productivity. Except for superiors' ratings of subordinates' performance, it is not even intended for use in such predictions. Accordingly, the theory is less useful than it might be for guiding a manager's behavior. It does, however, provide insights that can be very useful to a subordinate. If the subordinate wishes to establish either an in-group or an out-group relationship, the theory spells out quite clearly what is involved. Furthermore, there is evidence that establishing frequent in-group relationships with superiors, at least in Japan, can contribute to more rapid managerial career progress (Wakabayashi, Graen, Graen, & Graen, 1988).

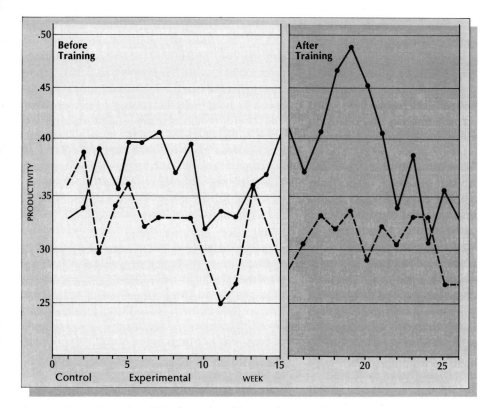

EXHIBIT 10-4   **Quantity of Work Produced by Employees Who Were Out-group Members Originally, before and after Their Managers Received Training in In-group Relationships**
After managers were trained to develop in-group relationships, their subordinates who had been out-group types showed a sharp rise in productivity; but they soon reverted to their original level of productivity.
SOURCE: Terri A. Scandura & George B. Graen (1984). Moderating effects of initial leader–member exchange status on the effects of a leadership intervention. *Journal of Applied Psychology, 69,* 434.

☐ Training toward In-group Relationships

A training program has been developed to guide managers in cultivating in-group relationships with subordinates. This training includes lectures, group discussions, and role modeling, where the managers take turns role-playing superior and subordinate in one-on-one sessions. Discussions cover the nature and use of the vertical-dyad linkage model and exchanges between superior and subordinate; practice is given in using the model. The objective is to encourage managers to hold a series of one-on-one discussions with each of their subordinates, so that they may exchange views and perhaps move their relationship toward an in-group status.

One application of this training, within a government agency, achieved particularly strong results for subordinates who were initially out-group members. Once an in-group relationship was formed, various aspects of job satisfaction improved substantially. Quality of productive output showed little change but quantity improved, as shown in Exhibit 10-4. Several aspects of the results are worth noting. A control group that did not receive the vertical-dyad linkage training showed very little change in productivity over the twenty-six weeks of the study. The experimental group that did receive the training dramatically increased in output during the weeks immediately after training, and this was the period during which most of the discussions between superiors and subordinates, stimulated by the training, occurred. Yet productivity began to decline after only a few weeks, so that before long the experimental group was down with the control group again, at the same level as before training. For some reason the training effects were short-lived; either the former out-group members resumed that status or, more likely, they adjusted to their new status, maintaining it without the need to increase production. It should also be noted that the training had no impact on the productivity of those subordinates who had been in-group members even before the training.

☐ The Idea of Mentoring

Mentoring involves a dyadic relationship where an experienced older individual coaches, guides, and helps a protégé in the same type of work (Hunt & Michael, 1983). Mentors serve as role models, as the younger person learns the ropes and plans an approach to his or her career. The mentor relationship clearly has much in common with the in-group relationship of vertical-dyad linkage theory. Thus it is reasonable to regard what is known about mentoring as relevant to the evaluation of vertical-dyad linkage theory.

Data from a survey conducted by Heidrick and Struggles, a major management-recruiting firm, indicate that senior executives who had mentor relationships earlier in their careers do somewhat better than those who did not (Roche, 1979). Those who had mentors tend to receive higher salaries and bonuses, are likely to stay with a company longer,

and report considerably greater career satisfaction and pleasure in their work. All this sounds very much like the in-group relationship. What is different is that although a mentor frequently is the individual's immediate supervisor, mentors often can be farther up the line—at the department or division level, or even top-level officers of the company. Perhaps vertical-dyad linkage theory, to achieve the best results, should incorporate relationships of this kind. In any event, it appears that, in the world of corporate management, mentor relationships occur more than 60 percent of the time.

Research on mentoring indicates that mentors serve a career function, helping to prepare the protégé for advancement, and also a psychosocial function, serving to enhance the protégé's sense of competence and self-efficacy (Kram, 1985). In general, those who have mentors in an organization perceive themselves as having greater power (Fagenson, 1988). Some organizations have experimented with formally assigning mentors, rather than letting such relationships emerge informally. This approach appears to yield psychosocial benefits, but it accomplishes little insofar as the career function is concerned (Noe, 1988).

■ ATTRIBUTION THEORY AND LEADER PERCEPTIONS OF POOR PERFORMANCE

Attribution theory has been applied widely in a number of problem areas within psychology (Harvey & Weary, 1984; Shaver, 1983). Our concern is with the applications of attribution theory in the area of leadership which is the major place within industrial-organizational psychology where the theory has been utilized. Within leadership, attribution concepts have been used primarily to deal with a rather narrowly focused topic: the poor performance of a subordinate and how superiors perceive it, and thus with processes related to

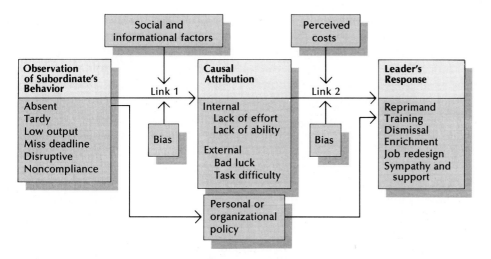

EXHIBIT 10-5   Model of Leader Response to Subordinate's Poor Performance, Involving Causal Attribution
A leader will attribute a subordinate's poor performance to internal or external causes, influenced by rational information or by bias, and will then select a type of behavior in response. The leader's behavior should be appropriate to the causal attribution, but may be affected by policy or bias instead.
SOURCE: Terence R. Mitchell (1982). Attributions and actions: A note of caution. *Journal of Management, 8,* 67.

performance appraisal. In Chapter 9 the role that implicit theories of leader behavior play in influencing subordinates' perception, and misperception, of leaders' behavior was considered. Similar implicit theories may influence leaders' perception of their subordinates. Both these considerations are involved in the application of attribution theory to leadership.

☐ Attribution Theory and the Individual Employee

Exhibit 10-5 outlines the operation of attribution processes in leadership. There are two primary linkages. At link 1 the leader diagnoses the causes of the behavioral problem, determining, first, the factors leading to an **internal attribution** of the subordinate's poor performance, such as a lack of ability or effort, and, second, the factors leading to an **external attribution** of the poor performance,

such as a difficult task or bad luck. This judgment is influenced by various rational factors as well as by errors and biases—often yielding misattributions of causation.

Link 2 involves the choice of a response to the poor performer. If the attribution at link 1 was essentially an internal one, then the response is expected to focus on the subordinate—reprimand or dismissal in the case of a lack of effort, training or transfer in the case of a lack of ability. If the attribution at link 1 was external, then the response is likely to focus on the environment—job enrichment or redesign when a difficult task is the problem, or sympathy and support when bad luck is causing the poor performance.

Behavior-Attribution Links. Leaders are likely to perceive a poor performer's behavior as caused by internal factors; this tendency is sufficiently strong that it can well represent a bias. The subordinate involved, however, is likely to attribute the problem to external factors. These conflicting perceptions and biases can make communication difficult. In any event, when faced with a poorly performing subordinate, leaders tend to bias their judgments toward internal causes, for which the leaders cannot be blamed, and away from external causes, for which they might be blamed (Mitchell, Green, & Wood, 1981). This problem of blame and bias is illustrated in Box 10-4, which describes the failure of Atlantic-Richfield's accounting manager in Venezuela. The retiring boss was partly to blame for the performance problem, but he attributed the problem entirely to the new manager.

When a leader is similar to, likes, and understands the feelings of a poorly performing subordinate, the two are more likely to make similar attributions as to the cause of the problem. But when the two are very distant, as when the leader has great power and the subordinate does not, leader attributions are likely to be different from those of the poorly performing subordinate, focusing heavily on internal causes, especially lack of effort.

Personal characteristics of the subordinate can also influence attributions. Women, minorities, and those in lower-level jobs are thus expected to elicit an unwarranted degree of attributions that emphasize internal causes of failure. Furthermore, if a leader expects a certain person to fail and that person does indeed fail, the cause tends to be seen as internal. However, if success is expected but failure occurs, leaders may well attribute the poor performance to some external cause, such as the unexpected difficulty of the task.

Attribution-Response Links. The potential sources of bias noted for link 1 are matched by others at link 2. If the poorly performing subordinate is considered to be personally responsible for the problem at link 1, then there is greater likelihood of a response at link 2, and that response is disproportionately likely to be punishment, as in the case described in Box 10-4.

If the consequences of the subordinate's poor performance are great—if the work of the whole group is disrupted or a major piece of equipment is broken—a punitive response from the leader can be anticipated, quite possibly an overreaction. In contrast, if the effect is unimportant, the response will probably be disproportionately mild.

Subordinates who can come up with good explanations for their poor performance can neutralize the leader's response. This neutralization may result either from a shift in attributions at link 1, so that the leader blames external forces rather than internal ones, or from a change in response patterns at link 2. Leaders who are unsure of their knowledge or who are susceptible to sincere persuasion are more likely to be influenced in these ways.

Finally, leaders appear to prefer responses that try to change subordinate behavior over those that try to change the environment. Environmental change requires leader action, while subordinate change is viewed as a subordinate responsibility. This tendency to ignore environmental problems can be a source of error.

Limitations on Attributional Processes. Exhibit 10-5 shows a tie between "Observation of Subordinate's Behavior" and "Leader's Response" labeled "Personal or organizational policy." This tie can bypass or substitute for the whole attribution process. When decisions about how to deal with poor performance are handled by policy, attribution theory does not apply. In many cases substitutes for leadership are mobilized so that the poor performance is handled in some way that is outside the leader's control or so that the discretion of the leader is severely limited. Company policy may say that a person cannot be fired for a given offense, overriding the

BOX **10-4**   I/O PSYCHOLOGY IN PRACTICE

Misattribution and the Failure of Atlantic-Richfield's New Accounting Manager in Venezuela

When the long-time incumbent was about to retire, Atlantic-Richfield needed someone to take charge of accounting activities in Venezuela. Most of the work was done in Caracas, but accounting for the drilling and producing operations at Lake Maracaibo was also part of the job. The plan was to hire someone from one of the Big Eight accounting firms and send this person to Venezuela to learn the position from the retiring manager before he actually retired. The person selected was ideally qualified from an accounting standpoint but lacked managerial experience with a large company and knowledge of Spanish; he was simply the most qualified candidate the executive-recruiting firm could come up with at the time.

Once in Caracas, the new manager picked up the accounting part of the work rapidly. However, his progress in learning Spanish was very slow. It also became apparent that the memos and letters he wrote were not communicating effectively, often causing recipients to misinterpret their intent or to go back for further explanations. In meetings and discussions the new manager did not handle himself well; sometimes he got confused about what others were saying, sometimes he had trouble explaining things.

The retiring manager soon became convinced that his replacement really was not trying very hard. His solution was to keep after the new manager and watch his work closely. When errors occurred or problems arose, the new man was told to stop being lazy and slipshod and to concentrate on his work. The retiring manager did not believe in mincing words, so the criticism sometimes got quite personal. The result was that the new manager became harried and depressed, and stopped talking at all except when absolutely necessary. His boss interpreted this as even further evidence of motivational difficulty, and put on even more pressure.

This downward spiral finally produced repercussions at company headquarters in the United States, and the new manager was brought back for "discussions," which included an evaluation by a company psychologist. This indicated that the man was scared to death of his superior in Venezuela and did not want to go back to face him again. Also, test results revealed a rather high level of numerical ability but very low verbal ability, which almost surely was the root cause of the initial problems. At the Big Eight firm the accountant had found ways to compensate for this disability, but the move to Atlantic-Richfield had not given him enough time to develop new tactics before the retiring manager's onslaught began. Yet the latter remained convinced that the new manager was entirely to blame for the communication problem. Given the way things had developed, the best solution seemed to be to go back to the executive-recruiting firm for another candidate. The initial effort clearly had not worked out, and the retiring manager would have to stay on a while to train his replacement.

---

leader's decision to terminate as a result of his or her attribution processes. Similarly, leaders may deliberately bypass the diagnostic and attributional process and apply their own personal policies and rules: "Absenteeism should be punished regardless of the cause," for instance, or "All employees who break equipment should be threatened with reprisal." Such personal policies may embody even more error than attributional approaches, but they are frequently used nonetheless.

☐ Extensions to Group Poor Performance

Attribution theory of leadership mainly concerns the individual leader–subordinate dyad, but it can be extended to the leader–group relationship and to the matter of **group poor performance**. However, this shift in focus introduces several new considerations (Brown, 1984, p. 54):

1. *Serious consequences.* If several employees perform poorly, the results are probably felt by the organization more than if an individual employee performs poorly.
2. *Indication of major problems.* Decline in group performance may indicate major problems in the organization. Isolated instances of individual poor performance, in contrast, are less likely to be evidence of major system deficiencies.
3. *Reflection on the supervisor.* The poor performance of an individual employee will reflect far less on the supervisor than will the poor performance of a group. As a result, a group performance problem can impede the supervisor's ability to make objective diagnoses.

Exhibit 10-6 sets forth certain hypotheses that indicate how causal attributions at link 1 involving poor group and individual performance might operate.

☐ Significance for Improving Performance

Attribution theory of leadership is potentially very important in improving performance and productivity. Ineffective performance at either the individual or the group level is a major threat to organizational effectiveness. Leaders need to diagnose causes of performance failures and select appropriate corrective responses—that is, to engage in effective performance control (Miner, 1985). If attribu-

tion theory can detect any biases existing in this process and can reduce them, then overall organizational effectiveness will improve. Performance control will be functioning more effectively in the organization.

There has been very little evidence about attributions in group poor performance. These ideas make sense, but solid research on the subject is in its infancy. At the individual level, however, much more is known.

Research on Behavior-Attribution Links. Research on the causal attributions that occur at link 1 of Exhibit 10-5 tends to confirm that a potential source of bias does exist here. Unfortunately, the research has been almost entirely of a laboratory nature, and more often than not has failed to involve any actual supervisors and managers.

However, one finding, obtained from practicing managers, deserves attention: Discussions between leader and subordinate subsequent to poor performance tend to make a leader more lenient (Gioia & Sims, 1986). In particular, lack of effort on the subordinate's part is less likely to be perceived as the cause of the problem; instead, external factors such as task difficulty and the supervisor's own behavior are more likely to be emphasized in attributions. Since these discussions of poor performance can be expected to provide a leader with more information, even if self-serving for the subordinate, they probably contribute to more valid assessments of causality. On this evidence, it appears that leader and subordinate alike would benefit from having a face-to-face discussion of the problem before corrective action is undertaken. Managers should set up discussions or counseling sessions of this kind; subordinates should welcome them, and try to initiate them if their superiors do not.

Research on Attribution-Response Links. As Exhibit 10-7 shows, the responses chosen to correct poor performance at link 2 do tend to

EXHIBIT 10-6   Managerial Attributions regarding Poor Group and Individual Performance Hypothesized from Theory at Link 1

Attributions about Poor Group Performance	Attributions about Poor Individual Performance
External attributions are made about the work environment.	Internal attributions are made about the poorly performing subordinate.
Internal attributions are made about employees' poor attitudes. These attitudes are viewed as having developed because of the negative influence of one or more "bad apples" in a cohesive or interdependent group.	External attributions are made about the work environment. Attitude problems are viewed as being more likely as causes of group poor performance and less likely as causes of individual poor performance.
Internal attributions are made by upper-level managers, regardless of whether poor performance is associated with one individual or an entire group. This results from a lack of task experience and direct contact and also from the fact that these upper-level managers take a broader system perspective and compare groups rather than individuals in assessing performance.	
Attributions are made that remove blame from the supervisor. These can include internal attributions about employees and external attributions about system factors that are outside of the supervisor's control.	External attributions are more likely here because individual poor performance is less relevant to the supervisor and, therefore, less likely to elicit a defensive or self-protecting diagnosis.
Internal attributions about group members escalate over time when poor performance persists, particularly when group failure is viewed as a personal failure by the supervisor.	External attributions about system or supervisory factors may be more comfortably made because the accumulated failures of one employee are less likely to be viewed as personal failures for the supervisor.

SOURCE: Adapted from Karen A. Brown (1984). Explaining group poor performance: An attributional analysis. *Academy of Management Review, 9,* 58.

depend on the cause of the problem attributed at link 1. These relationships tend to make considerable logical sense: Training can correct a lack of ability; transfer to a simpler task can solve the problem of a too-difficult task; discipline can deal with a lack of effort; and so on. Leaders do seem to rely on their attributions in selecting responses, as the model shown in Exhibit 10-5 indicates. In general, research supports theoretical expectations regarding what responses will be chosen at link 2.

However, these findings must be taken with a grain of salt. Terence Mitchell (1982, p.

71), the major contributor to theory and research about attribution theory and leadership, offers the following caution:

> The overwhelming conclusion we have drawn is that attributions are only part of the picture. . . . Not only are attributions only one contributor to action—a conclusion with which most people would agree—according to our findings attributions play a minor role. That is, there are many settings where action may be simply determined by personal, social, or organizational policies. Attributions would be completely by-passed. . . . In many settings attributions may be weakly related to action at best.

Exhibit 10-7   Corrective Responses Most Often Recommended for Various Attributed Causes of Poor Performance

Corrective Responses	Attributed Cause of Poor Performance				
	Effort	Ability	Task Difficulty	Working Conditions	Supervision
Additional training	—	Frequently recommended	—	—	Frequently recommended
Transfer to less difficult task	—	Frequently recommended	Frequently recommended	—	—
Disciplinary warning	Frequently recommended	—	—	Rarely recommended	—
Modified work environment	—	—	Frequently recommended	—	—
Encouragement and support from supervisor	—	Rarely recommended	—	—	Frequently recommended
Hiring of people with more ability	Frequently recommended	Frequently recommended	—	—	—

SOURCE: Adapted from James W. Smither, Richard B. Skov, & Seymour Adler (1986). Attributions for the poorly performing blackjack dealer: In the cards or inability? *Personnel Psychology, 39,* 129, 134.

This bypass process is noted in Exhibit 10-5. It clearly does play an important role, yet in organizations, where superiors are attempting to deal with the performance problems of subordinates, it is unfortunate. Attributions surely do have major potential for error and bias. But the solution is not to short-circuit their impact entirely by using standardized responses unrelated to cause. Rather, leaders need to be sensitized to potential sources of bias so that they can avoid error in determining causes of subordinate performance failures and in deciding what to do about them. That is exactly what **managerial role-motivation training** (as discussed in Chapter 3 and described in Box 3-3) attempts to accomplish. The route from observation of behavior to response often circumvents causal attributions, but this approach does not lead to an effective response and ultimately to increased productivity; a route through causal attribution is more likely to do so.

■ PATH-GOAL THEORY

During the early 1970s, when a great deal of the research in motivation focused on expectancy theory, this type of formulation was extended into the leadership area first by Martin Evans and then by Robert House. The result was what came to be called **path-goal theory.** This theory is also closely related to the consideration and initiating-structure views, although it has moved away from them somewhat in recent years.

☐ Evans's Views

The basic concept is that leaders influence subordinates' performance and satisfaction by first influencing their motivation. Specifically, leader behavior, in the form of consideration or initiating structure or both, affects subordinates' perceptions of their own behavior and its consequences: Will a given behavior (a path) help or hinder them in attaining something that they desire (a goal)? Thus, initiating-structure leader behavior which clearly indicates that frequent absences could result in termination is likely to cause a subordinate to view good attendance as a path to the goal of continued employment.

Working from this **path-goal instrumentality** approach, Evans (1979, p. 229) notes three elements that leaders should keep in mind:

1. The subordinate must perceive that it is possible to attain his or her goals. (S)he must envision a situation in which there exists a supply of rewards and punishments. In most organizations, the supervisor is an important source of such a supply. The level of consideration exhibited by the supervisor affects the abundance of this source and the appropriateness of the reward to the individual. The highly considerate supervisor has a large range of rewards, since esteem and social rewards as well as pay, promotion and security rewards are available. The highly considerate supervisor can also ensure that rewards are distributed selectively to subordinates in accordance with their individual desires, while the less considerate superior will not make such sophisticated discriminations.

2. The subordinate must perceive that rewards and punishments derive directly from his or her specific behaviors. It is upon the strength of this perception that leader initiating structure can have its greatest impact. The highly structuring supervisor indicates to subordinates the path (s)he wants followed and links rewards to successfully following this path.

3. Implicit in the above is a third way in which supervisory behavior affects the subordinate's role. The type of path deemed appropriate by the supervisor may be a function of his or her consideration. Presumably all supervisors see "good performance" as an appropriate pursuit, whereas only considerate supervisors view "helping fellow workers" as an equally appropriate activity.

A number of additional considerations have been made part of the theory since these views were first stated, but the emphasis on the coaching-guiding-helping role of the leader has remained. The additional considerations are best treated in terms of House's formulation.

☐ House's Views

House's amplification of path-goal theory involves two basic propositions:

1. Leader behavior is acceptable and satisfying to subordinates to the extent that they see it either as an immediate source of satisfaction or as instrumental to future satisfaction.

2. Leader behavior will be motivational to the extent that:
   a. It makes satisfaction of subordinate needs contingent on effective performance; and
   b. It complements the environment of subordinates by providing the coaching, guidance, support, and rewards which are necessary for effective performance and which may otherwise be lacking in subordinates or in their environment.

In this view the role of the leader is to:

1. Recognize or arouse those subordinate needs that the leader can act to satisfy.
2. Increase personal payoffs to the subordinate for goal achievement.
3. Make the path to these payoffs easier to travel by coaching and direction.

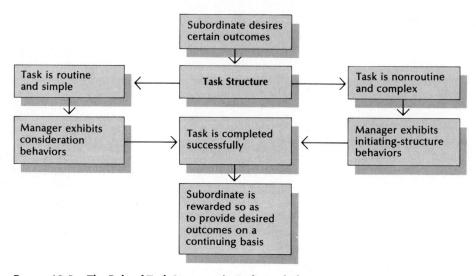

EXHIBIT 10-8   The Role of Task Structure in Path-Goal Theory
When subordinates desire specific outcomes, they will complete their tasks most success-fully if managers use an initiating-structure leadership style with complex tasks and a consideration style with simple tasks.

4. Help subordinates clarify expectancies.

5. Reduce frustrating barriers.

6. Increase opportunities for personal satisfaction contingent on effective performance (House & Baetz, 1979, pp. 385–386).

Initially the leader-behavior factors operating in this process were consideration and initiating structure, but House has now refined these concepts, calling them *supportive leadership* and *instrumental leadership*, respectively, and measuring them with a limited set of items from the original scales. He has also added two more types of leader behavior—*participative* and *achievement-oriented*—which appear to pick up certain other aspects of the consideration and initiating-structure measures, respectively.

Finally, two broad groupings of situational factors are said to operate much like the three situational factors that produce the octants of contingency theory (discussed in Chapter 9). One grouping consists of per-sonality characteristics of subordinates, such as their internal or external locus of control (see Chapter 6), their tendency to be or not to be authoritarian, and their perception of their abilities as high or low. The other grouping consists of environmental aspects such as the formal authority system of the organization, the primary work group, and the nature of the task. Exhibit 10-8 shows how the task factor can operate and explains how the theory generally treats situational factors.

Where the work is of a routine nature and relatively easy to learn, a strong initiating-structure leadership style would constitute overkill; the work itself is sufficiently structured so that any more structuring would do more harm than good. In this case, however, consideration can help reduce any stress in the environment and maintain good leader–member relations. Conversely, where the task is nonrepetitive and complex, so that learning is difficult, consideration must take second place to initiating structure; in order to cope with the difficulty of the work, the individual needs the guidance and direction that the initiating-structure leadership behavior provides.

□ Evidence

Unlike other theories incorporating the consideration and initiating-structure concepts, path-goal theory has been tested. However, the testing has not been comprehensive; research has focused on a limited set of leader behaviors, and has studied them in only one or a few situations. The early work utilized consideration and initiating structure as its leader behaviors. More recently, research has used House's more limited concepts of supportive and instrumental behaviors, but has paid very little attention to other leader behaviors such as the participative and achievement-oriented types. Situational factors involving the task, such as those indicated in Exhibit 10-8, have received by far the most attention.

It is now clear that many of the difficulties inherent in the consideration and initiating-structure measures have carried over into tests of path-goal theory. As a result, support of both Evans's and House's views has been spotty at best. Even the inherently appealing formulations about task structure, set forth in Exhibit 10-8, have occasionally been found not to apply. These inconsistent results have led some to suggest retaining the path-goal logic but applying it using different leader behaviors and situational factors. In fact, movement in that direction has occurred, with encouraging results (Fulk & Wendler, 1982; Keller, 1989; Schriesheim & DeNisi, 1981). It looks now as if starting out with consideration and initiating structure was a mistake—historically understandable, but nevertheless a mistake. Yet the newer approaches have not been studied sufficiently to yield definitive conclusions either.

At present, then, aspects of path-goal theory appear promising, but the approach is not yet ready for meaningful practical application. The theory remains important, however, because it may provide the road to a real understanding of leadership in the future. Its cousin, expectancy theory of motivation, took a long time to demonstrate its true value, but it eventually did so. Path-goal theory may well be following the same route.

■ CHARISMATIC AND TRANSFORMATIONAL LEADERS

A final approach to leadership, one that is truly at the frontier, takes several forms. But all these forms share a concern with the leadership exhibited by a very few, highly visible individuals. Many of the examples cited in this section are world leaders. This is an extremely rarefied view of leadership, as contrasted with the other approaches we have been considering. The numbers involved are small, although the effects produced appear large.

□ Formulations Regarding Charismatic Leadership

Although charismatic leadership is widely discussed, it has been the subject of very little objective study. Recently, however, there has been a major increase in understanding about this topic.

Weber's Charismatic Authority. Writing in Germany in the early 1900s, Max Weber differentiated several types of authority and related organizational forms. In this context he developed the concept of *charismatic authority* (Weber, 1968). Charismatic authority is a personal attribute of the leader; followers believe that charismatic leaders have supernatural, superhuman, or at the very least exceptional powers. These powers must be demonstrated often and must benefit the followers in some way. On occasion, a charismatic community emerges over which the leader exercises arbitrary control; communes and religious communities may be like this. Irrationality and emotional ties between leader and followers are typical. Charismatic leadership is not bound by rules, whether rationally or traditionally derived, so it can be a major force for change.

House's Propositions. To make Weber's formulations more precise, House has produced a series of propositions in a form that would permit them to be subjected to research tests. Although this research has not been conducted, the propositions themselves provide a clearer picture of **charismatic leadership** as exercised by such famous figures as Mahatma Gandhi in India, Winston Churchill in Great Britain, and Martin Luther King, Jr., in the United States. House's (1977) propositions are as follows:

1. Characteristics that differentiate leaders who have charismatic effects on subordinates from leaders who do not are dominance, self-confidence, the need to exert influence, and a strong conviction of the moral righteousness of their beliefs.
2. The more favorable the perceptions of the leader (as attractive, supportive, successful, competent, etc.) by followers, the more followers will model in themselves
   - The values of the leader,
   - The expectations of the leader regarding relationships between effective performance and desired outcomes,
   - The emotional responses of the leader to work-related stimuli, and
   - The attitudes of the leader toward work and toward the organization.
3. Leaders who have charismatic effects are more likely to engage in behaviors designed to create the impression of competence and success than leaders who do not have such effects.
4. Leaders who do have charismatic effects are more likely to state ideological goals than leaders who do not have such effects.
5. Leaders who communicate both high expectations of and confidence in followers are more likely to have followers who accept the goals of the leader, who believe that they can contribute to goal accomplishment, and who strive to meet specific as well as challenging performance standards.
6. Leaders who have charismatic effects are more likely to engage in behaviors that arouse motives relevant to the accomplishment of the mission in followers than are leaders who do not have charismatic effects.
7. Leaders are more likely to have charismatic effects in situations that are stressful to followers.
8. For leaders to have charismatic effects, followers must find appealing the ideologies and values that determine their own roles.

These propositions begin to reveal the substance of the relatively nebulous concept of charismatic leadership. It is important to recognize, however, that both Weber's and House's views derive from analyses of political and religious leaders much more than from leaders in the business world.

Bass's Extensions. Bernard Bass added propositions to House's list in order to capture more of the luster and excitement of charismatic leadership. Bass also noted as examples people from business, such as Lee Iacocca at Chrysler and Charles Revson at Revlon, in addition to numerous political leaders. Some of his propositions are as follows (Bass, 1985, pp. 56–57):

1. The charismatic leader fosters attitude and behavior change in followers by arousing emotional responses toward the leader and also a sense of excitement and adventure which may produce restricted judgment and reduce inhibitions.

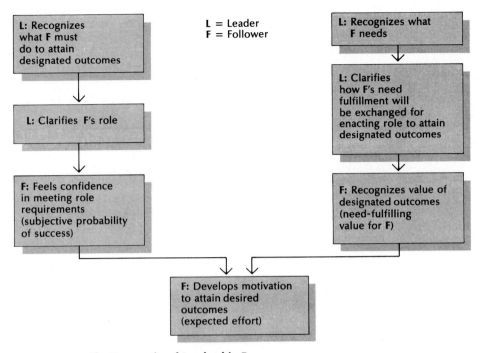

L = Leader
F = Follower

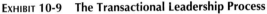

EXHIBIT 10-9   The Transactional Leadership Process
This type of leadership involves recognizing what followers (F) want from their work and
then the leader (L) giving it if performance warrants.
SOURCE: Bernard M. Bass (1985). *Leadership and performance beyond expectations,* p. 12. New York:
Free Press.

2. The larger-than-life status of charismatic leaders makes them useful targets of their followers' projections and provides a catalyst for the emergence of various types of emotional immaturity.

3. Shared norms and group fantasies among followers facilitate the emergence of charismatic leaders and their success.

4. Charismatic leaders tend to influence others and justify their position by displaying superior debating skills, technical expertise, and ability to appropriately muster persuasive appeals.

5. The very behaviors and qualities that transport supporters into extremes of love, veneration, and admiration of the charismatic personality, send opponents into extremes of hatred, animosity, and detestation.

☐ Transactional and Transformational Leaders

Bass goes on to make a distinction between two types of leaders—transactional and transformational—in which charismatic leadership constitutes just one component of the transformational form.

The Transactional Alternative. According to Bass, most leadership is transactional. **Transactional leaders** recognize what followers want to get from their work and try to see that they get what they want if their performance warrants it. They exchange rewards and promises of reward for followers' efforts. They are responsive to the immediate self-interests of followers, if followers can fulfill these by getting the work done. Exhibit 10-9

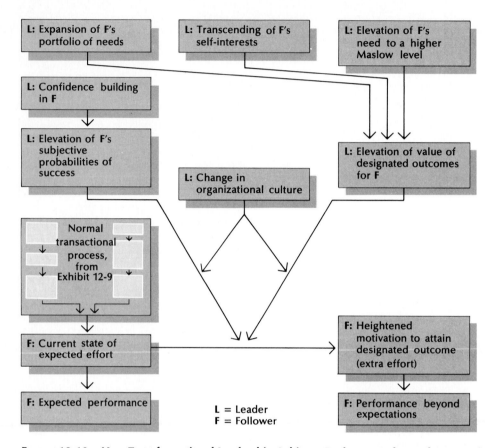

EXHIBIT 10-10   How Transformational Leadership Achieves Performance beyond Expectations
The usual transactional process results in ordinary levels of performance, while the behaviors involved in transformational leadership modify followers' motivation in various ways so as to produce extraordinary levels of performance.
SOURCE: Bernard M. Bass (1985). *Leadership and performance beyond expectations,* p. 23. New York: Free Press.

describes the process by which transactional leaders mobilize followers' efforts. The process follows path-goal theory quite closely.

Transformational Leadership and Performance beyond Expectations.   In a sense, Bass introduces the concept of transactional leadership to provide a baseline against which to gauge the transformational form. His primary interest is clearly in the latter. Exhibit 10-10 shows how transformational leadership works. The exhibit incorporates the transactional model

of Exhibit 10-9 in order to contrast the two forms and the performance that results from each.

Transformational leaders motivate their followers to do more than they originally expected to do. They accomplish this in three ways:

1. By raising followers' levels of consciousness about the importance and value of designated outcomes and about ways of reaching them

BOX 10-5   I/O PSYCHOLOGY IN PRACTICE

Transformational Leadership in Historical Perspective: Lorenz Iverson at Mesta Machine Company

Lorenz Iverson was a transformational leader who consistently exhibited charisma, individualized consideration, and intellectual stimulation.

Starting in 1902, Iverson rose through the staff ranks of the Mesta Machine Company to become its president in 1930. He regularly demonstrated inspirational leadership. He would bellow from a platform on the shop floor, "We got this job because you're the best mechanics in the world." The charismatic effect was still remembered in 1984 by a worker who had joined the company in 1933; "I get goose bumps just thinking about it. He really knew how to instill pride. We had then what the Japanese are bragging about now."

Iverson's individual consideration was expressed in many ways. Layoffs were rare. When there were downturns in demand, workers took salary cuts and worked four-day weeks. He practiced "walkaround management" on the shop floor, talking with employees about their work and family problems, not only on the day shift, but also on nights, weekends, and holidays. But he was a perfectionist and needed to be involved in and in control of all details of the business.

His intellectual stimulation gave rise to many patented inventions for the equipment used by Mesta and led to heated arguments with associates on the best ways for tasks to be accomplished.

SOURCE: Bernard M. Bass (1985). *Leadership and performance beyond expectations*, pp. 115–116. New York: Free Press.

2. By getting followers to transcend their own self-interest for the sake of the team, organization, or nation
3. By altering followers' need levels on Maslow's need hierarchy or by expanding their portfolio of needs and wants

About charisma as a component of transformational leadership, Bass (1985, p. 31) has the following to say:

The deep emotional attachment which characterizes the relationship of the charismatic leader to followers may be present when transformational leadership occurs, but we can distinguish a class of charismatics who are not at all transformational in their influence. Celebrities may be identified as charismatic by a large segment of the public. Celebrities are held in awe and reverence by the masses who are devoted to them. People will be emotionally aroused in the presence of celebrities and identify with them in their fantasies, but the celebrities may not be involved at all in any transformation of their public. On the other hand, with charisma, transformational leaders can play the role of teacher, mentor, coach, reformer, or revolutionary. Charisma is a necessary ingredient of transformational leadership, but by itself it is not sufficient to account for the transformational process.

Exhibiting transformational leadership, Alfred Sloan reformed General Motors into divisional profit centers. Henry Ford revolutionized the Ford Motor Company, and much of U.S. industry as well, by offering then-generous wages of $5 a day and by introducing the assembly line for production of automobiles. William Paley of CBS and Steven Jobs of Apple Computer were transformational leaders, shaping company policies, norms, and the values that dominated company cultures, often as a reflection of their own personalities. Box 10-5 describes how Lorenz Iverson manifested aspects of transformational leadership

BOX **10-6** I/O PSYCHOLOGY IN PRACTICE

Transformational Leadership Today: Lee Iacocca at Chrysler Corporation

One of the most dramatic recent examples of transformational leadership and organizational revitalization is the leadership of Lee Iacocca, the chairman of Chrysler Corporation. In the early 1980s he provided the leadership that pulled the company back from the brink of bankruptcy and brought it to profitability. He created a vision of success and mobilized large factions of key employees to make that vision a reality, while simultaneously reducing the work force by 60,000 employees. As a result of Iacocca's leadership, by 1984 Chrysler had earned record profits, had attained high levels of employee morale, and had helped employees find meaning in their work.

Until Lee Iacocca took over at Chrysler, the company's basic internal political structure had been unchanged for decades. It was clear who reaped what benefits from the organization, how the pie was to be divided, and who could exercise what power. Nonetheless, Iacocca knew that he needed to alter these political traditions, starting with a new definition of Chrysler's link to external stockholders. Therefore, the federal government was given a great deal of control over Chrysler in return for guaranteeing the huge loan

that staved off bankruptcy. Modification of the political system required other adjustments, such as "trimming fat" in the management ranks, limiting financial rewards for all employees, and arranging major concessions from the union.

Equally dramatic was the change in the organization's cultural system. First, the company had to deal with the stigma of needing a federal bailout. Thus Iacocca had to change the company's cultural values from a loser's mentality to a winner's. He realized that employees were not going to feel like winners unless their cultural norms could inspire them to be more efficient and innovative than their competitors. The molding and shaping of the new culture was clearly and visibly led by Iacocca, who signaled change not only through internal communications but also by appearing in Chrysler's print ads and television commercials. The new internal culture quickly transformed Chrysler's work force into a lean and hungry team looking for victory.

SOURCE: Noel M. Tichy & David O. Ulrich (1984). The leadership challenge—A call for the transformational leader. *Sloan Management Review, 26* (1), 59–60.

---

at Mesta Machine. Box 10-6 tells the story of Lee Iacocca's transformation of Chrysler Corporation. Other business leaders said to exhibit transformational characteristics are Michael Blumenthal at Burroughs Corporation, J. Jeffrey Campbell at Burger King, and Mary Ann Lawlor at Drake Business Schools (Tichy & Devanna, 1986). Clearly, transformational leadership can be found in a variety of settings.

Research Evaluations. Almost all the research on transformational leadership theory available to date has been conducted by

Bass and his coworkers (Avolio & Bass, 1988; Hater & Bass, 1988; Waldman, Bass, & Einstein, 1987). The results given in Box 10-7, which describes a study using a management simulation, are typical. As in other studies, the data give support to the idea that transformational leadership is effective, but the findings are not as compelling as the construct itself appears to suggest. Perhaps the problem is that transformational leadership as exhibited by MBA students and most practicing managers is quantitatively less and qualitatively different from the transformational leadership of, say, a Lorenz Iverson or

BOX 10-7 RESEARCH IN I/O PSYCHOLOGY

Management Game Performance under Transactional and Transformational Leaders

Twenty-seven teams of MBA students participated in a management game simulation over the course of a semester. The teams comprised from seven to nine members and each selected its own president. The president worked with team members in deciding who would take responsibility for various functions. How each team operated depended in large part on how the president made decisions and coordinated team efforts.

The game was a complex simulation of a medium-sized, publicly held manufacturing firm. Throughout the semester, teams made decisions concerning all aspects of company operations, including new market ventures, capital improvement projects, and securing loans: The simulation covered eight quarters of operation.

Team performance was evaluated in terms of market share, debt-to-equity ratio, return on assets, earnings per share, and stock price. These measures were averaged over the eight quarters. In the final quarter, team members completed a questionnaire describing their president in terms of the extent to which he or she operated in a transformational, active transactional, or passive

transactional manner. Average scores for these measures were calculated for each team. It was anticipated that the transformational leadership measure would show the closest relationship with team performance. Differences in intellectual capability were ruled out as a factor in the results by virtue of the fact that the teams did not exhibit meaningful average differences in either Graduate Management Aptitude Test scores or grade-point averages.

As hypothesized, transformational leadership showed frequent and substantial correlations with the various indexes of team performance; to this extent the theory was confirmed. However, the measure of active transactional leadership produced equally impressive relationships. Passive transactional leadership was unrelated to team performance. It was not possible to say from the findings that transformational leadership represented a superior form.

SOURCE: Bruce J. Avolio, David A. Waldman, & Walter O. Einstein (1988). Transformational leadership in a management game simulation: Impacting the bottom line. *Group and Organization Studies, 13,* 59–80.

---

a Lee Iacocca. Perhaps also the effects of transformational leadership have been exaggerated.

☐ The Romance of Leadership

The concepts of charismatic and transformational leadership are intuitively compelling. Yet there is a body of research rooted in attribution theory which says that we often attribute more to leadership-as-cause than is warranted: that when organizations are transformed, we tend to search for and find a great leader to explain the transformation (Meindl, Ehrlich, & Dukerich, 1985). We emphasize

leadership more when productivity changes are occurring, even though the changes may stem from other causes. There is a disproportionate tendency to explain extreme and unexpected performance changes as leadership effects.

None of this means that leadership does not make a difference, but, as the discussion in Chapter 9 suggests, it seldom makes as much of a difference as we think it does. This error appears to be particularly likely in the emotion-laden situations that characterize charismatic and transformational leadership. This is exactly the kind of context in which perceptual distortions are most likely to occur. Accordingly, there is good reason to believe that much of what is attributed to great leaders in these instances is not their doing at all. In **romanticizing leadership,** we see more than is really there, whether we are followers or mere observers. Charismatic and transformational views of leadership will need to take this phenomenon into account before they can be considered major contributions to knowledge in the leadership field. This conclusion is somewhat disillusioning, as the romantic view is more appealing. Unfortunately, science and truth do not always yield the results we prefer.

KEY TERMS

Decision tree

TELOS training

Influence–power continuum

Vertical dyad

In-group relationship

Out-group relationship

Mentoring

Attribution theory

Internal attribution

External attribution

Group poor performance

Managerial role-motivation training

Path-goal theory

Path-goal instrumentality

Charismatic leadership

Transactional leaders

Transformational leaders

Romanticizing leadership (romantic bias)

SUMMARY

A number of focused approaches have been developed that may be thought of as the modern generation of leadership theories. In general, these theories have fared somewhat better at the hands of research than earlier, more comprehensive theories of leadership.

A particular concern of these theories has remained participative leadership. This is characteristic of the various managerial-choice approaches and in large part is true of the *vertical-dyad* linkage model. The managerial-choice theories describe a series of possible leadership styles, ranging from complete control of the decision process by the superior to almost complete control by subordinates. The various managerial-choice approaches, moving from the original Tannenbaum and Schmidt views to the Vroom and Yetton decision tree and its most recent revisions, provide increasing degrees of precision in stating when each style should be used. It is apparent that the managerial-choice approach is far superior to the unilateral endorsement of participative management inherent in the Theory X/Theory Y formulation and in Systems 4 and 4T. Furthermore, research on the *influence–power continuum* indicates that major cultural differences exist in the use of participation and that higher-level, strategic decisions are best made with little power sharing.

Vertical-dyad linkage theory is concerned with manager–subordinate dyads. *In-group* dyad rela-

tionships, which are more participative in nature, are viewed as having more positive consequences than *out-group relationships.* In general, the research supports this conclusion, although effects involving the quantity and quality of output are not frequent. Training to foster in-group relationships has been conducted, with some evidence of positive consequences. *Mentoring* has much in common with the in-group dyad, although it may extend across multiple hierarchic levels, not just the manager–subordinate dyad.

Attribution theory of leadership focuses on the causes leaders attach to the poor performance of subordinates and on the responses leaders adopt to deal with performance failures. Attributional biases can be expected in both areas. In large part these biases are predictable, and *role-motivation training* for managers, as well as direct discussions between leader and subordinate, appear to be useful ways to reduce them. Most of the research in this area has dealt with individual performance, but the theory has been extended to *group performance* as well.

Path-goal theory, like expectancy theory of motivation, has been the subject of considerable research; in many respects it has been found wanting. The initial reliance on consideration and initiating-structure constructs and measures appears to have been a mistake. However, some aspects offer promise: the meshing of leader behaviors with subordinates' motivation and the use of situational moderators. Although not yet ready for practical application, path-goal theory may eventually provide answers to the complex riddles of leadership.

Building on Weber's early views, *charismatic-leadership* theory has achieved more precision in recent years. Charismatic leaders elicit highly emotional and often distorted perceptions from their followers. The concept of charisma has also been incorporated in *transformational-leadership* theory. Transformational leaders exert special motivational pressures on followers, thus producing performance beyond what would be expected under the more common conditions of *transactional leadership.* In both charismatic and transformational leadership a *romantic bias* appears to exist, which attributes more to the leader than the leader actually achieves.

QUESTIONS

1. How can attribution theory contribute to more effective performance and greater productivity in a company? What does it tell us about the role of supervisor–subordinate discussions in these outcomes?

2. What is the role of training in managerial-choice approaches to participation? How does the training work?

3. Why are in-group versus out-group distinctions important? What differentiates the two?

4. What is charismatic leadership, and what role does it play in transformational leadership?

5. How does the organizational level at which a decision is made relate to the effective use of participative approaches?

6. What specific biases are likely to appear at the behavior-attribution link? at the attribution-response link? (See Exhibit 10–5.)

7. Why does research on attribution theory and the romance of leadership bring charismatic concepts into question? What issues are involved here?

8. How do path-goal theory and the Vroom and Yetton formulations relate to other theories of organizational behavior?

9. What is the influence–power continuum, and how has it been studied?

10. How does training that involves vertical-dyad linkage relationships operate? Does mentoring produce a similar result?

CASE PROBLEM

PHYLLIS MCCARTHY GLAZE
Factory Inspector

Prior to beginning work at the factory, Phyllis McCarthy's work experience had been limited to a variety of summer jobs. She indicated on her application that, of these jobs, she had particularly enjoyed working as a grocery clerk. She had done reasonably well in high school and had considered going to college. She had taken the state university's admission tests and had done sufficiently well on them to be admitted. However, financial pressures and apparently a certain amount of parental apathy eventually discouraged her. She came to the factory seeking work with the idea that she might save enough money to go to college full-time later on. In the meantime she intended to begin by taking evening courses at a local university. The factory's personnel interviewer had seen a number of similar cases over the years. Many of these persons continued to work at the factory for a long time; their good intentions about college often seemed to fade before such responsibilities as marriage, child rearing, and increasing financial needs.

For four years Phyllis worked at various semi-skilled positions at the factory. Her supervisors generally had a positive view of her. She was considered dependable, accurate, and alert. She made suggestions for improvements and learned new tasks quickly. Typically the supervisors liked her, and she clearly liked them. She did require a little more time than the average employee, but she was pretty, bright, and pleasant to be with. The men all liked her. She had a way of making her male superiors feel that she viewed each one as a font of wisdom. She was always asking questions and talking to people. Even when she did make mistakes, she was so concerned and contrite that her supervisors often found themselves reassuring rather than criticizing her.

Phyllis did not start her college courses right away, as she had planned. In fact, it was almost two years before she finally enrolled, taking one or two evening courses per semester. During her second year of college she married one of her fellow students, Jim Glaze, whom she had known since

he was a senior in high school and she was a freshman.

Not long after her marriage, Phyllis became pregnant and took a maternity leave from work. She was away for a number of months, but finally her mother agreed to take care of the new grandson and it became possible for her to return to the factory. There was no way she could continue her college work, however, so that was delayed indefinitely.

When she came back to work, Phyllis Glaze was assigned to an inspection group under one of the factory's most experienced female supervisors. She had not done inspection work before and was not sure she would like it. However, she indicated that since she had never been an inspector, she didn't feel she could object to the assignment. She assumed that if she didn't like the work after she had tried it for a while, she could transfer to some other position.

It turned out that Phyllis did not like inspection work and, in fact, did not like anything about her new position. This came out quite clearly when she first returned to the personnel department to ask for a lateral transfer. The inspection job required a great deal of concentration, and because of the incentive payment system one did not do very well financially without concentrating for long periods of time. This left very little opportunity to talk with people, so Phyllis told the personnel interviewer that she found the work dull. In addition, she did not like working under the incentive system, she did not feel that being an inspector was what she wanted to do, and she considered her supervisor a tactless and unpleasant person who resembled an automaton more than a human being. She complained that the supervisor would not give her the time she needed for training and would not answer questions about the job. Even though Phyllis was brand new, the supervisor treated her just like the other inspectors, all of whom had years of experience.

At this point in the interview with Phyllis, the personnel representative felt compelled to say that the factory pretty much operated on an unwritten policy against granting lateral transfers at employee request. Granting such requests was often viewed by the supervisor involved as a slap in the face. That not only caused a lot of difficulty, but often the slap was unjustified because the problem was the employee's, not the supervisor's. Phyllis said that it had been her understanding that she could try out the inspection job and could transfer if she didn't like it; otherwise she wouldn't have accepted the position in the first place. The personnel representative pointed out that no one in either the personnel or the inspection department had confirmed Phyllis's assumptions. It was something she had wanted to believe, and so she had believed it without ever obtaining official agreement from the company.

At first Phyllis was aghast. Then she became extremely upset. She felt this was the most unfair thing she had ever heard of. She thought she had been promised the right to transfer to another job at the same pay, but even if she hadn't, the company owed it to a long-term loyal employee to grant such a request. In her opinion this was a horrible injustice; people simply should not be forced to work at a job they hated, with an inhuman supervisor, and among coworkers who had no understanding of their problems. It amounted to involuntary servitude, to slavery. The company had no right to make her work at a job she didn't want. This was a violation of constitutional rights to individual freedom. It was inequitable, unjust, and unfair. The company had no respect for either human dignity or individual freedoms.

This same conversation was repeated with increasing emotional intensity on several occasions over the next six months. Phyllis wanted a transfer out of inspection work; the company had an unwritten policy against granting such requests; Phyllis viewed such a policy as totally unfair and contrary to everything she had been brought up to believe in.

All this interaction with the personnel department had happened without the knowledge of Phyllis's supervisor, but the fact that there was a problem was clearly evident. Phyllis's performance, after the first few weeks, when she was trying her best, had declined steadily. She was constantly seeking attention, demanding the supervisor's time and asking for instructions. She was indifferent and uninterested in the work, and yet at the same time she was very disturbed. The supervisor believed in setting high standards and then leaving people to do their jobs on their own. This had worked out well until now; the other people in the group seemed to prosper under such a regime. For Phyllis, however, it was disastrous.

Phyllis made errors, and in inspection work that was the worst thing that could happen. The supervisor felt that Phyllis had never reached a satisfactory level of performance; she felt that the basic problem was an indifference to inspection work. The supervisor felt it was important to level with subordinates and to confront them with their inadequacies. She told Phyllis that what was needed was to give more of herself to her work and to be less thin-skinned. The result was a continuing decline in effectiveness and an even more disturbed employee. Obviously her approach, which had worked well with others for many years, was not achieving anything with Phyllis. All Phyllis ever said was that the company was being unfair with her and was not doing the right thing. The supervisor never quite understood what this meant, but it was clear that things were getting steadily worse and that something would have to be done.

Questions

1. To what factors did Phyllis attribute her poor performance?
2. To what factors did Phyllis's supervisor attribute Phyllis's poor performance?
3. Exactly how did the supervisor respond to Phyllis's poor performance? What factors influenced the supervisor to respond as she did?
4. What problems in communication do you see here? How did they arise?
5. Ideally, what should the supervisor have done to deal with Phyllis's poor performance? Why? Were any biases present in her actual assessment of the situation?
6. Did Phyllis exhibit any biases in her assessment? What should she have done? Why?

11 Organization Development

Datavision, a rapidly growing computer company that specializes in manufacturing process-control monitoring, had begun to suffer from high turnover, a lack of collaboration between departments, and a decline in its backlog of orders. The president and the vice president for finance became interested in using some type of organization development intervention to solve these problems after they attended a two-week management development program at a local university. Through contacts made at that program, they met and hired an organization development consultant who they thought might be helpful.

The idea was to introduce a team-building effort in three stages:

1. The consultant would interview each of the five top-level managers who reported to the president.

2. An off-site workshop would be held for two days with all members of the top-management team and the consultant present.

3. The consultant would meet with the twenty-five or so managers reporting to the top team, first without and then with the top people present.

The initial interviews identified six problems to be addressed at the workshop.

1. A lack of trust among the top people and throughout the organization

2. Confusion regarding company goals

3. Difficulties regarding decision-making policy and an overabundance of spontaneous decision unmaking

4. A lack of clarity regarding the organization's structure

5. Excessive cronyism involving the president and his friends

6. Conflicting management styles at the top level

The role of the consultant at the workshop was that of an unbiased outsider whose major function was to help those present listen to and talk to one another more effectively.

The discussion of the six problems at the workshop brought out the fact that the president often made and unmade decisions without adequately considering the views of the other people. However, a major focus centered on the inadequacies of the vice president for marketing. His management style was clearly in conflict with that of the others, and much of the distrust related to him. Because the consultant encouraged open discussion, the marketing vice president took quite a verbal beating. Nonetheless, the group was successful in preparing planning strategies of various kinds. Most of the participants viewed the workshop as a success.

This was much less true of the session with lower-level managers at stage 3. There, a great deal of distrust of top management came out. The lower managers were sure top management could not work as a team, and the issue of the vice president for marketing came up again. No one seemed to believe that the organization development effort would really produce any changes. The consultant was unable to dislodge this negative view.

After much soul searching, the president came to the conclusion that team building, and in fact the organization development effort as a whole, was doomed as long as the marketing vice president was part of the firm. Ultimately, he was asked to resign, which he did.

Source: Michael Beer (1980). *Organizational change and development: A systems view,* pp. 286–305 and 342. Santa Monica, Calif.: Goodyear.

The Datavision experience provides an example of the early stages of an organization development intervention. To say that it is typical would be an oversimplification. As we shall see, organization development comes in a wide range of forms (Glassman & Lundberg, 1988). However, the Datavision example does provide a general idea of the kinds of activities in which organization development practitioners engage.

Organization development involves change at the organization level. Changes in individuals and groups typically are part of this process, but the goal is to bring about changes that are widespread, extending beyond the individual group to the organization as a whole, or a major portion of it.

The discussion in this chapter deals entirely with change. In the process we shall look at organization development as it has occurred in a number of companies, including Datavision, Citibank, Herman Miller, and Shell Refining. Changes of this kind are often carried out or assisted by industrial-organizational psychologists, and a major proportion of the research and writing in the field derives from this source. Yet it is important to recognize that organization development is an eclectic field whose practitioners have origins scattered across the social sciences (Massarik, 1990).

■ CONCEPTS AND VALUES

□ What Is Organization Development?

Many changes occur naturally as organizations pass through their life cycles. Generally, these changes are initiated and directed by those who hold power, such as top management in a bureaucratic organization. **Organization development (OD),** however, is a process of data collection, diagnosis, action planning, intervention and change, and evaluation of results applied to a whole organization or a large component of it. Although there has been continuing uncertainty as to what methods and procedures should be included in the concept of organization development, in general its aims are to:

1. Increase the degree of integration or fit among structures, processes, strategies, people, and culture in the organization
2. Develop new and creative organizational solutions
3. Develop the organization's capacity to

renew itself so that it continues to cope effectively with environmental forces

Some organization development efforts encompass only one or two of these aims. While the process is almost always guided by a change agent (an internal specialist or an outside consultant who possesses relevant knowledge and skills), organization development always is collaborative in form, involving organization members at varied levels (Beer, 1980, p. 10).

The following points amplify this definition:

1. In order to bring about self-directed change to which all company members are committed, as many people as possible—not just top management—are expected to collaborate in the change.
2. The assumption is that organizations are complex, interacting systems, so that if a change is made in one component, such as structure, other changes will reverberate through the organization.
3. The organization development process may concentrate on short- or long-range problems, or both. If the aim is to develop the organization's long-range capacity to renew itself, then members must be encouraged—and have the competence—to plan strategies for organizational improvement and change.
4. In comparison with other approaches, such as hierarchically initiated change, organization development places more emphasis on collaborative efforts in data collection, diagnosis, and action.
5. Organization development seeks, and often leads to, new organizational arrangements, power relationships, and structures that break with traditional bureaucratic patterns. Thus some variant of the professional, task, and/or group structures replaces at least part of the preexisting hierarchic structure.

6. Change agents bring both knowledge about organizational structures, processes, and interpersonal dynamics, and skills in working with individuals and groups.

Although organization development has undergone major changes over the years, it continues to focus on bringing into the open concerns, attitudes, and values not normally discussed. Plans of action are then developed to cope with the problems that surface. Efforts are made to bridge the communications gap between those who are powerful and influential and those who are not. In the end, the organization becomes more open and, ideally, more effective.

☐ Organization Development and Quality of Work Life

Social scientists have had difficulty defining the much-discussed concept called **quality of work life (QWL).** As a result, the precise relationship of quality of work life to organization development has been a matter of some debate (Faucheux, Amado, & Laurent, 1982). A widely used definition of quality of work life specifies that (Nadler & Lawler, 1983, p. 26):

> Quality of work life is a way of thinking about people, work, and organizations. Its distinctive elements are (1) a concern about the impact of work on people as well as on organizational effectiveness, and (2) the idea of participation in organizational problem solving and decision making. . . . The focus is not only on how people can do better work, but on how work may cause people to be better.

Certainly, the concern for introducing participation and decision sharing is the same in organization development, as is the emphasis on improving organizational effectiveness. What appears to be new is concern for the individual, which is of greater interest to

quality-of-work-life exponents, who have been known to stress this point with an almost religious zeal. Frequently, however, the organization development approach also underscores the well-being of the individual organization member. Some—though certainly not all—joint union-management cooperative projects have been labeled quality-of-work-life efforts. But the difficulty of defusing longstanding antagonisms between management and union (Mohrman & Lawler, 1984) has made projects of this kind among the least successful of those attempted under either the quality-of-work-life or organization development banner. A major problem has been that union leaders often view these projects as techniques for reducing union power. These fears now appear to have been unjustified. There is recent evidence that the risk to a union undertaking a quality-of-work-life effort is not very great (Thacker & Fields, 1987).

In any event, it does not appear possible to make a clear distinction between organization development and quality of work life, although many theorists believe that a difference exists. Throughout this chapter, therefore, organization development is used broadly to include both concepts.

☐ The Matter of Values

Humanistic values represent a problem for the field of organizational psychology because these features can conflict with the objectivity required of a science and because they can dilute a strong concern for performance effectiveness and productivity. This matter is particularly relevant to our discussion of organization development, because its practitioners have often been influenced by strong humanistic values (Miner, 1990).

The Values of Organization Development. Exhibit 11-1 presents three statements of the values that underlie practice and theory in

EXHIBIT 11-1   The Values of Organization Development: Three Approaches

---

Warren Bennis—A humane and democratic social philosophy

1. To improve interpersonal competence
2. To encourage a shift in values so that human factors and feelings come to be considered legitimate
3. To develop increased understanding among and within work groups
4. To develop more effective team management
5. To develop better methods of conflict resolution involving rationality and openness to replace the usual bureaucratic methods (suppression, compromise, unprincipled power)
6. To develop organic systems to replace mechanistic—group emphasis, mutual trust, shared responsibility, multigroup membership, shared control, extensive bargaining

Anthony Raia and Newton Margulies—A humanistic ethic

1. To provide opportunities for people to function as human beings rather than as resources
2. To provide opportunities for each organization member, and the organization, to develop to full potential
3. To seek to increase the effectiveness of the organization in terms of *all* its goals, not only profit
4. To create an environment in which it is possible to find exciting and challenging work
5. To provide opportunities for people in organizations to influence the way in which they relate to their work, organization, and environment
6. To treat each human being as a person with a complex set of needs, *all* of which are important

Michael Beer—The values of informed choice

1. To help organizations generate valid data about the state of the organization in relation to its environment
2. To help those with a stake in the organization to clarify the outcomes they desire
3. To help organizations make strategic choices based on a diagnosis of the current situation and desired outcomes

---

SOURCES: Adapted from Warren G. Bennis (1969). *Organization development: Its nature, origins, and prospects.* Reading, Mass.: Addison-Wesley. Anthony P. Raia and Newton Margulies (1979). Organizational change and development. In Steven Kerr (Ed.), *Organizational behavior*, pp. 355–378. Columbus, OH: Grid. Michael Beer (1980). *Organizational change and development: A systems view.* Santa Monica, CA.: Goodyear.

organization development. As might be expected, given the difficulty of defining organization development, the three sets of values in Exhibit 11-1 are not the same. The values emphasized by Warren Bennis tend to promote group systems at the expense of hierarchic. Anthony Raia and Newton Margulies stress values that are more individual in nature and thus more humanistic. The values emphasized by Michael Beer stress very different concerns: He underscores knowledge and rationality rather than humanism.

The application of Beer's values, as he notes, could yield greater centralization of decisions, more bureaucracy, and more directive managerial styles. Few organization

development advocates would endorse these values alone, but it is important to note that organization development can be viewed simply as a means of changing organizations to make them more effective, not just more humanistic.

Values and Performance. Can implementation of any of the value sets of organization development listed in Exhibit 11-1 lead to improved performance and productivity? No clear answer to this question has yet emerged. Potential means of boosting work output are inherent in Bennis's views, and Raia and Margulies's vision of a humanistic ethic is certainly appealing, but whether or not either

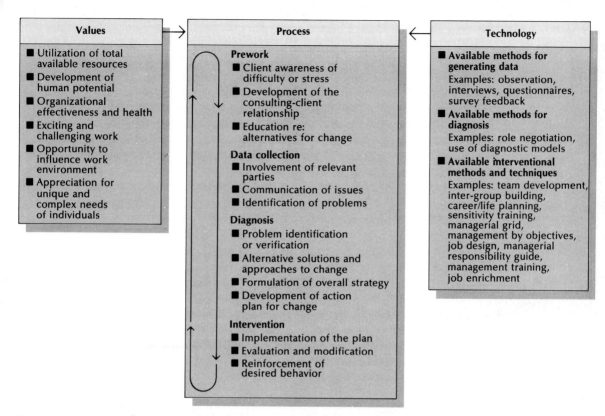

Values	Process	Technology
■ Utilization of total available resources ■ Development of human potential ■ Organizational effectiveness and health ■ Exciting and challenging work ■ Opportunity to influence work environment ■ Appreciation for unique and complex needs of individuals	**Prework** ■ Client awareness of difficulty or stress ■ Development of the consulting-client relationship ■ Education re: alternatives for change **Data collection** ■ Involvement of relevant parties ■ Communication of issues ■ Identification of problems **Diagnosis** ■ Problem identification or verification ■ Alternative solutions and approaches to change ■ Formulation of overall strategy ■ Development of action plan for change **Intervention** ■ Implementation of the plan ■ Evaluation and modification ■ Reinforcement of desired behavior	■ **Available methods for generating data** Examples: observation, interviews, questionnaires, survey feedback ■ **Available methods for diagnosis** Examples: role negotiation, use of diagnostic models ■ **Available interventional methods and techniques** Examples: team development, inter-group building, career/life planning, sensitivity training, managerial grid, management by objectives, job design, managerial responsibility guide, management training, job enrichment

EXHIBIT 11-2   How Values Enter into the Process of Organization Development
In this view values combine with organization development's available technology to produce the actual organization development process.
SOURCE: Anthony P. Raia & Newton Margulies (1979). Organizational change and development. In Steven Kerr (Ed.), *Organizational behavior,* p. 371. Columbus, OH: Grid.

of these value sets contributes to performance and productivity depends on numerous other factors. Beer's set of values, involving informed choice, seems most consistent with achieving higher levels of organizational effectiveness, but this set of values has not gained wide acceptance.

The possibility exists that the values of organization development, if implemented, can be most useful in yielding increased job satisfaction for those people whose needs the values meet. The values of organization development, in and of themselves, do not represent solutions to an organization's ills.

Exhibit 11-2 shows how values influence what is done in organization development. Later in this chapter we will discuss the technology of organization development and take a more detailed look at the process itself.

☐ Resistance to Change

Before turning to how organization development is carried out, we need to look at some of the forces that may impede or subvert efforts of this kind. Changes do not always go according to plan, as anyone who has ever tried to modify a rule or a policy, or anything else, knows (Hermon-Taylor, 1985). Many Presidents of the United States have been unable to restructure the federal bureaucracy, despite their campaign promises and best efforts to do so. Former astronaut Frank Borman, although successful in making some changes as chief executive of Eastern Airlines, was repeatedly blocked in other areas by the unions and their members; ultimately he had to leave the company.

Individual Sources. Some theorists imply that **resistance to change** is irrational and that it invariably arises from personality patterns that are rigid, authoritarian, and insecure. Although such resistance does occur, not all efforts to block change are without foundation. Some changes are simply ill-advised. Furthermore, because changes tend to bring about shifts in the power balance (indeed, this is the aim of most organization development), those in positions of influence may resist change, not out of rigid negativism, but in order to retain as much power as possible should the matter get down to hard bargaining.

There are, to be sure, people who can be counted on to oppose change. These people, who tend to be somewhat anxious and lacking in confidence, see order, rules, and standard procedures as important goals. They are usually submissive with superiors, yet very directive with subordinates. If enough such people are clustered together, especially if they operate in a culture that values stability and tradition, change of any kind may be very difficult to achieve.

Group Sources. Cohesive groups often can effectively resist change, as shown in the British coal-mining studies conducted by Eric Trist and a team of coworkers some years ago. In this instance the introduction of a new technology of mining, the longwall method, broke up preexisting work groups and spread the miners out along the coal face. The result was reduced productivity, rather than the technology-based improvement that management had anticipated. Group resistance led to increased absenteeism and a fall-off in productivity. In short, the groups found ways to thwart changes that threatened their very existence. Subsequently ways were found to reintroduce group work—in the form of autonomous work groups (see Chapter 7)—while maintaining the new longwall technology. The results reported were very positive (Trist, Higgin, Murray, & Pollock, 1963).

Organizational Sources. Resistance to change may also stem from the nature of an organization itself; it may even be built into certain organizational cultures. Any type of organizational structure, once entrenched, can become resistant to change simply because it is there and specifies certain power alignments (Greiner & Schein, 1988). However, the argument that bureaucracies are inherently resistant to change has little validity. That bureaucracies and their hierarchic structures can spawn considerable change has been demonstrated by Alfred Chandler (1962) in his studies of American corporations, particularly Du Pont and Sears, Roebuck. Even the initiation phase of change in bureaucracies can be at a high level under certain circumstances (Aiken, Bacharach, & French, 1980).

Given that resistance to change can stem from individual, group, and organizational sources, what can be done to overcome it? That is a matter that various organization development approaches have addressed in different ways. We will consider them in the following section.

■ PROCESS AND TECHNOLOGY STEMMING FROM INDIVIDUAL AND GROUP-MEMBERSHIP CONCEPTS

There are a number of different approaches to organization development; the strategy employed varies with the situation, the change agent, and the feasibility of the strategy. A recent review identified five general types of approaches: organization development as a consultant-centered intervention, as general management, as creating adaptive organizations, as human resource management, and as implementing change (Beer & Walton, 1987). Within these broad categories a wide range of techniques may be employed. The point is that there is a very sizable diversity traveling under the organization development umbrella. We can consider only some of the better-known techniques here; of special concern are techniques that relate to topics we have considered in previous chapters.

In some cases, an organization development effort utilizes a single technique; more commonly, especially in recent years, a variety of procedures have been combined. A full understanding of these techniques will require frequent reference to earlier chapters. This section deals with processes and technologies that have their origins in the theories and concepts of Chapters 4 through 8.

☐ Management by Objectives

In our discussion of goal setting in Chapter 4, we considered **management by objectives (MBO),** a process that involves a superior and a subordinate setting and recording goals, the subordinate working toward the goals, and a subsequent review of performance. When used in organization development, MBO is a highly participative procedure. The goals are set primarily by the subordinates themselves, who are then expected to be more personally committed to achieving these goals and less likely to exhibit resistance to change. Furthermore, the subsequent review of performance is also done by the subordinate; it is largely a matter of self-evaluation. When applied throughout a management hierarchy, this approach has the effect of moving decisions down one level.

The MBO format originated independently of organization development, but the two were brought together in their infancy by Douglas McGregor. McGregor (1957) found the highly participative form of MBO to be entirely consistent with his concept of Theory Y management. Today, most organization development efforts involve some type of goal setting, although not always in the context of a full-scale MBO process (Lippitt, 1982). When goal setting is incorporated into an organization development program, it is likely to extend down to lower levels of the organization and to include a means of measuring goal attainment. It is not uncommon for the goal setting to be done by committees composed of representatives from all levels in the company.

☐ Work Redesign

Various approaches to **work redesign** were considered in Chapter 4. All of these have been incorporated into organization development efforts on occasion, but the Hackman-Oldham approach appears to be most attractive to organization development practitioners.

Job Enrichment.   Box 11-1 describes an organization development project that is devoted exclusively to a **job enrichment** effort at Citibank. In many organization development projects, this kind of program is combined with other approaches. In particular, it is inherent in the multiskill aspect of sociotechnical projects, where workers learn to perform a number of different jobs within their work group.

Alternative Work Schedules.   Another type of work redesign, **alternative work schedules,** has been incorporated in organization development programs on occasion. An example is the organization development project initiated at the Tennessee Valley Authority (TVA), which extended over almost five years (Nurick, 1985). In this case a number of committees, each consisting of both managers and workers, were formed to make

BOX **11-1** I/O PSYCHOLOGY IN PRACTICE

Work Redesign at Citibank

Citibank faced a major problem: Its back office, where all financial transactions were processed, was not working well to serve customers. For years, the work had been split up so that each person performed a single, routine task over and over; no one person handled the flow for a given customer. Severe backlogs developed, and error rates were unacceptably high.

Accordingly, a major reorganization, structured around types of customers, was initiated. The idea was that clerical staff members would be given complete processing and customer-service responsibility for a small group of customers in a defined product area, which would complement the overall decentralized structure. The new multifaceted job in the letter of credit unit, for example, would be designed as in the accompanying diagram. The question was how to implement this radically changed type of job. How could the bank shift from what was essentially an assembly-line job structure to a work-station structure?

An outside consultant was engaged to act as a change agent on the project, and interviews were conducted with managers, supervisors, and clerical employees. There was clear dissatisfaction with the existing job structure at all levels. However, management blamed the problems on the workers, and the workers saw management as the culprit. Management was unanimous in its belief that the current workers were incapable of performing the enriched, work-station job as it had been proposed. Workers tended to feel that their capabilities had been underestimated for years and that they could contribute much more than they had been expected to in the past. They also felt that they could train one another so that each would ultimately become familiar with all the functions that were now being performed by different people.

Management agreed to experiment with what the workers proposed. Training was initiated for managers and supervisors in work redesign that would increase skill variety, task identity, task significance, autonomy, and feedback from the job (see Exhibit 4-4). Workers collaborated in the redesign of specific jobs. Change was slow, occurring over several years; each new job was studied carefully in an experimental context before going on-line. The changes were carried out initially in the letter of credit unit and then extended gradually to other units of the back office. As this occurred, all measurements indicated that the organization development effort was a success.

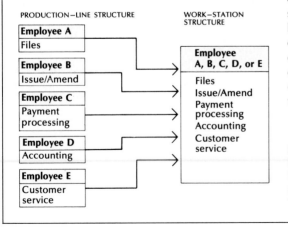

PRODUCTION–LINE STRUCTURE

WORK–STATION STRUCTURE

Employee A
Files

Employee B
Issue/Amend

Employee C
Payment processing

Employee D
Accounting

Employee E
Customer service

Employee A, B, C, D, or E
Files
Issue/Amend
Payment processing
Accounting
Customer service

SOURCE: Roy W. Walters (1982). The Citibank project: Improving productivity through work redesign. In Robert Zager & Michael P. Rosow (Eds.), *The innovative organization: Productivity programs in action,* pp. 109, 117, and 120–121. Elmsford, NY: Pergamon.

proposals for change. One of these committees suggested that a field surveying unit be permitted to work four days a week. The committee negotiated with the appropriate managers, and the four-day work week was introduced. Another committee proposed a voluntary system of flexible working hours that was adopted and utilized by 18 percent of the work force. At the TVA, as is the case generally, these alternative work schedules were not the core aspects of the organization development effort, but they did emerge from it.

☐ The Scanlon Plan

The last section of Chapter 4 touched on the use of group and organizationwide reward systems. One such approach, which has been closely associated with organization development for many years, is the **Scanlon plan.** This approach was developed by Joseph Scanlon in close association with the Massachusetts Institute of Technology during Douglas McGregor's tenure there, and he advocated it strongly as a method of moving to Theory Y management.

Box 11-2 describes an application of the Scanlon plan at Herman Miller Company, a nonunionized firm. Joseph Scanlon, however, came from a union background, and numerous similar success stories involving unionized operations have been reported (Schuster, 1984). In most cases, the Scanlon plan has been installed at relatively small companies, a fact that perhaps facilitates the necessary communication. If the plan is to be effective, employees must fully understand the nature of the company's operations and the environment in which the company operates. The employees must also care what happens to the company. This kind of knowledge and understanding was crucial to the informed vote that occurred at Herman Miller. Voting like this is practically unheard of in business firms other than professional companies, such

as law firms. A bonus system, which in the case of the Herman Miller Company has paid as much as 23 percent above base salary, is a typical feature of a Scanlon plan. Yet, as is evident from Box 11-2, the Scanlon plan is much more than a compensation system. It represents a means of allowing employees to determine methods of reducing costs and increasing productivity.

☐ From T-Groups to Team Building

In Chapter 7, considerable attention was given to **T-groups** and the more recently developed **team building** approach (see Boxes 7-3 and 7-4 for descriptions of their use at TRW and Mead Corporation). T-groups were once used extensively in organization development programs, but now team building is the favored approach (Dyer, 1987).

Unfreezing, Moving, and Refreezing. Many organization development efforts utilize a change process originally proposed by Kurt Lewin (1952). Douglas McGregor and Kurt Lewin were at MIT together, and both contributed to the development of the early T-group ideas. McGregor saw the potential of these ideas for organization development. The initial concept was that T-groups would serve to unfreeze existing thinking and behavior and foster the realization that change is needed. Then agents of change and consultants would move in to establish new, more participative systems. Finally, these new systems would be reinforced—or refrozen—by a new set of rewards and sanctions. In the end, a changed organization would result. Exhibit 11-3 outlines the process. It is a key ingredient of organization development today (Schein, 1987).

The Argyris Views. The movement of organizational theorists away from T-groups and toward team building is perhaps best illustrated in the writings of Chris Argyris (1962,

BOX 11-2 I/O PSYCHOLOGY IN PRACTICE

The Scanlon Plan at Herman Miller Company

Herman Miller Company, a furniture manufacturer, introduced a Scanlon plan in 1950, when it was small and having difficulty growing. That plan was created and implemented with the aid of a consultant. It included a bonus system, a participation structure, and a communication system. Bonuses were paid companywide, and were based on labor productivity above and beyond wage and salary costs. The participation structure consisted of committees, made up primarily of elected representatives who operated an extensive suggestion system and also reviewed, analyzed, and evaluated the company's production performance. The communication structure utilized employee meetings to review performance as well as written memos dealing with bonus calculations.

In 1978, after many years of successful operation, the Scanlon plan ran into difficulty. Sales had increased dramatically, and the company was having difficulty meeting demand. Customer service became deficient, and the bonuses decreased. Finally, a decision was made to approach the employees regarding change. The consultant was brought back, and meetings were held with all 2300 employees in the United States to explain the problems. A subsequent companywide vote indicated that over 95 percent supported change. Then an ad hoc committee of elected employees was established to design the change. Meeting as three subcommittees, this group struggled with the issue for ten months. Finally a revised plan emerged, and this too was voted on by all employees; over 95 percent endorsed it.

In broad outline, the new Scanlon plan was similar to the old, but it had many new features. It incorporated a planning process, introduced employee goal setting, expanded the participation structure, created a sophisticated performance-monitoring system, and revised the bonus formula. Suggestions for improvements were handled within the work group first. If this did not prove effective, another group composed of workers in similar jobs became involved. A third group was composed of elected representatives from the other two. The result of all these groups, committees, and meetings was much-improved communication. Problems in implementing the new plan were minimized because the employees voted for it in overwhelming numbers. In terms of both company performance and bonuses paid, the new plan was an outstanding success.

Source: Judith Ramquist (1982). Labor-management cooperation—The Scanlon plan at work. *Sloan Management Review, 23*(3), 49–55.

1982). Argyris originally recommended extensive formation of T-groups as a means of moving decision making down the hierarchy, so that all organization members had equal influence on the course of events. According to Argyris's plan, consultants or internal agents of change would work with the groups to unfreeze commitments to current ideas and values, thus producing a readiness for the values of organization development. The intent of the training was to unfreeze by encouraging participants to

1. Give feedback on others' behavior and receive feedback on how their behavior is perceived by others.
2. Accept their own values, attitudes, and feelings.
3. Be open to new values, attitudes, and feelings.
4. Experiment with new values, attitudes, and feelings.
5. Take risks with new values, attitudes, and feelings.

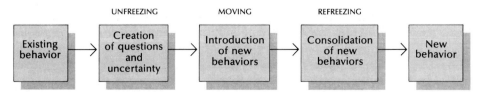

UNFREEZING   MOVING   REFREEZING

Exhibit 11-3   The Unfreezing-Moving-Refreezing Model for Change
Unfreezing creates doubt and uncertainty; moving provides new behaviors; refreezing puts
new behaviors in place.

As T-groups became less popular in the business world, Argyris, along with many others, moved to a team building approach, which focused less on interpersonal processes within a group and more on real organizational problems and methods of coping with them. The example at the beginning of this chapter considers the early stages of an organization development program of this type at Datavision. Interestingly, vestiges of the early T-group procedures can be discerned, and it is possible to identify aspects of the unfreezing–moving–refreezing model in this modern approach.

☐ Sociotechnical Interventions and Autonomous Groups

While T-groups have long been important organization development tools, sociotechnical systems have only recently come to be viewed as part of organization development technology. **Autonomous work groups** were discussed in Chapter 7; Box 7-5, describing events at ALMEX in Sweden, presents a successful application of the sociotechnical systems approach.

Initiating Intervention. Organizational psychologists have developed specific guidelines for using **sociotechnical systems** to restructure work situations or redesign organizational social structures (Cherns, 1977):

1. If structural reorganizations such as the creation of autonomous work groups are to be effective, organization members must share in the design of these groups.

2. Only those aspects of system design that need to be specified at each stage should be specified—for example, it may be necessary to stipulate what has to be done, but not how it should be done.

3. Problems should be dealt with as close to where they occur as possible. Inspection, for example, should be incorporated into production so that work is inspected by those who do it rather than by a distant quality-control unit.

4. The organization should be designed to achieve its results in more than one way; through multiskilling it should be possible for members to perform in a wide range of positions.

5. Roles that require shared access to similar knowledge should be placed within the same grouping.

6. Work groups should be able to obtain directly the information and feedback they need to control their own work.

7. Reward systems should be designed to reinforce desired behaviors. Thus, if there are group-based systems, there should be group-based rewards.

8. A primary objective should be to provide a high quality of work life to organization members.

9. Restructuring of work methods should be preceded by a period of rehearsal of new work roles.

10. A multifunctional, multilevel, multidisciplinary team is needed to redesign organizational structures, and this same team should be used for evaluation and review as well.

Lack of trust and communication between management and workers can hinder the application of sociotechnical approaches. For example, the decision to move to autonomous work groups should be a group one, and usually committees are established to help in unfreezing and to create commitment to change. But rarely do these committees have the authority to reject the organization development effort, because top management has already committed itself to change, and consultants with a clear idea of what the administrators want have already been engaged. When sociotechnical interventions are introduced in a hierarchic manner, as they typically are, real support for the changes may never develop. Some workers may find the new work system incompatible with their motives and values (Anderson & Terborg, 1986; Goodman, 1979). Others may give only lip service to the change, or resistance may emerge within a union. Thus, the seeds of failure are present from the very beginning. This was apparently the case in the application of sociotechnical intervention at Shell Refining Ltd., described in Box 11-3.

One solution to problems of this kind is to make participation in the autonomous work groups voluntary. Both autonomous and more traditional structures can operate at the same location, as occurred at ALMEX (see Box 7-5), giving individuals the opportunity to opt for one or the other. Another strategy is to establish new plants on a sociotechnical basis and hire only those who prefer this type of work system. In existing operations, sociotechnical organization development should be introduced only if and when widespread support exists for doing so.

Diffusion. As at Shell Refining, sociotechnical approaches have often been introduced through pilot projects, or in some of a company's locations and not others, in the hope that the success of these initial efforts will produce a gradual **diffusion** through a whole company, or even a whole society. The idea is that the organization development process will not have to be sold over and over again, but rather will spread by selling itself, once originally established. Obviously, if the initial efforts are not perceived as successful and as substantially different from what existed before, diffusion is unlikely. Shell Refining is a case in point.

Ironically, however, success does not guarantee diffusion, either. A number of sociotechnical projects were undertaken in various companies in Norway starting around 1970. These projects were initiated as part of a concerted effort by the Norwegian government to introduce autonomous work groups on a broad scale, with the ultimate objective of transforming the whole society. The hope was that diffusion throughout Norway would occur from the demonstration projects. Yet in spite of some initial successes that were widely publicized, little diffusion resulted (Emery & Thorsrud 1976; Sorensen, 1985). Twenty years later, few if any traces of these efforts could be found, even in the demonstration locations. Individual and union resistance appear to have been a major factor in this outcome. These same sources of resistance appear not to exist just across the border, in Sweden. There, sociotechnical organization development has diffused and produced major changes in the society. We have already noted the ALMEX application (Box 7-5). Another widely publicized example is the success of autonomous work groups at the Volvo automobile plant at Kalmar (Gyllenhammar, 1977).

A similar comparison can be made between the lack of diffusion within General Foods and the very considerable diffusion at General Motors. General Foods has made only sporadic use of sociotechnical interventions. Nonetheless, a widely heralded application occurred at the corporation's plant in Topeka, Kansas. This project had its ups and downs, and there may well have been some exaggeration in describing its success (Walton, 1982; Whitsett & Yorks, 1983), but the program continued and production costs remained low; multiskilling proved very successful. The company culture as a whole, however, simply was not receptive, just as Norwegian culture was not.

General Motors, in contrast, has introduced varying degrees of sociotechnical intervention into many of its operations: Cadillac at Livonia, Michigan, Lordstown in Ohio, the Pontiac Motor Division, and the Project Saturn effort, among others. What is done at General Motors in the name of this type of organization development is highly flexible and depends in large part on local needs and desires (General Motors Corporation, 1984). Perhaps this is why diffusion has occurred. Although General Motors has drawn upon a variety of organization development ideas, it appears to be moving increasingly toward sociotechnical strategies. Yet diffusion has not spread throughout General Motors. Overall, the company culture appears to be conducive to this type of change, but in any given location individuals and union forces may inhibit it.

☐ Quality Circles

As indicated in Chapter 8, **quality circles** came to the United States from Japan. The process by which they are typically introduced in a company was set forth in Exhibit 8-9; their application was considered in Box 8-5. Although quality circles did not have their origins in organization development, there is an element of participation and decision sharing in the approach that appeals to many organization development practitioners. Accordingly, quality circles are occasionally incorporated in organization development programs, especially if the problem that is under consideration might be solved through improvements in manufacturing methods.

Exhibit 11-4 shows the structure of a quality circle program. The facilitators, who may be either internal or external organization development consultants, usually direct problem-solving training sessions and help with forming the circle. Although ultimate responsibility for the circle resides in the steering committee, the coordinator oversees the program on a day-to-day basis. The steering committee consists of people from all levels and areas of the company. In many respects, quality circles are like team building extended to the shop floor. In fact, there may well be a gradual merger of quality circles and team building to the point where they are indistinguishable from each other.

■ PROCESS AND TECHNOLOGY STEMMING FROM LEADERSHIP CONCEPTS

In this section we consider organization development processes and technologies that have their origins in leadership theories.

☐ Grid Organization Development

Grid organization development utilizes the **managerial grid** concept (described in Chapter 9). It occurs in six phases, although not all applications proceed to the later phases.

Because of the problems inherent in using authority to install a participative procedure, those who are considering adopting a grid approach often attempt to test the strategy. This may involve reading the literature, pilot exposures to aspects of the procedure, or spe-

BOX **11-3** I/O PSYCHOLOGY IN PRACTICE

Sociotechnical Intervention at Shell Refining Ltd.

The accompanying diagram shows what was intended at Shell Refining Ltd. Action plan 1 was the sociotechnical intervention introduced with the aid of several of the founders of sociotechnical theory. Action plan 2 was a joint union–management effort dealing with related issues. It is clear that the two plans were intended to foster each other's objectives.

The intervention started with a wide-ranging series of meetings and workshops intended first to develop a sociotechnical philosophy for the company and then foster commitment to it. The

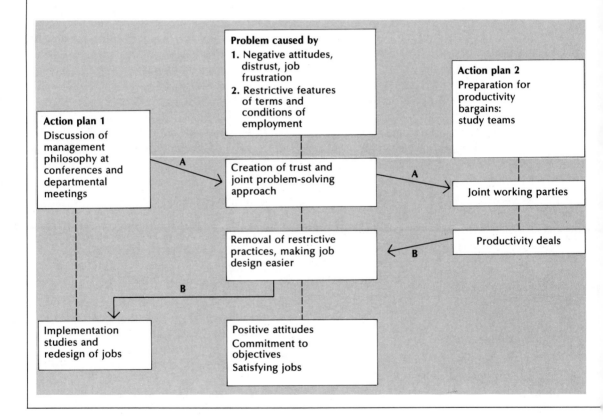

cial training for a few key individuals. Companies that decide to proceed then establish a steering committee to consider long-term involvement. The committee generally includes people from all levels of the organization, but top-level management is heavily represented (Blake & Mouton, 1985).

Phase 1 of grid organization development involves extensive, systemwide training in grid leadership theory and practice. The goals of grid seminars include increased self-understanding, learning how to solve problems in teams and how to manage interface conflict, and comprehending the organizational implications of the training. Seminars last a week. Although teams work together during a semi-

written philosophy that emerged included the following statements:

> The company must manage both a social system, of people and their organization, and a technical system, of physical equipment and resources. Optimization of its overall operations can be achieved only by jointly optimizing the operation of these two systems.

> Implicit in the fact that the company's resources are part of the total resources of society is the objective of creating conditions in which employees at all levels will be encouraged and enabled to develop and to realize their potentialities.

> The company will seek the fullest involvement of all employees and will make the best use of available knowledge and experience of the social sciences.

In line with the philosophy statements, a number of job-redesign projects were undertaken in the company's two existing refineries, looking to the eventual installation of autonomous work groups. A new refinery was launched in the spirit of participation and shared involvement. Joint union–management efforts to increase productivity were initiated via meetings and committees.

In a few cases, the redesign projects produced some downward shift in the locus of decisions. However, most proposals spluttered to eventual silence without being missed; there was much talk, but action follow-through was often lacking. Real autonomous work groups never did appear. The new refinery operated in a somewhat more participative manner than the others, but the differences were slight. Some increase in union–management collaboration occurred, but it did not last. After roughly a year and a half, top management's attention had clearly turned to other matters; accordingly, enthusiasm for change throughout the organization waned.

A follow-up on the intervention several years later yielded the following conclusions:

1. The project never really took off and, in a number of important respects, soon faded away.
2. Top management and their sociotechnical advisors had somewhat different aims and expectations.
3. In terms of the manifest aim of the sociotechnical consultants to change the philosophy of management, the project was a failure.
4. Despite the broad failure to introduce long-term change, certain benefits did accrue to the company.
5. The change strategy was ill-conceived and poorly executed. It led to a betrayal of people's expectations.

SOURCE: Frank H. M. Blackler & Colin A. Brown (1980). *Whatever happened to Shell's new philosophy of management?*, see especially p. 94. Westmead, England: Teakfield.

nar, they are not composed of people from the same work group. All managers and frequently other organization members ultimately participate in this phase 1 effort.

Phase 2 entails actual team building. It is focused on diagnosing specific barriers to teamwork and identifying opportunities for improvement within existing work teams of manager and subordinates. Team building, which is carried out on the job, generally takes five days, but it may be spread over a longer period.

Phase 3 is concerned with intergroup conflict. Only those groups in which real barriers to effective cooperation exist are involved. Group members are taught to apply problem-

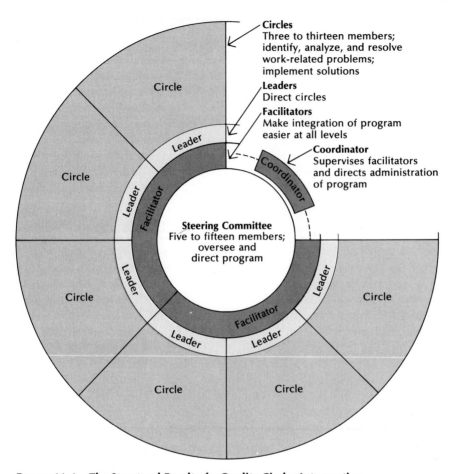

Circles
Three to thirteen members;
identify, analyze, and resolve
work-related problems;
implement solutions

Leaders
Direct circles

Facilitators
Make integration of program
easier at all levels

Coordinator
Supervises facilitators
and directs administration
of program

Steering Committee
Five to fifteen members;
oversee and
direct program

Exhibit 11-4   The Structural Result of a Quality Circles Intervention
This diagram shows how a quality circles effort looks when organization development of this kind is in full force—that is, the structural relationships among circles,
leaders, facilitators, coordinator, and the steering committee.
Source: Joseph Hanley (1980). Our experience with quality circles. *Quality Progress.* February,
pp. 22–24.

solving and decision-making skills more effectively, utilize confrontation to identify focal
issues needing resolution, and plan steps to
achieve improved cooperation between units.

Phase 4 involves the organization's highest-
level managers, or the top team engaged in
organization development. This group studies, diagnoses, and designs an ideal model
of what the organization should become. Included are a statement of financial objectives,
a description of the business activities to be

pursued, a definition of future markets, a
revised organization structure, a statement of
requirements for maintaining active pursuit
of goals, and a delineation of policies to guide
future decision making.

Phase 5 designs and carries out a plan to
shift to the model developed in phase 4.
Phase 5 includes:

Examining existing activities to identify gaps
between how the organization is now being

BOX 11-4   I/O PSYCHOLOGY IN PRACTICE

Grid Organization Development at Exxon's Baton Rouge Refinery

The results of a grid organization development effort at Exxon's refinery in Baton Rouge, Louisiana, were summarized in the following manner:

- The shift is from a situation where the refinery was operating at a serious deficit to one in which the refinery is returning a substantial profit. . . . the organization development effort accounts for approximately 30 percent of the gain.

- The number of people employed in the refinery has decreased at a faster rate than for the industry as a whole.

- A more or less continuous revision and modernization of the organization structure has occurred.

- From these changes has come a more mature organization—more planning-oriented, deliberate, and self-assured.

- The change is away from trying to force people to fit the structure toward trying to fit organization structure to the needs and capabilities of individuals.

- Organizational improvement has been striking through increased cooperation between groups,

where past relationships have involved invidious comparison and competitiveness.

- Relations between the refinery and headquarters have improved.

- Improvement in union–management relationships is evident. . . . This change is clearly the result of the organization development effort.

- Fewer unilateral decisions affecting subordinates are made and then announced out of the blue; more pretesting of the impact of a given decision is now undertaken. Greater effort is made to ensure understanding of problems and to get solutions that result in agreement.

- The improvement activity has increased awareness of and skill in the use of team action.

- A substantial number of interpersonal tensions and blockages have been cleared up.

This list of improvements represents a very strong testimonial to the value of organization development.

SOURCE: Robert R. Blake & Jane S. Mouton (1964). *The managerial grid,* pp. 291–307. Houston: Gulf.

---

operated and the way it is expected to operate according to the ideal strategic model

Specifying which activities are sound, which can be changed and retained, which are unsound and need to be replaced or abandoned, and what new or additional activities are needed to meet the requirements of the ideal model

Designing specific actions necessary to change to the ideal model

Continuing to run the business while simultaneously changing it toward the ideal model.

Phase 6 is where stabilization and consolidation of progress occurs. Involved are a critique of the change effort to determine that everything is proceeding according to plan; the identification of problems, followed by corrective action; and continued monitoring of the business environment to identify trends that have implications for the company.

Grid organization development is an ongoing process extending over many years. Box 11-4 describes the results over five years of application at Exxon's Baton Rouge refinery.

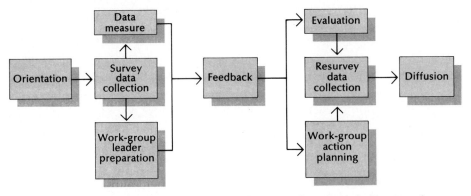

EXHIBIT 11-5 Overview of the Survey-Feedback Approach to Organization Development
Feedback of survey data is the bridge between the initial measurement phase and the ultimate move to action.
SOURCE: David A Nadler (1977). *Feedback and organization development: Using data-based methods,* p. 26. Reading, MA: Addison-Wesley.

☐ The Survey-Feedback Approach

The **survey-feedback** approach to organization development is an outgrowth of Rensis Likert's **System 4 and 4T theory** (discussed in Chapter 9). Previously this theory had been implemented in various ways, among which Box 9-2, describing an application in General Motors' Lakewood plant, provides a good example. Survey feedback involves moving companies along the System 1-to-System 4 continuum (see Exhibit 9-5) with the hope that they will eventually become System 4 organizations, in which work groups are equipped to make some of the decisions once made by administrators. Other organization development approaches use attitude-survey data as one aspect of the overall process, but the survey-feedback procedure gives these data a focal role. The approach is outlined in Exhibit 11-5. A detailed statement of the steps involved follows (Bowers & Franklin, 1977, p. 117):

1. Initial planning sessions are held involving consultants, managers, and selected nonmanagers.
2. A questionnaire is administered to all organization members. The questions deal with managerial behavior, organizational climate, group processes, job satisfaction, supervisory needs, job challenge, aversion to bureaucracy, and integration of goals.
3. Selected individuals are trained to act as knowledgeable persons in the data feedback sessions.
4. Organization members are trained in basic concepts of organizational functioning and, in particular, in System 4 functioning.
5. Analyzed questionnaire data are returned to group supervisors.
6. Group feedback meetings are conducted during which problems unearthed by the questionnaire data are discussed.
7. A systematic organizational diagnosis is presented to all involved.
8. Resources are allocated to carry out change in accordance with the needs indicated by the feedback meetings and the systematic diagnosis.
9. Additional questionnaires are administered and analyzed to monitor the change process.

10. The organization is formally reassessed to evaluate change, again using questionnaire data.

The information obtained from questionnaires is given not just to managers but also to the work groups. Indeed, the name "survey feedback" arises from the fact that data are fed back to the groups from which they were obtained initially, in order to permit the groups to identify problems and develop solutions. Often a "cascade" procedure is used, with each level preparing data for presentation to the groups below.

In early applications of the survey-feedback approach, all the data came from the survey questionnaires. More recently, the groups have been given other data as well: information on productivity, cost and accounting records, behavioral inputs from payroll and personnel records, and the like. The idea has been to get as much relevant information as possible to the groups in order to improve the quality of participative decisions. As decisions that were formerly made well up in management shift down to the work groups, System 4 becomes increasingly implanted.

■ ORGANIZATION DEVELOPMENT AND PERFORMANCE

The preceding discussion dealt with a number of approaches that matured with or ultimately became part of organization development. It did not systematically consider how good these approaches are or how helpful organization development itself is in changing organizations to make them more effective. The issue of how well organization development fares in practice is, naturally, of great concern to organization development practitioners (Burke, 1987; Lawler, Mohrman, Mohrman, Ledford, & Cummings, 1985). It is a matter to which we now turn.

□ Overall Evaluations of Research

Many organization development efforts utilize several approaches, and it is very hard to disentangle the effects of each. Analysts seeking to evaluate organization development programs have been more successful in judging an overall effort than in looking at the different processes and techniques separately.

Performance Changes. Exhibit 11-6 represents an effort to summarize the results of organization development research by relating the approach taken to various indexes of performance. Given the limited number of studies dealing with each approach, we cannot say definitively that one is better than another for a particular purpose. Exhibit 11-6 does indicate, however, that survey feedback alone and straight job redesign are among the least effective procedures. Overall, the organization development approaches measured here have something over a .500 batting average in boosting performance. Organization development appears to be particularly effective in improving the quality of work performance.

The results presented in Exhibit 11-6 are for hard measures of performance, not judgments, perceptions, or feelings. When we consider performance measures of all kinds, roughly 75 percent of the studies on the effectiveness of organization development yield evidence of an improvement. Organization development interventions unquestionably can have an impact on performance (Guzzo, Jette, & Katzell, 1985; Woodman & Wayne, 1985). The chances of success are substantially increased if several different processes or technologies are incorporated in these efforts to change.

Changes in Intervening Processes. Researchers have found evidence that the performance changes that occur as a result of organization development efforts may be due

EXHIBIT 11-6   Percent Effectiveness of Organization Development Approaches in Producing Changes in Various Aspects of Performance and Productivity

	Improved Results			
Organization Development Approach	Reduced Turnover, Absenteeism, or Grievances	Reduced Costs; Increased Profits or Sales	Increased Effectiveness, Efficiency, or Quantity	Improved Quality of Work Performance
Laboratory training	100%	50%	100%	50%
Team building	50	50	50	Insufficient data
Survey feedback	0	Insufficient data	50	Insufficient data
Team building and survey feedback	60	100	0	50
Sociotechnical systems	50	60	64	100
Job enlargement	0	75	25	60
Job enrichment	50	0	38	50
Job enrichment with a participative emphasis	100	0	75	100
Two or more of these approaches used together	50	57	38	60
Average value	51	49	49	67

SOURCE: Adapted from John M. Nicholas (1982). The comparative impact of organization development interventions on hard criteria measures. *Academy of Management Review, 7,* 534–537.

to various intervening factors, such as improved organizational climate, greater perceived participation and influence, higher levels of job satisfaction, better communication, less stress, and more cohesive groups. Frequently, the studies that report changes in intervening processes use questionnaires administered before or early in the organization development effort and again after the change effort has been in effect for a time. These studies may not include any attempt at all to measure performance changes. Box 11-5, describing an organization development effort at the Tennessee Valley Authority, presents a typical study of this kind. Note that in this instance there was an improvement in organizational climate, perceived influence, and aspects of job satisfaction. These changes did not occur in the control unit that was not exposed to organization development.

The research dealing with intervening processes typically involves questionnaires that require participants to report on their own organization development experience. Yet training and other factors that are a part of that experience may in themselves cause participants to perceive their situation very differently; accordingly, comparisons of pre- and postmeasures may not be valid. Perceptual problems of this kind can be overcome (Millsap & Hartog, 1988; Randolph, 1982; Van de Vliert, Huismans, & Stok, 1985); but many studies have not concerned themselves with this matter and may thus be over- or underestimating the amount of change resulting from intervening processes. In any event, it is apparent that improvements in intervening processes are much more likely when multiple organization development techniques are used (Neuman, Edwards, & Raju, 1989).

☐ The Problem of Positive-Findings Bias

A certain amount of the research on the effects of organization development leaves much to be desired; we cannot be absolutely certain that the results reported are correct (Nicholas & Katz, 1985). For instance, many evaluation studies have been carried out by the same consultants who introduced the organization development program they were evaluating. Even when this was not the case, those conducting the research were likely to be favorably disposed toward organization development, and this bias may be reflected in the research findings.

Several analyses of existing research have looked into this issue (Bullock & Svyantek, 1985; Terpstra, 1981; Woodman & Wayne, 1985). Overall, **positive-findings bias** is apparently not a major factor in organization development research. However, in studies of T-groups, sensitivity or laboratory training, team building, and the survey-feedback approach only—procedures that historically have been central to organization development—evidence of a positive-findings bias has been found. Much research on these techniques is poorly rather than rigorously designed, and the resulting tendency is to report a more favorable outcome than might be warranted. In short, the value of these approaches has been overestimated.

A related problem is that analyses of research on organization development rely primarily on studies published in the professional journals, which tend to select reports of positive findings for publication. A study that yielded no evidence of change from an organization development intervention would be less likely to find a publication outlet. Again, we appear to be somewhat overestimating the positive impact of organization development. It should be noted, however, that this particular problem is no more likely to characterize organization development research than re-search in other areas of industrial-organizational psychology.

Even taking these considerations into account, a large body of evidence indicates that organization development, if carried out correctly—especially if multiple techniques are included—can be an effective force for high performance and satisfaction.

☐ Quantum versus Incremental Change

One key to why the effects of organization development often are not as great as might be hoped is provided by research into quantum versus incremental strategies for change (Hoskisson & Galbraith, 1985; Miller & Friesen, 1982). **Quantum change** involves making numerous changes all at once; the period of change is kept as short as possible, but a great deal of realigning of the organization occurs in that brief period. Then the organization stabilizes to absorb what has occurred. **Incremental change** is more piecemeal and gradual. Changes are made as they come to seem feasible. One part of the organization may change long before other parts do, and changes may be carried out in stages extending over a considerable period.

The evidence indicates that quantum changes are more effective in contributing to organizational goal attainment. Thus, General Motors improved its financial performance substantially when it made a quantum change to a decentralized division structure. Moving to this structure in a piecemeal manner, Sears, Roebuck did not experience nearly the same results (Chandler, 1962). Thus, incremental change does not appear to have as positive an impact.

Because group processes usually move slowly, organization development is generally characterized by incremental change. In procedures such as those implemented at Shell Refining (see Box 11-3), Exxon (see Box 11-4), and the TVA (see Box 11-5), change

BOX 11-5 RESEARCH IN I/O PSYCHOLOGY

Evaluating Organization Development at the Tennessee Valley Authority

Organization development was initiated in the Transition Planning and Engineering Division of the Tennessee Valley Authority (TVA). This division was responsible for creating the transmission and communication systems required to produce and deliver electric power to consumers. For purposes of control in the experimental design, the Division of Engineering Design was also studied. The organization development effort was assisted by consultants, extended over almost five years, and required union cooperation. The consultants conducted extensive interviews, fed back their results at off-site workshops, and participated in the meetings of a variety of task forces. These task forces were headed by a multilevel steering committee.

A variety of recommendations for change came out of these task forces and committees: more two-way performance appraisals, a procedure for delegating technical decisions, flexible working hours at some locations, instituting a suggestion system, attempts at restructuring, fostering affirmative action, and more. A number of these changes were put into effect.

The evaluation process involved administration of questionnaires to survey attitudes at both experimental and control sites at three time intervals. In addition, extensive in-depth interviews were conducted. Clearly, changes did result. In the division where organization development occurred, there was an increased feeling of personal influence and the organizational climate improved. Satisfaction with rewards intrinsic to the work increased. Overall, this group came to view their unit as a better place to work, and employee influence over key decisions affecting their lives increased.

In many respects, however, the consequences were mixed. On the positive side were the following:

1. Participation emerged as the single most important intervention.
2. Several important technical and structural problems—duplication of work, for instance—were resolved.

3. The division began to explore long-term issues.
4. Management was viewed by employees as more open and responsive to new ideas.
5. The organization development effort became built into the organization, so that a continuing structure for change was created.

Yet there were negative features as well:

1. A clear statement of goals and objectives was never developed.
2. An implicit power struggle between certain top-level managers and the organization development steering committee was never resolved.
3. Communications between the task forces and committees, and the division as a whole, were inadequate.
4. A problem of inequity between people at different salary levels who performed comparable work was addressed but never resolved.
5. The project had minimal effects on the unions, which continued to represent a major source of resistance to change.
6. An accurate measure of productivity was never developed, and therefore the impact of organization development on productivity could not be assessed.
7. Although the change program became a permanent part of the division, it was not diffused to the rest of the TVA.

It is not possible to say whether the changes observed were sufficient to justify the costs. The lack of data on productivity represents a major shortcoming.

SOURCE: Aaron J. Nurick (1985). *Participation in organizational change: The TVA experiment.* New York: Praeger.

occurred only when task forces and committees finally came together and agreed on a course of action. As a result, organization development can keep a firm in constant flux.

If organization development could be used to a greater extent to produce quantum change, its positive effects would probably increase dramatically.

KEY TERMS

Organization development (OD)
Quality of work life (QWL)
Humanistic values
Resistance to change
Management by objectives (MBO)
Work redesign
Job enrichment
Alternative work schedules
Scanlon plan
T-groups
Team building
Autonomous work groups

Sociotechnical systems
Diffusion
Quality circles
Grid organization development
Managerial grid
Survey feedback
System 4 theory
System 4T theory
Positive-findings bias
Quantum change
Incremental change

SUMMARY

Organization development is a process of data collection, diagnosis, action planning, intervention and change, and evaluation of results intended to increase integration, devise new solutions, or develop a capacity for renewal. The change process is collaborative in nature and includes people at multiple levels. *Quality of work life* is a similar concept that appears to place somewhat more consistent emphasis on the welfare of the individual. In the eyes of many practitioners, the objective of these procedures is to instill *humanistic values* in the workplace. Humanistic values may or may not contribute to organizational effectiveness, however. In any event, organization development practitioners are faced with the problem of overcoming *resistance to change*, whether stemming from individual, group, or organizational sources.

Organization development is in fact a collection of techniques or approaches that may be used separately or in combination. *Management by objectives*, with a highly participative emphasis, was absorbed at an early point. Various *work-redesign* procedures, such as *job enrichment* and *alternative schedules*, also came to organization development from outside. The *Scanlon plan* has been very attractive to organization development practitioners because of its strong participative emphasis. *T-groups* were at the heart of early organization development practice, but have increasingly given way to *team building*. *Sociotechnical interventions* moving to *autonomous work groups* have been particularly popular in recent years. *Quality circles* came originally from Japan and are now included in many organization development interventions in the United States. *Grid theory* of leadership also has generated a specific way of approaching organization development. The *survey-feedback* approach has its origins in Likert's *System 4 and 4T theory.*

More often than not, *organization development* efforts do change people and organizations. Performance and productivity may well be improved; in particular, it seems, quality increases can be expected. Research in the field appears to suffer from several sources of bias that in all probability serve to exaggerate the overall success of organization development programs. Even so, it is apparent that successes do occur with some frequency. One of the major problems still unsolved is the long-drawn-out, *incremental* nature of most organization development efforts. If a way could be found to bring about more *quantum change,* the success rate could be expected to increase substantially.

QUESTIONS

1. What appear to be some of the factors that make for diffusion of organization development efforts in some contexts but not in others?

2. Why are values an important consideration in organization development, and how do they operate?

3. There appear to be a number of factors that may serve to exaggerate the positive findings reported on the value of organization development programs. What are these factors, and how do they operate?

4. What is grid organization development, and what stages does it move through?

5. Among the wide range of approaches used in organization development, which ones originated in some other context? Why do you suppose each of these approaches appealed to organization development practitioners?

6. What is known about the effectiveness of the various organization development approaches and of organization development overall?

7. It has been argued that resistance to change is inherently an irrational process. What appears to be the true state of affairs in this regard?

8. Exactly how do survey questionnaire data operate within the context of the survey-feedback approach?

9. What is meant by organization development and quality of work life? Are these different concepts?

10. How does the concept of unfreezing relate to T-groups? Can you identify processes of this kind embedded in any other organization development techniques?

CASE PROBLEM

W. WARNER BURKE
Organization Development Consultant

[W. Warner Burke is a professor at Columbia University and heads a consulting firm—W. Warner Burke Associates. This is his story of an organization development project.]

The client organization was a division of a large U.S. manufacturing corporation. The division consisted of two plants, both of which manufactured heavy electrical equipment. The division was in trouble at the time. There were quality and control problems and customers were complaining. The complaints concerned not only poor quality but late delivery of these products—inevitably weeks, if not months, later than promised. Several weeks prior to my arrival at the divisional offices, a senior vice president from the corporation's headquarters had visited with the division's top management team, a group of six men. The corporate vice president was very much aware of the problems, and he was anything but pleased about the state of affairs. At the end of his visit, he made a pronouncement. In essence, he stated that unless this division was "turned around" within six months, he would make the necessary arrangements to close it down. If he carried through with this threat, it would mean loss of jobs for more than 1000 people, including, of course, the division's top-management team. Although the two plants in this division were unionized, the vice president had the power and the support from his superiors to close the division if he deemed it necessary.

Over a period of several months prior to my arrival as a consultant, the division general manager had taken a variety of steps to try to correct the problems. He had held problem-solving meetings with his top management team; he had fired the head of manufacturing and brought in a more experienced man; he spent time on the shop floor talking with first-line supervisors and workers; he authorized experiments to be conducted by the production engineers to discover better methods; he even conducted a mass rally of all employees at which he exhorted them to do better. After the rally, signs were posted throughout the plants announcing the goal: to become number one among all the corporation's divisions. None of these steps seemed to make any difference.

The general manager also sought help from the corporate staff of employee relations and training specialists. One of these specialists made several visits to the division and eventually decided that an outside consultant with expertise in organization development could probably help. I was contacted by this corporate staff person, and an initial visit was arranged.

My initial visit, only a few weeks after the corporate vice president had made his visit and his pronouncement, consisted largely of (1) talking at length with the general manager, (2) observing briefly most of the production operations, (3) meeting informally with the top-management team so that questions could be raised and issues explored, and finally, (4) discussing the action steps I proposed. I suggested we start at the top. I would interview each member of the top-management team at some length and report back to them as a group what I had diagnosed from these interviews; then

Organization Chart: Top-Management Team of Manufacturing Division

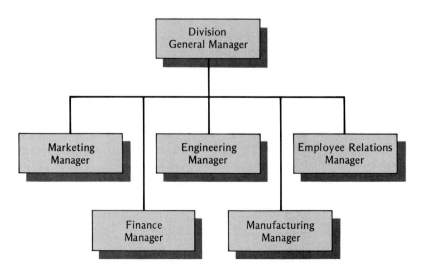

we would jointly determine the appropriate next steps. They agreed to my proposal.

A couple of weeks later, I began by interviewing the six members of the top-management team for about an hour each. They gave many reasons for the division's problems, some of the presumed causes contradicting others. What did emerge was that, although divisional goals were generally understandable, they were not specific enough for clarity about priorities. Moreover, there were interpersonal problems, such as the head of marketing and the head of employee relations not getting along. (The marketing manager believed that the employee relations manager was never forceful enough, and the employee relations manager perceived the marketing manager as a "blowhard.") We decided to have a two-and-a-half-day meeting at a hotel some 90 miles away to work on clarifying priorities and ironing out some of the interpersonal differences.

The meeting was considered successful because much of what we set out to accomplish was achieved—a clearer understanding of the problems and concerns and a priority for action. The key problem needing attention did indeed surface. It was as if a layer or two of an "organizational onion" had been peeled away and we were finally getting at not only some causes but specifics that we could address with confidence that we were moving in the right direction. The specific problem that surfaced from this off-site meeting of the top team was the lack of cooperation between the two major divisional functions—engineering and manufacturing.

The next step in my consultative process was to deal with this problem of intergroup conflict. Another off-site meeting was held about a month later with twelve attendees, the top six people from engineering and the equivalent group from manufacturing. These men were predominantly engineers, either design engineers assigned to the engineering function or production engineers working in the manufacturing operation. These two functions had interacted closely, or they were supposed to. The design engineers sent plans (similar to blueprints) to manufacturing to have the specified electrical equipment produced. The manufacturing people complained that the designers established specifications for tolerances that were significantly more stringent than their machinery could handle. The manufacturing department stated further that the

machinery was too old. In order to meet the design specifications, new machinery would have to be purchased, and the cost would be prohibitive. "And besides," they added, "those design guys never set foot on the shop floor anyway, so how would they know?"

Using a standard intergroup problem-solving format from organization development technology, I worked with the two groups (1) to understand and clarify their differences, (2) to reorganize the two functional groups temporarily into three four-person cross-functional groups to solve problems, and (3) to plan specific action steps they could take to correct their intergroup problems. The purpose of this kind of activity is to provide a procedure for bringing the conflict to the surface so that it can be understood and managed more productively. The procedure begins with an exchange of perceptions between the two functional groups about how each group sees itself and the other group. This initial activity is followed by identifying the problems that exist between the two groups. Finally, mixed groups of members from both functions work together to plan action steps that will alleviate the conflict and solve many of the problems.

The outcome of this intergroup meeting clearly suggested yet another step. A major problem needing immediate attention was that the manufacturing group was not working well as a team. The design engineers produced evidence that they often got different answers to the same design production problem from different manufacturing people. Thus, the next consulting step was to help conduct a team-building session for the top group of the manufacturing function. Approximately two months after the intergroup session, I met off-site for two days with the production engineers and general foremen of manufacturing. In this session, we set specific manufacturing targets, established production priorities, clarified roles and responsibilities, and even settled a few interpersonal conflicts.

By this time I had been working with the division on and off, from my initial contact, for close to nine months. After my team-building session with the manufacturing group, I was convinced that I had begun to see some of the real causes of the divisional problems; until then I had been dealing primarily with symptoms, not causes. I noticed, for example, that the first-line supervisors had no tangible way of rewarding their hourly workers; they could use verbal strokes—"Nice job, Alice," or "Keep up the good work, Joe"—but that was about it. They could use negative reinforcement, however, if they so chose—for example, threatening a one- or two-week layoff without pay if performance did not meet standards. This type of action was within the bounds of the union contract.

The hourly employees were paid according to what is called a measured day-work system. Their pay was based on what an industrial engineer had specified as an average rate of productivity for a given job during an eight-hour day. Incentive to produce more for extra pay was not part of the system.

I suggested to the division general manager that a change in the reward system might be in order. At that suggestion, the blood seemed to drain from his face. What I then came to understand was that the present president of the corporation was the person who, years before, had invented the measured day-work system. He did not believe in incentive systems. The division general manager made it clear that he was not about to suggest to the corporate

president that the measured day-work system should perhaps be scrapped. I discussed this matter with my original corporate contact, the staff specialist. He confirmed the situation and stated that the change in the reward system was not in the offing. I became extremely frustrated at this point. I thought that I had finally hit upon a basic cause of divisional, if not corporate, production problems, but it became apparent that this root of the problem tree was not going to be dug up. My consulting work with the division ended shortly thereafter. What I urged as a next step in the overall problem-solving process—to change some elements of the reward system for hourly employees, if not the entire system—was not a step the divisional general manager was willing to take. The corporate staff person was also unwilling to push for change in this aspect of the system.

SOURCE: W. Warner Burke (1987). *Organization development: A normative view*, pp. 2–6, 8. Reading, MA: Addison-Wesley.

Questions

1. This chapter has considered a number of instances of process and technology in organization development. What aspects of these approaches can you identify in this case?

2. To what extent does the consultant's effort appear to be a success? To what extent a failure?

3. Are there any among the processes and technology considered in this chapter that, if applied in this case, might have produced a better result for the company? Explain.

PART THREE Industrial Psychology

12

The Role of Individual, Group, and Cultural Differences

Duke Power Company employed ninety-five people at its Dan River Steam Station in Draper, North Carolina; of these, fourteen were black. For many years the company had restricted black employees to low-paying jobs in the labor department. With the passage of the Civil Rights Act the company instituted a requirement that no one could be promoted out of the labor department unless he or she passed two standardized tests of verbal and mechanical abilities. No evidence was developed by the company to show that these tests had a relationship to job performance, that high scorers performed well or low scorers poorly. Furthermore, it was immediately evident that very few blacks in the labor department could pass the tests, whereas most whites could. Thus blacks remained essentially barred from promotion to the more desirable and higher-paying jobs.

In reviewing this situation the Supreme Court of the United States came to the following conclusions:

The Civil Rights Act proscribes not only discrimination but also practices that are fair in form, but discriminatory in operation. The touchstone is business necessity. If an employment practice which operates to exclude Negroes cannot be shown to be related to job performance, the practice is prohibited.

. . . Good intent or absence of discriminatory intent does not redeem employment procedures or testing mechanisms that operate as "built-in headwinds" for minority groups and are unrelated to measuring job capability.

At Duke Power the Court found that (1) passing a standardized test was not shown to be significantly related to successful job performance, (2) the test requirement operated to disqualify Negroes at a substantially higher rate than whites, and (3) the jobs in question formerly had been filled by white employees as part of a longstanding practice of giving preference to whites. The tests, to be used, should measure the person for the job and not the person in the abstract. At Duke Power this requirement was not met, and consequently the company was found guilty of illegal discrimination by the Supreme Court.

SOURCE: *Griggs v. Duke Power Co.* 401 U.S. 424 (1971), 3 FEP Cases 175.

Cases like Duke Power have engaged the attention of industrial psychologists on many occasions since 1971. In some instances companies have been found guilty of discrimination, as Duke Power was; in other instances they have been found not guilty. But throughout, industrial psychologists have been continuously in demand to conduct studies designed to determine whether tests are performance-related, to serve as expert witnesses in court, and to advise on matters related to discrimination. At the center of these efforts, and of nearly everything that industrial psychologists do in practice, is the fact that individual and group differences exist. At Duke Power the key consideration was the substantial difference between blacks and whites in their test performance. Understanding differences of this kind is very important to the practice of industrial psychology.

As we move now from the theories and research of organizational psychology to the field of industrial psychology, the discussion will become even more concerned with applications and with methods of achieving organizational objectives. Yet at the base of nearly every subject considered is the underlying concept of **individual differences.**

People differ from one another in an almost infinite number of respects, including aspects of their intelligence, learning and decision-making capabilities, motivation, attitudes, commitments, values, personality, perceptual skills, and physical makeup—the areas considered in the first five chapters of Part Two. This fact of difference is something of which we are all so aware that we tend to take it for granted. Yet industrial psychology is influenced more by this diversity of human characteristics than by any other factor.

The individual differences among employees determine in large part what a company can and cannot do. With certain knowledges, skills, abilities, and motives it is easy to carry out certain jobs and accomplish a given set of objectives. But if the goal is to do something else, then the people may well have to change, or new individuals may have to be hired; either way a new arrangement of individual differences is acquired. Thus, when AT&T changed from an end-to-end provider of telephone service to become a major source of computerized systems, it needed many new people with new capabilities. There was also a considerable retraining process. Many skills were no longer needed. In short, the mix of individual differences shifted dramatically.

■ THE IMPORTANCE OF INDIVIDUAL AND GROUP DIFFERENCES

The importance of individual differences is attested to by the fact that, even in areas such as goal setting (as discussed in Chapter 4), where many theorists have considered individual differences irrelevant, an increasing body of evidence indicates that different kinds of people set goals differently (Hollenbeck & Brief, 1987). To understand how individual differences of this kind operate, the best starting point is a frequency distribution of scores on some measure of a human characteristic. Box 12-1 provides such a distribution of scores on a measure of verbal ability administered by Public Opinion Surveys (Gallup Poll) interviewers.

The important thing to note is that the scores are spread out over a very wide range—19 of the possible 21 score points. There are not many people at the extremes of the distribution, but there are some. In addition, the data follow the **normal distribution**, with its typical bell-shaped form, which has been found with very high frequency in the field of industrial-organizational psychology.

□ Group Differences

Box 12-1 contains not only the distribution of test scores for the total sample, but within this, two other distributions—one for the people with the least education and another for those with the most. Neither of these group distributions spreads over as large a range as the total sample distribution. On the average these distributions differ by 6.5 points; this is what is meant by a group difference. A **group difference** is the difference between measures of central tendency, usually the means, for two groups.

Group differences are smaller than individual differences, and they are not as important (Plomin, 1988). In the case of the low- and high-education groups, the individual differences within each group (15 and 13 points, respectively) are about twice as large as the group difference. The individual differences in the total sample are almost three times the group difference. Generalizing from knowledge about a group to specific individuals within that group can be quite hazardous.

This may be illustrated in the case of the data presented in Box 12-1, where the differences in the means for the groups are unusually large. Forty-five percent of those with very little education appear to have the verbal ability to make it through college (assuming that a score of 9 represents a bare minimum requirement). Furthermore, if a company was in search of raw intellectual talent, if it wanted trainability rather than the knowledge a particular college degree might provide, the place to look would not necessarily be among college graduates. There are 105 people with six years of schooling or less who score 9 or above and only 83 college graduates in this category. Clearly there are many more individuals with the needed ability in all educational groups below the college level than among the college graduates, and these individuals can in all probability be recruited more easily and hired at less expense.

BOX 12-1   RESEARCH IN I/O PSYCHOLOGY

Verbal Ability in the United States as Determined by Gallup Poll Interviews

As part of an extensive study conducted under a research grant from the U.S. Department of the Army's Office of the Surgeon General to Princeton University, Public Opinion Surveys of Princeton, New Jersey (the Gallup Poll organization), administered a brief verbal ability test to a cross section of the U.S. population. The test included twenty items, and when attention was focused on adults no longer in school, the number of items answered correctly extended across almost the entire possible range. As the first two columns in the table show, there are people who get only two items right and others who get twenty right:

Test Score	Frequency in Total Sample	Frequency among Those with Six Years of Schooling or Less	Frequency among College Graduates
0			
1			
2	4	3	
3	10	8	
4	20	15	
5	36	23	
6	58	23	
7	85	21	1
8	105	33 ← Median	
9	126	29	3
10	125	25	5
11	139 ← Median	18	3
12	128	12	4
13	114	10	7
14	98	4	13
15	65	3	12 ← Median
16	60	3	13
17	35	1	10
18	27		9
19	8		1
20	6		3
Mean score	10.95	8.23	14.73

A comparison of people at the extremes, those with scores below 4 and those scoring 18 or more, would reveal very different kinds of people with sharply differing work capabilities; substantial individual differences in verbal ability are involved. Yet it is also true that over 50 percent of the people score in the five-point range from 9 through 13. Here differences are less pro-nounced. This is typical of the so-called normal distribution that so many individual differences follow.

The data for individuals who left school with only six years of education and for college graduates also take the normal form with major differences between the extremes. There are high-intelligence people who for various reasons leave school early, and there are relatively low-intelligence people who make it through college by dint of very hard work. In spite of the fact that individual differences for the low-education people range over sixteen scores and the college graduates over fourteen scores, the two groups differ sharply in the points at which the majority are concentrated. The major concentration of low-education people is around a score of 8, and the high-education individuals concentrate around 15; thus, even though substantial individual differences exist *within* each group, there is a sizable group difference *between* groups as well.

SOURCE: John B. Miner (1973). *Intelligence in the United States,* pp. 148–149. Westport, CT; Greenwood Press.

A similar point may be made with regard to the data of Exhibit 12-1. Here the group difference is smaller and of a magnitude more commonly found. The scores were obtained on a measure of motivation to manage, the central construct of the hierarchic role-motivation theory considered in Chapter 3. The average manager, regardless of level or function, has a test score of zero; this is roughly the average for top-level human resource managers in Exhibit 12-1. Thus, there appears to be a somewhat higher level of motivation to manage outside the human resource field (Miner, 1976). However, within the samples considered, 57 percent of the top-level group have the average amount of motivation to manage or more (a score of 0 or higher), whereas 41 percent of the middle-level group score at that level.

These two managerial groups do differ in mean motivation levels (with a high degree of statistical significance), but there remains so much overlap that it would be misleading to substitute knowledge of a person's position level for an actual measurement of motivation to manage. Only a small part of the individual differences on any human characteristic can be expected to be accounted for by membership in a particular group.

☐ How Groups Are Formed

The prior discussion is not meant to imply that some kind of grouping for purposes of comparison is not occasionally useful. Yet serious questions may be raised regarding the usefulness of many of the traditional bases for grouping that have been used in industrial-organizational psychology (Ghiselli, 1974). These include factors such as gender, race, age, geographic area, and educational level. In practice these types of categories turn out to be very broad, and the range of human variation on important work-related characteristics within such groups is often nearly as large as in the population as a whole. Groupings of this kind are so far removed from the characteristics that matter for performance, such as intelligence and motivation, that they have only very limited value for industrial psychology as it seeks to improve performance and effectiveness in organizations. On the other hand, legal enactments over the past thirty years have made certain groupings of this kind important for other reasons.

The relative usefulness of different ways of forming groups can be illustrated with reference to research on the relationships between job satisfaction and the degree to which a job contains variety and freedom, two aspects of job enrichment (see Chapter 4). Variety and freedom are a major source of satisfaction to some people but not to others. The best way of describing people who react positively to variety and freedom is that they possess strong motives involving self-expression and autonomy in the use of skills. People without these strong motives are much less likely to enjoy enriched jobs (Wanous, 1974). An earlier attempt to use rural, as opposed to urban, origins to identify those who would respond

EXHIBIT 12-1   **Distributions of Motivation to Manage Scores for Middle- and Top-Level Human Resource Managers in a Nationwide Sample**

Test Score	Middle-Level Managers	Top-Level Managers
−8		
−7	2	
−6	1	
−5	3	1
−4	4	1
−3	7	5
−2	6	8
−1	6 ← Median	7
0	10	7 ← Median
+1	6	4
+2	3	7
+3	1	4
+4		2
+5		
+6		1
+7		
+8		
Mean score	−1.55	−0.04

well to enriched jobs proved much less successful. A rural background provided only a rough indicator of who might be expected to react favorably to an enriched work context.

Groupings based on factors that are close to on-the-job attitudes and behaviors, factors that are internal to the person in a psychological sense, are much more useful in industrial psychology than groupings in terms of more remote characteristics such as rural–urban origins. This is another way of saying that it is the individual differences directly underlying job attitudes and behavior that are of real importance.

■ GROUP DIFFERENCES MADE IMPORTANT BY LEGISLATION

The gist of the discussion thus far is that primary attention should be given to individual rather than group differences, and if group differences are to be used the groups should be constituted using psychological variables

that are close to actual work behavior and attitudes. Yet industrial psychology has been forced by **legislative enactments** in the area of fair employment practices to give substantial attention to certain other group differences as well (Schmitt & Noe, 1986). An example of one such legislative intervention, Title VII of the Civil Rights Act, is considered in the case of Joyce Greenberg at the end of Chapter 8. In particular, the legal concern has been with gender differences between males and females: racial differences between whites and other minorities, especially blacks: and age differences involving people under 40 and those above that age. The following discussion considers these group differences.

□ Gender Differences

A comprehensive review of **male–female differences** notes a number of "unfounded beliefs" that turn out not to be true. There appear to be no consistent group differences with regard to factors such as sociability,

EXHIBIT 12-2   **Significant Differences between Males and Females**
(number of +s indicates relative size of difference)

Characteristic	Males Higher	Females Higher
Verbal ability		+
Visual-spatial ability	+++	
Numerical ability	++	
Aggressiveness	+	
Activity level	+++	
Performance on laboratory tasks	++	

SOURCES: Diane F. Halpern (1986). *Sex differences in cognitive abilities,* pp. 61–64, Hillsdale, NJ: Erlbaum; Alice H. Eagly & Valerie J. Steffen (1986). Gender and aggressive behavior: A meta-analytic review of the social psychological literature. *Psychological Bulletin, 100,* 322; Warren O. Eaton & Lesley R. Enns (1986). Sex differences in human motor activity level. *Psychological Bulletin, 100,* 24; Wendy Wood (1987). Meta-analytic review of sex differences in group performance. *Psychological Bulletin, 102,* 57.

suggestibility, self-esteem, role-learning ability, analytical skills, achievement motivation, and managerial motivation (Maccoby & Jacklin, 1974). As Exhibit 12-2 indicates, however, there are areas where differences do exist.

In the intellectual sphere, females tend to be somewhat higher than males in the crucial verbal abilities. Yet in the visual-spatial area, including mechanical ability, males tend to score substantially higher. This same difference appears also in the numerical area, although it is somewhat less pronounced. Men tend to be somewhat more aggressive than women, especially when it comes to physical aggression. Women are particularly likely to feel guilty about aggression and to be concerned about the harm that aggression might bring to themselves and others. At least in the early years, males are much more active and appear to possess a stronger activity drive. In laboratory studies, all-male groups and males individually perform better on a variety of tasks. But this may be because the tasks are more male-oriented.

This whole matter of gender differences is in considerable flux at the present time. Increasing numbers of women in the labor force and/or preparing for business careers appear to be associated with a narrowing of gender differences. The overall consequence of more and better employment for married women has been an improved level of mental health. However, their spouses' employment is associated with higher levels of psychological distress among married males (Kessler & McRae, 1982). An example of the latter point is the case of Adele Jones at the end of Chapter 3.

☐ Black–White Differences

Considerable controversy has surrounded the issue of **black–white differences** in the intellectual sphere. This controversy has centered on the matter of environmental versus hereditary causation, and in particular, on the appropriateness of standardized general intelligence tests for black people. A full discussion of these issues would take us far afield and is beyond the scope of this book. What is relevant for present purposes is that measures now in use do tend to yield higher scores for whites on the average. The following summary of a comprehensive review in the area conducted some years ago remains true today:

BOX 12-2 RESEARCH IN I/O PSYCHOLOGY

Numerical Ability Test Scores for Black and White Employees at Georgia Kaolin Company

For many years Georgia Kaolin Company used numerical ability tests to select workers for promotion to higher-level jobs in its clay mining and processing operations. The company operated in a section of rural Georgia where the labor force included more blacks than whites; this disproportionality was reflected in the company's work force as well.

The black employees the company was able to recruit had substantially lower levels of education than the whites. This difference was reflected in performance ratings. Blacks, on the average, were rated less favorably than whites, and this discrepancy was present whether the ratings were made by white foremen or by one of the four black foremen the company employed.

The numerical ability tests were deemed appropriate in selecting workers for higher-level crafts because these jobs required more, and more complex, mathematical calculations. The tests showed a clear relationship to performance ratings in this mathematical area: Those with higher test scores tended to perform better. During the 1980s, scores on a test of intermedi-ate difficulty used to promote workers into middle-level plant jobs were

Blacks: 22 of the 40 items correct

Whites: 31 of the 40 items correct

On a more difficult test used for promotion into the higher-level crafts these scores were

Blacks: 10 of the 35 items correct

Whites: 24 of the 35 items correct

This picture had remained essentially constant since the 1960s. It presented the company with a real dilemma. Should management promote more blacks, even though many would inevitably have rather low numerical ability test scores, and could be expected to perform less well; or should management hold out against continuing pressures from the federal Equal Employment Opportunity Commission and attempt to retain existing performance standards?

The results are almost identical across all age samples: blacks, on the average, earned a mean IQ about 11 points lower than whites. Wide individual differences around this mean were found in all samples, however (Matarazzo, 1972).

Box 12-2 describes how this black–white differential has operated at Georgia Kaolin Company over many years. It is apparent that white employees do test higher in numerical ability, and that this differential presents the company with a problem in maintaining performance levels. This is true because the black employees perform less well also. Other studies have found similar performance differen-tials in favor of whites (Ford, Kraiger, & Schectman, 1986). Interestingly, however, the performance decline is not as great as the intelligence difference would predict.

This chapter began with a now-famous case in the early history of employment discrimination law. At Duke Power Company intelligence tests were introduced and used to screen blacks out of the promotion process, even though these tests had not been shown to relate to job performance; thus the company could not claim the defense of **business necessity.** The tests operated as they did to produce discrimination because blacks scored below whites on them.

EXHIBIT 12-3   Significant Black–White Personality Differences

Personality Characteristic	Mean Scores for	
	Blacks	*Whites*
Social dominance—self-confidence, a good leader, a strong personality	1.53	1.37
Fundamentalist religious belief	1.63	1.49
Compulsive orderliness—prefers planned activities, neatness, and routine	1.64	1.45
Self-criticism—feelings of guilt, self-reproach, discouragement	1.64	1.52
Psychological toughness—unconcerned about others' opinions and being liked	1.60	1.31
Proneness to take risks—disregard for danger, adventuresomeness	1.35	1.63
Power orientation—mistrust of others, material ambition, decisiveness	1.56	1.34
Psychological vulnerability—timidity, sensitivity to criticism	1.50	1.60
Unconventional morality—behavior beyond conventional mores	1.56	1.66
Conformity—conventional attitudes toward dress, propriety, right and wrong	1.55	1.41

SOURCE: Adapted from E. E. Jones (1978). Black–white personality differences: Another look. *Journal of Personality Assessment, 42,* 247–249.

Numerous personality differences between blacks and whites have been noted as well. The results of one study are given in Exhibit 12-3. A number of the characteristics that predominate among blacks—social dominance, psychological toughness, power orientation, and reduced psychological vulnerability—are of the kind found to exist in more successful managers. The research in general supports the conclusion that blacks often possess the drive and motivation that make for good managers.

Other characteristics that distinguish blacks from whites in Exhibit 12-3 appear to be unrelated to managerial performance, but may contribute to effective performance in other jobs—compulsive orderliness, avoidance of risks, and conventional morality, for example.

☐ Age Difference

Although there was some controversy in the past regarding the path that intellectual abilities take over the average life span, the picture is now becoming quite clear. Increases in verbal ability and general intelligence can be expected with age at least up to the normal retirement age (Birren, Cunningham, & Yamamoto, 1983). This pattern is most pronounced at higher occupational, educational, and intellectual levels; it is true of males and females. Managers in large corporations may actually be expected to improve in verbal ability with age. Research conducted in companies such as AT&T, Sears, Roebuck, and Exxon has consistently found that verbal ability is a major factor in managerial performance (Campbell, Dunnette, Lawler, & Weick, 1970). Thus it seems likely that managerial performance often improves with age, contrary to what many companies with early retirement programs for managers have assumed.

In areas other than the verbal, people may well become less competent as they advance beyond age forty. A rather pronounced decrement with age is likely to occur on tasks that emphasize speed. Here there is no doubt that significant decreases occur—partly because of reduced efficiency in visual perception, partly as a result of a falloff in the rapidity with which muscular responses can be carried out. Furthermore, there is a concomitant decline in visual-spatial ability with age, a decline that on occasion has been found to be more pronounced among females (Halpern, 1986).

None of this should be taken to imply that older workers cannot be taught new skills. The problems that do arise in this area appear to be attributable primarily to inappropriate motivation rather than to a lack of abilities required for learning. Older people often develop rather definite attitudes as a result of their extensive work experience. Beliefs regarding the correct way to do things are reinforced again and again over the years, to a point where they can become firmly entrenched. For this reason those who have been in the labor force for a considerable period may fail to see any value in new techniques and procedures that younger people view quite positively; they may even be right on occasion.

Older people often fail to learn new skills largely because they do not believe the learning is desirable, rather than because they lack ability. The following quotation illustrates what may happen when age-based differences in attitudes exist (Korman & Korman, 1980, p. 125):

> As a result of corporate pressures, an increasing number of young managers and executives with MBA-level training have joined the company. This has created a managerial force consisting of two very different types of managers: the new, younger people and the oldtimers who date back to preacquisition days. There is now conflict in the company as these mutually antagonistic groups work together. Open hostility at staff meetings and nasty backbiting are common. One illustration of the problem is that despite the fact that an expensive computer system has been introduced, it is not being utilized at maximum effectiveness because of the antipathy of the two groups toward each other. The old line sales-marketing executives are unwilling to work with the young manager in charge of the electronic data processing facility. Throughout the company similar conflicts to these are taking place.

Age and Performance. Insofar as work performance is concerned, it is apparent that problems arise most often when an older worker is employed in a factory job or similar work that requires extensive physical activity. Beginning sometime in their forties, people may well have increasing difficulty carrying out repetitive physical activities at a rapid pace. The quality of work done may be maintained at a high level, but quantity is likely to fall off. Where the work is less physical in nature and verbal ability is an important factor, improvement with age can be anticipated. A recent survey of age–performance relationships overall found a generally upward trend in productivity with age (Waldman & Avolio, 1986). However, ratings of performance by superiors tended to be slightly lower for older employees, suggesting a possible source of bias. This departure from the productivity results did not occur among those working in the professions, and it was not characteristic of ratings by an individual's peers. The data as a whole indicate that older workers more often than not perform better.

Obsolescence. The view that older workers are generally more satisfied with their jobs has been confirmed many times (Rhodes, 1983). However, when **skill obsolescence** is involved, so that people feel the pace of advancing knowledge in their field is more rapid than their capacity or opportunity to absorb it, they are likely to experience much stress and less job satisfaction. Obsolescence has been defined as follows (Fossum, Arvey, Paradise, & Robbins, 1986, p. 364):

Obsolescence of this kind occurs when the person requirements of a job which are demanded by its tasks, duties, and responsibilities become incongruent with the stock of knowledge, skills, and abilities currently possessed by the individual; given that the knowledge, skills, and abilities were previously congruent with job demands.

This is not a matter of motivation or attitude: It is a matter of no longer knowing how to do the job. Engineers may become less satisfied as they grow older if they remain in a rapidly changing engineering occupation. Often these individuals return to school to start a new career or reinvigorate an old one. Although obsolescence can be overcome with sufficient ambition, it remains a major problem for those who specialize in the merchandising of knowledge, such as professionals (Kaufman, 1982).

☐ The Reason Legally Specified Group Differences Are Important

Industrial psychologists need to know about the types of group differences we have been considering because the very existence of these differences may serve to hamper the hiring and upgrading of women, blacks, and older workers. And companies may be under considerable pressure from many sources to hire and promote just these individuals. The important point is that when a constant hiring standard is maintained and no special recruiting efforts are mounted, groups that are significantly lacking in a given characteristic, whatever it may be, will not show up in large numbers in a company work force.

If measures of visual-spatial ability and activity level are used in the employee selection process, fewer female applicants and many more male applicants will be hired. Similarly, using verbal ability and general intelligence measures tends to yield disproportionately fewer black hires. Use of highly speeded and visual-spatial tests will yield

fewer people over age 40 under normal circumstances. In all of these cases, the lower average scores in a group mean that there are likely to be fewer members who will exceed any minimum acceptable standard.

To eliminate this effect and hire more females, blacks, or older workers, it would be necessary either to recruit a disproportionately large number of applicants from these population groups while maintaining existing standards, or to lower the standards for the specified groups. In any event, to adopt either of these strategies it is necessary to know what existing group differences may be anticipated. This is why a knowledge of legally specified group differences is important.

It is important to recognize that there are three possible approaches to removing group differences within a company work force if it is necessary to do so:

1. Go outside the company and find people within a specified group who have the needed characteristic.
2. Change existing employees within the specified group so they have the characteristic.
3. Change existing job requirements so that the characteristic that appeared to be in short supply in the specified group is no longer so crucial.

■ CULTURAL DIFFERENCES

Knowledge as to how differences in national culture may influence company management is of considerable importance to U.S. companies. Large numbers of firms are faced with the need to staff overseas offices and in many cases the prospect of manning major production and distribution facilities in foreign countries. If these international operations are to be managed effectively, a very high priority must be given to the development and uti-

BOX 12-3   I/O PSYCHOLOGY IN PRACTICE

The Internationalization of Dow Chemical Company

When Zoltan Merszei, who grew up in Hungary, left Dow Chemical Company, he shifted from CEO of Dow to the same position at Occidental Petroleum. Paul Oreffice then took over as Dow's chief executive. Oreffice was born in Italy and spent much of his career in Europe and Latin America, particularly Brazil.

In the early 1950s Dow's only foreign subsidiary was in Canada. At this time work in other countries was generally viewed negatively, a place for managers whose careers had fizzled in the United States. Selling in world markets was primarily for the purpose of dumping excess capacity. Similar views were held within many U.S. companies of that period.

As Dow's foreign sales escalated during the 1960s and 1970s, and on through the 1980s, to a point where over 50 percent of its market was outside the United States, the company undertook a deliberate campaign to internationalize its managers. One approach used was to give individuals who were considered to be on a fast track to top executive levels considerable international exposure. Accordingly, C. B. Branch was shifted from head of the company's fastest-growing division to manager of foreign operations. Herbert Doan, a member of the Dow family, went to Europe on a fact-finding mission. Both Branch and Doan subsequently became presidents of Dow. Clearly international experience was important. The image that had prevailed in the 1950s rapidly dissipated. The appointments of Merszei and then Oreffice were merely a reflection of the change that had occurred.

lization of knowledge that indicates how managing should be varied in the light of differing cultural considerations. In moving to this level of intercultural competence, U.S. firms have often had to overcome a type of provincialism that held international knowledge and experience in low regard. Box 12-3 describes what happened at Dow Chemical Company as it moved into the international arena.

That important **cultural variations** do exist can no longer be doubted. In a study conducted throughout the international operations of IBM, comparisons were made involving employees in forty countries or regions around the world. Certain aspects of this research were considered in Box 5-5. Additional aspects emphasizing cultural differences are treated in Exhibit 12-4. There are tendencies for certain countries to group together and exhibit a degree of cultural homogeneity—the Scandinavian countries, for instance, and certain countries in South America. However, the differences are more pronounced. Yugoslavia emphasizes hierarchic differences, risk avoidance, collectivism, and more feminine behavior patterns. Great Britain is just the opposite, tending toward reduced authority differences, risk taking, individualism, and a masculine behavior emphasis. These kinds of differences can have a major impact on what types of human resource programs employees will accept and a society condone. From the data of Exhibit 12-4, it is not surprising that Sweden has often been very receptive to programs of a sociotechnical nature involving shared decision making.

An example of the relevance of cultural differences for industrial psychology comes from research on collective bargaining between management and labor. Sizable differences in basic strategies and approaches to dealing with a labor union were found

EXHIBIT 12-4 Country Differences on Four Values

Rank	Emphasis on Power Distance and Hierarchic Inequality	Emphasis on Avoiding Uncertainty and Risk	Emphasis on Individual Rather than Collective Action	Emphasis on Masculine Rather than Feminine Behavior
Ten countries or regions with the highest values scores				
1.	Philippines	Greece	United States	Japan
2.	Mexico	Portugal	Australia	Austria
3.	Venezuela	Belgium	Great Britain	Venezuela
4.	India	Japan	Canada	Italy
5.	Yugoslavia	Yugoslavia	Netherlands	Switzerland
6.	Singapore	Peru	New Zealand	Mexico
7.	Brazil	Argentina	Italy	Ireland
8.	France	France	Belgium	Great Britain
9.	Hong Kong	Chile	Denmark	Germany
10.	Colombia	Spain	France	Colombia
Twenty Intermediate countries or regions				
Ten countries or regions with the lowest values scores				
31.	Great Britain	Canada	Yugoslavia	Spain
32.	Switzerland	United States	Hong Kong	Thailand
33.	Finland	Philippines	Chile	Portugal
34.	Norway	India	Thailand	Chile
35.	Sweden	Ireland	Singapore	Finland
36.	Ireland	Great Britain	Taiwan	Yugoslavia
37.	New Zealand	Hong Kong	Peru	Denmark
38.	Denmark	Sweden	Pakistan	Netherlands
39.	Israel	Denmark	Colombia	Norway
40.	Austria	Singapore	Venezuela	Sweden

SOURCE: Adapted from Geert Hofstede (1980). *Cultures consequences—International differences in work related values*, p. 315. Beverly Hills, CA: Sage.

EXHIBIT 12-5   How French and American Managers Differ in Their Perceptions of the Limits of Managerial Authority

Activities that French managers believe should be less *subject to managerial authority, in contrast with American managers:*

How many drinks, if any, a subordinate has at lunchtime
Whether a subordinate uses profane language at work
The type of clothing worn at work
The amount of time spent talking to the subordinate's family on the telephone at work
What clubs or organizations a subordinate belongs to
How much alcohol, if any, a subordinate consumes during the working day
The amount of company work a subordinate takes home
Whether a subordinate uses the company's products in preference to those of competitors
How active a subordinate is in recruiting others to join the company
The amount of time spent in job-related reading at work
How a subordinate divides the working day among various duties
How much a subordinate competes with peers for promotion
How much leisure time the subordinate spends with his or her subordinates
How a subordinate supervises a secretary
Whether a subordinate wears a beard or mustache
How faithful a subordinate is to his or her spouse
The amount of additional education obtained in job-related areas

SOURCE: Adapted from G. Inzerilli (1980). The legitimacy of managerial authority—A comparative study. *Academy of Management Proceedings, 40,* 61.

between American managers on the one hand and Danes, Dutch, Germans, and Britons on the other. The Americans were likely to settle more rapidly, thus avoiding deadlocks, to give up more in cash settlements, and to resort to trade-offs among items under consideration more frequently (Shapira & Bass, 1975). The differences suggest that injecting an American bargaining team into German negotiations could very well produce some startling results.

Almost any area that industrial psychology concerns itself with may be influenced by cultural and national differences of the kind described above. People in various parts of the world may view things very differently, and in particular they may have widely varying value-based conceptions of what is right and what is wrong. The following examples provide a sampling of these differences from two countries widely dispersed across the globe.

☐ Managerial Authority in French Culture

Exhibit 12-5 makes an important point with regard to company operations in France. The French, much more than Americans, are likely to view various uses of managerial authority as lacking legitimacy and beyond the point of being proper or appropriate. Consequently, there may be resistance to many managerial actions that in the United States would be viewed as entirely appropriate. In the study of Exhibit 12-5, there was only one activity where American managers rejected authority more. American managers were more likely to believe a manager had no right to influence the amount of leisure time a subordinate spends at company social functions. Thus the French are more rejecting of managerial authority by a ratio of 17 to 1.

Some of the activities noted in Exhibit 12-5 should make little difference in running a

EXHIBIT 12-6   A Comparison of Japanese and American Work Values and Behaviors

	Japanese Pattern	American Pattern
Employment term	Lifetime for males	Primarily short, but varies
Decision making	Consensus among many	Individual by managers
Responsibility	Held collectively by many	Resides in the individual
Evaluation and promotion	Slow and based primarily on loyalty	Rapid and based primarily on performance
Control system	Informal and not stated explicitly	Formally stated and written down
Career path	Movement through many areas	Within a specialized area
Breadth of supervisory concern	The whole person and all aspects of life	Segmented and focused on performance

SOURCE: Adapted from William G. Ouchi (1981). *Theory Z: How American business can meet the Japanese challenge.* Reading, MA: Addison-Wesley.

business, although the overall implication is that it may be harder to get many things done in France. However, the tendency for the French to be less receptive to company efforts to control work behavior (allocation of time at work, work taken home, etc.) can have direct implications for productivity. Authority will be less effective in France and presumably that is why the French are particularly likely to resort to participative and decision-sharing approaches to get the work done (Heller & Wilpert, 1981).

☐ Paternalism in Japanese Culture

Japanese culture repeatedly has been found to differ from the cultures of other countries. Because it is very homogeneous, the controlling effects of cultural values can be strong. The key element appears to be an intense organizational **paternalism.** Life off the job and the world of work are closely melded, so that the authority of the organization extends far beyond that in the United States. In return, employees expect considerable job security. There are strong values placed on the subor-

dination of the individual to the group, acceptance of one's place in the hierarchy, conformity, and the view that membership in the national family results in basic duties and obligations (Kleinberg, 1989). This is, however, an essentially masculine ethic. After marriage, females historically have not been an important factor in the workplace. The differences between Japan and the United States in these regards are pointed up in Exhibit 12-6.

Under conditions of this kind, ties to the organization tend to be strong and turnover, at least among males for whom the system is designed, should present few problems. Companies can expect a highly motivated and loyal work force, but careful attention must be given to meeting cultural expectations. Because of the emphasis on shared decision making, many decisions in Japanese firms are long drawn out. Once a decision is made, however, acceptance is widespread and implementation presents few problems.

Exhibit 12-7 presents a model of the type of human resources program that meshes best with Japanese culture. Training is emphasized, turnover is discouraged, pay levels are

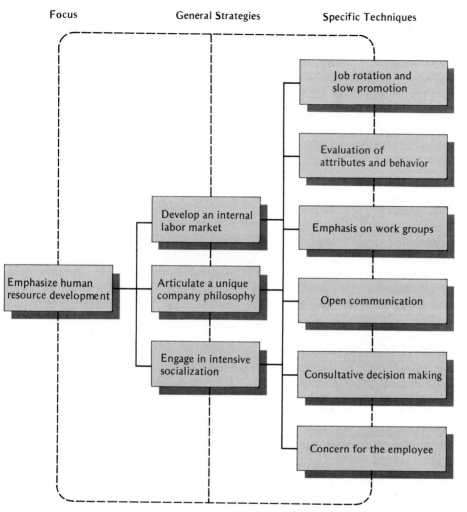

Focus   General Strategies   Specific Techniques

Emphasize human resource development

Develop an internal labor market

Articulate a unique company philosophy

Engage in intensive socialization

Job rotation and slow promotion

Evaluation of attributes and behavior

Emphasis on work groups

Open communication

Consultative decision making

Concern for the employee

EXHIBIT 12-7   Human Resources Model of Japanese Management
The flow is from a focus on human development, to general strategies, to specific techniques.
SOURCE: Nina Hatvany & Vladimir Pucik (1981). An integrated management system: Lessons from the Japanese experience. *Academy of Management Review, 6,* 470.

low initially and very high after experience is gained, fit with company values is important in selecting new employees, performance evaluation stresses team capability and conformity, and a wide range of employee and family benefits are provided.

☐ Dealing with Cultural Differences

Industrial psychologists are often concerned with the process of dealing with cultural factors of the kinds we have considered. They may develop and operate selection procedures for filling positions in foreign countries.

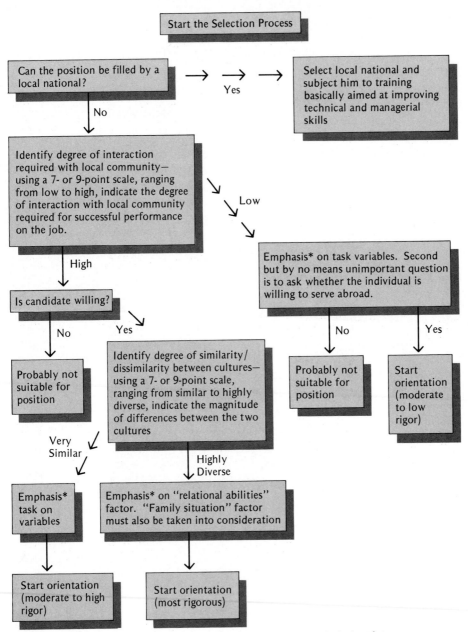

Start the Selection Process

Can the position be filled by a local national? → → → Yes → Select local national and subject him to training basically aimed at improving technical and managerial skills

No ↓

Identify degree of interaction required with local community—using a 7- or 9-point scale, ranging from low to high, indicate the degree of interaction with local community required for successful performance on the job. ↘ Low

High ↓

Is candidate willing? ↘ Yes

No ↓

Emphasis* on task variables. Second but by no means unimportant question is to ask whether the individual is willing to serve abroad.

No ↓   Yes ↓

Probably not suitable for position

Identify degree of similarity/dissimilarity between cultures—using a 7- or 9-point scale, ranging from similar to highly diverse, indicate the magnitude of differences between the two cultures

Probably not suitable for position

Start orientation (moderate to low rigor)

Very Similar ↙   Highly Diverse ↓

Emphasis* task on variables

Emphasis* on "relational abilities" factor. "Family situation" factor must also be taken into consideration

↓

Start orientation (moderate to high rigor)

Start orientation (most rigorous)

*"Emphasis" does not mean ignoring the other factors. It only means that it should be the dominant factor.

EXHIBIT 12-8   The Selection Decision Process for Multinational Operations
Staffing foreign positions requires an understanding of personal capabilities, interaction requirements, training needs, cultural similarities, and family situations.
SOURCE: Rosalie L. Tung (1988). *The new expatriates: Managing human resources abroad,* p. 25. Cambridge, MA: Ballinger.

BOX 12-4 I/O PSYCHOLOGY IN PRACTICE

How the Olivetti Group Trains for Foreign Assignments

Olivetti is the world's leading maker of electronic typewriters; it also produces office automation and data processing equipment. An Italian firm, it markets heavily in Europe, but it also has substantial sales and operations throughout the world. The company has an alliance with AT&T which provides the latter with a 25 percent ownership interest in Olivetti.

Because management turnover is very low, the company has few qualms about investing in training programs to develop an international orientation. These programs are extensive.

1. Language training—up to six months of training in any language needed

2. The international executive program—a two-week course for top executives, conducted in England, dealing with the firm's international strategies

3. The Olivetti management development program—a two-week course for senior managers, conducted in Switzerland and England

4. Environmental briefing—provided as needed by sending managers to various university programs dealing with specific cultures

Olivetti's comprehensive training programs prepare expatriates for their new assignments. Accordingly there is very little need to bring people back to Italy. When repatriation is needed it is because of incompatibility of cultural systems and values, health reasons, or strains within the family. The company has many managers who spend almost their entire careers in foreign assignments, moving from one country to another as promotion opportunities occur.

SOURCE: Rosalie A. Tung (1988). *The new expatriates: Managing human resources abroad*, pp. 93–105. Cambridge, MA: Ballinger.

They may be involved in training and developing managers and others for multinational assignments. Both of these activities require a comprehensive understanding of cultural differences. Exhibit 12-8 shows how selection and training activities interact with a knowledge of cultural differences to produce decisions regarding what should be done in various situations. Note that an evaluation of family circumstances is important here. Companies not only send managers to foreign assignments, they send whole families. Failure in the assignment can be as much a family matter as an employee matter. If any family member cannot cope, it is probable that the whole family will need to be repatriated.

Box 12-4 describes how Olivetti, an Italian office machine company, trains for foreign assignments. The training in languages and cultures is geared specifically to the degree of difference between Italy and the country involved. In general, European firms such as Olivetti, and Japanese firms, do much better in staffing foreign operations than U.S. firms. While among U.S. firms as many as 30 percent of the people sent overseas are dismissed or recalled home because they or their families cannot function effectively in a foreign environment, the top rate for European and Japanese firms is 15 percent, and for most of these companies it is under 5 percent.

KEY TERMS

Individual differences
Normal distribution
Group difference
Legislative enactments
Male–female differences

Black–white differences
Business necessity
Skill obsolescence
Cultural variations
Paternalism

SUMMARY

Individual differences are the basic element from which industrial psychology operates. They are more important than *group differences,* which span a smaller range. When groupings need to be made, it is generally more fruitful to use internal factors such as intelligence and motives that are close to the actual behavior of individuals, rather than global constructs such as education or gender. Individual differences available in a company's work force serve to determine what strategies and policies can be implemented effectively, and even what strategies can be formulated.

Legislative enactments have made groupings based on race, color, religion, national origin, gender, and age of considerable importance to industrial psychologists. There clearly are major group differences in intelligence and personality that can relate to performance. A major challenge is to find ways of overcoming any performance deficiencies in legally protected groups. Techniques available

include expanded recruiting, changing existing employees, and altering jobs.

Groupings in terms of culture are also significant for industrial psychology. There are major *differences between cultures,* and these differences may limit not only the types of talent available, but also the ways in which people may be managed and business activities carried out. Examples of how this occurs may be derived from the very limited legitimizing of authority in French culture and the *paternalism* of Japanese culture. Cultural differences play a particularly important role in staffing decisions and in specifying training needs. It is important to select managers for foreign assignments who can function effectively in the new cultural environment. It is also important to provide training and development that will prepare individuals for new cultures and protect them against culture shock.

QUESTIONS

1. How do cultures differ in their values regarding the use of authority and power in organizations? What are the implications of these differences?
2. In what sense are group differences relatively unimportant to industrial-organizational psychology, and in what sense are they, or at least

some of them, very important? Support your answer with examples.
3. What approaches may be taken to deal with cultural differences?
4. How does the concept of business necessity relate to group differences?
5. Under what circumstances might individual dif-

ferences that are imposing limitations internally within a firm serve to limit external recruiting decisions as well?

6. What is unique about the Japanese system of managing human resources?

7. What is a normal distribution, and how does it relate to individual differences?

8. In what ways do workers in the United States appear to differ from workers in other parts of the world?

9. What group differences in the intellectual or cognitive area have been identified by research? What are the implications of these differences?

CASE PROBLEM

Caught between the Courts and Organizational Values: A Bank in Trouble

A bank operating in a medium-sized city had developed some major human resource problems, largely because of its history. From its very beginnings, the bank had had close ties to the local Polish community and also to the union movement. The two relationships were in fact closely bound together. The city had been settled by a large number of Polish immigrants, who went to work in the local manufacturing plants. These plants became unionized in due course and, at about the same time, the bank was founded. Although there was no official designation, the bank actually operated to serve the Polish community. Most of its depositors came from that community, and most of its loans were for real estate and businesses acquired by Polish residents. In essence, the bank grew as the Polish community moved up in socioeconomic status.

Because in the early years many of the people the bank dealt with were union members, the bank itself became unionized at a time when this was not very common. In this period, there were a number of banks established and owned by unions. Although not in quite this category, our bank was strongly influenced by organized labor from its beginnings.

Out of these origins a stable set of human resource policies emerged. The bank favored members of the local Polish community in its hiring. Many new employees were recruited by family members already employed. All this was simply good business. Furthermore the union supported this policy and placed strong emphasis in contract negotiations on job security and seniority as a basis for

promotion. As a result, Polish recruits tended to stay with the bank; there was little turnover. Over time, many moved up into senior management positions. At the same time, other members of the Polish community became financially successful in business ventures and joined the bank's board of directors. Through them, pressures from the Polish subculture to maintain the favorable hiring status of its members were mediated to the bank itself.

All this was working well, until the bank unexpectedly found itself faced with a court order to drastically increase its hiring and upgrading of blacks. As the Poles had moved out of the plants and up in socioeconomic status, they had been replaced by blacks. Thus, the local labor force came to include a high proportion of blacks who, because of the bank's long-established hiring practices, were only minimally represented among its employees. The court order presented particular difficulties because the bank was not growing, had an average employee age of roughly 45—with an overall high level of seniority but with few people close to retirement—and thus was doing very little hiring or promoting.

As a consequence of the bank's lack of growth in recent years (and in fact of some financial problems) as well as changes in the banking regulations and the court order to increase the proportions of blacks at all levels, serious consideration began to be given at top-management levels to expanding into new markets, perhaps by acquisition, as well as to undertaking new types of investments. The bank had never had a strong trust department, and this was an area where there was a clear opportunity for growth. The problem was that all of these growth strategies required technical and managerial talent that the bank did not have; it was hard to implement these kinds of strategy in the face of the homogeneous internal values that the bank had acquired. There were a lot of people, many at the highest levels, who simply did not want change.

Questions

1. What are various limitations or constraints on the actions the bank might take in this situation?

2. What actions might be taken to deal with each of these limitations?

3. What specifically should the bank do to cope with its human resource problems?

13

Job Analysis and Job Evaluation

Rubbermaid, Inc., faced a difficult situation involving two jobs. One position, entitled "sales representative," was filled primarily by males, while the other, which females usually performed, was called "market representative." Originally the sales representative position was established as a full-time job dealing with retail and wholesale trade. The market representative position was to provide part-time work at the retail level for women whose children were in school. The pay for the latter position was at a substantially lower rate.

Over time, there was some movement in certain parts of the country which produced a narrowing of the gap between the two positions without a significant reduction of the pay differential. In one of the affected areas a group of women came together and filed a suit against the company claiming that the sales representative and market representative positions were really the same, and that accordingly the women doing market representative work were entitled to the much higher pay of the sales representatives. The company had no job analysis data to refute this claim that the two jobs were the same.

Subsequent to the filing of the suit, a psychologist was hired by Rubbermaid to study the situation. He recommended that district managers who supervised both sales and market representatives be administered a job analysis questionnaire in which they could describe the work performed in both positions. A list of job duties performed in both positions was compiled from many sources; there were eighty questions. District managers were asked in a face-to-face interview to indicate how much time people in each position spent performing each duty. Half the managers described the sales manager position first and the marketing manager position second, while the other half discussed the positions in the reverse order.

The resulting analysis indicated that there remained major differences between the positions of a kind which would justify the pay differential. The responses of the district managers to certain of the job analysis questions were as follows:

	Percent of Time			
	None	*Small*	*Medium*	*Large*
Sell cold to new accounts				
Market representatives (female)	21	79		
Sales representatives (male)		50	36	14
Hold sales meetings for wholesalers and retailers				
Market representatives (female)	100			
Sales representatives (male)	14	50	36	
Straighten, clean, and inventory merchandise on counter				
Market representatives (female)			14	86
Sales representatives (male)		7	57	36
Create "plan-o-grams" for store layouts				
Market representatives (female)	86	14		
Sales representatives (male)		64	21	15
Deal with accounts having above-average dollar volume				
Market representatives (female)	65	14	14	7
Sales representatives (male)		28	36	36

	Percent of Time	
	No	Yes
Work trade shows at a national level		
Market representatives (female)	86	14
Sales representatives (male)	0	100
Spend nights away from home		
Market representatives (female)	79	21
Sales representatives (male)	0	100
Work on a part-time basis		
Market representatives (female)	36	64
Sales representatives (male)	100	0

	Low	Medium	High
How would you describe the level of ability required to perform the job?			
Market representatives (female)	86	14	
Sales representatives (male)		36	64
How would you describe the responsibility level of the job—the accountability, the importance of the job obligation to the company?			
Market representatives (female)	50	43	7
Sales representatives (male)		21	79

Although an after-the-fact job analysis of this kind is hardly a substitute for preexisting job analyses, Rubbermaid did obtain an out-of-court settlement that it considered satisfactory based on these data.

In the Rubbermaid case, the discrimination charge was filed under Title VII of the Civil Rights Act and the Equal Pay Act. Job analysis data are used frequently in court cases of this kind to establish what employees actually do in their work. In this instance it was most appropriate to obtain the needed information using standardized interviews with those individuals who supervised the jobs being studied. As we will see, this is only one among many approaches in job analysis.

Industrial psychologists rely heavily on knowledge of the existing job structure in carrying out many aspects of their work. In large part this knowledge comes from job analysis.

Job analysis is a method of establishing a base against which the actual behavior of a firm's employees may be evaluated. It serves to provide a picture of each job and of the interrelationships among jobs. Taken as a whole, the results of job analyses yield a comprehensive and detailed picture of how a company has structured itself to achieve its objectives. As we will see, job analysis provides the underpinning and the unifying force behind almost everything industrial psychologists do.

A number of the theories and ideas considered in Part Two deal with job analysis and design in important respects. These views are typically related to aspects of motivation and involve inputs to the design of jobs from incumbents and work-group members. Chapter 4 includes discussions of management by objectives, motivation-hygiene theory, job characteristics theory, and alternative work schedules, all of which relate to the design of jobs in some manner. Chapter 7 takes up the concept of autonomous work groups. Chapter 11 extends many of these ideas into the realm of organization development, which may also concern itself with restructuring work. It is apparent that these ideas from organizational psychology represent some of the major advances in the field of job analysis in recent years (Algera, 1987; Wall & Martin, 1987).

■ JOB ANALYSIS: DEFINITIONS, APPLICATIONS, AND SCOPE

□ Terminology of Occupational Study

Before discussing the methods and procedures of job analysis, it is essential to establish an understanding of the terms to be used. The definitions that follow come as close as possible to a generally accepted terminology (McCormick, 1979).

A **task** is a distinct work activity carried out for a specific purpose. An example is a retail clerk in a department store dusting merchandise. Another example is the same clerk setting up the same merchandise in an attractive display. When there are enough such related activities, a position is created.

A **position** is a specific set of tasks and duties performed by a given individual in a given firm at a given time. The number of positions in a company at one time is equal to the number of employees at the same time.

A **job** is normally made up of a number of similar positions in a given company. However, a job may involve only one such position at a given time. For example, a store may have one retail hardware clerk or many,

depending on the size of the store and the scope of its business.

An **occupation** is a number of similar jobs existing in different companies and at different times. Examples of occupations are carpenters and civil engineers.

A **job description** is a written statement of the tasks, duties, and behaviors required in a given job, plus the personal qualifications that all candidates for the job must possess. (The latter aspect is often referred to separately as the job specification.)

A **job family** is a collection of two or more jobs that either require similar worker characteristics or contain parallel tasks, as determined by the job analysis.

When a study is made of the tasks performed by a single person, the term *position analysis* is usually employed. When the scope is broadened to include two or more positions that are similar enough to be considered one job, it is more characteristic to speak of **job analysis.** Because in the business world, at least at lower levels, there are usually two or more similar positions within a firm, the designation *job analysis* is typically used. This analysis provides information about the job, the necessary activities and personal requirements involved, and its relationship to other jobs. It results in the job description and job specification.

Although the job analysis frequently utilizes the actual behavior of incumbents, the job description provides a statement of what should be: It is a set of role prescriptions or requirements. Job analysts usually develop their descriptions from information that is derived from people actually doing the work, but this does not mean that the final result is a specific statement of what any individual actually does. It is instead an idealized statement of what that person and others holding the position are expected to do.

On occasion, job descriptions are written well before the company has actually employed anyone in the position. In such

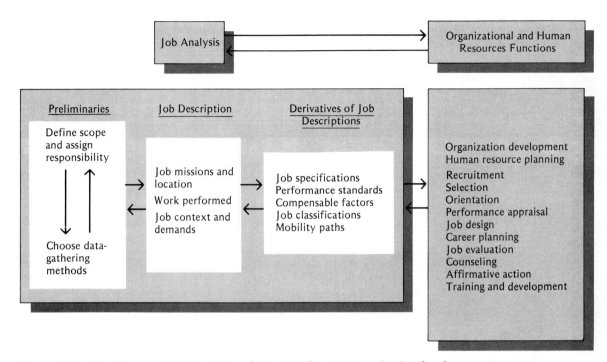

EXHIBIT 13-1   The Process of Job Analysis and How It Relates to Organizational and Human Resource Functions

Preliminaries result in a job description, which in turn yields various derivatives, and this total job analysis process then feeds into the performance of a wide range of organizational and human resources functions. At each step there may be a feedback process which modifies the preceding step.

SOURCE: J. V. Ghorpade & Thomas J. Atchison (1980). The concept of job analysis: A review and some suggestions. *Public Personnel Management, 9,* 137.

instances, the role prescriptions cannot be based on the actual behavior of incumbents. Perhaps the most striking example of this derives from the field of space travel in its early days. Before each astronaut started out on a flight, a detailed job description was developed, specifying exactly what the person was expected to do and when. Because of the physical and psychological stresses involved, a great variety of factors had to be considered in constructing such role prescriptions. In many instances, simulated conditions were devised to determine which behaviors would contribute most effectively to goal attainment. Here there can be no question but that an ideal behavior pattern was developed.

☐ Applications of Job Analysis

We have already noted how job analysis data may be used in connection with court cases. Exhibit 13-1 outlines the wide range of other uses to which job analysis information may be put, and shows how the job analysis process contributes to, and may be influenced by, these ends.

The data derived from job analyses aid considerably in evaluating the behavior of individual employees. Are they doing what they are supposed to do? Jobs are structured with the objective of contributing as much as possible to implementing company strategies; then individual behaviors are compared against these expected patterns. In this way, an evaluation of individual performance is obtained. This contribution to the appraisal and evaluation process is an important function of job analysis.

Job evaluation is perhaps the most widespread application of the data of job analysis, and in fact job analysis activities typically are housed in a compensation unit (Levine, Sistrunk, McNutt, & Gael, 1988). Job descriptions are used to evaluate jobs in terms of their worth to the company. Wage and salary differentials are then established to reflect the existing differences in job requirements. In this connection, it is important to make a clear distinction between job analysis, job evaluation, and individual evaluation. The first refers to the establishment of role prescriptions; the second to the rating of jobs for payment purposes; and the third to the rating of people in relation to role prescriptions.

Job descriptions are of considerable value as guides to hiring, placement, and promotion practices. People who will be most successful, who will most closely approximate role requirements, should be selected for employment and assigned to appropriate kinds of work. Therefore, selection procedures must be developed on the basis of a detailed knowledge of position requirements. The use of job analysis in this manner is not only good practice; it is also a necessary step in establishing the job-relatedness of selection procedures under equal-opportunity laws and executive orders (Thompson & Thompson, 1982).

Job analysis provides an indication of the needs that training and management development must fulfill. Training programs should be devised to provide skills, knowledge, and motives that are lacking but that are required for effective or outstanding performance. Training should be along the lines required to generate a close match between actual and expected behavior.

The data of job analysis can be used to identify job hazards and dangerous working conditions. In fact, many job descriptions include this information as an integral aspect. With this information, steps can be taken to minimize the possibility that an accident will occur.

By providing a means for common understanding between management and labor unions with regard to the duties of each position, job analysis helps reduce employee grievances. Suspicion of favoritism is reduced to the extent that pay differentials are based on clear differences in job duties. Thus, job analysis contributes to reduced internal conflict once the program is well established and widely accepted.

The data of job analysis provide an index of what are presumed to be the most appropriate work procedures, given the existing equipment. But after a job has been studied this minutely, it may become apparent that certain changes in the person–machine balance are economically feasible and desirable. Automatic equipment may be introduced or, on occasion, human actions may be substituted for machinery. Thus, job analysis can provide a basis for reengineering the positions involved.

Job descriptions from different companies provide a method of comparing rates of pay within occupations. With such information, it is possible to be reasonably certain that the jobs compared are in fact similar. A company may determine how its pay scales for similar work jibe with those of others in the community and adjust its rates to a desired level.

Counseling, of course, is often an application outside the company itself. Yet job descriptions, such as those developed by the U.S. Employment Service, and occupational information based on extensive job analyses, can have considerable value in areas such as vocational guidance and rehabilitation counseling. With this type of data, it is possible to guide the inexperienced and the disabled into occupations where they are most likely to succeed.

☐ Elements of the Job Description

Box 13-1 presents a very different type of job description than the one in Box 13-2. In the former instance Georgia Kaolin needed the job description only for purposes of selecting individuals to be promoted. What was desired was a clear picture of the performances required by the job, so that those with the requisite capabilities could be identified. Atlantic-Richfield, on the other hand, needed a more traditional job description that could be used for many purposes, including the test selection process described in Box 13-2.

Diversity of this kind is characteristic; job descriptions vary because they are needed for different purposes, different tasks are salient, and different methods of obtaining data were used. Yet there is some tendency to emphasize a certain set of elements. Beyond this, consistency is hard to find. Where a particular item will appear is subject to considerable variation. A specific item may initiate one job description and come at the end of another. There are almost as many variants as there are companies. In some order, then, the following are most likely to be considered.

Job Title.   Job descriptions typically contain a specific job title or name. These titles are needed for internal purposes, and also to facilitate reporting of the firm's activities to the government and to other data-collection agencies. On occasion, alternative or slang titles are noted also.

Work Activities and Procedures.   The segment of the job description covering work activities and procedures is devoted to describing, in whatever detail is necessary, the tasks and duties to be performed on the job; the materials used in carrying them out; the machinery operated, if any; the kinds of formal interactions with other workers required; and the nature and extent of the supervision given or received.

Physical Environment.   The section on physical environment contains a complete description of the physical working conditions where the work is to be performed. Among the factors that should be noted are the normal heat, lighting, noise levels, and ventilation in the work situation. In addition, it is sometimes desirable to indicate the location of the work in terms of some geographic designation, because this may be of relevance in recruiting and for other purposes. Any particular accident hazards are also described.

Social Environment.   An increasingly common part of the job description is a section devoted to specifying the social conditions under which the work will be carried out. The types of information included tend to vary considerably from one company to another. Often there is a statement regarding the number of individuals in the working environment of the particular job, as well as information on certain characteristics of these work associates.

Physical aspects of the job that have a bearing on the social aspects may also be noted— time of work hours (night or day), work location (city, suburban, or rural), availability of noncompany facilities (stores, restaurants, and so on), and availability of recreation (company-sponsored or not). Role prescriptions in the areas of conflict minimization, cooperation with superiors, maintaining continued employment uninterrupted by excessive absenteeism, and the like always exist, even though these requirements may not be stated explicitly in the job description. Knowledge of the social environment can be extremely helpful in minimizing disparities between prescriptions of this kind and actual behavior.

Conditions of Employment.   The aspect of the job description dealing with conditions of employment is concerned with the place of the job in the formal organization, in such

BOX 13-1   I/O PSYCHOLOGY IN PRACTICE

A Job Description Used to Analyze Employee Performance for Promotion at Georgia Kaolin

Georgia Kaolin Company operates plants that process clay for various purposes, including the coating of fine-grade paper. Many of the plant jobs involve the operation of sophisticated equipment and require considerable skill. The company is concerned that those promoted possess sufficient verbal, mathematical, and judgmental abilities so that the best possible product will be produced and the expensive equipment will not be damaged. Accordingly, written job statements focus on these areas. The following job description deals with the skills required of operators of filtering equipment.

Number 6 and 7 Filters Operator
 I. Verbal
   A. Read—The ability to read comprehensively.
     1. Mill Production Schedule.
       Daily production schedule indicates grades to be produced and disposition of same on the various production units.
     2. Special Written Instructions.
       Operator's lineup and activity report, foremen, general foremen, etc., instructions.
     3. Test Instructions and Results.
       a. Specific Gravity.
       b. Ph.
     4. Charts and Recorder—Controllers.
       a. Temperature controllers and recorder.
       b. Feed Timer (6 and 7 Eimco).
       c. Vacuum Gauges.
       d. Lubrication.
     5. Units of Measure.
       a. Linear Measure.
         Inches and Feet—Production rates.
       b. Unit of Time.
         Seconds and Minutes—Production rates.
       c. Temperatures.
         Degrees C & F—Feed slip.

   B. Write—The ability to write legibly, express ideas, and record operating data on the following reports.
     1. Daily Operation Reports—Filter and Reblunger.
     2. Shift Operator's Lineup (Relief Operator).
   C. Oral Communications—The ability to express oneself clearly and accurately when receiving or conveying information to others on subjects pertaining to the operation.
     1. Exchange operating information with other operators.
       a. Line up the appropriate storage tank to supply the proper grade to the proper production unit.
       b. Line up filter product to proper dryer, reblunger, or slip tank.
     2. Mill Foremen.
       To keep both operator and foreman advised of any changes, delays, etc., in the operating schedule.
     3. Maintenance Personnel.
       Contact maintenance personnel for machine repair.
     4. Laboratory Personnel.
       Exchange information concerning quality values—grade changes and check out.
   D. Written Communications—The ability to express oneself in writing clearly and accurately on all facets of the operation.
     1. Remarks concerning the operation delays.
     2. Disposition of substandard materials.
     3. Explanation of changes.
     4. Operator's Lineup (Relief).
 II. Math
   A. Fractions, Decimals, Whole Numbers.
     1. Add.
       Total tons.

2. Subtract.
    Tank inventories.
3. Multiply.
    Production rate.
III. Judgment—This job requires good judgment to operate the equipment efficiently and coordinate the operation with other connecting production equipment.
    A. Grade Changes.
        Anticipate grade changes, which requires knowledge of inventory level and production rates.
    B. Chemical and Water Addition.
        Recognize and adjust chemical or water addition to maintain pH control within specifications.
C. Dryer Production—not in operation.
    Recognize and adjust filter variable necessary to maintain maximum dryer feed (6 and 7 Eimco).
D. Filtration.
    Associate filtration variables with filter performance and adjust to maintain maximum efficiency.
E. Equipment Maintenance.
    Must exercise judgment as to when it would be most advantageous to maintenance equipment without delaying the operation.
F. Make adjustments to maintain maximum production rate of good quality material.

---

terms as the wage structure, working hours, method of payment, permanency of the positions, seasonal or part-time nature of the work, allowable fringe benefits, relation to other jobs, and opportunities for promotion or transfer. Although efforts should always be made to write statements in a job description clearly and precisely, this is particularly important when the conditions of employment are being described because of the possible legal implications of many of the items.

☐ The Job Specification

The **job specification** part of the job description may not be labeled separately or, if it is, it may well appear under the heading of qualifications. The job specification contains information on the personal characteristics that are believed necessary for the performance of the job. Included are such factors as educational background, experience, and personal qualifications.

Although the job specification is not universally treated as a separate entity within the job description, there are strong arguments for doing so. The reason is that it performs an entirely different function from the other components. The job specification neither states role prescriptions nor describes the conditions of work. Instead, it attempts to indicate what kinds of people can be expected to approximate the role requirements most closely. Thus, it is basically concerned with matters of selection, screening, and placement.

Job specifications are often written with little real knowledge as to their actual relationship to work performance. Thus, it has become common practice to require high school graduation for a great variety of positions. Yet this is often done without trying out individuals who have not graduated from high school in the particular type of work to determine if they are capable of effective performance. In most jobs, it seems likely that a person of reasonable intelligence and emotional maturity who has not finished high school will do at least as well as the graduate who lacks one or both of these characteristics.

Numerous other examples could be noted. The point is that job specifications often serve to restrict the labor market artificially, so that it is more difficult to find a person who meets all the requirements. This is fine—if the specifications must in fact be met to assume satis-

BOX 13-2   RESEARCH IN I/O PSYCHOLOGY

Using a Job Description to Develop a Testing Program for the Selection of Dealer Sales Supervisors at Atlantic-Richfield

Atlantic-Richfield's personnel research unit had been requested to propose a battery of tests that might be used to identify those dealer sales employees who should be considered for promotion to Dealer Sales Supervisor. From an analysis of the literature it was apparent that personality and interest measures should prove particularly useful for this purpose. The next step was to study the job description that had been developed for the position. This read as follows:

Title: Dealer Sales Supervisor

Salary grade: 12

Department: Domestic Marketing

Title of immediate supervisor: District Manager

Duties: Under direction, supervises 6–15 sales employees engaged in selling and stimulating resale of company products to and/or by assigned accounts, acquiring new business, and in developing stations. Plans and supervises direct marketing activities within district or assigned territory in order to acquire and maintain maximum amount of profitable business by securing and retaining superior operation of service stations, developing dealers, acquisition of new direct marketing accounts, etc.

1. Performs supervisory duties; assigns work, answers questions, etc.; follows current activities by review of reports, discussions with subordinates, etc. Interviews job applicants and makes selection subject to district manager's approval. Handles minor disciplinary matters. Is consulted relative to promotions, transfers, salary treatment, etc. Endorses expense and mileage accounts.

2. Plans and supervises direct marketing activities within the district or territory in order to acquire and maintain maximum amount of profitable business by securing and retaining superior operation of service stations, developing dealers, acquisition of new direct marketing accounts, etc. Receives occasional special assignments from district manager, consults as necessary on policy problems, and keeps DM advised as to direct mar-

keting activities; otherwise works independently in accordance with established policies. Keeps informed of current activities by field observations, advice of subordinates, etc.

a. Recruits new dealers through personal contacts, newspaper ads, etc.; interviews candidates in conjunction with sales employees and recommends selection to district manager. Gathers necessary credit information and personal references. Schedules trainees in training school and reviews periodic progress reports. Attempts to place graduate trainees awaiting station with established dealer for further training. Indoctrinates and motivates new dealers; makes in-station inspections to check on training, answer questions, etc. Upon request, arranges for dealer employee clinics to be held within the district and assigns service sales employees as instructors; acts as faculty member of dealer training schools.

b. Reviews monthly profit-and-loss statement and housekeeping reports prepared by sales employees on each financed dealer; looks for possible trouble spots, such as excessive personal accounts receivable expenses, personal loans, unbalanced sales, etc.; discusses weak points with sales employees, recommends remedial measures, and follows for correction. Participates in annual district reviews of dealers for purpose of discussing past performance, planning future programs and goals, pointing out weak spots in operation, and offering advice relative to elimination. Prepares dealer lease analysis forms recommending future rental treatment and discusses with district manager.

c. Trains, coaches, and assists sales employees in selling and acquiring accounts, training their dealers, investigating and settling complaints, overcoming problems, negotiating contracts, planning and executing sales promotions, etc., by double teaming with them in the field. Requests assistance from regional staff personnel and supplier's representatives and handles necessary liaison duties.

d. Inspects stations in conjunction with district

manager; checks on appearance, service rendered, personnel's working knowledge, customer contacts, etc.; prepares written report and follows for correction of noted deficiencies. In daily travels around territory, makes casual inspections of stations and advises others of items needing correction. Follows closely and handles nonroutine matters in connection with dealer changeovers.

e. Performs sundry related duties; plans and may conduct periodic sales meetings. Attends district's staff meetings. Handles correspondence with regional and home office personnel, dealers, etc., relative to matters supervised. Contributes to district's monthly marketing letter. Assists district manager in preparation of service station site justifications, budgets, quotas, performance reports, etc. Speaks at local service organizations and may serve as member of various industry and trade associations and committees.

3. As individually assigned, substitutes partially for district manager during vacations and other absences to the extent of signing forms, reports, etc., normally signed by DM, and handling familiar matters according to district manager's known views or his handling of similar problems in past; refers questionable matters to regional office for advice or decisions; advises district manager of matters handled.

Educational requirements: High school graduate.

Specific knowledge to start: General knowledge of dealer marketing; company products; district organization and facilities; company marketing policies and procedures; service station operation. Supervisory experience.

Where experience acquired: 4–5 years' experience in dealer marketing with at least 1–2 years as dealer salesperson.

Knowledge acquired on job: Experience in motivating, training, and supervising sales employees: learn to develop and apply effective selling programs; familiarity with company and competitive marketing activities in district; learn responsibility limits of positions. (6–9 months to acquire)

Physical effort: Semiactive; drives car approximately 1100 to 2000 miles/month.

Responsibility:
People—Supervision of 6–15 sales employees.
Materials—Economical use of office supplies.
Equipment—Care and use of office equipment; inspection of service stations.
Markets—Acquiring and efficient servicing of accounts; occasional public relations contacts.
Money—Economical use of company expense funds by self and subordinates.
Methods—Execution, selection, and control of methods used in direct marketing.
Records—Preparation, analysis, and endorsement of records, reports, and forms relative to direct marketing activities.

Working conditions:
Regular working hours five days a week.
Surroundings and hazards:
10–60 percent normal office conditions.
40–90 percent field and travel conditions, with related hazards.

The job description suggested to the psychologists that mental ability tests emphasizing verbal and numerical skills as well as personality and interest measures which focused on various types of interpersonal relationships and energy level were most likely to prove useful. The instruments actually selected for trial were:

Mental ability tests
Terman Concept Mastery Test
Vocabulary Test G-T
Wesman Personnel Classification Test
Wechsler Adult Intelligence Scale subtests as follows: Information, Comprehension, Arithmetic, Similarities, and Digit Span

Personality and interest measures
Kuder Preference Record—Vocational
Tomkins-Horn Picture Arrangement Test
Thematic Apperception Test
Miner Sentence Completion Scale—Form H

Subsequent analyses indicated that the expectations generated from the literature review and study of the job description possessed considerable validity.

factory performance. But frequently the information that would indicate whether this is true or not has not been obtained. Specifications often are written without the intensive study that should precede the introduction of any selection procedure. If under these conditions they operate to exclude disproportionate numbers of minority-group members or females, they may very well be declared illegal by the courts.

■ METHODS OF JOB ANALYSIS

The methods used to gather information about a job vary greatly in comprehensiveness and systematic rigor. In the discussions that follow, an effort is made to explain some of the more commonly used techniques. Emphasis is placed on the advantages and disadvantages of each approach, and an attempt is made to cite typical occupations for which the particular procedure is most useful.

We have already noted one approach, supervisor descriptions, in connection with the Rubbermaid case at the beginning of this chapter. In that instance data from supervisors were used alone. More frequently, information from this source is combined with some other method, either to supplement it or to check on its accuracy.

☐ Observation of the Job Occupant

Observation of the job occupant is frequently used as a method of identifying the tasks and duties actually involved in fulfilling the demands of a particular job. It requires merely that the job analyst observe a number of job occupants as they perform the job in a normal, workaday manner and that these observations be recorded in some systematic manner. This may be done either by writing down what was done in narrative form or by selecting what is relevant from among alternatives on some sort of checklist. The checklist approach, of course, requires some prior knowledge of the particular job and jobs closely related to it. The job description is then written to include any new role prescriptions that may be desired. It is important that more than one job occupant be watched at work, because to do otherwise might result in the highly idiosyncratic and unique behaviors of a specific individual being written into the description.

Unfortunately, the simplicity of this approach is somewhat misleading. There are related problems that can be very significant. First, the use of this method requires the assumption that the act of observing an individual at work does not have an impact on the work behavior itself. For the method to be of value, workers must do the same things in the same way when they are being watched as when they are not. In many instances, this requirement is clearly not fulfilled. At the very least, the type of social facilitation effects noted in Chapter 7 can be expected to occur. Many people tend to show off under circumstances such as this; others become anxious. Activities that are expected to yield approval often are exaggerated. If workers feel they are being observed in order to set wage rates (as may well be the case), it is very likely that they will pattern their activities so as to obtain as favorable a rate as possible. These difficulties can, of course, be avoided by setting up a procedure whereby workers may be observed without their knowledge. However, if the subterfuge is found out, labor relations and other problems can be anticipated.

A second difficulty with the direct-observation method of job analysis is that it becomes almost meaningless in the case of work that is primarily mental. There are many positions, ranging from secretary to chief executive officer, that are not really subject to this type of study. Observation alone will not yield a clear and meaningful picture of what the individual is doing. It should be noted, also, that the general trend with the introduction of technology is for the amount of physical behavior to decrease, whereas mental activities increase as a factor in job performance.

A final problem is that observation is not very practical when the job cycle is rather long; that is, when the time from the beginning to the end of a specific task extends over a considerable period of time. For example, punching holes in some material with the aid of a machine may have a cycle of ten or twenty seconds. But the skilled machinist who is making up an extremely complex and sensitive die may have a cycle of three to six months. In any instance where a specific action occurs only infrequently, it is very uneconomical to attempt a complete job description based on observation alone.

For the reasons stated, it appears that the observation technique should be employed only when the work is largely automatically controlled (as with a conveyor-belt system), when it is primarily physical, and when the job cycle is rather short (as with certain lower-level clerical jobs and many unskilled and semiskilled factory jobs).

☐ Interview of the Job Occupant

Many of the objections to observation as a method of establishing the tasks, duties, and responsibilities of a job can be overcome by utilizing the interview as a source of information. The job-cycle problem is largely eliminated, because the workers can observe themselves and briefly summarize, in words, behaviors that were spread over a long time span. Similarly, individuals can monitor their own mental processes even though an observer cannot. As a result, the difficulty with nonphysical tasks is minimized; mental and behavioral activities can both be described. Furthermore, the employee becomes an active participant in the information-gathering process, with the result that negative attitudes and resistances are much less likely to develop. Finally, this procedure utilizes the often considerable information that workers have about their jobs, information that may not be available to the job analyst from any other source.

It is desirable that this procedure be utilized only after considerable preplanning and forethought. The individual doing the interviewing, the job analyst, must be thoroughly trained in the techniques of interviewing. Questions need to be worked out in advance, and there should be a clear concept of exactly what information is desired.

The job analyst has to gain rapport with the worker whose job is being studied. Confidence must be elicited, and the worker must be induced to accept the usefulness of the job analysis procedure. This is not easily done. Sometimes it is impossible. But the difficulties are compounded when, for instance, a college-trained job analyst goes into a plant to interview a blue-collar worker with only a minimum of formal schooling and uses a vocabulary that is well above the level the worker can adequately comprehend. In such cases, misunderstanding is inevitable and resentment very likely.

A second possible source of difficulty is the distorted picture of a position that the person being interviewed may present, consciously or unconsciously. Workers may, for example, attempt to portray their work as more difficult and important than it really is, in the hope that pay and status will be increased accordingly. To a degree, interview data derived from a number of individuals performing the same or very similar tasks can be used to correct this tendency. The important thing is that job analysts keep constantly in mind the fact that they are supposed to establish a set of role prescriptions. These will only rarely be identical with any one incumbent's statements regarding his or her work behavior. Thus, job descriptions must go beyond mere interview data to effectively structure the whole pattern of work within the organization.

It is important to note that observation and interview procedures do not consistently yield the same results (Jenkins, Nadler, Lawler, & Cammann, 1975). Agreement is best on such matters as the variety inherent in the work and the level of skills required; it is least good on the extent to which the work is perceived as uncertain in nature and on the extent to which cooperation with others is required.

Since individual interview and observation procedures tend to be expensive, some companies have employed group interviews with job incumbents. Usually, four to six people are included. The job analyst may interview a cross section of incumbents, or a technical conference approach may be utilized, with the job analyst coordinating a discussion among highly experienced personnel, including trainers and supervisors. Undoubtedly, these approaches lose something as against a composite derived from individual interviews, but they do conserve the time of job analysts.

☐ Job Occupant Description

Job occupant description is similar in intent and procedure to the interview, except that the occupant either writes a narrative description or fills out a questionnaire, rather than giving the information orally. Usually, individuals are expected to go into considerable detail regarding the tasks performed, the conditions of work, and the materials and equipment employed. Examples of items used by the U.S. Department of Labor in a checklist to be filled out by job occupants are given in Exhibit 13-2. Such measures are often called **task inventories.**

Some large organizations have utilized the task-inventory approach to develop computerized systems on a major scale. The task inventories are completed by job occupants at many locations and then processed via computer. Box 13-3 describes a system of this kind that was developed by AT&T prior to the divestiture of the operating telephone companies.

Techniques of this type have many of the advantages and disadvantages of the interview. They are somewhat more economical of time and effort because the services of an interviewer are not required. On the other hand, there is a loss in flexibility, which means that mistaken impressions can go uncorrected or require considerable time to correct. Also, the benefits of a face-to-face discussion, as they may contribute to rapport and consequently to the correctness of the information obtained, are lost.

Both the interview and the written description suffer from the fact that job occupants may report incorrectly regarding their work. Probably the most effective way to compensate for this bias is to have the data obtained from the incumbent reviewed by the immediate superior. If superiors have actually performed the work in the past, they are likely to be particularly helpful. Although studies have indicated that job occupants tend to be quite consistent from one to another in their descriptions of the same job, investigations dealing with the degree of agreement between job incumbents and their superiors have not produced evidence of as high a relationship. Workers and managers may see and stress somewhat different aspects of the work (Banks, Jackson, Stafford, & Warr, 1983).

In general, the methods involving the securing of information directly from the job occupant have a considerable advantage when the job analyses cover positions at middle or relatively high levels, where the work is not very repetitive. Individuals in these types of jobs are also those with whom the typical job analyst is likely to be most capable of gaining rapport. At lower levels, an approach that has proved useful is to have an immediate superior provide a number of instances of good and poor job performance among subordinates. These **critical incidents** are then analyzed to establish what behaviors are important in the job.

☐ Examination of Previous Job Descriptions

Another way of gathering information about a job is to determine what is already known about it. This cuts down on duplication of effort and can provide a substantial base for subsequent study. Thus, for those companies that have them, previous job descriptions can be of real benefit. Before utilizing such information, however, or any job descriptions that may be available from other firms, it is important to look into the analysis procedures employed. A poorly prepared job description may well do more harm than good. Also, the possibility that technological and other changes may have altered the job considerably should be considered. Many job descriptions prepared in the past are in fact obsolete insofar as present-day activities are concerned, even though the job titles may have remained the same.

There are several other sources of occupational information that can be of help. Perhaps most important among these is the *Dictionary of Occupational Titles* (DOT), published by the U.S. Department of Labor (1977). This volume contains brief job descriptions of over 28,000 jobs. Almost any job title in normal usage can be found there. In addition to the 1977 volume, supplements have been issued periodically.

The job descriptions in the *Dictionary of Occupational Titles*, however, are short and are based on multicompany studies. Thus they may well not be appropriate for establishing role prescriptions in connection with a specific job in a specific company. There are problems as well in that matters such as authority relationships are not considered. Nevertheless, the DOT can prove a very useful place to start in carrying out a job analysis (Cain & Green, 1983; Cain & Treiman, 1981). Two other sources are the *Alphabetical Index of Industries and Occupations*, put out by the Bureau of the Census (U.S. Department of Commerce, 1982), and the *International Standard Classification of Occupations*, published by the International Labour Office (1975). Both are intended primarily for use in connection with a census of population and thus provide only minimal information about each job in the sense of a job description. However, by providing classification information, they do indicate the general type of work to which each job title refers.

☐ Examination of Work Materials

In some cases it is possible to gain important information concerning the tasks and duties of a particular job by examining the materials that are typically used during work performance. A good example would be the tools of a carpenter, or perhaps the programs used by a computer operator. Various records and design specifications for equipment used can also be employed in the same way. The usefulness of this method is, of course, quite limited, but it can be of considerable supplementary value in certain instances.

☐ Performance of Work Activities

It has long been said that the best way to learn about something is to do it. More recently, this assumption has received considerable support from laboratory research in psychology. Thus it seems apparent that one of the best ways to obtain information about a job is to take on its duties.

In many cases this is entirely feasible. Such jobs as retail clerk and truck driver can be learned rather rapidly, as can many others requiring relatively limited skills. However, it is obvious that this is a technique of rather restricted usefulness and generality, because many jobs take years of training. For positions of the latter type, the procedure is obviously of little value. Probably, as the complexity of knowledge increases, there will be fewer and fewer jobs that can be studied by actually performing them, but the advantages of the approach where it can be used are considerable.

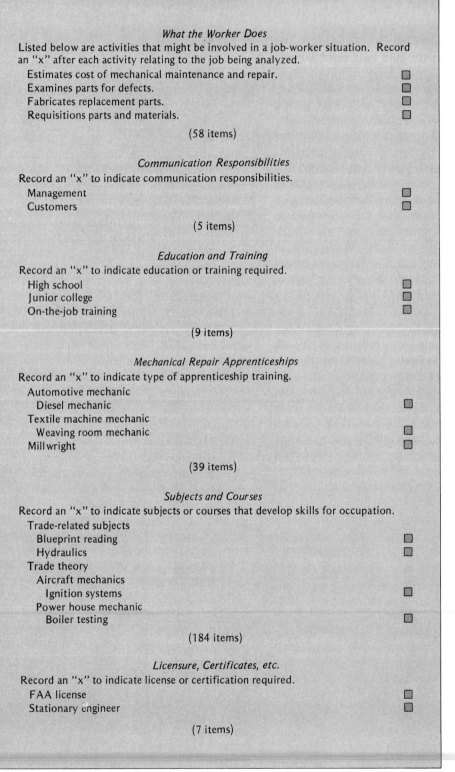

What the Worker Does

Listed below are activities that might be involved in a job-worker situation. Record an "x" after each activity relating to the job being analyzed.

Estimates cost of mechanical maintenance and repair. □
Examines parts for defects. □
Fabricates replacement parts. □
Requisitions parts and materials. □

(58 items)

Communication Responsibilities

Record an "x" to indicate communication responsibilities.

Management □
Customers □

(5 items)

Education and Training

Record an "x" to indicate education or training required.

High school □
Junior college □
On-the-job training □

(9 items)

Mechanical Repair Apprenticeships

Record an "x" to indicate type of apprenticeship training.

Automotive mechanic
  Diesel mechanic □
Textile machine mechanic
  Weaving room mechanic □
Millwright □

(39 items)

Subjects and Courses

Record an "x" to indicate subjects or courses that develop skills for occupation.

Trade-related subjects
  Blueprint reading □
  Hydraulics □
Trade theory
  Aircraft mechanics
    Ignition systems □
  Power house mechanic
    Boiler testing □

(184 items)

Licensure, Certificates, etc.

Record an "x" to indicate license or certification required.

FAA license □
Stationary engineer □

(7 items)

EXHIBIT 13-2

Union Affiliation

Record an "x" to indicate union affiliation.

Aluminum Workers International Union ☒

United Rubber Workers Union ☒

Company union ☒

(19 items)

Machines and Equipment

Record an "x" to indicate type of machines or equipment repaired.

Oil field machinery and equipment ☒

Film laboratory equipment ☒

Auxiliary systems

Pneumatic systems ☒

(132 items)

Tools and Work Aids

Record an "x" to indicate tools and work aids used.

Handtools

Blow torches ☒

Box wrenches ☒

Measuring devices

Depth micrometer ☒

Technical manuals ☒

(74 items)

Environmental Setting

Record an "x" after each item to indicate where the work is performed.

Agriculture ☒

Commercial

Business service ☒

Printing and publishing ☒

Military ☒

Other (specify) ☒

(32 items)

EXHIBIT 13-2   Examples of Items from a Job Description Checklist for Mechanical Repairing and Related Work

SOURCE: U.S. Department of Labor (1973). *Task analysis inventories,* pp. 77–85. Washington, DC: U.S. Government Printing Office.

■ DEVELOPING JOB FAMILIES

One of the primary goals of a job analysis program is to develop systematic knowledge of how the jobs in a given company are related to one another in terms of either the required tasks, the necessary personal characteristics, or both. Such information can be of considerable value in planning training programs, selection, transfer, promotion, and other human resource activities. If certain jobs can be shown to group together, the occu-

BOX 13-3   RESEARCH IN I/O PSYCHOLOGY

Development of the Work Performance Survey System at AT&T

The Work Performance Survey System was created within the AT&T system to standardize jobs
throughout the country, thus eliminating substantial variations from one location to another. It is a
computerized system that stores and analyzes
task inventory questionnaire data provided by
large numbers of respondents within the company. The process involved is indicated in the adjacent diagram.

The questionnaires provide information on the
importance of different tasks for a given job
based on estimates of time spent on the tasks. A
page from the questionnaire for Service Representative is reproduced on page 359.

In addition to permitting control of jobs so
that variations in activities performed in different
locations can be eliminated, the system can be
used to establish training requirements for jobs
and to develop performance rating systems
which emphasize tasks known to be important in
the work.

SOURCE: Sidney Gael (1983). *Job analysis: A guide to
assessing work activities.* San Francisco: Jossey-Bass.

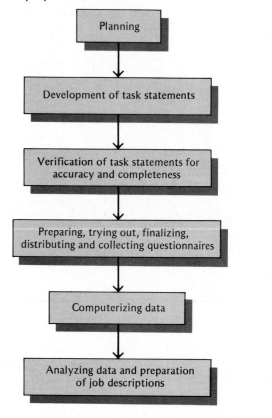

Planning

Development of task statements

Verification of task statements for
accuracy and completeness

Preparing, trying out, finalizing,
distributing and collecting questionnaires

Computerizing data

Analyzing data and preparation
of job descriptions

---

pants of these similar positions can be treated
as a unit for a number of purposes. Groupings of this kind are particularly valuable as a
guide in the placement of employees and in
developing compensation schedules.

A wide variety of methods for grouping
jobs into families has been developed. Some
approaches are essentially conceptual, whereas others rely on various statistical procedures to establish similarities and differences
among jobs. Recently there has been considerable emphasis on the statistical approaches.
The following discussion focuses on two

methods that have been the subject of substantial study. It should be recognized,
however, that numerous other approaches
are available (Harvey, 1986; Pearlman,
1980).

☐ The Position Analysis Questionnaire

One of the more promising approaches to
developing job groupings is the **Position
Analysis Questionnaire** (PAQ) (McCormick,
1979; McCormick, DeNisi, & Shaw, 1979).

	Part B								Part C
	SIGNIFICANCE								TIME SPENT
Task List	Not Part	Minor		Substantial				Most significant	0 - No time 1 - Very small 2 - Small 3 - Slightly less 4 - As much 5 - Slightly more 6 - More 7 - Very much more

A. Completing Forms

001 Authorize refund of deposit to customer.   0 1 2 3 4 5 6 7   _____

002 Change treatment history or treatment class.   0 1 2 3 4 5 6 7   _____

003 Note treatment and follow-up action.   0 1 2 3 4 5 6 7   _____

004 Phone service order in English to order writer.   0 1 2 3 4 5 6 7   _____

005 Prepare a contact memo on an incoming business sales call.   0 1 2 3 4 5 6 7   _____

006 Prepare adjustment voucher to adjust a billing error or to reconcile records.   0 1 2 3 4 5 6 7   _____

007 Prepare and send form to AT&T Long Lines on overseas calls appearing to be billed in error.   0 1 2 3 4 5 6 7   _____

008 Prepare and send to customer a Transfer of Service (Billing Responsibility) Agreement form.   0 1 2 3 4 5 6 7   _____

009 Prepare change of address record, worksheet, or order.   0 1 2 3 4 5 6 7   _____

010 Prepare contact memo on intracompany or intercompany contact.   0 1 2 3 4 5 6 7   _____

011 Prepare final account write-off voucher.   0 1 2 3 4 5 6 7   _____

012 Prepare form to order office supplies, machine supplies, or forms.   0 1 2 3 4 5 6 7   _____

013 Prepare form to transfer money or debit between accounts.   0 1 2 3 4 5 6 7   _____

014 Prepare Full Station Detail form.   0 1 2 3 4 5 6 7   _____

015 Prepare Key System diagram (worksheet or graphic).   0 1 2 3 4 5 6 7   _____

016 Prepare note to inform others of changes of phone numbers, people, or locations called within the company.   0 1 2 3 4 5 6 7   _____

017 Prepare programming sheets for CENTREX or other programmable equipment.   0 1 2 3 4 5 6 7   _____

This questionnaire contains 187 job elements presented in checklist form that incumbents or other knowledgeable individuals evaluate relative to a given job. The elements are of six types—information input (e.g., use of written materials), mental processes (e.g., coding/decoding), work output (e.g., use of keyboard devices), relationships with other persons (e.g., interviewing), job context (e.g., working in high temperature), and other job characteristics (e.g., irregular hours). The approach has the advantage that a large range of jobs may be studied and described in terms of the extent to which the various elements are or are not present.

Through the use of the mathematical technique known as factor analysis, thirty-two basic dimensions on which jobs vary have been identified. Scores on each of these dimensions may be computed for any job using responses to the job-element items. The result is a profile that describes the job on each of the thirty-two dimensions, which range from Watching Devices/Materials for Information to Being in a Hazardous Job Situation to Working on a Regular versus Irregular Schedule. Jobs may then be grouped on the basis of the degree of similarity of their profiles. Box 13-4 describes some of the work that has been done using the PAQ in the U.S. Navy.

The extent to which this technique can be used effectively with all workers has been questioned. The developers of the questionnaire indicate that it can be completed by individuals with as little as ten years of formal education. However, analyses of its reading level indicate that some of the words used are sufficiently difficult so that full understanding should not be anticipated below the college level (Ash & Edgell, 1975). It therefore appears that the instrument should not be used with individuals who have little formal education. In such cases it can be completed by a job analyst on the basis of interview/observation data; the latter approach

has been found to be entirely satisfactory (Sparrow, Spurgeon, & Barwell, 1982). Recently also, a questionnaire that appears to be analogous to the PAQ, but which imposes less arduous educational demands, has been developed (Harvey, Friedman, Hakel, & Cornelius, 1988).

Although the PAQ was developed as an all-purpose procedure to be used with all jobs, there is some question as to whether this objective has been obtained (DeNisi, Cornelius, & Blencoe, 1987). There appear to be certain jobs for which many of the PAQ questions turn out to lack relevance. In at least one study, however, dealing with clerical occupations, an abbreviated version of the PAQ with irrelevant items deleted was shown to be an adequate substitute for the full questionnaire (Ziering & Raju, 1988). In any event, the PAQ appears to be as close to an all-purpose job analysis approach as currently exists, and it is for this reason that it is very useful in identifying job families.

☐ Career Ladders and Functional Job Analysis

Approaches such as the Position Analysis Questionnaire tend to emphasize job families constituted on a horizontal basis. An alternative procedure, illustrated in Exhibit 13-3, establishes grouping on a vertical basis to constitute **career ladders.** Jobs are viewed as varying in the extent to which they require dealing with data, people, and things. Within each of these areas, levels of activities exist. Higher-level activities are presumed to incorporate all those within the area that are placed at a lower level, but lower-level activities preclude those above them. **Functional job analysis** requires slotting the activities of a job on the three scales.

Thus, career programming is viewed as movement upward in one or more of the three areas to the performance of higher-level activities and thus to a higher-level position.

BOX 13-4   RESEARCH IN I/O PSYCHOLOGY

A Test of the Position Analysis Questionnaire in the U.S. Navy

As part of a program of research undertaken by the U.S. Navy to evaluate the Position Analysis Questionnaire (PAQ) for use on Navy jobs, the PAQ was completed by 223 incumbents of twenty-five different jobs. One phase of this research dealt with the physical-strength requirements of the jobs. The PAQ yields several different indexes of strength requirements—among them static strength, dynamic strength, explosive strength, and lifting strength. The question under investigation was whether these requirements as derived from a PAQ job analysis matched the strength requirements of jobs as established by a much more extensive study including actual strength tests of incumbents and observation of work behavior.

Certain of the twenty-five jobs were identified as requiring considerable muscular strength; these were jobs such as Aviation Structural Mechanic, Boiler Technician, Machinist's Mate, and Aviation Boatswain's Mate, and Aviation Ordnanceman. Other jobs did not require much strength—Mess Management Specialist, Hospital Corpsman, Personnelman, Quartermaster, and the like. When the PAQ data of incumbents of these two types of jobs were compared, it was found that the PAQ consistently indicated much higher strength requirements for the high-strength jobs. The findings from this study and several others of a similar nature combined to indicate that questionnaire data such as that provided by the PAQ could be used to provide valid job analyses of Navy positions.

SOURCE: Robert C. Carter & Robert J. Biersner (1987). Job requirements derived from the Position Analysis Questionnaire and validated using Military Aptitude Test Scores. *Journal of Occupational Psychology, 60,* 311–321.

Education and training are means for movement to higher-level activities. This approach is of particular value in eliminating dead-end jobs at lower levels, from which upward movement is virtually impossible. Grouping jobs on a vertical basis into those requiring skills related to data, people, or things permits the specification of a career ladder extending upward from all entry-level positions. Of course, opportunities to engage in higher-level activities may be quite limited within any one organization.

Concern for the upgrading of minorities and others with limited occupational skills has sparked a sizable body of research on job families and on career ladders in particular. In certain industries, such as health care, these studies have raised serious questions regarding the essential nature of license, certification, and degree requirements that effectively block upward movement on the job and that may necessitate a greater investment in education than performance of particular tasks requires. These research findings have been embraced by a number of groups, resulting in a major attack on **credentialism,** including union-established apprenticeship standards. Functional job analysis has proved quite effective in establishing real job requirements in situations of this kind (Olson, Fine, Myers, & Jennings, 1981).

☐ Using the Approaches

Information on the relative value of the various job analysis approaches is limited, but research in this area does exist (Levine, Ash, & Bennett, 1980; Levine, Ash, Hall, &

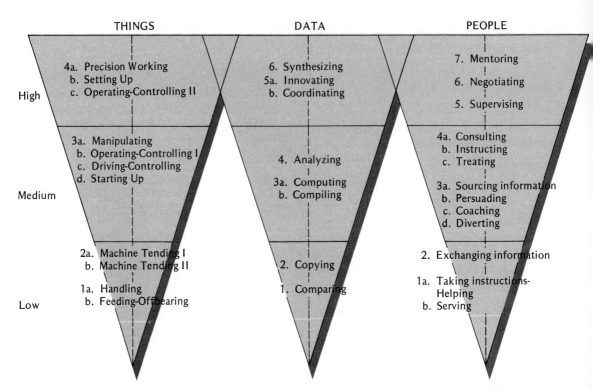

EXHIBIT 13-3   Scales Indicating Levels of Job Activities for Purposes of Establishing Career Ladders

- Each hierarchy is independent of the other. It would be incorrect to read the functions across the three hierarchies as related because they appear to be on the same level. The definitive relationship among functions is within each hierarchy, not across hierarchies.
- Data are central, since a worker can be assigned even higher data functions even though things and people functions remain at the lowest level of their respective scales.
- Each function in its hierarchy is defined to include the lower-numbered functions.
- The hyphenated functions, taking instructions-helping, operating-controlling, etc., are single functions.

SOURCE: Sidney A. Fine (1986). Job analysis. In Ronald A. Berk (Ed.), *Performance assessment: Methods and applications*, p. 58. Baltimore: Johns Hopkins University Press.

Sistrunk, 1983). Although not inexpensive, individual interviews of knowledgeable people, primarily job incumbents, appear to be the best way to obtain job analysis information. Technical conferences and a combination of observation and interview are almost as effective, but their total costs are even greater. Group interviews with incumbents and the various questionnaire approaches are less expensive, but they also yield less useful information. Consistently, combined approaches involving several methods are found to expand the amount of useful information obtained. More detailed analyses of specific procedures provide considerable support for the critical-incident approach, although it is costly. At the other extreme, using the Position Analysis Questionnaire can reduce costs, but its generalized language, necessary to cover all types of jobs, and high educational demand create problems.

Reports on specific methods by experienced job analysts indicate that the need served is an important factor in deciding which approaches to use. Thus, a job analysis program intended to serve many different functions would do well to include several approaches. Critical incidents are best for performance appraisal and safety-management purposes. The position analysis questionnaire is most useful for job evaluation and setting pay rates. Task inventories are widely useful, as is functional job analysis, but both excel for purposes of writing the job description. The overall conclusion remains, however, that in spite of the costs involved, it is best to use several different methods.

■ JOB EVALUATION

In Chapter 4 the section on reward systems provided a brief overview of compensation and the motivating effects of pay. Among the topics considered there, job evaluation is of particular concern to industrial psychology. Job analysis provides the essential information on which job evaluation is based. Job evaluation takes the data set forth in the job description, and sometimes in the job specification as well, and appraises these data in terms of their relationships to company objectives. Thus a rating of the job is obtained that is in many ways similar to the rating an individual might receive on his or her performance. In fact, the methods of job evaluation have much in common with the performance rating procedures considered in Chapters 14 and 15. They are not universally endorsed, but they are widely used (Lawler, 1990).

□ Methods of Job Evaluation

There are four methods that have been used extensively in job evaluation. Two of these—job ranking and job classification—are considered to be of a nonquantitative nature. The other two—factor comparison and point systems—are quantitative.

Job Ranking   In **job ranking,** the various jobs are arranged in order of merit, according to their worth as a whole. No attempt is made to separate out different factors within the jobs, although certain aspects, such as difficulty level, may be specified as criteria for the ranking. Usually, separate ranks are developed, using the job descriptions for each department and raters who know the work done in that department.

Either of two approaches may be used in developing ranks. The job descriptions may be sorted directly, so that a continuous ordering results, or the paired-comparison technique may be applied and a ranking developed from the various individual comparisons between each pair of jobs. In either case, the ratings made by two or more individuals must be averaged to produce the final ranking for the department. Then the data from all departments are dovetailed, either on the basis of the knowledge of a single individual who is well informed regarding the work done in the company as a whole or through committee action. The result is an ordering of all jobs in the organization.

Job Classification.   Grouping of jobs into various grades or levels may of course follow a ranking approach. It is, in fact, common practice to do this. A similar assignment of jobs to categories of worth is also frequently used with the other methods to be discussed shortly. But in the **job classification** method proper, grades are established first and then jobs are fitted into the appropriate classes, using preestablished grade descriptions or grading rules. Thus the various groupings are not developed after some type of ordering process has already been carried out, but at the outset.

Separate classification systems may be established for office, factory, sales, and managerial positions. Within each of these, descriptions are written that establish the bounds for the various grades. The number of grades so established will vary with the total range of job difficulty or complexity represented in the company, as well as with the fineness of differentiation desired. In general, between seven and fifteen classes will be required. The number of sales grades may, however, differ from those in the factory area, for instance. The crucial task of writing the grade descriptions or grading rules, against which individual job descriptions are subsequently compared, may be assigned to an individual or to a committee.

Factor Comparison.   Factor comparison is in reality a complex variant of the ranking approach, because jobs are compared with each other rather than against category descriptions. The rankings are not done on a global basis, taking the whole job into account, but individually, in terms of various component factors such as skill requirements, mental requirements, physical requirements, responsibility, and working conditions.

The initial step is to select fifteen to twenty-five key jobs that seem to be generally in the correct relationship to each other insofar as wage rates are concerned. Usually, these will be jobs that are widely distributed in level and that have not been a subject of controversy regarding payment rates. These key jobs are then rank-ordered on each of the five factors. Thus, in the case of the sixteen jobs noted in Exhibit 13-4, the jobs rated highest on the particular factor noted are:

1. Mental requirements—pattern maker
2. Physical requirements—common laborer
3. Skill requirements—pattern maker
4. Responsibility—pattern maker
5. Working conditions—common laborer

The jobs rated lowest are

1. Mental requirements—common laborer
2. Physical requirements—tool crib attendant
3. Skill requirements—common laborer
4. Responsibility—common laborer
5. Working conditions—pattern maker

Next, the present wage being paid on each of the key jobs is divided among the five factors, with the greatest proportion being given to the most important factor. This is as much a judgmental process as is the ranking. In both instances, averages of several independent ratings by different individuals should be obtained. With reference to the backup data for Exhibit 13-4, given a present wage for gauger of $15.40, this might be distributed among the factors as follows:

Mental requirements	$ 3.60
Physical requirements	1.90
Skill requirements	5.10
Responsibility	2.55
Working conditions	2.25
	$15.40

For pattern maker, the average of the judgments might be:

Mental requirements	$ 4.50
Physical requirements	1.95
Skill requirements	5.65
Responsibility	3.00
Working conditions	1.15
	$16.25

The money amounts thus established may then be used to set up a second ranking on each of the five factors. The two rankings, on difficulty and money, are then compared as in Exhibit 13-4. Where sizable disparities exist, as with gauger (working conditions) and blacksmith (skill and working conditions), these jobs are eliminated from the list of key jobs.

EXHIBIT 13-4 Rankings on Difficulty and Money for Sixteen Tentative Key Jobs

	Factors									
	Mental Requirements		Physical Requirements		Skill Requirements		Responsibility		Working Conditions	
Job	Difficulty	Money	Difficulty	Money	Difficulty	Money	Difficulty	Money	Difficulty	Money
Gauger	2	2	13	13	2	2	3	3	15	4
Pattern maker	1	1	12	12	1	1	1	1	16	16
Common laborer	16	16	1	1	16	16	16	16	1	1
Power shear operator	11	11	11	11	9	9	5	5	4	6
Plater	10	10	6	6	6	7	12	12	9	10
Riveter	12	12	3	3	12	12	14	14	8	9
Blacksmith	13	13	2	2	8	5	13	13	7	2
Punch press operator	14	14	4	4	13	13	15	15	5	7
Screw machine operator	4	4	8	8	3	3	2	2	13	14
Casting inspector	3	3	7	7	4	6	4	4	10	11
Millwright	9	9	10	10	5	4	6	6	11	12
Tool crib attendant	7	7	16	16	14	14	10	10	14	15
Arc welder	8	8	9	9	7	8	9	9	3	5
Electrical truck operator	6	6	15	15	11	11	8	8	12	13
Crane operator	5	5	14	14	10	10	7	7	6	8
Watchman	15	15	5	5	15	15	11	11	2	3

SOURCE: David W. Belcher & Thomas J. Atchison (1987). *Compensation administration*, p. 193. Englewood Cliffs, NJ: Prentice-Hall.

The remaining jobs are then put into a job-comparison scale. This scale indicates the money amounts associated with each job for each of the five factors. Thus the key jobs become benchmarks against which other jobs may be compared. The appropriate pay for each nonkey job is determined by establishing which jobs it falls between on each of the five factors. The five money amounts thus identified are added to obtain the wage rate for the job. Each job in the company is related to the job-comparison scale one factor at a time, using the job descriptions for key and nonkey jobs. The result is not only an evaluation, but an actual pricing of the firm's job structure.

Point System. The **point system** is an extension of the job-classification approach that utilizes a variety of factors as a basis for classification rather than a single dimension. In one variant or another, it appears to be the most widely used of the job-evaluation methods. As with job classification, point systems are usually developed separately for different categories of jobs—factory, clerical, sales, and the like. The reason is that the relevant factors may differ considerably from one category of job to another. Thus, a single system for the whole organization could be extremely cumbersome and at the same time yield some rather incongruous results. The number and type of factors on which ratings are made tend to vary considerably among companies and even within companies between job categories. Among the factors that often occur are education, job knowledge, mental demand, effect of error, personal contact skill, initiative and ingenuity, physical demand, responsibility (in various areas such as safety, work of others, equipment, and materials), working conditions, hazards, and level to which the job reports. It is not uncommon to use as many as ten or even more factors in a single system.

When the factors have been established and defined, degrees are determined for each factor, so that those who subsequently rate jobs using the point manual may identify the amount, or level, of a factor in the particular job under consideration. Different numbers of degree differentiations may be used on the various factors, but in any case the definitions for each degree should be stated in considerable detail and should include if possible the titles of several key jobs falling at that particular level.

Exhibit 13-5 provides an example of how points might be assigned after the appropriate factor and degree descriptions have been written. Judgments must be made on how the total number of points should be allocated among factors. A common procedure is to start with 500 points and split this up in accordance with the importance of the various factors, to set the point values for the highest degrees. Then the lowest degrees are set, equal to one-fifth of the number of points used at the highest levels. Intermediate degree points are allocated in terms of arithmetically equal intervals. These intervals vary in size, depending on the number of separate degrees identified on the factor.

Once a manual is developed describing factors and degrees and indicating points for each degree on each factor, jobs may be evaluated by comparing their descriptions against those in the manual. The points obtained on each factor are summed to yield a point total that indicates the value of the job. Usually, these point totals are then grouped to yield a series of job grades within each of which a single pay scale applies.

As indicated previously, a variety of point systems has been developed. Some use a few factors, some many. Some use more than 500 total points, some much less. Some use statistical procedures for weighting the various factors. Some assign points to the degrees, using a geometric rather than an arithmetic

Exhibit 13-5   Hypothetical Point Values for Job Factors

Factors	Lowest Degree	Next Degree	Next Degree	Next Degree	Highest Degree
Mental demand	15	30	45	60	75
Experience	20	40	60	80	100
Physical demand	15	35	55	—	75
Hazards	10	20	30	40	50
Education	10	20	30	40	50
Personal contact	10	30	—	—	50
Equipment responsibility	10	20	30	40	50
Initiative	10	23	37	—	50

progression. A point system that has been developed by a major consulting group in wage and salary administration, called the Hay plan, is used extensively for salaried and executive positions.

Although it seems desirable to develop a point manual that is adapted to a specific company situation, as the Hay plan is, there are many general systems that have achieved rather widespread use, particularly for lower-level jobs. Examples are the National Electrical Manufacturers Association and the National Metal Trades Association systems for factory jobs, the National Electrical Manufacturers Association system for salaried jobs, and the National Office Management Association system. In any case, it should be emphasized that no matter how great the statistical elaboration on the data, the point system, like other job-evaluation procedures, remains primarily a judgmental process.

This is clearly evident in the description given in Box 13-5. This is a point system for managerial jobs developed by Control Data Corporation. Only the procedures used in establishing and measuring factors are described in any detail, but even so it is apparent that judgments by groups and committees were widely used. One objective of including so many people in the judgment processes was to win acceptance of the results.

☐ Selecting a Job Evaluation Method

The most crucial consideration in selecting among the various methods described is that the plan actually yield a stable job structure that is viewed as equitable and therefore minimizes controversy over monetary payments. In all probability, the approach that will accomplish this in one company is not the one that will yield the same result in another. Employees in one firm may be conditioned to expect intensive study of each job along the lines of the factor-comparison and point systems. In other instances, the major requirement may be that the procedures employed be simple and easy to understand, as with the job-ranking and job-comparison procedures. Where there is a strong need to recapitulate the current situation in any newly established job structure, the factor-comparison method appears to offer some advantages because it is tied directly to existing wage rates. In a small company with a limited number of positions, job ranking may be all that is needed to achieve a sense of equity.

Given these situational differences that may overrule all other considerations, the results of studies bearing on the job-evaluation process can provide certain guidelines. For one thing, a single-factor, overall value accounts for the majority of the results

---

BOX 13-5 RESEARCH IN I/O PSYCHOLOGY

Identifying Compensable Factors for Management Positions: The Approach Developed by Control Data Corporation

The Control Data Corporation program began with a task-inventory questionnaire consisting of 300 items tapping different aspects of managerial jobs. This questionnaire was administered to a large number of people in various management positions.

Next a committee of twenty-six top personnel officials met to identify the factors and weights that would be applied in accordance with the existing company value system. In the first meeting these managers were asked to specify the compensable factors as well as the relative weights of these factors on a scale of 1 to 100 points. At the second meeting they were given feedback about the factors identified at the first meeting, as well as the means and standard deviations of the weights. They were then asked to review their previous judgments and to revise them as they now felt appropriate. As a consequence, greater unanimity was obtained. This process produced eight primary factors, which were, in order of the magnitude of their judged weights:

1. Internal contacts
2. Human resource responsibilities
3. Know-how/problem solving
4. Decision making
5. Planning
6. Impact
7. Supervising/controlling
8. Representing (external contacts)

To define the content of each of these factors more specifically, the task-inventory questions were allocated to them. This was done during several meetings with compensation specialists, human resource managers, and line managers. The initial judgments assigned a large number of questions to each factor—an average of thirty. Subsequently, using statistical analyses of the data, the questions were trimmed to an average of seven per factor. In this way the compensable factors were specifically anchored to a set of inventory items defining their content.

The final point totals for each management position were obtained using the task-inventory responses on the compensable factors and the weights previously assigned to the factors.

SOURCE: Luis R. Gomez-Mejia, Ronald C. Page, & Walter W. Tornow (1987). Development and implementation of a computerized job evaluation system. In David B. Balkin & Luis R. Gomez-Mejia (Eds.), *New perspectives on compensation,* pp. 31–42. Englewood Cliffs, NJ: Prentice-Hall.

---

obtained with the factor-comparison and point methods. Thus, the single-factor approaches, such as job ranking and job classification, do not produce a great loss in precision. One problem with the more complex job-evaluation plans is that it is difficult to accommodate new jobs or changes in existing jobs. With the increasing rate of change in the ways in which both production and clerical jobs are performed, traditional job-evaluation structures frequently are subject to criticism, particularly by union representatives. Additional approaches have been developed, some of which are based on a single factor, such as problem solving or decision making, on which all jobs in a company can be evaluated (Jaques, 1961). This type of job evaluation also eliminates the need for separate classification systems for the different categories of employees; however, there is little evidence that single-factor approaches have been adopted to any extent to date.

If a multiple-factor approach is used, there seems little reason to go beyond three factors under most conditions. Experience, or time to learn the job, seems to be of considerable importance in almost all situations. Hazards, education, initiative, safety responsibility, complexity of duties, and character of supervision may be added, depending on the company and the type of job covered. A major disadvantage of the use of multiple factors is the time and cost involved in rating jobs initially and in maintaining the system. Research has compared the results of the four traditional job-evaluation methods with a method using a number of job dimension scores from the Position Analysis Questionnaire (PAQ) used in job analysis. Although all five methods provided similar results, the method using PAQ data took less time and therefore was less costly than the point method used previously (McCormick, 1979).

Studies dealing with the degree of agreement obtained with different judges or raters suggest that this is not a major problem. Independent ratings of the same jobs by different individuals tend to yield similar results. Thus a large number of judgments need not be averaged. Four raters should be entirely adequate (Doverspike, Carlisi, Barrett, & Alexander, 1983). Furthermore, the raters need not be experienced in the field of job evaluation. Inexperienced raters can achieve at least as high a level of agreement as the experienced. In fact, some companies have turned job evaluation over to employees and have found that the resulting job hierarchy is then based on the factors that the employees themselves view as relevant and important. Where an employee group performs this task, this approach should result in increased equity of the system as perceived by the employees.

Some companies have introduced various statistical prediction formulas to continue a pay structure once it has been established. In essence, these formulas indicate the best combination of predictor variables when the current pay system is treated as a criterion. Predictors are taken from the job analysis. The advantage of this approach is that pay rates for new jobs can be generated without actually going through the judgmental processes of formal job evaluation. Although total costs may well be reduced when these statistical approaches are used, employee acceptance is likely to be lower, simply because it is harder to understand why the pay for a job is what it is. The statistical approaches are no more accurate than the basic methods, such as ranking and point systems. There is some reason to believe that a combination or hybrid approach utilizing both statistical and basic job-evaluation components provides the optimal solution (Gomez-Mejia, Page, & Tornow, 1982). This in fact is what was involved in the Control Data Corporation system described in Box 13–5.

☐ Bias in Evaluating Jobs

Relative to performance appraisal, the possibility of bias in job evaluation has been given very minimal attention. Yet any place that judgment enters into a process of this kind, there is the possibility that biases will influence the results. Clearly, job evaluation contains a number of points at which judgment enters in.

Research in this area to date has focused almost entirely on gender differences. There has been concern that because many jobs are predominantly male in occupancy while others are predominantly female, and the male jobs often pay more than the female jobs, a characteristic bias may be operating in the underlying job evaluation process, to the disadvantage of females. Some studies have in fact found certain evidence for such a bias against female jobs, but when found the effects have been small and the more frequent finding has been no evidence of bias at all (Arvey, 1986; Mount & Ellis, 1987; Rynes,

Weber, & Milkovich, 1989). It is clearly too early to write off the issue as of minor significance, and practically nothing is known about racial bias in job evaluation. Surely there are individual situations where stereotypes about group differences and jobs do operate to the disadvantage of one group or another. However, what is known to date does not indicate this is a major problem among well-trained and knowledgeable job analysts and evaluators (Hahn & Dipboye, 1988).

☐ The Comparable-Worth Issue

Given this background, it is important to understand the social issue involved. In many respects this is depicted in the case of Ann Mongio described at the beginning of Chapter 3, a case where inequity dominated the motivational picture. The issue has been dubbed the **comparable-worth controversy.** At the heart of this controversy is the fact that many jobs in our society tend to be segregated by sex, or sex-typed, and at the same time working women on the average are paid considerably less than men. In part at least, the lower pay level for women can be attributed to the fact that the jobs in which women are concentrated pay less than those in which males are concentrated. Exhibit 13-6 documents the fact of sex segregation and points out one aspect of the associated pay differentials. In order to understand fully what is involved in the comparable-worth issue, and the origins of the term, it is necessary to go back into the legal history.

Legal Background. The **Equal Pay Act** has served for a number of years to outlaw pay differentials between men and women who work in substantially equal jobs—either the same exact jobs or jobs that, although titled differentially, are really the same. This type of legal structure provides no basis for claiming discrimination when jobs are clearly not the same—even if the male and female jobs

can be shown on some basis to have essentially the same value to the organization or society.

With passage of the Civil Rights Act and certain amendments to it, however, a small window appeared to have been opened, looking to this latter issue. There was some feeling that, under **Title VII,** discrimination could be shown when a job occupied primarily by women paid less than one occupied primarily by men, and the two jobs could be shown to possess equal value—to possess comparable worth. Thus, in Exhibit 13–6, the prevailing monthly pay for maintenance carpenters is $1707 and that for secretaries is $1122, yet both are given 197 job-evaluation points under a common system; the jobs are not equal in a legal sense, but they do appear to be comparable based on job evaluation.

The window produced by Title VII has attracted a number of discrimination suits, and a legal history has begun to develop around the comparable-worth issue. Initially, at least, Title VII was interpreted by the courts in much the same manner as the Equal Pay Act. If well-conducted wage surveys demonstrated that the going rate of pay for one job was different from the rate for another job, then the jobs were neither equal nor comparable and no discrimination was involved—or at least existing laws gave no basis for a claim of discrimination. In this view, the Equal Pay and Civil Rights Act yielded the same legal results.

Then, in a landmark case, the U.S. Supreme Court opened the window a little wider (*Gunther v. County of Washington,* 1981). It indicated that pay discrimination could be claimed under Title VII even though the Equal Pay Act conditions of substantial job equality were not present. It did not, however, say exactly how such discrimination might be demonstrated. At present, market pricing of jobs continues to be an acceptable defense against claims of discrimination, but not without strong opposition from those who feel

EXHIBIT 13-6   Data from the State of Washington on the Gender Segregation of Jobs and Its Relationship to Compensations

	Pay Level Relative to Prediction from Job-Evaluation Points	
	Below	Above
Jobs that Are More than 80% Male		
Warehouse worker		X
Truck driver		X
Highway engineering technician		X
Correctional officer		X
Automotive mechanic		X
Maintenance carpenter		X
Civil engineer		X
Senior architect		X
Highway engineer		X
Senior computer systems analyst		X
Physician		X
Jobs that Are More than 80% Female		
Laundry worker	X	
Telephone operator	X	
Retail sales clerk	X	
Data entry operator	X	
Intermediate clerk-typist	X	
Word-processing equipment operator	X	
Licensed practical nurse	X	
Secretary	X	
Administrative assistant	X	
Registered nurse	X	
Librarian	X	

SOURCE: Adopted from Helen Remick (1981). The comparable worth controversy. *Public Personnel Management, 10,* 371–383.

that the market is just as biased as the employer who uses it as a defense.

Even though a number of states and localities have passed laws that incorporate the comparable-worth terminology, or that deal with the matter in one way or another, comparable worth does not possess an established legal status at the present time. It is, however, a major issue in a continuing debate, frequently argued within courtroom walls. Its legal status appears to turn first one way and then another (Heisler, Jones, & Benham, 1988).

EEOC Initiatives.   In late 1977, the U.S. Equal Employment Opportunity Commission initiated discussions with the National Academy of Sciences with a view to having the latter organization conduct studies and analyses in the area of comparable worth. The objective was at the very least to focus attention on the issues involved and perhaps to foster related legislation.

The initial consequence of this initiative was a staff review of job-evaluation concepts and practices in order to determine their relationships to comparable-worth discrimination claims. The report concludes:

> We have discussed three features of formal job evaluation procedures that render problematic their utility for job worth assessment in a labor force highly segregated by sex. First, the relative ranking of jobs tends to be highly dependent upon which factors are used in the evaluation and how heavily each factor is weighted. But the principal procedure for deriving factor weights pegs them to current wage rates and thereby reflects existing sex differences in wage rates. Second, job evaluation is inherently subjective, making it possible that well-known processes of sex-role stereotyping will be operative in this context as well, resulting in an underevaluation of jobs held predominantly by women. Third, many employers use several job evaluation plans—one for shop jobs, one for office jobs, etc.—a procedure that makes it impossible to compare the worth of jobs in different sectors of a firm (Treiman, 1979, p. 48).

In short, job-evaluation procedures were seriously questioned, and their potential for discriminatory application, along with that of wage surveys, was emphasized.

Stimulated by EEOC initiatives, the Equal Employment Advisory Council, working with the Business Roundtable, developed a series of position papers dealing with aspects of the comparable-worth issue; the objective was to present a reasoned analysis from an employer perspective. The following exerpts provide some feeling for the nature of this effort:

> Any attempted implementation of comparable worth would encounter substantial difficulties and would have disruptive and undesirable consequences.
> There is a viable alternative—the accelerated

promotion of women, which is being effectively pursued by many companies.

> Comparable worth is based upon a rejection of traditional job evaluation plans and market rate standards and would substitute in their place some undetermined form of bias-free or value-free job evaluation. Support for such an approach fails to appreciate the realities of how evaluation procedures actually operate.

> Given the success of upward mobility and the problems associated with the implementation of comparable worth, it is most doubtful that new legal or regulatory controls are appropriate (Livernash, 1980, pp. 19–21).

Subsequently, the National Academy of Sciences group published its final report. This contains detailed analyses of studies dealing with male–female pay differentials and the factors that might account for them—differences in the size of employing firms, educational levels, labor force experience, and the like. The viewpoint taken is primarily that of economic theory, and the research reviewed has been conducted almost entirely by economists.

Based on this review, certain conclusions were reached:

> The committee is convinced by the evidence, taken together, that women are systematically underpaid. Policies designed to promote equal access to all employment opportunities will affect the underpayment of women workers only slowly. Equal access to employment opportunities may be expected to be more effective for those who have invested less in skills than for those who have invested more. . . . For these reasons the committee believes that the strategy of "comparable worth" merits consideration as an alternative policy. . . . The viability of a strategy of paying jobs in accordance with their "worth" requires, first, that an appropriate mechanism, other than current market wage rates, can be found to measure the relative worth of jobs to an employer and, second, that wages commensurate with worth can be set and paid by the employer (Treiman & Hartmann, 1981, pp. 66–67).

Alternative Actions. It is apparent that widely differing perspectives and values related to comparable worth exist (Hill & Killingsworth, 1989; Killingsworth, 1990). Some believe that the solution is to reduce the amount of sex stereotyping of jobs in some manner so that females move into male jobs and males into female ones. Thus the sex differentials in job occupancy noted in Exhibit 13-6 would disappear, and the Equal Pay Act standards would be quite sufficient to protect against discrimination.

Another alternative advocated is to establish a single, nationwide job-evaluation system of a kind that does not rely on wage survey data and market pricing for its results. Then objective measures would be available to determine comparable worth and the wage structures of all employers. At this point, options still remain in pricing the structure. Most discussions appear to assume that wage rates for female jobs would be moved up to those of comparable male jobs. No one appears to have proposed the reverse—that the pay for male jobs be moved down to the female level. But there have been proposals for striking a realistic balance so that a common ground is reached without increasing the company's overall compensation budget.

Many employers are concerned about comparable worth not because they wish to discriminate but because they foresee a sizable increase in labor costs beyond their capacity to pay, and because they do not wish to experience further legal constraints on human resource decision making (Rosen, Rynes, & Mahoney, 1983). Unilateral action—to equate the pay of carpenters and secretaries, for instance—contains a number of pitfalls. As long as market-pay differentials remain essentially unchanged, one cannot realistically do anything to substantially lower pay rates for carpenters, because it is very likely that the result would only be a number of unfilled positions. This means that, to achieve comparable worth, a firm would have to raise secretaries' pay by some $600 a month (over 50 percent) to make their pay the equal of that for carpenters. Assuming that a firm has a large number of secretaries, and most do, this sort of thing represents a very drastic, one-time increase in labor costs.

Clearly, the comparable-worth issue will face American business, and the society as a whole, with major challenges for some time to come. It is something in which industrial/organizational psychology will continue to play a major role.

KEY TERMS

Task

Position

Job

Occupation

Job description

Job family

Job analysis

Job evaluation

Job specification

Task inventories

Critical incidents

Position Analysis Questionnaire

Career ladders

Functional job analysis

Credentialism

Job ranking

Job classification

Factor comparison

Point system
Comparable-worth controversy

Equal Pay Act
Title VII (Civil Rights Act)

SUMMARY

Job analysis establishes the role prescriptions that govern work. Job analysis data are used for purposes of compensation, hiring and selection, determining training needs, and in many other areas. Major components are the *job description* and *job specification*. Methods used by job analysts include observation, interviews, questionnaires, examination of previous job descriptions, study of work materials, and actual performance of the work. Various conceptual and statistical techniques may be used to create *job families* and *career ladders* once jobs have been analyzed. In recent years, traditional job analysis has been extended, or even on occasion replaced, by approaches such as job enrichment and management by objectives. Other innovations within the domain of job analysis serve to introduce changes in the hours of work. In general, research suggests that there are sizable advantages in combining data obtained from several different job analysis methods, especially if the job analyses are to be used for a variety of purposes, as is normally the case.

Although wage surveys may be used to price jobs within a company directly from the market, it is more common to develop an internal wage structure through *job evaluation,* an area in which industrial psychology has made substantial contributions. Methods of job evaluation include *job ranking, job classification, factor comparison,* and *point systems.* Which type of procedure is most appropriate depends on the specific company situation. Although bias in the job-evaluation process has not been widely studied, the evidence to date suggests that it is not a major problem. Even so, the *comparable-worth controversy* over whether women are typically paid less than their work would warrant, continues to burn brightly.

QUESTIONS

1. How does the job-ranking approach to job evaluation differ from job classification?
2. What is a job specification? What special problems are involved? Can you think of any laws a job specification might violate?
3. Distinguish between the following:
   a. The *Dictionary of Occupational Titles* and the *Alphabetical Index of Industries and Occupations*
   b. Position and job
   c. Job analysis and job evaluation
   d. Task inventories and the critical-incident method
4. What special problems is the Position Analysis Questionnaire designed to solve? What method of obtaining job analysis information does it employ? How might this approach be used as an aid in job evaluation?
5. What are the points at which judgment may enter into the job-evaluation process using the different methods?
6. Under what circumstances is observation of the job occupant an appropriate method of job analysis, and when is it not?
7. What is known about the impact of bias in job

evaluation? How does this relate to the comparable worth controversy?

8. What elements are usually included in a job description? How are these elements reflected in the job description given in Box 13-2?

9. How does job analysis contribute to the following areas?

   a. Labor relations

   b. Job evaluation

   c. Training need analysis

   d. Employee evaluation

   e. Selection

10. How does functional job analysis help to develop job families? For what purposes are these job families useful?

CASE PROBLEM

Job Analysis: Problems in New-Product Development

A research scientist who had made substantial contributions to her company in the area of new-product development had become increasingly upset because she believed her pay had not been increased in a manner commensurate with her contributions. She was one of a group of five scientists who had been spearheading the new-product work for a number of years. All five were paid at essentially the same level; the other four were males. All five were almost indispensible from a company viewpoint, and accordingly, their pay had been deliberately pegged at a level somewhat above normal market levels. The problem was that the products they had developed had proved immensely profitable for the company. It was like a professional athlete who performs before packed stands day after day. One begins to get the idea that it is only fair for the organization to give back a reasonable share of what one is bringing in. That kind of thinking can mean a very large amount of money indeed.

Among the five, the female member of the group appeared to have grasped this idea of equitable compensation first, and accordingly, she had taken the lead in pushing it. The others agreed with her, but they apparently did not feel so strongly or were not willing to push as hard, in any event. There was no feeling that any one of the five might deserve more than the others; they all did essentially the same work. What was at issue was the size of the pie to be divided among them.

For some time, the female scientist had been writing letters protesting the salary situation, which almost always found their way to the research and development vice president. Typically, she would receive a reply saying the matter would be looked into, and that was about all. The next round of raises would trigger another letter. The most recent of these contained a new element, however. This was a request for someone from the human resources department who was knowledgeable in the area to come over and actually study her job to see what she did. Perhaps with a fuller understanding of the nature of the work, the company would be in a better position to evaluate it and come up with an equitable compensation level.

This type of request is usually seen as reasonable in the business world, and accordingly, the research and development vice president contacted human resources for their reaction. Unfortunately, the company lacked a job analysis program because the company legal counsel had recommended against establishing one, on the grounds that the job descriptions might be used against the company in court. Yet everyone agreed that, in this particular instance, a job analysis of some kind should be carried out. There was no good reason for not doing it and, in any event, all that was involved was finding out in detail about the nature of the work. It was hoped that that, in and of itself, would be sufficient. Accordingly, an individual on the human resources staff was assigned responsibility for conducting the job analysis and writing it up.

Questions

1. If you were that individual, exactly how would you go about doing the job analysis? What methods would you use and in what manner?

2. How would you go about writing up your findings? What format would you use, and what factors would you consider?

14

Approaches to Performance Appraisal

At General Electric a unit known as the Executive Management Staff (EMS) has the responsibility for identifying and developing those who will rise to the highest levels of the organization. Of the 400,000 employees at GE, the EMS is concerned with the top 5000 and pays especially close attention to the top 600. The EMS is on a par with the corporate finance, legal, and planning staffs and is organized as shown in the accompanying chart.

The two executive management consulting units and the corporate executive resources unit all comprise consultants whose major duties include conducting what are called accomplishment analyses; these are evaluations of especially promising employees. These analyses provide an initial data base to the EMS and do not occur until well into a manager's career. Someone selected for analysis will be considered for ultimate movement to upper management, but the analysis is not tied directly to any particular promotion decision.

The process starts when a consultant from the EMS interviews the individual for as long as four hours. The discussion focuses on what the person accomplished in his or her past few jobs and did not accomplish but might have. The consultant conducts a similar interview with the person's present boss and contacts a number of former associates.

Former subordinates may provide additional information. An extensive report pulls together all this information. It presents the consultant's conclusions as to the achievements, management style, and development plans of the person analyzed, as well as the degree to which career goals are realistic, and so on. All this typically takes about a week of the consultant's time.

The completed report is given to both the person evaluated and the immediate superior, for the purpose of checking facts and eliciting comments. Errors are then corrected, and the report may be annotated to show points of disagreement. The report stresses both strengths and weaknesses, and accordingly its feedback to the individual can yield conflict. Nevertheless, the report goes into the EMS file on the employee, and can have a major impact on subsequent career development. It constitutes the most extensive appraisal that GE conducts on its managers.

SOURCE: Based on Stewart D. Friedman & Theodore P. LeVino (1984). Strategic appraisal and development at General Electric Company. In Charles Fombrun, Noel M. Tichy, & Mary Anne Devanna (Eds.), *Strategic human resource management*, pp. 183–201. New York: Wiley.

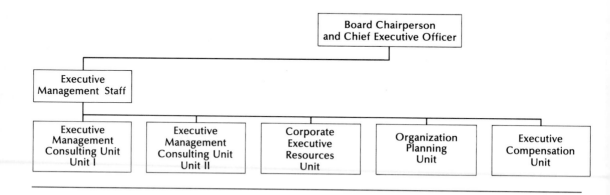

This is how one large corporation carries out the appraisal of its top-level people. As will become evident, this is only one approach among many that a company may use. It is apparent, however, that performance appraisal plays a very important role at General Electric. Much is invested in it, and much is expected of it.

■ THE ROLES OF PERFORMANCE APPRAISAL

□ The Nature of Performance Appraisal

To understand how performance appraisal works, it is necessary to start at the very top with overall organizational objectives and goals, and the strategies developed to attain them. Once what constitutes effective performance on the part of an organization as a whole has been established, so that a picture of what the organization is trying to do strategically can be drawn, it becomes possible to break that picture down into parts like a jigsaw puzzle. Group and individual contributions to the organization's overall effectiveness are the puzzle's component pieces.

The work to be done, as indicated by the organization's stated or assumed goals, is split up by means of some type of job analysis. This **division of labor** occurs because more work—and more complex work—is involved than one individual can handle. As a result, specific expectations are created for the behavior of groups and individuals in the organization.

After these expectations are established, it is possible to measure and evaluate behavior, assessing how well it matches the expectations. This is the process of **performance appraisal.** Behavior which matches the roles that have been created to pursue organizational effectiveness is valued positively; behavior which departs from what is expected is viewed negatively (Mohrman, Resnick-West, & Lawler, 1989).

A great number of performance appraisal approaches have been developed to determine if individuals and groups are doing what they are supposed to do. If the great majority of employees are behaving as expected (performing effectively) and the work has been divided up correctly (without omissions and overlaps), then the whole should fit together to yield an effective, productive organization. The most important function of performance appraisal is to identify where the parts do and do not fit together well as a result of individual and group behaviors. Performance appraisal helps the organization to maximize efforts, prevent problems, and maintain controls, so that performance throughout the organization can be improved and the jigsaw puzzle joined into a unified, productive whole.

Because any given position is likely to have a number of different role requirements, we can expect that job-related behavior will be evaluated in a number of different aspects. Particularly in the case of managers, it is not a matter of doing one or even a few things correctly, but of doing a great variety of different things, all designed to meet one role requirement or another. Accordingly, an individual may be considered a great success in one regard but fall down badly in some other area relative to some other requirement.

It is characteristic to evaluate people in terms of various aspects of their behavior, or dimensions of performance. Generally, the major concern is with actual behavior, with the things a person does or says. On occasion, however, evaluation systems move one step back into the individual and attempt to deal with the abilities, motives, and emotional patterns that cause or determine the behavior. The most general approach is to establish the extent of the match to a role requirement, or the degree of success. But often performance standards are introduced so that job behavior is considered only as it relates to some minimal acceptable level. Either the person is above standard in a particular regard or below it.

□ Uses of Performance Appraisals

Performance is evaluated in some manner in all organizations. Very small firms may not need formal systems of appraisal, but evalua-

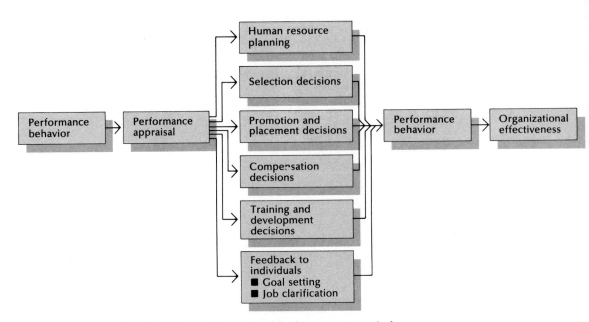

EXHIBIT 14-1   Organizational Uses and Impacts of Performance Appraisal
Appraisals can modify performance, increasing its effectiveness.
SOURCE: Allan M. Mohrman & Edward E. Lawler (1983). Motivational and performance-appraisal behavior. In Frank J. Landy, Sheldon Zedeck, & Jeannette Cleveland (Eds.), *Performance measurement and theory,* p. 176. Hillsdale, NJ: Erlbaum.

tion occurs nevertheless. And as firms experience a growing need to standardize, retain, and communicate appraisal information, they are increasingly likely to institute formal systems.

In many respects performance appraisal, in conjunction with job analysis, is the glue that binds together the human resource activities of an organization so that they can contribute forcefully to the attainment of organizational goals (Wexley & Klimoski, 1984). Exhibit 14-1 illustrates these relationships, showing how job performance leads to performance appraisal and is then modified by that appraisal in the direction of greater effectiveness.

Historically, the major uses of performance appraisals have been to allocate rewards such as pay and promotions in proportion to performance and to provide feedback in the hope of improving future performance (Cleveland, Murphy, & Williams, 1989). In both cases, the appraisals have been focused on the activities of employees being appraised and on ways of motivating them to higher performance levels. In line with this emphasis, the field of industrial psychology often considers performance appraisal in conjunction with rewards. Yet there are other uses of appraisals, as indicated in Exhibits 14-1 and 14-2. Although appraisals continue to be used more frequently as the basis for rewards, in many companies they are utilized in almost all aspects of human resource management. Industrial psychology is concerned not only with performance appraisal itself, but with the great majority of these uses to which performance appraisal data may be put.

Exhibit 14-3 presents an overview of the various factors that combine to determine how effective the performance appraisal process is in a given company, and of the relationships among the factors. We will be concerned with many aspects of this model in this chapter, and in Chapter 15 as well.

Exhibit 14-2   Uses to Which Performance Appraisals Are Put in Large Companies

A study of major firms revealed the range of performance appraisal uses shown here. Note, for example, that a majority of the companies reported using performance appraisals as the basis for promotions and merit salary increases, while relatively few used them in making decisions about such matters as bonuses and personnel planning.

Over 75% of Companies	Between 50% and 75% of Companies	Fewer than 50% of Companies
• Promotion • Merit increases • Feedback and job counseling	• Termination or layoff • Assessment of performance potential • Career planning • Transfer • Succession planning	• Bonuses • Personnel planning • Development and evaluation of training • Internal communication • Selection procedure validation • Expense control

Source: Adapted from Robert L. Laud (1984). Performance appraisal practices in the *Fortune* 1300. In Charles Fombrun, Noel M. Tichy, & Mary Anne Devanna (Eds.), *Strategic human resource management*, p. 119. New York: Wiley.

■ JUDGMENTAL APPRAISAL

The most widespread method of evaluation is to obtain some type of judgment about an employee's effectiveness, or the factors that influence it. Most frequently an immediate superior renders this judgment, at least in the kind of hierarchic organization that is most common in today's corporate world. However, multiple sources may be used; Exhibit 14-4 indicates these other alternatives. At the beginning of this chapter a method used at the highest levels of General Electric was described which involved human resource specialists, immediate superiors, the appraisee, and to a lesser degree peers and subordinates. The final evaluation consolidates views obtained from a wide range of sources, even though the evaluation itself is made by a human resource specialist.

☐ Appraisal by Superiors

In hierarchic organizations, communication and power tend to flow vertically, and thus it makes sense to use superiors to make evaluations. The evaluation process almost always includes the immediate superior, but it may also use ratings from further up the line. This makes sense only if these higher-level managers have observed the employee's performance independently.

A common practice in management appraisal, in the author's experience, is to convene a meeting of evaluators—the immediate superior, managers at higher levels, a human resource specialist, and perhaps several superiors in other units who interact with the manager being appraised. These group evaluations can be very effective, if the participants make their ratings independently and then refine and consolidate them in the course of the discussion, and if the final report incorporates any dissenting opinions. The highest-level manager present should be careful not to dominate the appraisal process and its outcome: because of physical distance from the employee's day-to-day work, that manager is often the least well informed of those present.

The Appraisal Summary.   In companies that maintain an ongoing appraisal system with periodic evaluations, the typical procedure is for a member of the human resources depart-

Input Variables   Process Variables   Outcome Variable

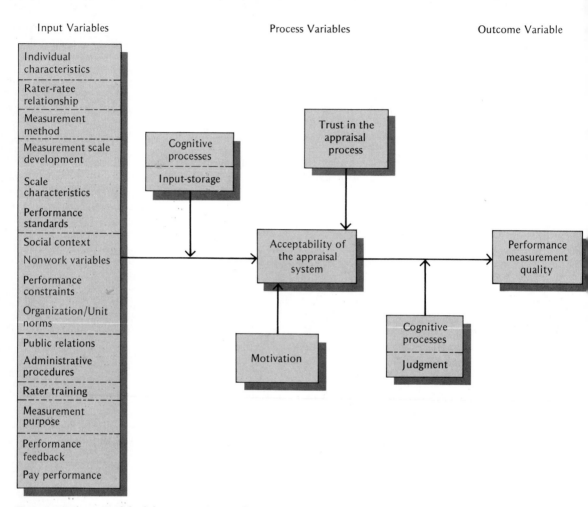

EXHIBIT 14-3   A Model of the Determinants that Influence Performance Appraisal Quality
Input variables consisting of characteristics of the measurement system, the organization, and the people are moderated by the acceptability of the appraisal system to determine appraisal quality. Cognitive processes, motivation, and trust enter into this process at various points.
SOURCE: Michael J. Kavanagh, Walter C. Borman, Jerry W. Hedge, & R. Bruce Gould (1987). Performance measurement quality. In Bernard M. Bass & Pieter J. D. Drenth (Eds.), *Advances in organizational psychology: An international review,* p. 60. Beverly Hills, CA: Sage.

ment to write up the findings in an appraisal summary. This summary may be merely a brief synopsis, but in some firms it takes the form of an extensive and detailed description of the individual. An outline for an appraisal summary of this latter type is pre-

sented in Exhibit 14-5; it derives from Atlantic-Richfield.

The data used to write the appraisal summary on a specific individual are derived in large part from the individual's superiors. In addition, however, the program may utilize

Exhibit 14-4   Sources of Performance Appraisal
The evaluation process may use information about an
appraisee's performance from any of the sources shown here.

psychological tests, a personal history form to be filled out by the managers themselves, and in many cases a personal interview with the manager conducted by a personnel representative. The summary itself is characteristically considered confidential and is made available only to the manager's direct-line superiors and to appropriate human resource managers.

The Management Inventory. Effective human resource planning requires making projections of internal supplies of various types of talents. At the management level, these projections are usually based on a composite analysis of data derived from the management appraisal process. When all the appraisal summaries are completed in a given company unit, it is common practice to prepare a **management inventory** indicating future replacement needs and listing the candidates who may qualify for anticipated vacancies, immediately or after further devel-

opment. Anticipated needs for at least five years are usually considered, based on performance, expected promotions, retirement schedules, health, and projected organizational changes.

Replacement candidates are obtained not only from the specific unit but from other segments of the company as well. It is entirely possible that an individual may appear as a candidate on inventory lists for several units, depending on breadth of training and experience. The lists are maintained on a continuing basis and are reviewed and updated frequently. On occasion, the management inventory is developed in chart form along the lines of Exhibit 14-6.

☐ Appraisal by Peers or Subordinates

During World War II, a technique known as **buddy rating** was developed by Navy psychologists. This procedure requires that each member of a group rate all other members on

Exhibit 14-5   Abbreviated Outline Covering Items Included in an Appraisal Summary at Atlantic-Richfield

1. Personal Background:
   Age
   Family background
   Education
   Military experience
   Work history
   Special accomplishments
   Special limitations
   Hobbies and recreational activities
2. Nature of Work:
   Generalized statement based on organization planning and job analysis data
   Committee assignments
   Number and titles of people supervised
3. Job Performance and Personal Qualifications:
   General statement of value to company and probable future contribution
   Technical performance
   Motivation in current position
   Intelligence as manifested on the job
   Emotional stability
   Leadership skills
   Three accomplishments in present job that indicate what he or she is capable of
   Summarizing "snapshot" covering major strengths and weaknesses
4. Overall Performance Rating:
   Individual rating relative to what is expected
   Ranking among others at same level doing similar work
5. Potentiality:
   Promotability and expected rate (or timetable) of progress
   Actual job or job types (job families) qualified for
   Long-range potential
6. Recommended Actions:
   Changes in placement
   Ideal duration of current placement
   Development needs and plans

---

certain aspects of their work performance. The ratings on each individual are then averaged to provide an index of the person's competence.

In the years since these initial applications, much has been written about the advantages of this technique, especially as an aid in the evaluation of managers. Either all managers at a comparable level in a given unit, perhaps all first-line supervisors in a small manufacturing plant, rate each other; or, as a variant, the managers are rated by their subordinates.

In this way it is possible to obtain evaluations from those who are likely to be well acquainted with the person being appraised, to have observed his or her work closely over a long period, and thus to be capable of making extremely accurate ratings.

Of the two approaches, peer ratings appear to be more useful than ratings by subordinates. On occasion, peer ratings have been found to yield results quite similar to those obtained when superiors do the rating; in other cases, the two have differed consider-

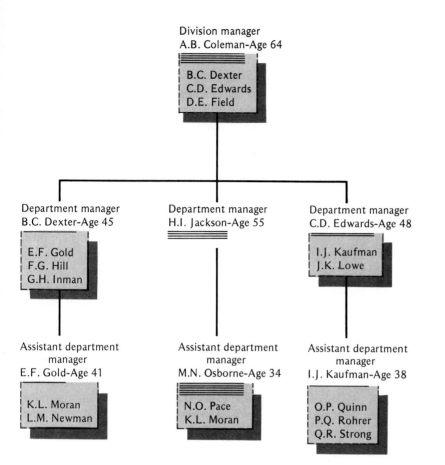

Division manager
A.B. Coleman-Age 64

B.C. Dexter
C.D. Edwards
D.E. Field

Department manager
B.C. Dexter-Age 45

E.F. Gold
F.G. Hill
G.H. Inman

Department manager
H.I. Jackson-Age 55

Department manager
C.D. Edwards-Age 48

I.J. Kaufman
J.K. Lowe

Assistant department
manager
E.F. Gold-Age 41

K.L. Moran
L.M. Newman

Assistant department
manager
M.N. Osborne-Age 34

N.O. Pace
K.L. Moran

Assistant department
manager
I.J. Kaufman-Age 38

O.P. Quinn
P.Q. Rohrer
Q.R. Strong

Code for underlining of incumbents:

——— Outstanding potential. Ready for job above. High promise for unit head.

══ Good potential. Fair promise for unit head.

═══ Potential for some growth. Not likely to make unit head.

═══ Not likely to advance beyond present position.

═══ Age or health make replacement necessary within five years.

═══ Unsatisfactory performance. Replacement needed.

EXHIBIT 14-6   A Management Inventory Chart

ably. There appear to be major variations among situations and companies that may serve to reduce or to increase the differences between perceptions of role behavior by peers and superiors. Nevertheless, across multiple studies there does appear to be a substantial correlation between ratings from the two sources (Harris & Schaubroeck, 1988).

It is apparent that peer ratings can also be used effectively to predict subsequent job performance and promotion. This is true even when those doing the rating are fully aware that what they say about individuals may have considerable impact on their future careers. These data, taken as a whole, indicate that many of the potential sources of bias inherent in the peer-rating procedure may not actually operate as frequently as has been assumed. The evidence to date indicates that peer ratings can serve very well as a useful adjunct to more traditional evaluations by superiors (Latham & Wexley, 1981).

One difficulty, however, and perhaps the major reason that peer appraisals are not more widely used in organizations, is that people tend not to like them. They can produce conflict, divisiveness, and bad feelings (DeNisi, Randolph, & Blencoe, 1983). This is a problem particularly when there is any doubt as to the confidentiality of the ratings (McEvoy & Buller, 1987). To provide honest evaluations of their peers and superiors, people have to be convinced that those being evaluated will not learn what was said or who said it.

☐ Alternative Approaches

Field Review. One variant on the standard method of appraisal, to which the name **field review** is often applied, involves much more active participation on the part of the industrial psychologist. In this approach, the appraisal data are collected orally rather than through the use of written forms. Normally, an industrial psychologist will go to the office of a person's superior with a specific list of questions. Answers to these questions are obtained in conversation and recorded in note form. The notes are then converted to a written description after the interview. A draft of this written description is reviewed by the superior, and then it is put in final form. All this can, of course, be a time-consuming and costly process.

The advantages of this approach are inherent in the fact that an oral procedure is more likely to elicit specific information regarding the person being appraised. Superiors will say things about a person in a free discussion of this kind that they will not put in writing. In addition, the fact that someone will actually spend an hour or more conducting the interview conveys the impression that the appraisal process is considered quite important. Thus, the kind of superficial, hurried response that written rating forms sometimes produce is much less common.

Finally, this technique has the advantage that similar standards of evaluation can be maintained across a large number of interviews. It is possible to establish what amounts to a set of ground rules, which are held constant for all managers appraised. This control over the general level of ratings and of the factors to be considered is much more difficult to exercise when written forms are used or when appraisal sessions are conducted by differing groups of managers, each constituted to judge a particular individual.

In the latter instance, it has become common practice for management appraisal specialists to sit in on the group meetings for just this reason. Usually, these people also write the appraisal summary. Such individuals can establish common standards for the ratings within a department or division or across the company as a whole. If they feel a particular group of superiors is being excessively lenient, or harsh, compared with other such groups, they can take steps to correct this variation in standards, either by inducing the group to change its views or by introducing compensating statements into the final appraisal summary.

Psychological Appraisal. A markedly different type of appraisal is typically carried out by personnel psychologists who have had some training in the techniques of personality assessment. These **psychological appraisals** usually involve extensive interviewing coupled with individual psychological testing.

They are often employed in conjunction with other evaluation procedures. But even if this is not the case, efforts are made to integrate the test and interview data with information available from personnel files and other sources. The psychologist attempts to get as clear an understanding as possible of the underlying intellectual, emotional, and motivational characteristics of the individual and then converts this into a picture of how such a person might be expected to behave. The resulting psychological description is not so much a summary of actual behavior as a prediction of anticipated behavior under certain specified circumstances. This is clearly evident in the appraisal from Atlantic-Richfield given in Box 14-1.

Evaluations of this kind are particularly helpful when decisions must be made regarding promotion or transfer, because they provide information regarding how the individual might be expected to act in the new position relative to revised role requirements. However, psychological procedures are also used by many companies in connection with a regular, periodic appraisal program. Although some companies do maintain an internal staff of industrial psychologists to conduct assessments of this type, a large proportion of the work is done by outside consultants. These psychologists utilize a wide range of techniques (Ryan & Sackett, 1987).

Research on the success with which subsequent performance has been predicted from such evaluations has yielded varied results. A number of studies have produced findings indicating that the psychological descriptions are highly accurate and that they can be used to identify those who will succeed or fail in a given company. However, it appears that whether these performance predictions will prove correct depends in large part on the psychologist's knowledge of the organization, its role requirements, and its value structure. When this knowledge is lacking, the psychologist may have to rely on misconceptions about what makes for success in the firm or may make judgments based on a view of the individual's emotional health alone. In such circumstances, there may be large differences among psychologists in the extent to which their recommendations are favorable, irrespective of any actual differences between individuals. Box 14-2 provides a good example of what can happen when organizational and job information are limited.

The data of Exhibit 14-7 are derived from an analysis of six psychologists' evaluations of candidates for consulting positions at McKinsey & Company. Psychologist 3 tends to make a disproportionately large number of favorable recommendations, whereas psychologists 2 and 6 tend to be unfavorable. These differences are statistically significant and suggest a generalized tendency for certain psychologists to respond positively or negatively independent of the qualifications of the person evaluated. As indicated in Box 1-3, psychological evaluations are not valid under these conditions.

Self-Evaluations. Self-appraisal occurs everywhere, even if it is not used formally in evaluations. People do develop perceptions of their own performance and compare them with feedback received from other sources. Organizations rarely collect this information on a formal basis, using standardized rating forms and the like. But self-evaluations do occur and do exert considerable influence on an individual's behavior. For this reason it is important to understand how self-ratings relate to appraisals obtained from other sources.

Self-evaluations are usually unrelated to other performance indexes, such as ratings by superiors; or else they show only a low positive correlation with them (Gladstein, 1984; Mount, 1984; Steel & Ovalle, 1984). Individuals tend to rate their own performance higher than others do. And self-evaluations do not agree with subordinates' appraisals any more

BOX 14-1   I/O PSYCHOLOGY IN PRACTICE

A Psychological Description of a Candidate for Promotion in Atlantic-Richfield's Marketing Department

Albert W. Woodworth, Sales Training Representative. Mr. Woodworth appears to be the outstanding individual among the four candidates for district marketing manager evaluated. The evidence suggests that Mr. Woodworth would not only make a major contribution in the position for which he is currently being considered, but that he also has the potential to perform very effectively at higher levels in the company. The following strengths are apparent.

1. Mr. Woodworth's general verbal intelligence level is very high. He has a Wechsler Verbal IQ of 136. This is the top score obtained among the thirty-one members of marketing management who have been evaluated to date. This showing is particularly surprising in view of the fact that Mr. Woodworth has no formal college education. Reasoning and problem-solving ability are also at a high level, as indicated by the results of the Terman Concept Mastery Test. Apparently, Mr. Woodworth has not only accumulated a great deal of knowledge—he is capable of bringing his intellectual abilities to bear in the solution of complex problems.

2. Mr. Woodworth is very strong on problem solving in the numerical area, being particularly adept in quickly grasping a problem and coming up with a solution. He should be outstanding in drawing inferences from an analysis of sales figures and in the accounting aspects of his work.

3. Mr. Woodworth's mechanical ability is at a very high level. In fact, his ability in this area is actually quite outstanding.

4. Mr. Woodworth has very wide interests and keeps himself informed in a great variety of fields. This breadth of interest plus his capacity for very rapid learning should permit Mr. Woodworth to adapt readily to new situations. It is unlikely that he will require a very long training period if promoted.

5. From the Picture Arrangement Test, it is apparent that Mr. Woodworth has very strong work motivation. He can be counted on to push himself hard. He has the capacity to get things done and will keep at a problem until he has it licked. He appears to be happiest when he is working hard and effectively.

6. Mr. Woodworth is a rather independent person. He is unlikely to lean on others and is quite capable of reaching his own decisions. He would much prefer to figure out problems himself and do things his own way. Although he will on occasion follow the advice of others, he tends to distrust it. However, he can be counted on to follow directions and company policy meticulously when this is necessary. There is little question that Mr. Woodworth will do his best work when given a free hand.

7. It is evident from the Thematic Apperception Test stories that Mr. Woodworth is an extremely competent planner and organizer. He will take risks but prefers to do so only after he has made a careful analysis of the alternatives. He has his own ideas about how things should be done, and these ideas are likely to be both original and practical.

Although these strengths taken as a whole seem to argue very strongly for Mr. Woodworth's selection as district marketing manager, there are two problems that should be mentioned:

1. At the present time, Mr. Woodworth is somewhat uncertain about his own ability. Although he seems to enjoy management responsibilities and likes to participate in the solution of complex marketing problems, he has no clear conception of his own capacities and tends to underestimate them. He realizes that he has never held a job that has really challenged him, but, on the other hand, perhaps because of this lack of challenge, he has

no idea of the level at which he might be able to function. It seems probable that Mr. Woodworth is the type of person who will perform more effectively the higher he rises in the organization. He needs to find out how good he really is, and only by facing greater challenges is he likely to gain confidence in his own ability. He needs to prove himself to himself, and only after he has done this is he likely to realize his full potential. This entire problem came out quite clearly during the course of the interview.

2. Mr. Woodworth tends to be rather impatient with mediocrity. He holds himself to very high standards and expects others to perform at the same high level. He may find it hard to delegate to people whom he feels are not as competent as he would wish. As a result, he may try to do too much himself and thereby

fail to develop his subordinates to the full. He is also unlikely to establish warm relationships with his subordinates, tending to remain somewhat at a distance from people. Mr. Woodworth is well aware of these problems but appears to be incapable of solving them at the present time. As Mr. Woodworth becomes more confident of his own abilities, he may well feel freer to let subordinates learn through an occasional failure and may become capable of greater freedom in his own emotional relationships. This problem, like the other, should largely solve itself if Mr. Woodworth rises to higher levels of management responsibility. Nevertheless, it should be recognized that Mr. Woodworth will probably never be as effective in his handling of people as he is in problem-solving and organizing efforts.

than they do with appraisals by superiors. In addition, group ratings of the group's own performance appear to be unrelated to performance measures determined by others, just as individual self-evaluations are.

Findings such as these suggest a major problem for organizations. We often do not view our performance as others view it. Our own evaluations may be quite different from the results of objective measures. Often we emphasize aspects of our work that others consider much less important. It is difficult to get people to consider ways of improving their performance when they are convinced that they are already doing an outstanding job.

However, there do appear to be certain circumstances where self-evaluations take on a somewhat higher degree of objectivity and validity (Farh & Werbel, 1986; Farh, Werbel, & Bedeian, 1988). If the self-ratings are not to be used for administrative purposes such as pay increases or promotions, that helps; they may, for instance, be useful in guiding personal development efforts. Also, where other, hard data on performance are collected and

highly visible, this fact does exert some pressure on people to bring their self-evaluations in line. All in all, it appears that having individuals evaluate themselves is practically useless if it is the only approach used, but in conjunction with other approaches it can yield some useful information. Also, as indicated in Box 1-4, it helps to have comparative performance information on others available to the self-raters.

Management-by-Objectives (MBO) Appraisal. Chapter 4 considered **management by objectives (MBO)** as a motivational technique, and in Chapter 11 the incorporation of MBO into organization development received attention. Since its inception, however, MBO has also been viewed as a method of appraisal. This tie between appraisal and MBO arose out of certain dissatisfactions with conventional procedures of evaluation by superiors, and in particular out of dissatisfaction with the consequences when managers were required to feed back appraisal data to their subordinates with a view to encouraging more effective performance.

BOX 14-2   RESEARCH IN I/O PSYCHOLOGY

Agreement among Psychologists in Making Assessments under Simulated Conditions

Three psychologists with extensive experience in carrying out psychological appraisals were recruited to assess the same three candidates for a position as "director of sales training and development." The three candidates all held sales training jobs at the time of assessment. There was no actual management position to be filled, and they were not paid for their work. The concern was to determine how well the psychologists agreed in their evaluations.

Information regarding the company and the

The three psychologists used whatever tests, interview formats, and background data they viewed appropriate. Thus the information each obtained on the candidates was not necessarily the same. Accordingly, the psychologists often emphasized different aspects in their written reports. However, all concluded with a statement regarding the candidates' suitability for the sales training director position. These recommendations may be compared to determine how well the psychologists agreed:

	Candidate 1	Candidate 2	Candidate 3
Psychologist 1	Marginally qualified; a strong candidate for a director's position at a later date.	Adequate, but not a strong candidate.	I am reluctant to evaluate as a strong candidate.
Psychologist 2	Not likely to be successful.	Has the potential to achieve a successful middle-management career.	A likely success.
Psychologist 3	Appears to have considerable potential.	Has considerable potential.	Has considerable potential.

job to be filled was available from a telephone contact in an actual company. This individual had been instructed to role-play for the psychologists. She did, however, currently hold a position as director of training and development in her company. The psychologists actually obtained only very limited information from her regarding the company, its culture, and managerial reporting relationships. They inquired more extensively regarding the position to be filled, but even here there appear to have been marked deficiencies in their understanding of the work to be performed.

Clearly the three psychologists were not in strong agreement. At least part of the problem appears to be that they did not have first-hand knowledge of the company and the job. Given this void, they could develop their own assumptions in this area. To the degree that these assumptions varied, their recommendations would also vary.

Source: Ann Marie Ryan & Paul R. Sackett (1989). Exploratory study of individual assessment practices: Interrater reliability and judgment of assessor effectiveness. *Journal of Applied Psychology, 74,* 568–579.

EXHIBIT 14-7   Mean Psychological Evaluation Scores and Hiring Recommendation Percentages for Six Psychologists Serving as External Consultants to McKinsey & Company

Psychologist	Individuals Evaluated	Mean Evaluation Score (range 1–4)	Percent Favorable Recommendations (scores of 3 and 4)
Firm A			
Psychologist 1	38	2.26	53
Psychologist 2	25	1.76	32
Firm B			
Psychologist 3	32	2.88	69
Psychologist 4	29	2.28	55
Psychologist 5	20	2.40	55
Psychologist 6	12	2.08	25

Intensive studies of appraisal interviews conducted at General Electric indicated that criticism by a superior is usually rejected as incorrect (Meyer, Kay, & French, 1965). Defensiveness was the characteristic attitude among the subordinates, and indications of a desire actually to improve performance occurred less than once per interview. Without the development of carefully stated goals for improvement, criticism was unlikely to produce an increase in effectiveness. Clearly, feedback procedures may well yield a considerable loss insofar as employee satisfaction is concerned and very little, if any, improvement in productivity. More recent research, as indicated in Box 6-3, appears to indicate that destructive criticism is particularly detrimental.

In addition, the experience of many companies has been that it is very difficult to get managers to conduct appraisal interviews with their subordinates. Because the situation is perceived as an unpleasant one, managers avoid it, and the interviews are held only after considerable pressure and dissension. Many are never held in any real sense at all.

Another response to the anticipated unpleasantness of feeding back negative evaluations is a distortion of the ratings. In an early study, the average rating on 485 supervisors moved from a score of 60, under normal non-feedback conditions, to 84 when a rerating to be combined with appraisal interviews was obtained two weeks later (Stockford & Bissell, 1949). More recent studies confirm this result, indicating that when feedback is required, ratings tend to be consistently higher, and there is a tendency to delay feedback sessions with poorer performers. These patterns are more pronounced for females, but they occur among male evaluators as well (Benedict & Levine, 1988). One way of making the ratings easier to report to others is to make them more favorable. This suggests that evaluations that are to be used for development purposes in an appraisal interview should not be used for other purposes, such as pay or promotion.

Because of these deficiencies in the feedback approach, it has been suggested that the development goal can be better served if managers appraise themselves in an MBO context (McGregor, 1957). Although the various advocates differ somewhat on the specifics, the usual approach is for individuals to sit down with their immediate superiors and establish a series of targets or objectives for the next six months or for some other appropriate time period. Then, at the end of the specified interval, the two have a second

Exhibit 14-8   Frequency with Which Different Methods of Management Appraisal Are Used

Method	Percent Use for Organizations with Management Appraisal Systems
Written essay	61
Rating scales	52
Management by objectives (MBO)	49
Checklists	25
Critical incidents	19
Ranking	7
Assessment centers	7

SOURCE: Adapted from Bureau of National Affairs (1983). *Performance appraisal programs,* Personnel Policies Forum Survey No. 135, pp. 6 and 21. Washington, DC: BNA.

discussion, during which individuals evaluate their performance relative to objectives, attempt to solve any problems that are now recognized, and set new objectives for the next period. Throughout this process, the superior assumes the role of a listener, and on occasion a guide, but never that of a critic. Because there is no external criticism, there is no defensiveness. To the extent that individuals criticize themselves, the basis for a change in behavior has presumably been established.

With this type of emphasis, management appraisal and MBO become primarily procedures for developing the individual. However, self-established role requirements and self-appraisal are not essential to the use of an MBO approach to evaluation. Thus MBO-based appraisals can be conducted in such a way as to serve other goals than those of personal development. A number of companies utilize procedures under which higher levels of management above the individual exercise considerable control over the role requirements that are established. The evaluation of performance against objectives subsequently is done by the superior, not by the individual. Thus the MBO approach to performance

appraisal should not be identified entirely with self-appraisal; it may involve appraisal by superiors as well.

Even so, there appears to be a widespread consensus among managers that MBO appraisals should not completely replace the more traditional approaches. There is considerable feeling that the fact that MBO is tailored to the individual makes it less satisfactory as a method for making comparisons across managers. According to this view, MBO's greatest strengths are in goal setting, and thus in motivation and development, and its emphasis on planning for the future. A frequently mentioned problem with MBO among those using it is that the measurement process tends to partially distort the realities of the job (Muczyk, 1979). Thus there is a tendency to establish objectives in areas where measurement of accomplishments is relatively easy, especially quantitative measurement. These may not be the most important areas. Objectively defined MBO goals may be relatively unrelated to overall assessments of effectiveness. In short, MBO assessment, as practiced, does not cover all that should be expected from an appraisal system.

From Exhibit 14-8, it is apparent that MBO, although not the most frequently used appraisal method, is widely employed. At the same time, most companies rely on multiple methods. It is not at all uncommon for an MBO procedure to be coupled with some other approach in order to obtain comprehensive coverage of major aspects of the job and to provide the comparative data needed for promotion decisions.

A major factor contributing to the use of MBO-type appraisal systems, at least within the federal government, is the wording of the Civil Service Reform Act of 1978. This act not only mandates some form of performance evaluation for all agencies, but requires the use of objective performance criteria to the extent possible, evaluation on factors that are known to be job-related, and participation by employees in the establishment of their own performance standards. Although other types of appraisal can be combined with various job analysis approaches to meet these requirements, MBO procedures appear particularly suited to the legislated needs (Thompson, 1981).

In fact, the federal legislation has fostered MBO-type appraisal systems in many state and local governments as well. In at least one such instance, however, involving the state of Kentucky, the difficulty of incorporating all aspects of the work into an MBO system has continued to plague the program (Fay & Clark, 1987).

Assessment Centers. We have considered **assessment centers** previously in several different contexts. Chapter 2, and in particular Box 2-2, dealing with the ITT experience, focused on the role that intelligence plays in assessment center performance. Chapter 6 provided additional detail on how assessment centers operate to provide measures of personality characteristics. The way in which Gerstein, Reisman & Associates uses assessment center data to profile the personality characteristics required in various strategic situations is described in Box 6-2. As indicated in Exhibit 14-8, assessment centers are not widely used for management appraisal purposes. They are most likely to be found in larger companies. In some instances, assessment centers are used for the purposes of initial hiring, and in these cases they function as selection techniques. However, a much more frequent application is in connection with the appraisal process, where the purposes served are essentially the same as for any other evaluation method (promotion, for example). The only major difference is that assessment center results are less likely to be used as a direct input to compensation decisions.

Although assessment centers have a relatively long history in the field of psychology, the impetus for their current popularity in the appraisal of managers derives from applications initiated at AT&T in the mid-1950s (Howard & Bray, 1988). Since that time, a number of variants on the initial procedures have emerged, to the point that it is difficult to say what a typical approach is. A hypothetical description of a comprehensive approach with multiple measures will provide an idea of what may be involved, however.

In such a situation, managers would participate in the assessment process over a three-day period, followed by two days during which the assessors actually make their evaluations. In this program, twelve managers are evaluated each week by three managers several levels above them and by two psychologists. The evaluations are not made on the job, but rather are based on observations of behavior and on test results obtained in a special setting designed specifically for the purposes of appraisal. The ratings are made from personal history forms completed by the assessees, the results of interviews conducted by one of the management representatives, observed and recorded performance on the situational exercises, analyses of personality tests made by clinically trained psychologists, other psychological test results, peer evaluations of other assessees, and personal impressions derived from both formal and informal contacts during assessment. Thus, elements of superior appraisal, peer ratings, and psychological evaluation are all involved.

The end result is a set of composite ratings made by the superior managers and psychologists on various job-related factors bearing on placement considerations, the appropriate supervisory climate for the person, developmental needs, and potential for advancement. For each individual assessed, there is a written report for managers throughout the company, a quantitative output adapted for computer storage for human resource planning, and a technical file for use by personnel managers and psychologists. Box 14-3 provides an idea of what is included in the written report.

BOX 14-3   I/O PSYCHOLOGY IN PRACTICE

Summaries and Evaluations from an Assessment Center Report Developed from the Consensus Judgments of Assessors

Plum-Lyne, Inc.
Participant: Pat Urn
Date: November 7–9, 1983

Summary. Ms. Urn was something of an enigma to the assessors. In group exercises, which required no complex preparation, she showed a lot of initiative, was very assertive, and was willing to accept the responsibility for the group's accomplishing its task. In these situations, Ms. Urn was seen as showing a great deal of behavior on the required dimensions. However, in exercises that required analysis and deliberation prior to accomplishing them, her performance fell precipitously. Perhaps one of the most obvious examples of this situation occurred in the in-basket exercise. Here, in contrast to her behavior in spontaneous group situations, she was very tentative and seemed unsure of herself. This exercise, plus others that required analysis and deliberation in complex managerial situations, led the assessors to believe that although Ms. Urn has good "street sense," she needs to pay a considerable amount of attention to management principles and techniques in analyses and administrative situations.

Ms. Urn threw herself into the exercises in a very deliberate and aggressive manner. This resulted in the assessors being able to generate a considerable amount of data on her performance. They were, therefore, quite confident in their analysis of the rather complex behavioral pattern that emerged.

Listening. Use of information extracted from oral communications: Above Average.

Problem analysis. Identifying problems, securing relevant information, relating data from sources, and identifying possible causes of problems: Above Average—spontaneous situations; Below Average—less spontaneous, analytical situations.

Judgment. Making decisions based on logical assumptions that reflect the factual information available: Below Average.

Planning and organizing. Establishing a course of action for self and/or others to accomplish a specific goal; planning proper assignments of personnel and appropriate use of resources: Below Average.

Management control. Establishing procedures to monitor or to regulate processes, tasks, or activities of subordinates and job activities and responsibilities; taking action to monitor the results of delegated assignments and projects: Below Average.

In the in-basket exercise, Ms. Urn did not use any standard control procedures. She set up no tickler file, on only two occasions assigned due dates to items that she delegated, and was often unspecific in what she wanted her subordinates to do with items. In the interview simulation, no time goals were set for a follow-up, and no behavioral objectives were given.

Overall Evaluation. Based on behavior relevant to the supervisory dimensions determined to be important in the position, Ms. Urn's present level of potential as a District Sales Manager could best be described as marginal. Major development in a number of critical managerial dimensions is necessary before satisfactory performance could be expected.

SOURCE: George C. Thornton & William C. Byham (1982). *Assessment centers and managerial performance,* pp. 332–335. New York: Academic Press.

In the Plum-Lyne, Inc., example the ratings were developed out of rather lengthy group meetings in which the assessors developed a consensus. Experience at the Dade-Miami Criminal Justice Assessment Center indicates, however, that just as good results can be obtained by simply averaging individual assessors' ratings without the need for consensus meetings; this latter approach can produce substantial cost savings (Pynes, Bernardin, Benton, & McEvoy, 1988).

The unique aspect of assessment centers is the use of situational exercises such as special interviews, management games, in-basket performance, leaderless group discussions, case analyses, individual fact-finding and decision-making exercises, and oral presentations as a basis for assessment. These are often tailored to the particular corporate environment. Many have proved to be highly predictive of subsequent managerial performance.

Although such special exercises have often proved to be good indicators of on-the-job effectiveness in later years, so have the other aspects of the total assessment center process. Reviews of the extensive research that has been done in the area consistently conclude that the procedure appears to be very effective in the identification of managerial potential (see Chapter 6). On the other hand, the process is extremely costly, in terms of both the time of the raters and the lost work of managers who are assessed, and there is reason to believe that equally effective results may be achieved with less costly procedures (Brush & Schoenfeldt, 1980; Hinrichs, 1978; McEvoy, Beatty, & Bernardin, 1987; Pynes and Bernardin, 1989). It is probably most beneficial for large firms, where communication regarding sources of managerial talent across units is difficult. In smaller firms, other appraisal methods and more informal communication procedures may be quite adequate. Although experienced managers are widely used as assessors, on the assumption that they best reflect the values of the organization, the actual evidence is that psychologist assessors do a better job than managers. Also, the assessment-center approach to evaluation appears to work at least as well when applied to females as it does with males (Ritchie & Moses, 1983; Walsh, Weinberg, & Fairfield, 1987).

■ OBJECTIVE MEASURES

What are usually referred to as **objective measures** of performance derive directly from the measurable actions of the individual rather than from subjective judgments about job behavior. But many jobs do not have outputs that can be counted in this objective manner; furthermore, important aspects of the work may not yield objective measures, while unimportant aspects do. In such cases it is crucial that easy measurement not be substituted for painstaking job analysis.

Some objective measures may be used as indexes of both individual and group performance. Thus the number of days a person is absent from work in a given period may be used to evaluate that person; and an absenteeism figure for a whole work group can also be computed and used to evaluate that group. In hierarchic contexts, a group performance index of this kind is considered the responsibility of the person in charge, and thus it is treated as a measure of the manager's performance. Group performance measures per se, independent of managerial evaluation, are relatively rare in the business world.

☐ Quality and Quantity of Work as Performance Standards

Companies have developed and utilize a wide variety of output measures, which vary with the particular job considered. In manufacturing, measures often focus on number of units produced, number of units rejected, training time to reach a set standard output rate, success in meeting production schedules, machine downtime, scrappage, and the like. In sales, it is typical to use some index of volume, which may be compared to past performance in the same territory, along with the number of customer complaints. In clerical work, evaluation uses number of words typed, number of errors in filing, amount of material entered into the computer, and the like.

In many cases these measures are established by industrial engineers using time-study and work-sampling methods. They may develop a single **performance standard,** which would represent the minimum acceptable level of performance. Or they may introduce various numerical standards at intervals above the acceptable minimum, against which an individual's performance may be compared. Measures of this kind have been developed more extensively for some types of work than for others (Landy & Farr, 1983).

The usual approach to assessing quality and quantity focuses on typical output over an extended period of time. However, it is also possible to use **maximum performance,** where the individual is measured after being stimulated to do the best job possible, over a relatively brief time span. Both approaches may be useful for certain purposes, but it is important to recognize that they are only minimally related (Sackett, Zedeck, & Fogli, 1988).

☐ Cost and Profit

Businesses use a variety of cost and profit measures, particularly to evaluate managers; these are often developed by accountants. Budget performance measures are used widely. The cost of wastage, equipment maintenance, and labor input may be evaluated. Profit centers may be distributed throughout the organization and managers held accountable for their performance.

Increasingly, these procedures are being moved down through the managerial hierarchy, so that the contributions to profit achieved by lower-level managers, especially those within the line organization, can be determined. Standard costs are established for labor, materials, and overhead on the basis of prior experience and judgment. Cost variances are then computed by comparing actual figures with these standards, and managers are evaluated in accordance with the direction and amount of these variances. The technique requires a detailed organization plan with clear-cut designation of areas of responsibility. Also, there is a very considerable element of subjectivity inherent in setting the standard costs. Yet variance analysis of this kind does appear to provide an extremely valuable tool in appraising managers.

An extension of this approach involves the use of data derived from **human resource accounting** in the evaluation of managers. Such a procedure serves to give a manager credit for increasing investments in human resources and charges for using up that investment. Thus managers who recruit and develop outstanding people whose current performance and performance potential have considerable value to the company are in fact credited with these contributions in the calculation of the profitability of their operations. At the same time, managers who squander human resources, whether by failing to utilize personnel effectively, by provoking high turnover rates among their more talented subordinates, or by failing to train and develop people to their full potential, are penalized in the calculation of profit performance. This procedure has the advantage that it tends to forestall, or at least devalue, managerial approaches that achieve high short-term profitability at the cost of using up the organization's human capital, and thus at the expense of the long-term profit potential of a unit. Although human resource accounting in general, and in particular its applications in management appraisal, are still in a developmental stage, progress has been made.

Evaluation criteria relating to cost are widely advocated because they often correlate closely with organizational effectiveness. Yet they are also criticized, for these reasons (Latham & Wexley, 1981):

1. Cost-related measures almost always omit important factors for which a person should be held accountable (for instance, team playing, as when a superintendent in one district lends equipment to a superintendent in another).

2. Cost-related measures are not relevant to the work of many employees. What cost-related measures exist for a personnel manager, an engineer, or a newspaper reporter?

3. Cost-related measures may take into account factors for which the individual is not responsible, as employee performance is often affected by the performance of others.

4. Cost-related measures, if relied on exclusively, can encourage a results-at-all-costs mentality that can run counter to both corporate ethics and legal requirements.

5. Cost-related measures of performance outcomes by themselves do not inform employees what they need to do to maintain or increase productivity.

☐ Productivity Measurement

Effective performance in organizations may also be evaluated through **productivity measurement** (Brinkerhoff & Dressler, 1990). While their roots lie in economics and econometric models, productivity measures are important for personnel psychology as well, especially as they relate directly to labor output. Productivity measurement originated at the national level with macroeconomic indexes—Gross National Product and the like (Levitan & Werneke, 1984). Similar measures

were then refined for use at the industrywide level, and the approach was extended to individual companies. Company indexes were first developed in the United States and were subsequently exported to Japan and the countries of Europe, where major refinements occurred. At present the United States possesses no particular superiority in this area.

Approaches to Measurement. It is common practice to measure productivity in some broad ratio such as sales per employee or sales relative to labor costs. The disadvantage of such ratios is that they do not directly reflect inflation, changes in product mix, variations in accounting policies, and the like. Simple ratios do not explicitly incorporate inputs such as financial capital, materials, and energy. They also assume that all labor inputs are equal. For these reasons, more sophisticated indexes have been developed and are used by a number of firms.

This new approach remains one of calculating a ratio of outputs to inputs, but the ratio is then used comparatively: Ratios may be compared over a period of time; or units within the company may be compared; or data may be compared between different companies or throughout a whole industry. In short, many kinds of relationship can be determined. Data are typically translated into monetary terms, making it possible to combine different types of information. By using monetary figures consistently throughout the calculations, it is possible to counteract the effects of inflation.

Four major types of input costs may be considered:

1. Labor compensation
2. Cost of materials and contractual services
3. Capital costs
4. Indirect business taxes

In any year measured after the base year, the productivity gain or loss is the difference

BOX **14-4**   RESEARCH IN I/O PSYCHOLOGY

Calculation of a Productivity Index (PI) at General Foods

General Foods (GF) has long used productivity calculations to evaluate the effectiveness of its plants. The company has found the approach to be very useful.

The PI for an individual plant portrays the overall management effectiveness at the plant. Since productivity is defined as output divided by input, the productivity index is the ratio of output and input with both factors adjusted for inflation. The output (the numerator of the productivity calculation) is conceptually the cost value that should have been added by converting raw and packaging materials into finished goods if plant operations were carried out at base-year efficiency levels. It is, therefore, the value (in base-year dollars) added to the raw materials that are put into the production process.

The input elements that combine to form the total input amount include:

- Direct labor
- Service labor—maintenance, quality control, etc.
- Administration and clerical labor
- Purchased services and supplies
- Raw and packing materials lost in production
- Energy
- Depreciation, property taxes, and insurance
- Cost of capital—investment in land, buildings, machinery and equipment, and inventories

All of these elements add to the value of the raw materials being processed. Therefore the value of the product equals the value of the raw materials plus the value of these input elements.

Since both the output data and the input data are converted to base-year dollars, the productivity index becomes a simple ratio of (1) the current productivity (output/input) stated in base-dollar terms and (2) the base-year productivity (output/input for the base). The base-year PI, of course, equals 1.0, since the base-year productivity figure would be divided by itself. If the pro-

ductivity index for years subsequent to the base year is greater than 1.0, the productivity (output/input) for that year exceeded the base-year productivity. Similarly, productivity deteriorated for the year if the PI for the year is less than 1.0.

To demonstrate the method of computing the PI, assume that a product requires two inputs— labor (including overhead and associated costs) and raw materials. To compute the output, GF determines for labor and materials the cost of a unit of output during the base year. For example, assume the following data:

Cost Elements	Base-Year Cost ($)
Labor cost/unit of output	0.24
Materials-lost cost/ unit of output	0.20

GF receives this type of data from its cost accounting system for each product. Basically, GF is interested in representing the output as the value added to the raw materials that are put into the production process. For example, how much more valuable is a pound of processed and canned coffee than a pound of raw coffee beans ready for processing? Notice that GF employs a materials-lost measurement for productivity measurement as opposed to a materials-used approach. There are two primary reasons for employing this approach:

- Materials lost represents the cost reduction opportunity at the plants. The purchasing of materials and the related price management is not a plant function but is carried out at the corporate level.
- Using materials lost reduces the impact of raw materials cost on the PI. Raw materials represent a high proportion of the cost of GF products. Changes in total materials cost caused by the volatility of commodity prices would distort

the PI. Moreover, if materials-consumed data were included in the output figure, they would have to be eliminated in order to arrive at value added.

We can summarize as shown in the accompanying table the calculations involved in determining current-year productivity indexes, for material and labor separately and for overall value.

Without going into great detail on the calculations involved, it is apparent from the current-year measures at the lower right that the plant has improved productivity over the base year, especially in the use of materials.

SOURCE: John W. Kendrick (1984). *Improving company productivity: Handbook with case studies*, pp. 151–155. Baltimore: Johns Hopkins University Press.

	Base Year			Current Year		
Output	Total Cost ($)	Units Produced	Cost/ Unit ($)	Base-Year Cost/($)	Units Produced	Total Cost ($)
Material (lost)	100,000	500,000	0.20	0.20	600,000	120,000
Labor	120,000	500,000	0.24	0.24	600,000	144,000
Total	220,000					264,000

	Base Year			Current Year		
Input	Units of Input	Purchase Cost /Unit ($)	Cost of Input ($)	Base Year Purchase Cost /Unit ($)	Units of Input	Cost Base-Year Prices ($)
Material (lost)	200,000	0.50	100,000	0.50	190,000	95,000
Labor	10,000	12.00	120,000	12.00	10,800	129,600
Total			220,000			224,600

Base-Year PI

$$\frac{\text{Output}}{\text{Input}} = \frac{\$220,000}{\$220,000} = 1.0$$

Current-Year PI

$$\text{Material PI} = \frac{\$120,000}{\$\ 95,000} = 1.26$$

$$\text{Labor PI} = \frac{\$144,000}{129,600} = 1.11$$

$$\text{Total Factor PI} = \frac{\$264,000}{\$224,600} = 1.18$$

between total inputs and total outputs (both stated in terms of base-year prices). This method thus compensates for inflation. The productivity index for a company's specific year is obtained by dividing measured output by input (both in base-year prices). Box 14-4, describing the calculations of a productivity index (PI) at General Foods, shows how such an approach may be applied to a single product as manufactured at one plant.

Uses of Measures. Productivity measurement is used much like other objective appraisal approaches in organizations. It is in one sense a group measure; in hierarchic organizations, it is also an individual measure applicable to the person in charge at that level. This approach does not specify why productivity is high or low, but breakdowns by factors of production, company units, locations, products, and the like enable the analyst to determine where positive or negative forces are operating.

Productivity measurement, like the other measures, provides feedback on results, and it does so in both broad and specific terms. Productivity measurement can be closely related to national concerns, or it can be tied directly to the performance accountability and rewards of specific managers, as is the usual practice in Japan (McInnes, 1984). It can have tremendous incentive value, as the following quotation indicates. An executive vice president of the Mill Products division at Aluminum Company of American (ALCOA) points out (National Center for Productivity and Quality of Working Life, 1976, p. 40):

> It was a terrible shock to discover that although output per man hour in ALCOA had increased 20% from 1958 to 1965, the increase in the industry for the same period was about 60%. Believe me, that stimulated real action on our part. The record since 1968 would indicate that the mechanism used in Mill Products to insure productivity growth has been relatively effective. . . . Measured against our 1968 base, output per man hour in ALCOA's Mill Products has increased more than the output per man hour of the aluminum rolling and drawing industry as a whole. If that were not the case, I might not be here to tell you about it.

☐ Measures of Withdrawal

As with productivity, organizational maintenance measures taken within the group or unit that is a particular manager's responsibility may also be used for purposes of appraisal. This assumes that a major factor contributing to any lack of job satisfaction, or sense of attachment to the work organization, may be the behavior of the manager in charge. If the various objective indexes suggest that a certain manager has a highly dissatisfied group, the undesirable situation can be attributed to that person, and an unfavorable evaluation can result.

Unfortunately, the use of this type of infor-

mation in evaluating individual managers has not been developed to the level of sophistication achieved in the productivity and profit areas. Immediate supervision is not the only factor that must be considered in identifying sources of variation in satisfaction indexes.

Clearly, policies and decisions made at a variety of managerial levels can have an impact. Yet very few companies have worked out their role requirements and allocations of responsibility among the various levels of management with the same precision in this area as they have achieved when dealing with productivity and profits. There appears to be a tendency to exaggerate the role of immediate supervision, when higher-level management may actually be exerting greater influence. Therefore, the various **withdrawal indexes** should be used with caution when appraising individual managers. It is important to know who or what is actually responsible for the existing state of affairs. Yet some measures of this kind are essential because of their relationship to an important company goal. Such measures may be combined into an overall employee relations index (Cash, 1979).

There are a number of indexes that seem to reflect the tendency of people to avoid or escape from what they experience as unpleasant. In units where dissatisfaction is marked and there is little sense of commitment, employees may be expected to seek out various ways of leaving the specific work situation, either temporarily or permanently.

Absenteeism. As indicated in Chapter 5, such factors as job dissatisfaction and organizational commitment levels can contribute to absenteeism; the more people are absent, the more their output is threatened in quantity and quality. It is also assumed that lost work days, temporary replacements, and overstaffing to cover absenteeism all result in extra costs. Thus absenteeism undermines the efficiency of production. Although it is probably true that in many situations absenteeism has a serious negative impact, surely in some cases this does not happen (Staw, 1984). For instance, absence from work may reduce stress so that the employee subsequently does more and better work. In this case, subsequent efforts may compensate for the loss occasioned by the employee's absence. How often this happens we do not know.

In any event, as Exhibit 14-9 indicates, absenteeism can have different consequences depending on the perspective from which it is viewed. Furthermore, absenteeism can be measured in different ways; it is always a function of definitions, regulations, and policies established by the employing organization. To the extent that these vary, absenteeism rates will vary as well. For example, not coming to work on Martin Luther King, Jr.'s birthday may or may not be absenteeism, depending on the company. Thus absenteeism is an objective index, but with imprecise bases for measurement. It is included here as an index for performance appraisal because it can be so pervasive as to threaten the attainment of organizational goals. The amount of absenteeism that is tolerable will vary with the situation. But many companies clearly have been harmed by absenteeism and have sought to reduce it. Not the least of these harms, to company and individual, is the fact that absenteeism often brings less experienced workers to a job, with the result that accident rates increase (Goodman & Garber, 1988).

Companies use a variety of formulas to indicate absence rates. One common approach is:

$$\text{Absenteeism} = \frac{\text{number of person-days lost through job absence during period}}{\text{average number of employees} \times \text{number of work days}} \times 100$$

Some firms keep records covering not only the number of days lost, but also the number of times. Usually, older work groups will have a higher number of days lost from work than those containing largely younger employees, but the actual frequency of separate incidents of absenteeism may not be as great.

Closely related is the use of tardiness statistics, which may well reflect a similar withdrawal tendency and which are easily obtained for any group where time cards are used. However, measures of lateness are probably much less frequently maintained on a regular basis than absenteeism data. Certainly, they are less commonly used to evaluate managers.

Separations and Turnover. Leaving a company permanently can well be the final result of the same forces that produce excessive absenteeism; rates of turnover and of absenteeism have often been found to be closely related (Gupta & Jenkins, 1982; Kanfer, Crosby, & Brandt, 1988; Keller, 1984). Furthermore, like absenteeism, turnover can be viewed from both positive and negative perspectives (Mobley, 1982). From an individual viewpoint, being fired with no immediate prospect of a new position can only be considered negative, but leaving to take an attractive new job at higher pay is another matter. Many companies experience continuing high turnover among newly hired employees, who leave long before hiring and training costs can be recovered through the new employees' productive work. For these firms, turnover is a major problem and reflects an accumulation of individual performance failures. But high turnover rates among long-term, higher-paid employees whose output has declined significantly can be a boon to a company. New employees with greater potential can replace them at much lower cost.

Exhibit 14-10 indicates how important it can be for a firm to monitor the performance levels of those who leave. McKinsey and Company has an up-or-out policy intended to retain only the best performers, who will eventually become partners. Thus reasonably high turnover rates are anticipated, but not among the better performers who appear to

Exhibit 14-9   Possible Consequences of Absenteeism

Who Is Affected	Positive Effects	Negative Effects
Individual	Reduction of job-related stress Meeting of non-work-role obligations Benefit from compensatory nonwork activities Compliance with norms to be absent	Loss of pay Discipline, formal and informal Increased accidents Altered job perception
Coworkers	Job variety Skill development Overtime pay	Increased workload Undesired overtime Increased accidents Conflict with absent worker
Work group	Crew knowledge of multiple jobs Greater crew flexibility in responding to absenteeism and to production problems	Increased coordination problems Decreased productivity Increased accidents
Organization management	Greater job knowledge base in work force Greater labor-force flexibility	Decreased productivity Increased costs More grievances Increased accidents
Union officers	Articulated and strengthened power position Increased solidarity among members	Weakened power position Increased costs in processing grievances
Family	Opportunity to deal with health or illness problems Opportunity to manage marital problems Opportunity to manage child problems Maintenance of spouse's earnings	Lower earnings Decline in work reputation Aggravated marriage and child problems
Society	Reduction of job stress and mental health problems Reduction of marital-related problems Participation in community political processes	Loss of productivity

Source: Paul S. Goodman & Robert S. Atkin (1984). *Absenteeism: New approaches to understanding, measuring, and managing employee absence,* p. 280. San Francisco: Jossey-Bass.

Exhibit 14-10   **Percentage of McKinsey and Company's Consultants Employed Each Year Who Separated during the Year, Broken Down by Performance Level**

	Year 1	Year 2	Year 3	Year 4	Year 5	Year 6
Total firm						
High performers	6	4	8	6	5	7
Low performers	11	7	5	8	6	9
Total	17	11	13	14	11	16
A high-turnover office						
High performers	0	0	13	25	0	19
Low performers	23	23	0	6	0	25
Total	23	23	13	31	0	44
A medium-turnover office						
High performers	10	4	9	8	11	10
Low performers	8	8	1	8	7	11
Total	18	12	10	16	18	21
A low-turnover office						
High performers	0	7	0	0	6	8
Low performers	0	0	5	0	0	5
Total	0	7	5	0	6	13

have partner potential. The data indicate that throughout the firm the system is working—more low performers than high performers leave. But in some of the offices in certain years, turnover has been very high among the better consultants; this is cause for concern.

Different procedures are used to compute turnover. For purposes of evaluating managers, it is generally desirable to eliminate involuntary separations, such as those caused by death, illness, and mandatory retirement, from the statistics, because these causes are not normally subject to managerial influence. Often a ratio such as the following is computed for each unit:

$$\text{Turnover} = \frac{\text{number of separations}}{\text{midmonth employment}} \times 100$$

It is important in evaluating statistics of this kind to utilize data collected over a period of time, to eliminate the effects of seasonal and other temporary fluctuations. Only when managers have consistently high turnover fig-

ures month after month should the possibility that they are ineffective be actively considered. Also, it is important to hold the general type of occupation and certain employee characteristics relatively constant in evaluating these figures. Turnover among younger employees, for instance, is almost invariably higher than among older workers (Tsai, Bernacki, & Lucas, 1989).

Other measurable data may be considered as indexes of withdrawal as well—injuries, dispensary visits, and the like, for instance. Absenteeism and turnover, however, are the most frequently used measures of this type.

☐ Measures of Resistance

Another way in which internal stress may manifest itself within a work unit is through direct resistance and conflict. Group members who are dissatisfied may not avoid the situation that disturbs them; rather, they may attack the management that they see as causing their difficulties. Such resistance may be covert or overt. In any event, managers who head units where **resistance indexes** are numerous may find themselves judged to be less competent; whether this is justified or not must depend on the degree of influence exerted over the situation.

Disciplinary Actions. One way in which dissatisfaction may appear is through overt flouting of work rules and intentional deviation from role requirements. Such behavior characteristically results in a warning, suspension, or discharge, after a formal disciplinary hearing. When such formal disciplinary actions occur frequently within a given unit, it may well be that the manager has provoked considerable resentment. Among the behaviors that may elicit formal action of this kind by the company are the following:

1. Unauthorized absence
2. Insubordination or impertinence
3. Loafing or sleeping
4. Misrepresentation, such as tampering with time cards or records
5. Smoking when forbidden
6. Drinking or carrying liquor
7. Dishonesty or stealing
8. Fighting on the job
9. Gambling
10. Willful breach of safety rules
11. Repeated lateness
12. Leaving the job without permission
13. Immoral conduct
14. Drug abuse

The processes through which formal disciplinary actions operate were discussed in Chapter 4. Where such actions are needed frequently, a manager may be judged less effective.

Grievances. Another commonly used index is the number of grievances filed by employees within a given time period. Although complaints of any kind can theoretically be used, the usual procedure is to count the number of separate, formal grievances filed in writing under the terms of a union contract.

By filing a grievance, employees are taking an action that they are well aware management does not wish them to take. Furthermore, in most cases the grievance statement is directly critical of some managerial behavior. The union may make this particular outlet for dissatisfaction readily available and may even take the action itself. Yet it is doubtful that many grievances occur in the complete absence of some measure of discontent. Thus, a manager with a high grievance rate may be presumed to have a group that represents some threat to the integrity of the firm.

There are several other possible measures that may or may not be appropriate, depending on the company and situation. Among these are the number of hours lost from work due to work stoppages, strikes, slowdowns, and the like—or the total number of separate incidents of this kind. Managers who experience a high incidence of such occurrences may not be fulfilling the requirements of their jobs, whether or not the resistance behavior is union-inspired—provided that they are in a position to exert some influence over such events.

Actually, any failure to behave in ways that management is widely known to desire, if it is prevalent enough in a group, may yield evidence regarding the extent of dissatisfaction. Thus, a consistent refusal to join a company retirement system or to participate in group insurance plans might be used as an index in evaluating managers. So, too, may the extent of participation in suggestion systems and in company-sponsored recreational programs.

Box 14-5 describes a method of using withdrawal and resistance data to evaluate unit

BOX 14-5   RESEARCH IN I/O PSYCHOLOGY

Use of Measures of Withdrawal and Resistance at Atlantic-Richfield to Evaluate Managers

As part of a program by industrial psychologists to identify managers whose actions might be contributing to labor union militancy and unrest, measures of withdrawal and resistance were developed and studied. One focus of the program was to identify instances of intense union activity and see if the measures would have predicted the militancy.

The measures studied were:

Withdrawal

1. Days absent per 100 employees in the unit
2. Times absent per 100 employees in the unit
3. Percent of employees in the unit separating for any reason
4. Initial visits to the dispensary for a new disorder per 100 employees in the unit

Resistance

1. Disciplinary actions per 1000 employees in the unit
2. Grievances reaching at least the second level per 1000 employees in the unit
3. Percentage of eligible employees enrolled in the company retirement system
4. Percentage of eligible employees enrolled in the group life insurance plan

Four categories were established on each measure, ranging from little evidence of withdrawal or resistance against management to substantial evidence. The scores were interpreted as follows:

1. Good to outstanding
2. Average
3. Poor
4. Extremely poor

Among the problem areas studied was a distribution terminal which was ultimately organized by the Teamsters Union. In this particular instance, dispensary visit information was not available; thus withdrawal scores across the three measures ranged from 3 to 12, with a score of 8 or more considered critical. Resistance scores ranged from 4 to 16, with a score of 9 or more considered critical. Scores for the years preceding the certification of the Teamsters as bargaining agents and the year of the election were as shown in the table below.

Clearly the scores were consistently elevated, especially the resistance scores. Similar results were obtained at other trouble spots, but not in more peaceful contexts. With hindsight it was evident that certain managers had not been doing a very good job of handling employee dissatisfaction in their units.

	Days Absent	Times Absent	Separations	Withdrawal Score	Disciplines	Grievance	Retirement Membership	Insurance Membership	Resistance Score
Two years before	4	3	2	9	3	2	4	4	13
Year before	4	2	2	8	3	1	4	4	12
Year of union certification	4	3	2	9	3	3	4	4	14

managers that was developed at Atlantic-Richfield. A similar approach was first introduced at General Electric more than 35 years ago (Merrihue & Katzell, 1955).

■ APPRAISAL BY ATTITUDE SURVEY

An approach to managerial evaluation that is in fact an extension of appraisal by subordinates has been used by companies such as Sears, Roebuck for many years. In this approach, attitude survey data are obtained from unit members and used to evaluate management of the unit. Chapter 5 provides information on what is involved in this type of program, and the introduction to the chapter as well as Box 5-2 provide examples from the Sears, Roebuck experience.

When used to evaluate managers, attitude surveys are normally handled on a group basis. That is, it is not the feelings of a particular individual that are of concern, but the overall level of satisfaction in a given unit. For this reason, the surveys are usually conducted on an anonymous basis, and on occasion only a sample of the employees in a group is measured. In the latter instance, it is important that the sample be truly representative. The usual procedure is to select the sample **at random,** so that each individual in the unit has an equal chance of showing up in the survey group.

Surveys of this kind normally contain questions dealing with working conditions, supervisory behavior, attitude toward the job itself, loyalty to the company as a whole, company policies, and other considerations. If the questionnaire is this broad in scope, it is inappropriate to use the total result to evaluate immediate supervision. The various sections of the survey form must be sorted out in terms of the particular level of management with the appropriate responsibility. One cannot expect a manager whose role requirements do not call for action in a given area to exert influence over attitudes in that area.

Second, a decision as to whether a particular unit is satisfied or dissatisfied should be based on information that can be presumed to be valid and that is characteristic of the group as a whole. To do otherwise can only produce a biased evaluation of the unit's management. Thus, there must be reason to believe that the people surveyed have in fact given evidence of their true feelings. And the survey should include all, or nearly all, members of the unit. If a sample is used, the respondents should not be permitted to select themselves. Replies obtained from the 30 or 40 percent who may take the trouble to return a mailed questionnaire may well reflect only the attitudes of those who have extreme views. It is essential to obtain evidence regarding the attitudes of those who did not reply originally and to correct the results accordingly, or to obtain something very close to a 100 percent response rate initially.

■ CAREER APPRAISAL

Although much appraisal is concerned with determining how well a person is doing on the present job relative to a given set of role prescriptions, there are instances where a measure of overall career success to date is desired. This is a particularly important consideration when evaluation data are being used to provide a criterion for use in developing selection procedures (Meyer, 1987). Usually, for example, it is more desirable to select management trainees who will achieve continuing success in a variety of positions, rather than those who will do an outstanding job only as trainees or in their first subsequent assignment.

Perhaps the most frequently used **career appraisal index** is the position level attained. Most firms maintain a system of salary grades, with each job assigned to some point on the scale. The particular grade for the position held by an individual then becomes a measure of success.

Because these grade levels may be closely related to age or seniority, and because they are strongly influenced by the level at which a person started with the company, it is more desirable to employ some index of grade progression than the absolute level. Thus, a promotion rate measure such as the following may be used:

$$\text{Success} = \frac{\text{present grade} - \text{starting grade}}{\text{total years of employment}}$$

There has also been some interest in the use of direct salary data as a basis for evaluation. Certainly such a measure is consistent with popular sentiment. It appears to offer a number of advantages for employees within a single company that awards salary increases on grounds of merit and that maintains a stable salary scale utilizing comparable standards for all. Usually, when salary is employed as a success index, some correction for age or tenure is introduced to produce a change rate rather than an absolute amount. On occasion, more complex statistical proce-dures are developed to provide data on the degree to which each person's salary deviates from the figure to be expected for people of this age and experience.

Rating procedures may also be used to evaluate career success as well as success on the current job. The most commonly used technique is some kind of promotability index of the type described in Exhibit 14-6. When a person is said to have outstanding potential for advancement, a major determinant of this evaluation is likely to be a pattern of consistent accomplishment in prior positions. Thus, predictions of future progress are in large part predicated on past success. Of course, **potential ratings** are conditioned to some degree by age and thus should not be used to evaluate career success among individuals in late career. An individual of age 60 may have little prospect of progressing further in the remaining years with the company and yet have had an outstanding career. Also, potential ratings derived from assessment centers should not be considered as indexes of career success, since they are not a direct function of past experience (Dulewicz & Fletcher, 1982).

KEY TERMS

Division of labor

Performance appraisal

Management inventory

Buddy rating (peer rating)

Field review

Psychological appraisals

Self-evaluations

Management by objectives (MBO)

Assessment centers

Objective measures

Performance standard

Maximum performance

Human resource accounting

Productivity measurement

Withdrawal indexes

Resistance indexes

At random

Career appraisal index

Potential ratings

SUMMARY

Appraisal procedures are used to compare role behaviors to role requirements, however established. Many approaches involve some type of judgment, usually by superiors, but in some instances by peers, subordinates, or even the appraisees themselves. In addition, evaluation data may be processed by human resource managers using a *field review* approach or by psychologists using various techniques of personality assessment. A *management-by-objectives* program may be utilized so that managers essentially evaluate themselves in terms of objectives they established at an earlier time. *Assessment centers* may be introduced for purposes of evaluation. In this instance, performance on certain standardized instruments and exercises replaces actual job performance as the basis for judgment.

Although these subjective procedures are widely used, it is also possible to utilize a more *objective approach*. Various indexes of output may be obtained and used to evaluate individuals or their superior. Industrial engineers have done much to develop such measures, whereas accountants have done more to facilitate the costing of individual managers' contributions to profits. Although objective procedures often focus on *productivity* and profit considerations, they can be extended to other areas as well. Examples are turnover and absenteeism rates among the subordinates of a particular manager, as well as *indicators of resistance* such as the number of disciplinary actions or grievances.

Some firms have introduced periodic attitude surveys for the specific purpose of obtaining information from subordinates that can be used to evaluate managers. Finally, indexes of overall managerial *career success* may be developed using rates of progression up position or salary hierarchies. Judgmental evaluations of *promotion potential* may also be employed for this purpose and then keyed into a *management inventory* chart.

QUESTIONS

1. How do the fields of industrial engineering and accounting contribute to management appraisal?
2. What special cautions should be exercised when collecting and analyzing attitude survey data for management appraisal purposes?
3. How may career success levels, turnover rates, and absenteeism rates be calculated? Which among these three might enter into an employee relations index?
4. What special problems are associated with ratings by the following groups?
   a. Superiors several levels up
   b. Peers
   c. Subordinates
   d. Immediate superiors who feed the ratings back to the employees
   e. The employees themselves

5. Evaluate management by objectives as an appraisal procedure. How might objective measures be utilized with this approach?
6. How widely are management appraisals used? Are there any situations where they are used less? Are there any major differences in the frequency with which different methods of appraisal are used? Explain.
7. If self-appraisals are used, under what circumstances would they be expected to be most effective?
8. How do psychological appraisal and assessment centers differ from other approaches to appraisal?
9. Distinguish between the following:
   a. Measures of withdrawal and measures of resistance
   b. Field review and the appraisal by superiors

c. Career appraisal and the management inventory

10. What special advantages does human resource accounting appear to offer in connection with management appraisal? Would you expect this approach to be used widely? Explain.

CASE PROBLEM

Management Appraisal: MBO and Alternatives

The person in charge of management appraisals for a large corporation had been receiving an increasing number of complaints about the existing management-by-objectives system. Part of the problem was that many managers found the paperwork involved very burdensome—so burdensome, in fact, that they often did not complete it on schedule, necessitating numerous phone calls, memos, and the like just to keep the system going. Underlying all this appeared to be a substantial amount of resistance to the MBO process itself, resistance that seemed to be gradually accelerating. The MBO program had been in place for almost three years now, and over the entire period, the management appraisal director had been checking on its effectiveness by conducting interviews on the subject with various managers throughout the company as the opportunity presented itself. She did not like what she had been hearing recently.

The initial reactions had been quite favorable. People did appreciate the opportunity to participate in setting their own objectives, and doing so seemed to spark them to extra efforts. But the appraisal process, as it later served to hold them accountable for achieving those objectives, was another matter. Many reacted by saying that they had been tricked into agreeing to objectives that were not realistic by the argument that something had to be put down just to satisfy the personnel people—then a year later their salaries were based on those very same objectives. Others thought they were agreeing to an ideal state of affairs and then found themselves held to that ideal. Still others had wanted to change their objectives because circumstances had changed, only to find they could not. In short, one way or another, people felt the MBO program had become a way to manipulate them into agreeing to certain

things and then later to hold them to agreements that they had made without fully understanding what they were doing. Not surprisingly, the objectives they would agree to on the next round were at a substantially lower level. More and more people had to be told what their objectives were, and some clearly viewed what they were told as unrealistic. The objectives set were probably less difficult, and it was apparent that they were becoming less specific, so that it would be hard to say for certain whether they had been achieved or not. Furthermore, the MBO program was becoming a real source of controversy.

Another problem came down from higher levels of management. The MBO program was not working effectively to establish promotion priorities. There was a management inventory, but the data on which it was based were not convincing. The feeling was that whatever its benefits, MBO was not an adequate method of guiding replacement decisions; too many bad decisions had been made in the last few years. Eventually the management appraisal director knew he had to make a change.

A study carried out with the aid of her staff initially convinced the director that the best alternative was some kind of assessment center. However, it was apparent that to use the assessment center method as it should be used would be quite costly. Calculations of costs were made and budget requests were put in. The net result was that the management appraisal director saw no possibility of conducting an adequate assessment center program with the money available to her.

Consequently, a decision was made to introduce a system using a panel of people who knew the assessee's work, primarily superiors, to develop a comprehensive data base regarding each manager and to appraise the manager using that data base. It was felt that such an approach would most nearly approximate an assessment center while still remaining within cost limitations.

Questions

1. How closely does such a group appraisal system approximate an assessment center?

2. If you were assigned responsibility for designing such an appraisal system, what would you recommend? Why would you include the various features?

3. Considering yourself as a manager appraised, write an appraisal summary that might derive from such a system. Assume that you are a dealer sales supervisor.

15

Performance Rating Systems

The dean of arts and sciences at a large state university has been notified of his probable selection as the new vice president for academic affairs. The promotion has cleared the university itself but must be acted upon by the Board of Regents for the university system as a whole. Approval at this level is normally automatic, but it can take some time. In the meantime the dean wants to take steps to name his own successor, since that person would be reporting directly to him in his new position. The problem is that the successor will be picked by a search committee composed of faculty and administrators, and he is not at all sure he can control the actions of that committee. It seems almost certain that the successful candidates will come from inside the university, since a number of strong candidates are available.

Among these candidates is one whom the dean favors; in fact, this is the person he strongly prefers for the job. As a strategy to achieve his ends, the dean decides to utilize the upcoming round of performance evaluations. All the candidates are department heads, and he will be evaluating all of them. His idea is to evaluate his preferred candidate very positively, the other candidates negatively, and to put these evaluations in the respective personnel files. The forms will be presented to the dean search committee at the appropriate time. Since the department heads have to sign their evaluations, there is an implication that they accept what is said there. Some of them might even decide not to let themselves be considered for the deanship for fear the negative evaluations will come out.

The strategy goes very well through the preferred candidate and most of the others. Everyone signs the evaluation form as originally presented, although there are some very unhappy people. Only the discussion with the chemistry department chairperson remains, and that is where the trouble starts. The woman simply will not sign the form. She contends that charges such as that she spends too much time in the research laboratory rather than in the departmental office, is not available to students, does not get needed papers in on time, and the like, simply are not true. The dean agrees to revise the evaluation to make it more palatable, and they will meet again.

This second round goes no better; in fact, it is worse. The evaluation remains quite negative, although somewhat toned down. The department chairperson says she has been talking with some of the other people, and there is a strong feeling that the performance evaluation process is being misused. They have seriously considered going to see the university's president about the matter; that could very well still happen. The dean agrees to make another try at drafting an acceptable evaluation document.

The next meeting produces a new problem. After looking over the revised performance statement, which again has shifted to a slightly less negative view, the department chairperson produces a formal letter requesting that the whole matter be placed before the Committee on Faculty Evaluation, Compensation, and Tenure for a public hearing. She indicates that if this appeal fails she might very well have to take the whole matter to the courts for resolution. In any event, under existing regulations the dean is required to put her case in the hands of the committee within forty-eight hours—unless they can come to a mutual agreement on the performance evaluation document, in which case she will withdraw the appeal. Given the fact that the dean's promotion itself is not yet final, this turn of events has him a little worried.

This is an example where bias and error have been introduced into the evaluation process deliberately and quite consciously. Probably this sort of thing does not occur very frequently, but there are all kinds of errors that can creep into evaluations and produce results that deviate from true performance, in much the same manner as occurred with the dean of arts and sciences' ratings. The preceding chapter considered various approaches to judgmental evaluation, but it did not take up these sources of error in any detail, and it did not consider how various types of rating methods relate to these sources of error.

These are of primary concern in this chapter. One of the tasks that nearly every industrial psychologist must perform at one time or another is to construct a new rating form or to revise an old one that is not working properly. At first glance, this may seem to be a relatively simple task, but there are a number of pitfalls. It is extremely helpful to have some familiarity with the relevant research and with the experience of others.

In addition, we will be concerned with the various obstacles and resistances that may obstruct the effective utilization of these techniques. For various reasons, the systematic evaluation of employee behavior relative to role requirements may face a number of difficulties and may itself become a source of considerable internal conflict. It is important that an industrial psychologist be sensitive to these problems, especially as they relate to seniority provisions in union contracts and legal issues.

■ BEHAVIORAL SPECIFICITY IN RATING SYSTEMS

An important dimension on which rating systems vary is the degree of specificity with which actual behavior on the job is described. The rating measure itself may incorporate detailed descriptions of behavior derived from job analysis. In this situation, all important formal role prescriptions are spelled out, and evaluation becomes a matter of merely indicating the extent to which these desired role behaviors are exhibited. At the other extreme is the rating measure that simply asks whether an individual is a good or bad performer, with very little reference to the specific role requirements for the job. Generally, rating systems that are highly **behaviorally specific** have been viewed as preferable. It has been assumed that different raters will be more likely to agree when more specific measures are used and that the various errors to which rating systems are prone will be less likely to occur. In actual practice, however, less behaviorally specific measures may prove as effective in some respects as those that are closely tied to formal role requirements. It appears that scales with varying degrees of behavioral specificity can be used with profit, although the different types of scales may in fact turn out to be measuring quite different things. For many purposes it is best to use both.

□ Evaluation Against Highly Behaviorally Specific, Formal Role Requirements

The behaviorally specific measures that incorporate formal role requirements invariably are based on some kind of job analysis. Frequently the role requirements are grouped into rating dimensions by the mathematical technique of factor analysis, which identifies those behavior descriptions that are most closely associated with each other.

Examples of some behavior descriptions associated with the role requirements for centrifuge operation in a chemical plant are:

1. Can be expected to vary the centrifuge speed in order to obtain the best speed for unfamiliar material, constantly monitoring evenness of cake

2. Can be expected to forget to turn on centrifuge pump or open proper outlet valves, frequently tearing bags or not reporting holes in them until end of shift (Baird, Beatty, & Schneier, 1982, p. 59).

Examples for a waiter or waitress are:

1. Makes suggestions to customers, for example, "Would you like another cup of coffee?"

2. Smokes a cigarette before checking to see that counter, tables, floor, bar stools, and

shelves are clean (Latham & Wexley, 1981, pp. 211, 213).

One requirement for rating systems of this kind is that the evaluations be made by a person who has had ample opportunity to observe job behavior closely over a considerable period. Furthermore, separate rating forms must be constructed for each job because each job has different role requirements. Where there are some overlapping role requirements across jobs, the magnitude of this task may be reduced, but it is nevertheless true that to develop behaviorally specific measures for all jobs in a company is a time-consuming and costly process. It may well be worth all the time and money involved, however. It may also prove to be a valuable asset should company performance evaluation procedures be subjected to judicial scrutiny. Box 15-5 provides an example of a highly behaviorally specific measure, as does Exhibit 15-3.

☐ Evaluation against Low Behavioral Specificity Criteria

At the other extreme is the global rating system, which asks whether an individual is outstanding, average, or unsatisfactory; whether performance is above standard or below; and/or whether potential is high or low. There may be many gradations or few in the scale used, but there is little to indicate which role behaviors are associated with a high rating and which with a low one. This is up to the rater. Although the rater may utilize formal role requirements based on an extensive job analysis in making judgments, these are likely to be tempered to a marked degree by any generalized concepts of good and bad performance or good and bad people existing in the organization. If aggressive selling, for instance, is valued generally in a company, such behavior will contribute to a high rating, but so too might such factors as nationality,

church membership, educational background, race, or sex. Obviously, there is a potential for illegal discrimination in the use of such procedures. On the other hand, discrimination is not an inevitable concomitant: It depends on the value system of the organization and of the individual rater; organizational culture plays an important role.

Measures of this type can be used effectively for a great variety of jobs with little or no modification. This is partly because raters are being asked to take into account their perceptions of the role requirements for each job as they make their evaluations; thus, the rating scale does not change from job to job, but the rater's reference points may. Perhaps even more important, however, is the fact that many informal role prescriptions do not vary much across jobs. If high intelligence, or a tendency to work hard, is valued in a company, this will be true regardless of the particular job held; thus, no revision of the rating measures used is needed in shifting from evaluations of sales personnel, for example, to those of clerical workers.

Although some companies use only a single rating of overall performance, perhaps supplemented by a rating of potential for promotion, others move slightly farther in the direction of behavioral specificity by utilizing several measures dealing with various aspects of performance, such as quality of work produced, quantity, cooperativeness in dealing with others, and the like. Many of these are aspects of all jobs; some, such as effectiveness in dealing with customers, which is important for all sales personnel, are associated with job families. Generally, ratings of an individual on the separate dimensions are highly correlated with each other. It is as if the employees were really being rated on the same dimension each time. They probably are—the dimension being the degree of fit with the organization's value structure. The labels, such as quantity of work, quality, or generalized descriptions of areas of work, that are attached to measures that have little behavioral specificity do not seem to be very meaningful in and of themselves.

Box 15-1 describes a minimal behavioral specificity rating system which differentiates only a few very general role requirements. It is typical of measures with little behavioral specificity in that in all four school districts—Portland, Oregon; Eugene, Oregon; Vancouver, Washington; and Beaverton, Oregon—the generalized measures are all highly correlated with one another. It appears likely that the values that are guiding ratings here are characteristic of the educational profession generally and of administration in that profession; the same values appear to pervade all four districts.

■ ERROR AND BIAS IN RATINGS

A number of different types of rating methods have been developed. Some tend to be quite behaviorally specific, others are not, and a few can be one or the other depending on how they are used. Since most of the newer methods in the field have been introduced in an effort to reduce or eliminate various presumed sources of error or bias in the rating process, the discussion turns to these types of error first. It should be recognized, however, that error is a relative matter and need not be pervasive. There is sound evidence that actual performance can be the major determinant of ratings (Bernardin & Beatty, 1984; DeNisi & Stevens, 1981; Smither, Barry, & Reilly, 1989). Whether it is so in a particular situation depends on numerous factors.

□ Halo

Halo is the tendency to evaluate a person in a similar manner, favorably or unfavorably, on all or most of the dimensions of a rating form because a general overall impression colors the ratings. There is thus a bias that causes the independent dimensions to be less measures of what their labels state than of a single pervasive view of the individual. When correlations among the various component measures of a rating form are consistently high, there is reason to suspect halo error, although other statistical indexes of this factor may be used as well with somewhat different results (Fox, Bizman, & Hoffman, 1989).

Whether a halo effect should really be considered error, however, depends on several considerations. If the rating scale does in fact measure characteristics that are important to job success, the selection and retention process can be expected to produce in its own right rather sizable correlations that are not due to bias. Also, error is involved only to the extent that a true measure relative to a specific role requirement is desired. Thus, for behaviorally specific measurement, halo is a problem; for more general ratings that attempt to evaluate congruence with organizational value systems of an informal nature, the high intercorrelations are no problem at all. In fact, they may be one indication of a desirable degree of integration within the firm.

Recently, the matter of halo has been the subject of considerable study. There has been an increasing understanding of the fact that high correlations among rating dimensions do not reflect merely rating error; there can be a set of real relationships operating that accounts for much of the correlation. Nevertheless, the fact that halo effects are greater when the raters know less about the people rated indicates the existence of at least some potential for halo error (Kozlowski, Kirsch, & Chao, 1986). From the evidence, actual halo error now appears to be rather infrequent, although always possible (Murphy & Reynolds, 1988). As Box 15-2 demonstrates, ratings made when the rater is in an elated mood are more likely to contain halo error than ratings made when the rater feels depressed.

BOX 15-1 RESEARCH IN I/O PSYCHOLOGY

The Development and Use of a Rating Scale with Low Behavioral Specificity as a Criterion for Test Validation

As part of a study to identify tests that might be used to select school administrators, a rating form was developed to be used as a criterion of administrator success. The study was carried out in the administrative components of four school districts in the Pacific Northwest.

School Administrator Evaluation Form

Name of Person Being Evaluated   _____

Name of Person Making Evaluation   _____

    Please check the one category for each of the following six job-related factors which best represents your considered judgment regarding the individual being evaluated.

    The three scales which follow deal with the individual's level of performance on the job—his or her contribution to the basic task of getting the children and youth of the community educated.

1. Performance in relation to subordinates. Ability to elicit effective work from his or her subordinates.	2. Performance in relation to community. Ability to draw on the resources of the community and its representatives in a way which facilitates the attainment of educational objectives.	3. Performance in relation to students. Ability to develop and implement policies, rules and procedures with reference to students which contribute to student learning.
Outstanding + _____	Outstanding + _____	Outstanding + _____
Outstanding _____	Outstanding _____	Outstanding _____
Outstanding − _____	Outstanding − _____	Outstanding − _____
Good + _____	Good + _____	Good + _____
Good _____	Good _____	Good _____
Good − _____	Good − _____	Good − _____
Satisfactory + _____	Satisfactory + _____	Satisfactory + _____
Satisfactory _____	Satisfactory _____	Satisfactory _____
Satisfactory − _____	Satisfactory − _____	Satisfactory − _____
Unsatisfactory _____	Unsatisfactory _____	Unsatisfactory _____
Not Relevant _____	Not Relevant _____	Not Relevant _____

The next three scales deal with the individual's capacity to elicit positive feelings and attitudes in others—his or her contribution to the maintenance of the school system as a stable, ongoing structure which is relatively free of conflict and dissatisfaction.

4. Effect on attitudes of subordinates. Ability to create and maintain high levels of satisfaction among subordinates and to keep dissension to a minimum.

5. Effect on attitudes in the community. Ability to deal with the community and its representatives in a way which fosters a favorable public feeling toward the school system and minimizes overt conflict between the schools and the community.

6. Effect on attitudes of the students. Ability to develop and implement policies, rules and procedures with reference to students, which lead to student satisfaction and a generally favorable feeling toward school.

Outstanding +	_____	Outstanding +	_____	Outstanding +	_____
Outstanding	_____	Outstanding	_____	Outstanding	_____
Outstanding −	_____	Outstanding −	_____	Outstanding −	_____
Good +	_____	Good +	_____	Good +	_____
Good	_____	Good	_____	Good	_____
Good −	_____	Good −	_____	Good −	_____
Satisfactory +	_____	Satisfactory +	_____	Satisfactory +	_____
Satisfactory	_____	Satisfactory	_____	Satisfactory	_____
Satisfactory −	_____	Satisfactory −	_____	Satisfactory −	_____
Unsatisfactory	_____	Unsatisfactory	_____	Unsatisfactory	_____
Not Relevant	_____	Not Relevant	_____	Not Relevant	_____

Insofar as possible, this form was completed by two superiors of each administrator and these evaluations averaged. In the Portland, Oregon, School District the ratings were done by the superintendent, two assistant superintendents, and three directors of elementary education. In the Eugene, Oregon, School District the superintendent, the assistant superintendent, the director of secondary education, and the director of research did the ratings. In the Vancouver, Washington, School District the raters were the superintendent, the assistant superintendent, the director of personnel, the director of elementary education, and the director of secondary education. In the small Beaverton, Oregon, School District, only the superintendent and assistant Superintendent completed ratings.

The ratings on each of the six factors turned out to be very similar in all four districts. Clearly the raters were not discriminating among the factors. The Portland ratings averaged at the "good" level; the Eugene ratings midway between "good" and "good +," the Vancouver ratings midway between "good +" and "outstanding −," and the Beaverton ratings at the "good +" level.

These low behavioral specificity ratings did prove useful as criteria in the validation study. Certain test measures were identified that exhibited substantial association with the ratings.

SOURCE: Based on John B. Miner (1967). *The school administrator and organizational character.* Eugene, OR: University of Oregon Press.

BOX 15-2   RESEARCH IN I/O PSYCHOLOGY

Laboratory Studies of the Effects of Emotional Moods on Halo at Pennsylvania State University

Prior research had suggested that judges in good moods make broad categorizations, differentiate less, assimilate more information into fewer categories, and inappropriately categorize different job-related behaviors in the same performance category. In contrast, judges in depressed moods make more narrow, discrete categorizations, discriminate among behaviors, and see behaviors as falling into different performance categories. These differences in cognitive processes suggest that good moods will yield high halo and depressed moods less halo.

The subjects studied were introductory psychology students at Pennsylvania State University. The students started out by reading a series of descriptions of the behavior—both good and bad—of a fictitious college professor. Then they participated in an ostensibly unrelated exercise designed to induce different moods in different students. Equal numbers of students read a series of statements designed to produce either elation, a neutral mood, or depression; after they read a statement, they wrote it out. After writing out the last statement, they closed their eyes in order to concentrate on events in their own lives that made them feel like the mood represented by the statements. A questionnaire given subsequently clearly indicated that the three groups differed in mood as anticipated.

Finally, the students all completed a rating form on the fictitious professor. The ratings were based on the behavior descriptions provided previously, and utilized a seven-point scale. There were eight dimensions of behavior rated:

Answering questions
Delivering lectures
Preparation and organization
Availability

Sensitivity
Friendliness
Setting expectations
Generating student involvement

Correlations were calculated between each pair of dimensions separately for the elation group, the neutral-mood group, and the depression group. The hypothesis predicted that the correlations should be highest in the elation group (halo) and lowest in the depression group (less halo).

The hypothesis was confirmed. Of the twenty-eight correlations between scales, twenty-five were smaller in magnitude in the depression group than in the elated group. The median correlation in the elation group was 0.53, while in the depression group it was 0.36. In the neutral-mood group the median correlation was 0.48. The author interprets these results as indicating that halo error will be minimized and accuracy increased if ratings are made when the rater is depressed and thus experiencing a mood state that fosters more discriminating cognitive processes. Taking this one step further, it would seem to follow that people who are frequently depressed should make more effective raters.

Source: Robert C. Sinclair (1988). Mood, categorization breadth, and performance appraisal: The effects of order of information acquisition and affective state on halo, accuracy, information retrieval, and evaluations. *Organizational Behavior and Human Decision Processes, 42*, 22–46.

☐ Constant Error

There is a tendency for superiors to use somewhat different sets of standards in judging subordinates. The situation is essentially the same as that in colleges and universities, where every student knows that there are difficult and easy graders. When evaluations made by different managers are compared, as they must be, this tendency can introduce considerable error. All those rated by one manager may score below all those rated by another, even though the two groups may be in fact very similar. The differences obtained are due to differences in managerial standards, not in performance. Although the literature tends to devote more attention to **leniency errors,** it should be recognized that **severity errors** can occur as well.

As noted in Chapter 14, leniency occurs frequently when ratings must be fed back to employees. There are, in addition, certain other conditions that tend to contribute to leniency (Bernardin, Orban, & Carlyle, 1981; Ilgen & Feldman, 1983). One is the mere use of a performance rating system over a period of time. There is a marked tendency for the average of ratings to creep up, even though on other evidence there has been no overall change in performance. Possibly related is the tendency for raters to be more lenient if they do not trust the appraisal process. What appears to happen is that some raters come to distrust the rating system after they have had a chance to see what happens as a consequence of their evaluations. As a result of this experience and the resultant distrust, they inflate their ratings in order to protect against higher-level administrative actions that might take control of their employees out of their hands.

☐ Errors of Central Tendency and Range Restriction

Whatever the level of the standards employed by a given superior, there is a possibility that all subordinates will be rated within a narrow range. For one reason or another, the difference between the best and the worst employee on a particular scale often turns out to be minimal, even though much larger differences do in fact exist. In small units, it is not unheard of to find the whole group clustered around one point on the scale. Errors of this kind tend in large part to obviate the value of the evaluations. This clustering is commonly toward the middle of a scale, and it is this particular tendency that is implied by the **error of central tendency.** The rater does not place anyone very far from the midpoint, in either a positive or a negative direction.

Thus it is important to distinguish between errors of central tendency and errors of range restriction (Saal, Downey, & Lahey, 1980). Central tendency errors involve a restriction of range, but only to the center or middle of the scale. **Range restriction errors** may involve such clustering around any point on a scale, often in combination with leniency errors at the very top. What is distinctive in both cases is a failure to distinguish real performance differences, either intentionally or because of insufficient attention.

☐ Recency Error

Most ratings are intended to cover a preceding period of time, perhaps six months or a year. Ideally, they should represent the average or typical behavior for this period. There is a tendency, however, to base ratings on what is most easily remembered, that is, the most recent behavior. This may well not be characteristic of the total period, especially if employees are aware of the approximate date when they will be evaluated and perform at a maximal level just prior to it. The existence of **recency errors** of this kind argues for the use of more frequent appraisals which are averaged over time (Steiner & Rain, 1989). There is also evidence that diary keeping can provide a useful antidote to recency error (DeNisi, Robbins, & Cafferty, 1989).

☐ Similar-to-Me Errors

Similar-to-me errors are the tendency for raters to give more positive ratings to individuals who are more like themselves, perhaps to enhance their own status. Males may rate males higher, blacks may rate blacks higher. This does not always happen, but it can.

☐ Personal Bias

Perhaps the most important error of all arises from the fact that few people are capable of carrying out objective judgments entirely independent of their values, prejudices, and stereotypes. All kinds of inappropriate criteria and standards may be introduced into the evaluation process, with the result that, on occasion, ratings relate not so much to company goals as to the personal goals of a particular manager. Thus, evaluations can be influenced by factors such as an employee's racial or ethnic background, physical attractiveness, religion, manner of dress, alcohol consumption, social standing, treatment of wife and children, and ancestry, which are normally of little significance for the achievement of organizational goals. Biases of this kind can operate without the rater being aware of what is happening, or the biases may be conscious and intentional.

Furthermore, an individual rater may permit personal feelings to weigh heavily in evaluations, as in a case of sexual harassment. Superiors may try to use their control over the evaluation process to get even with subordinates whom they believe have hurt them in some way or to reduce the threat posed by a highly effective subordinate; this threat may be real or imagined. There are even those who get some perverse enjoyment out of seeing others suffer and use the evaluation process for this purpose. Personal biases of these kinds may not operate often, but it is important to recognize their existence and the fact that ratings can contain this type of error. The example of the dean of arts and sciences at the beginning of this chapter demonstrates how performance ratings can be used quite consciously to achieve personal goals, and in a biased manner.

Ethically, it matters a great deal whether the bias is intentional or unintentional, but often it is hard to say. There is evidence, for instance, that whether one likes or dislikes a person can influence appraisals (Cardy & Dobbins, 1986). Furthermore, a person who argues for the hiring or promotion of an individual will rate that individual higher subsequently, presumably to justify the original decision (Schoorman, 1988).

☐ Bias and Equal Employment Opportunity

To the extent that race, sex, age, and the like enter into ratings, so that certain kinds of people are consistently rated lower than their true performance would warrant, with the result that promotions are denied and pay raises are not forthcoming, bias is transformed into illegal discrimination. Court-ordered back-pay awards can result, and in the case of class-action judgments, these may be very large indeed. Bias of this kind in performance evaluations may also be transformed into discrimination in hiring if the performance measure is used as a criterion in a validity study to identify measures for use as selection instruments.

A comprehensive review of the literature in this area concluded that:

> The sex stereotype of an occupation interacts with the sex of the ratee, such that males receive more favorable evaluations than do females in traditionally masculine occupations but that no difference or smaller differences in favor of females occur in traditionally feminine occupations. Ratees tend to receive higher ratings from raters of their same race, although this may not occur in highly integrated situations (Landy & Farr, 1980, p. 81).

But what happens as sex stereotypes break down and the number of integrated situations increases—and perhaps as age differentials become less important? Recent studies conducted in actual operating situations where some degree of control over the performance evaluation system was exercised indicate that, although biases against certain groups may operate, they tend to be quite limited in extent and have very little influence on the ratings given (Guion & Gibson, 1988; Latham, 1986; Pulakos, White, Oppler, & Borman, 1989). There is reason to believe that, whatever the situation in the past, biases against groups protected by law are not now a very important factor in the area of performance appraisal.

☐ Reducing Error through Training

A procedure that has been used to reduce the various types of errors that may plague ratings involves training raters to recognize and counteract biasing tendencies, and to observe performance more effectively. Such training may take a variety of forms, including lectures, group discussions, and videotape feedback. The key objective in the training is to provide an opportunity to identify and learn about sources of error and bias and to stimulate motivation to improve evaluations. Far too often, performance evaluation systems are introduced merely by distributing the necessary forms within the company.

Where training programs of this kind have been studied effectively, the results have been mixed (Athey & McIntyre, 1987; Hedge & Kavanagh, 1988; Pulakos, 1986). Usually, but not always, the types of errors on which the training focused have been reduced. However, it appears that the training may reduce some biases only to introduce others. Thus, accuracy may not be improved overall. Furthermore, any positive effects that are achieved may dissipate over time, requiring retraining. Nevertheless, there is good evidence that training can improve rating quality if the training is done appropriately. For that reason, it is to be recommended.

■ TYPES OF RATING METHODS

Although there are a variety of classifications of judgmental procedures, the one used here employs rating scales, employee comparison systems, behavior lists, and free-written essays as the primary categories. This approach covers all of the techniques that are in widespread use.

☐ Rating Scales

Rating scales may take numerous forms, but the essential characteristic is that a checkmark is placed along a scale of value. In the graphic-scale approach there is a line along which a mark is placed; or there may be a set of numbers, one of which is to be circled. The scales of Box 15-1 are rating scales. In any event, the high and low ends of the scale at a very minimum are identified, and intermediate points may be defined through the use of appropriate adjectives or phrases. However identified, the distinct scale points should number at least five to obtain sufficient dispersion of ratings.

Many firms use **trait rating** scales to gauge whether individuals possess certain traits assumed to help them work effectively. Industriousness, trustworthiness, cooperativeness, leadership ability, decisiveness, and the like, are examples. Exhibit 15-1 provides instances from a form that Perry Ice Cream Company has used to rate managers. These ratings emphasize means rather than ends. A problem arises because the factors rated may not have a strong relationship to performance. It is assumed that they have a positive relationship, but no empirical evidence to this effect is typically obtained. Thus trait ratings risk that the factors are irrelevant to actual job

	0	1	2	3	4
	Cannot Rate	Needs Improvement to Attain Executive Level Competence	Approaching Executive Level Competence	Executive Level Competence	Outstanding Executive Level Ability
Conceptual Ability: Ability to understand and create a range of alternatives for reaching goals and objectives and in the problem-solving process.					
Decisiveness: Ability to make decisions in a timely manner, and follow up on the decision.					
Entrepreneurial Ability: Willingness to take calculated risks or initiate actions to capitalize on business opportunities from a strategic or tactical standpoint.					
Impact: Ability to create a good impression, command attention and respect, and convey an air of confidence.					
Initiative: Self-generated actions to take charge of situations and make things happen with a sense of urgency.					
Judgment: Selecting among alternative courses of action to maximize desired outcomes.					
Stress Tolerance: Reliability and stability of performance under pressure.					
Ability to Handle Power and Influence: In an effective and responsible manner.					
Ability to Work with Executive Management: Includes political sensitivity and sense of timing.					

EXHIBIT 15-1   Trait Rating Items from a Form Used by Perry Ice Cream Company to Evaluate Managers

performance, and in addition that the factors may be difficult to evaluate accurately and consistently. For these reasons they leave something to be desired in performance appraisal, and industrial psychologists have often argued against using them. Yet they appear to have remarkable staying power. A likely reason is that people appear to prefer thinking in terms of personality and personality traits when carrying out performance appraisals (Krzystofiak, Cardy, & Newman, 1988).

Rating scales of some kind are widely used, primarily because they are so simple to construct. Yet in most cases no provision is made for reducing halo, constant error, and errors of range restriction, all of which can have a considerable impact. To the extent that they become behaviorally specific, error may be reduced, but simplicity of construction is lost as well.

Given an adequate awareness of the factors that introduce bias and a desire to overcome them, rating scales apparently can be employed effectively by managers in evaluating their subordinates. In actual practice, this degree of freedom from error may not be too common. This is particularly true if the rater is asked to mark a great variety of scales, which frequently appear to overlap, on each individual. When the number of dimensions is more than ten, the prospect of appropriate motivation in the rater becomes rather low.

Exhibit 15-2 presents a rating scale that has been constructed to obtain information regarding whether or not an employee should be retained at the end of an initial probationary period, usually from two to six months. It has a strong negative orientation, because the major concern is to identify those who will not be capable of effective performance. Perhaps the greatest value of scales of this kind is that they help to remind a manager of the great variety of behaviors that must be compared against role requirements in reaching a decision on retention. Notice that this decision is not actually requested of Atlantic-Richfield managers until the end of the scale, after all the various aspects of the employee's behavior have been considered.

☐ Employee Comparison Systems

Employee comparison systems do not require the use of an absolute standard, as do rating scales. Instead of comparing each worker against some generalized concept of acceptable behavior, the rater makes comparisons among the various individuals being evaluated. Thus, other workers provide reference points for the ratings, and the result is a relative evaluation.

Ranking. With **ranking,** the manager merely orders subordinates on as many dimensions, or characteristics, as are required. Each dimension is treated separately. Various aids have been developed for this purpose, because ranking may not be an easy task when a relatively large number of employees is involved.

One of these, called the alternation-ranking method, represents an attempt to get the easier discriminations, those involving the poorer and better individuals, out of the way first so that the rater can concentrate on the middle range, where decisions are more difficult. Thus the best person is selected first, then the worst, then the next best, the next worst, and so on, working inward, until the last person noted is the one in the median position.

An alternative approach involves having managers assume a hypothetical role as the head of a newly formed firm. They are then asked to select the one individual from among present subordinates whom, on the basis of performance and potential, they would like to have as their vice president. This name is recorded. Next, the manager is asked to assume that this particular individual has refused the appointment and to select a second person from among the remaining group. This procedure is repeated until all members have been ranked. The problem with this and similar nomination techniques is that they provide only a single measure on an overall effectiveness scale.

The major advantage of any type of ranking is that it spreads individuals out over the whole range of performance. The error of central tendency is eliminated, and constant errors cannot occur as such. In addition, halo appears to be minimized when the dimensions are ranked separately and person-to-person comparison made on each. The big-

Name: Current Date:
Department: Date Probationary Period Ends:
Job Title:

Please check the appropriate statement or statements in each area to indicate
extent of employee's progress.

Quantity of Work:
  Slow to learn _____
  Has to be pushed on occasion _____
  Consistently meets requirements _____
  Does more than required _____
Quality of Work:
  Not really very good _____
  Sometimes drops below acceptable level _____
  Acceptable _____
  An accurate worker _____
Personal Characteristics:
  Does not cooperate with other workers _____ Cooperates _____
  Is absent frequently _____ Is rarely absent _____
  Wastes time _____ Does not waste time _____
  Is not a safe worker _____ Is a safe worker _____
  Demands frequent supervision _____ Can work along _____
  A troublemaker _____ Does not stir up trouble _____
Are you satisfied to have the employee remain working for you? _____
If not suitable for retention in present job, would you recommend another job?
_____

Comments:

**EXHIBIT 15-2   A Rating Form Used for Probationary Employee Evaluation
at Atlantic-Richfield**

gest problems arise when there is a need to combine ratings made by different supervisors on different groups. It is always possible, although not probable, that the best person in one group is actually below the poorest in another. One solution is to supplement the rank ordering with a rating system; these rated ranks can then be used to telescope the various groups.

Paired Comparisons. A second method of employee comparison produces a ranking as a final result but requires only that the superiority of one individual over another be established by judgment. From a series of such comparisons of pairs, a rank ordering may be constructed. The nature of the **paired-comparison** technique is illustrated in Box 15-3. The machine operators in the four units at

Atlantic-Richfield were evaluated by their supervisors and, where possible, by their assistant supervisors as well.

Forced Distribution. One of the difficulties with ranking, and particularly with paired comparisons, is that when the unit to be evaluated is large—for example, over twenty-five—it is often necessary to break down the total group into subgroups for purposes of evaluation. An alternative to this is a **forced distribution.**

In a sense, forced distribution is a variant of the rating-scale procedure, with a provision eliminating constant errors and errors of range restriction. Managers are instructed to place their subordinates in categories on each dimension according to certain predesignated proportions. The common distribution is

low 10%   next 20%   middle 40%   next 20%   high 10%

Thus, for a unit of forty-six people, the foreman would be asked to sort them as follows:

low 5   next 9   middle 18   next 9   high 5

Notice that no assumption is made regarding the absolute level of performance. The lowest five ratings are not necessarily unsatisfactory; they are only relatively less effective. If there is any reason to believe that the performance distribution chosen does not reflect the true state of affairs, forced distribution is not recommended.

Combining Employee Comparison Data. The major difficulty with all the techniques discussed in this section is that although the relative position of each person within a group is established, there is no provision for determining the relative status of various groups. Two rankings on separate work units by their separate supervisors do not reflect any existing differences between the groups. One unit may have many more outstanding performers than the other, yet the ranking data will not indicate this fact. Another problem is that

since the real level of performance remains unknown, training and development needs are not served.

The most common approach has been to assume that the groups to be compared or combined do not differ appreciably. If the groups are of different sizes, the ranks obtained from ranking or paired comparisons are translated into a set of common scores through the use of conversion tables and then combined into a single list. This, however, does not solve the underlying problems.

An approach that does solve those problems is first to obtain alternation rankings within each employee group from supervisors. Then, using a rating scale with, say, seven points, extending from outstanding to poor, the supervisors are asked to assign descriptions to each person ranked, repeating the alternation procedure. The key is that they must follow the earlier rankings in making the ratings; employees ranked higher must be rated either higher than or equal to those ranked below them. Thus the ranks are converted to rating values for purposes of combining groups and establishing developmental needs. This **rated ranking** approach serves to minimize many of the common sources of error and yields substantial agreement between two raters (Miner, 1988). The same procedures can be applied to paired-comparison and forced-distribution data.

☐ Behavior Lists

The essential characteristic of **behavior list** procedures is that they deal with on-the-job behaviors; they are by definition very behavior specific. The manager actually reports on or describes the behavior of subordinates rather than merely evaluating it. This means that separate lists must be developed for each position that differs to any significant degree in role requirements from other positions.

Because the manager provides only a number of behaviors that serve to describe a par-

BOX 15-3 I/O PSYCHOLOGY IN PRACTICE

A Paired-Comparison Rating System to Evaluate Machine Operators at Atlantic-Richfield

The purpose of the rating system was presented to the machine group supervisors as follows.

> The purpose of these rating forms is to see how the various members of the group you supervise compare with each other in important aspects of machine operation.
>
> In making the ratings, compare the employees under you on the following aspects of machine operation:
>
> 1. *Application.* Which employee is stronger in application to the job? Which shows more interest in the work and strives to do well in it?
>
> 2. *Accuracy.* Which employee produces more consistently accurate work? Which do you feel you do not have to check on as much?
>
> 3. *Speed.* Which employee gets assigned jobs done faster? Which one can produce more in a given time?
>
> 4. *Cooperation.* Which employee demonstrates a greater spirit of cooperation with co-workers and supervisors? Which gets along better with people on the job?
>
> 5. *Overall effectiveness.* Considering the four factors above, and others not mentioned that are important in the work, which employee would you say is a more effective machine operator?
>
> A separate form for each of these aspects on which you will rate your employees is attached. In completing these forms, you are to compare each employee with every other employee once on each of the five aspects.
>
> 1. In the column running down the left side of each form are the names of employees in your group who do the machine work. The same names in the same order appear in the row running across the top of the form.
>
> 2. No ratings are required in the blanks below the diagonal line running from the top left to the bottom right corner of the sheet, because you cannot compare individuals with themselves.

> 3. Beginning with the name of the first employee in the left column, you are to compare that person with each of the other employees whose names appear in the upper row. If, in your opinion, the employee whose name is to the left is better in the aspect of the job that is being judged, place a "1" in the square made by the intersection of the column and the row. If you feel the employee whose name is in the upper row is better, place a "0" in the square.
>
> 4. Repeat the process for the succeeding names in the left column until the form is finished.
>
> 5. Even though two employees may be nearly equal on any characteristic, you must decide who is better and assign a "1" or "0."
>
> 6. Leave no blank spaces and use only "1s" or "0s."

One of the rating forms came back from one of the supervisors as follows:

Aspect: *Overall effectiveness.* If you consider application, accuracy, speed, cooperation, and any other aspects that are important in the work, which employee would you say is a more effective machine operator?

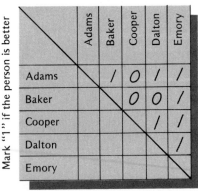

Mark "0" if the person is better

	Adams	Baker	Cooper	Dalton	Emory
Adams		1	0	1	1
Baker			0	0	1
Cooper				1	1
Dalton					1
Emory					

Mark "1" if the person is better

If the number of "better" evaluations is totaled for each person, the results are:

Cooper	4
Adams	3
Dalton	2
Baker	1
Emory	0

These data provide a ranking within this particular group, with Cooper the most effective worker and Emory the least. The actual study involved the combining of similar information on four different machine units, most of them considerably larger than this one.

Results obtained from pairs of supervisors within the same machine unit indicated good agreement. Also, a repetition of the ratings after one year yielded very similar ratings.

ticular person, the actual evaluation process must be carried out elsewhere. The behavior descriptions included in the list must be categorized in terms of the degree to which they match role requirements. This is normally done by people who are familiar with the specific type of work—various levels of supervision, job analysts, industrial psychologists, and perhaps industrial engineers or others who serve in a staff capacity relative to the positions under consideration.

These evaluations of items may be carried out in a rough manner or by using more precise scaling techniques. In any event, the result is a designation of certain behaviors as good or desirable and others as less so. If the good behaviors are consistently checked by the superior of a particular employee, and the less desirable behaviors are not, then the employee is considered to have been given an outstanding rating. The weights or evaluations attached to items may or may not be known to the supervisors doing the rating.

Forced-Choice Procedures. A variant of the behavior list technique has been developed that can almost eliminate the personal bias problem and most other sources of error as well. Unfortunately, it accomplishes this result while introducing a situation in which those doing the rating have no idea whether they are evaluating a person favorably or not. The consequence has been that many managers have developed considerable resistance to this approach—called the **forced-choice procedure**—so much so that very few firms now use it. Yet it is desirable to have some familiarity with the forced-choice procedure, if only because of the extensive discussions it has provoked within industrial psychology.

The basic elements of the measure are a series of blocks of two or more behavior descriptions. The descriptions within each block are selected to be approximately equal in their degree of favorableness but markedly different in the degree to which they have been found in prior studies to be associated with effective or ineffective performance, as defined by some other, external criterion. Thus, a block of items used in one of the early developmental studies for rating training skills and containing favorable descriptions is

1. Patient with slow learners
2. Lectures with confidence
3. Keeps interest and attention of class
4. Acquaints classes with objective for each lesson in advance

A block of unfavorable items is

1. Does not answer all questions to the satisfaction of students
2. Does not use proper voice volume
3. Supporting details are not relevant

BOX 15-4 RESEARCH IN I/O PSYCHOLOGY

A Critical-Incident Rating System for 3M Company Sales Personnel

The critical-incident system was developed in the following manner. Initially, sales managers in the various divisions were asked to submit short stories or anecdotes, called critical incidents, that illustrated what they considered particularly effective or ineffective sales behavior. The result was sixty-one instances of effective performance and thirty-five instances of ineffective performance. Analysis of these data revealed that fifteen basic types of behavior were involved, such as following up, carrying out promises, and communicating all necessary information to sales managers.

A rating sheet was then constructed covering these fifteen areas, based on items as closely allied to the original critical incidents as possible.

The raters were to indicate what would be the extent of their agreement or disagreement if they were to hear a particular statement used to describe the salesperson being evaluated. Examples of these statements based on critical selling incidents are

1. Follows up quickly on requests from customers.

2. Promises too much to customers.

3. Writes poor sales reports.

SOURCE: Wayne K. Kirchner & Marvin D. Dunnette (1957). Identifying the critical factors in successful salesmanship. *Personnel, 34* (2), p. 54–59.

Within each of these blocks, certain items have been found to discriminate between poor and good teachers, whereas others have little relation to success (Berkshire & Highland, 1953).

Checklists. **Checklists** contain a number of descriptors, usually job behaviors but in some cases personal traits as well, which are to be checked if they apply to the individual. Often adjectives or descriptive phrases are used. The descriptors are not linked to any specific aspects of job performance. However, the items checked may be scored in some manner so that certain responses receive greater weight than others. For example, some items might be:

Does good-quality work. _____

Requires excessive instruction. _____

Is attentive to detail. _____

Does not interfere with others' work. _____

Critical Incident Rating. The essential feature of the **critical incident procedure** is that incidents of effective and ineffective performance are obtained to serve as a basis for rating. Box 15-4 describes the development of such an approach at 3M Company.

Often the incidents are presented to the rater in checklist form. Thus, a performance rating for a human resources representative might offer the following examples of effective and ineffective incidents:

In discussions to fill a difficult position, will explore all possible approaches and attempt to determine why it is difficult to locate applicants. _____

In classifying a position, fails to consider other functions in the organization that have an impact on the position being classified. _____

The major advantages of this technique are in establishing comprehensive definitions of role requirements if these are not available from other sources and in providing items that, because they are close to on-the-job behavior, can serve to reduce personal bias.

Methods of Scaled Expectation. An approach that has achieved considerable popularity is the scaled expectation, or behaviorally anchored, procedure. There are several variants of this method, but all have much in common with the critical-incident and other behavior-list rating systems, while retaining certain common elements with the rating scales as well.

Although the order in which they are carried out may vary, the following steps are characteristic in the **scaled expectation method:**

1. Managers with knowledge of the work to be rated identify and define a number of dimensions or aspects of the job, such as communicating relevant information, diagnosing problems, and meeting day-to-day deadlines. In essence, this is a type of job analysis.

2. These same managers develop a number of statements illustrating effective and ineffective job behaviors along each of these dimensions. This step is analogous to the critical-incident rating procedure.

3. Another group of managers, equally knowledgeable regarding the work, is given the definitions of dimensions from step 1 and the critical incidents from step 2 separately and asked to assign each incident to the most appropriate dimension. This is a matter of retranslation to see if the original incident-dimension fit will hold up. If it does not, the incident is discarded.

4. The second group of managers scales each remaining incident as to the degree of effectiveness of the behavior, usually on either a seven- or a nine-point scale. Where disagreement regarding scale values is pronounced, the incident is discarded.

5. The final rating form contains a series of scales, perhaps ten, anchored by behaviorally specific incidents at points along each scale obtained by averaging the values obtained in step 4. The rater evaluates the ratee by indicating what behaviors could be expected of the person.

Box 15-5 serves to illustrate the approach as applied to the evaluation of engineers. This is a particularly complex application using four groups of experts (managers).

Typically the anchoring incidents are recast in an expectation format, and the rater is to check the scale value that best describes the worker. Alternatively, incidents of the employee's behavior are recorded on the appropriate scales throughout a rating period. At the end of the period, summary ratings are made from these recorded incidents. Although it is not widely used, this latter approach is preferred (Bernardin & Smith, 1981).

Constructing scaled expectation measures, in any form, is a time-consuming and costly process. It is intended to drastically reduce errors such as halo, leniency, and central tendency. Yet the accumulated research evidence does not always support such a conclusion (Jacobs, Kafry, & Zedeck, 1980; Kingstrom & Bass, 1981). Improvements over the simpler rating scale and employee comparison methods may occur; but the amount of error reduction is not as great as had been anticipated, and it may not be sufficient to justify the time, effort, and cost involved. This is particularly true if adequate job analysis data are already available, and the use of the scaled expectation method accordingly contributes little extra to an understanding of job requirements and performance. Furthermore, there are conditions under which the behavioral anchors may actually add to bias (Piotrowski, Barnes-Farrell, & Esrig, 1989).

One problem that can arise is that the behavioral statements used are so specific that raters have difficulty using them with

BOX 15-5   RESEARCH IN I/O PSYCHOLOGY

The Process of Developing a Behaviorally Anchored Rating Scale for Engineers in Industry (BARS)

Numerical scale		Examples of activities related to this factor
9 8 7	More than usual amount of typical activity or effort related to this factor	Seeks information about all technical areas
		Seeks involvement in relevant technical developments
		Works extra hours on own initiative to learn about new developments
6 5 4	Usual amount of typical activity or effort related to this factor	Occasionally reads journals in related technical areas
		Interest in new technology is usually limited to own area only
		Sometimes displays a negative attitude toward new ideas
3 2 1	Less than usual amount of typical activity or effort related to this factor	Is pessimistic and cynical about new technical developments
		Has little curiosity about technologies related to own specific area
		Adopts an attitude of "if it's important, someone will tell me about it" toward developments

Specific instances of this individual's work activities related to this factor: _____

_____ Numerical description for this factor

SOURCE: Frank J. Landy & James L. Farr (1983). *The measurements of work performance: Methods, theory,* *and applications,* pp. 61 and 65. New York: Academic Press.

their own subordinates. Consider the following behavior anchor for the ineffective performance of a first-time supervisor:

When a manager requested that this supervisor instruct one of her clerks to provide another unit with some data on an exception basis, the supervisor agreed to this, but explained that there would be a week's delay owing to the clerk's heavy workload.

If this type of situation has not arisen, it is hard to know what a person might do, and thus hard to carry out the evaluation.

A method of dealing with this difficulty, termed **behavioral summary scales,** is to anchor the performance ratings with somewhat more general or abstract behavioral benchmarks. The approach develops specific behavior anchors as in the scaled expectation method generally, but then the highly specific incidents representing a given level of performance effectiveness on a particular performance category are examined for an underlying thread of common behavioral components. Benchmarks may then be written to represent the wider range of scaled behaviors common to the specific incidents. Exhibit 15-3 provides an example that was developed to evaluate U.S. Navy recruiters. Note that these statements are more general than the usual behavioral anchors, and that they attempt to reflect a variety of ways to perform at each performance level. Behavioral summary scales represent some movement away from extreme behavioral specificity.

Behavioral Observation Scales. A procedure that has much in common with the methods of scaled expectation has been proposed as a superior alternative (Latham & Wexley, 1981). The procedure, called **behavior observation scaling** to distinguish it from the behavioral expectation approach, develops a series of items in the following format for each component or dimension of work:

Works overtime when asked:

Almost never   0   1   2   3   4   Almost always

The rater selects one of the five scale values, and these are set equal to percentage frequencies of occurrence, usually ranging from 0 to 64 percent for "0," to 95 to 100 percent for "4." Overall ratings on a dimension are obtained by totaling the circled values for all items in the behavior list. Note that a graphic scale as in Box 15-5 is not used, and reference is made to actual, not expected, behavior.

Measures of this kind suffer from the same problems in the areas of cost and time to construct as the scaled expectation methods. To date they have not been found superior to those methods in reducing error, and it is possible that they may introduce certain special problems of their own in their demands on raters (Fay & Latham, 1982; Murphy, Martin, & Garcia, 1982). Nevertheless, raters appear to like them, and the scales have been found useful in situations where performance data are fed back for developmental purposes (Tziner & Kopelman, 1988).

Mixed Standard Scales. The **mixed standard approach** has much in common with the other behavior lists. Job incumbents help to develop sets of behavioral statements in groups of three. These three statements represent a scale of favorableness, and each statement is used to rate an individual's behavior as better than, equal to, or worse than that described. In a study with state highway patrol officers, one of the scales was (Rosinger, Myers, Levy, Loar, Mohrman, & Stock, 1982):

Stops vehicles for a variety of traffic and other violations.

Concentrates on speed violations but stops vehicles for other violations too.

Concentrates on one or two kinds of violations and spends too little time on the others.

In the state trooper study, twenty-six sets of behaviors that were known to involve critical and frequently performed activities were developed—a total of seventy-eight behaviors.

The next step in this approach is to scramble the individual behavior statements so that the nature of the individual scales is not apparent. Since actual scoring is done after the ratings are obtained, raters may not be sure how they have rated a given individual, as with the forced-choice procedure. Also, inconsistencies in responses to the three statements of a scale can be noted and thus poor raters identified.

Good results have been obtained with the mixed standard approach, as in the highway patrol officer study. However, comparative research fails to demonstrate a meaningful superiority to other well-developed rating methods (Bernardin, Carlyle, & Elliott, 1980). Again, cost and time to develop remain major considerations.

☐ **Essay Evaluations**

In the **essay evaluation**, superiors merely write out what they think of the subordinate, usually with very little in the way of guide-

Exhibit 15-3 A Behavioral Summary Scale Devised to Rate U.S. Navy Recruiter Performance

Establishing and Maintaining Good Relationships in the Community

Contacting and working effectively with high school counselors, newspaper editors, radio and TV personnel, and others capable of helping recruiters to enlist prospects; building a good reputation for the navy by developing positive relationships with persons in the community; establishing and maintaining good relationships with parents and family of prospects; presenting a good navy image in the community.

9 or 10
Extremely Effective Performance

Is exceptionally adept at cultivating and maintaining excellent relationships with school counselors, teachers, principals, police, news media persons, local business persons, and other persons who are important for getting referrals and free advertising.	Is innovative in informing the public about the navy; actively promotes the navy and makes friends for the navy while doing it; always distributes the most current navy information.	Volunteers off-duty time to work on community projects, celebrations, parades, etc.

6, 7, or 8
Effective Performance

Spends productive time with individuals such as police, city government, or school officials; may lunch with them, distribute calendars, appointment books, buttons, etc., to them, and/or invite	Arranges for interested persons such navy activities as trips to the Naval Academy; keeps relevant persons informed of navy activities.	Encourages principals, counselors, and other persons important to a prospect to call if they have any questions about the navy.

3, 4, or 5
Marginal Performance

Contacts school officials only sporadically; keeps them waiting for information they want; relationships with counselors, teachers, etc., and persons important to an applicant or recruit are distant and underdeveloped.	Is not alert to opportunities to promote the navy; rarely volunteers off-duty time to promote the navy and is unenthusiastic when approached to do something for the community; rarely accepts speaking invitations.	Is, at times, discourteous to persons in the community; for example, sends form letters to persons who assisted him or other navy recruiters; is not always alert to the family's desire for more information about the navy and the program in which their son or daughter enlisted.

	1 or 2 *Ineffective Performance*	
Does not contact high school counselors; does not accept speaking engagements; drives around in car instead of getting out and meeting people.	Alienates persons in community or persons important to an applicant or recruit by ignoring them, not answering their questions, responding rudely, demanding information, encouraging high school students to drop out of school; sometimes does not appear at recruiting presentations for which he or she is scheduled.	Presents negative image of the navy by doing things like driving while intoxicated or speeding and honking impatiently at other drivers; may express dislike for the navy or recruiting.

SOURCE: Walter C. Borman (1986). Behavior-based rating scales. In Ronald A. Berk (Ed.), *Performance assessment: Methods and applications,* pp. 106–107. Baltimore: Johns Hopkins University Press.

lines concerning what points should be covered. An example is presented in Exhibit 15-4.

This approach does little to reduce the various types of error that may influence the evaluation process. Personal bias, in particular, may be marked, because managers select their own grounds for judging subordinates. Comparisons between individuals become difficult because one person may be evaluated in one regard and another person on a completely different basis.

Specific role requirements may be introduced, and free-written statements requested, in each area. If this is done, however, a rating scale is normally much easier to employ. Yet essay evaluations completed with reference to job descriptions can prove to be useful adjuncts to other methods.

☐ Performance Simulations

Because of the many possible sources of bias and error that may serve to distort evaluations based on performance in the actual workplace, there has been some tendency to utilize various kinds of work simulations as a source of evaluation. These often are similar to the situational exercises employed in assessment centers; in fact, ratings derived from the in-basket exercise, which is widely used in assessment centers, have been used as independent performance measures.

Advocates of the simulation approach to evaluation argue that day-to-day performance is not usually a good measure of what a person can do, because it is influenced by such factors as the nature of supervision, peer pressures to control output, individual motivation, and the like. Factors of this kind can be held at approximately the same level for all who participate in the simulation, and thus valid comparisons can be made between one person's proficiency and another's.

Although some simulations are little more than knowledge tests indicating how much the individual knows about the job, others go far beyond this, providing an opportunity to perform most of the tasks that would be performed in the actual work setting. The difference is that performance occurs in a highly controlled, or "purified," environment, estab-

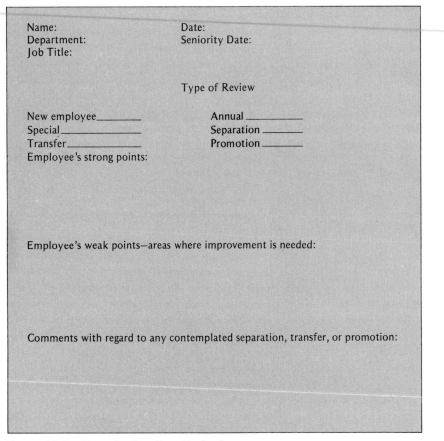

Name: Date:
Department: Seniority Date:
Job Title:

                          Type of Review

New employee_____   Annual _____
Special_____   Separation _____
Transfer_____   Promotion _____
Employee's strong points:

Employee's weak points—areas where improvement is needed:

Comments with regard to any contemplated separation, transfer, or promotion:

EXHIBIT 15-4   **Example of an Essay Evaluation**

lished in order to facilitate accurate measurement.

The problem with this type of purification of the evaluation situation is that it may emphasize the effectiveness of measurement at the expense of what needs to be measured. The simulation may in fact be unreal and artificial. It may have little to do with the actual job, and even if it is highly job-related, the employee is most likely to exhibit maximum performance capability rather than what might be expected to be typical on a day-to-day basis. These considerations suggest that simulation evaluations should not be considered as identical to error-free on-the-job eval-

uations unless some evidence to this effect is available. In many instances, the two will be measuring somewhat different things. Nevertheless, indexes derived from simulations can prove useful for certain purposes, such as determining the extent to which learning has occurred in a training program.

■ RESISTANCE TO EVALUATION

In spite of the obvious significance of employee evaluation for the attainment of company goals, there are a number of sources of resistance that may make it difficult to install and maintain systems of this kind (Beer, 1981). This problem appears to be particularly acute among production employees. Although the majority of other employee groups is covered by some kind of performance evaluation system, this is much less true of production workers.

One major difficulty is that employees who do not anticipate a favorable rating are likely to be opposed to the whole evaluation process, which is perceived as a personal threat. Managers and supervisors may experience considerable group pressure in this regard, with the result that many of them, especially those who are particularly sensitive about such matters, may find it very difficult to actually do the ratings. Thus, there may be delays and other difficulties that, although probably not intentional, do reflect the conflicting pressures to which managers are exposed. It should be emphasized, however, that the problems for raters and ratees alike revolve around negative evaluations. Both parties appear to react positively when the outcome is positive. Yet the sources of the resistance among raters and ratees are not the same overall. It would be difficult to make everyone happy (Dipboye & dePontbriand, 1981; Mount, 1983; Russell & Goode, 1988).

☐ Seniority and Union Resistance

Perhaps the greatest present source of difficulty in the area of employee evaluation stems from the unions. Rating procedures are almost universally condemned as being inconsistent with the longstanding labor union commitment to the seniority principle.

When seniority holds for purposes of layoff, promotion, shift selection, eligibility for overtime, work assignments, and the like, it is the senior employee in terms of service with the company, or in the seniority unit, who gets the preferred treatment. This tends to eliminate most, if not all, need for a merit rating system and accounts for the low frequency of performance evaluation in unionized production situations.

Union contracts contain a variety of provisions insofar as seniority is concerned. In the most extreme case, seniority only is mentioned. Other contracts say that seniority governs, provided the senior employee is minimally capable of doing the work. Still others indicate that seniority shall be the deciding factor where ability is equal. This, of course, places the burden of proof on management. Evidence must be presented that those with less seniority are more capable, if, for instance, they are to be promoted. Even in the latter case, close inspection of actual practices often reveals that merit characteristically takes a position secondary to seniority.

Union contracts contain widely varying provisions regarding the date that seniority starts to accumulate, loss of seniority, individuals who are exempt from the standard seniority provisions, and so on. It is almost impossible to generalize on these matters. There are also wide differences in the way the seniority unit is defined. Seniority may be companywide or plantwide. It may hold only within certain occupational groups or departments or even pay ranges.

In general, management prefers to keep the seniority unit as small as possible. The reason for this is that when layoffs must occur and higher-level positions are eliminated, it is common practice to permit **bumping** within the unit; that is, an employee with seniority may demand the job of another employee with less seniority. This can extend down through the unit until the person with the least seniority, in the lowest-level job, is the one laid off. Where seniority is companywide and a highly skilled position is eliminated, the amount of dislocation occasioned by successive bumping can be considerable. Where the seniority unit is small, changes in the job structure are much more easily accomplished. Nevertheless, many companies have been forced to move to plantwide seniority in recent years because of court actions and government pressure related to equal employment opportunity considerations.

Even where seniority provisions have not eliminated the need for employee evaluation, the union may exercise a certain degree of control over an existing rating system. Thus, some contracts call for a review procedure under which a combined union–management committee reconsiders certain supervisory evaluations and may in fact change them. Among office employees, many have access to some kind of appeal procedure; among production workers, when an evaluation system does exist, appeal or protest safeguards are even more prevalent. In a number of cases, the regular grievance machinery is used for this purpose.

All this would not be important if seniority and performance effectiveness were closely related. But this is not the case; seniority is not the same as effective performance (Gordon, Cofer, & McCullough, 1986). Accordingly, seniority is a form of resistance to evaluation; it yields quite different results than would be obtained with an effective appraisal system.

☐ Overcoming Resistance

Resistance may serve to block the initiation of an evaluation system, but it is also likely to emerge after the system has been established and there are specific details to attack. The result may well be a gradual erosion of the program and in some cases eventual abandonment.

The greater the resistance exhibited, the more those who are administering the program need to move toward those who do the rating if the program is to survive. One method of moving toward the raters involves having human resource representatives actually go out and collect the data in a face-to-face situation, as in the field-review method, rather than merely sending out forms and waiting for

them to come back. Such an approach demonstrates the willingness of industrial psychologists to do a sizable share of the work in order to ensure a successful program. Rater training may achieve a similar objective.

Another approach is to involve those who will do the rating in the construction of the evaluation system. In this way it becomes their system, and they have an investment in its success. Such an approach is built directly into the scaled expectation and similar methods, but it can become a part of the development of other types of performance evaluation systems as well. Resistance can also be avoided by deliberately designing the evaluation system with a view to minimizing it, as indicated by the following examples.

1. Managers often oppose peer and subordinate ratings but will accept superior ratings.
2. Whereas a procedure requiring the feedback of results to subordinates may elicit major resistance, one without the feedback requirement is much less likely to be opposed.
3. Forced-choice and forced-distribution methods are often a source of resistance because managers feel manipulated and forced into something they may not want to do. Where resistance is anticipated, the system can be tailored to gain maximum acceptance.

Finally, there is evidence that where a performance evaluation program is initially acceptable, it can be maintained over a number of years as a viable, functioning entity by training managers in its use and by constant monitoring for evidence of erosion. This latter process involves a higher-level review of all ratings made by a given manager with a view to early identification of any shift toward errors of central tendency, leniency, severity, and the like. Summary data for all ratings made in a given period are fed back to each

EXHIBIT 15-5   **Performance Appraisal System Characteristics Showing a Significant Relationship with the Outcomes of Employment Discrimination Cases**

	Percent of Cases with	
Appraisal System Characteristic	*Successful Defense*	*Unsuccessful Defense*
1. Job analysis used to develop system	100	0
Job analysis not used to develop system	21	79
2. System focused on job behaviors of employees	70	30
System focused on personal traits of employees	32	68
3. Evaluators given specific written rating instructions	92	8
Evaluators not given written rating instructions	7	93
4. Results of appraisal reviewed with employees	78	22
Results not reviewed with employees	0	100
5. Appraisal system exists in a nonindustrial organization—largely universities	64	36
Appraisal system exists in an industrial organization	22	78

Appraisal System Characteristic Showing No Relationship to the Success of a Defense

Validity information available and presented in case
Reliability information available and presented in case
Frequency with which evaluations were conducted
Use of multiple evaluators to rate individuals

SOURCE: Adapted from Hubert S. Feild & William H. Holley (1982). The relationship of performance appraisal system characteristics to verdicts in selected employment discrimination cases. *Academy of Management Journal, 25,* 397.

manager. Given continuing attention of this kind, the various sources of resistance need not be insurmountable.

☐ Legal Considerations

An increasingly important consideration in developing employee evaluation systems is how the courts might react to what has been done if a discrimination suit should be brought. Exhibit 15-5 provides an overview of

how courts reacted in sixty-six employment discrimination cases. It is apparent that employers should do certain things if they wish to win such cases, even though on other grounds they might not wish to do some of these things. It is also apparent that evidence of psychometric sophistication in developing measures does not seem to exert much influence on the courts.

A recent review of court cases that focused specifically on the use of performance appraisals in the discharge of employees came to the following conclusions:

1. Conduct a job analysis to ascertain characteristics necessary for successful job performance.
2. Incorporate these characteristics into a rating instrument. Written definitive standards should be provided to all raters.
3. Train supervisors to use the rating instrument properly. This involves instructions on how to apply performance appraisal standards when making judgments.
4. Formal appeal mechanisms and review of ratings by upper-level personnel are desirable.
5. The organization should document evaluations and reasons for the termination decision. Credibility is enhanced with documented performance appraisal ratings and instances of poor performance.
6. Provide some form of performance counseling or corrective guidance to assist poor performers in improving their performance (Barrett & Kernan, 1987).

Although at one time it appeared, in a case involving the Zia Company, that the courts were going to enforce very difficult, perhaps impossible, standards for measurement sophistication in performance appraisal cases, this has not proved to be the case. In fact, there have been some instances in which measures with very little behavioral specificity have been considered acceptable (Brito v. Zia Co., 1973).

■ USEFULNESS OF APPRAISAL METHODS

□ Judged Usefulness

It has become apparent that some approaches to performance appraisal work better for one purpose and other approaches for another.

Exhibit 15-6 considers some of the purposes for which various performance appraisal techniques discussed in this and the preceding chapter may or may not be used. The opinions of a number of human resource management professionals, professors, and consultants were averaged to produce these results. On this evidence, the procedures most generally useful are management by objectives, checklists, and performance standards. BARS (Behaviorally Anchored Rating Scales) and critical incidents come next, followed by ranking (which in this case is considered without reference to the rated-ranking approach). Trait ratings and forced-choice ratings are viewed quite negatively, although for different reasons. Performance standards were discussed as objective measures; all the other techniques are methods of rating.

Several of these purposes—particularly counseling and development, and communicating performance expectations—may be served by formal performance-appraisal reviews where superiors feed back their evaluations to subordinates. These reviews can improve employee motivation and satisfaction levels. However, actual improvements in performance itself have not been documented (Dorfman, Stephan, & Loveland, 1986). Thus the evaluations of these techniques given in Exhibit 15-6 cannot be extended to the matter of performance improvement.

This discussion, and work in the area of performance appraisal generally, emphasizes the value of various procedures and techniques for reducing error and bias, without considering differences among the users of these approaches. It is becoming increasingly apparent, however, that raters differ in how they think about performance and in the approaches they take to the rating task (Nathan & Alexander, 1985). As a result, some raters do a better job of judgmental evaluation than others, no matter which appraisal techniques they use. We are just beginning to learn about this phenomenon.

Exhibit 15-6 Expert Opinions Regarding the Usefulness of Various Appraisal Techniques

Purposes Considered	Appraisal Techniques							
	Trait Ratings	Management by Objectives	BARS	Checklists	Critical Incidents	Forced Choice	Ranking	Performance Standards
Validation of selection procedures	– –	+	+	+	0	+	+	+
Allocating merit pay	– –	+	0	+	0	0	+	+ +
Documentation for discharge decisions	– –	+	+	+	+ +	– –	0	+ +
Promotion and transfer	– –	+	0	+	+	0	+	+
Identifying training needs	– –	+ +	+	+	+	– –	– –	0
Counseling and development	– –	+ +	+	+	+ +	– –	– –	–
Communicating performance expectations	– –	+ +	+ +	+	–	– –	– –	+ +
Obtaining rater acceptance	+	+	+	+ +	+	– –	+	+ +
Obtaining ratee acceptance	–	+	+	0	0	– –	– –	+
Cost of development	+ +	–	– –	–	–	– –	+ +	–
Cost of administration	+ +	–	–	+	0	+	+ +	+

+ + Very useful for this purpose.
+   Somewhat useful for this purpose.
0   Neither very useful nor a source of problems.
–   Introduces some problems if used for this purpose.
– – Introduces major problems if used for this purpose.

SOURCE: Adapted from Stephen J. Carroll & Craig E. Schneier (1982). *Performance appraisal and review systems: The identification, measurement, and development of performance in organizations*, pp. 232–233. Glenview, IL: Scott, Foresman.

☐ Use as a Criterion

Within industrial/organizational psychology, the measures described in this and the preceding chapters are often referred to as criteria. A **criterion** is any measure of success. What is an appropriate measure of success in a given instance depends on the results of job analysis and on the specific purpose for which the criterion data will be used—validation of selection procedures, allocating merit pay, and the other purposes noted in Exhibit 15-6.

Criteria typically serve as **dependent variables** in that they are the major object of a researcher's interest; they are what the researcher wishes to predict. **Independent variables,** in contrast, are what a researcher manipulates or controls or measures for purposes of predicting. As we turn now to matters of validating selection procedures, many of the performance appraisal methods we have been considering will emerge as criteria. Tests, interviews, and the like are independent variables which may serve as predictors of these criteria.

KEY TERMS

Behaviorally specific

Halo

Leniency errors

Severity errors

Error of central tendency

Range restriction errors

Recency errors

Similar-to-me errors

Rating scales

Trait rating

Employee comparison

Ranking

Paired comparisons

Forced distribution

Rated ranking

Behavior list

Forced-choice procedure

Checklists

Critical incident procedure

Scaled expectation method

Behavioral summary scales

Behavior observation scaling

Mixed standard approach

Essay evaluation

Bumping

Criterion

Dependent variables

Independent variables

SUMMARY

Behaviorally specific evaluation procedures are closely tied to job analysis and vary sharply from job to job. In contrast, evaluations may be of a global nature, related largely to less formal role prescriptions, and be applied in essentially the same format to a wide range of positions. Both approaches have the potential for error, although the possibility of bias in the form of discrimination is generally considered to be less in the former instance. Other types of error commonly encountered in performance evaluation are *halo,* constant deviations such as *leniency, recency, central tendency, range restriction,* and *similar-to-me.* Errors of these kinds can be reduced through appropriate training.

A wide range of rating methods exists, each with advantages and disadvantages. A major concern is to minimize the different sources of error. The methods used are *rating scales; employee comparison* systems such as *ranking, paired comparisons,* and *forced distributions; behavior lists* such as *forced-choice procedures, critical incidents,* methods of *scaled expectation, behavioral observation scales,* and *mixed standard scales;* and *essay evaluations.* In recent years, the major research emphasis has been on the behavior list procedures. On occasion, performance simulations similar to the situational exercises used in assessment centers are introduced into the evaluation process.

Performance evaluation programs almost invariably encounter various types of resistances, both from those being evaluated and, on occasion, from those doing the evaluating. Unions have long sought to replace merit considerations with seniority, and in many production situations they have been successful. Yet procedures such as field review, rater training, constant monitoring of results, and higher-level review can help to maintain effective programs. It may also prove necessary to use different types of approaches for different purposes. In any event, it is well to be aware of the possible legal pitfalls that can arise in connection with performance evaluation.

QUESTIONS

1. What is the evidence on the value of rater training programs? Should they replace detailed written instructions to raters?

2. How can mixed standard scales, behavioral observation scales, and behavioral expectation scales be differentiated from one another? Which appears to be superior?

3. It has been claimed that the best rating methods are the least widely used, and the worst methods are the most popular. Why might this be?

4. What special problems are associated with the use of ranking and paired comparisons? How can these be overcome?

5. If you were faced with the problem of introducing a performance evaluation system into a unionized production unit where high levels of resistance were to be anticipated from first-line supervision and the union, what approach would you take?

6. How may discrimination against minorities or women become manifest in performance ratings? What may be the consequences when this occurs?

7. When might it be appropriate to use simulations in evaluation? When would essay evaluations seem to be desirable?

8. Distinguish between constant errors and errors of central tendency. Would you expect one to yield more halo error? Explain.

9. What can be done to minimize the probability that a performance rating system will be judged negatively by the courts?

10. Distinguish between the following rating methods:
    a. Paired comparison and forced choice
    b. Scaled expectation and forced distribution
    c. Rating scales and employee comparison systems

CASE PROBLEM

Performance Appraisal: The Rated Ranking Technique at Georgia Kaolin

A plant manager needed a performance appraisal system for hourly employees; there had been no such system in the past, and promotions to more skilled positions had been based on seniority and test scores. Based on recommendations by an industrial psychologist, an appraisal system was introduced. The objective was to provide a criterion for validating the tests.

Job analyses covering the forty-seven jobs involved produced results much like those for filter operators listed in Box 13-2. These job analysis results were the basis for the appraisal system. The appraisals were obtained in face-to-face interviews with the twenty-one foremen, each of whom described the six to nineteen hourly employees reporting to him. The instructions went as follows:

Initially, I will ask you to rank your employees in order, on an aspect of their performance, and then to give a rating for their performance on that aspect. Thus there will be both a ranking and a rating for each of the five kinds of performance: verbal task performance, mathematical task performance, judgmental task performance, new task performance, and overall task performance. Two things are important:

1. You should evaluate the individual only on the specific job aspect under consideration (verbal, mathematical, etc.).
2. You should evaluate the individual relative to the specific job noted (i.e., filter operator).

The foreman then received a sheet such as the following, indicating the aspect of performance to be considered and the individuals to be evaluated:

Verbal Task Performance

Relative to the requirements of the particular job noted, how effective is the individual in performing the various verbal tasks involved? This may include reading job-related materials, writing as necessary, oral expression to others on subjects related to the work, and understanding oral communications from others.

The instructions were:

Here are the employees to be evaluated and the first aspect of performance. [The names and the description of the first aspect were then read.]

James Anthony, 6 & 7 Filters Operator

Sanford Davenport, Chemical Mixer—Forklift

Maxwell Freeman, Cage Dryer Operator

John Lloyd, Extra Operator

Talbert MacIntosh, 12 & 13 Filters Operator

Stanley Patterson, Extra Operator

O. T. Reilley, Centrifuge Operator

Donald Santini, Assistant Centrifuge Operator

Albert Vance, Assistant Leaching Operator

M. V. Wasco, Leaching Operator

Of those listed, tell me who is the highest on this aspect. [Once the name was recorded, the process continued.] Now tell me who is the person who is not as good as any of the others on this aspect. [After recording] Now, of those remaining, who is the highest on this aspect? [And again, after the name was recorded] Who of the remaining is not as good?

When this ranking process was completed, the recorded results looked as follows:

Foreman _____ Greenberg _____

Verbal

	Rank	Rating
1.	Santini	
2.	Anthony	
3.	Reilley	
4.	Lloyd	
5.	Wasco	
6.	Freeman	
7.	Patterson	
8.	Vance	
9.	MacIntosh	
10.	Davenport	

Then the following rating scale was given to the foreman.

Rating Scale

An outstanding performer	Performance is entirely satisfactory but no
A very good performer	more than that
A good performer	Performs at somewhat
Performs at somewhat above a satisfactory level	below a satisfactory level
	A poor performer

The instructions were:

> Now we have a comparative ranking of these employees' performance in this particular regard. But we still need to know how good each one really is. Here is a rating scale I want you to apply to these people. Let's take Santini, whom you have ranked at the top. Is he outstanding?

If the "outstanding" label was rejected, each one below it was tested until a suitable designation was found. The rating process then shifted to Davenport at the bottom, Anthony at the top, MacIntosh at the bottom, and so on until all were rated. The resulting ranks and ratings as recorded on the evaluation form then looked as follows:

Foreman _____ Greenberg _____

Verbal

	Rank	Rating
1.	Santini	Outstanding
2.	Anthony	Very good
3.	Reilley	Very good
4.	Lloyd	Good
5.	Wasco	Above satisfactory
6.	Freeman	Above satisfactory
7.	Patterson	Above satisfactory
8.	Vance	Satisfactory
9.	MacIntosh	Satisfactory
10.	Davenport	Poor

Each foreman carried out an identical evaluation process using the following additional aspects of performance and applying them to the same employees:

Mathematical task performance. Relative to the requirements of the particular job noted, how effective is the individual in performing the various mathematical tasks involved? This may include counting and various types of numerical calculations required by the work.

Judgmental task performance. Relative to the requirements of the particular job noted, how effective is the individual in performing the various judgmental tasks involved? This may include making decisions regarding equipment operation and maintenance, product quality, production levels, and in other areas.

New task performance. Relative to the requirements of the particular job noted, how effective has the individual been in learning to perform new tasks? This may involve the initial learning of the job or the learning of new tasks as job changes occur.

Overall task performance. Relative to the requirements of the particular job noted, how effective is the individual in performing the job as a whole? This would include the performance of verbal tasks, numerical tasks, judgmental tasks, new tasks, and any other aspects of the job that you consider important for overall performance.

The order in which the four task-performance dimensions (verbal, mathematical, judgmental, and new) were presented was varied to eliminate any order effects. The overall task performance measure always came last. The foreman gave each employee a score between 1 (poor) and 7 (outstanding) for each rating dimension, thus producing the rated ranks. For Sam Greenberg's crew the results were those indicated in the table on page 444.

Clearly, Don Santini and Jim Anthony were the top performers. Although no one was less than satisfactory overall, Sandy Davenport had some major problems in the areas of verbal and new task performance. When all twenty-one foremen had completed their work, scores like these were available for 185 individuals. Of these, fourteen had scores of 7 overall and thirteen had scores of 1. On balance, Sam Greenberg's group was somewhat above average.

Analysis of the data from all foremen indicated the following:

1. When different foremen rated the same people (because of rotating shift assignments), agree-

	Verbal Performance	Mathematical Performance	Judgmental Performance	New Task Performance	Overall Performance
Santini	7	5	7	7	7
Anthony	6	6	6	7	7
Reilley	6	6	5	6	5
Lloyd	5	6	5	6	5
Wasco	4	5	4	5	5
Freeman	4	4	5	3	5
Patterson	4	5	3	5	5
Vance	3	4	3	3	3
MacIntosh	3	3	3	3	3
Davenport	1	3	3	2	3

ment was reasonably good on the four aspects of performance and very good for overall performance.

2. The rated rankings showed some tendency to concentrate on the middle scores, with fewer extreme 1s and 7s. However, this tendency was not pronounced and in general scores were well spread, with the average just above 4.

3. Groups working for different foremen showed differences, as average overall-performance scores for a group ranged from 3.3 (somewhat higher than satisfactory) to 5.4 (above good). Sixty-three percent of the groups scored from 3 to 4, 21 percent from 4 to 5, and 16 percent from 5 to 6.

4. The various types of performance were positively related to each other and to a substantial degree, although no more than is typically found with other ratings procedures. Of the four dimensions, mathematical performance showed less correlation.

5. When the test of mathematical ability used previously in selecting individuals for promotion was compared with these rated rankings, it showed a good relationship with the mathematical rated ranking score, but considerably lower relationships with the other performance measures.

6. The performance measures were unrelated to age and company seniority, but blacks consistently scored below whites.

7. Comparisons of performance evaluation data obtained from black and from white foremen indicated that they all tended to rate their black employees as average, and to approximately the same degree. The black employees generally had fewer years of education than the whites.

8. Although the company had not previously collected performance information, the foremen had no difficulty in following the instructions and providing the necessary data.

Questions

1. How effective is this rated ranking procedure in dealing with the various types of error and bias that may plague rating scales? Be specific.

2. What do you think the results would have been if, instead of foremen doing the ranking and rating, individual employees had scored themselves?

3. How would you evaluate the rated ranking technique, as contrasted with ranking alone, for the various purposes noted in Exhibit 15-6?

16

Research Designs and Selection Models

Research was carried out among clerical workers operating different types of office machines at Atlantic-Richfield. Study 1 was concurrent in nature. The objective was to determine the validity of various tests and background factors as predictors of success. The criteria, obtained at essentially the same time as the tests, were supervisory ratings. Analyses produced evidence of meaningful predictor–criterion relationships for a personality test, the Tomkins-Horn Picture Arrangement Test, and the number of years of prior experience working with office machines that the individual possessed. The personality measures dealt with such characteristics as work motivation, conformity, conscience, and emotional pathology. The validity coefficients obtained when test data and years of experience were combined into a single predictor score were as follows for the various paired-comparison rating measures used (see Box 15-3):

Cooperation with peers and superiors	0.58
Application to the work	0.66
Accuracy of work	0.82
Speed of production	0.53
Overall effectiveness	0.82

Study 2 extended the preceding analyses forward in time. The thirty-five individuals from study 1 who were still with the company a year later were rerated at that time. In addition, twenty-three people who assumed machine operator positions during the intervening year were tested at the time they assumed their positions and their performance rated along with the thirty-five. On the average, this longitudinal analysis extended over an interval of 9.5 months from testing to performance evaluation. The predictive validity coefficients were:

Cooperation with peers and superiors	0.43
Application to the work	0.50
Accuracy of work	0.69
Speed of production	0.40
Overall effectiveness	0.61

On the average, predictive validity is approximately 0.15 point lower than concurrent validity, but it is still substantial and the coefficients all remain statistically significant. At least in this instance, a personality test remained effective when validated using a longitudinal model.

These are examples of various approaches to the selection process and the validation of predictors that will subsequently be used to make hiring decisions. We will consider these and other selection models in this chapter. The focus is on research approaches used to improve selection. Before turning to these specifically selection-oriented research designs, however, it may prove helpful to review what has been said about research design generally throughout this book.

As indicated in Chapter 1, discussion of research and research design is not concentrated in one place in this book. The objective has been to discuss various design considerations as they arose, thus making them as relevant as possible. However, this chapter does contain a substantial dose of research design. The reason is that the entire logic of the selec-

tion process is embedded in design considerations.

A comprehensive understanding of research design in industrial-organizational psychology requires much more than is contained in this chapter. Discussions are sprinkled throughout Part Two. Chapter 2 contains a treatment of how pretest–posttest control group designs are used to evaluate training (see Exhibit 2-3) and an example of the after-only approach to training evaluation (Box 2-4). In Chapter 3 the pretest–posttest control group design is described as applied to the evaluation of achievement motivation training (see Exhibit 3-3). Chapter 4 also treats control group designs, first as used at Georgia Kraft Company to evaluate goal setting (see Box 4-1) and then as used by Florida state government to evaluate flextime (see Exhibit

4-7); also in this chapter is an explanation of the ABAB design as it is used in organizational behavior modification (see Exhibit 4-9). In Chapter 5 moderator analysis is described using growth-need strength as a moderator variable (see Exhibit 5-3). Chapter 6 contains a description of a study conducted at Sears, Roebuck using the longitudinal prediction model (Box 6-1); this model is discussed in much greater detail in the present chapter.

Chapter 7 develops moderator analysis further, describing a study of group processes where self-esteem was used as a moderator (see Exhibit 7-6). In Chapter 8 testimonials based on subjective appraisal are distinguished from research studies; Box 8-5 provides examples of testimonials regarding quality circles emanating from Hughes Aircraft. Chapter 9 contains two more instances of studies in which control group designs were used to evaluate training—leader match at Sears, Roebuck (Box 9-3) and human relations approaches at International Harvester (Box 9-4). In Chapter 10, Exhibit 10-4 plots changes in experimental and control group productivity as they relate to training in cultivating in-group relationships. In Chapter 11 a control group design used to evaluate an organization development intervention at the Tennessee Valley Authority (Box 11-5) is described. These are not all the points at which design factors are considered, but a review of them in conjunction with the treatment in this chapter can provide a good overview of the topic.

This chapter is devoted to a general treatment of the logic of selection. It should be read with a full understanding of the material covered in the Statistical Appendix at the end of the book. Much of our knowledge in this area was originally developed with reference to psychological testing. However, these approaches have much wider applicability, and the considerations involved are just as relevant for interviews, application blanks, and the other selection procedures as they are

for psychological tests (Schmitt & Klimoski, 1991). Basically, we shall be concerned with the various methods used to relate the preemployment, or preplacement, data on an individual to indexes of the degree of matching between actual role behaviors and role expectations. As noted in Chapter 15, the latter measures usually are referred to as **criteria** in the selection context.

Increasingly in recent years, practice in this area has been influenced by various guidelines issued by federal government agencies and by certain principles set forth by the Society for Industrial and Organizational Psychology. Because these two sources serve different purposes—the one legal and the other professional—they differ in various respects (Bartlett, Grant, & Hakel, 1982). Yet both make clear the massive impact that legal issues have had on the selection context.

■ THE LONGITUDINAL PREDICTION MODEL

The logic of the selection process has been most completely developed in what has been called the classical longitudinal prediction model (Guion, 1987). When a selection measure meets the requirements of this model, it is said to possess **predictive validity.** There are two major variants, or cases, involved, although each may be applied in several different ways.

□ Case 1: Single Predictor

Step 1. Study the job or group of related jobs for which selection is to occur in order to identify characteristics that might be related to success. These might be intellectual abilities, personality factors, types of prior experience, physical attributes, or anything else that can be measured prior to actual job placement.

Step 2. Decide on the specific measures of these characteristics to be used. If verbal ability is a potential predictor, is it to be estimated from an interview or measured by a test? If a test, which one?

Step 3. Obtain these predictor measures on a relatively large group of job applicants or candidates. Then hire from this group without reference to the predictor data. That is, select the individuals to be employed without looking at the measures obtained and without taking this information into account in any way. This ideally means random selection; otherwise employment decisions should be made by a person other than the one conducting the study. If the measures are used to select those who will be hired at this initial stage, and these predictors do have some validity, only relatively good performers will be found on the job, and the possibility of identifying predictors that differentiate between good and poor performers will be to that degree lost. The sample may be accumulated over time as hirings occur, but there should be a bare minimum of thirty individuals in the hired group and preferably many more—ideally over 100.

It is important to recognize that when using the predictor to select in the validation study cannot be entirely avoided, there are statistical approaches that can be applied to compensate for the effects. This type of so-called **correction for restriction of range** has been found to be quite useful in a variety of contexts (Lee, Miller, & Graham, 1982; Linn, Harnisch, & Dunbar, 1981).

Step 4. Gather criterion data on the individuals hired after such information becomes available. The measure used may be any of those discussed in Chapters 14 and 15. Usually these data are not suitable for use as criteria until after the individual has been on the job long enough for performance levels to stabilize.

Step 5. Determine the degree of relationship between the predictor values and the criterion values. Usually, a correlation coefficient is used to indicate the degree of this

relationship. The specific statistical index of correlation may vary, depending on the distribution of predictor and criterion values in the group, but in any event, the result will be a coefficient ranging from -1.00 through 0 to $+1.00$, with the larger values, both negative and positive, indicating a closer relationship between predictor and criterion. The larger the coefficient, the greater the predictive validity of the measure taken before hiring.

A simple chart of the relationship may be established if a summary statement of the kind a correlation coefficient provides is not needed. Thus, at each level on the predictor index, the number of people falling at each point on the criterion would be indicated as follows, assuming a sample of fifty:

	Criterion Values				
Predictor Values	*1*	*2*	*3*	*4*	*5*
5			1	2	2
4		2	1	4	3
3	2	2	12	4	
2	1	5	4		
1	2	1	2		

It is not necessary to compute a correlation coefficient from this chart to ascertain that a predictor is rather closely and positively related to a criterion.

Box 16-1 provides an example of how this single-predictor model was used by the U.S. Army to validate an instrument for selecting officer candidate school trainees.

☐ Case 2: Multiple Predictors

Most jobs are not so simple that a single measure of a single predictor is sufficient to yield maximum results. Normally, the best predictions are obtained when a number of predictors measuring a variety of characteristics are combined in some manner.

Steps 1 through 4 are essentially the same

BOX 16-1   RESEARCH IN I/O PSYCHOLOGY

Prediction of Success in Completing the U.S. Army's Branch Immaterial Officer Candidate Course at Ft. Benning, Georgia

The objective was to determine whether a measure of managerial motivation developed in accordance with hierarchic role-motivation theory (see Chapter 3) would predict failure to complete the Army's officer training program. For a variety of reasons, including voluntary withdrawals and poor performance, a number of candidates did not complete the fifteen-week course and thus failed to receive appointments as commissioned officers. The Army wanted to identify as many of these so-called attrittees as possible before the program started, so that they could be weeded out and the expense of investing in them avoided. This was the objective of the validation research.

The single predictor used was a multiple-choice instrument containing seventy items covering the various motivational patterns of the hierarchic role-motivation theory. This instrument was administered to two consecutive previously selected classes at the very beginning of the training. In all, 251 candidates were tested in this manner prior to starting training. At the end of the fifteen weeks, 222 remained and were appointed as commissioned officers.

The correlation between test scores and the criterion of graduation–nongraduation was 0.36. It appeared that attrittees were less competitive, less assertive, and less desirous of standing out from a group in a unique role. The evidence clearly indicated that the predictor could make a useful contribution to identifying those unlikely to complete the training.

SOURCE: Based on Richard P. Butler, Charles L. Lardent, & John B. Miner (1983). A motivational basis for turnover in military officer education and training. *Journal of Applied Psychology, 68,* 500–503.

---

under multiple prediction as they are when predictors are validated separately. The major difference emerges in step 5. Some solution must be developed to the problem of combining the various factors in such a way as to maximally predict job success. There are a number of approaches to this problem.

Multiple Correlation. In multiple correlation, the correlations between the predictors are computed, as well as the correlations between various predictors and the criterion. A multiple-correlation coefficient is then derived that represents a maximal index of the relationship, one that automatically weights the separate predictors in order to yield the best prediction of the criterion. So-called **regression weights** may then be developed. The values obtained by an individual on the

various measures may be multiplied by these weights and then combined to produce an estimate of the chances for job success.

Additive Correlation. Additive correlation is essentially an approximation procedure for the multiple correlation coefficient. It involves adding the values obtained by an individual on all the predictors together and then computing the correlation between this composite index and the criterion. Rather surprisingly, this technique does yield a close approximation to the results obtained from the multiple-correlation approach when the predictors have much the same standard deviations.

Multiple-Cutoff Prediction. In multiple-cutoff prediction, the predictors are utilized one at a time rather than in combination. Thus, correlations are computed as in case 1 for each of the predictors. Then the predictor that consistently produced the highest relationship with the criterion is identified, and some value is established as minimally satisfactory for employment. All candidates who fall below this value are screened out; all others continue as candidates. These remaining individuals must then meet a similar test based on the predictor having the second highest correlation with the criterion. This process of successive screening out is continued until all predictors exhibiting a consistent relationship to the criterion are exhausted. Those who at least equal the minimum satisfactory value on all predictors are hired. Normally, three or four such hurdles are all that are required. Beyond that, very little predictive power is added.

Profile Matching.   In profile matching, the scores on all valid predictors for those particular employees who prove to be successful are averaged. These average scores then serve to describe what a successful employee would look like; they may be used to constitute an ideal profile for comparison purposes. Candidates are matched against this profile, and those whose scores most nearly approximate the ideal on the predictors included in the profile are selected for employment. The degree of match may be calculated by simply adding the absolute values of all deviations from the ideal values.

Clinical Prediction.   With clinical prediction, the combining of predictors is accomplished on the basis of personal experience and without resort to statistical aids. The result is a decision that takes into account all the information available but weights the different measures and factors on a largely intuitive basis.

A study of decision processes used by experienced managers in selecting individuals for international assignments provides an example of clinical prediction (Miller, 1973). Such considerations as proved performance in a similar job, leadership skills and the ability to command respect, general perceptiveness and grasp of problems, and administrative skills were consistently weighted heavily in reaching the selection decision. In contrast, spouses' attitudes toward overseas assignment, past performance overseas, ability to work with foreign employees, and potential for advancement to a more responsible position were viewed as much less important and had relatively little influence on the assignment decision. Whether or not these are the most appropriate priorities, it is clear that the process involved here operates in a manner not unlike the use of statistical regression weights. However, when feasible, the statistical procedures are to be preferred.

Cross-Validation.   The approaches noted do not cover all possible ways of combining predictors, but they do provide an idea of the methods used and the issues involved. From what has been said, it should be apparent that if the number of predictors and/or criteria considered is rather large, some predictors may emerge as statistically significant by chance alone in their relationships to criteria; when actually used for day-to-day selection, they would not operate with the same validity as the validity study implied. This raises the issue of cross-validation, a sixth step beyond those considered in the single-predictor case. Normally, cross-validation is not needed in the single-predictor situation because capitalization on chance fluctuations is less of a problem.

If the results of step 5 indicate a relatively good validity, then under most circumstances a second study should be carried out on the same job using the same predictor and criterion measures. This is called the **cross-validation** and is undertaken because any relationship established in the first group might have been due to a mere chance fluctuation. A sec-

BOX **16-2**   RESEARCH IN I/O PSYCHOLOGY

Using Cross-Validation in the Development of an Integrity Test at Intergram, Inc.

Intergram, Inc. wished to develop an integrity (or honesty) test to replace its polygraph (lie detector) business, which had fallen off substantially due to state and then federal legislation restricting the use of the polygraph. Possible test items were written and then administered to samples of people who had passed and people who had failed the polygraph. By comparing the responses obtained in the two groups, it was possible to identify certain test items that discriminated between the two groups—that seemed to identify the more honest people as determined by the polygraph, and the less honest. Included in this initial study were 200 people who passed the polygraph, and another 200 who did not.

The test items that discriminated the best were made into a new test and administered to a new, cross-validation sample of 100 people who also took the polygraph. The resulting correlation between test score and polygraph result was 0.34. This result, although statistically significant, was deemed to be capable of improvement.

Accordingly, a new pool of possible test items was developed and the whole procedure repeated. This time the test–polygraph correlation in the cross-validation sample of 100 was 0.51.

The next step was to combine the results of the two studies. The best items from each, the ones that discriminated the most effectively between those who passed and those who failed the polygraph, were put into a single test of eighty-two items. Then another cross-validation study was undertaken with this composite measure, again using polygraph results as the criterion. Again 100 individuals were studied. The correlation now obtained, when the best items from the previous two studies were included, was 0.64. Based on this result, the eighty-two-item test was considered to be suitable as a substitute for the polygraph. Subsequent improvements in scoring raised the validity coefficient to 0.69. When the test was administered to a group of prison inmates, the scores were very low, as anticipated.

ond study is done to be more confident that the relationship is there and that it can be relied on subsequently when people who obtain high values on the predictor are actually selected for employment.

Obtaining a cross-validation sample is not always easy, especially if there is some urgency about getting the selection procedure into use as soon as possible. Under these circumstances, it has been relatively common practice to collect data on both groups at once. Thus, if 100 persons are hired for a job, the total group may be split in half, with the initial validation done on one subsample and the cross-validation on the other. In any event, step 6 should be carried out.

A preferable procedure to splitting the original sample is to study two independent groups—two shifts, two locations, early and late applicant groups, and the like. This is more consistent with the idea of seeing if predictors established in a validity study hold up in practice.

It should be noted also that there are statistical procedures for predicting how well a set of predictors might work out in a cross-validation analysis; under some circumstances, these may be preferable to actual cross-validation. However, the evidence is mixed on this point, and it is not possible to give a carte blanche endorsement of the obviously much easier to use statistical approaches (Cattin, 1980; Mitchell & Klimoski, 1986; Murphy, 1983).

Box 16-2 provides an example of how cross-validation was used at Intergram in the

EXHIBIT 16-1   Original Validation and Cross-Validation Results for Various Predictors of Success among Females in Officer Training

Predictors	Correlation with Subsequent Success in Officer Training	
	Original Training Group	Cross-Validation Group One Year Later
Intelligence test	0.18	0.19
Peer ratings from noncommissioned officer training	0.34	0.26
Superior ratings of noncommissioned officer performance	0.13	0.18
Selection interview ratings of officer potential	0.17	0.12
Multiple correlation	0.39	0.33

SOURCE: Adapted from Aharon Tziner & Shimon Dolan (1982). Evaluation of a traditional selection system in predicting success in females in officer training. *Journal of Occupational Psychology, 55,* 271–272.

development of an integrity test. In this instance validity coefficients were not even computed in the initial samples of 400, because it was assumed that only what happened in the cross-validation analyses would be truly meaningful. Exhibit 16-1 provides another example of how cross-validation works. Here it is possible to compare validation and cross-validation results. Note the often-found tendency for the highest correlation, and in particular the multiple correlation, to decrease with cross-validation. Yet all values in Exhibit 16-1 are statistically significant.

■ THE CONCURRENT MODEL

The **concurrent validity** approach is identical to that of longitudinal prediction, with one very important exception: The predictor and criterion measures are obtained at roughly the same time, usually on individuals who have been employed for a considerable period in the job to be studied. Thus, there is no long wait after the predictor data have been obtained to collect the criterion information. Either case 1 or case 2 may be applied, and

the cross-validation is done on a second sample selected from among current employees.

This procedure is admittedly a shortcut and as such has certain deficiencies. For one thing, the motivation of present employees in taking a test or filling out a questionnaire or even in an interview situation may be quite different from that of job applicants: They may not try as hard. Yet the results are to be applied to an applicant group. This can introduce considerable error into the selection process, especially when measures of interests and certain kinds of personality tests are used. With physical examinations, intelligence tests, application blank data, and the like, it probably matters little.

Second, the results obtained from certain measures may be largely a function of job tenure. Thus, indexes of job knowledge may yield higher scores the longer the person has been on the job. This can produce rather misleading results when the job-knowledge measure is used as a predictor in an applicant group, none of whom have had prior experience in that particular type of work. If, however, one is aware of this problem, appropriate statistical procedures can be used to take the effects of job tenure out of the results.

Thus, this potential source of error can be eliminated. Also, cognitive ability tests appear to be relatively free of this source of error (Barrett, Phillips, & Alexander, 1981).

It is also possible with some predictors that success or failure on the job may serve to determine the predictor values obtained, rather than the reverse. In a study conducted among AT&T managers, consistent decreases in personal satisfaction were found over eight years of employment among the less successful managers, while personal satisfaction increased among the more successful managers (Bray, Campbell, & Grant, 1974). Clearly, any predictor–criterion correlation involving personal satisfaction established from a concurrent study would not necessarily be replicated under the more exacting conditions of a longitudinal prediction study; nor would a concurrent study conducted early in the eight-year period yield the same result as a concurrent study carried out later, when the satisfaction effects had begun to emerge.

The example from Atlantic-Richfield at the beginning of this chapter describes a research program in which both concurrent and predictive validity data were obtained. In this instance the concurrent correlations were higher, but the selection measures remained effective with a longitudinal analysis. Nevertheless, it is true that measures of attitudes, interests, and certain personality characteristics are vulnerable to substantial changes in validity when shifts from concurrent to predictive measurement are made.

This discussion of longitudinal and concurrent models has covered the major variants in each case. However, it is well to recognize that a variety of approaches of both kinds exists. Some differ little from one another, but the differences may be sufficient to make it desirable to use one or the other in specific instances. A recent review noted eleven different criterion-related validation designs that can be used for selection (Sussman & Robertson, 1986).

■ OTHER APPROACHES TO VALIDATION

Although the methods just described are the most widely used in personnel selection, certain other approaches to validation require discussion. Several of these approaches have taken on particular significance because they have been mentioned in the various guidelines for compliance with equal employment opportunity legislation issued by federal enforcement agencies. Others represent extensions or variants of the basic criterion-related approaches that have particular value in special circumstances or for solving certain kinds of problems.

☐ Content and Construct Validity

There are two types of rational validation for selection procedures that are recognized in compliance guidelines. The first of these, **content validity,** involves a systematic study of a job to establish the knowledge, skills, and behaviors that are required; an appropriate selection procedure is then developed on a judgmental basis. Most of the tests of job knowledge utilized by the government in connection with meeting civil service requirements rely on such content validity. Another example might be a typing test used to select people for jobs in a typing pool. Typically, content validity is strongly grounded in job analysis (Schmitt & Ostroff, 1986; Schneider & Schmitt, 1986).

It is important to distinguish this approach from **face validity.** Content validity involves a judgment by an expert that the selection procedure is in fact job-related. Face validity, on the other hand, involves merely an impression of appropriateness on the part of the person completing a measure. Thus, numerical items may be written with reference to actual store products and prices to make them look appropriate to applicants for positions as retail sales clerks. This is face validity. But the computations involved could be so much more complex than those actually required on the job that the test items are totally irrelevant. Under such circumstances, one would have face validity without content validity. Normally, content-valid procedures do appear face-valid, but the reverse need not be true.

Construct validity refers not so much to job behaviors and skills as to underlying characteristics of the job performer, such as verbal ability or achievement motivation. For construct validity to apply, the theoretical construct must be well defined. The selection procedure must be known to be a measure of the construct, and an important aspect of job behavior must involve the construct. Establishing such validity involves rational inference from a body of research. Thus, a measure of achievement motivation must be shown to relate to other measures of the same construct while having less relationship to other motivational constructs—social motivation, conformity motivation, and the like. At the same time, there must be good reason to believe that the construct is important in a certain kind of work, as achievement motivation is in entrepreneurial activities, for instance.

Although it is recognized in federal guidelines, content validity has proved difficult for the courts to comprehend and utilize effectively (Barrett, 1980; Scharf, 1980). Judges' opinions and expert testimony are often contradictory and confused. Thus it is difficult to predict the outcome of a case in which the defense is based solely on content-validity evidence. Construct validity as such has rarely been used alone as a defense. In a basic sense, construct validity underlies the other types. Both content- and criterion-related validity evidence can be used to contribute to the understanding of constructs. In this sense, the three types of validity are really one, and construct validity is the primary concept.

What is added in construct validation per se is a rational, theoretical understanding of basic constructs and how they may be used and influenced.

☐ Moderator Variables

Moderator variables are characteristics used to divide a sample of employees into two or more groups, so that predictor–criterion correlations may be calculated in each group separately. The reason for doing this is that a predictor may be very effective in one group, but when this group is combined with another in which the predictor is not effective, the overall result may be useless for selection purposes. Thus, for a group as a whole, the predictor–criterion correlation might be 0.19. When this group is divided into two subgroups, however, on the basis of some moderator variable, the results might be as follows:

Subgroup 1: $r = 0.48$

Subgroup 2: $r = 0.04$

In this instance, the initial correlation (r) of 0.19 would appear to be of little practical significance; the correlation of 0.04 for subgroup 2 is even worse. But for subgroup 1, a truly effective predictor has been identified (provided that cross-validation yields a similar result). Thus, one would use this predictor for selecting among job applicants of the type represented by subgroup 1 and then would attempt to identify some other predictor that could be used with applicants of the subgroup 2 type.

A number of different types of moderator variables have been used. Under the impact of equal employment opportunity legislation, race has been used often, with separate validities calculated for blacks and whites. Work satisfaction has been utilized to separate out subgroups that are more and less satisfied. Various measures of motivation have also been used in order to permit validation of predictors separately for highly motivated workers and for those with less motivation.

Perhaps the greatest problem with this approach is that it may identify a number of good predictors for one subgroup yet leave another subgroup practically without useful measures for selection purposes. It may prove impossible to find procedures that can be shown to be valid for a sizable subset within the normal applicant population. In addition, the use of moderator variables requires a large number of individuals to start with. By the time two or three subgroups have been formed for both first and cross-validation samples, each group may be so small that the results have little meaning.

A possible solution to the sample-size problem involves the use of multiple-correlation procedures that combine predictor, criterion, and moderator data in a manner which approximates the moderator variable research design. Such an approach has been rather widely used. However, there are certain remaining statistical problems with this approach which raise questions regarding its use to identify moderator effects under at least some circumstances (Dunlap & Kemery, 1987).

☐ Utility Analysis in Selection

Another approach that has fostered considerable discussion, even though because of its complexity it has not been widely applied in practice, derives originally from mathematical decision theory (Cronbach & Gleser, 1965). According to this view, the ultimate purpose of any predictor is to assist in making a decision as to what should be done with a given applicant or candidate, and therefore the soundest approach to evaluating a measure is through determining the benefits that accrue to the total organization as a result of a particular decision. The utility concept is used to provide an index of value. **Utility** is defined in terms of the benefits that accrue from a given set of decisions, less the total costs incurred in the decision-making process.

Although a detailed mathematical treatment is not contemplated here, it is possible to describe the basic elements of this approach. There is, first, certain information regarding the individual—interview data, a completed application blank, test scores, and the like. Second, there are various treatments that may be utilized depending on the decision made—hire the applicant, reject the applicant, collect further information. Third, the outcomes of decisions are expressed in terms of various criterion values, which may be based on ratings and objective indexes. Finally, there are the utilities attached to the various outcomes: the benefits, less the costs, derived from having an individual perform effectively in a given type of work or the net benefit derived from rejecting an individual with somewhat different characteristics.

Probabilities are attached to these factors and a matrix constructed so that it is possible to evaluate each applicant in terms of expected value to the firm should the person be hired for a particular position. One difficulty with this approach is that good measures of the utilities associated with various decision outcomes often are not available. Solutions to this problem have been proposed, but there has been little agreement on which is best, or even whether any are appropriate. In spite of widespread expectations that utility analysis would become the major approach in selection, it has not progressed very rapidly over the years. A recent comment based on an extensive review of the literature appears appropriate (Guion & Gibson, 1988, p. 355):

> We find the research on utility theory diverse and disjointed, and we wonder where it is leading. Should the emphasis be upon making accurate predictions of utility gains? . . . we do not see this as an achievable purpose at least at present. Should the purpose be to determine rela-

Exhibit 16-2   Overview of Descriptive Statistics for Validity Generalization Analysis of Law Enforcement Officer Selection Studies

	Criteria	
	Success in Training	*Success on the Job*
Number of validity coefficients	138	242
Percentage of coefficients taken from published studies	55	43
Percentage of coefficients from predictive as opposed to concurrent studies	71	30
Mean sample size	142	92
Mean observed validity for all tests studied (primarily cognitive abilities)	0.36	0.13

SOURCE: Adapted from Hannah R. Hirsh, Lois C. Northrup, & Frank L. Schmidt (1986). Validity generalization results for law enforcement occupations. *Personnel Psychology, 39,* 401.

tive utilities of alternative selection procedures? We suspect that such comparisons will do little more than favor the more valid procedures over those that are less valid.

At the present time it seems that we may have expected more of utility analysis in selection than it can deliver. The procedure relies on highly subjective judgmental decisions at various points, and it is here that appropriate solutions have proved most elusive (Mathieu & Tannenbaum, 1989; Orr, Sackett, & Mercer, 1989).

☐ Validity Generalization

The general implication of federal selection guidelines has been that selection measures should be validated in every situation where they are used. Transportability of a validation from one context to another—say, one plant or one company to another—is viewed as appropriate only when the contexts can be shown to be substantially the same.

This type of formulation increasingly has come under attack. Formulas have been developed that make it possible to determine whether differences in results obtained with a

particular predictor or type of predictor across a number of studies can be attributed to statistical artifacts and chance variations (Hunter, Schmidt, & Jackson, 1982). Thus, when a predictor has been used a great deal in research, it is possible to say whether a real relationship exists between that predictor and criteria and thus whether **validity generalization** to unstudied contexts is warranted. Exhibit 16-2 provides an overview of what goes into a validity generalization analysis.

Findings from this type of analysis have been striking (Schmidt, Gast-Rosenberg, and Hunter, 1980; Schmidt, Hunter, & Pearlman, 1981). Cognitive ability tests, such as those of general intelligence, numerical ability, and perceptual speed, have been shown to possess good validity across a wide range of clerical jobs. A cognitive measure of aptitude for computer programming has been found to be highly valid over a great diversity of contexts and settings. These findings do not preclude the operation of situational effects and moderator variables of various kinds. They do suggest that such contingent differences may be fewer and smaller in size in the selection area than many have thought.

In actuality there are a number of different analytical procedures used in validity generalization. One review identified nine distinct procedures (Linn & Dunbar, 1986). However, where these variants have been compared they generally have been found to yield quite similar results (Burke, Raju, & Pearlman, 1986). On the other hand, there do appear to be certain problems remaining to be solved before the validity generalization approach can be relied upon fully (Kemery, Mossholder, & Roth, 1987; Spector & Levine, 1987). Some of the statistical formulas need further development. Under certain circumstances, transportability is indicated when it appears not to be warranted. Analyses based on too few studies (and coefficients) can prove misleading. There is no question that validity generalization continues to generate its share of controversy (James, Demaree, Mulaik, & Mumford, 1988; Schmidt, Hunter, & Raju, 1988).

■ RELIABILITY

In validation research, reliability may be at issue both in the predictor and in the criterion. To the extent that unreliability is present in either measure, it tends to reduce the size of the validity coefficients rather than inflate them.

Reliability means that if one makes the same measurement twice, the same result will be obtained both times. To the extent that this is not true, the measure is said to be unreliable. Thus, if one uses a ruler made of wood or metal to measure a distance twice, it is probable that almost identical results will be obtained. But if one tries to do the same thing with a thin rubber ruler, the results will depend on the tension induced, and the two measures may not yield the same results at all. Unfortunately, psychological measurement often seems to be like the situation with the rubber ruler: Consistency or stability of

measurement may be quite low, making it very difficult to achieve successful prediction. Prediction with unreliable predictor and criterion measures is like trying to hit a target that is in constant, erratic motion—with a rifle that cannot be aimed consistently. There is a good chance of missing.

A variety of procedures have been developed to measure reliability, although the typical outcome, a correlation coefficient, is the same in all cases. The various procedures tend to yield somewhat different values for this reliability coefficient, but the results should be sufficiently close so that the procedures may be considered interchangeable for practical purposes.

□ Test-Retest Reliability

The **test-retest approach** requires a second measurement at some time subsequent to the first and then correlation of the scores obtained in the two time periods. Thus a manager might rate subordinates on two different occasions, or the same test data might be collected over two different time periods. A major question relates to the interval between measurements. It is essential that the two measures be independent of one another in the sense that one does not directly determine the other. Thus the interval should be sufficient so that memory effects are unlikely to determine the results. On the other hand, too long an interval increasingly confounds true and valid change in people with unreliability of measurement; this makes the reliability seem less than it is. The answer to the interval question, then, is that the measures should be taken as close together as possible without compromising independence.

□ Parallel-Form Reliability

One way of avoiding the independence problem is to use two different measures of the same construct. Because the measures are actually different, memory effects cannot operate, and the two forms may be used with a relatively short time interval between them.

The problem, of course, with the **parallel-form approach** is that two measures must be developed and shown to yield the same results before one can go on and do a reliability study. Precise statistical definitions establishing the requirements for a parallel form have been advanced. However, for working purposes, parallel forms are said to exist where (1) the number of items of each type is the same, so that the measures concentrate equally on the same aspects of the individual; (2) the average scores tend to be essentially the same; and (3) the distributions of actual scores through the range of possible scores are roughly comparable. Whether these conditions can be met, and in fact whether a parallel measure can be developed at all, depends largely on the nature of the measure involved.

☐ Internal Consistency Reliability

A widely used approximation to the parallel-form approach involves splitting up an existing measure into two equal parts and then correlating the scores on these parts to obtain an estimate of reliability. It is common to use the odd-numbered items as one measure and the even-numbered ones as another. An example would be where individual production data are calculated on a daily basis. The first day's data would go in one measure, the second day's in the other, the third day's back with those for the first day, and so on. At the end of six weeks one could compute the average or total production for each person in the sample using both measures separately. The correlation between these two measures is a reliability coefficient. The scores obtained from the odd and even items of a test provide another example.

However, where **split-half reliability** is used, one additional step remains. It is a statistical fact that a measure becomes more reli-

able as one includes more individual measurements. A rating form can be made more reliable, for instance, by increasing the number of rating variables used in calculating a composite score from, say, ten to twenty. But when one uses the split-half method the number of measurements included in the reliability coefficient is actually cut in half. Thus, with the production data just mentioned, the reliability estimate is really based on three weeks of data, not six. If one intends to use a six-week measure as a criterion in a validity study, it is the reliability of that measure that is desired; the three-week coefficient that has been calculated needs to be corrected to make it equal to what would have been obtained over six weeks. Such a correction may be made statistically by applying the **Spearman-Brown prophecy formula** to the reliability coefficient calculated from the two halves (Guion, 1965). The resulting value is the best estimate of actual criterion reliability.

There are other approaches to internal consistency reliability which utilize statistical combinations of multiple measures within a single test. However, there are serious questions as to whether any of the internal consistency measures impose the same restrictions on validity that the test-retest and parallel-form approaches do (Miner, 1992). One difficulty is that, in responding to one item one way, a person may predispose the response to another item. Thus measured internal consistency reliability may not compromise validity.

☐ Interrater Reliability

An approach to reliability measurement that is frequently used with rating procedures is to obtain independent ratings of each individual from two, or perhaps more, sources. These ratings are then correlated across a sample of employees to obtain a reliability coefficient. For this approach to be used, of course, there must be at least two individuals who have comprehensive, firsthand knowledge of those aspects of the employee's performance to be rated. In **interrater reliability,** the two measures used do not utilize different instruments as such, or measures taken at different points in time. The rating forms are identical and the timing can be identical also. However, the measuring instrument is varied in the sense that two different people complete it based on what may well be somewhat different samples of the employee's job behavior. The same type of situation arises when two selection interviews or test protocols are scored independently by two psychologists.

When two or more independent ratings of this kind are to be averaged or totaled to obtain the actual criterion values used in a validity study—and this should be done whenever possible to increase reliability—a situation much like that with the split-half coefficient is created. The number of measures (people making ratings) is reduced in calculating the initial reliability coefficient. Although it is often neglected in practice, it is usually appropriate and in fact desirable to apply the Spearman-Brown prophecy formula to correct for the proportionate reduction in number of independent raters involved in calculating the interrater coefficient over the number of raters to be used in the actual measurement.

☐ Reliability and Validity

One factor that contributes to failure to demonstrate validity when validity is in fact present is a restriction of range in the predictors, usually caused by the fact that the predictors are used to select the validation sample and thus scores below a given cutoff point are few or nonexistent. This factor is best corrected for by letting a full range of candidates go on to employment. If necessary there is a statistical correction for restriction of range that can be employed. This formula serves to adjust the validity coefficient to what it would be if the spread of scores on the predictor in the validation sample were as large as the spread in the candidate group.

The second factor that limits validity is the size of the validation sample. If the sample is small, even rather sizable coefficients may not reach acceptable levels of statistical significance. Furthermore, there is some tendency to look askance at the practice of using a correction for restriction of range to raise a validity coefficient over the line into statistical significance. Raising one that is appreciably too low is another matter. Thus the best solution to problems created by too small a sample is to increase the sample size.

Additional factors that may contribute to a failure to show validity are associated with the criterion. One is a restriction of range in the criterion caused by predictor restriction. If validity really is present and predictor-score distributions are truncated by the use of the predictor in selection, then the criterion-score distribution will be restricted too. Normally this problem cannot be handled through a statistical correction for restriction of range in the criterion, because data on what the spread of scores on the criterion should be is lacking. The best answer is to have the full range of predictor scores in the validation sample, and then the full range of criterion scores should be present also.

However, the major criterion-related factor limiting a demonstration of validity is unreliability in the criterion. Unreliability in a predictor can of course be a problem, but any unreliability there will also extend into the subsequent selection process itself and thus predictor unreliability should rightfully be included in the validity coefficient. But unreliability in a criterion represents a defect of the measurement process, not of the practical result. When validity is established with a rather unreliable criterion and then the predictors are used, one actually gets a better result than one bargained for. The problem is that the unreliable criterion measure may not yield a validity coefficient large enough to be acceptable. There are, however, statistical procedures available to correct for this unreliability.

■ SELECTION AND FAIR EMPLOYMENT

At various points in this chapter, and in preceding chapters as well, the significant role played by the law in the conduct of the selection process has been noted. The ways in which laws operate as constraints and facilitators for selection decisions appear to undergo continual change as courts render their decisions and new scientific evidence is developed. Certain aspects of the current situation in this area, however, require explanation.

☐ Validation Requirements

The consideration that has contributed most to the implication of selection procedures in fair employment matters is the finding that minority applicants on the average usually score below whites on various ability tests. Research on this point was discussed in Chapter 12. As a consequence of this situation, an employer who wished to minimize the number of blacks on the payroll could do so simply by requiring that all people hired score above a given level on a test of intellectual ability, without regard to whether the test was job-related (had validity) or not. By setting the cutoff score quite high, one can ensure in many labor markets that a much greater proportion of white than black applicants will "pass." In some instances, it might even be possible to hire no blacks at all, because none who apply score at the required level in a period during which enough whites are screened to fill the available openings.

It should be emphasized that a low proportion of minority-group members is not in and of itself evidence of discrimination. Only if the relevant labor market for a given occupational group, when defined in a reasonable manner, proves to contain a considerably higher proportion of minority-group members than a company's labor force is there a basis for a charge of unfair hiring practices. If under such circumstances the company is using selection procedures that contribute to this situation, it must show that they are in fact job-related—that is, that any tendency that the use of the selection procedure introduces to screen out minority-group members is justified because these individuals could not be expected to perform the work effectively. In practice, this has been interpreted to mean that the company must demonstrate validity among both whites and minority-group members for all predictors used in selection.

However, recent decisions by the Supreme Court have served to reduce the pressure on companies to conduct comprehensive validity studies to support the job relatedness of their hiring practices (Potter, 1989). Whereas in the past it was essential to show the business necessity of these practices, which stacked the cards very heavily in favor of validation studies, it is now sufficient to produce evidence that the hiring practice serves in a significant way the legitimate business goals of the employer. This clearly can be accomplished in ways other than through validation research; however, validation remains a very effective means of rebutting charges of discrimination.

☐ Differential Validity

One response to governmental pressures was to cease using techniques such as psychological tests or to suspend their use temporarily. Some companies chose this route on the grounds that they were not sure what would satisfy legal requirements and that complex validation studies of the type required were too expensive to justify the costs. On the other hand, if validity for blacks and whites can be demonstrated, a company is then in a good position to protect itself against any charge of discrimination that a government examiner may bring. Thus, a strategy that emphasizes validation can well be a much more effective approach than merely abandoning tests or application blanks. In view of the sizable

BOX **16-3**   RESEARCH IN I/O PSYCHOLOGY

Differential Validity at AT&T

In connection with a fair employment practices case against AT&T, the U.S. Equal Employment Opportunity Commission required the company to provide extensive information on test validation research throughout the Bell System. Review of these studies indicated that differential validity had been investigated frequently. In the one study where validities were calculated separately for males and females, significant results were obtained in both groups. Similarly, in two studies involving Hispanics and whites, significance was obtained in all groups. There were nine studies in which validities were calculated separately for blacks and whites, and in eight of these studies the predictors were valid for both groups. In the one remaining study a statistically significant validity coefficient of 0.32 was found among the 113 whites, but among the 26 blacks the figure was a nonsignificant -0.04. In this instance there appeared to be a differential validity problem. The percentage distributions of test and criterion scores were as follows in the two groups:

In this instance, a high proportion of black candidates was eliminated by the test, and 57 percent of those who made the cutoff score were just above it—in contrast to 31 percent of the whites. This means that the blacks tended to be bunched (restriction of range), whereas the whites were spread over all four test-score categories. With so few blacks in the upper score ranges, it is not surprising that their validity coefficient was minimal. This is a statistical artifact, associated with the restriction of range occasioned by the use of the same cutoff score for both groups and the overall lower scores of the blacks.

Overall, differential validity did not appear to represent a problem at AT&T, and this fact was recognized by the Equal Employment Opportunity Commission as it continued to pursue the case.

SOURCE: Adapted from John B. Miner (1974). Psychological testing and fair employment practices: A testing program that does not discriminate. *Personnel Psychology, 27,* 57–58.

	Criterion Performance							
	White Employees (r = 0.32)				Black Employees (r = −0.04)			
	Low	Medium	High	Totals	Low	Medium	High	Totals
Test scores								
High	1	4	10	15	0	0	4	4
Medium high	10	4	12	26	8	11	4	23
Medium	11	8	8	27	11	0	4	15
Just above the cutoff point	11	11	9	31	23	19	15	57

increases in validation research over the years, it appears to be a strategy that has achieved widespread acceptance.

In essence, validating separately for blacks and whites or for males and females involves the use of the moderator variable design where race or gender is the moderator. One might ask why this is necessary. Would not a

measure that proves valid for one group be expected to be valid for the other? The answer is that, over a wide range of circumstances, this does turn out to be the case (Schmitt & Noe, 1986). However, there are exceptions.

Box 16-3 provides an example from one company, AT&T of how frequently **differen-**

tial validity occurs, i.e., a predictor that is valid in one group turns out to be valid in the other as well. This was true in eleven of twelve studies. In the one remaining instance, extreme restriction of the test score range among blacks was sufficient to reduce the validity coefficient to essentially zero. Typically validity generalization analyses introduce corrections for these kinds of statistical artifacts, so that even this one study would not be treated as a departure from the general result should validity generalization procedures be applied to the twelve studies as a whole.

■ LIMITATIONS ON SELECTION

It should be apparent from the correlations between predictors and criteria noted previously that available selection techniques are not a panacea. Utilized effectively, they can increase the level of performance in a company, but instances of performance failure and individual discontent will inevitably remain. There are certain inherent limitations in selection models and technology that may never be overcome completely.

□ Sources of Failure

One major problem, and this will become increasingly apparent after the discussions in Chapters 17 and 18, is that the available predictors are far from perfect. They do not always reveal a characteristic that is important in determining job behavior, nor do they consistently specify correctly the degree to which it may be present. Interviews, psychological tests, physical examinations, and all the other techniques may not yield the information they should, and on occasion they may produce erroneous information.

Another difficulty is associated not so much with the techniques themselves as with the people who use them. Human error is almost inevitable, even though it can be reduced through effective selection and training. In one instance, the author instigated the subsequent rescoring of a sample of several hundred answer sheets for the psychological tests used in Atlantic-Richfield's selection battery. Although in most cases the divergence was not large, there were tests that had clearly been scored with considerable error—sufficiently so to produce an inappropriate selection decision. Similar errors, because of the misunderstanding of an interview statement or the misreading of some physical measure, occur more often than is generally recognized. They certainly are not limited to Atlantic-Richfield.

Considerations of economy are also relevant. The physical exam is a good example. Increasingly, medical science is developing complex procedures for the detection of various diseases. Many of these diagnostic aids are extremely costly and require highly trained personnel to use them; some necessitate hospitalization during the period in which tests are carried out. There can be no question that these techniques have considerable value in predicting subsequent events. Yet companies rarely use them in connection with the preemployment physical examination. They are too costly in time and money, and the disorders they identify are generally relatively rare. As a result, a decision has been made in many instances to risk future absenteeism and perhaps ineffective job behavior rather than invest in the available selection techniques.

The investment decision here is analogous to that involved in a deferred maintenance policy as applied to equipment and machinery. Instead of attempting to spot potential breakdowns and correcting the situation, one allows the breakdown to develop, on the assumption that the resulting costs will be less than those that preventive maintenance would necessitate. Many companies have failed to adopt psychological testing programs and other selection procedures for much the same type of reason. They assume that a sizable investment in selection procedures is not warranted because any difficulties that develop can be handled later.

In addition to these limitations associated with the selection procedures themselves, there are other problems. One of the major reasons for the failure of selection predictions is that people change in unexpected ways. A physical disorder may develop, personality changes may occur, and so on. Marital difficulties may produce discontent that is subsequently transferred to the job. Or financial problems may arise that could not have been anticipated but that leave the employee preoccupied and upset. The list of possibilities is endless. The point is that things happen to people over the years of employment that leave them changed individuals. When these are added to the normal alterations associated with aging, it is obvious that selection procedures have a potential that realistically must be considered somewhat limited. Certainly, prediction in the short run is much better than it is over a long period.

This problem of change is not restricted to the individual, however. Jobs change, too. A person who was quite effective on an assembly line may not do so well when the job is computerized. A salesperson who can sell one type of product in one market may run into difficulty when competitive pressures force the company to shift to a somewhat different market or product. It is difficult if not impossible to select for the jobs of the future, especially when at the same time one must select for the jobs of the present.

Change may also occur across jobs rather than within them. That is, a person may shift from job to job within the company rather than be faced with a change in the role prescriptions of a given position. Some amount of career change is the general rule rather than the exception. Certainly, this is the case among college-educated employees and with-

in the ranks of management. This matter of career prediction is one of the most difficult in the entire field of personnel selection. It requires that predictors be validated against career criteria and that longitudinal studies extend over long time periods. It is not too difficult to predict whether a person will do well during a training period or in the initial placement with the company. It is quite another matter to predict that the person will perform effectively twenty years hence in a position whose level and nature are something of a mystery. Yet there is no question that career selection of this kind is what most companies need, at least for some proportion of the people they hire.

A final source of error has already been mentioned in a different context. Two managers may not evaluate their subordinates in exactly the same way, using the same criteria and standards. This is particularly true when organization planning and job analysis have had only minimal application, with the result that role requirements are ambiguous and uncertain. Workers who are considered satisfactory by one superior may be rated considerably lower by another, even though their behavior is no different. Two employees whose work behaviors are almost identical can be evaluated quite differently. When criteria are unstable and unreliable in this manner, selection techniques will not come out looking very effective (Maier, 1988).

Exhibit 16-3 uses data from the Georgia Kaolin research described in the case analysis of Chapter 15 to provide an indication of the level of agreement that can typically be expected when two superiors with equal access to information rate the performance of subordinates. Usually, as here, there is better agreement on overall performance than on specific aspects. But even with overall performance there is not the complete agreement that a correlation of 1.00 would reflect.

All these limitations are superimposed on the constraints imposed by the available

EXHIBIT 16-3   **Agreement between Two Foremen Rating the Same Subordinates at Georgia Kaolin**

Performance Measure	Ranking Measure	Rated Ranking Measure
Verbal task performance	0.71	0.58
Mathematical task performance	0.73	0.60
Judgmental task performance	0.75	0.62
New task performance	0.79	0.76
Overall task performance	0.85	0.81

human resource pool and the restrictions created by the nature and extent of the recruiting process. No selection procedure can yield an effective work force if the recruitment procedures cannot, or do not, provide an adequate group of candidates from which selection can occur. Recruitment, then, becomes the sine qua non for selection. If the number of possible hires equals the number of positions to be filled, there is no selection. Therefore, it is crucial to develop recruiting procedures that will provide a sufficiently large and varied candidate pool so that the selection techniques can achieve their maximum potential. Actually, any valid selection technique will perform quite effectively if it can be used to skim the cream off a very large candidate group. As the number of candidates available begins to approach the number to be hired, however, a human resource strategy emphasizing selection becomes less and less appropriate.

□ Self-Selection and Realistic Job Previews

The procedures considered to this point assume that the decision to hire is made by an individual other than the candidate, who possesses information regarding the candidate, the job, and the relationship between the two. But what if the candidate makes the decision? What if the candidate is provided with de-

tailed information regarding the job and perhaps even regarding validity relationships? How is this kind of self-selection likely to work out? Here we are in a kind of no-man's land between recruiting and selection, where the candidate supply could be severely restricted simply because those who might otherwise be candidates are no longer candidates because they possess information that causes them to select themselves out. Clearly, selection on the part of the company can be limited under such circumstances, if it occurs at all, as a result of the reduced number of people who really want the job.

One method of providing candidates with the requisite information for self-selection is through a computerized information system. In other cases, **realistic job previews** have been made available in the form of written booklets, films, or job visits (Wanous, 1980; 1989).

Whether such procedures actually serve to reduce the candidate pool appears to depend on the unemployment rate. If there are few jobs available, the provision of detailed job information makes little difference; candidates will accept the job if it is offered, even if they know enough about it to have serious doubts regarding their interest. On the other hand, even under conditions of limited employment opportunities, providing information to permit valid self-selection can relate to job survival. Those who make realistic self-selection decisions based on compre-

BOX 16-4 RESEARCH IN I/O PSYCHOLOGY

The Effects of Realistic Job Previews on Turnover during U.S. Army Basic Training

The U.S. Army has a problem in that many basic trainees leave the Army during training voluntarily. To look into this matter, realistic job previews of various kinds were given to four companies of trainees as training began, and separations were then tracked throughout the seven-week program. Two types of previews were studied as follows:

The first preview was a twenty-seven-minute, professionally produced, videotaped overview of basic training, including a pictorial and verbal description of relevant activities and events. Some of these, which were typically overestimated in their difficulty, were the daily schedule of training activities, including the amount of free time; living and training conditions; the type and duration of daily physical training; long marches; firing live ammunition, including rifles and hand grenades; gas chamber training; living in field settings; and the standards to be met for graduation.

The second preview was a twenty-four-minute, videotaped presentation, also professionally produced, that covered the emotional aspects of basic training. This presentation emphasized that the biggest challenge facing trainees was not specific events in training, but the adjustment to Army life. The presentation then identified five specific adjustment problems that new trainees do not normally anticipate, and

presented suggestions for dealing with each. These problems and suggestions were presented by recruits (actors) themselves. Modeling and graphics were used to reinforce the major points. The five areas covered were as follows: the adjustment to living and working with a group of "strangers" and having no privacy; homesickness; dealing with authority and taking orders; concerns over not being able to meet physical requirements; and anxiety over discussing problems with the drill sergeant.

When the two previews were both given to the trainees, the net effect was a reduction in voluntary turnover over the control condition where the trainees saw neither. The previews appeared to increase trust in and commitment to the Army, and job satisfaction. Generally, the first preview had a positive effect as well. The second preview alone produced a dramatic increase in turnover, and a decrease in job satisfaction. Clearly, the type of realistic job preview used makes a substantial difference; it is possible to be too negative.

SOURCE: Bruce M. Meglino, Angelo S. DeNisi, Stuart A. Youngblood, & Kevin J. Williams (1988). Effects of realistic job previews: A comparison using an enhancement and a reduction preview. *Journal of Applied Psychology, 73,* 259–266.

hensive knowledge of the job are more likely to want to stay.

The answer to our question appears to be that self-selection is no more valid than any other approach. People take jobs they do not want because of pressures in the labor market, and they may miscalculate their own interests and capabilities. Ultimately, those who make employment decisions based on realistic information are somewhat more like-

ly to stay on (Dilla, 1987; Reilly, Brown, Blood, & Malatesta 1981), but there is no certainty that they will make valid self-selection decisions. In spite of the inherent appeal of the self-selection approach, the limitations of selection are no less in evidence when the approach is used.

Box 16-4 describes two realistic job previews used in a study conducted for the U.S. Army. The first preview is more typical of what is usual practice. The second preview is quite negative regarding the Army experience. If given before hiring (or enlistment), the second preview could be expected to cause many people to select themselves out of an organization. Consequently, a firm might have difficulty recruiting sufficient candidates. The study appears to indicate that how realistic job previews operate depends a great deal on the content of the previews themselves.

☐ The Invasion-of-Privacy Question

Industry generally has been under considerable ethical pressure with regard to selection. Several congressional investigations have been conducted with a view to imposing constraints on the use of psychological tests, although no federal legislation has been passed. Legal constraints have been imposed at the state level, however.

A major concern is that personality testing and other selection techniques represent an invasion of privacy: that individuals are called upon to reveal things that they might not wish to reveal; that they often do not even know what they are revealing about themselves; that information obtained is not held to a confidential psychologist–applicant relationship but imparted to a third party, the company's management. These actions are felt to be unethical. Those who attack such procedures and who feel that perhaps legal constraints should be imposed in this area believe that individual freedoms are being violated.

What does not seem to be clearly understood in all this is that the selection situation is not synonymous with the physician–patient relationship or that of lawyer and client. Except with self-selection, it is not the applicant who wants information or assistance, but the company. Furthermore, applicants are aware of the purpose of the various selection

procedures. If they take tests, they recognize that this experience is germane to being considered for employment. The applicants presumably want something from the potential employer and understand quite clearly that they must provide certain information to have a chance of obtaining what they want. Thus they trade information about themselves for the opportunity to be hired. This is a long way from coercion, and it is coerced invasion of privacy, where the individual has no choice, that is normally considered unethical.

This is not to say that information obtained from psychological tests, application blanks, physical examinations, or other selection tools, whether stored in a computer data bank or not, cannot be misused by unscrupulous individuals. There are important security problems here, and there can be a major ethical problem as well if information is used for some purpose other than that anticipated by the applicant—that is, the evaluation of qualifications for employment. To protect the public against such misuse of employment data, psychologists and others have devoted considerable time and energy to the formulation and the enforcement of appropriate ethical controls. Nevertheless, the pressures in this area are real, and should they derive from sources, such as consumers, lending institutions, and the like, that are of central significance to a company, they can be sufficiently strong to influence company selection procedures.

☐ Union Influence

Unions may provide another source of pressure to limit or eliminate the use of tests, and on occasion other selection techniques as well. A union may wish to establish seniority as the only basis for promotion, assignment, and layoff. The existence of test data would provide objective support for ability or merit claims and thus might be used to override seniority considerations. In addition, some unions have been able to exert considerable influence, if not outright control, over the hiring process, in spite of the outlawing of the closed shop. To the extent that selection techniques might threaten this influence, they have been opposed.

Some firms have agreed to labor contract terms that effectively proscribe testing and other selection techniques as well. In general, such agreements usually appear in a context of minimal selection emphasis, and thus the company is giving away something it cares little about, probably to gain some concession it views as more significant. On the other hand, agreeing to severe constraints on selection procedures can prove to be self-defeating if at some later time a more selection-oriented strategy appears to be called for. Certainly, if a company desires to utilize a selection strategy for unionized jobs, every effort should be made to retain as much freedom in the use of selection techniques as possible.

□ Return on the Investment

Throughout this chapter, a considerable amount of evidence regarding the validity of various measurement procedures has been presented. There can be little doubt that selection tools offer an opportunity to regulate human input in such a way as to make a very sizable contribution to organizations. These procedures do work: not perfectly, but they work.

Further evidence on this point, in dollars-and-cents terms, comes from an early study carried out on the selection of telephone operators for AT&T in the San Francisco area (Rusmore & Toorenaar, 1956). A test battery containing numerical and clerical ability measures was used as a predictor. Calculation was made of the savings attributable to the fact that many operators who would ulti-

mately have failed were not hired and therefore did not have to be trained. The following figures correct these training savings for the additional recruiting costs that the tests introduce. Scores on the test battery may range from 0 to 80, and the minimum score for hiring could, of course, be set at any point between, depending on the availability of applicants in the labor market and the degree of selectivity desired. This study was published in 1956; the savings would be many times greater today because of inflation.

Minimum Score for Hiring	Net Savings ($)
30	8,000
40	35,000
50	47,000
60	50,000

A study carried out in the U.S. Office of Personnel Management provides data on the savings to the federal government from the use over a one-year period of the previously mentioned cognitive test for computer programmers (Schmidt, Hunter, McKenzie, & Muldrow, 1979). Obviously these savings will vary depending on how high a test score is required for hiring; they go beyond the AT&T study in that productivity considerations, not just training costs, are taken into account. In any event, the potential savings over simply random hiring range from $16.5 million to $97.2 million. If only the top half of all candidates are hired, the value is $37.6 million.

Savings of this magnitude are possible only when a great many people are hired. Yet this happens in industry, too. An analysis of the consequences of using a strength test to hire steelworkers in one company indicates a yearly saving of $6.3 million in the presence of a court order to hire 20 percent female workers. If only the highest scorers on the test were hired, without reference to gender, the yearly savings would be $9.1 million (Arnold, Rauschenberger, Soubel, & Guion, 1982).

It is apparent from these data that good selection procedures developed with reference to organizationally meaningful criteria can yield very sizable savings. The real strength of human measurement techniques in selection is that, when validated correctly, they place primary emphasis on merit rather than on the biases and moods of the person doing the selection.

Given this potential for both validity and savings, when should a major investment in selection strategies be attempted? At least one such condition occurs when people are prepared for their work primarily outside the organization. This would normally be true of professionals, secretaries, and many other occupational groups who learn most of what they will do on the job in some segment of the educational system. Here stress should be placed on attracting the best possible people and selecting from among them those most likely to succeed, thus investing disproportionately more in selection processes. On the other hand, when jobs requiring considerable knowledge and skill that are practically unique to the particular company or industry are involved, the selection emphasis can be decreased considerably. What is most needed in this situation is the best possible internal training effort.

Another consideration is whether a selection emphasis can really be made to work. Is it possible for the company to recruit top talent? Can really effective selection devices be developed and applied? In many instances, accomplishing these goals at reasonable cost is much easier for larger firms than for small ones. Larger companies are more likely to be widely known and thus have a recruiting edge based on goodwill. They are also more likely to be able to justify the personnel research staff or the consulting expense needed to conduct fruitful validation studies. In small companies, such research is more difficult because of small numbers of employees in the various occupations and limited numbers of new hires. Also, the total number of employees and hires may not be sufficient to warrant the investment in research.

KEY TERMS

Criteria

Predictive validity (longitudinal prediction)

Correction for restriction of range

Regression weights

Additive correlation

Cross-validation

Concurrent validity

Content validity

Face validity

Construct validity

Moderator variables

Utility

Validity generalization

Reliability

Test-retest approach

Parallel-form approach

Split-half reliability

Spearman-Brown prophecy formula

Interrater reliability

Differential validity

Realistic job previews (self-selection)

SUMMARY

Validation of selection procedures, although important in its own right, has taken on increased significance under the impact of equal employment opportunity legislation. The ideal research procedure calls for criterion-related validation in a *longitudinal prediction* design. When multiple predictors are used, they may be combined in several ways, but multiple correlation seems preferable on a number of counts. In any event, the use of multiple predictors may require *cross-validation* of results in a second sample to eliminate the possibility of capitalization on chance. Under certain circumstances, it may be necessary to substitute the *concurrent model,* where predictors and criterion measures are obtained at the same time, for the predictive model.

Federal agencies recognize both *content and construct validity* as additional approaches that may be acceptable under certain circumstances. *Utility* analysis has been used on occasion to establish the expected value to the firm of hiring different people. Sometimes *moderator variables* are introduced to identify specific groups in which predictors work well. *Validity generalization* is an approach that permits extending the results of prior research to new contexts. *Differential validation* involves conducting studies separately for blacks and whites, males and females, and the like.

In spite of the tremendous potential inherent in the use of selection processes coupled with appropriate validation, selection still has its limitations. It is not perfect, and the use of *self-selection* procedures does not make this any the less true. Furthermore, certain selection procedures tend to arouse fears regarding invasion of privacy and to elicit various types of union resistance. Yet it is becoming increasingly apparent that major cost savings can be achieved through the use of appropriate selection techniques.

QUESTIONS

1. What is validity generalization? How does it relate to federal selection guidelines?

2. What are the major limitations of selection? Self-selection has been proposed as a panacea for these limitations of selection. Compare it to each of the limitations and indicate your conclusions.

3. Which validation concept is basic to the others? How does criterion-related validity operate in this regard?

4. Under what circumstances do the courts require evidence of the validity of a selection procedure?

5. What is the usual union position on selection procedures? What is the union alternative?

6. Why do you suppose the matter of differential validity has become such a source of controversy? Why should the Equal Employment Opportunity Commission favor it and many employers oppose it?

7. What is cross-validation? When is it not necessary? What alternatives are available?

8. What are the major differences between concurrent and predictive validity? What possible sources of error in interpreting results does the predictive approach avoid?

9. How may multiple predictors be combined? What are the advantages and disadvantages of the various approaches?

10. Differentiate among construct, content, and face validity. Which is more likely to elicit employee acceptance of a testing program? Which is more likely to elicit acceptance by an industrial psychologist?

CASE PROBLEM

Selection Processes: City Government Priorities

A human resource manager who had served for many years as director of hiring and selection for a large city government subsequently moved up to head the city's human resource operations. In this capacity he assumed responsibility for a wide range of activities, of which selection was just one. He also found himself working much more closely with elected officials at the policy-making level.

In discussing his experiences as a top human resource administrator, in relation to his background in selection, before a meeting of the International Personnel Management Association, the man had this to say (Springer, 1982, p. 9):

> I have come to the conclusion that selection and the activities of selection specialists represents a relatively low priority in the viewpoint of elected officials. Selection is not the subject of discussion, dispute, or controversy at the finance committee or council meeting unless a problem exists of the magnitude of a class action EEO suit with large cash settlements or the with-

holding of federal revenue sharing funds. Here, the political leaders will undoubtedly be concerned, not with the merit system selection or testing per se, but with the financial consequences of what they may perceive as mismanagement on our part.

The issues that do receive attention are labor relations, wage and salary administration, and fringe benefit management. It is not hard to see why. All of these personnel issues are cost-related items, and all involve big money. For example, health-related benefits alone amount to approximately $22 million per year and are increasing. A 9 percent pay raise for members of one union will cost the city approximately $22 million over two years, and we have over twenty unions with which we negotiate. Clearly, financial constraints at all levels of government have made economic concerns paramount to policymaking officials. It is, therefore, understandable that the areas within personnel management which receive the greatest attention are the areas which the elected officials see as being most directly related to productivity, cost containment and control.

Questions

1. If you were this human resource administrator and were convinced that good selection was a major factor in "productivity, cost containment and control," how would you go about demonstrating that fact to the elected officials who hold the pursestrings?

2. How does "the logic of selection" relate to this issue and how may it be used to deal with questions regarding the value of selection?

17

Interviews, Application Blanks, and References

Zale Corporation was faced with a situation in which it needed to hire a number of people for retail jewelry sales positions. To facilitate this, a decision was made to develop and validate a structured interview keyed specifically to this type of work.

The first phase was to obtain a large number of critical incidents from salespeople and their managers describing jewelry sales performance. The best incidents were culled from this group and cast in a form whereby the people interviewed could be expected to indicate how they would behave if the incident should happen to them. Most of the items dealt with basic sales and customer service situations. Some focused on security and prioritizing sales over nonsales tasks. For each incident there was a rating scale of five points, and verbal anchors indicating below-average, average, and above-average performance were developed. A typical interview item might look as follows:

> A customer comes into the store to pick up a watch he had left for repair. The repair was supposed to have been completed a week ago, but the watch is not back yet from the repair shop. The customer becomes very angry. How would you handle this situation?

1 ■ Tell the customer it isn't back yet and ask him or her to check back with you later.
.
.
.
.
.
2 ■
.
.
.
.

3 ■ Apologize, tell the customer that you will check into the problem and call him or her back later.
.
.
.
.
.
4 ■
.
.
.
.
5 ■ Put the customer at ease and call the repair shop while the customer waits.

In the interview the candidate is told the incident and asked the question but is allowed to respond in an open-ended manner without knowledge of the anchors. The interviewer scores the response from 1 to 5 using the anchors as a guide. There are sixteen incidents in the interview.

In a predictive validity study extending over nine months, interview scores were correlated with subsequent sales volume per hour worked. The validity coefficient obtained was a very respectable 0.45. On the evidence from this finding the structured interview of sixteen incidents was put into use.

SOURCE: Jeff A. Weekley & Joseph A. Gier (1987). Reliability and validity of the situational interview for a sales position. *Journal of Applied Psychology, 72,* 484–487.

This is one way in which industrial psychologists work to develop selection procedures. They create and validate standardized interviews, application blanks, and reference-checking techniques. As we move now to discussion of actual selection processes, we need some basis for differentiating among them.

Two broad categories may be distinguished within the overall framework of selection decision making. One relies heavily on the assumption that a candidate's **past behavior** can serve as a guide for predicting the future. Accordingly, extensive information is collected regarding the person's previous behavior in various educational, occupational, and perhaps other situations. Then this information is evaluated relative to the role requirements of the position to be filled—or of several positions, if career considerations are involved. The expectation is that individuals will remain much the same people in the future that they were in the past—that they

Exhibit 17-1   Use of Interviews, Application Blanks, and References for Selection in the United States

Procedure	Variations in Percentage Use across Occupational Groupings	Comments
Interview		
Unstructured	71–72%	All occupations the same
Structured	30–36%	Somewhat more for clerical, professional, and managerial jobs
Application blank		
Weighted blanks	7–9%	All occupations the same
Reference checks	83–96%	Somewhat more for professional,
Reference and record checks		sales, and managerial jobs; very low for less skilled
Outside agency investigations	6–22%	Highest for executives; low for blue-collar and clerical positions

Source: Bureau of National Affairs (1983). ASPA-BNA survey no. 45—Employee selection procedures. *Bulletin to Management,* May 5, p. 3.

will retain the same or similar characteristics and will behave in accordance with previous patterns.

This rationale underlies many of the procedures that are regularly employed in selection interviews. It also underlies most biographical inventories, application blanks, medical history forms, and reference-checking techniques. In all these instances, the primary, although not exclusive, emphasis is on accumulating valid information about the past to provide a basis for selecting the particular human inputs to the organization that will maximize future effectiveness.

A very different rationale underlies most psychological testing, the physical examination, and certain adaptations of the interview and the application blank. As we shall see, these adaptations make the particular interviews and application blanks very similar to psychological tests. The structured interview for retail jewelry sales jobs at Zale Corporation is an example. This second approach relies heavily on the sampling of **present behavior** as a basis for prediction. Relatively

standardized situations that presumably have some relation to the job or jobs are established, and candidates are asked to behave within these contexts. It is assumed that their behavior in these limited situations will be typical of their total present behavior and that they will remain sufficiently unchanged in the future to permit effective prediction.

The present chapter will take up the selection procedures that have their primary roots in an evaluation of the candidate's past: the interview, the various adaptations of the application blank procedure, and reference checks. In the next chapter, attention will be focused more directly on techniques of sampling current behavior to obtain information on intellectual and physical functioning and on personality characteristics.

Information on the frequency with which methods considered in this chapter are used in organizations of all types and sizes is given in Exhibit 17-1. The same preferences for interviews and reference checks have been found in Great Britain (Robertson & Makin, 1986).

■ THE INTERVIEW

Although it is evident that interview procedures are widely used for a variety of purposes, the primary concern here is with specific applications in the evaluation of human inputs to a business organization. Therefore, applications in such areas as marketing research, employee counseling, management appraisal, and attitude surveys receive little attention. We are concerned here with **employment interviews.**

Even within the input context, the interview serves a number of purposes: It is much more than a selection device. This is probably why it has survived and even thrived in the face of extended attacks by industrial psychologists and others and in the face of considerable evidence that, as commonly used, it is often not a very effective selection technique (Eder & Ferris, 1989).

There are, in fact, a number of requirements connected with the input process that at present cannot be accomplished in any other way, although telephone and written communication might be substituted in certain instances. Interviews are used as often to sell the company and thus recruit candidates for employment as to select. A single interview frequently involves both selection and recruiting aspects. Furthermore, terms of employment are characteristically negotiated in the interview situation, and an important public relations function is performed. Applicants who must be rejected are particularly likely to leave with very negative attitudes toward the company if they have not had an opportunity to talk with a responsible representative.

Even when the focus is directly on the selection process, the interview appears to possess certain unique values, which may account for its continued widespread use. For one thing, the great flexibility of the technique, which can contribute to limited validity in some selection situations, may represent a major asset in other instances. The interview is the method *par excellence* for filling in the gaps between other selection techniques—gaps that could not have been foreseen until the other techniques were actually applied. Responses on the application blank may make clear the need for further information regarding the circumstances surrounding certain previous employment and separation decisions. An interview can be of considerable help in providing such information.

It is also clear that the interview is widely used to determine whether an applicant is the type of person who can be expected to fit in and get along in the particular firm, who will adapt to the organizational culture. There is something about the process of personal judgment that produces a strong feeling of validity, even when validity is not present. It is not surprising, therefore, that many companies place heavy emphasis on interviewing when attempting to predict whether a person will be a source of conflict, will have a negative impact on others, or will be an extremely unhappy employee. Furthermore, interviewer judgments appear to have some validity as measures for assessing personality (Paunonen & Jackson, 1987).

Finally, there are situations, especially when managerial and professional positions are involved, where the interview is the only major selection technique that can realistically be used. When people who already have a good job and do not have a strong initial incentive to make a move, but who give every evidence of being good prospects, are faced with extensive psychological testing, a physical exam, and an application blank (above and beyond the résumé already submitted), they may shy away. If this seems likely, it is often wiser to rely on the interview, reference checks, and the like in spite of their shortcomings, rather than risk losing the individual.

☐ What Is Known

A great deal has been written regarding the techniques of interviewing for various purposes (see, for example, Zima, 1983). Much of this, however, derives from the expertise and opinion of specific individuals. What is really known, in the sense that it is based on studies using selection models of the kind discussed in Chapter 16 and on other scientific research procedures, is considerably less.

At the outset, it should be noted that validity studies overall have not yielded very strong support for the employment interview. Reviews of published studies have produced somewhat different results depending on the sample of studies considered, the criteria employed, and the degree to which statistical artifacts were considered, but in no case was the average validity coefficient above 0.20 (Hunter and Hirsh, 1987; Muchinsky, 1986). Because of such results, which have been found over many years, industrial psychologists have not looked on the interview with great favor.

Recent findings, however, serve to temper this conclusion. There is reason to believe that past research underestimated the validity of the interview (Dreher, Ash, & Hancock, 1988). In particular, there appear to be substantial differences in the effectiveness of individual interviewers, and these differences have not been taken into account fully in previous research. Second, structured interviews, of which the Zale Company procedure described at the beginning of this chapter is a good example, consistently yield far superior results. It now appears that these structured interviews can be expected to produce validities twice those of the unstructured interviews studied previously (Wiesner & Cronshaw, 1988; Wright, Lichtenfels, & Pursell, 1989). Thus the validity coefficient of 0.45 reported for the Zale Company study is not at all out of line.

Consistency of Interviewer Judgments.   There is considerable evidence to indicate that, although interviewers will themselves exhibit consistency in successive evaluations of the same individual, different interviewers are likely to come to quite disparate conclusions when the interview is not structured. Thus, when two employment interviewers utilize their own idiosyncratic interview procedures on the same applicant, the probability is that they will come to differing decisions. They will normally elicit information on different matters, and even when the topics covered do overlap, one individual will weight the applicant's responses in a way that varies considerably from that employed by another (Zedeck, Tziner, & Middlestadt, 1983).

These problems can be overcome. Interviewers can be trained to follow similar patterns in their questioning and to evaluate responses using the same standards. When these more **structured interview techniques** are used, when the questions asked are standardized and responses are recorded in some systematic manner, the consistency of the judgmental process increases markedly, as shown in Exhibit 17-2. Within limits, it does not matter which interviewer is used; the results tend to be similar. This kind of reliability of decision is sharply increased by providing the interviewer with detailed information regarding the nature of the jobs to be filled. Unfortunately, structuring of a kind that will increase the consistency of judgments appears to be the exception rather than the rule in most human resource contexts. Thus, where strong reliance is placed on the unstructured interview, the final selection decision often depends as much on which interviewer conducts the interview as on the characteristics of the applicant. On the other hand, agreement does not guarantee accuracy of prediction; there can be great consistency while still picking the wrong people.

Box 17-1 describes the interview process used at McKinsey and Company to hire new consultants. It provides a good example of the results to be expected when interviews are unstructured. Without the standard interview form and the pooling of multiple interviews, even less useful results would have been obtained.

EXHIBIT 17-2   Agreement between Interviewers Involved in Hiring Production Workers When the Evaluations Are Based on Factors Derived from Job Analysis

Job Analysis Factors	Range of Correlations between Interviewers in Different Groups	Overall Correlations
Stamina and agility	0.42–0.72	0.71
Willingness to work hard	0.62–0.71	0.72
Working well with others	0.51–0.70	0.66
Learning the work	0.39–0.67	0.67
Initiative	0.65–0.70	0.70

SOURCE: Adapted from David A. Grove (1981). A behavioral consistency approach to decision making in employment selection. *Personnel Psychology, 34,* 61.

Accuracy of Information.   Studies to determine the accuracy of work history statements made in the interview indicate that reporting errors may occur. Thus, in one instance, when a check was made with employers, information given by the interviewees regarding job titles was found to be invalid in 24 percent of the cases. Job duties were incorrectly reported by 10 percent, and pay was incorrectly reported by 22 percent (Weiss & Dawis, 1960). In general, the tendency was to upgrade rather than downgrade prior work experience.

In many employment situations, interview distortion may not be as prevalent as the preceding figures suggest. In any given instance, however, an interviewer may be faced with an applicant who deliberately, or perhaps unconsciously, falsifies a report. In such cases, the usual tendency is for people to make their records look better than they are. It can be assumed, also, that many applicants will attempt to avoid discussing previous instances of ineffective work performance. Where valid data are essential, it is usually desirable to check interview statements against alternative sources.

Accuracy of Judgments.   The inevitable conclusion derived from a number of investigations is that interview judgments, as they are usually made in the unstructured employ-

ment situation, are not closely related to independent measures of the characteristics judged. Nor are they closely related to measures of success on the job.

Yet there are conditions under which the interview exhibits considerable strength as a selection device. Evidence on this point is contained in Box 17-2, based on the selection interviews conducted at McKinsey and Company. The most valuable predictor proved to be the tone (whether positive or negative) of the overall comments the interviewer wrote in at the end of the report form—a "gut" reaction to the fit between individual and organization. What appears to be involved here is that the partners and personnel administrators, with substantial knowledge of consulting work and the McKinsey culture, have knowledge of the kind a job analysis can provide. The junior associates lack comparable knowledge, and therefore do not produce valid interview judgments; they do not really know what they are selecting for.

Other studies in which interviews produced good accuracy as predictors suggest more about the conditions under which this type of outcome may be anticipated (Arvey, Miller, Gould, & Burch, 1987; Campion, Pursell, & Brown, 1988). Interview questions developed from job analysis and focused on specific, known aspects of the job clearly do

BOX 17-1   RESEARCH IN I/O PSYCHOLOGY

Agreement among Interviewers at McKinsey and Company

At McKinsey and Company, a major factor in the selection of new consultants to work in the firm is an interview. Candidates are typically interviewed by three or four people, who may be junior associates in the firm who are not partners, partners in the firm, or personnel administrators. Interviewing is something that almost everyone in the firm does at one time or another.

The average interview lasts a little over an hour. Although a standard interview form is used, the interviews are by no means structured. Each interviewer uses his or her own approach, although all attempt to answer the same questions on the form at the end. There is no formal interviewer training, and criteria for employment remain quite subjective. The interview form contains questions dealing with the following:

Personal impression of the candidate

Effectiveness with people (potential for client acceptance)

Likelihood of firm acceptance

Mental ability for problem solving

Imagination

Initiative and sustained drive (motivation)

Practical judgment

Technical competence

Character and habits

Self-confidence, maturity, and emotional stability

Writing skill

Pattern of success in the past

Flexibility

Oral communication skill

Potential as a clientele builder

Promotion potential (to partner)

Overall recommendation as to employment

Special comments as to the candidate's match with the firm's culture

From the responses to these questions, each form could be scored as to the percentage of items that elicited an entirely favorable response from the interviewer. Because multiple interviews were used with the same candidates, it was possible to compute the reliability or overall agreement among these scores across large numbers of candidates. In one major office this correlation coefficient was 0.43. In a group of small offices it was 0.30. Among some forty-two individuals who ultimately became partners, it rose to 0.56. By most standards, agreement among the interviewers was not very high.

help. This means a different interview for each job or at least job family. Also, questions should relate to observable behavior and be essentially factual, rather than requiring interviewers to make conjectures about future plans. The interviewer should work from a specific set of questions dealing with aspects of the job under consideration, in addition to having a job description and specification at hand.

It is evident that the interview can be quite effective when used in a relatively standardized manner and when individualized interviewer approaches and biases are controlled. Under such standardized conditions, the interview takes on certain characteristics of

BOX 17-2   RESEARCH IN I/O PSYCHOLOGY

Validity of Selection Interviews at McKinsey and Company

From Box 17-1 it is clear that McKinsey and Company did not have a very reliable interview program, although for some reason the program worked a bit better among the one-in-six employed candidates who later became partners. This suggests that if validity was to be found, it would be when the promotion-to-partner decision was used as a criterion. This proved to be the case.

Using promotion versus separation from the firm short of partnership (a natural consequence of the up-or-out policy) as a criterion, the interviews as a whole produced a predictive validity of 0.17—not a very impressive figure. However, the problem appeared to be that the junior associate interviewers did not know the nature and culture of the firm very well. The more experienced partners did much better as interviewers, with a coefficient of 0.23, and the personnel administrators did very well indeed, with a validity of 0.52.

Among the questions on the interview form noted in Box 17-1, there were some that predicted subsequent success quite well in the hands of the partners and personnel administrators, and

others that did not. In the order of their effectiveness, with validity coefficients in parentheses, the really useful questions were:

Special comments as to the candidate's match with the firm's culture (0.54)

Self-confidence, maturity, and emotional stability (0.40)

Practical judgment (0.37)

Promotion potential (to partner) (0.36)

Overall recommendation as to employment (0.28)

Imagination (0.27)

Mental ability for problem solving (0.23)

Neither the interview measures dealing with social relationships nor those related to motivation at work were effective predictors. On the other hand, items dealing with cognitive processes and mental ability, as well as those dealing with emotional adjustment, worked rather well.

---

the application blank or a psychological test. It becomes in many respects an oral version of common written selection procedures, though with greater flexibility. Also, it should be recognized that, even though an interview procedure can be created to fill a particular selection need, it does not follow that this is the best procedure to use. There is ample evidence that questionnaires, tests, and the like may prove to be as good or better predictors, doing the same job often at substantially less cost (Guion & Imada, 1981; Tubiana & Ben-Shakhar, 1986).

In considering the accuracy of the interview, it is important to recognize that there are good interviewers and bad interviewers. The McKinsey data suggest one reason for this, degree of knowledge of the work, but there are other factors as well. In one instance three very experienced interviewers were compared in terms of their evaluations of 120 job applicants and the accuracy with which they predicted subsequent performance. While one of the three exhibited a very consistent ability to predict later performance, another evidenced no such ability at all; the third was in between (Dougherty, Ebert, & Callender, 1986). A company that could identify and consistently use interviewers like the first one would have a very useful selection process.

Decision Making in the Interview. Certain other conclusions regarding the decision-making process in the interview have been developed as a result of a series of studies initiated at McGill University (Webster, 1964, 1982). The early research found that in the actual interview situation, most interviewers tend to make an accept–reject decision early in the interview. They do not wait until all the information is in. Rather, a bias is developed and stabilized shortly after the discussion starts. This bias serves to color the remainder of the interview and is not usually reversed. However, other research indicates that this temporal bias can be reduced when interviewers have detailed information regarding the job and what makes for success in it, as well as when the time allocated for the interview is longer and when the candidate is of higher quality (Peters & Terborg, 1975; Tullar, Mullins, & Caldwell, 1979).

Interviewers are much more influenced by unfavorable than by favorable data. If any shift in viewpoint occurs during the interview, it is much more likely to be in the direction of rejection. Apparently, selection interviewers tend to maintain rather clear-cut conceptions regarding the role requirements of the jobs for which they are interviewing. They compare candidates against these stereotypes in the sense of looking for deviant characteristics and thus for negative evidence with regard to hiring. Positive evidence is given much less weight.

These findings suggest certain guidelines for maximizing the effectiveness of employment interviewing. For one thing, the data repeatedly indicate that if interviewers know a lot about the job they are interviewing for and what kind of people tend to succeed in it,

they will be more objective and the result will be better. If it is intended that the interview should make a unique contribution to the selection process, however, the interviewing ought to be done with relatively little foreknowledge of the candidate. Thus, contrary to common practice, application blanks, test scores, references, and the like should be withheld until after the initial selection interview.

Personal history data needed should be obtained directly from the candidate in oral form. This approach will serve to delay decision making in the interview, with the result that information obtained during the latter part of the discussion can be utilized in reaching a judgment. It also tends to reduce the likelihood of a **self-fulfilling prophecy,** where pre-interview expectations determine what happens in the interview (Dipboye, 1982).

If data are needed to fill in the gaps between the various selection techniques, these can be obtained from a second interview. Thus, the interview as an independent selection tool should be clearly differentiated from the interview as a means of following up on leads provided by other devices. Interviewers should be clear in their own minds as to which objective they are seeking.

Employment Discrimination in the Interview. Articles in the personnel management literature over the past ten or fifteen years have frequently set forth lists of the kinds of questions that should and should not be asked in the employment interview if charges of discrimination are to be minimized. To be avoided are such things as (Koen, 1980):

Inquiries about a name that would indicate the applicant's lineage, ancestry, national origin, or descent

Information on child-care arrangements

Questions about an applicant's height or weight

Names and relationship of persons with whom applicant resides

Birthplace of applicant

Inquiry as to how foreign language ability was obtained

Any inquiry relating to arrests

The names of organizations to which the applicant belongs

The list is long and includes many more items. Where **bona fide occupational qualifications (BFOQs)** are involved in the job, this may affect the use of some questions; an actress does need to be female, for instance. The BFOQ exemption applies to a very narrow range of situations involving authenticity or genuineness, such as an actress, and to situations involving universally recognized standards, such as a ladies' room attendant. Also, if it can be shown that a question does not produce a disparate effect in the hiring of a protected group—or, when it does, that the factor involved is validly related to job performance—then avoidance is not necessary. In any event, questions used should be used with all applicants. The net effect of this legal constraint has been that many companies have decided to avoid a number of questions, and that in turn has contributed in its own right to a greater standardization of the interview process.

Given this legal pressure, it becomes important to determine what is likely to happen in the interview situation, insofar as employment discrimination is concerned. Is there a likelihood of bias? A considerable amount of research has been done on this topic, and the conclusions from reviews of this research are relevant (Arvey, 1979):

1. The evidence from résumé research is fairly consistent in showing that women tend to be evaluated more poorly than men.

Moreover, the degree of differential evaluation appears to be related to the type of job for which women are considered; a more prominent bias occurs when women are considered for typically masculine-oriented jobs.

2. Qualifications of job candidates show a powerful main effect; the research did not support the notion that highly competent women are prone to more negative evaluations compared with highly competent males.

3. The data do not support typical a priori assumptions about the interview's providing a ready mechanism by which to discriminate against blacks.

Most, although not all, of the evidence for bias against females comes from research using résumé and application blank data, not interviews per se. However, to the extent that these data are seen before the interview, résumé reactions can be expected to influence interview outcomes. In any event, the bias effect against women is not strong relative to the effect of actual qualifications, and there is little reason to believe that highly competent women will be discriminated against. What bias does exist could probably be eliminated by appropriate selection of interviewers. In one study, it was found that bias in favor of male candidates for a management trainee position did exist—and it existed equally for male and female interviewers. But the bias was evident only among those interviewers known to have highly authoritarian personalities; if these people had been eliminated from the study, no bias effect would have been found (Simas & McCarrey, 1979).

Another point relates to changes in proclivities for bias over time. The more recent studies have found less evidence of interviewer bias than the earlier ones, and strong support for the role of ability and skill in interviewer decisions (Gilmore, Beehr, & Love, 1986; Raza

& Carpenter, 1987). It seems likely that a real change has occurred in this respect, especially insofar as females are concerned.

As noted, the research does not indicate that discrimination against blacks in the interview is characteristic. In fact, there have been several studies that obtained the reverse finding. A bias in favor of blacks appears to be most likely in the larger corporations that have been under the greatest legal pressure to hire blacks. Age-related bias has not been studied as extensively. However, there is evidence that where it does exist, information designed to remove stereotypes can prove quite effective (Singer & Sewell, 1989).

☐ Types of Employment Interviews

It is evident that the content of the selection interview may be varied. Different interviewers may ask different questions, concentrate on different parts of the person's prior experience, and attempt to develop estimates of different characteristics. It is also true that the basic technique or procedure may be varied.

Patterned, or Structured, Interviews. The structured approach has been noted in connection with the discussions of the consistency and accuracy of interviewer judgments. Often a detailed form is used, with the specific questions to be asked noted and space provided for the answers. The form is completed either during the interview or from memory immediately afterward. In other cases, only the areas to be covered are established in advance, and the order of coverage and actual question wording are left to the interviewer. Either way, the more structured approach offers distinct advantages over the usual procedure, in which different interviewers may go off in completely different directions, depending on their own and the candidate's predilections. On the other hand, it should be recognized that information loss may occur because of a lack of flexibility. The ideal may

be to combine a structured interview with a more free-wheeling interview later.

Nondirective Procedures. The **nondirective approach** derives originally from psychotherapy and counseling. It permits the person being interviewed considerable leeway in determining the topics to be covered. The basic role of the interviewer is to reflect the feelings of the other person and to restate or repeat key words and phrases. This tends to elicit more detailed information from the interviewee, especially with reference to emotional reactions, attitudes, and opinions. Because the candidate actually controls the content of the interview, this procedure may take the discussion far afield from what the interviewer might wish to treat. It frequently yields a great deal of information about the prior experiences, early family life, and interpersonal relationships of the individual, but much of this often has no clear relationship to the employment decision. For this reason, the nondirective technique is usually mixed with a more directive, questioning approach when it is used in the selection interview.

Multiple and Group Interviews. Another procedure, which has on occasion proved to yield very good validity, involves the use of more than one interviewer. Either the candidate spends time talking to several different people separately, or the candidate meets with a panel, or board, whose members alternate in asking questions. The latter approach can easily be integrated into a patterned or structured format, and when this is done, the resulting decisions and evaluations appear to maximize prediction of subsequent performance. Normally, the group evaluation is derived after discussion among the various interviewers, but independent estimates can be obtained from each person, and these then can be averaged to achieve a final decision. The major disadvantage of any multiple-interviewer procedure is that it can become very costly in terms of the total number of working hours required. For this reason, it is usually reserved for use in selecting people for the higher-level positions in a company.

Stress Interviews. The **stress approach** achieved some acceptance in the business world after World War II as a result of its use during the war to select people for espionage work with the Office of Strategic Services. As used in industry, this procedure usually involves the induction of failure stress. The interviewer rather suddenly becomes quite aggressive, belittles the candidate, and throws him or her on the defensive. Reactions to this type of treatment are then observed.

Because it utilizes a sample of present behavior to formulate predictions, rather than focusing on past behavior, the stress interview is in many ways more like a situational test than a selection interview. It has the disadvantage that rejected candidates who are subjected to this process can leave with a very negative image of the company, and even those whom the company may wish to hire can become so embittered that they will not accept an offer. This does not happen often, and usually a subsequent explanation can serve to eradicate any bad feelings. Yet when the fact that there is little positive evidence on the predictive power of the stress interview is added to these considerations, it seems very difficult to justify its use under normal circumstances. The selection situation alone appears to be anxiety-provoking enough for most people.

Computerized Interviews. A recent innovation in interview technique is the **computerized interview.** The applicant is questioned from the computer screen and no other person is present. This approach is a logical extension of the proliferation of inexpensive microcomputers and the development of relevant software designed to collect self-report data by interactive computers. Branching

logic allows promising areas to be explored and less promising topics to be bypassed. As the study described in Box 17-3 indicates, computerized interviewing is more suited to lower-level positions. However, in the appropriate context it can prove cost-effective, and it has the advantage of introducing a high degree of structuring.

☐ The Interview and Selection Models

It seems absolutely essential that interviewers receive some systematic feedback on the validity of their decisions if a company is to make effective use of the selection interview. To accomplish this, written evaluations of each candidate must be recorded. These interview ratings can be compared at a later date with criterion information provided by the employee's immediate superior or derived from some other source. In this way, interviewers can modify their techniques over time to maximize predictive validity. Furthermore, more effective interviewers can be identified.

This approach suffers from the fact that no follow-up can be made on applicants who are not hired. Yet interview recommendations are not followed religiously in most companies. For various reasons, those recommended for rejection are still hired on occasion. In addition, other selection procedures may outweigh a negative interview impression. Thus, there will be individuals in the follow-up group who have received rather low interview ratings, although the preponderant number will have had generally favorable evaluations in the interview.

One should not expect perfect success from these studies. Yet an interview should contribute something above what might be obtained by chance alone and from the use of other techniques. Also, if a standardized interview form is used, individual questions can be analyzed to see if they differentiate

BOX 17-3 RESEARCH IN I/O PSYCHOLOGY

Emotional Responses to Computerized Interviews among Georgia Institute of Technology Students

Undergraduate students at Georgia Tech were assigned at random to one of three conditions where they played the role of a job applicant:

1. In-person interview
2. Computerized interview
3. Paper-and-pencil form only

The students were told that those who did the best would receive extra class credits. In each experimental condition, half interviewed for a clerical position (low level) and half for a management trainee position (higher level). All students had had some prior experience interviewing for jobs. The overall content of the interview was the same across experimental conditions.

After the interview, the students completed a questionnaire in which they indicated on a twelve-point scale how angry and resentful they felt about their interview.

The emotional reactions were essentially the same across the three conditions for those stu-dents who interviewed for the low-level clerical position. In all cases the mean level of anger and resentment was quite low. This was also true for the applicants for the higher-level position inter-viewed face to face by an actual interviewer. However, substantially higher levels of resent-ment occurred when the applicants were being considered for the management trainee job and received either a computer interview or the paper-and-pencil form. Clearly there was a feel-ing that the higher-level position warranted more personal attention. There is a definite implication that computerized interviewing, or any approach devoid of social interaction, can make people angry when the job involved is of higher status; thus they may not accept the job if it is offered. At lower levels, computerized interviewing seems to be viewed as appropriate.

SOURCE: Christopher L. Martin & Dennis H. Nagao (1987). Some effects of computerized interviewing on job applicant responses. *Journal of Applied Psychology*, 74, 72–80.

---

between effective and ineffective employees, as in Box 17-2. If certain questions appear not to be contributing to the predictive process, others can be substituted and evaluated in a similar manner.

■ APPLICATION BLANKS AND BIOGRAPHICAL INVENTORIES

Probably the most widely used selection device is some type of written statement regarding the applicant's prior experiences and behavior. This may take the form of the conventional application blank, or an extend-ed biographical inventory utilizing a great variety of multiple-choice questions may be employed. On occasion, the form and content of the statement are determined by the appli-cant rather than the company. Such résumés are particularly likely to be used when the applicant is at the professional or managerial level.

☐ Application Blanks

The actual items included on the **application blank** vary considerably from company to company. Many firms maintain several differ-ent versions for various positions. It is partic-ularly common to have a separate blank for professional and technical employees, but it may be expedient to develop special forms for any group of jobs that are similar in their requirements and for which applications are received frequently.

In constructing an application blank, it is important to obtain only data that will be used. There is a tendency for these forms to grow in length over the years, to the point that they may well discourage applicants who, at least initially, are not strongly motivated toward employment. It is also important to be sure that the information requested is not in violation of federal or state fair employment practices legislation. Items such as arrest history, educational level, and children born to unmarried mothers may be interpreted as discriminatory unless clear evidence can be presented that they are job-related. Data for minority-group members may well be different, and an employer has to show that these matters are as important to job performance for one group as for the other.

The important consideration insofar as legal restrictions are concerned is that data related to race, sex, national origin, religion, and age not be used to discriminate against certain groups. In order to clear themselves of any suspicion in this area, employers have eliminated many application blank items that had previously been standard.

An additional problem arises because some states have more stringent fair employment legislation than does the federal government, and accordingly, these states place what amounts to an outright ban on the asking of certain questions. Where company forms are used nationwide or standardized forms provided by business forms companies are used, there is a risk of being in compliance insofar as federal laws and the laws of other states are concerned, but not in the state where a particular operation is located.

Although the accuracy of information reported in application blanks has been studied less frequently than the accuracy of inter-view information, the findings are much the same (Goldstein, 1971). In some instances, previous employers listed by the applicant indicate that the individual never worked for them. Reasons for leaving are at variance in 25 percent of cases. Time spent in previous employment often is overestimated, as is the rate of payment. At least among applicants for lower-level positions, some degree of distortion of application blank statements can be anticipated.

☐ Weighting Application Blank Items

The scoring of application blanks in accord with the demands of the selection model dates back to the early 1920s. The basic requirement is that responses to the various items on the blank be related to some criterion of job success. Studies have been done using job tenure, success ratings, salary increases, and a variety of other indexes. Application blank data are widely used in predicting turnover. One advantage of this approach is that, because application blanks are filled out by almost all applicants, it is possible to carry out weighting studies at any time. All that is required is a search of the files for the application blanks of people hired for a given type of work during a specified period. These blanks may then be related to available measures of success or turnover.

A variety of techniques for weighting application blank items has been developed, some of them quite statistically complex. In general, however, the more involved procedures do not add a great deal as long as the number of cases used in the analysis is sufficiently large. The much simpler horizontal percent method, as illustrated in Exhibit 17-3, appears to be perfectly adequate for most purposes. All that is needed is a sample of employees that may be divided, usually at the median, into a high and a low group on some criterion index. Application blanks filled out previously, at the time of employment, are

EXHIBIT 17-3   Example of Weighting Application Blank Responses by the Horizontal Percent Method

Response Categories	Low Group	High Group	Total Number	Percent High	Weight
Education					
Grade school	13	14	27	52	5
High school incomplete	28	23	51	45	5
High school graduate	56	46	102	45	5
College incomplete	18	16	34	47	5
College graduate	16	25	41	61	6
Graduate work	9	16	25	64	6
	140	140	280		
Most recent work experience					
None	18	5	23	22	2
Production	40	30	70	43	4
Clerical	38	28	66	42	4
Sales	8	35	43	81	8
Managerial	5	17	22	77	8
Professional	13	16	29	55	6
Other	18	9	27	33	3
	140	140	280		

then checked to determine how many in the low and high groups selected each alternative on a given item. The percentage of those responding in a particular way who also fall in the high group on the criterion is then computed. This percentage is converted to a weight by rounding to a single number. High values are associated with the desired performance, and low values with that which is not desired. A total score for the blank is obtained by adding up the weights on the individual items.

In the example of Exhibit 17-3, the two items have been selected to illustrate both effective and ineffective predictors. The education item does little to differentiate and probably would not be included in a final instrument. The most recent work experience item does differentiate, with sales and managerial experience being preferable and thus weighted more highly.

After weights have been developed in this manner, it is important that the scoring be cross-validated on another sample. This is essential in constructing a weighted application blank, because many of the differences in weights may not reflect real differences but only chance fluctuations. When a large number of items is weighted in this manner, cross-validation may yield validity coefficients well below what the analysis of the original sample seemed to suggest; these coefficients may even shrink to zero.

Additional cross-validations should also be conducted at periodic intervals after the weighting procedure has actually been introduced into the selection process, especially if any major changes in the jobs involved, in personnel policies, or in the labor market have occurred in the interim since the weights were established. In one instance a weighted application blank used to predict turnover had an original validity of 0.74. After three years this figure fell to 0.38, and five years after the initial research it was down to 0.07. At this point only three of the original fifteen items were found to be working effectively (Muchinsky, 1986).

Continuing studies of the relationship between weighted scores and job performance should also be made when the weights used are widely known in the company. A validity that was initially entirely satisfactory can shrink to zero if managers, anxious to find replacements and familiar with the weights, are tempted to guide applicants into the desired responses.

It should be emphasized that studies done to date do not yield support for the view that certain responses on an application blank are universally maximally predictive of future success, irrespective of the job, company, and situation (Brown, 1981). In fact, the responses that contribute the most to the relationship with a criterion are often difficult to explain in any rational manner.

On the other hand, some studies have produced very significant patterns of predictive responses. In Box 17-4, findings from McKinsey and Company highlight what can be achieved. Individual items often produced validity coefficients in the 0.50s in one sample or another, and the average validity for the items selected for use in the final measure was in the low 0.40s. The construction of this measure is described in Box 17-5; the cross-validation coefficient was 0.58. These results at McKinsey and Company are generally typical of what has been achieved in other similar studies. In this instance a cutting score between 11 and 12 would virtually assure that practically no potentially successful candidates would be lost.

☐ Biographical Inventories

The distinction between a weighted application blank and a biographical inventory is by no means clear-cut. However, the typical **biographical inventory** contains a somewhat larger number of items, utilizes a multiple-choice format exclusively, and deals with

matters that would not normally be covered in an application form. Often there are questions dealing with early life experiences, hobbies, health, social relations, and so on, that go well beyond the application blank in their detailed coverage of prior experiences (Mumford, Stokes, & Owens, 1990). In some instances, questions on attitudes, interests, values, opinions, and self-impressions are included. When this occurs, the biographical inventory begins to approximate a test. Thus, selection instruments of this kind, although they tend to place primary emphasis on the past as a predictor of the future, may also serve to sample present behavior and functioning to achieve their predictive purpose. Examples of the various kinds of items currently in use are presented in Exhibit 17-4.

Biographical inventories appear to have validities at essentially the same levels as weighted application blanks. They have been found to be quite stable, with retest correlations averaging in the mid 0.70s, over up to five years. When compared against others' observations, at least the hard-data items exhibit substantial accuracy (Fleishman, 1988; Shaffer, Saunders, & Owens, 1986).

Biographical inventory data have been used to develop classification systems for individuals on essentially historical grounds and to implement these systems as a basis for selection and placement (Brush & Owens, 1979; Owens & Schoenfeldt, 1979). Here the initial thrust is to establish constructs by logical and statistical methods and then to group responses to biographical inventory items into meaningful categories. Only after this construct-establishment process is completed is validation initiated. Comparisons of this approach and the weighted application blank procedure as applied to the same basic items indicate that the more rational item-grouping approach does have the advantage of establishing meaningful constructs (it is possible to explain what is going on), and shrinkage on cross-validation is minimal (there is little cap-

BOX **17-4**   RESEARCH IN I/O PSYCHOLOGY

Investigating Application Blank Items at McKinsey and Company

As part of its effort to develop procedures for selecting new consultants, McKinsey and Company undertook a study relating application blank data in the files to the subsequent success levels of consultant candidates who were hired. Although data were available on forty different application blank items, a decision was made to focus on fifteen items relating to (1) a previous life pattern of success and (2) previous exposure to corporate top-management culture. Many of the firm's partners felt that these areas would be the most fruitful. Success criteria utilized were an overall rating of performance effectiveness by the partner in charge of the office, the mean yearly increase in compensation received by the consultant, and whether or not the consultant was promoted to partner.

The fifteen items selected for investigation were:

Class standing in college

Class standing in graduate work

Advanced degree (including law) versus no advanced degree

Commissioned officer in service versus a lower rank or no service

Experience in a managerial capacity in business versus experience in a nonmanagerial capacity

Father's educational level (years completed)

Father held a high-level position in a corporation versus only lower-level positions or a position as a small businessman

Graduate of a private preparatory school versus high school graduate

Undergraduate degree from an Ivy League school versus another type

Undergraduate degree from a small, private college versus another type

Harvard Business School graduate versus advanced degree from elsewhere

Advanced degree from a school given priority in the firm's recruiting efforts (Harvard, Columbia, Pennsylvania, Chicago, MIT, and Stanford Business, Yale Administrative Science, Harvard Law, and Cambridge) versus advanced degree from elsewhere

Service in the Navy (Marines) or Air Force versus service in the Army

Years of prior business experience (for those with business experience)

At least one officer of a business corporation listed as a reference versus no corporate officers

Some of these items were found to be unrelated to any success criteria in the firm—the class-standing items, advanced degrees, an undergraduate degree from an Ivy League college, and company officer references. In several other cases the results were the opposite of what had been expected; those whose fathers had *less* education were rated higher ($r = -0.21$) and consultants whose fathers held *lower*-level positions were rated higher as well ($r = -0.52$). Years of business experience was related to success in a curvilinear manner, with very little and much experience both exhibiting positive relationships.

There were some strong relationships of the kind expected, however. Having been a commissioned officer in the military was associated with being promoted ($r = 0.43$), and prior management experience went with higher performance ratings and larger salary increases (both $r = 0.37$). Graduating from prep school correlated 0.26 with the ratings, from a small private college 0.44 with compensation increases, from Harvard Business School 0.37 with promotion, and from a school given priority in recruiting 0.44 with the ratings. Service in the Navy or Air Force was associated with positive ratings ($r = 0.25$). The study clearly unearthed a great deal of information that could be used to improve selection of new consultants.

BOX 17-5 RESEARCH IN I/O PSYCHOLOGY

Developing a Weighted Application Blank at McKinsey and Company

Based on the data developed from the analyses described in Box 17-4, steps were taken to create and test a weighted application blank for use in selecting new consultants. Only items that had shown a statistically significant relationship to some success criterion were used. Responses to these items were then weighted using the horizontal percent method. The resulting scoring system looked as follows:

1. Extent of prior business experience

    Less than 1 1/2 years—3 points

    1 1/2 to 5 1/2 years—0 points

    More than 5 1/2 years—2 points

2. Type of prior business experience

    No business experience—3 points

    Business experience without managerial responsibility—0 points

    Business experience with managerial responsibility—3 points

3. Branch of service

    No active-duty service—1 point

    Service in the Army, Air Force, or Coast Guard—1 point

    Service in the Navy or Marines—3 points

4. Type of military experience

    No active-duty service—1 point

    Active duty without commissioned rank—0 points

    Active duty with commissioned rank—3 points

5. Type of secondary schooling

    Public or Catholic high school—1 point

    Private preparatory school—3 points

6. Type of college graduated from

    State college or university—0 points

    Small college—3 points

    Large private or municipal college or university—2 points

7. Graduate education

    No advanced degree—1 point

    Business or law degree from a recruiting-priority school—2 points

    Harvard Business School degree—3 points

    Advanced degree other than those noted above—0 points

8. Extent of father's education

    Did not graduate from high school—3 points

    High school graduate or some college—1 point

    College degree—0 points

9. Father's highest occupational attainment

    Small businessman or corporate manager below middle level—3 points

    Nonprofessional, outside business—2 points

    Professional, outside business—1 point

    Middle- or upper-level corporate manager—0 points

Scores could range from 2 to 27. For purposes of cross-validation, all junior associates employed in a single office of the firm were studied. The application blank scores were correlated with performance ratings made by partners in the office. The resulting validity coefficient was 0.58. Application of the scoring procedure to the data of the original study, when promotion to partner was the criterion, yielded the following results:

Score Range	Percentage of Those in Score Range Promoted
22–26	62
17–21	47
12–16	23
7–11	6
2–6	0

Given these results, a brief measure was devised to tap the items contributing to the application blank score.

Biographical Information—Consulting Staff
(Brief Form)

Name _____   Date _____

Address _____

Telephone _____

Date of Birth _____

Work Experience. Please note all regular, full-time employment (not summer) starting with the most recent position.

1. Name and nature of organization _____

   Dates of employment (month & year) _____

   Titles of positions held _____

   Duties (highest level position) _____

2. Name and nature of organization _____

   Dates of employment (month & year) _____

   Titles of positions held _____

   Duties (highest level position) _____

   (Note additional positions on the back of this sheet using the same format.)

Military Experience. Please note active duty service only.

Nation _____ Branch (Army, Navy, Air Force, etc.) _____

Dates of service (month & year) _____

Rank at separation _____

Education.

Type of School	Name and Location	From	To	Degree	Major
High School					
Prep. School					
College					
Grad. School					

Early Background.

Place where spent childhood (longest residence) _____

Father's education (level and type) _____

Father's highest position _____

   Name and nature of organization _____

Other positions held by father _____

Mother's education (level and type) _____

italization on chance). Nevertheless, the type of procedure described for weighted application blank data produces higher validity coefficients and thus is more practically useful—in spite of uncertainty as to exactly what is behind the predictive measures and consider-able chance fluctuation in the results prior to cross-validation (Mitchell & Klimoski, 1982).

In short, weighting items of an application blank or biographical inventory nature against subsequent performance outcomes appears the preferable practical approach

EXHIBIT 17-4   Typical Biographical Inventory Questions

Habits and Attitudes
  How often do you tell jokes?
    1. Very frequently
    2. Frequently
    3. Occasionally
    4. Seldom
    5. Cannot remember jokes
Health
  Have you ever suffered from:
    1. Allergies?
    2. Asthma?
    3. High blood pressure?
    4. Ulcers?
    5. Headaches?
    6. None of these.
Human Relations
  How do you regard your neighbors?
    1. Not interested in your neighbors
    2. Like them but seldom see them
    3. Visit in each others' homes occasionally
    4. Spend a lot of time together
School and Education
  How old were you when you graduated from high school?
    1. Younger than 15
    2. 15 to 16
    3. 17 to 18
    4. 19 or older
    5. Did not graduate from high school
Self-impressions
  Do you generally do your best:
    1. At whatever job you are doing?
    2. Only in what you are interested?
    3. Only when it is demanded of you?
Values, Opinions, and Preferences
  Which one of the following seems most important to you?
    1. Having a pleasant home and family life
    2. Obtaining a challenging and exciting job
    3. Getting ahead in the world
    4. Being active and accepted in community affairs
    5. Making the most of your particular ability
Work
  How do you feel about traveling in your work?
    1. Would enjoy it tremendously
    2. Would like to do some traveling
    3. Would travel if it were necessary
    4. Definitely dislike traveling
Personal Attributes
  How creative do you feel you are?
    1. Highly creative
    2. Somewhat more creative than most in your field
    3. Moderately creative
    4. Somewhat less creative than most in your field

right now, and it clearly does serve to validate items in accord with legal mandates at an early point in the process. On the other hand, one has to keep validating over time because it is often difficult to understand and predict events. The more rational, construct-related approaches to the use of biographical data involving classification systems do not suffer from these problems; thus, they may well be the hope of the future. In fact, recent findings indicate that this approach can be effective in predicting career success across multiple occupations (Childs & Klimoski, 1986). There is even some preliminary evidence that theories regarding jobs may be used with success to determine which items should be selected for validation (Breaugh & Dossett, 1989). This represents a major break with the prevailing empirical approaches.

■ REFERENCES AND BACKGROUND INVESTIGATIONS

A final method of obtaining information on an applicant's prior behavior utilizes not the individuals themselves, but those who have associated with them and been in a position to observe them. Often, a written evaluation is obtained, but telephone interviews appear to be frequent also.

☐ Validity Considerations

Although the use of **references,** usually individuals named by the applicant, is widespread in the business world, the available research does not provide much basis for optimism insofar as this approach to the selection problem is concerned. One study related scores obtained from a standardized recommendation questionnaire to subsequent supervisory ratings of performance. The questionnaire contained items on occupational ability, character and reputation, and employability. On the average, two complet-

Exhibit 17-5   Correlation of Employee Recommendation Scores with Supervisor's Ratings in the U.S. Government

Trade	N	r
Carpenter	51	0.01
Equipment repairman	40	0.23
Machinist	100	0.24
Machine operator	108	-0.10
Ordnanceman (torpedo)	125	-0.01
Radio mechanic	107	0.29
Aviation metalsmith	94	0.24
Highlift-fork operator	108	0.21
Auto mechanic	98	0.09
Painter	70	0.07
Ordnanceman	100	0.10
Printer	116	0.11

SOURCE: James N. Mosel & Howard W. Goheen (1958). The validity of the employment recommendation questionnaire in personnel selection. *Personnel Psychology, 11,* 484.

ed questionnaires were returned on each individual included in the study, and the scores on these were averaged for the purpose of computing validity coefficients. The recommendations came from previous employers, supervisors, personnel managers, coworkers, and acquaintances. The people evaluated were all civil service employees of the U.S. government working in various skilled trades. Results are presented in Exhibit 17-5.

Only the correlations in the 0.20s have any predictive significance, and these are still low. Since only five of the twelve values reach even this level, the findings cannot be interpreted as providing much support for the use of recommendations. The major difficulty is that the responses were, almost without exception, very positive. Thus the range of scores was narrow and discrimination among applicants minimal. This appears to be a typical difficulty with recommendations (Baxter, Brock, Hill, & Rozelle, 1981).

A question may arise concerning the source of the recommendations. Is it possible that certain types of people, having had par-

EXHIBIT 17-6 **Correlations of Reference Ratings with Subsequent Performance Ratings in Terms of the Source of References for Teachers in the Montgomery County, Maryland, Public Schools**

Reference Source	N	r
Last superintendent	147	0.08
Last principal	340	0.19
Last supervisor	96	0.23
Other superintendent	111	0.22
Other principal	407	0.07
Other supervisor	53	0.06
Head of college education department	150	0.21
Professor of practice teaching	68	-0.03
Cooperating teacher of practice teaching	184	0.09

SOURCE: Rufus C. Browning (1968). Validity of reference ratings from previous employers. *Personnel Psychology, 21,* 391.

ticular kinds of relationships with an applicant, will provide more valid information than other types? A study to check on this hypothesis has been conducted among public school teachers. Employment recommendation questionnaires were correlated with performance ratings given at the end of the first year of employment by each teacher's principal. The results, given in Exhibit 17-6, are similar to those of Exhibit 17-5. Only correlations of about 0.20 and higher have any predictive significance, and there are few of these. The data do not suggest that any particular sources are clearly preferable.

Somewhat more encouraging results have been obtained from a study that attempted to determine whether references might yield substantial validity under certain circumstances but not others (Carroll & Nash, 1972; Nash & Carroll, 1970). This proved to be the case. The references were most accurate when they were received from immediate supervisors who supervised the candidate for a considerable period in a job much the same as that in which the later employment occurred. However, references from supervisors of the

same sex, race, or country of origin as the individual evaluated often had an upward bias that made them less useful. Thus, if characteristics of the source and of the relationship between the applicant and the reference source can be taken into account, the reference check does appear to have some value. Unfortunately, as with many moderator variable studies of this kind, the findings of this investigation provide no guides with regard to the large group of candidates whose references have a very good chance of being inaccurate.

Much of the validity research cited was carried out some years ago, and in fact there has been little done more recently. However, one study has the added distinction that rather favorable results were obtained without resort to moderator variables. The study was conducted in England and involved references provided by school principals prior to students' admission for officer training at the British Royal Naval College (Jones & Harrison, 1982). An overall validity of 0.36 was obtained. What appears to be involved here is that the accountability of the principals for the accuracy of their ratings was high. This is much less true in most business situations, where commitment to the candidate may be much stronger than to the potential employer, and the consequences of providing an inaccurate reference are minimal. If, however, accountability can be assured, results comparable to those of the Royal Naval College study can be anticipated.

☐ Written Recommendations and Field Investigations

An important question involves the relationship between written recommendations and more intensive **field investigations,** which attempt to develop a picture of an individual's background from personal interviews with a variety of people who have known him or her. A study in this area dealt with

U.S. government employees hired to fill positions as economists, budget examiners, and training officers. Field interviews were conducted with from three to six people who knew the applicant, and the results of these interviews were combined into an overall field evaluation. The latter investigation report ratings were then correlated with previously obtained ratings on a standardized recommendation questionnaire dealing with the applicants' personality, skill, knowledge, human relations competence, and occupational development.

As Exhibit 17-7 indicates, there was a positive relationship between the written recommendations and the more intensive field investigations. What the exhibit does not indicate is the amount of information that came out in the interviews but not in the letters. Such matters as gross incompetence and alcoholism were practically never mentioned in writing. Yet the field interviews often led to the identification of such factors. It seems clear, therefore, that the more effort one puts into an investigation of an applicant's background, the greater the probability that meaningful results will be obtained. Letters to friends identified by the applicant are in all probability not even worth the cost of mailing. Intensive interviews with former superiors, and others who know the person well, may be worth the effort.

It should be emphasized that field investigations of the type described are not restricted to government employees. Bonding and security clearance investigations are frequently carried out on industrial employees. Many firms regularly obtain credit evaluations on applicants, and the credit agencies often provide detailed information on other matters as well. For a rather nominal price, checks are carried out on court records, educational credentials, prior work experiences, and places of residence. On occasion, detective agencies are used to investigate managerial candidates. It is common practice to speak either

EXHIBIT 17-7 Correlation between Employee Recommendation Scores and Field Investigation Reports among U.S. Government Employees

Position	N	r
Economist	41	0.22
Budget examiner	21	0.54
Training officer	47	0.45

SOURCE: Howard W. Goheen & James N. Mosel (1959). Validity of the employment recommendation questionnaire: II Comparison with field investigations. *Personnel Psychology, 12,* 300.

on the telephone or in person with mutual acquaintances, especially those with occupational skills similar to the applicant's. Although the evidence on the matter is sparse, it seems likely that all these techniques, if they are used in a systematic manner with cross-checks between sources, will be more valuable and valid than written references. Nevertheless, it is important to maintain an ongoing validation effort to determine whether all types of preemployment information are related to subsequent success. This is particularly important because of the pronounced tendency that people have to rely on reference data in making selection decisions when such data are available to them (Paunonen, Jackson, & Oberman, 1987).

☐ Legal Considerations

Various laws and court decisions increasingly are constraining the use of references and background investigations in order to protect individual rights to privacy and to prevent blacklisting in employment. There are not only the federal limitations on the use of credit investigations without adequate reporting to job candidates, but also a number of state laws that make former employers liable for damages under certain circumstances. Such liability may occur when statements by a former employer can be shown to have wrongfully barred a candidate from a subsequent position with another employer as a result of blacklisting, false statement, or misrepresentation.

At one point, it appeared that the legal constraints surrounding the area might well serve to effectively discourage the use of references and background checks entirely (Muchinsky, 1986). Yet employers do need information on a candidate's past from sources other than the candidate, if only to certify information provided in interviews and on application blanks; in certain sensitive positions, such information may be absolutely essential. The current resolution appears to be that employers are hesitant to give reference information in written form, while at the same time continuing to request such information from other employers regarding their own candidates. This means that the reference check continues to survive while achieving what appears to be an even lower degree of accuracy than it had in the past.

It does seem now, however, that the legal threat in this area may have been somewhat overestimated. Courts have not always held companies liable or considered them to be engaged in discriminatory practices with regard to references. Thus, the legal climate appears to be improving. Nevertheless, the need to assure accountability of the source and to use procedures more nearly approximating those of a field investigation is greater today than it has ever been.

KEY TERMS

Past behavior

Present behavior

Employment interviews

Structured interview techniques

Self-fulfilling prophecy

Bona fide occupational qualifications (BFOQs)

Nondirective approach

Stress approach

Computerized interview

Application blank

Biographical inventory

References

Field investigations

SUMMARY

The common feature underlying most selection interviews, *biographical inventories, application blanks,* and *reference checks* is that *past behavior* is assumed to predict future performance. *Employment interviewing* is of particular importance because of its widespread application. Although these interviews can produce reliable and valid results, they often do not do so in practice. It is particularly important that questions be structured in advance, factual in nature, and derived from job analysis. Interviewers need to know the job they are interviewing for and to counteract tendencies to make decisions too early in the interview. Although discrimination can occur in the interview setting, particularly against women, it can be counteracted. A variety of approaches to interviewing has been developed. There are advantages and disadvantages to each, but in general the more *structured approaches* seem preferable in the employment context, especially when questions are individually validated.

Application blanks and *biographical inventories* also work best when items are validated directly against performance. Weights may thus be attached to individual items. A number of approaches have been devised for this purpose, but it is important to carry out continuing studies to be sure that changing circumstances have not intervened.

Validation is also important in the use of *references* and background investigations. Without it, these approaches have often proved of little value. An important consideration in using references appears to be the degree of accountability of the person providing the reference. For similar reasons, intensive *field investigations* have generally proved preferable to letters of reference. Although there are legal threats to the use of reference checks and similar procedures, there appears to have been some easing in pressures of this kind recently.

QUESTIONS

1. In what ways are the construction and use of application blanks constrained by legal considerations? Explain.

2. What things can be done to increase the reliability and validity of decisions based on selection interviews?

3. How and to what extent can it be said that discrimination is characteristic in the interview? In the use of application blanks and résumés?

4. What can be said about the accuracy of information given in interviews, application blanks, and references? How might accuracy be assured?

5. Define what is meant by each of the following and evaluate the effectiveness of each:
   a. Nondirective interview
   b. Stress interview
   c. Biographical inventory
   d. Field investigation

6. What is the evidence on the validity of the reference check? Under what conditions is it likely to prove most valid?

7. Why is cross-validation so important with weighted application blanks? How would you go about constructing and cross-validating such a measure?

8. A number of considerations bear on the view that written reference checks are becoming a thing of the past. What are these considerations, and what is their current status?

9. Why might the use of multiple selection interviews by different interviewers be expected to have advantages over a single interview? Would the same types of advantages hold for the use of multiple references?

10. What appears to be the relationship between the validity of the various selection procedures considered in this chapter and the frequency of their use? Explain.

CASE PROBLEM

Validation of Selection Procedures: Comprehensive Analysis in an Oil Company

A large oil company had for many years been using a wide array of selection techniques to guide hiring decisions for new employees at all levels. There were several different application blanks used for different employee groups—all of which had a great deal in common. These blanks had grown in size over the years as one person or another became enamored of a particular type of item and added it; since deleting items might offend someone else, it was simply easier to let the application blanks grow. They had all become what amounted to biographical inventories.

Multiple interviews were conducted for all positions, using several different interview forms that had been provided by a consulting firm at some time in the past. There were separate forms for clerical, blue-collar, and managerial and professional positions, but they were all standardized, having been developed by the consultants in their prior practice. Company policy required at least two parallel interviews on each candidate—one by human resources and one by management in the employing unit. Considerable attention was given to assuring that completed forms were received from all interviewers. As with the application blanks, no overall scoring procedures had been developed for the interview forms.

At least three written references were to be obtained for each candidate. A standard set of questions was used. Usually, the reference form was completed and mailed back to the company. However, in some cases it was filled out by a human resources representative, who took the answers over the telephone. Sometimes the reference-checking process was not completed by the time a hiring decision had to be made. Even so, three completed reference forms were obtained eventually on all people employed.

Finally, there was a test battery consisting of a general intelligence test, a personality inventory, and an interest measure. The same three tests were used with all candidates, although different expectations regarding performance held for different employee groups.

None of these selection procedures had ever been validated in any way. The company had a small personnel research unit, but involvement in selection was limited to establishing norms for the tests and occasionally interviewing candidates. The vice president in charge of human resources had concluded that a heavy investment in validation research was not warranted. Because the vice president was a lawyer, all records collected in connection with the selection process were retained— whether the person was hired or not—against the possibility that they might be needed in connection with some legal action.

All this remained essentially the same up to the time that the realities of federal fair employment legislation began to become apparent. At this point, the vice president concluded that all psychological testing should be suspended indefinitely. At the same time, the personnel research unit was assigned responsibility for developing the necessary evidence so that the company could defend itself against a discrimination charge in the selection area, should it be forced into court. The ban on validation research was suspended for this purpose.

Questions

1. How should the personnel research unit go about carrying out its charge? What specific steps should be taken and why?

2. In what ways might this situation provide an opportunity to improve the company's selection procedures regardless of legal considerations? What new approaches could be introduced?

18

Employment Testing

For a number of reasons, Sears, Roebuck became interested in developing a computerized method of generating written reports from results of test batteries (see Box 6–1). The existing clinical write-ups by psychologists were not cost-effective, and it was felt that greater standardization and accuracy could be achieved with a computerized approach.

Much of the work on the system was done by a committee of testing experts. This committee developed a comprehensive list of questions that a good interpretive report should answer. Then scales were selected from the existing test battery that were judged appropriate to answer each question. Finally, a computer statement library was written to provide descriptive phrases answering the questions for the various score levels on the scales. The list of questions dealt with mental ability (overall, quantitative, and verbal), business motivation, personal characteristics, and emotional adjustment. The question list for quantitative skills was as follows:

1. Quantitative ability
   a. How does his/her quantitative ability compare to that of other company executives?
   b. Can he/she handle complex quantitative material?
2. Does he/she like to use his/her quantitative skills?
   a. Does he/she enjoy computational tasks?
   b. Can he/she tolerate routine, detailed, or repetitive work?
   c. Does he/she have careful work habits?
   d. Does he/she like to have variety and change in his/her work?

The statement library was composed primarily of different answers to each question based on the score level of a single scale, although there were some instances where combinations of scores on several scales were used. An example of the computer-generated result for a specific individual in one area follows:

Quantitative Skills and Their Use

Mr. Alpha has exceptionally fine quantitative ability. He is capable of working with highly complex and abstract numerical material, reasoning through problems and solving them very rapidly.

Despite his good numerical ability, Mr. Alpha very strongly dislikes computational work and will avoid numerical tasks whenever possible. He also strongly dislikes repetitive, detailed, or routine tasks and will have no tolerance for such assignments. When he does engage in quantitative work, his need for change and variety is likely to interfere with careful and conscientious attention to detail.

Outputs from the final system were compared with individually written clinical reports to determine how well the objectives had been accomplished. Expert judges indicated that the computer-written reports were more thorough and accurate (and longer). The individually written reports were somewhat more coherent and better integrated. Overall, the computerized system was judged a success.

SOURCE C. David Vale, Laura S. Keller, & V. Jon Bentz (1986). Development and validation of a computerized interpretation system for personnel tests. *Personnel Psychology, 39,* 525–542.

The Sears test scores thus converted to words are from a variety of instruments—for mental ability, from the American Council on Education Psychological Test; for personality, from the Guilford-Martin Personality Inventories; for values and interests, from the Allport-Vernon Scale of Values and the Kuder Preference Inventory. The following discussion attempts to provide a greater understanding of instruments of these kinds.

This whole subject of testing is a topic with which psychologists have been involved for many years. In fact, at one time industrial psychology was practically synonymous with psychological testing, and most psychologists working in industry owed their jobs to their knowledge of testing. Testing, unlike the selection approaches considered in Chapter 17, places primary stress on samples of current activity for the prediction of future behavior. **Testing** attempts to develop an estimate of future effectiveness from an analysis of present functioning in a particular sphere.

In its present form, testing has been markedly influenced by the computer. The test-interpretation program developed at Sears, Roebuck is a good example. For many years it has been common practice to use computers to score tests. Increasingly now, computers are being used to administer tests. An example is **tailored testing,** where the individual answers a specially selected series of questions displayed on a computer screen by keying responses directly into the computer. Tailored testing is defined as follows:

> A process in which examinees interact with a computer to answer a series of items, each prompted by the correctness or incorrectness of answers to previous items. After each item is answered, the computer estimates the examinee's ability. Based upon this estimate, the computer selects the next item. As the series of items progresses, the estimate of ability becomes increasingly precise. Because each series of items or test is tailored to the individual examinee, significantly fewer items (and consequently less testing time) are required (Tenopyr & Oeltjen, 1982, p. 60).

Approaches like this are costly, and the costs may be recoverable only if a large number of people are hired for a particular job or job family; yet for large employers they make a great deal of sense. There is obviously a substantial parallel between tailored testing and computerized interviewing.

As we discuss various test procedures, it may be helpful to keep in mind the numerous ways in which the computer may assist the testing process. The tests considered are some of the most widely known and most extensively utilized.

■ TESTING ABILITIES

Chapter 2 included a general discussion of intelligence, the abilities that comprise it, and the contributions that mental abilities make to performance. Here we will take up the tests that have been developed to measure intelligence in its various aspects, and also tests of other types of abilities.

□ Multiability Tests

One approach in psychological measurement has been to incorporate a number of quite varied subtests in a comprehensive test battery. The batteries typically yield an overall index of intelligence plus subscores for specific mental abilities.

Wechsler Adult Intelligence Scale. The Wechsler Adult Intelligence Scale is an individually administered test, with questions asked orally by a psychologist of the person tested and answers recorded on a special test form (Matarazzo, 1972). Because it is time-consuming and costly to administer, the Wechsler is not widely used for personnel selection except at the higher levels. There are eleven subtests in all:

Verbal

1. *Information.* A series of open-ended questions is asked, dealing with the kinds of factual data that people normally pick up in their ordinary contacts.
2. *Comprehension.* Another series of open-ended questions is presented, covering the individual's understanding of the need for social rules.
3. *Arithmetic.* All the questions are of the story, or problem, type. Scoring is for the correctness of solutions and the time to respond.
4. *Digit span.* A group of numbers is read off, and the subject is to repeat them from memory, sometimes backward.

5. *Similarities.* Pairs of terms are read off, and a common property, or characteristic, must be abstracted.

6. *Vocabulary.* A series of words must be defined in the subject's own terms.

Performance

7. *Picture completion.* A number of pictures is presented for which the subject must identify the missing component.

8. *Picture arrangement.* Items require that a series of pictures be arranged as rapidly as possible in the order that makes the most sense.

9. *Object assembly.* Jigsaw puzzles must be put together within a given time limit.

10. *Block design.* Working with a set of small blocks having red, white, or red and white faces, the subject attempts to duplicate various printed designs as quickly as possible.

11. *Digit symbol.* Subjects are given a series of paired symbols and numbers as a code. They are to write as many correct numbers as they can for each of a whole series of scrambled symbols within a set time period.

Differential Aptitude Tests.   One of the most carefully constructed sets of tests currently available is the Differential Aptitude Tests, which take about four hours to administer. Eight separate aptitude measures are included. With the exception of the clerical test, all have liberal time limits, with the result that older applicants are not unduly penalized. For most purposes, it would probably not be necessary to administer the entire battery, but only those tests that have proved to have relevance for the particular position under consideration. The aptitudes measured are:

1. *Verbal reasoning.* These are a series of verbal analogies. A good background of general information is required.

2. *Numerical ability.* Arithmetic computations with a multiple-choice format. The choices are structured in such a way that the answers must actually be computed.

3. *Abstract reasoning.* The items are made up of sets of four "problem figures" that constitute a logical sequence of some kind. A fifth figure must then be selected from among five "answer figures" to complete the sequence.

4. *Space relations.* A series of items requiring visualization of forms in space is presented. A key pattern must be matched in some way with one or more of five multiple-choice forms.

5. *Mechanical reasoning.* Pictures are shown that depict various mechanical problems. A number of questions are then asked to determine if the subject understands the mechanical processes involved. This is typical of mechanical ability measures.

6. *Clerical speed and accuracy.* Five pairs of numbers and/or letters are shown, one of which is underlined. On an answer sheet, the same pairs are shown but in a different order. The task is to pick out the underlined pair on the answer sheet. The test is timed, and the score is based on the number of items completed correctly.

7. *Language usage, spelling.* A series of words, some spelled correctly and some not, is shown. The subject must indicate which are correct.

8. *Language usage, sentences.* This test is a measure of the degree to which an individual understands the formal rules of grammar.

General Aptitude Test Battery.   A battery of psychological tests constructed by the U.S. Employment and Training Administration, the General Aptitude Test Battery has had wide distribution because of its use in state employment offices (Hartigan and Wigdor, 1989). It is aimed primarily at lower job levels

Exhibit 18-1   Correlations among General Intelligence Tests in a Sample of Sales Employees at Atlantic-Richfield

Test	Mean Score	Vocabulary Test G-T		Concept Mastery	WAIS Score
		Form A	Form B		
Vocabulary Test G-T, Forms A and B (40 items)	27.64	0.89	0.89	0.73	0.56
Vocabulary Test G-T, Form A (20 items)	13.03		0.59	0.64	0.47
Vocabulary Test G-T, Form B (20 items)	14.61			0.67	0.54
Concept Mastery Test	61.50				0.54
WAIS Score	67.22				

and contains twelve separately timed tests. Scores from these tests are combined to yield measures of various individual aptitudes plus an index of general intelligence. The special aptitudes measured are verbal, numerical, spatial, form perception, clerical perception, coordination, finger dexterity, and manual dexterity.

The test has been used extensively in occupational research and in these studies has typically yielded good validity (Alexander, Carson, Alliger, & Cronshaw, 1989). However, it is clear that the aptitudes that are related to success in one type of work are not always the same as those that are associated with success in another (Gottfredson, 1986). Furthermore, the studies indicate that although success in training is best predicted with measures of general intelligence and of verbal and numerical ability, aptitudes such as coordination, finger dexterity, and manual dexterity are relatively more important in predicting job proficiency.

☐ Tests of Special Intellectual Abilities

A number of separately published tests measure one, or at most two, of the various mental abilities. In many respects they are similar to specific subtests of the multiability batteries. There are independent measures of clerical ability, mechanical ability, creative ability, spatial ability, numerical ability, verbal ability, and others.

Certain of these tests are considered **measures of general intelligence.** These usually are pure verbal ability tests, although in certain instances numerical items are included as well. Available evidence appears to support the general intelligence designation even when the verbal ability measures are quite short. In Exhibit 18-1, correlations among various versions of a short vocabulary test, the Concept Mastery Test (a much longer measure containing some numerical as well as verbal items), and the Wechsler Adult Intelligence Scale are reported. All the correlations are substantial. Thus, when a score is referred to as an index of general intelligence, either a verbal ability test score, a verbal and numerical score, or a comprehensive score derived from a multiability test may be indicated. The common bond appears to be a strong emphasis on material normally learned in school.

Box 18-1 describes efforts to validate several of the tests noted in Exhibit 18-1 as selection instruments at McKinsey and Company. As in this instance, conducting psychological

BOX 18-1   RESEARCH IN I/O PSYCHOLOGY

The Search for a General Ability Test at McKinsey and Company

For a number of years McKinsey and Company had been using a variant of a test originally developed for military screening to select consultants. The test had been used without empirical validation on the assumption that a problem-solving occupation such as consulting required bright people. When validation finally was carried out, the results were surprising. Only marginal evidence of validity was obtained, and that was due almost entirely to the superior performance of the better consultants on verbal analogies items.

Following up on this lead, and initially focusing entirely on the firm's central office, the Concept Mastery Test was given a trial. This is a very difficult, primarily verbal measure made up of analogies and synonym–antonyms. It seemed ideally suited to the McKinsey situation, where intelligence levels clearly are high. The pilot research on a small sample was encouraging.

The next step was to conduct a more comprehensive validation in the firm's various offices. The study was longitudinal and used ratings after the consultants had been employed for about eighteen months as a criterion. No evidence of validity was obtained in the sample as a whole, but in the central office the validity coefficient was 0.50.

These results were confusing at best. A decision was made to try another test—the Vocabulary Test G-T, which contains only vocabulary items. The study duplicated the previous one in terms of longitudinal design but utilized more extensive and probably better criterion measures. Superior ratings with good reliability, compensation changes, and changes in the level at which the individual's services were charged to clients were all utilized. Again the multioffice analysis produced nothing. Again, in the central office, intelligence was a very valid predictor ($r = 0.48$ with the ratings, 0.37 with the compensation change per year, and 0.55 with client charge change per year).

Why intelligence was so important to success among consultants in the central office and not to consultants in other offices remained a mystery.

research in business organizations often seems to raise more questions than it answers.

Some of the more commonly used ability tests are those of mechanical and clerical abilities. Measures such as the Bennett Test of Mechanical Comprehension and the Purdue Mechanical Adaptability Test have proved quite effective for various industrial jobs. They tap understanding of principles of a mechanical or electrical nature. Clerical tests are often short and highly speeded. Box 18-2 describes the use of these measures at AT&T. Whether these tests would exhibit the same validity in the actual job situation is unknown. Probably the posttraining work sample criterion served to inflate validity somewhat. But the courts have accepted this kind of criterion, and AT&T was interested primarily in showing that its selection tests were valid.

☐ Psychomotor and Physical Ability Tests

In addition to the coordination and dexterity tests of the General Aptitude Test Battery, other typical **psychomotor measures** are the MacQuarrie Test for Mechanical Ability and the O'Connor Finger and Tweezer Dexterity Tests. In addition, there are a number of special coordination measures and apparatus

BOX **18-2**   RESEARCH IN I/O PSYCHOLOGY

Clerical Ability Tests at AT&T

At the time of this study AT&T employed some 120,000 people in clerical jobs. Assignments ranged from messenger to computer console operator. The study was conducted in fourteen metropolitan areas across the country. Job analysis indicated that the work involved primarily posting, recording, record preparation, and maintenance; computing and machine calculation; checking; and filing.

The predictor tests of clerical ability employed, all of which were highly speeded (i.e., designed to be completed in a limited time period), were:

1. *Number comparison*—100 pairs of four- to nine-digit numbers.
2. *Arithmetic*—100 simple addition and subtraction problems.
3. *Number transcription*—twenty-five randomly arranged numbers and twenty-five names to be paired with the numbers.
4. *Filing*—fifteen randomly listed names to be interfiled with forty-four alphabetically arranged names.
5. *Spelling*—forty multiple-choice items with one of three spellings correct.
6. *Perceptual speed*—a 40×25 matrix of randomly arranged single digits in which pairs of like numbers appearing together in a row are to be circled.
7. *Area codes*—using a list of cities and their area codes, area codes are to be assigned to eighty-four cities.

8. *Marking*—Sixteen ten-digit telephone numbers are presented directly above a mark sense card; the task is to mark the numbered boxes that correspond to the ten-digit number above the card.
9. *Coding*—100 sets of three letters are presented and the task is to associate one of three symbols with each set depending on the degree of sameness of the letters.

At the time the company was under considerable pressure from federal agencies and wished to demonstrate the validity of these measures. The criterion was a work sample extending over two days, administered within a month of the employment date. Essentially these were post-training measures of accomplishment that could be scored directly.

All nine tests demonstrated significant validity when correlated with the criterion, with validity coefficients ranging from 0.24 to 0.61 and averaging 0.42. All nine tests were valid in a black sample, six in a Hispanic sample, and eight in a white sample. These results helped the company in its fight against charges of employment discrimination in employment.

SOURCE: Sidney Gael, Donald L. Grant, & Richard J. Ritchie (1975). Employment test validation for minority and nonminority clerks with work sample criteria. *Journal of Applied Psychology, 60,* 420–426.

tests that tap grosser muscular skills.

Although most psychomotor tests require some kind of special equipment, the MacQuarrie utilizes only pencil and paper. There are seven subtests:

1. *Tracing.* The subject draws a continuous line from a start through gaps in a series of vertical lines to a finish point.
2. *Tapping.* The subject makes dots on a paper as quickly as possible.

3. *Dotting.* Dots are made within small, irregularly placed circles.

4. *Copying.* Simple designs are copied by connecting the appropriate dots from among a much larger number.

5. *Location.* The subject is required to locate specific points in a smaller version of a large stimulus.

6. *Blocks.* Piled blocks are shown in two dimensions, and the total number in the pile must be determined.

7. *Pursuit.* The subject visually traces lines through a maze.

This type of test appears to measure something rather different from the psychomotor tests that utilize special equipment. There is also reason to believe that the latter are more likely to yield adequate predictions in the selection situation. Yet tests such as those in the MacQuarrie have proved valid for occupations as varied as aviation mechanic and stenographer.

The O'Connor tests require a board with 100 small holes in rows of ten and a shallow tray in which a number of pins are placed. The subject's job is to fill the holes with pins using either fingers or, in some instances, tweezers. The score is the amount of time required to complete the task. This is the traditional type of measure used to obtain an index of finger dexterity. Similar pegboards with screws, nuts and bolts, and so on, provide a measure of more comprehensive psychomotor skills of the kind subsumed under the title "manual dexterity."

The O'Connor measures have been found valid as predictors of success among power sewing-machine operators and also for dental students, as well as for a variety of other manipulative tasks. The pegboard format is the most widely used among the psychomotor tests. It has in general proved to be a highly effective one.

For coordination, the most typical measure probably is the pursuit rotor, which establishes aiming skill or, perhaps more appropriately, motor coordination. The task here is to follow a dot on a rotating disk, using a stylus. The test measures electronically record the number of seconds the stylus is actually on the moving point. Much more complex apparatus tests, requiring a subject to pull certain levers, push certain pedals, and so on, when a given pattern of lights appears, have also been developed.

Physical ability tests have been much less widely used in personnel selection but have shown good validity where jobs require considerable strength. The data of Exhibit 18-2 illustrate the measures used and give their validity in jobs requiring pole climbing. The measures predict success in training and, as shown, whether individuals last on the job beyond a probationary period. In many instances, the validities for the female employees are well above those given for the total group. This is something AT&T would want to demonstrate given the fair employment pressures it faced.

□ General Pattern of Validities: Abilities

The various measures of intelligence, and also spatial and mechanical abilities, seem to achieve their greatest predictive effectiveness when used to select individuals for training programs. Used in this capacity, they far excel other types of ability measures. However, when prediction goes beyond the training period and moves to actual on-the-job performance, tests of intelligence and of spatial and mechanical abilities appear to do only as well as the clerical and psychomotor measures. This would suggest that, generally, when there is particular concern about selecting people who will be able to get through a training period, emphasis can best be placed on intelligence, spatial, or mechanical measures, as appropriate to the particular jobs

Exhibit 18-2   Validity of Physical Ability Tests for the Prediction of Job Survival (Six Months or more) in Telephone Company Craft Jobs (Splicer, Installer/Repairer, Line Technician)

	r	Females Only
Grip strength—using a hand dynamometer, which records kilograms of force	0.26	(0.22)
Dynamic trunk strength—number of sit-ups with a weight behind the head	0.21	(0.33)
Reaction time—time to respond appropriately to one of three possible lights	0.19	(0.45)
Dynamic arm strength—number of revolutions achieved by pedaling a bicycle ergometer with the hands	0.36	(0.56)
Balance—time of balance on one foot on a balance beam	0.18	(0.21)
Static strength—force achieved by pulling a cable across the chest	0.18	(0.18)
Stamina—time achieved in stepping up and down on a low bench in time to a metronome	0.33	(0.37)
Extent flexibility—distance the arm is extended in a rotating stretch of the trunk	0.18	(0.22)

Source: Adapted from Richard R. Reilly, Sheldon Zedeck, & Mary L. Tenopyr (1979). Validity and fairness of physical ability tests for predicting performance in craft jobs. *Journal of Applied Psychology, 64,* 264–266.

under consideration. Tests of this kind deal with the capacity to learn and thus are particularly suited to predicting success in training or educational programs. Job effectiveness, on the other hand, does not require these "learning" abilities any more than abilities of other kinds.

When attention is focused on specific types of occupations and the tests that will predict success in training for these occupations, the differential significance of the various abilities begins to appear. Success in training for clerical positions is best predicted with intelligence measures and with job-specific clerical ability tests. In addition, indexes of spatial and mechanical abilities also yield good validities.

In selecting people for training in service occupations, such as waiters and hospital attendants, it seems best, in view of the validities obtained, to concentrate on intelligence, spatial, and mechanical tests. These measures are also effective in predicting training success for skilled industrial occupations, as are measures of clerical ability. At

the semiskilled level, the highest validities against training criteria have been obtained with psychomotor ability tests and with spatial and mechanical measures. At all levels of skill, physical ability tests of the kind noted in Exhibit 18-2 can prove useful.

With the shift from success in training to effectiveness on the job, a greater number of studies becomes available and more occupations have been investigated. At the managerial level, measures of intelligence and those of a clerical nature appear to work best. Success in clerical work is predicted about equally well by intelligence and clerical indexes. In the sales occupations, abilities are not generally very important. An exception to this generalization can be made, however, in the case of higher-level jobs, such as industrial and insurance sales, where intelligence and, to a lesser degree, clerical ability, are important. In lower-level positions, especially among sales clerks, ability tests do not seem to carry any validity at all. Effective performance in the protective service occupations is about equally well predicted by all types of ability measures. Performance in other service occupations, however, appears to be more closely related to intelligence. Success in various industrial positions at the skilled, semiskilled, and unskilled levels can be predicted with all types of ability measures, although generally the validity coefficients tend to be lower than those obtained with managers, clerical workers, and higher-level sales personnel.

Results of validity generalization analyses indicate that ability measures predict training success with a validity of 0.63, performance ratings with a validity of 0.47, and promotion with a validity of 0.40 (Hunter & Hirsh, 1987). These are substantial relationships, and when they are costed out they indicate major savings if tests are used to select employees (Cascio, 1991). Success as indicated by rapid advancement up the managerial ladder is well predicted by measured ability (Schippmann & Prien, 1989).

■ TESTING PERSONALITY

Chapter 6 introduced the subject of personality measurement in the context of a general discussion of the nature of personality and of some of the more commonly studied personality characteristics. Here we will consider various tests that are particularly applicable in the organizational context. In addition, there are other measures that are used primarily in the clinical or educational spheres; these have limited relevance for industrial psychology.

The majority of the personality tests currently available ask respondents to describe themselves in some way, and these **self-reports** are either taken at face value or related to some group with known characteristics to obtain a score. A second approach utilizes **projective techniques.** Tests of this kind obtain descriptions or reactions, not with reference to the self in the here and now, but to

some far-removed situation and stimulus. Inferences are then made back to the individual's personality pattern.

The major problem in personality testing is the tendency to portray oneself in the most favorable light. This problem becomes acute in the selection situation (Elliott, 1981). Although the desire to make a good impression may represent a positive contribution when abilities are measured, because it ensures that applicants will do their best on the tests, such a desire may produce only a distorted and atypical picture of personality. Much of the work that has been done in the field of personality testing over the years has been concerned with the effort to find a solution to this problem.

□ Self-Report Techniques

Perhaps the most widely used self-report measures are those that provide information about the degree of interest in various types of activities, primarily those of an occupational nature. The major titles are the Strong-Campbell Interest and Kuder Preference Inventories. There are, in addition, a number of tests that yield scores on several personality characteristics, usually at least four and in some instances as many as eighteen. Among these self-report tests are the Edwards Personal Preference Schedule and the Minnesota Multiphasic Personality Inventory.

Interest Measures. In the **interest measures,** items typically deal with what individuals like to do or with reports on their own behavior. The Strong-Campbell Interest Inventory is scored in terms of the similarity between an individual's responses and those of people actually in a given occupation. Thus, a high score on a particular scale means that the person has interests like those of people in that occupation. It does not necessarily mean that the individual has directly indicated a marked interest in performing in that occupa-

BOX **18-3**   RESEARCH IN I/O PSYCHOLOGY

Development of a Supervisory Interest Scale for the Kuder Preference Record at Atlantic-Richfield

As part of its regular management appraisal process, Atlantic-Richfield had been administering the Kuder Preference Record for some time. At one point a question arose as to whether this instrument could be used more effectively to identify effective supervisors and managers. The subsequent discussion led to a research project to look into the matter.

The first step was to see if the Kuder Preference Record currently in use contained items indicating a preference for leadership positions, managing activities, taking charge of things, and making decisions; thirty-four such items were identified. These items were submitted to twenty judges, who were asked to select those responses "for which you feel a person who liked to supervise and direct the behavior of others more than anything else would indicate a preference." On seven of the items the judges could not agree. No one (or two) of the three alternatives elicited a high percentage of responses. These items were eliminated from further consideration. Sixty-seven records were then taken from the files and scored on the twenty-seven-item scale. These records were split into high and low groups at the median. Response frequencies within groups were computed for each item. Any item that did not clearly discriminate in the appropriate direction was eliminated. On this basis an additional four items were removed from the scale.

The final scale of twenty-three items was then applied to all the records in the management appraisal files. A comparison of odd- and even-numbered items in the scale produced a reliability coefficient of 0.74, which was somewhat lower than for the standard scales of the Kuder Preference Record. A comparison of supervisory interest scores of first-level supervisors with those of middle managers indicated no significant difference. When the new scale scores were correlated with management appraisal ratings of present job performance and potential for advancement, the validity coefficients obtained were 0.14 and 0.24 respectively. These values are low but statistically significant. No other Kuder scale yielded significant validities with both criterion measures, and the value of 0.24 was the highest coefficient obtained with any Kuder measure. The new Kuder supervisory scale was positively correlated with persuasive (0.45) and social service (0.15) interests; it was negatively correlated with scientific (-0.39), outdoor (-0.33), artistic (-0.33), musical (-0.32), literary (-0.19), and clerical (-0.13) interests.

Although encouraging with regard to the existence of a construct that might be labeled supervisory or managerial interest, the overall results of the project indicated that the Kuder Preference Record would be of only minimal help in identifying effective managers. Accordingly, a decision was made to pursue alternative routes to that goal.

---

tion. This indirect measurement procedure is intended at least to reduce the amount of distortion. The Strong-Campbell measure still can be distorted to produce a desired picture; on the other hand, in the actual selection situation, the amount of distortion occurring may be less.

One of the Kuder measures yields occupational scores in much the same manner as the Strong. Another deals with interest areas, such as mechanical or artistic endeavors, rather than specific occupations. In both instances, people must select from three listed activities the one they like the most and the one they like the least. Of the two Kuder measures described, the latter appears more likely to be distorted.

Box 18-3 provides an example of how home-grown scales are often developed by personnel psychologists. This study with an interest measure, the Kuder, is fairly typical of what is often done with both interest and other self-report techniques. Unfortunately, the Atlantic-Richfield effort failed to produce as effective a measure as had been desired.

Personality Measures. The Edwards Personal Preference Schedule is a forced-choice procedure requiring the subject to choose between paired alternatives, the majority of which have been selected so as to be matched in terms of their social desirability. Thus, on most items, subjects cannot respond in a way that presents a "good" image because they must choose between two equally "good" alternatives. The test measures some fifteen motives: the need or desire for achievement, deference, order, exhibition, autonomy, affiliation, intraception, succorance, dominance, abasement, nurturance, change, endurance, heterosexuality, and aggression. It takes approximately forty minutes to administer.

The Edwards has yielded acceptable correlations when studied in relation to various indexes of occupational success. Yet, again, as with the Strong-Campbell measure, the procedures introduced to handle distortion do not appear to have been entirely successful. The test can be answered in such a way as to present a good impression.

The Minnesota Multiphasic Personality Inventory (MMPI) is a quite different type of self-report measure. Here, an attempt is made to handle distortion by including certain items intended to indicate whether the individual has understood what is to be done and cooperated in completing the test. When these items are answered in certain ways, the other scores obtained become suspect. These latter scores deal with various types of emo-

tional pathology—depression, hysteria, and the like. The items are scored in terms of the tendency to respond in ways differing from the responses of the normally adjusted. Thus the end result is a profile indicating similarity to the emotionally disturbed for different diagnosed disorders (Butcher, 1985). After many years of use in its original form, the MMPI recently has been extensively revised.

Honesty or **integrity tests** as discussed in Chapter 6 are also self-report personality tests. As noted in Box 16–2, tests of this kind can possess substantial validity. One validity generalization study obtained a validity coefficient of 0.53 for a test that contains questions on theft admission, attitudes toward theft, and knowledge of others' thefts (McDaniel & Jones, 1986). Although tests in this area tend to deal directly with matters related to theft, drug use, telling the truth, and the like, there has been some use of more general self-report personality test items keyed to predict criminal behavior (Sackett, Burris, & Callahan, 1989).

☐ Projective Techniques

The projective procedures approach the problem of bias in a very different manner than the self-report techniques. A projective test is constructed so that the uninformed person cannot determine what is being measured. The subjects simply do not know what they are revealing about themselves when they respond to a test item. As a consequence, they cannot bias their responses in order to present a socially desirable picture or a picture that seems to be congruent with job expectations.

In theory, at least, this would appear to be the ideal solution to the bias problem. The subjects do not describe themselves; they react and, by reacting in a particular manner, reveal what type of people they are. In practice, this approach has encountered considerable difficulties. The problem is that the very procedures that keep subjects from understanding their own responses also make it difficult for the test administrator to understand them. Thus the projective approach in conquering the bias problem introduces the new problem of interpretation. Work with techniques such as the Rorschach Test, the Thematic Apperception Test, the Rosenzweig Picture-Frustration Study, the various sentence-completion measures, and the Tomkins-Horn Picture Arrangement Test has resulted in some real progress in this area. Yet more needs to be learned about the various ways in which people reveal themselves through their test responses. The projective tests have tremendous potential as personnel selection techniques, but that potential has been only partially realized to date.

The Thematic Apperception Test (TAT). The TAT, as originally developed, contained twenty pictures, many of them quite ambiguous. In many instances, however, fewer pictures are employed, especially in industry situations. Furthermore, a number of special versions of the TAT have been conceived, often using pictures of a much clearer and more structured nature than those originally utilized in the test. In all instances, subjects are asked to tell a story using the picture as a starting point. They are to describe the people, tell what is happening, and develop both the past and the future of the scene depicted. Because they must go beyond the picture itself, their own personal imaginative and fantasy processes are brought into play.

Limited evidence is available regarding the relationship between the TAT in its original form and job performance. Furthermore, although the test may be given in a group situation, with the subjects writing their stories, analysis remains a time-consuming process. For these reasons, the original TAT cannot be recommended as a selection technique under most circumstances.

However, various abbreviated versions of the TAT have been utilized with consider-

able success (Lefkowitz & Fraser, 1980; McClelland & Boyatzis, 1982). In most instances, these measures are scored to obtain indexes of achievement, power, and affiliation motivation as well as certain related variables in accordance with the dictates of McClelland's achievement-motivation theory (see Chapter 3, and especially Exhibit 3–2). Used in this manner, the TAT has been found to yield good predictions of success in entrepreneurial occupations and in line management.

Another approach that is closely related to the TAT is the Tomkins-Horn Picture Arrangement Test (PAT). In this test, subjects are presented with three pictures at a time, which they must arrange to produce a sequence that makes a logical story. Then a brief story describing this pattern of events is written below the pictures. There are twenty-five such items. Impressive results have been obtained with this measure in predicting success in various occupations (Bass & Barrett, 1981). The introduction to Chapter 16 describes one application of the PAT at Atlantic-Richfield. Box 18-4 describes its use to select consultants at McKinsey and Company.

The Sentence-Completion Technique. Sentence-completion tests, of which there are a number available, present a series of verbal stems, or beginnings of sentences, that the subject is asked to complete. Usually, there is an additional request that, in finishing the sentences, real feelings be expressed. Although some of the items may elicit completions of a self-report nature, the tests are usually constructed so that inferences regarding personality characteristics can be made in terms of the symbolic significance of the responses. Thus the self-reports are not accepted at face value.

There is reason to believe that this technique can prove valuable as a selection device. Unlike most other projectives, it is easy both to administer and to score; further-

BOX 18-4   RESEARCH IN I/O PSYCHOLOGY

Using the Tomkins-Horn Picture Arrangement Test (PAT) to Select Consultants at McKinsey and Company

As part of the comprehensive evaluation of selection procedures at McKinsey and Company, the PAT was administered to new consultants during an orientation and training program conducted shortly after hiring. The test yields thirty-seven different measures in the areas of work motivation (ten), social motivation (ten), inner life (eight), self-confidence (three), dependence (three), conformity (two), and emotional instability (one). The PAT results were correlated with criterion measures obtained roughly a year and a half later to evaluate the instrument as a selection technique. The criteria were performance ratings, compensation changes, and changes in the charge to clients for the individual's services.

The more successful consultants in the United States were found to be characterized by:

Low work motivation when passivity at work is possible

Low work motivation when passivity at work is not possible

Low work motivation when work problems are present

Low work motivation when distractions are present

High avoidance of active work

Low total active work motivation

Low social motivation in nonwork situations

High social motivation with authority figures at work

Low social motivation with groups of peers

High social motivation when support is involved

Low avoidance of social interaction

High total social motivation

Low self-confidence

Low dependence on others

Using these findings, a composite score was developed for the PAT. Although the individual scale results typically produced correlations with success criteria in the 0.20s and 0.30s, the composite score validity coefficient was 0.65. A check on the composite score's effectiveness in predicting promotion was carried out with a small sample of partners. All senior partners had above-average scores, many of them quite high. The junior partners averaged at the same high level, but there were two who fell below average. In these two instances the individuals involved had greater difficulty than the others during their consulting careers and advancement had come slowly. The one with the lowest PAT score ultimately separated to take a position outside consulting.

The PAT results provided a clear picture of successful consultants. They are planners and thinkers, not active doers and implementers. They like social interaction with people in authority, and are generally highly socially motivated. They are independent but not always self-confident.

---

more, its validity is high (Rabin & Zltogorski, 1985). Studies with the Miner Sentence Completion Scale, devised specifically for use with management personnel, have consistently indicated that this instrument has both pre-dictive and concurrent validity when used with managerial groups. Exhibit 18-3 provides a summary of these findings, as well as a summary of certain results obtained with a similar sentence-completion measure

EXHIBIT 18-3   Validity Data for Sentence-Completion Scales Intended for Use with Managers and Professionals

Group Studied	N	Criterion Measure	Correlation
Managerial form			
Research and development managers	81	Potential rating	0.43
Marketing managers	81	Promotion rate	0.39
Varied managers	61	Rehire rating	0.69
Department store managers	70	Managerial level	0.42
School administrators	82	Performance rating	0.42
Government research and development managers	117	Peer rating	0.55
Personnel managers	101	Objective index of managerial success	0.28
Professional form			
University professors	112	Compensation level	0.57
		Number of books published	0.53

SOURCE: Adapted from John B. Miner (1977). *Motivation to manage.* Buffalo, NY: Organizational Measurement Systems Press. John B. Miner (1980). The role of managerial and professional motivation in the career success of management professors. *Academy of Management Journal, 23,* 487–508.

devised for use with professional personnel. Additional evidence on the validity of the three different sentence-completion measures developed to test various role-motivation theories is given in Chapter 3 (see, for instance, Exhibits 3-4 and 3-5 and Box 3-3).

☐ Graphology

Graphology, the analysis of handwriting to infer personality characteristics, is not widely used for selection in the United States, but it has achieved much greater popularity in Europe (Shackleton & Anderson, 1987). The focus is on the way in which people write and shape letters, not the content of what they write. Interpretations of various personality characteristics are made.

A problem in evaluating graphological predictions arises because graphologists typically use autobiographical essays to make their interpretations. Under such circumstances it is always possible that their predictions are based on essay content rather than

graphology per se. Exhibit 18-4 describes the results of a test of this hypothesis. There is a positive trend in the graphologist's predictions, although not a strong one. Yet a clinical psychologist focusing entirely on essay content did better than any of the three graphologists, and a score developed using nine nongraphological factors did too. Either the graphologists were using content to some degree, or graphology alone is not a very good predictor.

This result is typical of what has been found with the better-designed tests of graphology's effectiveness. It does not appear to be a good way to measure personality.

☐ Drug Testing

Many companies have experienced continuing problems because of drug use by employees. These problems relate to reduced productivity because of drug use at work, absenteeism because of drug use off the job, and theft in order to support drug purchases.

EXHIBIT 18-4 Validity of Graphology as Compared with other Nongraphological Predictors

	Validity Coefficient Using Supervisor Ratings
Graphologist A	0.21
Graphologist B	0.29
Graphologist C	0.08
Clinical psychologist without graphological skills	0.34
Composite score from nongraphological data (education, army rank, arrival in Israel, marital status, vocational interests, quality of essay, esthetics of script, language errors, overall impression)	0.30

SOURCE: Adapted from Gershon Ben-Shakhar, Maya Bar-Hillel, Yoram Bilu, Edor Ben-Abba, & Anat Flug (1986). Can graphology predict occupational success? Two empirical studies and some methodological ramifications. *Journal of Applied Psychology, 71,* 648.

Accordingly, companies have become increasingly interested in identifying drug users in order to avoid hiring them in the first place, and in some instances to deal with the problem in some fashion among those already employed. One approach to identification has been through the application of the polygraph and honesty-testing procedures discussed in Chapter 6. Now, with legal restrictions on the use of the polygraph, honesty or integrity tests have been utilized increasingly for this purpose. These tests can be quite effective in spotting drug users (Frost & Rafilson, 1989).

Another approach to drug testing utilizes some type of physiological testing procedure, usually analysis of urine samples, to identify drug residuals. This is what is typically meant when the term **drug testing** is used. Such testing can be quite accurate, although as used in actual practice it may very well not be (Crown & Rosse, 1988; Fraser & Kroeck, 1989). The more accurate procedures tend to be more expensive, and many laboratories do not have the needed capabilities. Overall, it appears that when errors do occur, they are most likely to involve a failure to identify the presence of drugs when they are in fact present. Thus the testing may fail to accomplish the task for which it was instituted; or, put more correctly, it may only partially accomplish that task.

These problems are further confounded by the ethical and legal issues surrounding drug testing (Faley, Kleiman, & Wall, 1988; Guastello, 1988). Many contend that drug testing represents an invasion of privacy. Although a few jurisdictions have enacted outright bans, the more frequent situations is that the legal status of the physiological tests is unclear. This means that companies may well face considerable legal expense as an adjunct to a drug testing program. Two things are clear, however: A substantial number of employers, both private and public, do utilize drug testing in some form, and drug use is indeed a major problem that impacts upon performance (McDaniel, 1988). What appears to be needed most is an upgrading of existing practice so that the level of validity that is technically possible is in fact obtained.

☐ General Pattern of Validities: Personality

Several recent reviews have reported low validities for personality tests (Hunter & Hirsh, 1987; Reilly & Chao, 1982). Others, however, have indicated validities of a very respectable nature, entirely comparable to those for abilities (Cornelius, 1983; Miner, 1985; 1992). In part these differences can be accounted for by the fact that different studies were reviewed. Probably more important, though, is the fact that many personality tests yield a number of scores covering a wide range of characteristics. Some characteristics may be relevant for a given job; many will not be. Yet when all the scores are thrown together, as in a validity generalization analysis, the net result is a low estimate of overall personality test validity. What should be done is to correlate only appropriate personality measures with success indexes, focusing on what makes sense in the particular job or situation. When this is done—using managerial motivation measures to predict managerial performance, professional motivation scores to predict professional success, honesty or integrity test data to predict criminal behavior, and so on—the personality tests prove quite valid. In other words, personality tests should be validated in the same focused way that special-ability tests have been; unfortunately, this often has not been done in the past.

It is true, however, that personality tests, whether self-report or projective, have not produced evidence of good validity during the training period (Ghiselli, 1973). In groups where a sizable amount of research has been done, which includes clerical, protective service, and skilled occupations, the reported validities have consistently been below those obtained with certain types of ability measures.

When the focus shifts to on-the-job performance, this picture changes. Managerial success is well predicted by clerical and general intelligence tests, but personality measures are equally effective. Among clerical employees, the personality measures again are right up with the intelligence and clerical tests. It is in sales, however, that personality tests have proved most useful, primarily because here their contribution is almost unique. Ability measures, except for the intelligence measure, appear to have little relationship to sales success among those in higher-level sales posi-

tions. Personality measures, on the other hand, have consistently turned out to be good predictors at all levels of sales employment. Among sales clerks, they are the only kind of tests that yield positive relationships.

Within the various service occupations, personality tests, although not as effective as in sales, achieve validities that are often superior to those reported for ability measures. Job performance in industrial occupations generally is no better predicted by personality measures than by ability measures, but comparable validities can be expected. In general, the evidence indicates that personality measures, used correctly, can make a valuable contribution to the selection process.

■ TESTING SKILLS AND ACHIEVEMENTS

Measures of skills and achievements are derived directly from the job and thus tend to be specific to the occupation for which selection is to occur. Either a work sample is developed, as with the various typing and stenographic tests, or a series of questions is asked regarding the job. In some instances, tests of this type are available on a commercial basis, but it is also common practice to construct home-grown measures that are suited specifically to the needs of a particular company. Although criterion-related validity may be studied, the primary emphasis is on content validity, especially in smaller firms (Robinson, 1981).

□ Work Sample Procedures

Work sample tests are feasible only when the role prescriptions for a job form a rather homogeneous unit. If the job is complex, requiring many different types of activities, all of which are equally important to success, any truly inclusive work sample test would be so lengthy and cumbersome that its use in a selection battery would not normally be expedient. Even with more homogeneous jobs, most such tests tend to be only similar to the actual work situation and not exact duplicates of it.

Traditionally, the use of work sample testing has been restricted to positions that have been designed with rather simple role requirements or for which only previously trained or experienced applicants are hired. This is because testing a group of inexperienced individuals on a complex work sample is of little value, since all will obtain low scores. Under such circumstances, ability measures are much more likely to discriminate within the groups and predict which individuals will learn rapidly and achieve job success. More recently, approaches have been developed that include an opportunity to demonstrate one's ability to learn certain parts of the job; thus, evaluation follows a brief learning experience. As a result, inexperienced candidates can be tested and meaningful differences among them established (Robertson & Mindel, 1980; Siegel, 1983). These **trainability tests** show very good validity against short-term training success, but are less effective predictors over the longer term (Robertson & Downs, 1989).

A number of firms have developed work sample tests for skilled and semiskilled positions. In some instances, special equipment simulating that used on the job has been constructed. In other cases, a standardized test situation utilizing actual equipment is employed. In any event, it is crucial that all people tested be required to perform the same tasks under the same conditions in the same period of time. Work samples of this kind have been developed for a variety of positions in such areas as punch-press operation, inspection, packaging, fork-lift operation, truck driving, certain kinds of special machine operation, and many more.

Work sample procedures have also had widespread use in the clerical field. Here, where jobs tend to be highly standardized across a great many firms, regular commercial tests are much more common than for blue-collar workers. Examples of those available are the Thurstone Examination in Typing and the Seashore-Bennett Stenographic Proficiency Tests. These require that applicants take dictation and/or type, using materials that are the same for everybody. Scoring procedures have been worked out, and the scores obtained by a given applicant can be compared with those for a large number of clerical workers who have taken the test.

Although managerial work is generally less suitable for work sampling, certain aspects of the work have been simulated with considerable success, as is the case with various situational exercises used in assessment centers (see Chapters 6 and 14). In many respects, the management games, in-basket exercises, and discussion groups used do represent work samples (Thornton & Byham, 1982).

Although the work sample approach is probably most widely used to screen initial applicants, especially those who have gone through apprenticeship, vocational, or secretarial training programs prior to applying for a job, it is also used in connection with promotions. Work sample tests have proved particularly valuable in instances where union contracts place limitations on the promotion process. If, for instance, the contract says that seniority shall govern, provided the senior person is qualified to perform the higher-level job, it is important to determine whether that person is qualified. Work samples can be very helpful in this regard. In other cases, management has more freedom of action and can promote the most qualified employee, provided that where capability is equal the senior person will be moved up. Here also the level of qualification can best be demonstrated with a work sample test. The advantage of using work samples in these situations is that they do tend to be predictive of subsequent performance, and they are usually acceptable to the union. An equally valid projective personality measure would normally be of much less value for this purpose because of the apparent disparity between the test and the job.

The advent of the equal employment opportunity legislation and its enforcement have provided a spur to the development of work sample procedures. The need for a preliminary job analysis, the content validity, and the fact that adverse effects are less likely all make the approach particularly attractive from a fair employment viewpoint. Typically, a good work sample measure will not yield the same disproportionately high ratio of white to minority hires that the conventional mental ability tests do. Furthermore, in many of the kinds of jobs for which work sample measures are characteristically developed, the work samples prove to be as good predictors of later success as ability and personality tests. Tests that involve actual physical manipulation rather than verbal performance appear to be particularly effective (Robertson & Kandola, 1982).

☐ Achievement Tests

Achievement tests (also called job knowledge tests) differ from work samples in that they deal with the knowledge or information required to perform a job. Instead of demonstrating their skills, applicants answer written or oral questions about the work. There is considerable overlap between the two procedures.

Measures of this kind have proved particularly useful in discriminating between those who are and those who are not qualified to perform a given type of work. Because these measures are relatively easy to construct and administer, they are usually more appropriate for this purpose than work samples. It is not at all uncommon for job applicants to claim prior work experience as a carpenter, machinist, engineer, or accountant when they have actually performed in a less skilled capacity. Either the person intends to bluff his or her way into a higher-level position, or there is some ambiguity about the true meaning of the occupational title. In any event, a test of job knowledge can be very helpful.

So-called **trade tests** have been developed along these lines by the U.S. Job Service for a number of skilled occupations. These are oral tests, usually containing fifteen questions. The questions were selected by administering a much larger number of questions to three groups of workers: journeymen, apprentices and helpers in the trade, and individuals employed outside the trade in positions that are part of the same job family. A good question, one that is retained in the final test, should yield consistently correct responses from the first group and practically no correct responses from the third group. When a number of questions of this kind are put together in a test, experienced journeymen can easily be identified because they will obtain total scores at a level almost never obtained by those in the other two groups. Tests of this type have also demonstrated considerable validity as predictors of the degree to which an individual's behavior actually matches the role requirements for a job.

Achievement testing need not be restricted to short oral tests. Written tests have been developed by a number of firms for a whole range of positions. Tests of accounting knowledge, policies and procedures, human relations, business law, and economics, which cover segments of a job rather than the totality of information required, have also been constructed. Many civil service tests are of this kind.

Although, in general, achievement measures are constructed by the company to fit its own specific needs, some commercial tests are available. Thus, the Purdue Vocational Tests were developed primarily for the skilled trades. They are measures of information regarding such occupations as electrician, lathe operator, carpenter, sheet-metal worker, and welder. More specific tests also deal with industrial mathematics, blueprint reading, and scale reading.

To the extent that achievement tests and work samples are thoroughly embedded in job analysis and represent a point-for-point correspondence with the actual work, measuring relative performance on them assumes many of the same qualities as performance evaluation. The overlap with job simulations is immediately apparent. In fact, achievement tests of this kind have been used on occasion as criteria in selection research (Distefano, Pryer, & Craig, 1980).

In fact, Box 18-5 describes a measure which has operated both as a criterion and a predictor. AT&T originally viewed LAP as a criterion, but legal pressures ultimately forced its further consideration as a predictor.

☐ General Pattern of Validities: Skills and Achievements

The types of measures considered here are very close to the work, very job-specific, and very limited in their domains. It is probably this factor that accounts for their high validities; they are as close to actually doing the work as one can get without it being the work itself. That is why their status as predictors and criteria is somewhat murky. That is also why they tend to have very high validities. The problem is that separate instruments need to be created for each job, and that can be very costly.

As to actual reported validities, the figures vary somewhat from one review to another, but at the worst they are in the high 0.30s and at the best in the mid-0.50s (Schmitt & Noe,

1986). These are averages; there is no question that if one wishes to go to the effort and cost of developing a measure of skill or achievement, the result may well be a very effective selection procedure. Probably this is what accounts for much of the effectiveness of assessment centers.

■ USING AND NOT USING TESTS

During the 1970s a number of firms eliminated the use of tests, primarily because they feared they could not defend them against charges of discrimination. By the mid-1980s, however, at least as many companies had introduced testing programs, and in many cases these were the same firms that had abandoned them earlier. Thus, testing appears now to be at least as widespread as it was earlier, although perhaps in more diversified form (Bureau of National Affairs, 1983). Companies seem to feel more confident of their capacity to deal with discrimination charges.

One factor in this decision is the obvious fact that tests can work very well. If the validity-generalization approach is correct, and there is every reason to believe it is, then a great many tests are much more valid than was previously recognized, and their utility in monetary terms is much greater as well. The evidence on this point appears to be well established for the use of ability tests in selecting for a wide range of jobs; evidence of the same kind is beginning to emerge for certain personality measures as well.

Exhibit 18-5 provides an overview of how tests of different kinds measure up on different dimensions in comparison with other selection techniques. What they clearly have is relatively high validity. On other dimensions they are equally or even less attractive in comparison with the other techniques. Yet if not for its validity, what reason is there to use any selection procedure?

BOX **18-5** RESEARCH IN I/O PSYCHOLOGY

The Role of the Plant Department Learning Assessment Program (LAP) within AT&T

The Learning Assessment Program (LAP) was originally developed by Michigan Bell Telephone Company as a work sample of training, and as a criterion for the validation of selection tests. The program consists of key segments of training courses for station installer and repairman occupations and for more complex occupations such as central office repairman, PBX installer, PBX repairman, and test deskman. The program is organized into seven levels of training, ranging from the more elementary to the more complex, including basic electricity, basic telephone, Bell System practices, station circuits, advanced circuits, and trouble location. Levels 1–4 sample training for the station installer and repairman occupations, levels 5–7 for the more complex, "top-craft" occupations.

Candidates are tested preceding each level on the content of that level. If they pass the pretest, they go directly to the pretest for the next level. If they fail to pass the pretest, they go through the training for that level and, when ready, take a posttest. For any given level the proficiency tests, pre- and post-, have been designed to be equivalent in content and difficulty. Standards on the tests are based on the performance of experienced craftsmen.

All of the training has been programmed. The candidates are given the materials they need by the administrator of the program and proceed through the sequence at their own pace. Other than help in getting started, the candidate receives no instructional assistance. The tests are administered and scored (objectively) by the program administrator or assistant.

Much of the training and testing involves performance with normal tools and especially adapted telephone equipment. A relatively small proportion of the program is verbal in content. The primary objective of the program is to assess a candidate's ability to perform, after adequate training, a sample of tasks regularly performed by Plant Department craftsmen.

Because of the self-paced nature of this program, the time required to complete it varies from candidate to candidate. On the average, candidates for station installer-repairman positions take approximately four days to complete levels 1–4, while those for "top craft" take approximately six days. For both groups the time required is, of course, considerably less than the full training programs for the occupations involved yet gives ample time to demonstrate ability to learn the work.

Used as a criterion with predictors consisting of general intelligence tests, mechanical ability tests, achievement tests, and dexterity tests, LAP produced validities ranging from 0.19 to 0.44 and averaging 0.36. Differential validity for minorities and nonminorities was good.

However, federal agencies questioned this use of LAP. They claimed it was not job-related, was not based on job analyses, and was deliberately overweighted with intellectual content to produce high validities for cognitive tests. In short, they said it was a test, not a criterion, and thus that the so-called validation studies were test–test comparisons.

To counteract this argument AT&T undertook studies to validate LAP against clearly job-related measures, to show that it was job related. Some of the findings were:

Versus number of days in plant schools	0.30
Versus level of performance in plant schools	0.28
Versus number of times absent	−0.22
Versus number of accidents	−0.23

The data indicated validity against training criteria, and that was what LAP was supposed to be a work sample of. It also was significantly related to absenteeism and accidents. The data gave support to the argument that LAP was indeed job-related.

SOURCE: Donald L. Grant & Douglas W. Bray (1970). Validation of employment tests for telephone company installation and repair occupations. *Journal of Applied Psychology, 54,* 7–14.

Exhibit 18-5   Assessment of Tests as Compared with Other Selection Procedures

	Validity— Predictive Accuracy	Fairness— Unbiased Predictions	Applicability— Wide Application	Cost
Intelligence tests	Moderate	Moderate	High	Low
Ability tests	Moderate	High	Moderate	Low
Personality tests	Moderate	High	Low	Moderate
Work sample tests	High	High	Low	High
Assessment centers	High	High	Low	High
Interviews	Low	Moderate	High	Moderate
Biographical information	High	Moderate	High	Low
References	Low	(Unknown)	High	Low
Self-assessments	Low	High	Moderate	Low

SOURCE: Adapted from Paul M. Muchinsky (1986), Personnel selection methods. *International Review of Industrial and Organizational Psychology, 1,* 60.

KEY TERMS

Testing	Integrity tests
Tailored testing	Graphology
Measures of general intelligence	Drug testing
Psychomotor measures	Work sample tests
Self-reports	Trainability tests
Projective techniques	Achievement tests
Interest measures	Trade tests

SUMMARY

A wide range of *tests of abilities*, both intellectual and physical, has been developed. These tests possess validity across a large number of occupations, especially in predicting outcomes from training. However, they are less effective in sales. In contrast, *personality tests* have less value in predicting training success but work well with on-the-job performance, particularly in sales and managerial occupations. Tests of *skills and achievements,* including *work samples* and knowledge measures, tend to be much more specific to particular jobs than are ability and personality tests. Usually, they are strongly grounded in job analysis and possess substantial content validity.

Although employment testing experienced major setbacks under the initial impact of equal employment opportunity legislation, it now appears to have reestablished itself, and on sounder ground, with the aid of increasing evidence of validity. Furthermore, the advent of computerized, *tailored testing* gives promise of representing a major breakthrough in predicting job performance.

QUESTIONS

1. How are interest inventories such as the Strong-Campbell constructed? Why might such measures prove very effective for purposes of vocational guidance and counseling but less effective for personnel selection?

2. During the 1970s a number of companies stopped using employment tests. What was the reason, and what considerations have prompted many to return to the use of tests?

3. What types of tests are most valid for predicting success in training, and what types for predicting on-the-job success? Why do you suppose these differences exist?

4. How are computers used in connection with testing?

5. Work samples appear to be increasing considerably in popularity. What factors might account for this?

6. How is clerical ability measured? Why are these tests often speeded?

7. How do self-report and projective personality tests differ? Can you give any explanation for the fact that many industrial psychologists prefer the former, and many clinical psychologists, the latter?

8. What are the strengths and weaknesses, the advantages and disadvantages, of the following as selection tests?
   a. General Aptitude Test Battery
   b. Physical ability tests
   c. Edwards Personal Preference Schedule
   d. Sentence-completion techniques
   e. Drug testing by urinalysis

9. How are such constructs as verbal ability, numerical ability, mechanical ability, and spatial ability typically measured in standardized psychological tests? Give examples of each type of measure.

10. What is known about the validity of graphology?

CASE PROBLEM

Introducing a Testing Program: Upgrading Sales Operations for a Publishing House

A psychologist who served on the faculty of a large university and taught courses in industrial psychology was retained by a textbook publisher to develop a testing program. She was contacted originally because the company did not have this type of expertise in-house, and the new head of the college division felt that something had to be done about the high turnover and questionable performance that plagued his division.

The major area of concern was among the sales representatives, whose jobs required them to call on faculty members and college bookstores in their territories to help obtain course adoptions and thus sell the company's books. This basic sales function was not operating as it should because people kept quitting; frequently, it was the better ones who left. As a result, the time of sales management was almost completely taken up with training replacements and trying to deal with problems created by the typically less effective sales reps who stayed on. The problem was not a lack of candidates or particularly poor pay; the work was generally attractive to college graduates because it kept them in the academic environment, and the company paid at least as well as other publishers. As far as could be determined, the biggest problem and the major contributor to turnover was sales management itself.

The process operating was really circular. Sales reps were hired almost at random, based on the happenstance of a candidate and a vacancy being in a given location at the same time—at best, there was some rather superficial interviewing. Some of these reps were good, some not so good. The good ones left because they did not like the way they were treated by their managers. The poor ones stayed on because they could not get another job. Since promotion from within was the rule, many of the poorer reps were ultimately promoted into management, where they performed equally poorly and contributed in their own way to the exodus of competent personnel. Furthermore, promotions into editorial positions also came from the sales rep ranks, and this further depleted the supply of qualified managerial talent.

The college division president understood all this, and his intended solution was first to pick, from among those who applied, an overall better group of sales reps. At the same time, his plan called for hiring sales managers, at least for a while, from other publishers, rather than promoting from within. He wanted to break the circle of mediocrity; there were several competitors known to have top-flight sales organizations, which he believed he could raid. If candidates could be attracted from these competitors by the prospect of promotion, then the company could select some really good managerial talent, and the circle would be broken. What he wanted the psychologist to do was introduce tests that could be used to identify really good people, both among the sales rep candidates and among the managerial candidates; at the same time, it was important to protect against possible discrimination charges in an area of employment that had only recently been opened to women and minorities.

Questions

1. What tests would you consider for use in selecting people for the sales rep jobs? Why?
2. Would you use the same tests in selecting for the managerial jobs? If not, why, and what tests would you use?
3. Exactly how would you go about using your tests in order to protect the publisher against any charge of discrimination?

19

Training and Development

The initiative for a training program for supervisors at the First National Bank of Athens, Georgia, came from the marketing vice president. His concern resulted from questionable customer service practices apparently attributable to inadequate departmental coordination and a lack of knowledge on the part of supervisors regarding bank service. The bank's personnel officer also had concerns regarding employees being promoted to managerial ranks who failed to demonstrate adequate human relations skills. The consequences of these perceptions was the establishment of a set of supervisory training needs identified as awareness in the accompanying diagram.

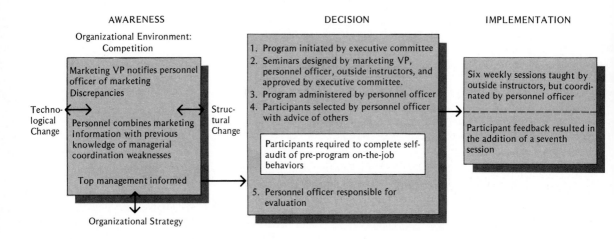

The program was administered by the personnel officer. She contacted faculty members at the University of Georgia, who taught the sessions. Meetings were held at bank headquarters immediately following working hours once a week. The content of the sessions was initially planned as follows:

Role of the Supervisor

In this introductory session, bank supervisors will learn how their performance on the job can be improved by management training. The supervisor's job is a demanding one with responsibilities toward upper management, subordinates, other bank employees, and the public. This session will review the transition into a supervisory position and the skills necessary to effectively manage bank employees.

Planning and Organizing

Supervisors tend to accomplish more when they are personally well organized. In this session, time management will be emphasized. Many supervisors lose control of their time because they do not delegate activities properly. Participants should leave this session with a better understanding of how much authority to delegate and when to do it. Also, the instructor will explain the organization's need for consistent rule enforcement.

Understanding Employees

The focus this week will be on employee satisfaction. Satisfaction and job performance influence each other, but the relationship is not always as clear as we may think. The needs of employees will be discussed. Participants will get a better idea of how they are perceived by their subordinates and how they affect the satisfaction of their work groups.

Motivating Employees

Among the many techniques for motivating employees, one that has been found useful for financial institutions is job enrichment. This session will concentrate on what job enrichment is and how bank supervisors can put it to use. The instructor will discuss other ways in which a manager influences employee motivation, including how consistent the manager's on the job behavior is toward the employees.

Training Employees for Customer Service

Each employee represents the bank to the public. Each employee, therefore, has a responsibility to market the various services of the bank to customers. In this session, the instructor will explain the importance of training personnel to perform as sales representatives of the full line of bank services. Techniques for training and for career development of employees will be discussed.

Communicating for Results
In these seminars, participants will learn a variety of techniques that they may wish to put to use to improve work group performance. Making changes on the job requires effective communication. In this final session, the supervisors will learn how to overcome communication barriers and will be exposed to ideas they can use to improve their ability to communicate.

The influence of the initial awareness of training needs is clearly evident in the training program content. Evidence from an extensive evaluation process suggests that the training did help to achieve the instructional objectives.

SOURCE: Bobby C. Vaught, Frank Hoy, & W. Wray Buchanan (1985). *Employee development programs: An organizational approach,* pp. 172–190. Westport, CT: Quorum Books.

This is a rather typical example of a management development program. It illustrates the roles played by the identification of a need, teaching methods, course content, and evaluation of results. These are the topics that are of concern in this chapter.

■ INTRODUCTION TO TRAINING AND DEVELOPMENT

The objective of training and development is to raise the level of performance in one or more of its aspects. This may be achieved either by providing new knowledge and information relevant to a job; by teaching new skills; or by imbuing an individual with new attitudes, values, motives, and other personality characteristics. Often these techniques are utilized with segments of a work force regardless of the existing performance level. Thus a given work group or managerial component may be given a particular course with a view to improving the role behavior of all members, the outstanding as well as the less effective. On occasion, training is focused on those who, either because they are new to the type of work or for other reasons, are not immediately in a position to achieve a successful level of performance.

□ Training versus Education

At the outset, it is important to differentiate training from education. Both relate to human change and learning, but they differ considerably in purpose. **Training** is basically role-specific. It attempts to help those who are or will be performing a certain job to achieve successful role behavior. **Education,** on the other hand, is tied to the goals of the individual more than to those of the organization, although some overlap between the two sets of goals can be anticipated. Thus, education tends to take individuals, their growth, and the multiple roles they may play in society as its starting point. Training starts with the requirements of a particular employing organization and, within that, of a given job.

Where students are expected to pay tuition to obtain a learning experience that they themselves desire, as in a university, we tend to speak of an educational process. Training normally is paid for by the employing organization, although both the individual and the company may benefit.

These distinctions leave some management development procedures in a position of considerable uncertainty. Clearly, management development is intended to be training, or at least it should be. But managerial jobs tend to have rather broad role prescriptions, especially at the very top levels, where the demand for the generalist is greatest. Furthermore, there are companies that do not place very clear delimitations on the scope of various managerial positions. The result is that management development can easily become transformed into something very close to education, even when it is paid for by the company; it can become oriented at least as much to the individual as to the company.

For most purposes, however, the training and development process is concerned with learning and change of a kind that is (1) specifically applicable to a job; (2) complete in its coverage of job requirements; and (3) efficient in terms of the time, money, and resources utilized. The latter requirement implies that the training should not be continued beyond the point where good on-the-job performance is possible.

Much of the discussion in this chapter relates to methods of achieving various types of learning. That means that the theoretical discussions in Chapter 2 often are directly relevant—particularly the treatment of learning concepts. It is important to keep these underlying concepts in mind as the various training and development approaches are considered.

☐ Approaches Previously Discussed

A number of training and development approaches have been considered in previous chapters, either because they are direct outgrowths of certain theories in organizational psychology, or because they relate to specific topics within organizational or industrial psychology that were of concern. A review of these treatments provides a good introduction to the discussion in this chapter.

Training in creative problem solving is discussed in Chapter 2. Box 2-4 describes the use of this training to stimulate creative research ideas.

Achievement motivation training receives attention in Chapter 3. Exhibit 3-3 shows the results obtained in developing entrepreneurship in India. Box 3-2 describes a training program utilized at Metropolitan Economic Development Association in the Minneapolis-St. Paul area.

Managerial role-motivation training has been the subject of previous discussion in Chapter 3, and Box 3-3 provides a specific example, the program at the University of Denver. Additional information on this approach is given in Boxes 19-1 and 19-2 of this chapter.

Behavior modeling is considered in Chapter 4. This is a direct extension of learning concepts as shown in Exhibit 4-12, which presents results obtained from an application developed by Mandev Training Corporation for retail sales personnel.

Stress-management programs of various kinds are considered in Chapter 6, and a typical training effort in this area is outlined.

Training that is variously referred to as laboratory, sensitivity, or T-group training is described in Chapter 7, and the schedule for a week-long program is given in Exhibit 7-7. Box 7-3 indicates how this approach has been utilized at TRW.

Team building, which is in large part an outgrowth of T-group procedures, typically includes training aspects and is treated in Chapter 7 as well. The use of team building at Mead Corporation is considered in Box 7-4.

Training is a major component of quality circle programs, and its use in this context is discussed in Chapter 8.

Leader match, the training application of contingency theory of leadership, is described and evaluated in Chapter 9; its application within Sears, Roebuck is the subject of Box 9-3.

Human relations training, which may take a variety of forms, receives attention in Chapter 9 also. The context is that of theories of consideration and initiating structure. Box 9-4 deals with a program designed to foster consideration among supervisors, which was developed for the International Harvester Company at the University of Chicago.

TELOS training, marketed by the Kepner Tregoe organization, is an application derived from the Vroom and Yetton decision-tree theory of leadership. The training is discussed in Chapter 10 and in Box 10-1.

Training in in-group relationships is an outgrowth of the vertical dyad theory of leadership. It too is treated in Chapter 10. Exhibit 10-4 shows the changes that can result from this type of training.

Organization development, although typically more than a training program, often contains a sizable training component. Grid organization development, based on the managerial grid theory of leadership, provides a good example. The use of training within grid organization development and in other such approaches is considered in Chapter 11. Box 11-4 provides an example taken from Exxon.

Culture training to help people adapt to foreign assignments is described in Chapter 12. Exhibit 12-8 shows how training fits into the staffing process as a whole, and indicates the role played by cultural similarity/dissimilarity. Box 12-4 depicts culture training in Italy's Olivetti Group.

Training efforts for the purpose of reducing error and bias in performance ratings are given attention in Chapter 15.

Much more often than not, these training programs were found to bring about changes in participants, and quite frequently these changes extended to performance, so that people did a better job as a result of the training. This result is not limited to the approaches discussed in previous chapters, however. Comprehensive reviews of the training literature indicate that a wide range of training efforts operate to produce learning and change (Burke & Day, 1986; Latham, 1988). Industrial psychology's, and also organizational psychology's, long-standing concern with the development and evaluation of

training methods clearly appears to have paid off.

■ EVALUATION OF CHANGE MODELS

Just as when a new selection procedure is introduced it should be validated against existing criteria of success in the organization, so when a new training program is introduced, it should be studied to determine whether it really is contributing to improved performance. There is a strong temptation to avoid this step, because the evaluation of a program always raises the possibility that it will turn out to have been worthless and thus a waste of time and money. From an overall company viewpoint, however, evaluation through research is essential if there is any prospect that the same or a similar course might be repeated in the future. As with validity studies in selection, however, there are cost considerations. Validation makes sense primarily if enough people are to be hired for the particular type of work to justify the expense of the research. Similarly, training evaluation is warranted when a sufficient number of people are to be trained in a particular way.

The section of Chapter 2 dealing with the identification of learning effects included a brief introduction to designs for the evaluation of training. The discussion here considers the subject in much greater detail.

☐ The Before–After Model

A basic question that may be asked with regard to any training effort is whether it does in fact yield a change in the people exposed to it. Normally, an experimental design for answering this question would involve a pretest, then exposure to training, and then a posttest. The pre- and postmeasurements are made using indexes that are closely related to what the course is expected to accomplish. Thus, an attempt to improve understanding of company policies might be evaluated by using a test of knowledge regarding policy before the course started and the same or a very similar test afterward. A statistically reliable increase in score for the group as a whole from pretest to posttest would provide the type of evidence for change that might permit generalization to other applications of the same course.

It would still remain to be demonstrated, however, that such a change had been caused by the course itself and not by some external factor. For instance, it might be that the change in knowledge of policy identified actually resulted not so much from the training as from the fact that a revised policy manual was issued to all management personnel shortly after the course started. To check on this kind of possibility, one would have to carry out the same pretest–posttest procedure on a **control group** consisting of managers like those exposed to training but differing in that they did not take the course in company policy. Should this control group increase in knowledge of policy as much as the **experimental group,** who had taken the course, this would support the view that some extra-training factor such as the new manual was the major cause of change. On the other hand, a statistically reliable increase in knowledge in the experimental group coupled with a lack of change in the control group would provide evidence that the training was in fact achieving its objective.

In selecting such a control group, it is important to use people as similar to those in the experimental group as possible and to make certain that the two groups have much the same types of experiences over the period of training. The only difference should be that one group is exposed to the course and the other is not. Ideally, people should be assigned to experimental and control groups on a random basis, so that there is as good a

chance that a specific individual would appear in one group as in another. In practice it is rarely possible to do this, because certain people need training and others do not. The best substitute is to construct the control group so that it is matched to the experimental group on several factors that are highly correlated with the pretest and posttest measures to be employed.

Exhibit 19-1 outlines the **before–after model.**

☐ The After-Only Model

Exhibit 19-1, in the lower half, also outlines the **after-only model.** This is an alternative approach that offers certain advantages, but also disadvantages. Here the experimental and control groups are selected in the same manner as in the before-after approach, but only posttests are administered. Change is presumed to have occurred if there is a statistically significant difference between the two groups at the time the measurement occurs. This assumes that the two groups were identical originally.

The problem is that in many ongoing business situations, it is extremely difficult to determine whether identical groups have been selected without employing a pretest to be sure. Thus there is always the possibility, when the after-only model is used, that any differences between the two groups established after training might have been present before. What appears to be change might be only a long-standing group difference.

Yet the simplicity of the after-only design is appealing, and there are circumstances under which one can feel reasonably confident that relatively good initial matching has occurred. Thus this approach is used on occasion, although probably not as frequently as the before–after model. The after-only design has the additional advantage that there is no possibility of a pretest's sensitizing those who take the course to certain specific aspects of

EXHIBIT 19-1   Models for Training Evaluation

		The Before–After Model	
Group	Time 1	Intervening Period	Time 2
Experimental	Pretest ⎯⎯⎯⎯⎯⎯→	Course ⎯⎯⎯⎯⎯⎯→	Posttest
Control	Pretest ⎯⎯⎯⎯⎯⎯⎯⎯⎯⎯⎯⎯⎯⎯⎯⎯⎯⎯→		Posttest
		The After–Only Model	
Group	Time 1	Intervening Period	Time 2
Experimental	⎯⎯⎯⎯⎯⎯⎯⎯⎯⎯⎯→	Course ⎯⎯⎯⎯⎯⎯→	Posttest
Control	⎯⎯⎯⎯⎯⎯⎯⎯⎯⎯⎯⎯⎯⎯⎯⎯⎯⎯→		Posttest

the training. Managers may learn certain things only because they get the impression from a pretest that they should learn these particular things. The posttest then reveals a change. But in subsequent administrations of the course, without a pretest (or a posttest either, for that matter), this learning does not occur, and the change may well be negligible. The after-only design avoids this source of error.

This **pretest sensitizing effect** can be a real problem, especially when the measures used contain items practically identical to material covered in training (Sprangers & Hoogstraten, 1989). In such cases, the ideal evaluation design is a combination of the before–after and after-only approaches, using at least three groups. This permits the identification of any pseudo-changes resulting from the sensitizing effects of a pretest through a comparison of the two experimental groups taking the course. Unfortunately, studies of this kind are rarely conducted. They are too complex and require more subjects for inclusion in the various experimental and control conditions than are normally available.

Box 19-1 illustrates the use of an after-only design to evaluate a management development program at Atlantic-Richfield. Note that, although random assignment to experimental and control groups was not possible (top management would not tolerate it), good

matching on appraised potential for advancement and managerial grade level was possible. Also, the posttest measures focused directly on managerial performance—what the training was intended to improve.

☐ Retention and Organizational Relevance Factors

Although the demonstration of a change caused by the educational process is the first step in any evaluation study, this is not all that is required. To be of much value to a company, the change must be retained, and it must be clearly of a kind that contributes to goal attainment.

Retention, Encapsulation, and Role Conflict. Retention is often determined by taking a third measurement, in the before–after context, at some time well after training has been completed, or the posttest itself may be delayed so that retention and change are measured at the same time. In the latter instance, if a pretest–posttest change is not found, there is no way of knowing whether the course was totally ineffective or a real change was vitiated by events occurring subsequent to training.

In the case of the evaluation described in Box 19-1, posttest data were collected over a period of more than five years after training.

BOX 19-1 RESEARCH IN I/O PSYCHOLOGY

The Use of an After-Only Design to Evaluate Managerial Role-Motivation Training at Atlantic-Richfield

The experimental group consisted of fifty-two career managers in the R&D Department at Atlantic-Richfield who had fifteen hours of managerial role-motivation training. A control group of forty-nine managers in the department did not undergo training. The managers had been assessed in connection with the company's management appraisal program shortly before the training occurred and given an advancement potential rating on a scale from 5 (low) to 1 (high). The mean potential rating was 2.9 in both the experimental and control groups. This evidence indicated good matching between the two groups prior to training. As a further check, the groups were compared as to managerial grade level at the time the training occurred on the company's scale running from grade 7 (low) to grade 18 (high). On the average, the experimental managers held positions at a grade of 11.6; the control managers averaged 11.8. Again the groups were virtually identical. As far as could be determined, the experimentals and controls not only began the race at the same starting line, but were judged to have an equal prospect of winning prior to the training.

Both experimentals and controls were followed for a period of five years and three months subsequent to the time the training had occurred.

Those who remained with the company throughout this period were evaluated in terms of their changes in grade level. Those who left the company at some point during the follow-up period were evaluated in terms of ratings given by their superiors at the time of separation.

Of the thirty-six managers in the experimental group who remained employed, 86 percent received at least one promotion; the average grade change was an increase of 1.9. Among the thirty-nine control managers who stayed, only 56 percent were promoted, and the average grade increase was 1.1. The sixteen managers from the experimental group who separated during follow-up were rated favorably in 69 percent of the cases. Only 30 percent of the control managers who separated were rated similarly. A comprehensive analysis combining data from all sources indicated that 81 percent of the experimental managers who had the training were subsequently successful with the company. Among the control managers without training, this figure was only 51 percent.

The after-training comparisons between experimentals and controls consistently supported the hypothesis that managerial role-motivation training contributes to managerial success.

Since change effects were found, the problem of identifying whether changes occurred over the period of the course did not arise.

It is clear that vitiation of change does occur. The consequence has been termed **encapsulated training.** Within the education situation itself, considerable change occurs, but none of this is actually carried back to the job. Because the training process is eventually terminated, all change will inevitably disappear also. Transfer of training as discussed in Chapter 2 does not occur.

This type of encapsulation seems to be particularly frequent when there is a disparity between the actual role prescriptions for the job and those taught in the course. Management development may emphasize being kind and humane toward subordinates, whereas the established role prescriptions for a manager, which are enforced by superiors, emphasize pressure for production and the frequent use of negative sanctions. One solution to the dilemma thus produced is to accept the training values, but only for purposes of training—not back on the job. Because the entire reward structure built around the job is calculated to obtain a close match between role behavior and the established role prescriptions, and because the training emphasis, if incorporated in behavior, would tend to widen this gap and thus reduce the chances of being considered a success, the manager is careful not to let any training effects manifest themselves in the actual work situation.

Box 9-4 describing the International Harvester training program conducted by University of Chicago faculty, provides a good example of encapsulated training.

Another type of reaction may occur when the role requirements presented in the training situation are distinctly different from those characterizing the job situation. On occasion, the two sets of expectations are carried into the work environment together, with the result that managers do not know what they are supposed to do and what kind of behavior will be considered as evidence of success. The result is role conflict. Under such circumstances, the changes produced by training are retained, but at considerable cost to the individual in terms of stress and confusion. The consequence for the organization is likely to be internal conflict and, in many cases, the eventual loss of a potentially valuable manager.

The solution to problems of encapsulated training and training-produced role conflict is to be sure that the role requirements taught in the course and those existing in the job situation are not divergent. This can be accomplished by synchronizing the course with existing role prescriptions. When this is done, it can be assumed that the training will be reinforced by subsequent work experiences, and changes will be retained. On the other

hand, if the training is intended as a procedure for introducing alternative role prescriptions and thus moving managerial behavior toward a new pattern of expectations, the new role prescriptions should be made part of the job context as well. Thus, the changes should be organizational in nature and not restricted to a given management-development experience. It is for this reason that an attempt is often made to expose the company's top management to any course emphasizing new role prescriptions. Then the training is applied down through the successive levels of the hierarchy. In this way, a climate favorable to the new behaviors is created from the onset, and retention of change is fostered.

Box 19-2 provides an example of how a third, retention test was used subsequent to a before–after study. In this case continued exposure to the professors and other aspects of the organizational climate in the University of Oregon's business school did not have much negative impact on the original changes. Substantial retention did occur, presumably because role conflicts between managerial role-motivation training and expectations existing elsewhere in the school were at a minimum.

Measuring Organizational Relevance. The final step in the evaluation model, and one that is often neglected, involves tying the change to organizational goals or to the role prescriptions that mediate goal attainment. Thus, if a knowledge change is produced, it must be demonstrated that the knowledge actually helps those who possess it to perform more effectively. If a change in attitudes occurs, there must be reason to believe that these attitudes are associated with success on the job.

Methods of accomplishing this final step vary considerably. The ideal is to use judgmental or objective appraisal measures such as those used at Atlantic-Richfield in the

BOX **19-2** RESEARCH IN I/O PSYCHOLOGY

Retention of Change after Managerial Role-Motivation Training among University of Oregon Business Students

Managerial role-motivation instruction was given to University of Oregon undergraduates as part of their regular coursework over a period of four quarters. In this period some 326 students underwent training. Of these, 287 completed a measure of managerial motivation at both pretest and posttest. This measure was developed in connection with the Atlantic Richfield research on managerial role-motivation training discussed in Box 19-1. At Atlantic-Richfield, among R&D managers, it had a correlation of 0.43 with the potential for advancement ratings assigned during management appraisals. It also correlated 0.29 with the subsequent grade-change index and 0.69 with the subsequent performance ratings at separation. Thus the managerial motivation measure appeared to possess both concurrent and predictive validity. Scores could vary from −35 to +35, although the actual range among the managers at Atlantic-Richfield was −10 to +20; this is typical.

Initial comparison of the pretest and posttest results for the experimental student samples at the University of Oregon indicated a consistent and substantial increase in managerial motivation over the period of training. Control samples taking courses in business law and educational foundations, and numbering 170 students, exhibited no change from pretest to posttest. This was a standard before–after analysis with a control group.

Subsequently an attempt was made to measure retention by testing the experimental subjects a third time, late in their university programs. Records of course registrations were obtained and students were contacted in their business classes. Some 129 students from the original 287 were located and tested. The retention period ranged from five to seventeen months subsequent to the posttest. Managerial motivation scores for this experimental retention group were as follows: pretest, +3.4; posttest, +6.6; retention test, +5.9. Roughly 78 percent of the initial increase was retained.

As a further check on these results comparisons were made with a control group consisting of fifty-five students just finishing their business programs, who were tested for the first time at the same point as the retention test was administered to the experimentals. For various reasons these students had not been exposed to any managerial role-motivation training. The mean score for this control sample was +2.3—well below the experimental retention sample and somewhat, although not significantly, below the pretest experimental result. This after-only analysis provides good support for the view that the motivational changes produced by role-motivation training were retained over a period averaging almost a year.

study of Box 19-1. In other instances the profit performance of cost centers or the turnover rate in work groups pre- and posttraining might be compared. Unfortunately, obtaining comparable objective measures for all members of both experimental and control groups is often difficult. And when ratings are obtained from superiors who know the com-

position of experimental and control groups, the possibility of bias exists. The wish, even though entirely unconscious, to justify the decision to invest in a training program can distort the posttest evaluations in favor of the experimental group. This could conceivably be a factor in the results reported in Box 19-1. However, the managers making the decision to undertake the training were only rarely those who made the performance ratings and decided on the promotions. Furthermore, justifying the training was not a matter of great concern in the R&D department.

The most common practice has been to use various tests or questionnaires as measures, as in the study of Box 19-2. However, these must be shown to have a positive relationship with success on the job. Thus, validity studies—in many cases predictive validity studies—must be carried out. The models discussed in Chapter 16 are the appropriate ones for this purpose. The point is that there must be good reason to believe that the development procedure has moved a number of individuals along some dimension that is known to yield role behavior that is positively valued within the organization. Box 19-2 contains data, from Atlantic-Richfield, on the validity of the managerial motivation measure used to evaluate training, and provides an example of the approach being discussed.

The ideal approach in establishing relevance probably is to measure change on a number of variables with varying degrees of proximity to organizational goal attainment. Thus, one might measure knowledge change, job performance change, unit productivity change, and overall profitability change in manufacturing plants serving in experimental and control capacities. When this sort of study is conducted, it is not always true that changes at one level are closely tied to what happens at other levels (Alliger & Janak, 1989).

A particularly difficult problem has appeared in some change evaluation studies when self-report questionnaires, similar to self-report personality tests, are used in pre- and posttests. Exposure to the training may cause a person to rethink responses given to the questionnaire at pretest and thus respond from different assumptions, or with different standards, or even with different perceptions of the meanings of words at posttest; thus, the same measure really may not be the same at all for that person. This problem was considered in Chapter 11 in connection with the evaluation of organization development programs. The ideal solution is to include measures that are not of a self-report nature.

A final point relating to retention and organizational relevance goes back to Chapter 2. Among the learning concepts considered there was transfer of training. In the past the encapsulation-of-training phenomenon and transfer of training (or the lack of it) have not been treated together. However, there are close parallels, and an increasing tendency to integrate the two concepts appears to be emerging (Baldwin & Ford, 1988).

☐ Subjects as Their Own Controls

An approach to evaluation that does not use control groups, but rather employs the experimental subjects in a control capacity at certain times, has begun to see use in recent years. It is not applicable to the evaluation of all types of training programs. The individuals to be trained are first studied under standard control conditions to establish a baseline; perhaps the quantity and quality of output from production units are monitored over a period of time, while their managers behave in their normal ways. Then an experimental training condition is introduced—thus the managers may be taught how to praise workers for behaviors that serve to improve output.

If this training is successful, quantity and quality should show increases as output continues to be monitored. At some point, the training effect should stabilize at a new level above what was obtained under baseline conditions. Next training is discontinued and the managers are instructed to stop using the skills in utilizing praise that they have developed; they are to restore the conditions of the baseline period. When a control situation is thus reasserted, output measures should drop back to the baseline level if the "praise training" was really the cause of the previous improvement. Finally, once a stable control level has been obtained, training is reintroduced and the praise condition reestablished. The output measures should return to the higher levels found under the previous experimental circumstances.

This is the ABAB design outlined in Chapter 4 and demonstrated in Exhibit 4-9. Although there are other, more complex variants of this design, they all have in common the fact that the subjects of the training also serve as their own controls. Accordingly, this approach can be used to evaluate a training effort applied to only a single individual. However, one can have more confidence in the results if multiple individuals are used.

■ ESTABLISHING TRAINING NEEDS

To operate efficiently, training must be focused on individuals and situations where the need is greatest. This means that large gaps between role expectations and existing role behaviors must be identified. Then a decision must be made on whether a significant reduction in the size of the gap might be achieved through training. Establishing **training needs** thus requires an answer to two questions: Is there a problem in terms of the level or type of performance? Can training be of any value in correcting such a situation?

In terms of sheer numbers, the training-needs problem is usually most pronounced among individuals just starting out on a new job. New employees, employees who have been shifted into a new position, and employees being retrained because the role requirements for a position have been changed can normally be assumed to have rather acute training needs. Fortunately, requirements of

this kind tend to be rather easy to identify, and the level of motivation to learn tends to be quite high.

A much more difficult problem arises in the case of existing employees who have been working on the current job for some time. Here, persistent deviations from role expectations must be identified on an individual basis. There is no single categorization, such as that of "new person on the job," to make employees with marked training needs highly visible. Furthermore, motivation for new learning may well be minimal. To be singled out for special training and to accept the need for this training represents a tacit admission that one has not been performing with maximum effectiveness in the past. Thus, "experienced" employees may go to great lengths to cover up any training needs and may resist any training that they do receive to prove that they have been performing the job correctly all along. This is not a universal occurrence, but it is well to be sensitive to the possibility.

Whether the training-needs analysis is directed toward individuals who are just starting on a job or those who have been there for some time, it remains a very important factor in a firm's total effort to utilize human resources effectively, and it may well become even more important in the future (Campbell & Campbell, 1988). Union pressure has produced many job-assignment systems based in large part on seniority. Furthermore, a number of companies are firmly committed to the concept of promotion from within. These plus other factors mean that job security is often greater today than it has been in the past, and training is often the major procedure for correcting deficiencies in selection and placement. If this training is to be applied in an efficient manner, it must be directed into areas where clearly identified training needs exist. Unfortunately, however, a great many companies appear to be deficient in this respect (Saari, Johnson, McLaughlin, & Zimmerle, 1988).

☐ Specific Techniques in Training-Needs Analysis

Because the process of identifying training needs depends at least in part on establishing disparities between role requirements and role behavior, any of the various appraisal and evaluation techniques discussed previously can be of value. In addition, achievement tests and job samples can provide information regarding the extent to which knowledge and skill are below expected levels.

Historically, however, training needs have been identified largely as a result of requests for training from line management, or through more protracted discussion with those responsible for the performance of the individuals considered for training, or through direct observation of actual job performance. Probably, the latter techniques remain the most common ones today, although group production records, turnover statistics, and the like are also widely used to pinpoint areas of difficulty.

The important thing, regardless of the approach employed, is to develop some conception not only of whether performance deficiencies are present, but also regarding the extent to which training can remedy such deficiencies, and the type of training that might be most appropriate for this purpose. Thus, a training-needs analysis should come before any attempt at establishing the method or content of training.

In attempting to develop a preliminary estimate of training needs in a particular group, it is very helpful to utilize some type of checklist along the lines of the one presented in Exhibit 19-2. Answers to the questions posed can be obtained using data and information from the various sources already noted. After possible training needs are estab-

EXHIBIT 19-2   A Checklist for Identifying Training Needs in a Particular Unit

Items to Be Considered for Training	Training Need?
Is turnover excessive?	_____
Are accidents excessive?	_____
Is absenteeism too high?	_____
Are grievances filed frequently?	_____
Are disciplinary actions excessive?	_____
Is production often behind schedule?	_____
Are there frequent production bottlenecks?	_____
Are quality control standards maintained without excessive costs?	_____
Are poor management practices in evidence?	_____
Are there problems in communication?	_____
Are there frequent interpersonal conflicts?	_____
Is supervision effective?	_____
Are objectives known and understood?	_____
Is paperwork done on time?	_____
Do supervisors use staff specialists effectively?	_____

lished, training specialists can then gradually narrow the analysis until they are able to deal with the specific needs of specific individuals in specific jobs.

Exhibit 19-3 provides an overview of the total training and development process, but more specifically it shows how training needs assessment fits into this process. Training needs must be established in some manner before instructional objectives and course content can be created. The example at the beginning of the chapter describes how the First National Bank of Athens, Georgia, established training needs in the areas of human relations, customer service, and departmental coordination. These needs were reflected in subsequent training content. The informal

EXHIBIT 19-3 Overview of a Training and Development System

Needs are assessed, objectives established, training carried out, and evaluation studies conducted; various types of validity are assessed as related to the training goal. The four types of validity are:

Training validity—whether the trainees learn during training

Transfer validity—whether what is learned in training transfers as improved performance on the job

Intraorganizational validity—whether the performance for a new group of trainees in the same organization matches the performance of the original trainees

Interorganizational validity—whether a training program validated in one organization will do as well in another

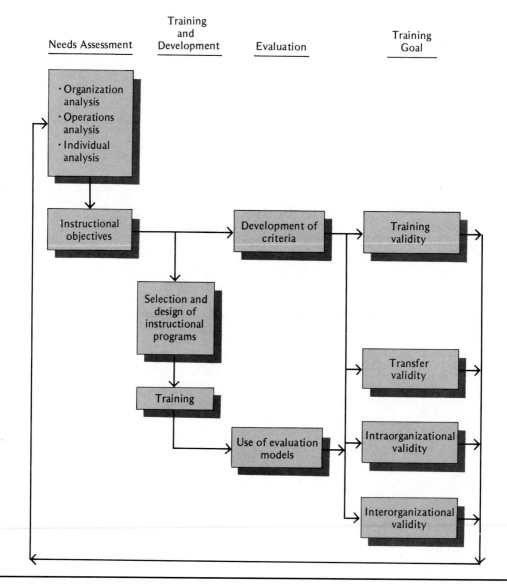

SOURCE: Adapted from Irwin L. Goldstein (1986). *Training in organizations: Needs assessment, development, and evaluation*, pp. 16–23. Monterey, CA: Brooks/Cole.

approach described is typical of much training-needs assessment in organizations today.

☐ Training Needs and Job Analysis

The content of training frequently is developed from detailed job analysis data. These data may have been prepared for other purposes as well, or the job analysis may be a special one to get at training needs only. In either event, the idea is to identify task components and then build these components into the training in the optimal sequence for positive transfer to on-the-job performance.

Various approaches have been used to analyze jobs into the component tasks that are to be taught. Critical incidents may be obtained and then a training program developed based on these incidents. Another approach utilizes the things–data–people categories for job activities discussed in Chapter 13 and illustrated in Exhibit 13-3. In this instance, the model serves to specify what kinds of skills must be taught if people are to be trained for higher-level positions and thus prepared for movement up a career ladder.

A related procedure deals with organization analysis, operations analysis, and individual analysis (McGehee & Thayer, 1961; Wexley & Latham, 1981). Organization analysis determines where in the organization the training emphasis should be placed. Operations analysis deals with what the content of training should be insofar as preparing an employee to perform specific tasks is concerned; this is the actual job analysis aspect. Individual analysis seeks to identify the skills, knowledge, aptitudes, and the like that a person needs to perform the tasks that constitute a specific job in the organization. Again, the emphasis is on pinpointing what needs to be taught.

The techniques of management by objectives also may be applied in establishing training needs. In this case the particular goals or objectives set for individual performance provide a basis for establishing what tasks need to be carried out and thus what needs to be learned. Also, management by objectives may well incorporate a self-assessment of training needs, and self-assessment can prove a useful method of determining what an individual needs (Ford & Noe, 1987).

■ METHODS AND APPROACHES IN MANAGEMENT DEVELOPMENT

Among the approaches to training and development, some are more frequently associated with management development and some with employee training. The differentiation is by no means clear-cut; there is considerable overlap. Yet the approaches considered in this section tend on the average to be used more often in management development. So too do a number of approaches discussed previously, such as behavior modeling, achievement-motivation training, managerial role-motivation training, T-group training, TELOS training, training in in-group relationships, culture training, and performance appraisal training, which are not considered further here.

☐ Lecture and Discussion

Changes seem to occur regardless of whether the training is conducted primarily by the lecture method or through group discussion. However, discussion techniques do appear to be more widely employed. The method uses a small group or groups who work with a leader to develop discussion. Actual practice differs considerably insofar as the role of the discussion leader is concerned. In some instances, leaders have the conference content outlined in advance and the major conclusions to be reached already clearly established in their minds. They then guide the groups by questions and comments so that the preestablished points are covered. In

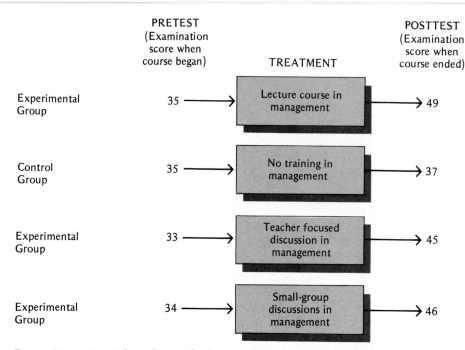

	PRETEST (Examination score when course began)	TREATMENT	POSTTEST (Examination score when course ended)
Experimental Group	35 ⟶	Lecture course in management	⟶ 49
Control Group	35 ⟶	No training in management	⟶ 37
Experimental Group	33 ⟶	Teacher focused discussion in management	⟶ 45
Experimental Group	34 ⟶	Small-group discussions in management	⟶ 46

EXHIBIT 19-4   How Discussion Methods May Operate to Produce Learning
This diagram shows the change in student performance on a seventy-five-item examination of management principles over a single course. All three experimental groups increased in knowledge, while the control group changed very little. The two approaches to discussion are equally effective, and almost as effective as the lecture course.
SOURCE: Adapted from Eliot S. Elfner (1980), Lecture versus discussion formats in teaching a basic management course. *Academy of Management Proceedings, 40,* 105–106.

other cases the approach is much more nondirective, with the group developing its own framework for discussion. Here the leader serves primarily to encourage members to participate and as a resource person. Which procedure is best depends on the goal of the training and the skill of the leader. The effective guidance of a discussion to a predetermined conclusion is a difficult art.

Exhibit 19-4 builds on results already considered in Exhibit 2-3. The top half of the exhibit repeats the previously described findings; the lower half adds further findings dealing with two discussion procedures. All courses were taught by the same instructor,

and change in the control group was minimal. Both discussion and lecture produced substantial increases in learning. Lectures were superior, but only by a small margin.

☐ Case Study

The case approach is one in which a problem is given in written form to a group for solution. The usual procedure is for group members individually to assume the role of the manager who is faced with the problem situation. The written statement stops short of a solution, and the participants in the training must then think through to the role behavior they feel to be desirable. The leader does not impose a specific solution. The emphasis is on individual or team problem solving, group discussion, and group critique (Reynolds, 1980).

The method is clearly more appropriate for certain purposes than others. It can be helpful in teaching managers to identify and analyze complex problems and to make their own decisions. It permits very rapid coverage of a great deal of ground in terms of diverse approaches, interpretations, and personalities. Making snap judgments and applying pat solutions to problems are discouraged at the same time that learning is fostered. When the participants are sufficiently sophisticated and knowledgeable in the subject areas involved, it can serve as a basis for the development of general principles that may then be used in solving actual on-the-job problems. If the trainees do not have the background knowledge to come up with meaningful case solutions, or they lack any real understanding of the role that the case requires them to assume, none of these objectives is likely to be achieved, and the use of the method should probably be avoided. Given such knowledge, case analysis can produce sizable improvements in performance. The extent to which creativity is fostered and the actual amount of transfer back to the job under normal circumstances are matters of some controversy, however (Argyris, 1980; Berger, 1983).

☐ Role Playing

Basically, the **role-playing** approach may be considered as a type of case study in which individuals play the roles of the various persons in the case. All participants do not assume the same role, the role of the responsible manager, as with the typical written case. The fact that participants behave in roles rather than merely think in them tends to create a more realistic learning situation.

Usually, role playing is done in groups of ten to twenty, with members taking turns acting and serving as analysts. The leader assigns individuals to roles. An oral or written briefing is given to put the audience and actors into the situation. Sometimes rather detailed role instructions are given; sometimes the actors actually read a skit up to a certain point; and sometimes there is practically no structuring of this kind, with the participants largely developing their own roles. In any event, the actors eventually take over, behaving as they see fit in the situation. The leader terminates the session when the audience has been emotionally involved and either the problem has been analyzed or an impasse has been reached. A lengthy discussion that attempts to point up the objectives of training normally follows.

There are a great many variants in technique used by different trainers, even to the point of employing professional actors to take certain parts in a skit. In addition, the approach has been used in a number of different contexts, although the training of managers in leadership behaviors is most common, often in conjunction with a human relations program. Specific applications have been made in connection with the handling of discharges, layoffs, merit ratings, and grievances, as well as in sales training.

Role playing can be very helpful in practicing role behaviors, provided a sufficient illusion of reality can be produced. Learning by doing is known to be an effective method of developing new skills, although it does not necessarily guarantee against encapsulation. The limited amount of research evidence available is generally favorable, but because role playing is typically used in conjunction with other methods, independent evaluations are few.

☐ Business Games

Another method of obtaining high levels of participant involvement is the business game,

EXHIBIT 19-5   Business Games and Case Study Compared

Knowledge Measure	Mean Pretest Score	Mean Posttest Score	Change
Overall test score			
Business game group	10.6	25.9	+15.3
Case study group	10.4	19.9	+9.5
Mastery of principles and concepts			
Business game group	8.8	22.0	+13.2
Case study group	9.4	16.6	+7.2
Mastery of specific facts			
Business game group	1.7	3.9	+2.2
Case study group	1.1	4.0	+2.9

SOURCE: Adapted from Joseph Wolfe (1973), The comparative learning effects of a management game vs. casework in the teaching of business policy. *Academy of Management Proceedings, 33,* 294–296.

which may be viewed as a case spread out over time, with the consequences of decisions made apparent. The usual procedure is first to inform the trainees regarding the business objectives to be sought, the decisions to be made, and the rules that apply. This may be done orally, but it is common practice to provide written instructions as well. Each competing team organizes itself, studies the available information on operations to date, and makes its initial set of decisions. Each decision period is set equal to a unit of time—a day, week, month, or even a quarter or longer. After the first decisions are turned in, the trainers calculate the operating results with the aid of a computer and feed them back to the teams, often with further environmental and competitive data added. This cycle is repeated several times, and the results are then discussed and critiqued at length.

Some of the available games deal with top-level decisions affecting the total enterprise. Others have been constructed with reference to specific functions and problems—personnel assignment, materials management, stock transactions, sales management, production scheduling, collective bargaining, inventory control, and bank management. The list is constantly increasing. Although the tendency is to deal with generalized and hypothetical business situations, there are a number of games constructed with specific reference to a particular firm or industry. In some instances, the decisions made by one team are **interactive** with the results obtained by other teams, in that constant mathematical probabilities have been built into the game as concomitants of particular types of decisions.

The results of a study evaluating the learning effects of a business game are given in Exhibit 19-5. Changes were identified from before training to afterwards in both groups—those who devoted most of their time to playing a business game and those who concentrated on analyzing and presenting cases. However, the important finding is that the change was significantly greater in the business-game group. Furthermore, the data indicate that the major effect of the game experience was to improve mastery of principles and general concepts, not specific facts.

In certain respects, assessment centers assume characteristics of business games, and other simulations too, when used for developmental purposes. Assessment centers with a development goal tend to include more exercises and to last longer. Unfortunately, little direct evidence exists on the value of assessment centers in this regard, although companies are using them to develop managers.

☐ University and University-Type Programs

Although much management development is carried out in classrooms located on company premises near the workplace, there is also widespread utilization of university facilities. In part, this involves enrollment in regular courses carrying degree credit. Many universities offer a large number of evening courses for the specific purpose of meeting the demand created by business firms and their employees. Some companies give time off during the day so that individuals may attend classes. Increasingly, policies are being developed that permit a person to take a leave to pursue graduate study on a full-time basis. Also, there are the various executive degree programs that meet primarily on weekends.

In some instances, the initiative behind this return to school comes from the employee; in some, from the company. Many firms pay a large proportion or all of the costs under tuition-aid programs. The number of such programs has been increasing. In many cases, the fact or amount of payment is tied directly to the grade received. Policies with regard to tuition aid vary tremendously, depending in large part on the company's need for individuals with various kinds of university training.

In addition, most universities are engaged in some type of management development effort on a noncredit basis. These are programs structured specifically to meet the needs of the business community. They vary from one-day conferences to year-long programs of the kind originated at the Massachusetts Institute of Technology in the early 1930s and since emulated by a number of other schools (Billy, 1988). In most instances, a company will send only one manager, or at most several, to a given university course, with the result that the groups tend to be quite heterogeneous in company representation. Sometimes a university will offer a program specifically for the managers of a single company, however.

The subjects taught vary a great deal but typically include some combination of the following:

Business policy and strategy

Human relations

General management functions

Communications

Financial management

Problem solving and decision making

Managerial economics

Quantitative approaches

Marketing

Accounting

Social responsibilities of business

Industrial relations

Government regulation

Human resources management

Organizational behavior

Very little information is available regarding the change-producing effects of these programs. Most are intended either to impart new knowledge, in an area related to career objectives and of a kind the managers do not currently possess, or to update existing knowledge. There is reason to believe that such learning does occur, but it may not be achieved as efficiently as in a regular university classroom. The reason for this is that in many instances examinations are not given, and no reports on the managers' level of accomplishment are sent back to the company. A manager who really wants to learn will no doubt do so, but without question some individuals attend these programs with very little gain to either themselves or the firms that send them.

EXHIBIT 19-6   **Percent of 250 Larger Companies Utilizing Various University and University-Type Management Development Activities**

Percent	Type of Activity
11	Reimbursement for *full-time* MBA degrees, but only for *selected* universities
15	Reimbursement for *part-time* MBA degrees, but only for *selected* universities
16	Reimbursement for *full-time* MBA degrees, for any university
63	Reimbursement for *part-time* MBA degrees, for any university
64	*In-house live-in* management development programs offered by *this organization* solely for its own managers
64	*External live-in* management development programs offered by *universities* for managers from a variety of organizations
53	*External live-in* management development programs offered by *nonuniversity vendors* for managers from a variety of organizations
69	*In-house major non-live-in* management development programs (i.e., programs of three or more working days)
52	*External major non-live-in* management development programs at *universities* (i.e., programs of three or more working days)
57	*External major non-live-in* management development programs at *nonuniversity vendors* (i.e., programs of three or more working days)

SOURCE: Lyman W. Porter & Lawrence E. McKibbin (1988). *Management education and development: Drift or thrust into the 21st century?*, p. 243. New York: McGraw-Hill.

A number of programs closely parallel those offered by the universities but are made available under other auspices. The American Management Associations conduct a great many such courses, as do a number of other professional and managerial societies and consulting firms. Most of these are very similar to university offerings, but they more frequently utilize business managers themselves as trainers. Often, instruction is given in hotel meeting rooms, at private clubs, or at special facilities maintained by the organization.

Another approach that is being utilized by a number of larger firms is for the company to establish what amounts to a "college" of its own. These facilities are generally located on former private estates or on similar properties. The teaching may be done by the company's own managers, by a special training staff, or by university professors hired as consultants. A group of managers may spend ten weeks or more on the premises, and a new group arrives shortly after the last has fin-

ished. Programs of this kind have been operated for a number of years by companies such as Shell Oil, General Electric, IBM, Motorola, and by the U.S. government for upper-level and high-potential managers (Storcevich & Sykes, 1982).

Exhibit 19-6 provides an indication of how frequently the larger corporations utilize these university and university-type programs.

☐ Job Rotation and Understudy Assignments

In job rotation, placements are not made so much with a view to selecting the individuals who will perform most effectively on the job as with the idea of exposing to new learning experiences individuals who are thought to have good prospects of moving to higher levels of responsibility. The extent to which these assignments carry full operating responsibilities varies considerably. In some cases the individual is rotated from one department to another, perhaps at yearly intervals, and takes over each job with all its role requirements. It is not uncommon for this sort of activity to occur at relatively high levels in the managerial hierarchy. The usual practice is to exercise rather close supervision over individuals who are being rotated for purposes of development and to give them a good deal of coaching. At the other extreme is an approach, used mostly with new management trainees, whereby the individual is assigned for varying periods to different types of work primarily for the purpose of observing and perhaps of carrying out special projects of a largely training nature. Here the development emphasis is primary, and there is only a very limited direct contribution to organizational goal attainment in the work the individual does; costs often are carried in a training budget.

Understudy assignments are normally used not so much for general broadening as to prepare a person for a specific position. Here the emphasis is not on obtaining a general understanding of the total company operation or of several important segments of it, as in rotation. Understudies may be in a direct-line relationship, serving as assistant managers, or they may hold positions as administrative assistants or assistants to a particular manager. In many cases these jobs are created specifically for the purpose of training a successor to an incumbent manager and are abolished after promotion occurs.

In evaluating the various developmental techniques involving the use of placement procedures, it is important to remember that training which seriously hampers present operations is not really of much value. The ideal is to be able to carry out the training process with a minimum of disruption on the job. This means that throwing people into jobs they know nothing about, purely to gain the advantage of rotation, is normally to be avoided. Even if they do eventually survive and begin to grow, the loss in present efficiency may well be too great.

Also, rotation and understudy assignments in and of themselves have little worth. It is because they can offer opportunities for new learning and change that these procedures are considered to be of value. If, however, because of the way an immediate superior handles individuals in such positions, or for some other reason, very little learning is possible, then techniques of this kind are likely to do more harm than good. Thus, such placements are probably best restricted to certain groups and departments where there is known to be a high probability that development will in fact occur. Furthermore, the kinds of individuals selected for rotation should be those who can be counted on to benefit from the experience.

It is a frequent practice to utilize rotation to develop so-called fast-track managers who are believed to have great potential for rising to high levels in the company. Several firms, such as AT&T and Anheuser Busch, are noted for these efforts. The intent is to identify individuals in the prime age group, late 20s and 30s, and give them numerous active learning experiences (Beatty, Schneier, & McEvoy, 1987; London, 1985).

☐ Committee Assignments

Another means of exposing managers to new experiences, and thus opportunities to learn, is through the judicious use of committee assignments. Work on salary and grievance committees and in groups set up to study special problems can be of considerable value if these committees are made up of representatives with varied backgrounds.

One such approach is multiple management as described in Box 19-3. McCormick and Company has been a leader in this area. Many firms that have adopted this technique have added factory boards, sales boards, and the like to deal with problems in particular

BOX 19-3 I/O PSYCHOLOGY IN PRACTICE

Multiple Management at McCormick and Company

Multiple management, as developed at McCormick and Company, involves establishing what amounts to a junior board of directors, made up of from ten to twenty members of middle management. Such a board deals with problems from the viewpoint of the overall company and makes recommendations directly to the board of directors in a variety of areas. Membership is rotated to a degree by virtue of the fact that the three least effective managers, as determined by peer ratings, are dropped off the board at regular intervals and replaced by new members. Recommendations to the board of directors must be unanimous, and if they are not accepted, the reasons for rejection must be stated in writing by the senior board. The primary purpose sought is the development of middle management.

Source: K. B. Watson (1974). The maturing of multiple management. *Management Review, 63*(7), 4–14.

functional areas. Subcommittees to handle such matters as executive actions, new products, human relations, training, and suggestions are often appointed. All this is done primarily for the purpose of development, although other objectives may be fostered as well.

■ METHODS AND APPROACHES IN EMPLOYEE TRAINING

Among the approaches to training and development considered in previous chapters, a number apply primarily below the management level whereas others apply more generally at all job levels. Among these are training in creative problem solving, stress-management programs, training within quality circle programs, and training within organization development efforts, as previously discussed. This leaves a number of approaches to be considered here.

☐ On-the-Job Training

The most common approach is for training to be done on the job, particularly for new employees. The individual becomes accustomed to the machinery and materials that will be used in the subsequent work and learns in the same physical and social environment in which job duties will be carried out later on. Usually, the training is done by an experienced employee or by a supervisor. On occasion, however, trained instructors are assigned for the specific purpose of teaching job skills.

Much on-the-job training still utilizes procedures similar to those developed for use in connection with the Job Instruction Training sessions conducted by the Training within Industry Division of the War Manpower Commission during World War II (see Chapter 1). The JIT guidelines are given here.

1. Pretraining steps:
   a. Have a timetable developed in terms of which skills are to be attained. Indicate the speed at which the various levels of attainment may be expected.
   b. Break down the job into its basic components.
   c. Have all materials and supplies necessary for the training process available and ready.

d. Have the workplace arranged in the same way that the workers will be expected to keep it.

2. Training steps:

   a. Prepare the workers by putting them at ease; find out what they already know and show them the relationship of this job to other jobs.

   b. Tell, show, and illustrate the job to be performed.

   c. Have the workers try to perform the job and have them tell and explain why they perform each specific operation of the job. This tends to clarify the key aspects.

   d. Follow up on trainees after they have been put on their own by checking them often and encouraging further questions.

On-the-job training of this kind is very attractive in a number of respects. It requires relatively little special attention, no extra equipment is needed, and the employees can do some productive work while learning. Furthermore, it is consistent with several principles of learning. There is active practice, motivation should be maximal due to the meaningful nature of the learning materials, and the problem of lack of transfer of training from the learning to the job situation is almost nonexistent.

Yet there are major difficulties. There is a risk that expensive equipment will be damaged by inexperienced employees, and the accident rate among on-the-job trainees tends to be high. In the absence of specially assigned trainers, the instruction is often haphazard or may be neglected entirely. The pressures of the workplace may in fact leave little time for effective training. Some activities may actually be more difficult to learn on the job because of their complexity or as a result of the regulated speed at which the machinery operates.

☐ Vestibule Training

An approach that is in a sense intermediate between on- and off-the-job training utilizes the **vestibule school.** Here the trainee uses equipment and procedures similar to those that would be used in on-the-job training, but the equipment is set up in an area separate from the regular workplace. The intent of this special installation is to facilitate learning, not to obtain productive output. A skilled trainer is in charge, and new workers receive detailed instruction while practicing their new skills at a rate appropriate to each individual.

From the learning viewpoint, this appears to represent an ideal approach. It does reduce training time and yield more skilled work performance. But it is also expensive, especially if the number of people to be trained on a particular type of equipment is small. Then, too, it is not suitable for many jobs. Unfortunately, some companies have placed obsolete or even broken machinery in vestibule schools in an effort to avoid the expense of purchasing duplicate equipment. This tends to limit severely the value of the training. It may even yield negative transfer effects.

☐ Orientation Training and Socialization

Orientation programs are established to provide new employees with information on such matters as company organization, the history of the firm, policies and procedures, pay and benefit plans, conditions of employment, safety practices, names of top executives, locations of various departments and facilities, manufacturing processes, and work rules. On occasion, brief orientation programs are offered for experienced employees to bring them up to date on current procedures.

Orientation training usually is conducted

BOX 19-4   I/O PSYCHOLOGY IN PRACTICE

Communicating Organizational Culture to New Employees in RCA's Video Disc Operations

RCA's Video Disc Operations facility in Indianapolis expanded over just a few months from 300 to more than 900 employees, as the company began gearing up to introduce the Video Disc system to the commercial video market. All these new employees needed to be socialized into the company's ways and to be taught the culture of the organization they had joined so that they could function effectively in it. To this end, RCA undertook a study of itself to determine what aspects of its corporate folkways should be incorporated into a videotaped orientation program for new employees.

Interviews were conducted with employees at all levels and in all functions. Printed materials such as annual reports, employee handbooks, recruiting pamphlets, and public relations materials were culled for recurring symbols and themes that reflected the internal culture. Stories about the company's history were collected. Many of these dealt with the charismatic leadership of David Sarnoff, who founded RCA and invented many of its early products; these stories often had a mythical quality. The organization was frequently described in figurative terms—RCA as a family, as a tradition on the move, as an industrial pioneer, and as an "ideas" company.

The videotape script that resulted was divided into four parts: "Introduction to RCA," "The History of RCA," "Introduction to RCA's Video Disc Operations in Indianapolis," and "Conclusion." The CEO, Dr. J. Brandinger, did much of the narrating. Every effort was made to keep the depiction of company culture as realistic as possible, even if that meant presenting some negative features.

The finished videotape has been used extensively. It has helped in assimilating the large numbers of new RCA employees, and it has proved successful in speeding up the processes by which employees come to understand their new organization. All in all, it appears to be a very effective communication tool.

SOURCE: Gary L. Kreps (1983). Using interpretive research: The development of a socialization program at RCA. In Linda L. Putnam & Michael E. Pacanowsky (Eds.), *Communication and organizations: An interpretive approach*, pp. 243–256. Beverly Hills, CA: Sage.

during the first few days of employment. Handbooks, films, and other materials may play an important part in this initial effort to provide the employee with knowledge regarding the salient features of a new environment. In those cases where immediate supervision has primary responsibility for these matters, the training tends to become more individualized, more variable, and on occasion more superficial. Standardized programs, including classroom sessions and group tours of facilities, appear to offer major advantages. Yet there is little solid research on the subject, and informal procedures may often be as effective as formal ones. In either event, orientation training initiates the process of socializing the employee to the culture of the organization. In some cases, as with the RCA program described in Box 19-4, the orientation process focuses directly on teaching new employees the organization's culture.

☐ Apprenticeship

Apprentice training offers an integration of on- and off-the-job learning that under ideal conditions appears to be extremely effective (Briggs & Foltman, 1981). It is used to prepare employees for a variety of skilled occupations. The apprentice agrees to work for a company, at a rate below that paid to fully qualified workers, in return for a specified number of hours of training. In many instances, the conditions of training have been negotiated with the relevant union and are specified in the union contract. Most such programs are registered with the federal Department of Labor, which has responsibility for promoting apprenticeship training throughout the United States, and with appropriate state agencies.

The actual content of the training is usually established by a local apprenticeship committee, which specifies the number of hours of experience for each machine or kind of work. The classroom part of the apprenticeship is conducted at a vocational school, with an experienced journeyman in the trade acting as instructor. These courses emphasize applied mathematics, the physical sciences, and the techniques of the occupation. The classroom instruction may be offered during the work day or after hours. It may also be by correspondence. The on-the-job training is also given by a skilled journeyman, and insofar as possible, it is integrated with the classroom material. Thus the apprentice is given an immediate opportunity to practice what has been taught.

Apprenticeships can be extremely effective where complex skills must be learned. Yet there is reason to believe that many apprenticeship programs have been unnecessarily long, with the result that a good deal of inefficient overlearning occurs. A number of trades represented are not as complex and difficult to learn as has been assumed. Evidence for the view that overlearning is widespread in apprentice programs comes from the fact that many individuals attain the same skilled positions through vocational high school and on-the-job experience. Also, a number of dropouts from apprentice programs nevertheless go on to enter the same trade, in spite of the abbreviated learning. A recent study conducted in the United Brotherhood of Carpenters and Joiners provided reason to believe that women are somewhat more likely to complete their apprenticeship than men (Latack, Josephs, Roach, & Levine, 1987). Also, carpentry apprenticeship appears to work equally well with both men and women.

It is important to recognize, however, that apprenticeship is not of the same significance in the overall employee-training picture in the United States as it is in many other countries. Data on this point are given in Exhibit 19-7. Most skilled workers in this country do not complete apprenticeships, and the dropout rate from apprenticeship training is high relative to that elsewhere.

☐ Individualized Instruction

The distinguishing characteristic of the various individualized instruction techniques is that individuals learn at their own rates, using materials prepared specifically to facilitate the instructional process. These materials include teaching machines, books, computer data banks, and workbooks. The earliest of the approaches is programmed instruction; in contrast, computer-assisted instruction programs of various kinds are relatively recent additions.

Programmed Instruction. **Programmed instruction** is an individualized procedure that utilizes training materials organized into a series of frames, usually of increasing difficulty, with each successive frame building on those that precede. Information, questions,

Exhibit 19-7 Proportion of the Labor Force Engaged in Apprenticeships in Various Countries

Country	Percent of Apprentices
Austria	6.2
Germany	5.7
Switzerland	5.4
Italy	3.4
New Zealand	2.7
Denmark	2.3
Australia	2.1
Ireland	1.6
Netherlands	1.4
Canada	1.0
France	0.9
Belgium	0.6
Norway	0.6
United States	0.3
Finland	0.2

Source: B. G. Ruebens & J. A. C. Harrison (1980). *Apprenticeship in foreign countries*, p. 12. Washington, DC: U.S. Government Printing Office.

and problems are presented to learners with the requirement that they either write in their answers or select answers from among multiple-choice alternatives. Then feedback is provided on the correctness of the answer. The material is developed in such a way that a high proportion of the questions will elicit the desired response and thus result in positive reinforcement. The frames are frequently presented in a teaching machine that utilizes film or sound tapes. There is also a variety of programmed books and other printed materials in which the trainee uncovers the successive frames manually.

Inherent in all programmed instruction, regardless of the way in which materials are presented, are such features as active practice, a gradual increase in difficulty level over a series of small steps, immediate feedback, learning at the individual's own rate, and minimization of error. Thus, learning principles are explicitly built into the technique. There is reinforcement, knowledge of results, active practice, and guidance. The material may be learned in a time period suited to the ability level of the trainee. If the material is selected from the job in an appropriate manner, there should be positive transfer.

Given this degree of synchronization with learning theory, one would expect that programmed instruction would provide an extremely efficient method of training. Such evidence as is available does yield a generally favorable result, but there are important reservations (Goldstein, 1986). Consistently, programmed instruction has proved to be a more rapid method of learning than conventional methods. On occasion, it has produced more learning as well. However, superior performance at the end of training is not a necessary result, and retention of what is learned appears to be about the same as with other approaches.

In general, the use of programmed instruction can be expected to prove most advantageous with individuals of rather high mental ability and also with those toward the low end of the intellectual range. The person in the middle range benefits less from this particular type of training. Furthermore, the advantages of programmed instruction are generally considered to relate to knowledge only rather than to attitude change, skill learning, and other common objectives of training (Neider, 1981). Finally, the approach is extremely costly if a new program must be written. A single frame takes up to an hour to write, and a total program can contain hundreds or even thousands of frames, depending on the complexity of the material and the desired size of the learning steps. This means that the approach is feasible only when a large number of employees must be trained for a given job.

Computer-Assisted Instruction.   Programmed instruction and **computer-assisted instruction** have much in common. However, the newer approach utilizes a computer to select and present material and evaluate responses. Interaction with the computer occurs through a teaching terminal. The computer adjusts instruction to known aspects of the individual; thus, the rate and nature of learning can be adapted to individual differences in abilities, prior knowledge, and the like. This flexibility and the great amount of information that can be brought to bear for learning, if needed, are major advantages. The computer can analyze mistakes and make the next presentation in such a way as to facilitate understanding of the reasons for error. Thus, with its capacity to select alternatives derived from multiple branching, computer-assisted instruction offers the possibility of a highly individualized and effective approach to learning.

Studies to date indicate that computer-assisted instruction yields outcomes very similar to programmed instruction, with much the same advantages and limitations (Pintrich, Cross, Kozma, & McKeachie, 1986). It has the appeal for industrial organizations that instructional quality can be maintained at many locations through a dispersed system of terminals. However, the expense to achieve this is sizable, and the complexity of the needed programming is such that progress to date has been slower than many had hoped.

Thus, the PLATO system developed by Control Data Corporation was some nineteen years in the making. Yet with this system computer program analysts were trained in nineteen days instead of the forty-four days of classroom instruction previously required. Improved training was achieved with a saving of $5000 per student. In connection with the maintenance of computer equipment, two new computerized courses reduced the cost of customer engineer training by approximately $700,000 per year (Norris, 1981).

Computer-assisted instruction combined with videotaped modeling of tasks to be learned has proved particularly effective (Gist, Rosen, & Schwoerer, 1988).

☐ Individual and Team Simulations

Equipment simulations are used most widely in situations such as airline pilot training, where the economic and human costs of error are substantial. This can be an extremely expensive type of training, but for certain purposes it is well worth it. The savings on fuel that would be used in flight, for instance, is a major consideration to the airlines. Simulations provide for active practice, knowledge of results, and, when appropriately constructed, transfer of training.

Types of Simulations.   Although the work done by the airlines in simulation is more widely known, there are a number of other uses that have been identified. The types of tasks involved are as follows:

Procedures—simulators designed to represent procedures for adjusting and calibrating complex electronic equipment

Motor skills—simulators used for teaching a skill such as climbing telephone poles, operating presses and lathes, and driving a truck

Conceptual tasks—simulators representing activities required in conceptual reasoning—equipment troubleshooting, aerial photo interpretation, navigation

Identification—simulators representing such activities as the identification of safety hazards, terrain features, and radar signals

Team functions—complex simulators emphasizing the coordination of effort among team members (air defense system crews, air traffic control tower operators, astronauts) toward the achievement of a common goal

Of these, training in team functions is of particular interest because it goes beyond what is attempted in most other types of training.

System or Team Training. The training of groups of individuals whose work tasks interact developed primarily within the armed services. However, various types of work-unit training are finding their way into industry, especially in air transportation.

In general, when the systems concept is applied as a basis for organizing work, the term **system** or **subsystem training** is applied. In other instances, one hears of team or crew training. In either case, complex person–machine interactions tend to be involved.

Training of this kind is normally introduced relatively late in the overall learning sequence, when individual workers are reasonably knowledgeable and proficient at their own individual jobs. A task is developed that requires role behavior from a number of employees in interaction. Usually, the task is selected to focus on special problem areas within the total work effort. At the end of the exercise, knowledge of results on total team performance is provided insofar as this is possible, and the team members discuss their own performance. To the extent possible, this feedback should be of both an individual and a group nature.

The intent is to develop a cooperative effort and thus overall levels of effectiveness beyond those that can be obtained from individual learning alone. As training progresses through successive trials on various tasks, individuals become increasingly aware of how their role behaviors may help and hinder coworkers. They also begin to view their own work in terms of its place in the total team effort. Thus team training can permit a group to develop solutions to various problems, such as the overloading of a single member, with the consequent formation of a bottleneck in production. Solutions of this kind are rarely learned when the training program relies entirely on individual instruction.

Evaluation of Team Simulations. Several arguments have been advanced against this type of team training. For one thing, it is often wasteful of time and money. Team training exercises almost invariably require role behavior from only a few members at a given time. The others act as observers or await their turn for participation. It is difficult to maintain alertness and motivation among these nonactive members. Thus, their time is often wasted, and labor costs increase with little return on the investment. In addition, there are the costs associated with the construction of adequate simulations.

Second, there are problems related to the identification of individual errors and the overall evaluation of results. It is often almost impossible to determine exactly what went wrong when difficulties arise. Thus, immediate feedback and knowledge of results may be hard to achieve, and the specific source of an error may not be identified. Also, suitable criteria of team performance must be established, so that an effective effort can be clearly differentiated from an ineffective one. This can be done, but an adequate backlog of information may not yet exist in this area, with the result that team standard setting can become a major problem. Thus, the knowledge-of-results requirement tends to run into difficulties both at the level of the individual team member and at the level of the total team.

On the positive side is the fact that where cooperative effort represents a major aspect of the work, clear gains in efficiency above those obtainable with individual training do appear to result from the team approach. There are factors in any actual work situation, with its flow of work activities and its patterning of social interactions, that cannot be adequately handled through individual training. When considerations of this kind are marked, group training seems to be a desirable adjunct to other procedures.

■ CAREER PLANNING AND DEVELOPMENT

Career planning is a process undertaken for the purpose of becoming aware of oneself, available opportunities, existing constraints, choices to be made, and consequences to be expected. It means identifying career-related goals, and it requires the programming of work, education, and developmental experiences in order to attain these goals. **Career development** follows; it is the process of actually carrying out what has been planned (Storey, 1979, p. 5). It may involve considerable retraining (Casner-Lotto, 1988; Rosow & Zager, 1988).

□ Activities Involved

Historically, career planning and development has been an individual matter. In recent years, prompted in part by equal employment opportunity concerns and pressures, companies have taken steps to create a closer alignment between individual career goals and organizational goals, to make individuals more aware of areas of common interest, and to assist in the planning and development process. Activities of this kind, such as tuition aid programs, job posting so that individuals learn about open positions, and job rotation for developmental purposes, have existed for many years. What is new, however, are the attempts to bring these activities together under the banner of career planning and development, and to add a wide array of career-related activities. There is not complete agreement as to what activities should be defined as existing primarily for career planning and development, but in any case the list is a long one (Burack & Mathys, 1980; Hall, 1986; Morgan, 1980). It includes:

Career counseling by managers as part of the appraisal process

Career counseling by staff specialists

Workshops on self-analysis and planning

Workshops on life or career planning

Workshops related to outplacement (job-hunting assistance provided by a firm to laid-off workers)

Training managers in career-counseling skills

Assessment centers for development purposes

Delineation of specific career paths within the firm through job analyses

Career-planning workbooks

Computerized job information systems.

Exhibit 19-8 shows one way in which a career plan might be designed. In this instance, the focus is on using assessment centers to evaluate an individual's strengths, aims, and concerns. Many firms accomplish much the same thing by using traditional vocational-guidance procedures. Upon entering the program, participants are interviewed extensively and given various tests of abilities, interests, motives, and personality traits. Participants frequently construct detailed career plans, using a variety of reference sources about the company and occupations in general. In-house or outside consultants may provide career counseling.

A typical career planning and development program, originally developed at Bell Telephone of Pennsylvania, has four steps:

1. Those invited and wishing to participate complete a self-assessment workbook dealing with identifying personal values, assessing training and job experiences, establishing general skills, measuring managerial potential, establishing career goals,

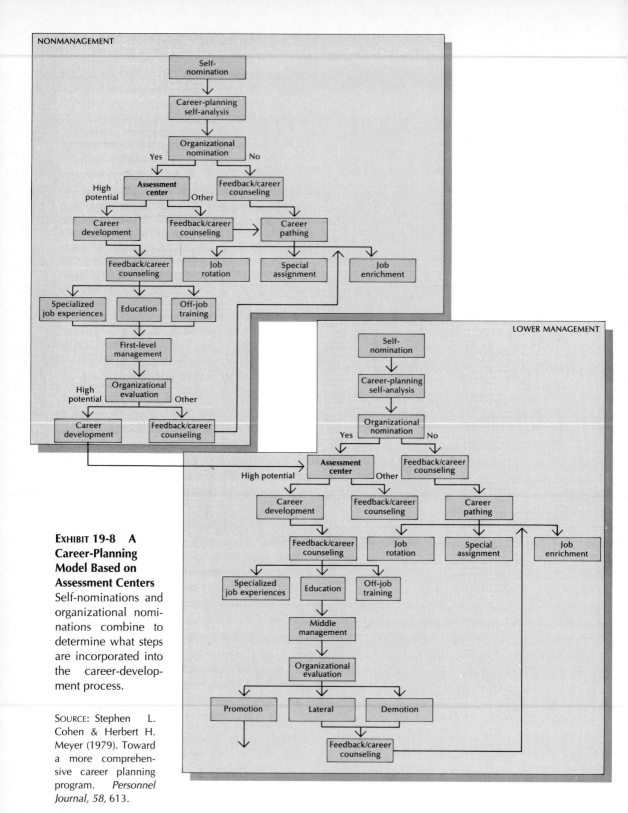

NONMANAGEMENT

Self-nomination

↓

Career-planning self-analysis

↓

Organizational nomination

Yes / No

Assessment center

High potential / Other

Feedback/career counseling

Career development

Feedback/career counseling → Career pathing

Feedback/career counseling

Job rotation

Special assignment

Job enrichment

Specialized job experiences

Education

Off-job training

First-level management

↓

Organizational evaluation

High potential / Other

Career development

Feedback/career counseling

LOWER MANAGEMENT

Self-nomination

↓

Career-planning self-analysis

↓

Organizational nomination

Yes / No

Assessment center

Feedback/career counseling

High potential / Other

Career development

Feedback/career counseling

Career pathing

Feedback/career counseling

Job rotation

Special assignment

Job enrichment

Specialized job experiences

Education

Off-job training

Middle management

↓

Organizational evaluation

Promotion

Lateral

Demotion

Feedback/career counseling

EXHIBIT 19-8 A Career-Planning Model Based on Assessment Centers
Self-nominations and organizational nominations combine to determine what steps are incorporated into the career-development process.

SOURCE: Stephen L. Cohen & Herbert H. Meyer (1979). Toward a more comprehensive career planning program. *Personnel Journal, 58,* 613.

Exhibit 19-9   Excerpt from a Personal Development Plan

Goal: To progress from a first-level supervisor of a research project team to a second-level manager and assistant director of the Research Department.

Plans for Development

Talents	Experiences	Job Assignments
Knowledge of technical domains	Develop oral communication skills; attend two-day workshop.	Volunteer for role of presenter at project review.
Good coworker relationships		Move to group leader of several project teams.
Forcefulness	Learn more about work scheduling; attend a course in operations management.	Seek task force leader role on XYZ project.
Effective written communications	Develop performance appraisal feedback skills; seek coaching from superiors.	Transfer for six months to Technical Development Department to broaden perspective.

Source: Manuel London & Stephen A. Stumpf (1982). *Managing careers*, p. 123. Reading, MA: Addison-Wesley.

and setting up a schedule for reaching goals.

2. Participants complete a career-exploration guide, which deals with clarifying career goals, using company-provided information on potential opportunities, obtaining help from career-development coordinators, and using company-provided resources.

3. Using a workbook, participants prepare for a career discussion with their superiors. Each person develops a preliminary work-action plan, summarizes his or her talents, and lists plans for developmental experiences, including preferences for job assignments. One such plan is presented in Exhibit 19-9.

4. The product of the career discussion with the superior is a five-year personal development plan and a corresponding work-preference document that contains choices for desired transfers in pursuit of developmental needs. These materials are fed into the company personnel data base for use in filling job vacancies when they occur.

A somewhat different approach, which makes more extensive use of the computer, was developed for use at IBM (see Box 19-5). Similar approaches are used at Corning Glass and Digital Equipment Corporation.

☐ Evaluation

How well do company efforts of this kind work? The evidence is generally positive, but research in this area often has been poorly designed. Whether or not people who would not have prospered otherwise have been identified and helped to advance their careers is still an unanswered question. It does appear, however, that career planning is a factor in the development of successful careers and that career-planning documents,

BOX 19-5   I/O PSYCHOLOGY IN PRACTICE

IBM's Computerized Career-Planning Information System

IBM has developed an Employee Development Planning System which is organized into five general sections. In Section 1, orientation and planning readiness assessment, employees receive an explanation of the system objectives and operating procedures and an inventory of items with which they assess their readiness for career decision making. Implications of their inventoried readiness are reviewed by means of an individualized interactive dialogue. In Section 2, employee self-assessment, the employees create a self-description profile based on their work-related interests, abilities, skills, and desired in-depth work experiences. In Section 3, system job search, the system permits searches through a file of generic job types that exist within the organization in order to identify those with profiles compatible with the employees' self-described profiles. A list of these job types is displayed to the employee. In Section 4, employees analyze jobs of interest; the employees select from a list of displayed job types those about which they would like to learn. While analyzing a job type, employees can express their likes and dislikes about various job features. Based on the employees' reactions in combination with their planning readiness scores, personalized messages are displayed to the employees. The messages describe potential planning problems, consistencies and

inconsistencies in the employees' response patterns to the job types analyzed. The employees are not limited to analyzing jobs in their list but can analyze any job type contained in the system. Section 5 summarizes personal development needs: After the employees have analyzed all job types of potential interest to them, the system helps them summarize their development needs. The summary reflects the employees' perceptions of how well their current skills and work experiences support the potential objectives they identified while using the system. The system organizes this information into a table useful for planning self-improvement activities.

The system enables employees to skip or return to selected modules. At critical checkpoints, the system automatically prints summary reports for the employees, which can be used for review with their managers and as a personal record of their activities with the system. The employees review with their managers their views, ideas, and preferences about goals, plans, and needs based on their experience with the system.

SOURCE: Frank J. Miner (1986). Computer applications in career development planning. In Douglas T. Hall (Ed.), *Career development in organizations*, pp. 209–210. San Francisco: Jossey-Bass.

when prepared conscientiously, reflect major motivational patterns of the individuals involved (Gould, 1979; Miner & Crane, 1981). Certainly, thinking through what one really wants and how these aims relate to other aspects of one's life, such as family considerations, can be of considerable value (Korman & Korman, 1980). Efforts of this kind by companies probably benefit all concerned. If nothing else, they make some people aware of com-

mon goals between themselves and their employers.

Anticipated negative effects of career planning and development programs have not materialized (Williams, 1981). Employees generally react positively and want to use the help provided. In general, career-development programs are not overwhelmed by the sheer number of participants. Expectations may be raised, but not unrealistically; no major increase in turnover occurs as a result of disillusionment. Given the importance for an employing organization of achieving an integration of employee career goals with the goals of organizational effectiveness, investments in career planning and development seem worthwhile.

KEY TERMS

Training
Education
Control group
Experimental group
Before-after model
After-only model
Pretest sensitizing effect
Encapsulated training
Training needs
Role playing

Interactive game
Multiple management
Vestibule school
Apprentice training
Programmed instruction
Computer-assisted instruction
Equipment simulations
System (subsystem) training
Career planning
Career development

SUMMARY

A wide range of *training* and development approaches has been considered throughout this book. Many of these approaches are applications of organizational psychology's theories. This chapter considers methods and approaches above and beyond those already considered.

There is an important need to conduct evaluation research for the purpose of determining whether training and development programs yield changes that contribute to improved performance. Various research designs for the conduct of such studies have been devised and used. The underlying logic of this type of psychological research is much the same as with the validation of selection techniques.

Training and development efforts should be constituted so as to be consistent with the concepts of learning theory. They should also focus on individuals and situations where the need is greatest—where a specific *training need* has been identified.

Many techniques for identifying training needs have been developed. Usually these techniques start from some type of job analysis information.

Among approaches widely used in management development, lecture and discussion both appear to be effective. Case study, *role playing,* and *business games* serve to simulate actual business situations with varying degrees of fidelity. Many management development programs are conducted by universities or at special centers operated by large businesses for their own employees. Also, companies often emphasize development outside the classroom—job rotation, understudy roles, committee work, and junior boards. All of these management development approaches appear to have the capacity to induce change. The important consideration is to select the appropriate procedure to solve a specific problem or achieve a given objective.

An early approach in employee training was

Job Instruction Training. Other approaches are *vestibule training* and *apprenticeships*. Orientation training begins the organizational socialization process. Individualized techniques such as *programmed instruction* and *computer-assisted instruction,* though costly, can be effective. *Simulations* are widely used in airline pilot training. However, they and the various expanded team or *systems approaches* may be used in other contexts as well. Government initiatives have sparked considerable activity in the area of company *career planning and development* programs. Included are career counseling, the establishment of career paths, and a variety of workshops dealing with careers.

QUESTIONS

1. There has been considerable controversy over the years regarding the relative value of the traditional lecture approach. Some of the techniques discussed in this chapter utilize a lecture approach; some do not. Review the research reported from this viewpoint. What is your conclusion regarding the lecture method?

2. How might subjects be used as their own controls in evaluating training? What problems remain with this approach?

3. What is it about simulations that makes them so attractive to the airlines for flight training? Would team training be important here? Explain.

4. It has been said that apprenticeship is the key to the American production system. In what sense is this true? In what sense is it not true?

5. In what ways do programmed instruction and computer-assisted instruction differ? What are the pros and cons of these approaches for training industrial production workers?

6. What is career planning and development, and why do companies become involved in it? What are the arguments for and against investments in such activities?

7. What is the role of training-needs analysis? Do you believe that all training programs are based on such an analysis? Explain.

8. On-the-job training for production workers, although widely used, has a number of deficiencies. What are the deficiencies, and what alternative procedures may be used to overcome them?

9. Why are control groups needed in evaluation of change studies? Can you think of any reason why it might be useful to have both a before-after control group and an after-only control group?

10. Describe and discuss each of the following:
    a. Tuition aid
    b. Multiple management
    c. Vestibule training
    d. Encapsulated training
    e. Pretest sensitization

CASE PROBLEM

Sales Training: The Needs of Department Store Clerks

A large retail department store chain had been experiencing increasing numbers of complaints, and more vehement complaints as well, from its customers regarding the quality of service provided by its store clerks. These complaints took a variety of forms—lack of knowledge regarding products, inability to handle returns without obtaining supervisory assistance, difficulty in using the computerized charge system, being uninformed regarding sales advertised in the newspapers, not knowing where various products were located in a store, failure to provide customers with information on how to obtain credit, and so on. It was not that the clerks were discourteous, although often they did not deal with customers in the ways that the company generally prescribed; rather, the problem was that they did not know what customers expected them to know, thus causing delays, mixups, and generally making it difficult for customers to consummate their business.

The store managers were pretty much agreed that the problem lay in the training area, but they could not agree on exactly what the training problem was. Some felt that the complaints actually reflected a generalized pattern of unhappiness with the clerks rather than any specific deficiency. Others would emphasize one area or another where they felt the clerks were uninformed. Although there was rather high turnover in the sales clerk positions, the problems did not appear to be limited to the new people.

These difficulties were particularly disturbing because the firm had always prided itself on its training. There was a strong emphasis on decentralizing training decisions down to the local store level and on having new sales clerks start dealing with customers as soon as possible so that they could learn on the job. Supervisors and experienced clerks were to work directly with the new people and explain procedures as they went along. There had, however, been some recent cutback in staffing at both the sales clerk and supervisory levels in many of the stores because of increased labor costs under the new contract; that might be part of the problem—maybe those who were supposed to train did not have time to do so.

The company had introduced a career-development program for all employees when that approach first became popular. A rather sophisticated package had been put together by the corporate training people, and detailed career paths had been worked out. In accord with standard company practice, this package had been turned over to the individual stores for implementation. There had been little follow-up beyond that, other than to monitor the number of people participating. Participation rates among the store clerks were generally low.

As the complaints continued over a considerable period of time, the corporate training people were finally brought in. The store managers were agreed that they had not been able to solve the problem on their own and that they needed help. They were willing to give the training people considerable freedom both in looking into the problem and in doing something about it. If needed, the corporate-level training budget would be increased to deal with the problem. Something really had to be done and fast.

Questions

1. If you were in charge of the corporate training group, how would you approach this situation? What would you do first?

2. What training methods or approaches would you utilize?

3. How would you evaluate the training initiatives you introduced?

20

Safety Psychology and Industrial Clinical Psychology

Psychologists from the St. Paul Insurance Companies introduced a stress-management program into a medium-sized Midwestern hospital with the objective of lowering worker compensation costs. The rationale was that high levels of stress contributed to employee injuries, and that training for the purpose of reducing stress would have an impact on the rate and severity of injuries.

The training started with management personnel in the hospital, who were encouraged to manage hospital stress better and were given feedback on how to reach this goal. A stress measurement instrument was administered to employees and the results fed back in group sessions. High-stress groups were given personal consultations to correct the underlying sources of their stress. Stress education tapes intended to teach employees how to prevent stress-related injuries were shown. Control Data Corporation's Stay Well program, a program of wellness education and training modules, was utilized. A director of health promotion was hired.

In the ten-month period prior to the stress-management program, paid worker compensation claims averaged well over $2000 per month. In the same period after stress-management training, these same claims dropped to under $1000 per month. Although certain attribution regarding the cause of this change would require a control group analysis, the evidence available suggested that the stress-management program was successful.

SOURCE: Lisa Kunz (1987). Stress intervention programs for reducing medical costs and accident claims in a hospital. *Journal of Business and Psychology, 1,* 257–263.

This is an example of the practice of both safety psychology and industrial clinical psychology. On the one hand, the program described represents an effort to reduce accidents and injuries, and at the same time reduce costly worker compensation claims. In this respect it is an application of safety psychology. On the other hand, the program focuses on emotional stress and its reduction. Stress measurement, personal consultation, and stress education are all part of the procedures employed. In this respect the approaches of industrial clinical psychology are brought to bear. The St. Paul Insurance Companies stress-management program clearly demonstrates the close ties between safety psychology and industrial clinical psychology that characterize the subject matter of this chapter.

Safety psychology and industrial clinical psychology have in common that they are concerned with preventing and correcting certain types of problems—problems which interfere with work and performance. In **safety psychology** the balance shifts in the direction of prevention. The goal is to head off accidents based on an understanding of why and how they occur. Once accidents occur, the matter of restoring the individual to work is primarily a medical concern. In **industrial clinical psychology** the major focus is on employees whose performance has fallen below acceptable levels, the factors that caused the performance failure, and what can be done to correct the problem. Preventing performance problems is of concern also, but in actual practice the diagnosis and correction of existing deficiencies is what takes up the majority of the psychologist's time.

Safety psychologists usually work in close collaboration with engineers and physicians. Industrial clinical psychologists have a strong tie to medicine as well. The reasons for these professional relationships will become more evident as we consider first the matter of safety and accidents, and then the diagnosis and treatment of performance problems generally.

■ SAFETY MANAGEMENT AND SAFETY PSYCHOLOGY

Although the usual practice in **safety management** is to administer an accident-prevention program out of a safety unit located within the human resources function, committees have become an important adjunct in this area, as they have in wage and salary administration. The primary reason for this development appears to be that widespread acceptance and cooperation are essential to the success of any safety effort. To the extent that a large number of individuals throughout the company can be involved in the program and made to feel a part of it, actual implementation of decisions related to safety is likely to be facilitated. It is important that those at the higher levels of management, as well as those at lower levels, feel this sense of involvement.

Under normal circumstances, the highest-level safety committee is established on an interdepartmental basis and is concerned primarily with policy matters. This committee has responsibility for establishing safety rules, for investigating particularly hazardous situations, for making expenditures related to accident prevention, and for resolving disputes.

In addition, there usually are a number of departmental committees to deal with inspection and the correction of unsafe conditions. Unlike the policy committee, the latter groups are not restricted to managerial personnel. In fact, they appear to function more smoothly and effectively if there is a heavy representation from below the managerial level.

The departmental committees may also handle safety training and publicity, although frequently a separate committee structure is devoted to the specific purposes of developing and implementing programs to promote interest in safety, to obtain compliance with safety rules, and to disseminate safety knowl-

edge. In some companies, safety training committees and those concerned with inspection have taken on a joint union–management character. Less frequently, the higher-level policy group also has union representation. In some instances, this joint approach is necessary and even helpful, especially if the union leadership is strongly concerned about safety matters, but it does tend to introduce a number of extraneous considerations into a group decision-making process that is often rather slow-moving and cumbersome even without this additional obstacle. The result is that joint union–management committees can become so bound up in conflict that they are incapable of action. For some years, union activity regarding safety has focused more on the bargaining process and grievance procedures than on joint decision making within the committee structure (Bacow, 1980). In any event, there is evidence that "health and safety committees may not only increase perceived effectiveness of safety interventions, but also increase safety on some objective criteria" (Sheehy & Chapman, 1987, p. 217).

□ Accident Statistics and Reports

Accident statistics are a valuable aspect of a total safety effort for two reasons. When calculated for the company as a whole, they permit comparison against the national and industry figures provided by such organizations as the National Safety Council and the U.S. Bureau of Labor Statistics. Thus a company can determine its position relative to other firms and set its accident-prevention goals accordingly. Where the comparative statistics suggest that a major problem exists, a sizable total investment in safety procedures may be warranted. Second, when rates are determined separately for the various work units within a firm, it is possible to pinpoint trouble spots and concentrate preventive efforts with these in mind. In this way, the accident-prevention process may be focused where it will do the most good. Most company accident statistics have been based on two rate formulas:

Injury frequency rate =
$$\frac{\text{number of disabling injuries} \times 1,000,000}{\text{number of employee - hours worked}}$$

Injury severity rate =
$$\frac{\text{number of days lost} \times 1,000,000}{\text{number of employee - hours worked}}$$

The usual practice is to use disabling or lost-time injuries only in these calculations, although rates for minor injuries may be determined separately. Lost-time injuries include deaths, permanent disabilities (whether partial or total), and injuries that render a person unable to do a job for at least an entire work shift subsequent to the accident. Minor injuries are those that do not meet the preceding criteria but that do require first aid or treatment in a dispensary or physician's office. Because they may be used for workers' compensation claims and reflected in absenteeism statistics, lost-time injury data tend generally to be valid. Minor injuries, however, may go unreported. In calculating severity rates, standard time charges are used in the case of deaths and disabilities and actual days lost for temporary conditions.

For many years, the U.S. Bureau of Labor Statistics published data using figures provided by employers participating voluntarily in the data-collection effort. With the passage of the Occupational Safety and Health Act (OSHA) in 1970, all employers except those with fewer than eight employees were required to keep accident records and to file an annual summary report of all accidents or injuries (Lofgren, 1989). Exhibit 20-1 is a guide for employers indicating when accidents or illnesses need to be recorded.

Accident rates have been consistently high in certain industries and low in others. Construction and agriculture, forestry, and fishing tend to have very high rates; rates in finance, insurance, and real estate have been the lowest. Rates are highest in smaller firms (a hundred or so employees) and decrease steadily with increasing company size, except that they tend to be relatively low among the very smallest firms.

Motor vehicle accident rates are normally recorded on a separate basis for all company-owned vehicles. For purposes of motor safety, an accident is defined as any contact with the company vehicle that causes either personal injury or property damage. The rate formula is:

Motor vehicle accident frequency rate =
$$\frac{\text{number of accidents} \times 100,000}{\text{number of vehicle - miles operated}}$$

An attempt is often made to compute separate rates for accidents that are chargeable against the company employee who was driving and those that do not appear to be chargeable in this manner. There is some question, however, whether such efforts at differentiation are ever entirely successful. Obtaining the required information is often difficult and almost always time-consuming, and accuracy cannot be assured.

Accident Reports. Statistics of the type discussed are developed from accident reports that are normally prepared by the immediate superior of the employee involved. The requirement that supervisors must fill out reports in this manner has the advantage that it makes the particular people who can do the most to promote safety aware of accidents occurring under their jurisdictions. Thus it not only provides necessary information but serves a useful educational purpose as well.

Many of the questions asked on an accident report form are noted in Exhibit 20-2. Several of these require explanation. For example, the accident is referred to as "alleged." This is done to protect the company against damage claims. Any report signed by a supervisor that refers in an unqualified

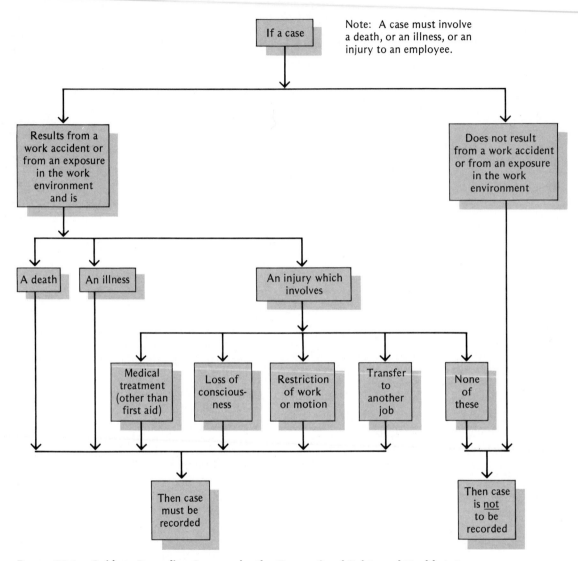

EXHIBIT 20-1   Guide to Recording Cases under the Occupational Safety and Health Act
SOURCE: U.S. Department of Labor (1975). Occupational safety and health statistics concepts and methods—Report no. 438, p. 2. Washington, DC: Bureau of Labor Statistics.

manner to a specific accident can serve as evidence in court that the employer acknowledges responsibility in the case, whether or not the employer actually wishes to do so. And, of course, all such records can be subpoenaed. Thus the use of "alleged" on a standard basis provides a defense against false claims.

The **agency** is the thing most closely associated with the injury. Examples are animals, boilers, chemicals, conveyors, dusts, electric apparatus, elevators, hand tools, flammable

Name of employee _____ Location _____

Address _____ Division _____

Sex _____ Age _____ Occupation _____

Married _____ Children _____ Wage rate _____

Date and time of alleged accident _____

Place of alleged accident _____

Description of alleged accident _____

_____

_____

_____

_____

Working on regular job? _____

Agency involved _____

Part of agency _____

Unsafe mechanical or physical condition of agency _____

_____

Accident type _____

Unsafe act _____

Unsafe personal factor _____

Safeguards provided _____

Safeguards in use _____

Nature and extent of injury _____

_____

_____

Days lost _____ Attending physician _____

Recommendations to prevent similar accidents _____

_____

_____

Prepared by _____ Date _____

EXHIBIT 20-2   **A Typical Accident Report Form**

substances, hoisting apparatus, machines, radiations, and working surfaces. The **agency part** is that specific part or aspect of the agency most closely associated with the injury. The **unsafe mechanical or physical condition** of the agency refers to the aspect of the agency that could have been guarded or corrected. The categories normally used are inadequate mechanical guarding, defective condition of the agency, unsafe design of the agency, hazardous processes or procedures, incorrect illumination, incorrect ventilation, and unsafe apparel.

The **accident type** refers to the type of contact of the injured person with the agency. Examples are caught in or between; struck by; struck against; fall of person; scratched; overexertion; and contact with either electricity, extreme temperatures, or noxious substances. The **unsafe act** is the type of behavior leading to the accident, such as working unsafely, performing unauthorized operations, removing safety devices, operating at unsafe speeds, using improper equipment, using equipment unsafely, horseplay, and failure to use safe attire. The **unsafe personal factor** is the characteristic of the individual responsible for the unsafe act—unsafe attitudes, lack of knowledge, bodily defect, or disturbed emotional state.

Unfortunately, reports of this kind do not always yield completely valid information. The persons involved in an accident, including the supervisor in charge, may well be strongly motivated to cover up certain aspects of the case to protect themselves against anticipated criticism from higher management. Thus it is often difficult to obtain objective data. Nevertheless, experience indicates that tabulations based on questions of the kind illustrated in Exhibit 20-2 can yield information that is at least sufficiently valid so that major sources of difficulty can be identified.

The Study of Near Accidents. The injury process may be described as a sequence running from a social environment or background, to a defect or fault of the person, to an unsafe act or conditions, to an accident, and finally to an injury. In the great majority of cases, this sequence does not run its full course, and therefore no actual injury occurs. Yet the preceding factors are much the same as when the sequence is completed. Thus the study of **near accidents** can provide useful insights that may be used to ward off future injuries.

Some companies go to considerable trouble to develop frequency and descriptive data on such near accidents. Either report forms or interviews with workers are used to collect the data. The approach has the advantage that because no actual loss occurs, attempts to cover up and protect against blame are less likely, and the true sources of danger can be established more easily. Furthermore, because near accidents are much more frequent, a study of them is particularly valuable in pinpointing those jobs, places, and individuals that require the greatest attention.

☐ Safety Training

One of the more important approaches in accident prevention is safety training. There is evidence that, where the work situation is relatively hazardous, injuries are particularly likely to occur during the first few months of employment, when workers have not yet learned how to protect themselves against dangers in the environment (Frenkel, Priest, & Ashford, 1980; Siskind, 1982). Under such circumstances it becomes apparent that any kind of training, whether directed toward orientation, skills, attitudes, or anything else connected with the job, can serve a preventive purpose insofar as accidents are concerned. To the extent that such early training makes a new employee more capable of coping with the work environment, it will inevitably contribute to the safety goal. Employees who are unfamiliar with their work contexts are vulnerable to injury.

This problem occurs most frequently among new employees, but it can develop among employees who have been absent from work as well (Goodman & Garber, 1988). Accidents are most frequent after periods of absenteeism. Accidents are also more frequent among replacement workers who work intermittently. Accidents are least common among regular workers who have not been absent recently. Apparently, continued, uninterrupted exposure to the work breeds familiarity, which in turn serves to prevent accidents.

In actual practice, training programs for new and unfamiliar employees do characteristically involve considerable safety content. Items covered are special hazards in the work situation, examples of previous accidents, nature and use of safety equipment, availability of medical services, accident reporting, and safety rules. Where the work is particularly hazardous, first-aid procedures are often included.

Techniques used for safety training include many of those discussed in Chapter 19, such as lectures, demonstrations, and films. The use of accident simulations may be quite effective. In accident simulation, operators perform an unsafe act and actually experience an accident, using equipment modified to prevent injury. This training effect can be successfully transferred to the use of unmodified equipment. Simulation training can be expected to be particularly effective in high-hazard situations. One study of the types of human error involved in underground accidents in gold mines indicates that the dominant types of errors involve failures to perceive warnings of danger and underestimations of hazards (Lawrence, 1974). Accident simulation should result in increased awareness of the dangers of the workplace.

Some firms introduce more general discussions of safety off the job into the training process. This is done because most larger companies, as a result of their safety efforts, have produced a situation where injuries at work are less frequent than during the rest of the day. Factories are often safer than the home. Time lost because of off-the-job injuries may well be greater than for work-connected injuries. Under such circumstances, the tendency has been to include a rather broad

treatment of accident prevention within the training context.

Another type of safety training is directed to specific situations where there has been a deterioration in accident rates. It is not uncommon for experienced employees to develop group norms that sanction the breaking of safety rules and a failure to use protective devices. When this happens, safety training becomes an important antidote. The usual procedure is to review safety rules in a series of discussions conducted by a safety specialist. Considerable opportunity is given for open criticism of existing rules and procedures, and on occasion, changes are introduced in response to group decisions. Every effort is made not only to impart safety information, but also to get employees personally involved in the safety effort.

A good example of using safety training to deal with problem situations comes from American Cyanamid Company (Eden, 1987). After a spate of chemical-plant disasters, and recent accidents at the major Linden, New Jersey, facility, the company stepped up its safety training substantially. Time for classes was blocked out, and workers were required to attend. Furthermore, extensive information on how chemical reactions occur was incorporated in the training. Training became a prime factor in the effort to improve the company's safety climate.

Some of the more interesting advances in the safety training context have involved adaptations of the organizational behavior modification approach. A number of studies have combined feedback on safety performance, rewards made contingent on reduced accident rates, competition between groups for rewards, and the like, to achieve substantial reductions in accidents (Haynes, Pine, and Fitch, 1982; Komaki, Collins, & Penn, 1982; Komaki, Heinzmann, & Lawson, 1980). Favorable results have been obtained among vehicle maintenance personnel working for a large city, employees in a poultry processing

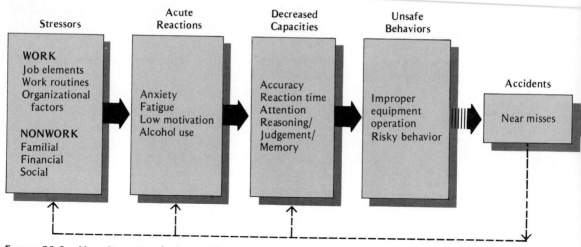

EXHIBIT 20-3   How Stress Results in Accidents

SOURCE: Lawrence R. Murphy, David DuBois, & Joseph J. Hurrell (1986). Accident reduction through stress management. *Journal of Business and Psychology, 1,* 12.

plant, and city bus drivers. Although much more needs to be learned about the long-term consequences of this approach, results to date indicate that it can bring about major safety improvements in situations of a high-hazard nature.

An approach to safety training that shows considerable promise is predicated on the fact, as discussed in Chapter 6, that one consequence of high stress levels is a propensity for accidents. Thus stress-management programs have been initiated with the specific objective of reducing accidents. The example at the beginning of this chapter describes one such program that the St. Paul Insurance Companies have been using. Exhibit 20-3 shows how stress may contribute to accidents.

☐ Safety Publicity and Contests

Safety publicity can take a variety of forms. Among those commonly used are posters, booklets, special memoranda, and articles in company publications. In many instances these media are used to advertise contests

that pit various work groups against each other in an effort to minimize the number of lost-time accidents.

A major source of posters for industry is the National Safety Council. Many companies also print their own posters and notices. Insofar as possible, these should concentrate on reminding employees of safe practices without arousing too much anxiety. Gruesome and disturbing material is simply avoided by many people; they do not look at it at all. The main function of a good poster is to attract attention and keep employees thinking about safety, not to scare them.

Company publications can be used to provide information on accidents that have occurred or on hazardous situations that have been corrected. Running accounts of the results of safety contests are often provided. All these serve to promote safety consciousness and, to the extent that employees are kept aware of the possibility of injury, they are likely to exhibit safer behavior.

Box 20-1 describes a safety publicity campaign initiated by Johnson and Johnson to foster seat belt use by company employees.

BOX **20-1** RESEARCH IN I/O PSYCHOLOGY

The Effects of a Seat Belt Use Publicity Campaign at Johnson and Johnson's Corporate Headquarters

A publicity campaign was initiated at the main parking lot for Johnson and Johnson's headquarters in New Brunswick, New Jersey. Results there were compared with those for another lot used by employees from several office buildings also located in New Brunswick. Observations of seat belt use were recorded at prespecified times at the lot entrances over five weeks prior to the one-week campaign, and then for six weeks after it.

The campaign itself started with the distribution of stickers to be posted on car dashboards which urged seat belt use. Those who actually used the stickers were given small gifts. During the week of the campaign, placards with various messages encouraging seat belt use were placed on tables in the employee cafeteria. Permanent signs reminding people to use their seat belts were placed in a variety of locations around the parking lot area.

Seat belt use was found to increase by 31 percent at one parking lot entrance and 7 percent at the other. Belt use at the central lot where there was no publicity campaign remained stable. A follow-up check six months after the campaign revealed a continued rise in use—up 61 percent at one entrance and 33 percent at the other. There is no plausible alternative to the conclusion that the publicity campaign was responsible for the substantial increase in seat belt use.

SOURCE: Neil D. Weinstein, Paul D. Grubb, & James S. Vautier (1986). Increasing automobile seat belt use: An intervention emphasizing risk susceptibility. *Journal of Applied Psychology, 71*, 285–290.

The evidence obtained from an evaluation study indicates substantial success.

Safety rules and regulations often are printed in a separate booklet that is given wide distribution. Unfortunately, these booklets rarely achieve a readership even approximating their distribution. Furthermore, some of them actually create disrespect for safety procedures rather than promote them. The reason is that there is a strong and, unfortunately, often valid temptation for management to absolve itself of responsibility in connection with accidents by proscribing all behaviors that might conceivably prove unsafe. As a result, many of the rules turn out to be entirely unrealistic, and employees break them without thinking, often with the tacit approval of their supervisors. When this happens, the whole system of safety regulation tends to become denigrated, with little differentiation being made between realistic and unrealistic rules. The only way to protect against this eventuality is to keep safety restrictions to a minimum. Given the current legal climate, however, this is difficult.

All manner of contests are conducted to foster safety, in most cases with considerable success. In general, the emphasis is on internal comparisons within a company, but there are some industrywide contests, such as those conducted by the National Safety Council. Perhaps most common is a competition between departments with similar accident potentials as indicated by national rates. These contests may stress maintaining a low-frequency rate, or they may be concerned with the number of days without an injury. Sometimes only lost-time injuries are counted; sometimes, minor injuries as well. Departments may also compete against their own records for certain periods in the past. Awards are often given to individual employees working in high-accident occupations, such as truck drivers, for remaining accident-free over an extended time span.

Although contests do appear to have a generally salutary effect on injuries, there are certain negative aspects that should be recognized. One is the tendency to let down when a long accident-free period finally comes to an end. A rash of injuries can occur at such a time if something is not done to divert interest to some new contest or record. Second, there is some tendency to cover up injuries when they occur in the context of a contest, especially if minor injuries are included. The result can be a failure to obtain needed first-aid and dispensary treatment. In addition, accident reports may not be filed when they should be, with a resulting distortion of statistics. Under certain circumstances, the harmful side effects of contests can outweigh the gains.

□ Control of the Work Environment

Design of the workplace, and of equipment used in it, is probably the major approach to accident prevention and the most effective one. Safety devices and the like have the advantage that they not only reduce accidents but also give employees a sense of confidence and security in the workplace. Anxiety levels are reduced accordingly, and a potential source of performance disruption and failure is eliminated. This is a particularly important consideration in situations that would be extremely dangerous without accident-prevention devices.

One of the major provisions of the Occupational Safety and Health Act calls for the government to set national standards for safety devices and other requirements related to a safe work environment. Much of the job of complying with these standards devolves on safety engineers.

The most crucial consideration is that equipment be constructed to introduce barriers that make it very difficult, if not impossible, for individuals to expose themselves to danger. Protective clothing, guards, covers, and the like can often isolate a person from a danger source so that, regardless of what is done, there is little chance of injury. In addition, controls should be designed and placed so that opportunities for erroneous use are kept to a minimum. Devices that will yield information regarding any malfunctioning or breakdown of equipment should be installed wherever possible, and they should be readily visible. Self-correcting mechanisms and automatic shutoffs are, of course, the ideal, because then danger is eliminated without the need for human intervention. But if these cannot be installed, all controls, releases, gauges, and the like should be built to mesh to a maximal degree with the capabilities and characteristics of the human operator.

Equipment design considerations probably constitute the major aspect of environmental control insofar as safety management is concerned, but there are other factors. Floors, stairs, ramps, elevators, and many other features can be constructed initially with safety in mind, and they can be inspected frequently. Both equipment design and work environment design are matters that often are of concern to engineering or human factors psychologists (Sanders & McCormick, 1987).

□ Inspection and Discipline

The Occupational Safety and Health Act calls for inspection of the workplace for hazards by representatives of the Labor Department. Such inspection may be initiated by the government or as a result of a complaint by an employee. If hazards are found, action can be taken to enforce a change. In its enforcement of OSHA, the government holds employers responsible for making sure that employees wear safety equipment such as hard hats,

BOX 20-2 I/O PSYCHOLOGY IN PRACTICE

Requirements from a Checklist Used by OSHA Inspectors at Construction Sites

The following are examples of requirements imposed by OSHA (Occupational Safety and Health Administration) inspectors from the U.S. Department of Labor at large construction sites:

1. The employer shall permit only those employees qualified by training or experience to operate equipment and machinery.
2. The employer shall instruct each employee in the recognition and avoidance of unsafe conditions and the regulations applicable to his work environment to control or eliminate any hazards or other exposure to illness and injury.
3. A person who has a valid certificate in first-aid training from the U.S. Bureau of Mines, the American Red Cross, or equivalent training that can be verified by documentary evidence shall be available at the worksite to render first aid.
4. The telephone numbers of the physicians, hospitals, or ambulances shall be conspicuously posted.
5. Welding torches in use shall be inspected at the beginning of each working shift for leaking shutoff valves, hose couplings, and tip connections. Defective torches shall not be used.

6. Employers shall instruct employees in the safe means of arc welding and cutting.
7. On suspension scaffolds designed for a working load of 500 pounds, no more than two men shall be permitted to work at one time.
8. The employer shall designate a competent person who shall inspect all machinery and equipment prior to each use, and during use, to make sure it is in safe operating condition. Any deficiencies shall be repaired, or defective parts replaced, before continued use.
9. The employer shall provide training or require that his employees are knowledgeable and proficient in procedures involving emergency situations and first aid.
10. All vehicles in use shall be checked out at the beginning of each shift to assure that the parts, equipment, and accessories are in safe operating condition and free of apparent damage that could cause failure while in use.

SOURCE: D. Petersen (1980). *Analyzing safety performance.* New York: Garland.

---

earplugs, and so forth. Employers, but not employees, are subject to legal citations and fines if hazards are found, even if there have been no accidents.

Box 20-2 provides examples of the requirements that U.S. Department of Labor inspectors impose at large construction sites such as where an office building is being erected. As noted previously, construction is an industry where accidents are particularly frequent. Consequently, OSHA inspections are likely to be very stringent.

Many companies conduct their own regular inspections with a view to providing an early-warning system against accidents and against OSHA citations. The inspections are carried out by supervisors, safety committee members, or safety engineers, or often by representatives of insurance carriers handling the company's workers' compensation policies. These inspections are much more effective in identifying unsafe working conditions than unsafe practices; even in the former instance, the inspector must have considerable knowledge of the particular operations in order to be effective. Furthermore, inspection does little good if there is no follow-up to make sure that sources of danger have been corrected. Unfortunately, inspection reports requested from supervisors often are subordinated to more pressing production considerations.

When unsafe practices are identified, either as a result of inspection or in connection with an accident investigation, the usual first thought is some form of discipline ranging from a reprimand upward, although in cases of serious injury the conclusion usually is that the individual has suffered enough already. Actually, however, discipline may have little value in the accident context. It may well only make things worse.

☐ Improved Safety Climate

A consideration that has to do with various aspects of safety management is the type of **safety climate** that has been created in a firm. Safety programs work best where this climate is positive (Denning, 1983; Zohar, 1980). Included in such a climate are a strong managerial commitment to safety—establishing safety-training programs, giving safety officials high status, participation of top executives in safety committees, designing jobs with safety in mind, and the like. Where employees believe that "safety makes a difference around here," the approaches we have been considering not only contribute to that perception, they work better as well. In short, a diversified, coordinated safety program that utilizes many approaches and that has considerable top-management involvement is most likely to work well. Unfortunately, and really not too surprisingly, this tends to happen most often when some safety consideration has taken on major significance for a company's survival—black lung disease among coal mining firms or asbestos poisoning among building materials manufacturers, for instance.

■ DIFFERENTIAL ACCIDENT LIABILITY

No matter how much effort is spent in training, controlling the work environment, or other aspects of safety management, there appears to be no way to eliminate on-the-job accidents or unplanned events that do or could result in personal injury. In large measure this is because people behave in ways that result in accidents. Although there is much disagreement about the concept, it is clear that some individuals do have more accidents than can be reasonably attributed to chance. It also would appear that a person might tend to have frequent accidents during one period of his or her life but not during another. As indicated by Exhibit 20-4, accidents are most frequent in the age ranges from 17 to 30 and decline steadily after that, reaching a low point in the late 60s.

Other evidence indicates that individuals who have high injury rates in one year are the ones who are most likely to have high rates the following year. The data of Exhibit 20-5 are typical. In this instance there is a steady increase in the number of accidents experienced during the second year as a function of the first-year frequencies. Those who had no accidents the first year had an average of only 0.69 the second year. Those who had nine accidents the first year averaged 5.14 the second year. The same trend appears in all the eleven separate departments represented in the combined data of Exhibit 20-5. Additional studies conducted to determine whether the hazards associated with specific jobs could account for these results produced negative results. When differences in job danger were controlled, the same pattern was still present in the data, as indicated by the dashed line in Exhibit 20-5. Consistent injury patterns of this kind have been found over periods of up to nine years (Boyle, 1980).

Findings of this type are consistent with

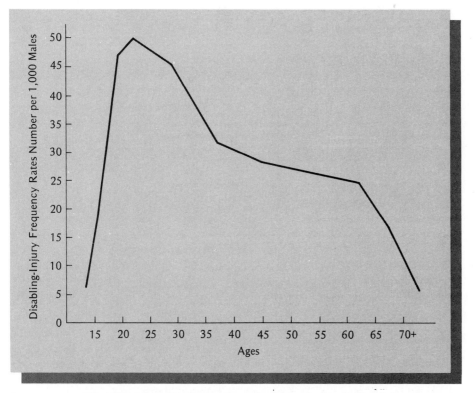

Exhibit 20-4   Disability Injury Frequency Rates for Males in the Civilian Labor Force
Rates rise rapidly in the early years, then by the late 20s begin to decline. This decline
continues throughout the life span, becoming quite sharp after age 60.
Source: J. B. Gordon, A. Akman, & M. L. Brooks (1971). *Industrial accident statistics: A reexamination*, p. 211. New York: Praeger.

the widely held opinion that injuries are not merely a direct function of the degree to which the working environment contains hazardous features. It is true that training deficiencies and the fact that younger workers are more likely to be new on the job account for part of the injury–age relationship. But these cannot explain all the findings. For one thing, the increase during the early years is far too marked. For another, the injury rates do not reach their highest level until age 21 or 22, even though skill deficiencies are most pronounced among those who are younger.

It seems, then, that, contrary to the view that differences in accident frequencies could be accounted for in terms of chance fluctuations, there are certain individuals who are consistently more susceptible to injuries than others. As noted, however, this tendency may well be more pronounced during a specific period of a person's life. Research into the personality characteristics of individuals with high injury-frequency rates tends to support this conclusion. There do appear to be some consistent differences between certain **accident repeaters** and those who do not have such a high injury potential.

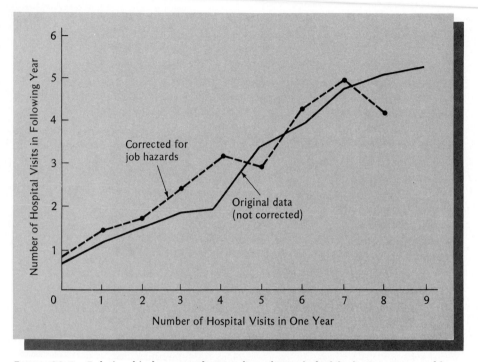

EXHIBIT 20-5   Relationship between the Number of Hospital Visits in One Year and in the Following Year among 9000 Steelworkers
Those who have few visits in one year tend to have few the next; those who have many visits in one year tend to have many the next. Correcting the data for hazard exposure does not change this pattern.
SOURCE: Ernest J. McCormick & Daniel R. Ilgen (1980). *Industrial psychology,* p. 413. Englewood Cliffs, NJ: Prentice-Hall.

☐ Characteristics of Accident Repeaters

An early study indicated that people with high injury-frequency and -severity rates are likely to act with a high degree of muscular speed, even though they lack the visual capacity to comprehend a situation with equal rapidity (Drake, 1940). Thus, action often precedes perception and thought; such people are often described as impulsive. This particular study was carried out in the metal-working department of a large factory, but similar findings have been obtained in other contexts.

Another factor in accident repetition appears to be the individual's characteristic reaction to monotony. Among long-distance truck drivers, those who tend to have difficulty concentrating and thus make more errors on a monotonous task also are those who have more accidents on the road (McBain, 1970). Again, the problem appears to be a difficulty in controlling thought processes to use them for effective action. Such people think less critically and become confused easily under stress. They do not think things through before acting.

Other research has focused more directly on personality characteristics rather than on perceptual and behavioral relationships (Davids & Mahoney, 1957; LeShan, 1952). In one such study, individuals who experienced a large number of accidents were found to be very negative in their attitudes. They disliked their superiors, their jobs, and work generally. Furthermore, they tended to be almost devoid of optimism and trust, and, in fact, had little positive feeling toward people at all.

Another investigation involved the testing of individuals with extremely high injury-frequency rates. The lack of warm emotional relationships with others was again apparent. Most had a number of acquaintances, but they were not really close to these people. In addition, negative attitudes toward those in positions of authority were once again present. These individuals exhibited a marked, and often unreasonable, aggression toward their superiors at work as well as toward other authority figures.

There were certain other findings. The high-accident group was characterized by a great deal of concern about health matters, even though actual illness tended to be rare. There was a strong desire for increased social status, coupled with very little accomplishment in this regard. Emotionally disturbing situations were often handled by misperceiving and distorting the world around them in order to make it less threatening. As a result, these people made bad mistakes in judgment rather frequently. Planning for the future was apparently minimal. They preferred to live from day to day and were, in fact, quite impulsive.

More recent research conducted at the duPont Company tends to confirm this picture of a high accident character structure (Denning, 1983). However, not everyone with a proclivity for injury fits the pattern.

Locus of control, as discussed in Chapter 6, appears to be a major factor in accidents (Montag & Comrey, 1987; Wuebker, 1986). Externality, especially when it involves accident situations specifically, is closely related

to high accident rates and more severe accidents. Externals believe that accidents are out of their control, a matter of luck and others' behavior; they themselves are not responsible. They do not exercise caution, and they suffer accordingly.

A recent review of personality-related factors and accident occurrences yields the following conclusions:

1. There is ample evidence that locus of control is related to accidents, specifically that an external orientation is associated with higher accident rates.

2. Extroversion has been strongly related to high accident rates.

3. Aggression has been strongly and repeatedly associated with accidents.

4. There is overwhelming evidence that social maladjustment is not only related to accidents, but is probably a primary factor in accident causation.

5. There appears to be a relationship between general neurosis and accidents.

6. Specific neurotic conditions such as anxiety and depression have been associated with accidents in the few studies done on these topics.

7. There is consistent and moderately strong evidence to link impulsivity with accident occurrences (Hansen, 1988).

These investigations yield a rather consistent picture, although it should be understood that many work injuries involve people who do not have frequent accidents and who do not possess the characteristics found among these accident repeaters. Accident repeaters seem to be rather socially irresponsible and immature. Because their high injury rates are not normally maintained throughout life, but only over a period of years, it seems most appropriate to view them as suffering from a transient personality maladjustment that is most likely to develop before age 30.

The major motivation behind the repeated

accidents themselves would appear to be a desire to impress others by resorting to sudden and impulsive decisions and behavior. This impulsiveness is usually combined with strong aggression toward people at higher levels in the organization and a consequent defiance of the rules and policies established by these people. Thus, safety regulations are deliberately flouted, not only as a way of impressing others with one's skill or bravery, but also as a means of attacking and resisting management. Under such circumstances, exposure to danger becomes unusually frequent for these employees. With an exposure level this high, it is not surprising that they are in fact injured on a number of occasions. By their own actions, they repeatedly place themselves in an extremely hazardous work environment, even though their jobs might not, under normal circumstances, be considered very dangerous.

In some instances this pattern may be supplemented as a result of certain additional personality processes. Anger toward one's superiors can on occasion generate considerable guilt and a wish, whether conscious or unconscious, to escape this guilt by being punished. To the extent that punishment is viewed as a means of atoning for one's sins, it may well be desired. For people such as this, an accident may be equated with punishment, and a real desire to suffer injury may develop at periodic intervals when guilt becomes too pronounced. Here the accident is not merely a chance event in a personally created hazardous environment, but a specific outcome that is unconsciously desired and directly caused. The need for self-preservation gives way before the need to expiate guilt, just as it often does in suicide cases.

☐ Dealing with High Accident Liability

The question remains: What can be done to reduce the frequency of personally created accidents of this kind? To some extent, selec-

tion procedures may be used to screen on this basis, although this has not been widely done (Jones & Wuebker, 1988). Such an approach seems particularly desirable in high-accident-rate injuries. It seems less appropriate in safer industries, where it may not be economically feasible to invest heavily in selection—to screen out a limited number of individuals who in all likelihood would not have an extremely high rate of injury in any event because of the lower danger level.

Given the fact, then, that because of a lack of, or the imperfections of, screening, accident-susceptible people are likely to be employed by any company at least in limited numbers, what can be done to deal with the problem? As the age–accident-frequency relationship suggests, the problem tends to correct itself eventually, but not until a number of injuries have occurred, large sums have been disbursed in disability payments, and, in many instances, sizable performance and equipment losses have accrued.

Thus, some kind of direct action does seem to be called for. One approach is to reduce the danger in the work environment as much as possible. This will have only limited impact on those who really want to injure themselves in order to reduce guilt, but it will yield results among the high-exposure group because there will be less chance for an accident to occur. In part, danger reduction can be achieved through equipment design and in part through transferring the individual to low-hazard work. Equipment design is of value, however, only to the extent that it takes control of the safety factor out of the hands of the employee. Protective clothing and warning devices are of little help. Automatic shut-offs and fixed barriers, on the other hand, can be much more effective.

The second point relates to aggression toward people in positions of authority, which is known to characterize the accident-susceptible. It is when they are forced into continuing close relationships with their superiors that these individuals are most likely to be injured. In view of this, managers should, insofar as possible, keep at a distance from those who have high accident rates. Everything possible should be done to minimize conflict and resentment. To the extent that employees can work on their own with only limited restriction, control, and discipline, the chances of injury will be reduced. Appropriate supervisory techniques can be taught as part of management development programs. If safety rules can be developed on a participative basis, rather than imposed from "on high," this too will help.

■ INDUSTRIAL CLINICAL PSYCHOLOGY: DIAGNOSIS

The various approaches taken to deal with high accident liability are preventive in nature. There are other similar approaches in industrial clinical psychology, such as employee health promotion programs. Exercise programs, smoking cessation efforts, health fairs, and fitness assessments fall into this category (Terborg, 1986). Yet industrial clinical psychology is primarily a matter of restoring effective performance to those who lack it— what has been termed performance control.

□ The Clinical Model and Performance Control

The overall process of **performance control** is outlined in Exhibit 20-6. This model is an adaptation of the general control model also used for purposes of budget, quality, production, and inventory control (Merchant, 1985). It is comparable to the clinical model used in clinical psychology and medicine. However, the latter applications are concerned with negative deviations from some acceptable standards of physical or emotional health. In industrial clinical psychology the concern is with negative deviations from acceptable standards of work performance. These deviations may be associated with problems of physical or emotional health, but performance problems arise out of a number of other causes, too.

The starting point in Exhibit 20-6 is establishing role prescriptions for the work, ideally by some type of job analysis; the process is the same as in performance appraisal generally.

Establishing Standards. Next, minimum acceptable standards are established using the various performance measures considered in Chapters 14 and 15. These minimum levels may be established in either of two ways. The most common practice is for immediate superiors to set standards in their own minds on a judgmental basis. Under such circumstances the minimum acceptable level of performance may vary somewhat from manager to manager and even at different times with the same manager. A second approach, which avoids this difficulty, involves a more objective standard-setting process carried out by some group, such as personnel research or industrial engineering, on a companywide basis. Unfortunately, however, suitable objective measures of the latter kind are not always available.

Performance standards, whether established judgmentally or in a more objective manner, almost always relate to the quantity and quality of output. Other important considerations are the extent of absenteeism, impact on the work of others, contribution to internal conflict, and dishonest behavior.

The Diagnostic Phase. Once performance standards exist, it is possible to compare an individual's performance against them. Should a person's behavior prove lacking in one or more respects, a need for diagnosis arises. Corrective procedures cannot be effective unless information is available regarding the causal factors that have operated to produce the performance failure. The situation is essentially comparable to the one that exists in medicine. Physicians must make a suitable

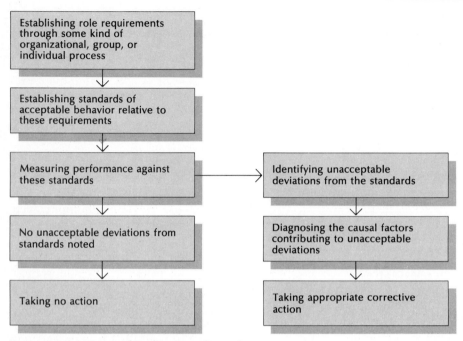

EXHIBIT 20-6   Nature of Performance Control
How measuring performance against standards leads to either no action in the absence of unacceptable deviations or diagnosis and corrective action when unacceptable deviations are present.

diagnosis, which identifies the cause of the failure to meet acceptable health standards, before they can select from among the numerous available treatments. They need to know what specific disease entity they are dealing with. Otherwise, treatment will be on a trial-and-error basis, and the chances for cure will be small.

Performance analysis is a name given to the process of identifying contributory causes, of diagnosing the factors that have combined to produce a given instance of performance failure. Basically, what is involved is that a series of hypotheses is formulated regarding the possible strategic factors. Each hypothesis is then checked against what is known about the individual and then either accepted or rejected. The result is a list of contributory causes that can serve to guide the

selection of an appropriate treatment or corrective procedure. Considerable research has demonstrated the validity of this type of clinical diagnostic model for understanding responses to subordinate ineffective performance (Mitchell, Green, & Wood, 1981; Mitchell & Wood, 1980; Pence, Pendleton, Dobbins, & Sgro, 1982).

Two additional points need to be made regarding the use of the clinical model. Chapter 10 treated attribution theory and its relation to leader perceptions of poor performance in some detail. As portrayed in Exhibit 10-5, there is substantial potential for bias inherent in the decision-making process at the point of diagnosis, and again at the point where treatments and corrective actions are tied to diagnoses (causal attributions). Attribution theory is a powerful tool for iden-

EXHIBIT 20-7   Reasons Given by Managers at Different Levels for the Retention of Ineffective Subordinates

Reasons from Which Managers Were Asked to Choose	Percent Giving Reason		
	Lower-Level Managers	Middle Managers	Upper-Level Managers
Maintaining adequate representation of women and minorities	87	39	6
Seniority or past work contributions of the individual	7	35	56
Nepotism or friendship for the individual	3	19	19
Perception of personal failure if the individual is dismissed	3	7	19

SOURCE: Adapted from Philipp A. Stoeberl & Marc J. Schniederjans (1981). The ineffective subordinate: A management survey. *Personnel Administrator, 26* (2), 72.

tifying where performance control may go wrong. To the extent that biases can be anticipated in advance, it is more likely that they can be eliminated.

Second, the diagnostic process is facilitated in several respects, and biases may well be reduced, by resorting to psychological appraisal. Appraisals of this kind typically utilize interview data, personal history forms, and ability and personality tests (Ryan & Sackett, 1987). The case at the beginning of Chapter 6 provides an example of this type of assessment involving an apparently alcoholic airline pilot. Box 14-1 provides another example of psychological appraisal, although in this instance not involving poor performance. Industrial clinical psychologists carry out these kinds of evaluations for many purposes, but one of the major ones is to identify factors contributing to ineffective performance. The process is analogous to what clinical psychologists do in diagnosing the causes of emotional and some physical disorders.

Firing as a Solution.   As indicated in Chapter 16, selection and screening are unlikely to prevent organizations from experiencing performance problems, although they may reduce them. Another possibility does

remain, however. Could not all those who become ineffective be immediately fired, thus eliminating any need for time-consuming and costly procedures such as performance analyses and corrective actions? The answer is that although firing is always a possibility, it has become hedged with so many constraints, both internal and external to the organization, that it is often not really feasible. In addition, it can well be as costly as taking corrective action. Thus it must be considered a last resort in most cases. Furthermore, the legal doctrine of termination-at-will is sufficiently threatened by changing social values that firing can be expected to become even more difficult in the future.

Pressures against firing emanate from the costs of unemployment compensation, legal actions, severance payments, and hiring replacements. Unions and employees may create obstacles. Exhibit 20-7 lists additional reasons why firing may be proscribed, in spite of poor performance.

Taken as a whole, a rather imposing array of factors exerts strong pressure for performance control rather than discharge. Certainly firing is not an impossibility, but it is often a last resort. As an all-purpose solution to ineffective performance, it is clearly inappropriate. As a solution when corrective action is known to be either impossible or inexpedient, it seems preferable to letting an employee stay on indefinitely while remaining entirely unsatisfactory.

☐ Individual Causes of Failure

Intensive study of cases where performance failures have occurred has resulted in the development of several schemata that cover many of the factors that may prove strategic (Miner, 1985; Miner & Brewer, 1976). The elements of such a schema are treated as hypotheses that should be considered either implicitly or explicitly in the process of diagnosis.

The number of confirmed hypotheses or strategic factors that will emerge from this process varies considerably from case to case. Job failure is rarely a result of a single cause. Usually, the number of contributory factors runs to something like four, but in an occasional instance it can be as high as seven or eight. People fail because with their own particular pattern of abilities and personality characteristics, they become enmeshed in a specific constellation of circumstances. The need is to spell out exactly which among these individual and environmental factors have in fact played a causal role.

We will consider the various potential causes in the order of individual, group, and organizational/contextual. A more extended treatment of many of these factors is given in Part Two of this book, although there the specific focus on contributions to performance failure is less pronounced. Where appropriate, the corresponding chapters from Part Two are noted.

Intelligence and Job Knowledge (Chapter 2)

Insufficient verbal ability. The higher up in the job hierarchy a position is located, the greater are its demands in terms of verbal ability or general intelligence. Given this circumstance, it is not surprising that on occa-

sion people attain a level where the role requirements are intellectually beyond them. At such times, failure is likely to be reflected in a high incidence of errors and incorrect decisions.

Insufficient special ability. Various jobs, regardless of their level in the hierarchy, require widely differing types of intellectual abilities. Numerical, spatial, mechanical, clerical, and other abilities are relevant for some types of work and not for others. To the extent that individuals lack whatever such abilities may be required, they are likely to fail through an inability to think effectively and learn rapidly.

Insufficient job knowledge. Insufficient job knowledge cannot be attributed to lack of ability. Individuals may have the intellectual capacity to learn the job, but either because of inadequate training or for some other reason, they have not done so. In some instances, the difficulty relates to a lack of desire to take advantage of learning opportunities or emotional blocks to learning.

Defect of judgment or memory. In most cases, defects of judgment or memory reflect the interference of emotional factors with intellectual processes. The individual may do well on standard intelligence tests, but when it comes to applying intelligence on the job, the results are not as good. Defects of this kind are particularly frequent among those suffering from some type of emotional disorder, but they can also result from a disturbance in brain functioning, such as might occur as a result of a head injury.

Individual Motivation (Chapters 3 and 4)

Strong motives frustrated at work. Probably the most common type of motivationally caused performance failure is the case where an individual wants something very much from a job and is unable to attain it. Among the things desired that seem to be important in this sense are success, the avoidance of failure, domination of others, popularity, social interaction, attention, and emotional support. When such motives are frustrated, the individual may leave the job, may stay on but make little effort, may become sullen and angry, or may attempt to achieve what is wanted through behavior that is antithetical to effective job performance.

Unintegrated means to satisfy motives. Workers who resort to behavior that is not job-integrated may not actually experience any frustration of a strong motive at work. Many people develop an approach to a job that permits motive satisfaction but at the expense of fulfilling role requirements. A secretary who desires social interaction may make friends rapidly and spend most of the time talking to others, to the detriment of the performance of everyone involved. Similarly, theft and other forms of dishonesty may represent a rapid route to the goal of success.

Excessively low personal work standards. Another possibility involves individuals who set very low work standards for themselves, standards well below those considered minimally acceptable. Individuals who have such low standards tend to be poor workers. They achieve a sense of personal success and accomplishment with a degree of effort far below that actually required.

Generalized low work motivation. These are individuals whose motivational systems are so structured that their important desires tend to be satisfied outside the work situation, or at least through behavior that is not intended within the role prescriptions for any job. In such cases there is practically no mesh between the individual and the world of work, and as a consequence the quantity, and probably quality also, of output will be low, quite irrespective of the position held.

Emotions and Emotional Illness (Chapter 6)

Frequent disruptive emotion. Emotions can, if intense enough and frequent enough, have a detrimental impact on many aspects of job behavior (Warr, 1987). This is particularly true of negative emotional states, such as anxiety and fear, depression, shame and guilt. But failure can also occur as a result of persistent anger, jealousy, and excitement. The individual need not be emotionally ill for a severe impact on the level of work performance to manifest itself. The result may be a number of errors; an inability to concentrate so that output is slowed; a tendency to be constantly immersed in controversy; or, and this is perhaps most frequent, a continuing avoidance of many required job behaviors. Stress is often at the heart of the problem.

Psychosis. **Psychoses** manifest themselves in a variety of symptoms that take on an inflexible character and serve to disrupt many of the ongoing processes of life. In a psychosis, the preoccupation with symptoms, emotions, and the warding off of unpleasant feelings becomes so intense that a break with reality occurs, at least at certain times and under certain circumstances. Symptoms vary from incessant emotional states to disorders of physical functioning, to pathological behavior and speech, and even to extreme distortions of perception and belief. Although the various psychotic conditions represent relatively rare phenomena insofar as the work environment is concerned, their impact on performance is generally marked. Often the individual cannot continue work at all while in the psychotic state.

Personality disorders. The **personality disorders,** although milder in their impact, may on occasion have just as detrimental an effect on work performance as psychoses. This appears to depend to a considerable extent on the job level. In lower-level positions of a repetitive nature, symptoms of emotional disorder are much more common, and in these particular jobs, the detrimental effects appear to be less. At higher levels, on the other hand, personality disorders are typically quite disruptive. Examples of managerial styles and symptoms, and how they may disrupt performance, are given in Exhibit 6-8.

Alcohol and drug problems. Alcoholism has been recognized as a major problem by many employers for a number of years. Because of drinking on the job, hangovers, and anxiety, alcoholics often turn out poor work. However, the major impact is in terms of absenteeism, where rates two to three times those of other employees are typical. In part, but only in part, these high absence rates are a function of accidents and physical disorders resulting from the alcoholic state. In some cases performance tends to deteriorate gradually to the point where employment is no longer possible.

Heavy use of any of the drugs currently in vogue, such as marijuana, amphetamines, the hallucinogens, and opiates, appears to have negative consequences insofar as employment is concerned. People under the influence of the drugs while at work can be expected to suffer performance decrements and to have more accidents. Drug users also have higher absenteeism rates (Heisler, Jones, & Benham, 1988). In addition, certain physical disorders have been found to result from drug use, and where the drugs are expensive and addictive, as with heroin, there is a considerable risk of theft (see Chapter 18). Quantity of drug use is a better predictor of drug problems than frequency. What really hurts is using drugs too much (Stein, Newcomb, & Bentler, 1988).

Physical Characteristics and Disorders

Physical illness or handicap. The major avenue through which physical disorders contribute to ineffective performance is absence from the job, although quantity and quality of output may also be affected. Handicapped employees have generally proved as competent as other workers if their handicaps do not bar working at all, but in some instances certain disabilities may contribute to failure in specific jobs. There are things that the deaf, the blind, those with heart conditions, epileptics, and other handicapped people just cannot do effectively.

Physical disorders of emotional origin. A number of physical symptoms, such as headaches, fainting, ulcers, high blood pressure, hay fever, backache, and skin disorders, may be caused by emotional factors. When this is the case, the symptoms and the work disruption are identical to those that would exist if no emotional element were present; only the cause is different.

Inappropriate physical characteristics. Inappropriate physical characteristics are the features of bodily proportion and esthetics that, although not widely significant, may become strategic in certain jobs. A large person may have difficulty working in a cramped space, as may a small person in a truck cab with the seat far removed from the controls, or an unattractive person in a modeling position. Many physical characteristics are less important today, what with the advent of **human engineering** and the consequent emphasis on designing equipment to fit the human operator, but these factors can become crucial at times.

Insufficient muscular or sensory ability or skill. A variety of muscular dexterities and abilities, as well as purely intellectual abilities, may influence job performance. Where there is a deficiency in some ability of this kind that is required by the job, ineffectiveness can result. Strength does appear to have decreasing relevance now, but it still can be a factor in failure on some jobs. Deficiencies of vision and hearing also remain a significant source of problems in many cases. Competence in driving a truck, for instance, is strongly influenced by such sensory abilities.

☐ Group Causes of Failure

Groups at Work (Chapters 7, 8, 9, and 10)

Negative consequences associated with group cohesion. Restriction of output within a cohesive group can yield a low level of production that is, nevertheless, socially sanctioned. Although it is common to observe a generally centralizing tendency among group members when restriction occurs, it is also true that some individuals may be forced below the minimum acceptable level of output by the restricted standard. Also, groups with a marked sense of cohesiveness may reject members whom they believe to be deviant. Although such ostracism may have no effect on some people, it is extremely threatening to others. The result can be intense anxiety or anger that constantly disrupts work.

Ineffective management. Varying managerial styles can influence performance in different ways. Managers who are extremely inconsiderate of subordinates and those who fail to establish and enforce standards may well have low-producing groups. Laissez-faire managing, where very little if any supervising occurs, is particularly detrimental. It is also apparent that these styles can contribute to the ineffective performance of specific subordinates. It is not at all uncommon for supervisory action to conflict with subordinate personality patterns—and as a result actually produce failure, even where just the opposite result is desired.

Inappropriate managerial standards and criteria. The criteria on which subordinates are judged are usually set by their superiors, as are the performance standards used to determine effectiveness. In certain cases these may be established without any reference to organizational goals. Thus failure may be embedded in the evaluative process rather than in the individual. Because of supervisory biases, standards may be set at an unrealistically high level. Or the criteria employed may be totally irrelevant to actual role prescriptions and the company's goals. In such instances the failure may be by definition only.

Family Ties

Family crises. There are a number of significant events occurring in the home environment that can have an impact on the personality of certain individuals that is sufficient to

disturb work performance. Among these are desertion, divorce, threatened divorce, illness of a family member, death, or criminal prosecution. Normally, these effects are transitory, but on occasion the performance decrement is maintained for a considerable period.

Separation from the family. The fact of extended separation from either the parental family or a spouse and children can produce a very intense homesickness in some individuals. Business trips, temporary assignments out of town, management development programs at universities, and the like induce considerable anxiety in some people, especially those who have rarely been away from home before. The result can be a severe disruption of performance during the period of absence, with frequent errors, poor decisions, and difficult interpersonal relationships.

Predominance of family considerations over work demands. These factors do not represent a threat to the family's unity or survival, yet they can have a considerable impact on performance. A demanding spouse can require so much of the marital partner's time that little time is left for work. Or a spouse may become disturbed at leaving the home town or going to a foreign country and may impose a severe burden. Certain family situations are little short of chaotic, and some carryover into the work situation is inevitable. Competition between father and son or wife and husband may well produce emotional reactions that permeate the job.

☐ Organizational/Contextual Causes of Failure

The Organization (Chapter 11)

Insufficient organizational action. Job failure may occur or be perpetuated because the company does not take the kind of corrective action required. Treatment, training, and the like simply may not be provided, either intentionally or through some oversight. In either case, the lack of action on the part of the company can become strategic. The decision not to invest in corrective action may be based on various considerations such as cost, chances of success, and the availability of potentially effective replacements.

Placement error. Placement error probably appears in more cases than any other. It is particularly prevalent where random assignment policies, seniority, or union pressures govern the placement process and where there is accordingly little effort to put individuals with known characteristics in appropriate jobs. If intellectual, emotional, motivational, or physical factors are strategic, there is nearly always a placement error as well.

Inappropriate organizational style. On occasion, a company will operate under such lax and permissive personnel policies and procedures that employees are actually encouraged not to work. When circumstances of this kind exist, individuals with certain types of motivational patterns may become ineffective as a result. A company may, for instance, encourage insubordination through a lack of discipline. Excessive training, far beyond that required for complete learning, can foster a feeling that actual on-the-job production is unimportant. Too liberal sick-leave policies can result in excessive absenteeism.

Excessive span of control. In some cases, managers may fail to deal effectively with a particular subordinate and thus contribute to a performance failure, not because of any inadequacy in themselves as managers, but because there simply is not sufficient time. The number of individuals supervised, the **span of control,** may be so great that the manager cannot deal with subordinates as individuals, carrying out performance analyses and the like. The organizational structure has been established in such a way as to preclude effective action by a superior aimed at preventing performance failure.

Inappropriate organizational standards and criteria. Inappropriate organizational standards

and criteria are the counterparts of the inappropriate managerial standards and criteria category discussed under the work group heading. In this instance, however, the focus is on standards set as a result of organizational policy or high-level decisions rather than on those established by individual superiors.

The Societal Context (Chapter 5)

Application of legal sanctions. These are cases in which individuals are unable to perform their job duties because they have committed a crime and have been sent to jail.

Enforcement of societal values. Although society obtains compliance with its values in large part through the agency of the legal process and police action, it is also true that pressure may be exerted outside the law. Thus, sales personnel may fail because no one will buy from them after they commit some act that potential customers consider unethical or immoral.

Conflict between job demands and values. The most frequent type of strategic factor involving societal values is the situation in which an individual holds strong convictions that are in conflict with the role requirements for a job. Intense commitments to equity and fair play, to individual freedom, and to morality can contribute to job failure. It is not uncommon for industrial scientists, for instance, with a strong belief in freedom of inquiry to become incensed at the restrictions of a bureaucratic organization.

The Work Context

Negative consequences of economic forces. Competing firms or economic conditions operate to produce a situation in which employees cannot achieve at a level consistent with their standards. As a result, they become emotionally distressed, and eventually performance does not even come up to what could realistically be expected under the existing circumstances. Problems of this kind are particularly common among salespeople.

EXHIBIT 20-8   **Relationship of Seniority and Performance Level on an Old Job to Performance Level on a New Job**

	Correlations		
Performance Level in the New Job	Total Seniority with the Company	Seniority in the Old Job	Performance Level in the Old Job
Over the first quarter after assuming the job	0.07	−0.09	0.34
Over the second quarter after assuming the job	0.08	−0.13	0.29

SOURCE: Adapted from Michael E. Gordon & William J. Fitzgibbons (1982). Empirical test of the validity of seniority as a factor in staffing decisions. *Journal of Applied Psychology, 67,* 315.

Negative consequences of geographic location. A similar type of reaction may occur as a result of being forced to work in an inappropriate geographic location. Being sent to a foreign country is very disturbing to some individuals because of the strangeness of the environment and people around them. Some people experience debilitating physical symptoms in certain climates, and a sailor who is prone to seasickness may well never achieve a satisfactory performance level when at sea.

Detrimental conditions in the work setting. These are cases involving physical characteristics of the actual working environment—the noise level, the amount and type of illumination, the temperature, and various aspects of the design of the workplace or the equipment in it. To the extent that this working environment contains features that do not mesh with the physical capacities and characteristics of individuals, or on occasion with their intellectual, emotional, or motivational make-up, it can contribute to employee performance failure.

Excessive danger. One aspect of the physical work context that appears to be sufficiently important to warrant separate attention is the danger level. A work environment with a high built-in accident potential can contribute to excessive absenteeism. It can elicit anxiety, too, and thus interfere with output. It is also true that an individual may read much more

danger into a situation than actually exists. Fears associated with heights, airplanes, closed places, and the like are common. Subjective danger situations of this kind stimulate sufficient anxiety in some instances to make work effort impossible. In other cases, the emotion serves to distract, producing errors and reduced output.

■ INDUSTRIAL CLINICAL PSYCHOLOGY: TREATMENT AND CORRECTIVE ACTION

Depending on the diagnosed causes of performance failure, a variety of treatments or corrective actions may be brought to bear. Many of these have been discussed previously in other contexts. For example, job redesign was considered in Chapter 4, and training and development approaches at a variety of points, but Chapter 19 especially. Rewards and punishments, the latter including formal discipline, were discussed at some length in Chapter 4.

It is relatively common to handle performance problems by shifting the individual to a more appropriate job. Transfers, demotions, even promotions may be utilized. On occasion, exceptions to existing assignment policies may be required. Exhibit 20-8 provides an example. In this company, seniority,

Exhibit 20-9 Extent of Use of Various Types of Counseling by Major U.S. Corporations

	Type of Counseling		
	Personal Problems	Retirement	Alcoholism and Drugs
Firms with various counseling programs currently in effect	71%	63%	63%
Sources of counseling used by firms			
Professional staff in-house	56%	69%	49%
Supervisors	26%	8%	11%
External counseling services	27%	13%	30%

Source: Adapted from Helen LeVan, Nicholas Mathys, & David Drehmer (1983). A look at the counseling practices of major U.S. corporations. *Personnel Administrator, 28* (6), 80.

whether calculated for company service as a whole or in the previous job only, has no relationship to performance in a new job, which represents either a promotion or a desired lateral transfer. Consequently, any job changes based on a strict policy of promotion according to seniority are going to produce a number of failures in the new job. In contrast, merit—performance level on the previous job—is significantly associated with a successful change, and accordingly, performance failures on the new job will be fewer if a merit-based policy is followed. In this case, policy change to emphasize merit is the ideal solution if the union can be convinced; if not, numerous after-the-fact policy exceptions and transfers back may be needed.

All of these approaches may be utilized with major involvement on the part of psychologists, but this is not necessarily the case. However, counseling procedures and employee assistance programs fall more directly within the industrial clinical psychology domain. Accordingly, they are given special attention here.

☐ Counseling

The history of counseling in industry began with a department established in the Ford Motor Company in 1914 to advise employees

on personal affairs and to assist them with health, legal, and family problems. The approach was strongly directive and permeated with Henry Ford's own personal philosophies. The result was considerable employee resistance and an eventual abandoning of the program. Similar large-scale efforts have been initiated in a number of firms, most notably the Western Electric Company, where counseling was introduced as an aspect of the Hawthorne studies (see Chapter 1). In almost every instance, these comprehensive programs have failed to survive over an extended period.

In recent years, industrial counseling has tended to focus more on specific types of employee problems and in the process has achieved renewed emphasis. Exhibit 20-9 provides figures on existing practice. Personal problems are most likely to be handled in-house, by specialists; retirement counseling is done primarily by the personnel staff; and alcoholism and drug problems are treated both internally and externally but usually by specialists. In spite of the renewed vigor of counseling programs, however, very little is known about their actual operational effectiveness in dealing with performance problems (Cairo, 1983). The general tendency is to extend research results obtained in the clinical context and in vocational work to the employment setting. To some degree this appears justified. In any event, increasing interest in business applications of counseling approaches is a reality, and it may very well yield an expansion of research in the area in years to come (Foley & Redfering, 1987; Oberer & Lee, 1986).

In recent years, industrial counseling has tended to focus more on specific types of employee problems, has involved the industrial clinical psychologist to a much greater extent, and has been more widely viewed as a corrective procedure for ineffective performance than as a means of increasing employee satisfaction or dealing with nonjob problems. Under these conditions, limited-scale programs have prospered and appear to have made sizable contributions. It is now recognized that the needs of an individual and the goals of an organization may well be in conflict, and for this reason certain kinds of counseling activities should usually be performed outside the employment context.

Counseling Technique. Although a psychologist must be somewhat directive in dealing with some types of problems, in that questions must be answered and information conveyed, the usual approach in industry where emotional or motivational factors are strategic has been to stress **nondirective counseling.** Under the nondirective approach, employees are encouraged to express their feelings to gain an understanding of themselves, and eventually to solve their own problems. The counselor listens and occasionally reformulates what the employee has said to permit greater understanding of the true emotional meaning of certain words. The counselor may also repeat certain phrases or sentences to stimulate the employee to continue and to lead him or her to concentrate on certain topics.

In the business context, counseling of this kind tends to focus on matters of performance and on social relationships at work, although family and other considerations may be treated also. Recently, an emphasis on career planning and guidance designed to correct inappropriate occupational choices has been added. Often, the counselor serves as an upward communication channel between the employee and the organization, correcting distorted communications and misunderstandings. The emphasis is on working out relatively mild problems that may be blocking performance effectiveness. More severe emotional disorders are normally referred to a psychotherapist working outside the company. If the problem appears to require more than perhaps ten or fifteen one-hour sessions, the employee is usually advised to seek help on a private basis. Some firms, in fact, reject all internal adjustment counseling of this type, on the grounds that such matters are the sole responsibility of the individual.

Executive Counseling. At higher management levels, counseling is often carried out by an outside psychological consultant rather than by a professional on the regular company staff (Speller, 1989). Although in some instances this counseling represents an attempt to cope with a performance failure, it is also true that many top-level managers are emotionally alone and thus in real need of someone with whom they can discuss problems. Under these circumstances, an industrial clinical psychologist may continue to work with an executive at intervals over an extended period of time. The approach, in contrast to that of a regular management consultant, tends to be nondirective, with the executives increasingly learning to understand themselves and the motives behind their actions.

Retirement Counseling. Most retirement counseling is intended to prepare employees for retirement, although on occasion it may be directed toward the rehabilitation of older

BOX 20-3 I/O PSYCHOLOGY IN PRACTICE

The Employee Assistance Policy of Georgia State University

The following policy statement was distributed to all Georgia State University employees.

It is the policy of the University to offer assistance to employees who have any personal problem that impairs their work attendance or performance.

Personal problems such as stress, depression, family concerns, drug dependency, or the disease of alcoholism often prevent employees from seeking or obtaining assistance. Timely intervention and assistance often can help to prevent further deterioration of performance and return an employee to productive employment. It is the goal of this policy to provide Georgia State University employees assistance with personal problems through initial assessment and, where necessary, referral to appropriate professional resources. Initial assessment and referral are also available to an employee's immediate family, since a troubled family member may also affect an employee's performance and well-being.

Responsibilities of Supervisory Personnel

It is the responsibility of all supervisory personnel to:

(1) Intervene where there is a documented pattern of deteriorating job performance.

(2) Ensure that an employee's job security or promotional opportunities will not be jeopardized by a request and/or referral for assistance.

(3) Refrain from making any diagnosis or judgment about the employee's problem. Referral for assistance shall be made only at the employee's request and/or on the basis of unsatisfactory job performance.

(4) Maintain rigorous confidentiality. No written records regarding a request or referral for assistance shall ever be a part of an employee's personnel file.

Responsibilities of Employee

The employee is expected to cooperate with a supervisory referral for assistance.

Implementation of this policy shall not require any special regulations, privileges, or exemptions from the standard administrative practices or disciplinary procedures applicable to job performance requirements.

---

workers whose performance has fallen off with the approach of retirement. The counseling tends to be rather directive, emphasizing information on pension plans and other benefits. Counseling of this kind may be initiated as much as five years before the anticipated date of separation, and it appears that such early initiation is a desirable procedure.

Alcoholism and Drug Problems. For a number of years, companies have been involved in programs for the treatment of alcoholic employees, involving various combinations of counseling by human resource staff and supervisors, Alcoholics Anonymous, and outside treatment facilities. In some cases the treatment facilities are under contract with the company; some are sponsored jointly by a group of companies; and some involve union participation. Supervisors are trained to deal with alcoholism problems. The major focus is on retaining the employees in the work context while at the same time making it clear that further alcohol-induced problems will lead to separation—thus fostering treatment. The results of programs of this kind have been widely touted. However, as with the area of counseling generally, there is only limited solid evidence at present that clearly substantiates the many glowing testimonials (Weiss, 1987). The evidence appears to indicate that these programs can be effective, but

BOX 20-4 I/O PSYCHOLOGY IN PRACTICE

The Employee Assistance Program Developed by Control Data Corporation

Control Data Corporation began its program in 1973 as an occupational alcoholism program. Before long it became apparent that the people seeking help for alcohol-related problems also were seeking help for a wide variety of other problems. Accordingly the program was expanded in 1974 to serve all troubled employees, not just one subset. With this broad-brush employee assistance program, the company began offering professional help to employees and their families twenty-four hours a day, seven days a week, 365 days a year. Before long the company received requests from other companies for information and assistance in setting up similar broad-brush programs. To fill these requests, Control Data began marketing its program in the Minneapolis-St. Paul area in 1977, and expanded to a national marketing effort in 1980.

At the present time over eighty companies are served, with a combined employee population of almost 200,000. When family members are included, close to a million people in the United States and Canada are served. What began with thirty new cases a month now averages 2000 cases a month. The program has a comprehensive array of professionals available, including attorneys, financial counselors, chemical-dependency specialists, industrial-relations specialists, and psychologists. When needed, referrals are made to many community resources.

Surveys of users of the program indicate a consistently favorable reaction.

SOURCE: R. Edward Bergmark (1986). Employee assistance programs: Trends and principles. *Journal of Business and Psychology, 1,* 61–62.

---

that to be effective they need substantial investments of company resources. Many programs fail this test, and accordingly do not seem to live up to their potential.

Efforts to deal with drug problems along these same lines are newer, and even less is known about their effectiveness. Yet employers are experiencing increasing difficulties related to drug use (Schreier, 1983). Performance effects tend to become much more prominent over extended periods of drug use and are now becoming a major area of company concern. Generally, the approach used has been to attempt to apply principles learned from dealing with alcoholics to drug abusers as well. In addition, companies are increasingly resorting to drug testing in the workplace, thus raising a number of legal issues (Heshizer & Muczyk, 1988). Chapter 18 considers some of these issues.

☐ Employee Assistance Programs

In recent years an increasing number of firms, especially the larger ones, have developed broad-brush **employee assistance programs (EAPs)** to deal with a multitude of problems. What has happened in many instances is a gradual evolution from alcoholism programs to alcoholism and drug programs to the more comprehensive employee assistance approach.

Nature of the Programs. Box 20-3 presents one view of a program via the organization's policy statement on employee assistance. Georgia State University's program has been active for a number of years. Box 20-4 describes the evolution of the Control Data Corporation program, which developed to a point where it was marketed to other compa-

Exhibit 20-10   Services Rendered through Employee Assistance Programs and Their Rated Effectiveness

Type of Service	Percent of Firms with EAPs Offering Service	Percent of Firms Providing Service Where That Service Is First or Second in Frequency of Use	Percent of Respondent Human Resource Managers Feeling Certain the Service is Effective
Alcohol program	100	70	85
Drug program	99	55	68
Emotional counseling	94	37	67
Family and marital counseling	91	33	65
Financial counseling	87	12	58
Legal assistance	79	2	47

Source: Adapted from Robert C. Ford & Frank S. McLaughlin (1981). Employee assistance programs: A descriptive survey of ASPA members. *Personnel Administrator, 26*(9), 32–33.

nies nationwide. Exhibit 20-10 provides a more detailed view of the services usually provided and how frequently they are used. Any given organization may have a different distribution of use, but alcohol and drug problems tend to remain a basic focus.

The list of services in Exhibit 20-10 is in fact somewhat restricted. Other services are often provided, including dealing with physical health problems, work problems and relationships, needs for employee benefit clarification, problems of sexual identification, career-related difficulties, requests for company policy explanations, and many more.

In some cases the services are provided entirely in-house by a regular professional staff. In other cases an outside consulting organization (community-based or privately run) operates the whole program, typically at a location removed from company premises. Most often, some services are provided internally and some externally, depending on demand and the expertise required. Many programs rely heavily on telephone counseling. Usually, both self-referrals and supervisory referrals are accepted, but some com-

panies hold to a performance-relatedness concept that limits referrals to instances where the supervisor deems the employee ineffective. In such cases, family members are not included. In any event, there is almost invariably a strong emphasis on confidentiality.

Program Effectiveness. As noted in Exhibit 20-10, human resource managers tend to view employee assistance programs as generally successful, although there are differences among services in this regard. Since most programs are headquartered in human resource departments, this source of evaluation is appropriate. However, users also tend to respond favorably (Sonnenstuhl, 1986).

One review of the literature notes ten conditions considered necessary for a successful program (Dickman & Emener, 1982):

1. Top-management backing
2. Labor union support
3. Confidentiality
4. Easy access

5. Supervisor training regarding the program

6. Union steward training regarding the program

7. Insurance involvement to cover outside costs

8. Breadth in the number of services available

9. Professional leadership from a skilled and accepted professional

10 Follow-up and evaluation

There is some fragmentary evidence, focused primarily on reduced costs associated with absenteeism, that investments in employee assistance programs may be worthwhile from a company viewpoint. Certainly from a social responsibility viewpoint they represent a major contribution. And insurance costs tend to be reduced, although whether in sufficient amounts to offset the costs of the employee assistance program is an open question.

Yet little solid evidence exists on the effectiveness of employee assistance programs. It may well be that, in the future, companies will refocus their efforts in this area to deal only with established instances of ineffective performance. At present, however, that is not the case.

KEY TERMS

Safety psychology

Industrial clinical psychology

Safety management

Agency

Agency part

Unsafe mechanical or physical condition of the agency

Accident type

Unsafe act

Unsafe personal factor

Near accidents

Safety climate

Accident repeaters

Performance control

Performance analysis

Psychoses

Personality disorders

Human engineering

Span of control

Nondirective counseling

Employee assistance programs (EAPs)

SUMMARY

A major feature of *safety management* is the formation of various committees to foster prevention. Another feature is a provision for accident reports whereby companies can identify particular problems and problem areas, in addition to fulfilling government reporting requirements. In some instances, *near accidents* are studied as well. Prevention is sought through safety training, publicity contests, control of the work environment (in large part through *human engineering* efforts), safety inspections, discipline, and an improved *safety climate*. The latter tends to be found where there is a diversified safety program in operation and considerable top-management involvement in it.

It is apparent that certain people are more likely to be *accident repeaters* than others and that this tendency is most common in the younger age groups. Certain personality characteristics involving negative attitudes to authority and impulsiveness are prevalent in such people. Preventive efforts should take these characteristics into account.

Performance control involves correcting instances of ineffective performance by first determining the causes of the difficulty and then instituting appropriate treatments and corrective action. This type of activity has become increasingly important as

firing has become more difficult to carry out. In determining the causes of performance failure, it is essential that a wide range of factors be considered. These include individual characteristics of an intellectual, emotional, motivational, and physical nature; influences from groups such as the work unit and the family; organizational factors; aspects of the societal context; and effects deriving from the work environment, including economic forces, geography, and the nature of the work setting.

A number of approaches already considered may be used for corrective purposes. In this chapter, special attention has been given to counseling and *employee assistance programs*. Taken as a whole, corrective efforts clearly can prove quite effective. However, counseling programs and the broader-ranging employee assistance efforts have not been adequately evaluated as yet.

QUESTIONS

1. Describe an instance of job or scholastic failure that you have observed. Using the schema for performance analysis as a checklist, see if you can identify the various key factors contributing to this particular failure.

2. Should a first-line supervisor be able to fire a worker as he or she desires? Discuss with reference to legal, company, and societal ramifications.

3. There are sharp differences among companies with regard to how they feel about the matter of employee counseling. Why should these disparities exist? What do the disparities imply about company attitudes toward the individual?

4. What is the relative effectiveness of safety training, contests, and control of the work environment in reducing accidents? Document your answer.

5. Why do firms retain ineffective employees?

Would you expect this to be as frequent now as in years past?

6. How did employee assistance programs develop? What advantages might they have over the various types of counseling programs?

7. What evidence would argue for and against differential accident liability as a psychological construct?

8. Exactly what do the following terms mean?
   a. Safety climate
   b. Unsafe personal factor
   c. Chargeable accident
   d. Lost-time injury

9. What major differences are there among employee assistance programs as introduced in different companies? How might these differences relate to the success of the programs?

10. What are the components of performance control?

CASE PROBLEM

ATHONY CICCELLI
Training Coordinator

From his record, there was every reason to believe that Anthony Ciccelli would be a competent training coordinator. He had come to the plant with very strong recommendations from the people at company headquarters, and with a background of experience that seemed almost ideal. After college, where he had obtained a degree in education, he had taught school for three years. Then, shortly before marrying, he had left teaching and enrolled in the MBA program at a local university. Much of his graduate work was apparently completed at night, as he held several different jobs during this period. He had joined the company as a junior job analyst immediately after obtaining his degree.

It was generally known that the training director had from the beginning had his eye on Tony as a possible addition to his group. The job analysis work was, however, a good way of learning about the company, and it was several years before Tony was actually transferred. For the past four years, Tony had worked as a training assistant on the staff at company headquarters, developing programs, arranging for the use of outside specialists, and occasionally doing some training himself. When the promotion to the job of training coordinator at the plant was offered, there had been some uncertainty as to whether he would accept. Tony's wife had been brought up in the city and had never lived anywhere else. At several parties attended by company personnel, she had even expressed the view that there was nowhere else worth living. Her sentiments on this matter were so clear that a number of people were absolutely sure that Tony would never accept a position out of town. Nevertheless, contrary to expectations, he agreed to take the plant job, which would move him and his wife to a city over a thousand miles from their former home. The betting was that Mrs. Ciccelli must be pretty sore at her husband.

The human resource director at the plant, who was the new training coordinator's superior, found him to be a very pleasant young man who seemed to be as well informed about industrial training and education in general as anyone he had ever met. Since the industrial relations staff at the plant was not large, the two men worked closely together on a variety of problems and soon became good friends. Several new programs were initiated during the first six months, including a course in coaching for supervisors and a complete retraining project for the people who were to operate some new equipment. Tony was well liked by nearly everyone. He had a convincing way of getting people to go along with him with very few objections.

Yet the human resource director became increasingly worried about him as time went by. His work was good, he was proving just as competent as everyone had expected, but every now and then he would do something that did not make sense. Also, he seemed very unsure of himself and lethargic. Except for an occasional lackadaisical job on a report, his work was customarily done well, but one would never have expected it from Tony's attitude. He acted as though every task was an insurmountable obstacle. The final product seemed to emerge out of chaos and disorganization so overwhelming that it seemed as though nothing could possibly be accomplished. Yet somehow the job would get done, although Tony himself would have been the last to say that anything other than pure luck could account for its completion. He was obviously not a happy young man.

In part his problems were financial. The Ciccellis had decided to keep their house in the city where the company headquarters was located, and they were currently renting it. They had, however, also bought another house to live in, and very shortly they found that they could not meet the mortgage payments. Tony tried to borrow money from the company's emergency fund, but was turned down. Subsequently he tried to sell the house in the other city, but he had permitted an option to buy to be written into the two-year lease. This option provided that the present tenants would have the first chance to acquire the property after the lease terminated if the house were put up for sale. The tenants now said they would be happy to buy, but only after the lease expired.

A second attempt to borrow money from the company proved successful, and a sizable loan was made from the emergency fund. There was, however, considerable discussion regarding Tony's business judgment. There were many who felt a company-employee at his level should have had sense enough not to get in such a mess. This negative feeling was considerably enhanced when it was learned that part of the loan money eventually went into the purchase of a new car. Furthermore, there were a number of stores in town that would not permit the Ciccellis to charge purchases because of large unpaid bills. Their telephone had been disconnected for some time because of the difficulty over the payment of charges for long-distance calls. Finally, in spite of the company loan, the Ciccellis did lose the new house and had to move into a small apartment.

All this did not help Tony's reputation in the company. There were many who presumed, although lacking any real knowledge of the facts, that he must exhibit a similar deficiency in judgment on the job. For a number of months the human resource director remained convinced that this was not the case and did his best to counteract the rumors, which persistently reappeared. There was a great deal of talk about Mrs. Ciccelli. The general feeling was that she was very bitter about having been forced to leave her home, friends, and family. She had not entertained anyone since their arrival, although the Ciccellis had been invited to the homes of a number of company people. On these occasions it was clear that the husband and wife did not get along well. Tony spoke very little and appeared dejected. His wife frequently criticized him for forcing her to leave everything that was dear to her, and this criticism apparently had an impact: Tony did consider himself to blame for his wife's unhappiness. Anything she wanted him to do, he did—as if to atone for bringing her there. Mrs. Ciccelli seemed to take an almost sadistic pleasure in forcing her husband to run errands for her, getting him to buy her presents, and otherwise reminding him of the debt he owed her. Some people said she drank very heavily at home. The human resource director was never sure about the truth of this.

By the time a year had passed, some evidence that Tony's difficulties were affecting his work did develop. On several occasions, often enough to make it a problem, other people at the plant had called his office during the afternoon, only to learn that he had left for the day. A check with his secretary revealed that these absences always followed a call from his wife. In addition, he consistently refused to take any trips out of town on business. There always seemed to be something at the plant that required his attention. On the one occasion when he did leave town, to attend a one-week development program required of all training coordinators, he had had to return home after two days because of his wife's severe illness.

Although the human resource director hated to do it, he finally forced himself to call his friend in and bring up these problems. He pointed out that in general the training function was being handled well, but that there was a question as to how much the company could permit personal problems to take precedence over job requirements. Certainly things had not yet come to the point where drastic action was required, but the way things were going, that day might not be too far off. Tony, as expected, did not want to talk about his problems. He mentioned that he had thought of getting a divorce but could not bring himself to do that to his wife. After all, he had forced her to leave her home and parents in order to advance his own selfish career objectives. It would be terribly unfair to leave her now. He did not know what to do. Things seemed rather hopeless. This thing had somehow gotten bigger than he was.

Several weeks later he called the human resource director and said he wanted to talk. It turned out that he wanted to transfer back to company headquarters. He would take anything that was available, even if it meant a demotion. Perhaps there was something in job analysis. He realized this would hurt his career, but he had to do it. The human resource director did not commit himself at this point, saying he would have to think it over. There were problems related to company interests, Tony's interests, Tony's wife's interests, and even his own interests. Matters of this kind were best given some time to think about.

Questions

1. What is the specific nature of Mrs. Ciccelli's problem, and what is its impact on her husband?
2. What factors have combined to produce Tony's reduced performance effectiveness, including his decision to seek a transfer out of the job where the company needs him most?
3. Given the nature of the causal factors involved, what should the personnel director do? What type or types of corrective procedures would seem to work best under these circumstances? Why?

Statistical Appendix

This appendix provides an overview of some of the statistical techniques used in industrial-organizational psychology. Particular attention is given to procedures used in connection with fair employment practices cases; thus the focus is primarily on statistics as related to validation research (Miner & Miner, 1978). In industrial-organizational psychology, statistical analyses are carried out for very practical purposes, such as convincing a judge or jury that an argument is valid (Ledvinka & Scarpello, 1991; Schmitt & Klimoski, 1991). It is important, therefore, to view them in this practical context.

The treatment of statistics here is intended to provide an understanding of the various techniques and a guide to when and how they should be used. Computational procedures and formulas are not included. Information related directly to computation may be obtained from software packages and from statistics textbooks. Understanding and interpreting research findings does not require this level of knowledge.

■ MEANS AND MEDIANS

The final output of data collection in the conduct of a validity study is a set or distribution of predictor scores and of criterion scores. Such a distribution can be developed for each measure or variable employed in the study. The distributions may take a variety of forms, and, as we shall see, the nature of predictor and criterion score distributions is a major determinant of the particular statistical techniques that should be used in the analysis. In the most common distribution, however, in which the scores spread out over a range of values, there is a sizable concentration of scores near the middle with gradually declining frequencies on both sides of the distribution, to the point where at the extremes there may be only one person with a given score value. A study of the scores obtained by eighty-four college graduates on a short, twenty-item vocabulary test yielded the following distribution, which is characteristic (Miner, 1973):

Test Score	Number of College Graduates
0–6	None
7	1
8	None
9	3
10	5
11	3
12	4
13	7
14	13
15	12
16	13
17	10
18	9
19	1
20	3

In instances such as the above, one typically needs some kind of overall summary statistic to provide a general index of how well the subjects do. Usually this summary statistic is an average, or measure of central tendency.

The most common procedure is to calculate a mean ($\overline{X}$) by totaling all the scores and dividing by the number of subjects (N). In the study of college graduates, the total of all scores is 1237; divided by 84 (the N for this study), the mean is 15.4.

Although the mean is the preferred measure, there are instances where it can be misleading. Say, for instance, that in the study of vocabulary test scores of college graduates a frequency of 3, not 0, had been observed for a score of 4. This would pull the mean score down sharply, providing a somewhat distorted picture. In such cases it may be better to use the middle score, or median, to summarize the data. The median is that point on the scale of scores where the frequency above or below is 50 percent of the total frequency. The mean and median are, of course, identical when the shape of the frequency distribution is perfectly symmetrical, but the median moves more slowly in either direction when scores begin to accumulate which are either extremely high or extremely low.

In any event, it is common practice to compute either the mean or the median for all predictor and criterion distributions obtained from a validity study. It is by comparing such indexes for male and female applicants, for instance, that the adverse impact of a predictor may be evaluated.

■ THE STANDARD DEVIATION

The second measure used to describe distributions, in addition to a measure of central tendency, is a measure of the spread or variability of scores. One could use the range from the lowest to the highest score for this purpose, but in carrying out statistical analyses this is rarely done. The range is a very unstable measure in that it may change from one group of subjects to another with practically no change in the overall distribution. Thus, among the eighty-four college gradu-

ates the range is 14 test score points, but in another separate sample of college graduates there is a good chance that the one low score of 7 would merge into the rest of the distribution, thus reducing the range by a full 2 points.

The most commonly used measure of the spread of scores is the standard deviation (SD or σ). A large SD means that the scores are widely spread around the mean or median; a small SD means that they are closely clustered. Using a predictor to select among candidates results in a restriction of range in the employed group and thus a smaller SD for the predictor scores of that group. An often-used derivative of the SD is the variance (v or σ^2), which is the SD value multiplied by itself (thus squared).

In the case of the normal, bell-shaped score distribution which is approximated so frequently in validation research, 34 percent of all scores will fall between the mean and the score which is one standard deviation above it. Since this type of distribution is symmetrical, the same holds for the score range between one SD below the mean and the mean. Thus, 68 percent of the scores are plus or minus one SD from the mean. If one goes out another SD, proportionately fewer additional scores are picked up even though the score range is doubled, because the frequencies decline as one moves to the extremes. Thus roughly 95 percent of the scores are between minus and plus two SDs, and well over 99 percent are between minus and plus three SDs.

It is not uncommon to express predictor or criterion scores in standard deviation. The result is a conversion of so-called raw scores to standard scores. One such standard score is the z score, which sets the mean equal to 0 and the standard deviation equal to 1. Using this approach, almost all scores will fall between the standard scores of -3 and +3. Another similar concept is the T-score, which sets the mean equal to 50 and the SD equal to

10; here the effective range is 20 to 80. Or one can establish the mean at 500 and the SD at 100, as is done with the familiar college entrance examination scores. Standard scores of this kind are often used in combining predictor or criterion scores. Thus the scores on two or more predictors might be converted to some kind of standard scores using the means and standard deviations for each measure's distribution; then those standard scores would be added to get a total score. This procedure serves to weight each predictor equally in the composite.

Standard scores provide a stable frame of reference for interpreting predictor and criterion data which is lacking when raw scores only are used. Another method of achieving the same result is to set scores equal to percentiles. Thus one starts at 0 and attaches percentages to scores by determining what proportion of the sample has scores equal to or below each successively higher score value. Thus the median becomes the 50th percentile; very high scores are at the 90th percentile and above.

On occasion a nine-point stanine scales is used for this same purpose. The first stanine contains the lowest 4 percent of all subjects in the score distribution. Each successive stanine encompasses successively higher score intervals, taking in the next 7, 12, 17, 20, 17, 12, 7, and finally, at the ninth stanine, 4 percent of the normative or standardization sample.

■ STATISTICAL SIGNIFICANCE

Government enforcement agencies have characteristically specified the 0.05 level ($P < 0.05$) as the maximum acceptable for demonstrating validity. Below the 0.05 level the relationship is said to be *statistically significant* or reliable; above that level it is not. What does this mean?

The concept of significance level relates primarily to generalization. To what extent can one be certain that a relationship (such as that between predictor and criterion) found to exist in one sample of employees will also appear in other samples? This is an important consideration in validation research, because the value of the research depends on generalization of the results to new samples of candidates for the positions studied.

This potentiality for accurate generalization of a result is typically expressed in terms of the probability (P) that a relationship in the same direction as that found in the experimental sample will appear in successive samples drawn from the same population. Thus, a positive validity coefficient significant at the 0.05 level means that the chances of obtaining a sample r value that high or higher when the r in the whole population is in fact 0.00 are less than 5 in 100. Clearly, a 19-out-of-20 bet is reasonably good one. On the other hand, if one is studying a large number of independent predictor–criterion relationships, chance alone will yield one "significant" relationship for every 20 studied. This is why cross-validation is so important in such multi-measure studies. It also points up the value of establishing even lower P values if possible—at the 0.01 level, for instance, where reversals can be expected only one time in a hundred.

☐ Establishing Significance Levels

The significance of the various statistical measures can be calculated directly using the appropriate formulas. Many of the standard statistical computer programs do this automatically and provide a P value for each statistic. However, P values for most commonly used measures also may be obtained from tables presented in most statistics texts.

One enters such tables with a number known as the *degrees of freedom* (df), which represents the number of values which are free to vary once other scores are fixed (usually $N - 1$). The specific df figure depends on the analytic approach used. In any event, the table then provides a value of the statistic above which significance may be assumed. Usually at least the 0.05 and the 0.01 levels are thus specified. If the value obtained in a study is above that tabled for the 0.05 level, the statistic is significant at $P < 0.05$; if it is in addition large enough to exceed the tabled value for the 0.01 level, it is significant at $P < 0.01$. Should the statistic's value be less than that required for the 0.05 level, it is generally considered not significant (n.s.).

☐ One-Tailed and Two-Tailed Tests

Although the 0.05 level as specified by government enforcement agencies, and as generally accepted in professional practice, might appear to provide a solid basis for decision-making, this is not entirely true. There is one additional complication. If one is absolutely sure about the direction, positive or negative, of any predictor–criterion relationship found, then there is little problem. Thus, if a mental ability test were being validated, an a priori decision might be made that only a positive relationship would be acceptable and result in actually using the test for selection purposes. In this case a statistically significant negative relationship has the same meaning as any nonsignificant negative relationship. The company simply is not interested in hiring people of low ability, even if, on the particular job studied, such individuals tend to do better than those with higher ability. In this case the lower 95 percent of the distribution of values of the statistic will yield a n.s. judgment (all values below 0, and the 45 percent next above 0). The 5 percent used to define the 0.05 level is all on the positive end.

However, in many cases either a positive or a negative value would result in a decision to use the measure in selection, provided significance is obtained. Personality tests and biographical data, for instance, are often studied with such an intention in mind. In such a case a significant negative relationship is not the same as nonsignificance, but is in fact comparable to a significant positive one. Yet if one applies the same definition of significance as used in the preceding one-tailed example at both the positive and the negative ends of the distribution, the result is that only a 0.10 significance level is being required (5 percent at each tail or extreme of the distribution). To obtain a true 0.05 significance, it is necessary to require larger values of the statistic, equal to the 0.025 level, when a two-tailed test is involved. This is because negative as well as positive values are to be accepted. The two-tailed test is clearly more conservative than the one-tailed, insofar as accepting the fact of a significant relationship is concerned. For this reason the enforcement agencies tend to favor it, and one must be prepared to justify a one-tailed significance test if a decision is made to use one.

■ CHI-SQUARE TESTS

The simplest of the statistics that may be used in the manner just described to determine the significance of a predictor–criterion relationship is chi-square (χ^2). The χ^2 test uses frequency data. An example of its use would be a situation where employee interviewers placed all hired candidates in one of two categories—recommended hire and recommended rejection—and where subsequent job performance was evaluated by supervisors as either satisfactory or not. The resulting four-fold table used to calculate χ^2 for 100 employees might look as follows:

Hiring Recommendation	Job Performance	
	Not Satisfactory	Satisfactory
Recommended hire	10 (25)	40 (25)
Recommended reject	40 (25)	10 (25)

In this instance it would appear to make considerable sense to follow the interviewer recommendations. The application of χ^2 is an appropriate way to confirm this impression statistically and to determine whether the distribution of frequencies is in fact significantly different from what would be expected by chance alone—indicated in parentheses above. If the frequencies expected by chance alone (those in parentheses in the example) are very low, certainly below 5 and conservatively below 10, many statisticians believe that χ^2 is not an appropriate statistic. For this reason it is often desirable to combine categories to achieve higher frequencies. One can even take variables with a sizable range of scores and split the distributions at the medians to create a fourfold table for computing χ^2. This is a particularly appropriate procedure when the distributions depart sharply from the normal, bell-shaped curve. On the other hand, it should be recognized that χ^2 yields only a P value indicating the degree of significance, not an estimate of the extent of the relationship, as in correlation.

■ THE t TEST AND ANALYSIS OF VARIANCE

Where it is feasible to compute means and where the data distributions approximate the normal form, with the larger frequencies in the middle and symmetrically smaller frequencies at the extremes, the statistics discussed in this section are most appropriate. The t test is used to compare mean scores in two groups to see if the difference between the means is large enough to warrant a conclusion that the groups differ in a statistically significant manner.

This type of analysis might be used, for instance, to evaluate adverse impact of a selection instrument as between males and females or between whites and minorities; a statistically significant t-value would be indicative of a real differential. The t test may also be used to compare the mean scores on predictors of those who do and do not complete training, or of those who do and do not perform satisfactorily, or of those who separate within a given period of time and those who remain employed. Like χ^2, such t tests yield information on significance levels only, not on the extent of the relationship involved.

Although the t test is the usual approach used in comparing two groups where the score distributions are continuous and normally shaped, there are some approaches which focus directly on the degree of overlap between the two distributions, such as Tilton's 0 statistic. In this case the extremes are complete overlap, where the two distributions are perfectly superimposed (n.s.), and complete separation, such that all scores in one distribution are below the lowest score in the other (highly significant).

When the number of groups to be compared increases above two and/or multiple continuous measures are involved, it is common to employ the analysis-of-variance technique (ANOVA) to determine whether overall significance is present. Analysis of variance yields an F statistic which may be evaluated for significance using the appropriate table and df values. Although it is an extremely powerful statistical tool, ANOVA is not widely used in validation research, primarily because the nature of research designs is such as to make correlational statistics more suitable.

■ CORRELATION TECHNIQUES

Here we will take up the various measures of correlation that may be used. In contrast to the techniques considered previously, these statistics provide an index of the degree of relationship present. This measure of degree may then be tested, using available tables for the statistic in many cases, to determine whether it is large enough to warrant the position that it is significantly different from 0. Thus correlation procedures can provide a measure both of the size of predictor–criterion relationships and their significance. It is also possible to determine through appropriate analyses whether one correlation coefficient is significantly different from another, not just different from 0 (this requires transforming the two correlation values to z values using a conversion table). All of these considerations argue strongly for using correlational techniques in validation research wherever possible; it is the usual practice to do so.

☐ Rank-Order Correlation

One of the simplest measures of correlation uses ranked data on both measures. It yields a coefficient known as rho (ρ). Since rankings are often used in developing criterion measures, as when supervisors rank their subordinates, the rank-order approach has had considerable application in validation research. If one variable—say, the criterion—is of a rank-order nature, the other must be converted to the rank form if it is not already so organized. When ties exist, the ranks are split between the individuals who are in tie positions. For example, if the second and third highest-ranking individuals have the same score, both are ranked as 2.5.

The rank-order approach becomes quite cumbersome when large samples are used. In addition, it tends to yield slightly lower values than the more conventional product–moment correlation coefficient. In general, the use of ρ should be restricted to those cases where the data for one or both measures are available only in the rank form.

☐ Product–Moment Correlation

The product–moment or Pearson correlation coefficient (r) is the most widely used validity index. It is appropriate when actual scores on

predictor and criterion are available and are spread over a number of values. When r has been calculated, it provides an index of the direct linear relationship between two variables. Thus the larger the value of r, the more accurately one can predict criterion values from a knowledge of predictor scores.

Prediction of this kind is achieved through the use of regression equations which define the best fit or regression lines between the two variables being correlated. Actually, there are two such equations which may be generated from any correlation relationship. One equation is for predicting criterion values from a knowledge of predictor scores—this is of most interest in validation research; the other equation yields best estimates of predictor values given a knowledge of criterion values. The accuracy with which such regression equations will predict in a particular situation may be stated in terms of a statistic known as the standard error of estimate. The smaller the value of this statistic, the more accurate the prediction possible.

One occasionally sees the value of r interpreted directly in percentage terms. Thus an r of 0.40 is interpreted to mean that a predictor can account for or explain 40 percent of the variance of variability in a criterion. This interpretation is incorrect. The appropriate statistic for determining how much of the variance in a criterion may be predicted from a knowledge of predictor values is the correlation coefficient squared (r^2). Thus an r of 0.40 actually permits an explanation of only 16 percent of the criterion variance, not 40 percent. For a number of reasons, however, this percentage of variance accounted for is not a good indication of the overall value of a predictor.

☐ Biserial Correlation

Product–moment correlation requires a spread of scores over multiple values of both predictor and criterion. However, there are instances where this spread does not exist. The most common instances involve predictors and/or criteria which are dichotomous, thus falling in only two categories. A number of correlation techniques are available to handle these situations. Each is appropriate to a somewhat different combination of score distributions, and it is important to understand when each type of correlation is appropriate.

Biserial correlation (r_{bis}) is used in the situation where one variable is continuous, in the same manner as when the product–moment coefficient is calculated, and the other, although potentially continuous also, has been dichotomized for convenience or some other reason. A common application is where there is a range of scores on a predictor but the criterion has been developed so as to yield only two categories, such as "effective" and "less effective," in some aspect of performance. Clearly such a criterion could be made continuous by specifying degrees of effectiveness; often, however, it is difficult to get supervisors to do this, and a dichotomous measure is used instead.

Where there is reason to believe that a graduated scale underlies the dichotomy, r_{bis} is the appropriate statistic. Such is the case in much validation research. However, on occasion one is faced with a dichotomy where the two categories are truly discrete and assigning a 0 to one and a 1 to the other is an entirely arbitrary process. This would be true of the male–female dichotomy, for instance. Usually in such cases one would compute means on the continuous variable for the male and the female groups and then test for significance using the t test. However, if a measure of degree of relationship is desired, the appropriate statistic is the point biserial coefficient (r_{pbis}). Biserial r and point biserial r are calculated in much the same manner. However, r_{bis} more nearly approximates the product–moment coefficient in its interpretation and thus should be used if possible.

☐ Tetrachoric Correlation and the Phi Coefficient

In some cases both variables are artificially dichotomized in the same manner as one is when r_{bis} is used. This would be the case, for instance, if one wished to correlate the above- and below-average ratings given by an interviewer with subsequent effective/ineffective ratings by a supervisor. Here the appropriate measure is tetrachoric correlation (r_{tet}). Like performance effectiveness, the hiring recommendation can be differentiated into degrees of suitability and would be expected to yield a distribution approximating the normal shape.

Because r_{tet} is easily calculated from available tables and graphs, there is a temptation to apply it in cases where the data permit the use of the product–moment r. All that is needed is to split both variables at the median, thus forming artificial dichotomies. This procedure is not recommended except in obtaining a preliminary picture of results. The product–moment r is a much more accurate statistic when it can be calculated appropriately, simply because it utilizes the full range of data.

An alternative to r_{tet} in some cases is the phi coefficient (ϕ). When both variables are true dichotomies, this is the appropriate measure; however, this is not a frequent situation in validation research. Another situation where ϕ is appropriate is when there are very few instances of one category of a dichotomy. In cases such as this, where there is a sizable imbalance between the categories of a dichotomy, neither the biserial nor the tetrachoric coefficient is very accurate. Thus, in one study ϕ was used to validate a telephone reference-checking procedure when it was found that over 98 percent of the applicants checked received favorable recommendations and less than 2 percent negative ones. Even with such an extreme imbalance, validity was established against a dichotomous termination criterion using the phi statistic in a very large sample. One disadvantage of using φ in such cases, however, is that the maximum values possible are not +1.00 and −1.00, but much smaller figures. Thus φ cannot be interpreted within the same frame of reference as *r*.

☐ Correlation Ratio

In most validation situations the primary concern is with linear relationships; as scores on the predictor get proportionately higher, so do scores on the criterion. That is what the correlation measures discussed to this point measure. However, should the relationship be other than linear, these techniques will underestimate its size. Major departures from linearity are not common in validation research, but they do occur. It is well to be aware of this potential and of methods for dealing with such departures when they occur.

An example of a nonlinear, curvilinear relationship would be where employees who scored low on a personality-test measure of conformity were rated low on job performance, those in the midrange of conformity were rated high, and those with high levels (excessive conformity) were again rated low—where both nonconformists and conformists do less well. In such situations the correlation ratio, eta (η), more correctly reflects the size of the relationship, and *r* may severely underestimate it. Thus a truly significant relationship may not be identified as such.

The best way to determine whether a deviation from linearity may be present is to inspect a scatter plot of the correlation data. If the data appear curvilinear this impression may be tested statistically to determine whether the deviation from linearity is significant. When it is, η is the preferred statistic. However, if a significant η is obtained, it is important to use the predictor in the manner the findings would indicate, not in a linear

fashion. Thus, individuals scoring both low and high on the measure of conformity should be rejected, not just low scorers. It is generally recommended that when η is used this way, the relationship be established by cross-validation or with quite large samples.

☐ Multiple Correlation

The correlation techniques considered up to this point deal with one predictor and one criterion. However, there are procedures for dealing with multiple measures in a single analysis. The use of these techniques has escalated considerably with the advent of computers and computer programs to facilitate calculations. The most common situation is one where there are a number of predictors to be related to a single composite criterion. Such a situation calls for multiple correlation (*R*) or multiple regression, and this is the technique that we will consider here. However, it should be recognized that the multiple-correlation approach can be extended to cases where a number of predictors *and* criteria are present through the use of canonical correlation.

R has the same basic characteristics and requires the same distribution types as *r*. It is interpreted in the same manner, except that it is always positive. *R* is an index of the maximum correlation between a set of predictors and the criterion, and it permits the development of a regression equation which combines the various predictors in a manner which maximizes the prediction of criterion values from a knowledge of the various predictors in terms of their relationship to the criterion. These weights, which maximize the overall criterion relationship, are known are beta (β) weights.

The ideal situation in multiple-correlation studies is to have a number of predictors which are significantly and sizably correlated with the criterion and which in addition are uncorrelated with each other. In this case each predictor contributes considerable unique criterion variance to the overall statistic, and multiple R goes up rapidly as new measures are added. Many computer programs provide for stepwise calculations so that the extent of the contribution made by each predictor may be determined; the best predictor is used first and the R is calculated at each step as predictors of decreasing value are added. In this process a predictor which is highly correlated with another and which relates to the criterion in roughly the same manner contributes very little to the R value, because the two predictors account for almost identical variance. To obtain a sizable R, the validation research should be designed to include a wide range of quite dissimilar predictors.

A question arises in multiple correlation as to how many predictors should be combined. There are procedures, such as the Wherry-Doolittle test-selection technique, for answering this question. Basically, the stepwise approach is used, along with a formula for calculating the shrinkage in R that might be expected if the multiple correlation were computed in a completely new sample. There comes a point at which the addition of another predictor yields a shrunken R value which is actually less than the value without that predictor; the increase in error contributed by the additional measure is greater than the increase in validity. At this point the predictor set is stabilized, and only those predictors already identified are actually applied in selection and entered into a regression equation.

In general, it is desirable to keep the number of predictors involved in computing R as low as possible. With a small number of subjects and a large number of predictors, one can almost always obtain an R value that is significant at the 0.05 level, but it may not hold up in a cross-validation sample because the underlying single predictor–criterion relationships themselves represent only chance fluctuations. For this reason, good multiple-correlation research requires quite large samples; usually five or six predictors are all that are needed, and little gain in validity is achieved with more.

☐ Expectancy Tables

The various statistics considered represent procedures for summarizing predictor–criterion relationships and determining their significance. As such these statistics should be calculated and utilized in presenting findings to enforcement agencies and the courts. On the other hand, it often is also useful to present findings in some manner which is more meaningful to the statistically uninitiated. One procedure for doing this is the expectancy table or chart. Such a table may be constructed as follows:

1. Where the criterion is not already a dichotomy, make one by identifying superior (effective, above average, successful) performers as appropriate.
2. Set up a frequency distribution with three columns: superior, other, and total frequency.
3. Divide the predictor distribution into roughly equal fifths in terms of number of subjects, not scores.
4. Count the total number of cases and the number of superior cases in each of the five predictor-score categories; then determine the percentage in each category that are superior.

The resulting expectancy table might look as follows:

Predictor-Score Range	Chances in 100 of Being Superior
18–20	86
16–17	75
14–15	58
12–13	22
0–11	20

Such a table may easily be converted into a bar chart if a graphic presentation is desired. The expectancy approach is a useful method of showing what a correlation may mean in practice.

■ FACTOR ANALYSIS

Although there are a number of different mathematical procedures that may be used in carrying out a factor analysis, the objective in all cases is to isolate and identify dimensions inherent in a correlation matrix, thus simplifying the matrix to make the information easier to use. Such a matrix is obtained when r values are calculated relating a number of measures each to the other. Thus, twenty different predictors might be employed in a validation study and one might desire to reduce these twenty down to a few key dimensions before calculating criterion relationships. Fac-

tor analysis is a method of doing this, and the starting point is a matrix showing the correlation between each of the twenty predictors and each of the nineteen others. The mathematical techniques extract a reduced set of factors, the number depending on the composition of the matrix and the technique, and indicate the relationship of each predictor with each factor extracted.

The usual practice is to describe each factor in verbal terms by abstracting out subjectively whatever the predictors with high loadings (relationships) appear to have in common. In addition, factor scores may be computed indicating an individual's relative position on each factor. The value of such an approach is that an original twenty predictor scores might be distilled down to from three to five factor scores. Some predictors are usually discarded. The remaining measures would be used in the validity study and thus correlated with criteria, but only as they contribute to the composite factor scores.

Glossary

The number(s) in brackets at the end of each entry refers to the chapter(s) in which the term is defined and discussed in detail.

accident repeaters Individuals who are consistently more susceptible to injuries than others. [20]

accident type A term often included in an accident report form which refers to the type of contact of the injured person with the agency. See **agency.** [20]

achievement motivation The desire to achieve success through one's own efforts and to take personal responsibility and credit for outcomes; the key construct of David McClelland's achievement-motivation theory. [3]

achievement-motivation theory David McClelland's view that human needs are learned and are arranged in a hierarchy of potential for influencing behavior that varies from one person to another. [3]

achievement tests These job knowledge tests differ from work sample tests in that they deal with the knowledge or information required to perform a job; the applicants answer written or oral questions about the work. See **work sample tests.** [18]

active practice The central concept in experiential learning, involving repetition of the task to be learned until proficiency is achieved. [2]

additive correlation An approximation procedure for the multiple correlation coefficient which involves adding the values obtained by an individual on all the predictors together and then computing the correlation between this composite index and the criterion. See **criterion; validation.** [16]

after-only model An experimental design in which both experimental and control groups receive a posttest only, after the time of experimental intervention. See **control group; experimental group.** [19]

agency A term often included in an accident report form which refers to the thing most closely associated with the injury. [20]

agency part A term often included in an accident report form which refers to the specific part or aspect of the agency most closely associated with the injury. See **agency.** [20]

alternative work schedules A type of work redesign involving adjustments in scheduled working hours. See **compressed work week; flexible working hours.** [11]

application blank A form completed by the applicant when applying for a job, which details past behavior. See **past behavior.** [17]

apprentice training An integration of on- and off-the-job learning used to prepare employees for a variety of skilled occupations; the apprentices work for the company at a reduced rate in return for a specified number of hours of training. [19]

assessment centers An evaluation technique in which individuals are asked to complete various types of exercises in order to identify personality characteristics needed for different strategic contexts. [6, 14]

at random A method of selecting individuals to study so that each individual in a larger population has an equal chance of showing up in the study sample; utilized for the purpose of ensuring that the sample is representative of the population. [14]

attitude Defined by Craig C. Pinder as "the degree of positive or negative feeling a person has toward a particular attitude object, such as a place, thing, or other person." [5]

attitudinal commitment Defined by Richard T. Mowday, Lyman W. Porter, and Richard M. Steers as the relative strength of an individual's identification with and involvement in a particular organization. Compare **behavioral commitment.** [5]

attribution theory In the area of leadership, the way superiors perceive the cause of a subordinate's poor performance. [10]

autonomous work group A work group to which some degree of decision-making authority has been shifted from management. [7, 11]

avoidance learning A contingency of reinforcement that involves the withdrawal or prevention of an unpleasant condition contingent upon the subject's manifestation of the desired behavior. [4]

before-after model An experimental design in which under ideal conditions both an experimental and a control group receive both a pretest and a posttest. See **control group; experimental group.** [19]

behavioral commitment A tendency of an individual

or a group to become increasingly committed to a job (or course of action) simply to justify the decision to take the position (or take the action) in the first place. Compare **attitudinal commitment;** see **escalation of commitment.** [5, 8]

behaviorally specific   The degree to which a performance rating measure incorporates detailed descriptions of job behavior itself derived from job analysis directly into the measure itself. [15]

behavioral summary scales   A variant of the scaled expectation rating method in which the performance ratings are anchored with somewhat more general or abstract behavioral benchmarks, rather than highly specific critical incidents; this represents some movement away from extreme behavioral specificity. See **behaviorally specific; scaled expectation method.** [15]

behavior list   A rating procedure that has as its essential characteristic that it deals with on-the-job behaviors; the manager actually reports on or describes the behavior of subordinates rather than merely evaluating it, with the result that separate lists must be developed for each position. See **behaviorally specific.** [15]

behavior modeling   An outgrowth of social learning theory that involves training people to perform tasks by observing and practicing the actions of others. [4]

behavior observation scaling   A variant of the scaled expectation rating method in which the rater indicates for a series of behavior descriptions or incidents how frequently the person being rated has been observed to exhibit the behavior. See **scaled expectation method.** [15]

biographical inventory   A form which utilizes a multiple choice format and deals with matters that extend beyond those covered in an application blank; often there are questions dealing with early life experiences, hobbies, health, and social relations, as well as attitudes, interests, values, opinions and self-impressions. See **application blank.** [17]

black-white differences   Group differences between blacks and whites in aspects of mental ability and personality. See **group differences.** [12]

bonafide occupational qualifications   An exemption contained in the law that eliminates certain occupations from a claim of employment discrimination; a very narrow range of situations involving authenticity or genuineness, such as an actress, or a situation involving universally recognized standards, such as a ladies room attendant. [17]

boundary spanners   Individuals who communicate extensively both with people inside the company and with external groups and individuals; frequently subject to stress as a result of role conflict. [6]

bounded rationality   The rational, narrow use of highly simplified models, working hypotheses, rules of thumb, and heuristics that characterizes the satisficing approach to decision making. [2]

brainstorming   A technique for solving problems and developing new ideas through unrestrained, spontaneous discussion. [8]

buddy rating (peer rating)   A technique developed by Navy psychologists during World War II which requires that each member of a group rate all other members; these ratings are then averaged to provide an index of the person's competence. [14]

bumping   A process utilized during layoffs when higher-level positions are eliminated whereby an employee with seniority may demand the job of another employee with less seniority. [15]

burnout   A phenomenon in which an individual's work effectiveness decreases as a result of negative emotionality (emotional exhaustion, depression, general dissatisfaction) combined with continuing stress. [6]

business necessity   A legal term used to describe a type of company defense against discrimination claims which relies upon the fact that a selection device is related to job performance. [12]

career appraisal index   Any measure of overall career success to date such as the position level obtained or salary progression. [14]

career development   The process in which an individual's career plans are actually carried out. [19]

career ladders   A procedure for constituting job families by grouping jobs on a vertical basis. See **job families.** [13]

career planning   The process of identifying one's career-related goals and programming work, education, and developmental experiences in order to attain these goals. [19]

charismatic leadership   Leadership based on strong emotional, irrational ties between followers and a leader who is believed to have supernatural powers and who demonstrates characteristics of dominance, self-confidence, the need to exert influence, and a strong conviction of the moral righteousness of his or her beliefs. [10]

checklists   A rating method which uses a number of descriptors, usually job behaviors but in some cases personal traits as well, which are to be checked if they apply to the individual. See **trait rating.** [15]

coalition(s)   Informal groups, usually composed of managers or professionals, who unite at least temporarily to pursue a particular objective. See **political coalitions.** [7]

codetermination   A form of participative leadership consisting of a legally mandated procedure whereby employees and employee representatives share in the top-level governance of the firm. [9]

cognitive processes   Those psychological processes which involve organizing information in our minds to help accomplish some desired end; included are learning, memory, concept formation, problem solving, intelligence, and the use of language. [2]

cognitive style An aspect of decision making that involves the characteristic ways in which people process and evaluate information. [2]

cohesion The extent to which members of a group desire to remain in the group because they are attracted to it and to one another. [7]

comparable worth controversy A dispute, now extended to the legal arena, which has arisen because many jobs in our society tend to be segregated by sex, or sex-typed, and at the same time working women on the average are paid considerably less than men. [3, 13]

compressed work week An approach to work redesign in which the standard number of working hours remains the same, but employees work more hours per day and fewer days per week. [4]

computer-assisted instruction A training procedure with much in common with programmed instruction, except that a computer is used to select and present material and evaluate responses. See **programmed instruction.** [19]

computerized interview An interviewing procedure in which the applicant is questioned from the computer screen, and no other person is present; branching logic allows promising areas to be explored and less promising topics to be bypassed. [17]

concurrent validity Identical to predictive validity except that the predictor and criterion measures are obtained at roughly the same time, usually on individuals who have been employed for a considerable period in the job to be studied. See **predictive validity.** [16]

conformity The process by which social pressures induce people to change their attitudes, perceptions, and behaviors; evidenced by the fact that even very diverse groups typically reach a consensus and endorse their decisions unanimously. [8]

consideration The degree of concern for subordinates and encouragement of their participation in decision making that is one of the two independent measures of leadership developed by Ralph Stogdill and others. See also **initiating structure.** [9]

construct validity Validation involving rational inferences from a body of research, and referring not so much to job behaviors and skills as to underlying characteristics of the job performer; to apply the theoretical construct must be well defined, the selection procedure must be known to be a measure of the construct, and an important aspect of job behavior must involve the construct. [16]

content validity A type of rational validation for selection procedures in which there is first a systematic study of the job to establish the knowledge, skills, and behav-

iors required, and second the development of an appropriate selection procedure on a judgmental basis. [16]

contingencies of reinforcement The types of reinforcements used in strengthening certain behaviors and weakening others. See **avoidance learning; extinction; positive reinforcement; punishment.** [4]

contingency theory Fred Fiedler's view that under certain circumstances (contingencies), but not others, leaders with certain characteristics elicit effective group performance. See **least preferred coworker.** [9]

control group A comparison group consisting of individuals like those exposed to an experimental condition such as training but differing in that they are not exposed. See **experimental group.** [19]

corporate codes of conduct Formal specifications of the types of behaviors that a company does or does not sanction across the myriad value systems and legal frameworks within which it operates. [5]

correction for restriction of range A statistical procedure, often used in validation research when a predictor has been used to select who is hired, to correct for the effect of the resulting restriction of range on the validity coefficient. See **validation.** [16]

creativity An aspect of decision making defined by Frank Barron and David M. Harrington as "socially recognized achievement in which there are novel products to which one can point as evidence such as inventions, theories, buildings, published writings, paintings and sculptures and films; laws; institutions; medical and surgical treatments, and so on." [2]

credentialism The tendency to establish license, certification, or degree requirements for jobs that effectively block upward movement on the job and that may necessitate a greater investment in education than performance of particular tasks requires. [13]

criterion A measure of success; what is appropriate in a given instance depends on the results of job analysis and on the specific purpose for which the data will be used—validation of selection procedures, allocating merit pay, etc. [15, 16]

critical incident procedure A rating method that has as its essential feature the fact that incidents of effective and ineffective performance are obtained to serve as a basis for rating. See **critical incidents.** [15]

critical incidents An approach to obtaining job analysis information, often used at lower levels, whereby a superior provides a number of instances of good and poor job performance among subordinates; these incidents are then analyzed to establish what behaviors are important in the job. [13]

cross-validation A validation procedure in which a second study is carried out on the same predictor and criterion measures in order to determine whether any relationship established in the first sample might have been due to a chance fluctuation. See **criterion; validation.** [16]

cultural variations Any difference existing between the people of one culture around the world and those of another culture which is caused by the different cultures. [12]

decision tree In Victor H. Vroom and Philip W. Yetton's managerial-choice theory, the series of questions a manager answers in deciding which leadership behaviors are appropriate in a particular situation. [10]

Delphi technique A variant of the nominal-group method of fostering creativity in which a panel of knowledgeable individuals, who never meet face to face, exchange proposed solutions and provide feedback in written form again and again until consensus is reached or until some voting procedure is imposed to reach a decision. See **nominal groups.** [8]

dependent variable A criterion that is the major object of a researcher's interest and thus represents what the researcher wishes to predict. See **criterion; independent variable.** [15]

devil's advocacy A group decision-making procedure in which a proposed strategy is turned over to a group whose job it is to determine what is wrong with it—to identify assumptions and biases inherent in the plan that jeopardizes its value. [8]

dialectical inquiry A group decision-making procedure that involves arguing logically about conflicting opinions regarding a problem in order to arrive at the best solution. [8]

differential validity The result of validating separately for two groups, such as blacks and whites or males and females, using a moderator variable design. See **moderator variables; validation.** [16]

diffusion The spread of organization-development processes from a successful pilot project throughout a whole company, or even a whole society. [11]

division of labor The creation of specific expectations for the behavior of groups and individuals within an organization by using organization planning and job analysis to split up the work to be done. [14]

double loop learning A learning or decision-making process in which the individual not only examines actions and their consequences but also questions the governing variables that underlie them. Compare **single loop learning.** [2]

drug testing A procedure for identifying drug use, either through honesty testing or through the use of some type of physiological testing procedure, usually analysis of urine samples, to identify drug residuals. See **honesty testing.** [18]

dual allegiance An idea set forth by Theodore Purcell that many employees are favorably disposed to both the company and the union. See **attitudinal commitment; union commitment.** [5]

education An approach to human change or learning which is tied to the goals of the individual more than those of the organization and which tends to take individuals, their growth, and the multiple roles that they may play in society as its starting point. See **training.** [19]

effort-to-performance expectancy The assessed probability that if effort is exerted, the result will be successful performance. Compare **performance-to-outcome expectancy.** [3]

employee assistance programs Programs provided by companies on a confidential basis to help employees with problems, especially alcohol and drug problems. [20]

employee-centered Referring to leaders who behave so as to foster work-group members' perceptions of the organization's supportiveness and high performance goals. [9]

employee comparison Rating systems that, instead of comparing each worker against some generalized concept of acceptable behavior as do rating scales, make comparisons among the various individuals being evaluated; thus other workers provide reference points for the ratings, and the result is a relative evaluation. See **rating scales.** [15]

employment interviews The use of interview procedures to evaluate human inputs to an organization, rather than for purposes of marketing research, employee counseling, management appraisal, or attitude surveys. [17]

encapsulated training Training which has its effects only within the training context, not back on the job. See **transfer of training.** [19]

entrepreneurs People who start and develop their own companies. [3]

Equal Pay Act A federal law that outlaws pay differentials between men and women who work in substantially equal jobs—either the same exact jobs or jobs that, although titled differentially for males and females, are really the same. [13]

equipment simulations Simulations of actual equipment developed for training purposes; used most widely in situations such as airline pilot training, where the economic and human costs of error are substantial. [19]

equity In equity theory, an individual's feeling that he or she is being treated in the same way as his or her chosen reference group. [3]

equity theory The view that certain aspects of motivation are rooted in the perceived fairness of the traditional employee–employer exchange whereby the employee gives something (inputs) and then gets something in exchange (outcomes) from the employer. [3]

error of central tendency A type of rating error in which all subordinates are rated in a narrow range and that clustering is restricted to the middle of the scale. See **range restriction errors.** [15]

escalation of commitment The tendency to increase allocation of resources to a decision that gives every indication of being wrong, in an effort to somehow justify the decision. See **behavioral commitment.** [5]

essay evaluation A performance evaluation method in which superiors merely write out what they think of a subordinate, usually with very little by way of guidelines concerning what points should be covered. [15]

expectancy theories The view that behavior and performance are a result of conscious choice and that people will choose to do whatever they believe will result in the highest payoffs for them personally. [3]

experiential learning The aspect of learning that involves practice and experience with the task. [2]

experimental group A group consisting of individuals who are exposed to some experimental condition such as training. See **control group.** [19]

external attribution According to attribution theory, superiors' perception of a subordinate's poor performance as caused by some problem beyond the subordinate's control, such as bad luck or difficulty of the task. Compare **internal attribution.** [10]

extinction A contingency of reinforcement that involves the withdrawal of a positive reinforcer so that undesired behavior gets weaker and eventually disappears. [4].

extrinsic outcomes Rewards that are provided or mediated by external forces, such as a superior, the organization, or other work-group members. Compare **intrinsic outcomes.** [3]

face validity An impression of the appropriateness of a selection procedure on the part of the person completing a measure. [16]

factor comparison A method of job evaluation which uses ranking but in terms of various component factors such as skill requirements, mental requirements, physical requirements, responsibility, and working conditions. See **job evaluation; job ranking.** [13]

family groups The unit—composed of a manager and the people who reported to him or her—to which early forms of team building, utilizing T-group procedures, were applied. See **team building; T-group.** [7]

field investigations A procedure for developing a picture of an individual's background from personal interviews with a variety of people who have known the individual. See **past behavior; references.** [17]

field review A method of performance appraisal in which appraisal data are collected orally from a person's superior using a specific list of questions. See **performance appraisal.** [14]

fixed interval reinforcement A schedule of partial reinforcement in which reinforcement occurs when the desired behavior appears after a fixed amount of time has passed since the preceding reinforcement. Compare **variable interval reinforcement.** [4]

fixed ratio reinforcement A schedule of partial reinforcement in which reinforcement always occurs after the same fixed number of desired behaviors have been exhibited. Compare **variable ratio reinforcement.** [4]

flexible working hours (flextime) An approach to work redesign in which the individual employee is given some choice about when he or she will put in the required number of working hours. [4]

forced-choice procedure A behavior list rating procedure that use blocks of two or more descriptions which are selected to be approximately equal in their degree of favorableness, but markedly different in the degree to which they have been found in prior studies to be associated with effective or ineffective performance. See **behavior list.** [15]

forced distribution A rating method in which managers are instructed to place their subordinates in categories on each dimension according to certain predesignated proportions. [15]

formal disciplinary systems Stated procedures for the use of punishment in an organization. [4]

formal work groups Groups of workers constituted by management for the purpose of combining their efforts, usually under a single supervisor, to get a particular job done. [7]

functional job analysis A procedure for developing career ladders created by Sidney Fine which groups jobs based on the extent to which they require dealing with data, people, and things. See **career ladders; job families.** [13]

goal setting An approach to arousing, directing, and maintaining motivation at work; the central propositions of this approach are (1) that difficult goals lead to higher task performance than easy goals and (2) that specific difficult goals lead to higher performance than no goals or vague goals. [4]

graphology The analysis of handwriting to infer personality characteristics; the focus is on the way in which people write and shape letters, not the content of what they write. [18]

grid organization development A process, initiated by top management, that utilizes the interface conflict-resolution model and the managerial grid concept to move the organization closer to their ideal model of what it should be. [11]

group Defined by Dorwin Cartwright and Alvin

Zander as "a collection of individuals who have relations to one another that make them interdependent to some significant degree." [7]

group decision making   Any of various methods—a report to the individual in charge, group consensus, or some kind of voting procedure—by which members of a group within an organization settle on a course of action. [8]

group development   A series of stages of internal conflict and harmony through which a group passes as it matures. [7]

group difference   The difference between measures of central tendency, usually the means, for two groups. [12]

group embarrassment   A result of individual or group failure that group norms are often specified in order to avoid. [7]

group norms   The informal rules or standards that groups adopt to regulate and regularize the behavior of group members. [7]

group polarization   The tendency of group discussion to cause a group to shift farther toward the extreme of an issue—either more risky or more cautious—that it already favored. See **risky shift.** [8]

group poor performance   An extension of the attribution theory of leadership to the leader–group relationship; involves more serious consequences for the organization, may indicate major problems in the organization, and reflects more on the supervisor, thus impeding the supervisor's ability to make objective diagnoses. See **attribution theory.** [10]

group similarity   A factor in the effectiveness of group decision making; the optimal degree of member similarity depends on the nature of the decision to be made. [8]

group size   A factor in the effectiveness of group decision making; the optimal group size depends on the nature of the decision to be made. [8]

groupthink   Irving Janis's term for the phenomenon whereby the desire of members of a cohesive ingroup for complete consensus overrides their motivation to evaluate alternatives realistically and often results in poor group decision making. [8]

growth needs   According to the Hackman-Oldham job characteristics theory, a primary moderator contributing to the success or failure of attempts at job enrichment; people with strong needs for growth respond to enriched jobs with more positive outcomes. [4]

halo   The tendency to evaluate a person in a similar manner, favorably or unfavorably, on all or most of the dimensions of a rating form because a general overall impression colors the ratings. [15]

hierarchic (managerial) role-motivation theory   John B.

Miner's view that certain strong motives contribute to success in specific managerial roles. [3, 10]

honesty tests   Assessments of attitudes and behavior related to theft, drug and alcohol use, sabotage, and other aspects of honesty in job performance. [6]

human engineering   The discipline concerned with designing equipment to fit the human operator. [20]

humanistic values   Conceptions of the desirable that emphasize the individual person and the goals of humanism. [11]

human relations   A movement in American industry, which served both to promulgate humanist values and to initiate the field called organizational behavior. See **organizational behavior.** [1]

human resource accounting   An accounting procedure used in evaluating managers that serves to give a manager credit for increasing investments in human resources and charges for using up that investment. [14]

human resource management   The process of developing, applying, and evaluating policies, procedures, methods, and programs relating to the individual in the organization. [1]

human resources model   In Raymond Miles's expanded view of Douglas McGregor's Theory X–Theory Y formulation, the rough equivalent of **Theory Y.** [9]

hygienes   In Frederick Herzberg's formulation, factors that are characteristic of the context in which work is performed and that can result in job dissatisfaction; they are: company policy and administrative practices, technical quality of supervision, interpersonal relations, physical working conditions, job security, benefits, and salary. See **motivation-hygiene theory.** [4]

hypothesis   A tentative proposition derived from a theory, advanced to explain something that is not understood. [1]

idea evaluation   An approach to fostering creativity that emphasizes the advantages of group procedures over individual decision making in assessing or choosing among proposed solutions to a problem. Compare **idea generation.** [8]

idea generation   An approach to fostering creativity that emphasizes the reduction or elimination of the inhibiting effects of social interaction, so that individual group members feel free to think up and present ideas. Compare **idea evaluation.** [8]

implicit theories   Ways of thinking often developed by subordinates in describing their leaders which occur because the descriptive process imposes excessive memory demands and taxes human information-processing capabilities; subordinates fill in forgotten details with stereotypes and assumptions about how a good leader ought to act, thus providing a description that is more a function of subordinate thinking processes than leader behavior. See **consideration; initiating structure.** [9]

incentive systems Contingent monetary rewards for employees who perform better; they may take the form of merit-pay or bonus systems. [4]

incremental change In organization development, the making of changes gradually, as they come to seem feasible, and in stages or over a considerable period. Compare **quantum change.** [11]

incrementalizing An approach to decision making that involves "muddling through," or making a number of small choices rather than one large one; its goal is primarily to alleviate existing problems. Compare **maximizing; satisficing.** [2]

independent variable That which a researcher manipulates or controls or measures for purposes of predicting a dependent variable or criterion. See **criterion; dependent variable.** [15]

individual decision making The process by which a person chooses a course of action. [2]

individual differences The differences that exist between individuals in various respects including aspects of intelligence, learning and decision-making capabilities, motivation, attitudes, commitments, values, personality, perceptual skills, and physical makeup. [12]

inducements-contributions balance A way of understanding the role of reward systems in organizations: the employer offers various inducements for the employee to continue making contributions to the organization's goals. [4]

industrial clinical psychology A field of industrial-organizational psychology which focuses primarily on employees whose performance has fallen below acceptable levels, what factors caused the performance failure, and what can be done to correct the problem. See **industrial-organizational psychology.** [20]

industrial-organizational psychology A component of psychology concerned with the application of psychological science, and thus its theory and research, to the problems of human organizations and in particular to the utilization of human resources within organizations. [1]

inequity motivation In equity theory, an individual's desire to act to restore equity in response to the guilt experienced when he or she is being overrewarded (that is, when outcomes are greater than inputs) or to the anger experienced when an individual is being underrewarded (that is, when inputs are greater than outcomes). [3]

influence-power continuum The view that managerial decision-making behaviors, reflecting the degree of influence and power exercised by the manager, vary with the situation. [10]

informal group A group that emerges in an organization to serve the personal goals of the members. [7]

in-group relationship A vertical dyad in which the behaviors exhibited by the leader and the subordinate depend on the interpersonal exchange between them, rather than on the use of formal authority. Compare **out-group relationships.** [10]

initiating structure The degree of focus on organizational performance goals and initiative in arranging and striving for their achievement that is one of the two independent measures of leadership developed by Ralph Stogdill and others. See also **consideration.** [9]

instrumentality The perceived probability that a first-level performance outcome (such as pay) will lead to a second-level outcome (such as a more affluent life style). [3]

integrity tests See **honesty tests; self-reports.** [18]

intelligence A capacity or readiness for learning; an ability to learn and reason. [2]

interactional view A theoretical perspective holding that behavior results from a continuous process of interaction or feedback between an individual and the situation. Compare **situationist view; trait position.** [6]

interactive game A business game where decisions made by one team of players affect the results obtained by other teams, in that constant mathematical probabilities have been built into the game as concomitants of particular types of decisions. [19]

interest measures A type of test in which the items typically deal with what individuals like to do or with reports on their own behavior which reveal interests. [18]

internal attribution According to attribution theory, superiors' perception of a subordinate's poor performance as caused by some flaw within the subordinate, such as lack of ability or lack of effort. Compare **external attribution.** [10]

interrater reliability An approach to reliability measurement, frequently used with rating procedures, where independent evaluations of each individual are obtained from two or more sources; these ratings are then correlated across a sample of employees to obtain a reliability coefficient. See **reliability.** [16]

intrinsic outcomes Rewards that come from within a person, such as feelings of accomplishment, of doing important work, of freedom. Compare **extrinsic outcomes.** [3]

job Normally made up of a number of similar positions in a given company; however, a job may involve only one such position at a given time. See **position.** [13]

job analysis A statement of performance expectations for employees below and occasionally at the managerial level. [13]

job attitudes Defined by Craig C. Pinder as the internal feelings people have when they think about their jobs, with different aspects of the job inevitably generating different sorts of feelings. [5]

job characteristics theory   An approach to job enrichment proposed by Richard Hackman and Greg Oldham which focuses on the characteristics of a job-skill variety, task identity, task significance, autonomy, and feedback from the job. See **orthodox job enrichment.** [4]

job classification   A method of job evaluation in which grades are established first and then jobs are fitted into the appropriate classes, using preestablished grade descriptions or grading rules. See **job evaluation.** [13]

job description   A written statement of the tasks, duties, and behaviors required in a given job, plus the personal qualifications that all candidates for the job must possess. See **job; job specification.** [13]

job enrichment   See **orthodox job enrichment.**

job evaluation   An analysis that makes possible a classification of jobs so that an equitable internal wage structure can be established. [4, 13]

job family   A collection of two or more jobs that either require similar worker characteristics or contain parallel tasks, as determined by the job analysis. See **job; job analysis.** [13]

job instruction training (JIT)   A program of job training developed by the War Manpower Commission's Training Within Industry Division during World War II which was highly successful in training inexperienced trainers; became the basis of many industrial on-the-job training programs. [1]

job ranking   A method of job evaluation in which various jobs are arranged in order of merit, according to their worth as a whole. See **job evaluation.** [13]

job satisfaction   Broadly, the equivalent of **job attitudes.** [5]

job specification   The part of the job description containing information on the personal characteristics that are believed necessary for the performance of the job. See **job description.** [13]

knowledge of results   The process of feeding back information on the effectiveness of responses so that people have a clear picture of how well they are doing. [2]

laboratory research   Research conducted not in the field with people working at the job which is under study, but in a more isolated setting which simulates the phenomenon being studied and simplifies it as well; the goal is to eliminate confounding factors so that it is relatively easy to determine what is causing what. [1]

laboratory training   An approach to enhancing work-group effectiveness through a program of lectures, experiential exercises, and, especially, T-groups. See **T-group.** [7]

law of effect   The principle, formulated by Edward Thorndike, that behavior that is viewed as leading to reward or that satisfies a need tends to be learned and repeated, and behavior that appears not to produce a reward or that leads to punishment tends not to be repeated. [2]

leader match   A self-taught method whereby a leader can engineer a situation so that it meshes with his or her leadership style, which contingency theory views as not easily changed. See **contingency theory.** [11]

leader–member relations   In contingency theory, a factor used, along with task structure and position power, to classify situations according to whether a high-LPC or low-LPC leadership style is more desirable. See **contingency theory; least preferred coworker.** [9]

leadership   Broadly defined in *Bass and Stogdill's Handbook of Leadership* as an interaction in which "one group member modifies the motivation or competencies of others in the group." [9]

learning   Defined by Alan W. Salmoni, Richard A. Schmidt, and Charles B. Walter as "a relatively permanent change, resulting from practice or experience, in the capability for responding." [2]

least preferred coworker (LPC)   A characteristic of leaders, used in contingency theory as a measure of their leadership style, which is seen as influencing their effectiveness in various circumstances; high-LPC leaders tend to be employee-oriented, while low-LPC leaders are much more performance-oriented. See **contingency theory.** [9]

legislative enactments   Laws passed by legislative bodies. For industrial-organizational psychology those in the area of fair employment practices such as Title VII of the Civil Rights Act are particularly important. See **Title VII.** [12]

leniency errors   Errors in ratings introduced by virtue of the fact that managers tend to use different standards, the tendency to rate all individuals at a high level. See **severity errors.** [15]

linking pins   Employee-centered leaders who serve to tie together the organizational groups to which they are superior and subordinate. [9]

locus of control   The degree to which an individual believes that his or her internal traits determine what happens in a given situation ("internal locus of control") or that he or she is at the mercy of chance, fate, other people, and outside events ("external locus of control"). [6]

male-female differences   Group differences between males and females in aspects of mental ability and personality. See **group differences.** [12]

management by objectives (MBO)   A motivational technique that involves a programmatic use of goal setting throughout an organization or major segments of it;

MBO is frequently tied in with decentralization of decision making, in which case individuals tend to have considerable discretion in setting their own goals. [4, 11, 14]

management inventory A projection, based on a composite analysis of data derived from the management appraisal process, indicating future replacement needs and listing the candidates who may qualify for anticipated vacancies, immediately, or after further development. See **performance appraisal.** [14]

management team A group consisting of a manager above the first level and that manager's immediate subordinates, who are also managers. [7]

managerial grid An approach devised by Robert Blake and Jane Mouton whereby a person's degree of concern for people and degree of concern for production are combined to yield his or her leadership style. [9, 11]

managerial role-motivation theory See **hierarchic role-motivation theory.**

matrix structure An integrating structure in which managers' responsibilities overlap along certain dimensions—such as product lines, geographic areas, and functional areas—so that complex, interdependent tasks requiring the processing of a large amount of information may be carried out under conditions of environmental uncertainty. [7]

maximizing An approach to decision making that involves maximizing the chances of achieving the desired objectives by considering all possible courses of action, explaining all conceivable consequences of taking these actions, and then making a choice. Compare **incrementalizing; satisficing.** [2]

maximum performance An approach to measuring the quality and quantity of a person's work which focuses on what is produced when the individual is measured after being stimulated to do the best job possible over a relatively brief time span, rather than being based on typical performance. See **objective measures.** [14]

measures of general intelligence A designation given either to a verbal ability test, a verbal and numerical test, or a comprehensive measure derived from a multi-ability test; the common bond appears to be a strong emphasis on material normally learned in school. [18]

membership groups Groups to which people actually belong. Compare **reference groups.** [7]

mentoring A dyadic relationship in which an experienced older individual coaches, guides, and helps a protégé in the same type of work. [10]

mixed standard approach A behavior list rating method in which sets of behavioral statements representing a scale of favorableness are developed in groups of three; these individual behavior statements are then scrambled across a number of sets so that the nature of the scales is not apparent. See **behavior lists.** [15]

moderator variables Characteristics used to divide a sample of employees into two or more groups so that predictor-criterion correlations may be calculated in each group separately. See **criterion.** [16]

motivating potential In Hackman-Oldham's approach to job enrichment, the aspect of a job that stems from five core job characteristics—skill variety, task identity, task significance, autonomy, and feedback from job—and that, in turn, results in internal work motivation, satisfaction of the need for growth, and overall job satisfaction. [4]

motivation-hygiene theory Frederick Herzberg's view (also known as "two-factor theory") that job satisfaction results from the presence of intrinsic motivators and that job dissatisfaction stems from contextual hygienes. See **hygienes; motivators.** [4]

motivators In Frederick Herzberg's formulation, the five intrinsic aspects of work whose presence enhances job satisfaction; they are: achievement, verbal recognition, the challenge of the work itself, responsibility, and opportunity for advancement. See **motivation-hygiene theory.** [4]

multiple management A training procedure developed by McCormick and Company that involves establishing a junior board of directors made up of members of middle management. [19]

near accidents Situations where the sequence from a social environment or background, to a defect or fault of the person, to an unsafe act or conditions, to an accident, and finally to an injury does not run its full course. See **unsafe act; unsafe personal factor.** [20]

need-hierarchy theory Abraham Maslow's view that human needs can be ranked in order of importance; lower-level (physiological) needs must be satisfied before higher-level (psychological) needs can operate as motivators for human behavior. [3]

nominal groups Collections of individuals, each of whom independently develops a solution to a common problem; a hierarchic superior or other designated individual decides which of the proposed solutions will be implemented. [8]

nondirective approach An interviewing procedure which permits the person being interviewed considerable leeway in determining the topics to be covered, and in which the basic role of the interviewer is to reflect the feelings of the other person and to restate or repeat key words or phrases. [17]

nondirective counseling A counseling approach where employees are encouraged to express their feelings to gain an understanding of themselves and eventually to solve their own problems. See **nondirective approach.** [20]

normal distribution A frequency distribution with a bell-shaped form and very few cases at both extremes which has been found with high frequency for characteristics studied in industrial-organizational psychology. [12]

objective measures   Methods of performance appraisal that derive directly from the measurable actions of an individual or group rather than from subjective judgments about job behavior. [14]

occupation   A number of similar jobs existing in different companies and at different times. See **job**. [13]

operant learning   B. F. Skinner's key concept that certain initially randomly produced behaviors are strengthened through reinforcement and thus come to occur more frequently. [4]

organizational behavior   The study of what people do in and in relation to organizations; the field that explores the factors within an organization that influence individual behavior, and how individual behavior in turn affects the organization. [1]

organizational behavior modification   A series of steps by which learning interventions are used to bring about changes in significant performance-related behaviors within an organization. [4]

organizational ethics   The rules of conduct and moral principles manifested by an organization. [5]

organizational science   A discipline whose subject matter is the study of organizations and their functioning, and what individuals do in and in relation to organizations. [1]

organization development (OD)   A process of data collection, diagnosis, action planning, intervention and change, and evaluation of results initiated and directed by top management and applied to a whole organization or a large component of it in order to increase the degree of integration, to develop new and creative organizational solutions, and to develop the organization's capacity to cope with environmental forces. [11]

orthodox job enrichment   An approach to work redesign devised by Frederick Herzberg; the theory's basic premise is that job satisfaction increases when certain motivators, called generators—the work itself, responsibility, and opportunity for advancement—are enhanced and when vertical loading is introduced. See **motivators; vertical loading.** [4, 11]

out-group relationship   A vertical dyad in which the leader and the subordinate behave according to the terms of a formal commitment, with the subordinate accepting the leader's legitimate authority in exchange for pay and benefits. Compare **in-group relationship.** [10]

paired comparisons   A method of employee comparison that produces a ranking as a final result but requires only that the superiority of one individual over another be established; from a series of comparisons of pairs a rank ordering may be constructed. See **employee comparison; ranking.** [15]

parallel-form approach   A method of establishing reliability using two different measures which meet statistical requirements for being indexes of the same construct; because the measures are actually different, memory effects cannot contaminate the results. See **reliability.** [16]

partial reinforcement   A behavior-modification approach to learning in which reinforcers are given after only some, not all, of the subject's manifestations of the desired behavior. [4]

participative leadership   An approach to leadership in which leaders are urged to share decisions and power with other members of their immediate group. [9]

part-time groups   Groups, such as committees and boards, whose members usually devote most of their time to their positions in other groups. [7]

past behavior   One of two broad categories used to distinguish within the overall framework of selection decision making; this one relies heavily on the assumption that a candidate's past behavior can serve as a guide for predicting the future. See **present behavior.** [17]

paternalism   When organizations are involved, a tendency for the organization to act like a father. In Japan this has meant that life off the job and the world of work are closely melded so that the authority of the organization extends far beyond that in the United States. [12]

path-goal instrumentality   In path-goal theory, a supervisor's use of behaviors such as consideration and initiating structure to influence subordinate's performance and satisfaction by helping them perceive that rewards and punishments derive directly from their own specific behaviors. See **path-goal theory.** [10]

path-goal theory   The concept, formulated by Martin Evans and Robert House, that leader behavior affects subordinate's perceptions of their own behavior and its consequences, inducing them to ask whether a given behavior (a path) will help or hinder them in attaining something that they desire (a goal). [10]

performance analysis   The process of identifying contributory causes, of diagnosing the factors that have combined to produce a given instance of performance failure. See **performance control.** [20]

performance appraisal   The process of measuring and evaluating the behavior of groups and individuals within organizations to assess how well their behavior matches the expectations set up by division of labor. [14]

performance control   An approach to elevating job performance levels that involves measuring performance against standards of acceptable behavior relative to role requirements, diagnosing the causes of unacceptable deviations from these standards, and taking appropriate corrective action. [20]

performance standard An objective measure that represents the minimum acceptable level of performance in a particular type of work. [14]

performance-to-outcome expectancy The assessed probability that should effort be successfully exerted, something that is desired will result, such as a financial reward. Compare **effort-to-performance expectancy.** [3]

personality A relatively stable set of characteristics that serve to determine how a particular individual behaves in various situations. [6]

personality disorders Emotional disorders of a milder nature than psychoses which may nevertheless yield symptoms which have a detrimental effect on work performance. See **psychoses.** [20]

personality traits Relatively stable individual characteristics, closely related to internal emotional states. [6]

point system A method of job evaluation which extends job classification to include a variety of factors as a basis for classification rather than a single dimension. See **job classification; job evaluation.** [13]

position A specific set of tasks and duties performed by a given individual in a given firm at a given time. [13]

Position Analysis Questionnaire An approach to developing job groupings created by Ernest McCormick which utilizes a questionnaire containing 187 job elements presented in checklist form that incumbents or other knowledgeable individuals evaluate relative to a given job. See **job families.** [13]

position power In contingency theory, a factor used, along with leader–member relations and task structure, to classify situations according to whether a high-LPC or low-LPC leadership style is more desirable. See **contingency theory; least preferred coworker.** [9]

positive-findings bias The unconscious tendency of researchers to conclude that their results support the position toward which they are favorably disposed. [11]

positive reinforcement A contingency of reinforcement that involves providing some reward contingent upon the subject's manifestation of the desired behavior. [4]

potential ratings Performance evaluations made of an individual's promotability or potential for advancement, usually based on the pattern of accomplishment in prior positions. See **career appraisal index.** [14]

predictive validity Validation achieved using the longitudinal prediction model, where a selection instrument such as a test is administered at one point in time and then related to a criterion measure obtained at a later date. See **criterion; validation.** [16]

prepotent Referring to the prevalence of physiological needs over all other human needs as motivators in Abraham Maslow's need-hierarchy theory. [3]

present behavior One of two broad categories used to distinguish within the overall framework of selection

decision making; this one relies heavily on the sampling of present behavior as a basis for prediction. See **past behavior.** [17]

pretest sensitizing effect This occurs when participants in training learn certain things only because they get the impression from a pretest that they should learn these particular things; the posttest then reveals a change, which would only be expected to occur when the pretest is present. See **before-after model.** [19]

principle of supportive relationships The essential proposition of Rensis Likert's System 4 theory; namely, that to be productive an organization must ensure that its leadership and other group processes maximize the probability that each member will view all interactions and relationships with the organization as supportive of his or her sense of personal worth. [9]

productivity measurement A procedure derived from economics which involves calculating a ratio of outputs to inputs and translating this into monetary terms; ratios may be compared over a period of time, or units within a company may be compared, or data may be compared between different companies, or throughout a whole industry. [14]

professional role-motivation theory John B. Miner's view that certain strong motives contribute to success in specific professional roles. [3]

programmable decision A type of decision for which a definite pattern exists and where the task is to find the right answer rather than the best possible one. [8]

programmed instruction An individualized training procedure that utilizes materials organized into a series of frames, usually of increasing difficulty, with each successive frame building on those that precede; feedback is provided on the correctness of answers to yield reinforcement. See **reinforcing.** [19]

projective techniques Methods of determining characteristics in which individuals are presented with some stimulus, in picture or word form, and are asked to react to it, thereby unconsciously projecting aspects of themselves. [18]

psychological appraisals A method of performance appraisal, involving extensive interviewing coupled with individual psychological testing, in which the psychologist attempts to get as clear an understanding as possible of the underlying intellectual, emotional, and motivational characteristics of an individual and then to convert this into a picture of how such a person might be expected to behave. See **performance appraisal.** [14]

psychomotor measures These include coordination and dexterity tests in the areas of finger and tweezer dexterity; in addition, there are a number of special coordination measures and apparatus tests that tap muscular skills of a grosser nature. [18]

psychoses Emotional disorders where the symptoms

take on an inflexible character and serve to disrupt many of the ongoing processes of life; a break with reality occurs. [20]

punishment A contingency of reinforcement that involves providing negative consequences upon the subject's manifestation of an undesired behavior, with the intent of decreasing the frequency of the behavior. [4]

quality circle Defined by Paul J. Wolff as "a voluntary employee group meeting regularly during working hours with the goal of identifying and solving task-related problems"; the group formally presents its solutions to management, which accepts, rejects, or modifies them. [8, 11]

quality of work life Defined by David A. Nadler and Edward E. Lawler as "a way of thinking about people, work, and organizations," the distinctive elements of which are "(1) a concern about the impact of work on people as well as on organizational effectiveness, and (2) the idea of participation in organizational problem solving and decision making." [11]

quantum change In organization development, the making of numerous changes all at once and within a short time. Compare **incremental change.** [11]

range restriction errors Errors in ratings in which all subordinates are rated in a narrow range; these errors may involve clustering around any point on a scale. See **leniency errors; error of central tendency.** [15]

ranking An employee comparison method of evaluation in which the manager merely orders subordinates on as many dimensions, or characteristics, as required; each dimension is treated separately. See **employee comparison.** [15]

rated ranking An evaluation method that first obtains rankings within each employee group from supervisors and then uses ratings which must follow the earlier rankings; thus ranks are converted to rating values for purposes of combining groups. See **ranking.** [15]

rating scales A rating method that may take numerous forms but with the essential characteristic that a check be placed along a scale of value. [15]

realistic job previews A procedure which makes information regarding a job available to applicants through booklets, films, or job visits so that they can make self-selection decisions on a realistic basis. [16]

recency errors The tendency in ratings to base the evaluations on what is most easily remembered, that is the most recent behavior, rather than the average or typical behavior for the rating period. [15]

reference group The people against whom a person weighs his or her attitudes and behavior; may or may not also be a membership group. In equity theory, the people—coworkers, relatives, or fellow professionals, for example—against whom an individual measures the

rewards he or she is receiving in exchange for his or her inputs. Compare **membership group.** [3, 7]

references A method of obtaining information on an applicant's past behavior which utilizes not the individuals themselves, but those who have associated with and been in a position to observe them; often these are individuals named by the applicant. See **past behavior.** [17]

regression weights Statistical values resulting from multiple correlation analysis which are multiplied times an individual's scores on various measures and then combined to produce an estimate of the chances for success. [16]

reinforcing A term describing any action that increases the likelihood of a particular behavior. [2]

reliability An index of the extent to which if one makes the same measurement twice, the same result will be obtained both times. [16]

resistance indexes Objective measures of performance which reflect a tendency for the subordinates of a given manager to either covertly or overtly resist that manager; examples are disciplinary actions and grievances. See **objective measures; withdrawal indexes.** [14]

resistance to change An impediment to organization development that some theorists regard as irrational and invariably arising from rigid, authoritarian, and insecure personality patterns, but that other theorists view as a reasonable response to ill-advised or destabilizing change. [11]

risky shift Group polarization toward the risk-taking extreme of an issue. See **group polarization.** [8]

role ambiguity A situation in which an individual does not know exactly how he or she is expected to behave because the expectations are set forth vaguely and abstractly. [6]

role conflict A situation in which an individual does not know how he or she should behave because the expectations of two or more other people differ. [6]

role playing A type of case study in which actual individuals play the various roles of the persons in the case; the fact that participants behave in roles tends to create a more realistic learning situation. [19]

romanticizing leadership (romantic bias) The phenomenon whereby perception of a leader's achievement is distorted so that much of what is attributed to that leader is not his or her doing at all. [10]

rotating shifts Work schedules in which employees change from one shift to another at intervals that are usually rather short, which tends to be very stressful. [6]

safety climate The degree to which there is a strong managerial commitment to safety in a firm including establishing safety-training programs, giving safety officials high status, participation of top executives in safety committees, and designing jobs with safety in mind. [20]

safety management The overall process of dealing with accidents and safety in an organization, which may include safety psychology and which often includes an extensive committee structure. [20]

safety psychology A field of industrial-organizational psychology concerned primarily with prevention, which is devoted to heading off accidents based on an understanding of why and how they occur. See **industrial-organizational psychology.** [20]

satisficing An approach to decision making that involves choosing a course of action that will result in reaching a desired goal without exploring all possibilities. Compare **maximizing; satisficing.** [2]

scaled expectation method A rating method in which managers with knowledge of the job define dimensions of the work, provide critical incidents, assign incidents to dimensions, scale incidents as to their effectiveness, and thus produce a series of rating scales anchored by behaviorally specific incidents. See **behaviorally specific; critical incident procedure.** [15]

Scanlon plan An approach to organization development formulated by Joseph Scanlon that uses bonus systems, participation structures, and communication systems to get employees involved in determining methods of reducing costs and increasing productivity. [11]

scientific validity An indication of whether good theory, and thus improved understanding and prediction, have been obtained; the key is the extent to which research tests have been carried out and have supported a theory. See **theory.** [1]

self-efficacy A person's self-perception of how well he or she can cope with situations as they arise. [6]

self-esteem A person's perception of his or her competence, self-image, and success expectancy. [6]

self-evaluations A method of performance appraisal in which individuals either formally or informally evaluate their own performance. See **performance appraisal.** [14]

self-fulfilling prophecy In interviewing, a situation where pre-interview expectations, often generated by personal history data, serve to determine what happens in the interview. [17]

self-management The tendency of people to manage their own organizational behavior so that less managerial control and influence are needed. [4]

self-reports Personality tests that ask respondents to describe themselves in some way; these reports are either taken at face value or related to some group with known characteristics to obtain a score. See **projective techniques.** [18]

severity errors Errors in ratings introduced by virtue of the fact that managers tend to use different standards; the tendency to rate all individuals at a low level. See **leniency errors.** [15]

sick organizations Organizations in which management generates stressors—especially work overload, role ambiguity, and role conflict—that cause outbreaks of physical symptoms among workers. [6]

similar-to-me errors The tendency for raters to give more positive ratings to individuals who are more like themselves, perhaps to enhance their own status. [15]

single loop learning A learning or decision-making process in which the individual examines only actions and their consequences, accepting the governing variables of prevailing assumptions and the status quo as given. Compare **double loop learning.** [2]

situational-leadership theory An approach to leadership style devised by Paul Hersey and Kenneth Blanchard in which the appropriateness of the leader's behavior—some combination of task behavior and relationship behavior—depends on the situation created by the task-relevant maturity of subordinates. [9]

situationist view A theoretical perspective holding that behavior is entirely a function of the situation—that all people will behave in the same way in situations they perceive to be the same. Compare **interactional view; trait position.** [6]

skill obsolescence Defined by John Fossum, Richard Arvey, Carol Paradise and Nancy Robbins as the process which occurs when the personal requirements of a job which are demanded by its tasks, duties, and responsibilities become incongruent with the stock of knowledge, skills, and abilities currently possessed by the individual. [12]

social facilitation The phenomenon whereby output tends to improve when individuals work in the presence of others. [7]

social learning theory The view that much learning occurs through modeling one's behavior on the actions of others. [4]

social loafing The tendency of certain people to obtain benefits from group membership while not sharing proportionately in the cost of those benefits. [7]

social support Encouragement and understanding from an individual's family, coworkers, superiors, and other people that can minimize or buffer stress. [6]

sociotechnical systems A theory of organizational design and organization development that regards autonomous work groups, management, technology, and the organization's environment as interacting parts of a single system. [11]

span of control The number of people reporting to managers at various levels. [20]

Spearman-Brown prophecy formula A statistical formula, applied when split-half reliability is considered, to correct the reliability coefficient for the fact that it has been calculated using measures only half as long as the one to be used in practice. See **split-half reliability.** [16]

split-half reliability A method of establishing reliability by splitting up an existing measure into two equal parts—perhaps odd and even numbered items—and then correlating the scores on these parts to obtain an estimate of reliability. See **reliability.** [16]

stress Defined by John M. Ivancevich and Michael T. Matteson as "an adaptive response, mediated by individual characteristics and/or psychological processes, that is a consequence of any external action, situation, or event that places special physical and/or psychological demands upon a person." [6]

stress approach An interviewing procedure which usually involves the induction of failure stress; the interviewer rather suddenly becomes quite aggressive, belittles the candidate, and throws him or her on the defensive; reactions are then observed. [17]

stress-management program A program, usually conducted by one of the larger firms, designed to reduce the stress reactions of individuals; programs often include muscle relaxation techniques, recognition of anxiety cues and training in how to deal with them, feedback of physiological measurements in order to control them, meditation, and time management. See **stress.** [6]

structured interview techniques Methods of interviewing where interviewers are trained to follow similar patterns in their questioning and to evaluate responses using the same standards; the questions asked are standardized and responses are recorded in some systematic manner. [17]

substitutes for leadership Characteristics—task, organizational, or subordinate—that make leadership both impossible and unnecessary; often applied as a general label to include leadership neutralizers which make it impossible for leadership to make a difference. See **leadership.** [9]

survey feedback An approach to organization development in which survey questionnaires and feedback sessions with organization members are used in initiating and evaluating changes intended to move the organization closer to System 4 functioning. See **System 4 theory.** [11]

System 4T Rensis Likert's expansion of his System 4 theory, adding other factors, beyond participative leadership, that contribute to an effective organization, such as the levels of performance goals desired and transmitted by leaders, and the leader's level of knowledge and skill. [9, 11]

System 4 theory Rensis Likert's formulation that there are four primary systems of organization, or leadership style, with Systems 1, 2, and 3 moving progressively closer to the ideal, participative-group System 4. [9, 11]

system (subsystem) training A method of training groups of individuals whose work tasks interact and where complex person-machine interactions tend to be involved. [19]

tailored testing A process in which examinees interact with a computer to answer a series of items, each prompted by the correctness or incorrectness of answers to previous items; as the series of items progresses, the estimate of ability becomes increasingly precise. See **testing.** [18]

task A distinct work activity carried out for a specific purpose. See **position.** [13]

task inventories A method of obtaining job information from occupants by having them complete questionnaires dealing with the tasks performed, the conditions of work, and the materials and equipment employed. [13]

task role-motivation theory John B. Miner's view that certain strong motives contribute to success in specific task-related roles. [3]

task structure In contingency theory, a factor used, along with leader–member relations and position power, to classify situations according to whether a high-LPC or low-LPC leadership style is more desirable. See **contingency theory; least preferred coworker.** [9]

team building A procedure, usually led by a trainer-facilitator, in which members of a work group learn to manage their problems and accomplish their goals, focusing on the actual tasks of the group and often using T-group procedures. See **T-group.** [7, 11]

TELOS training A program devised by Victor H. Vroom to help managers learn to use the Vroom and Yetton decision-making process. See **decision tree.** [10]

temporary groups Groups, such as project teams and task forces, that are formed for a finite, usually predetermined, period and are disbanded once their mission is accomplished. [7]

testimonials Subjective statements of approval and recommendation of a decision or course of action. [8]

testing A procedure which attempts to develop an estimate of future effectiveness from an analysis of present functioning in a particular sphere. See **present behavior.** [18]

test-retest approach A method of establishing reliability which requires a second measurement at some time subsequent to the first and then correlation of the scores obtained in the two time periods. See **reliability.** [16]

T-group A "training group" in which work-group members learn about group processes, interpersonal relations, and group processes, interpersonal relations, and group development in informal sessions, for the purpose of enhancing the group's effectiveness. [7, 11]

Thematic Apperception Test (TAT)   A projective test in which subjects tell stories in response to pictures selected to elicit the particular achievement, power, or affiliation motive being studied, and the stories are then analyzed. [3]

theory   A generalization that specifies relationships between factors; an attempt to make sense out of empirical observations that do not contain any inherent and obvious logic. [1]

Theory X   Douglas McGregor's term for a set of assumptions made by managers about their subordinates—essentially, that work-group members dislike responsibility and would be indifferent or even resistant to organizational needs without management's active intervention in motivating them and directing their efforts. Compare **Theory Y**. [9]

Theory Y   Douglas McGregor's term for a set of assumptions made by managers about their subordinates—essentially, that work-group members have a capacity for responsibility and a readiness to support organizational goals; and management's job is to arrange conditions and operations so that people can achieve their own goals best by directing their efforts toward organizational goals. Compare **Theory X**. [9]

Title VII (Civil Rights Act)   The portion of the federal Civil Rights Act that deals with discrimination in employment. Used to argue that discrimination is involved in comparable worth cases. See **comparable worth controversy**. [12, 13]

trade tests   A test of job knowledge for skilled occupations administered orally which serves to discriminate among journeymen, apprentices, and helpers in a trade. See **achievement tests**. [18]

trainability tests   Testing approaches that have been developed that include an opportunity to demonstrate one's ability to learn certain parts of a job; thus, evaluation follows a brief learning experience. See **work sample tests**. [18]

training   An approach to human change and learning that is role-specific and attempts to help those who are or will be performing a certain job to achieve successful role behavior. See **education**. [19]

training needs   Needs identified by virtue of the fact that problems exist in the level or type of performance *and* these problems can be corrected through training. See **training**. [19]

trait position   A theoretical perspective holding that a person has built-in predispositions which, because of their rigid, compulsive nature, result in the same kind of action, regardless of the situation. Compare **interactional view; situationist view**. [6]

trait rating   Rating scales used to gauge whether individuals possess certain traits assumed to help them work effectively such as industriousness, trustworthiness, cooperativeness, leadership ability, decisiveness, and the like. See **rating scales**. [15]

transactional leaders   Leaders who recognize what followers want to get from their work and try to see that they get what they want if their performance warrants it. [10]

transfer of training   The ability to apply what is learned in a training context to the actual work situation. [2]

transformational leaders   Leaders who motivate their followers to do more than they originally expected to do. [10]

Type A personality   A behavior pattern marked by extreme aggressiveness, hostility, time urgency, and competitive achievement striving; people with this behavior pattern tend to react to stress by developing problems and diseases of the heart. Compare **Type B personality**. [6]

Type B personality   A behavior pattern *not* marked by pressing conflict with other people or with time; people with this behavior pattern are not prone to coronary problems. Compare **Type A personality**. [6]

union commitment   A type of attitudinal commitment that is directed to a union rather than the employing organization. See **attitudinal commitment**. [5]

unsafe act   A term often included in an accident report form which refers to the type of behavior leading to the accident. [20]

unsafe mechanical or physical condition of the agency   A term often included in an accident report form which refers to the aspect of the agency that could have been guarded or corrected. See **agency**. [20]

unsafe personal factor   A term often included in an accident report form which refers to the characteristic of the individual responsible for the unsafe act. See **unsafe act**. [20]

usefulness in application   An indication of whether a theory has contributed applications that can be put to use in practice to achieve stated goals; the key here is whether applications have been subjected to research evaluation and shown to work. See **theory**. [1]

utility   An index of value defined in terms of the benefits that accrue from a given set of decisions, less the total costs incurred in the decision-making process. [16]

valence   The motivational value or attractiveness of an outcome. [3]

validation   The process of verifying that a test is actually measuring what it is supposed to measure. [6]

validity generalization   A statistical procedure that may be applied to a number of validity studies to say whether a real relationship exists between a predictor and criteria, and thus whether generalization to unstudied contexts is warranted. See **criterion; validation.** [16]

value judgment An interplay between cognitive and emotional elements of an individual's value system. [5]

values The explicit or implicit conceptions of the desirable that are held by an individual or a group and that influence selections from available modes, means, and ends of action. [5]

variable interval reinforcement A schedule of partial reinforcement in which reinforcement occurs after a desired behavior at some varying interval of time, but with the intervals distributed around a preestablished average. Compare **fixed interval reinforcement.** [4]

variable ratio reinforcement A schedule of partial reinforcement in which reinforcement occurs only after some set number of desired behaviors, with this number changing continually but varying around a preestablished average. Compare **fixed ratio reinforcement.** [4]

vertical dyad A pair consisting of a leader and a single subordinate. [10]

vertical loading An aspect of orthodox job enrichment that involves a qualitative, not merely quantitative, change in the work; may be achieved by such measures as introducing more difficult tasks and granting additional authority. [4]

vestibule school A training approach where trainees use equipment and procedures similar to those that would be used in on-the-job training, but the equipment is set up in an area separate from the regular workplace. [19]

wage survey Research that provides companies with information about wage levels in the various labor markets in which they compete for employees. [4]

withdrawal indexes Objective measures of performance which reflect a tendency for the subordinates of a given manager to avoid or escape from what they experience as unpleasant; examples are absenteeism and separations. See **objective measures; resistance indexes.** [14]

work ethic A value that defines work as important, virtuous, a source of dignity, and so inherently good that people should work even if their financial situation does not require it. [5]

work redesign A motivational technique that involves rewriting job descriptions and changing the nature of the work so as to engage higher levels of motivation. [4, 11]

work sample tests Measures developed by sampling from the work actually performed on a job, as with the various typing and stenographic tests. [18]

References

CHAPTER 1

Campbell, John P., Daft, Richard, & Hulin, Charles L. (1982). *What to study: Generating and developing research questions.* Beverly Hills, CA: Sage.

Cass, Eugene L., & Zimmer, Frederick G. (1975). *Man and work in society.* New York: Van Nostrand Reinhold.

Cederblom, Douglas, Pence, Earl C., & Johnson, Daniel L. (1984). Making I/O psychology useful: The human resource administrator's view. *The Industrial-Organizational Psychologist, 21*(3), 9–17.

Dansereau, Fred, Alutto, Joseph A., & Yammarino, Francis J. (1984). *Theory testing in organizational behavior: The varient approach.* Englewood Cliffs, NJ: Prentice-Hall.

Franke, Richard H., & Kaul, J. D. (1978). The Hawthorne experiments: First statistical interpretations. *American Sociological Review, 43,* 623–643.

Hakel, Milton D. (1988). Introducing the American Psychological Society. *The Industrial-Organizational Psychologist, 26*(1), 22–24.

Hakel, Milton D., Sorcher, Melvin, Beer, Michael, & Moses, Joseph L. (1982). *Making it happen: Designing research with implementation in mind.* Beverly Hills, CA: Sage.

Hall, Douglas T. (1986). *Career development in organizations.* San Francisco: Jossey-Bass.

Hinrichs, John R. (1984). I/O careers in consulting. *The Industrial-Organizational Psychologist, 21*(4), 17–23.

Howard, Ann (1984). I/O careers in industry. *The Industrial-Organizational Psychologist, 21*(4), 46–54.

Howard, Ann (1986). Characteristics of society members. *The Industrial-Organizational Psychologist, 23*(3), 41–47.

Howard, Ann (1990). *The multiple facets of industrial-organizational psychology.* Arlington Heights, IL: Society for Industrial and Organizational Psychology.

Howard, Ann, & Lowman, Rodney L. (1982). Licensing and industrial/organizational psychology: A summary of background and issues. *The Industrial-Organizational Psychologist, 19*(3), 10–18.

Howard, Ann, & Lowman, Rodney L. (1985). Should industrial/organizational psychologists be licensed? *American Psychologist, 40,* 40–47.

Kopelman, Richard E. (1986). *Managing productivity in organizations: A practical people-oriented perspective.* New York: McGraw-Hill.

Lindell, Michael K. (1990, 1991). Positions available. *The Industrial-Organizational Psychologist, 28*(2), 106–107; *28*(3), 124–129.

Locke, Edwin A. (1986). *Generalizing from laboratory to field settings.* Lexington, MA: Lexington Books.

Mankin, Don, Ames, Russell E., & Grodsky, Milton A. (1980). *Classics of industrial and organizational psychology.* Oak Park, IL: Moore Publishing.

McCormick, Ernest J., Jeanneret, Paul R., & Mecham, Robert C. (1972). A study of job characteristics and job dimensions as based on the position analysis questionnaire (PAQ). *Journal of Applied Psychology Monograph, 56,* 347–368.

Miner, John B. (1976). Levels of motivation to manage among personnel and industrial relations managers. *Journal of Applied Psychology, 61,* 419–427.

Miner, John B. (1980). *Theories of organizational behavior.* Hinsdale, IL: Dryden.

Miner, John B. (1982). *Theories of organizational structure and process.* Hinsdale, IL: Dryden.

Miner, John B. (1988). *Organizational behavior: Performance and productivity.* New York: Random House.

Münsterberg, Hugo (1913). *Psychology and industrial efficiency.* Boston: Houghton Mifflin.

Nord, Walter R. (1982). Continuity and change in industrial/organizational psychology: Learning from previous mistakes. *Professional Psychology, 13,* 942–952.

Rassenfoss, Sarah E., & Kraut, Allen I. (1988). Survey of personnel research departments. *The Industrial-Organizational Psychologist, 25*(4), 31–37.

Roethlisberger, Fritz J., & Dickson, William J. (1939). *Management and the worker.* Cambridge, MA: Harvard University Press.

Schmitt, Neal, & Howard, Ann (1989). American Psychological Society sets agenda. *The Industrial-Organizational Psychologist, 26*(3), 32–34.

Stagner, Ross (1982). Past and future of industrial/organizational psychology. *Professional Psychology, 13,* 899–902.

Stapp, Joy, Tucker, Anthony M., & Vanden Bos, Gary R.

(1985). Census of psychological personnel: 1983. *American Psychologist, 40,* 1317–1351.

Thayer, Paul W. (1984). I/O careers in academia. *The Industrial-Organizational Psychologist, 21*(4), 12–16.

CHAPTER 2

Argyris, Chris (1982). *Reasoning, learning, and action.* San Francisco: Jossey-Bass.

Argyris, Chris, & Schön, Donald A. (1978). *Organizational learning: A theory of action perspective.* Reading, MA: Addison-Wesley.

Barron, Frank, & Harrington, David M. (1981). Creativity, intelligence, and personality. *Annual Review of Psychology, 32,* 439–476.

Basadur, Min, Graen, George B., & Scandura, Terri A. (1986). Training effects on attitudes toward divergent thinking among manufacturing engineers. *Journal of Applied Psychology, 71,* 612–617.

Blustein, David L. (1987). Decision-making styles and vocational maturity: An alternative perspective. *Journal of Vocational Behavior, 30,* 61–71.

Driver, Michael J. (1988). Careers: A review of personal and organizational research. *International Review of Industrial and Organizational Psychology, 3,* 245–277.

Driver, Michael J., Brousseau, Kenneth R., & Hunsaker, Phillip L. (1990). *The dynamic decisionmaker.* New York: Harper & Row.

Driver, Michael J., & Rowe, Alan J. (1979). Decision-making styles: A new approach to management decision making. In Cary L. Cooper (Ed.), *Behavioral problems in organizations* (pp. 151–152). Englewood Cliffs, NJ: Prentice-Hall.

Fischer, Kurt W., & Silvern, Louise (1985). Stages and individual differences in cognitive development. *Annual Review of Psychology, 36,* 613–648.

Fotheringhame, June (1986). Transfer of training: A field study of some training methods. *Journal of Occupational Psychology, 59,* 59–71.

Gardner, Howard (1983). *Frames of mind: The theory of multiple intelligences.* New York: Basic Books.

Gingrich, Gerry, & Soli, Sigfrid D. (1984). Subjective evaluation and allocation of resources in routine decision making. *Organizational Behavior and Human Performance, 33,* 187–203.

Gordon, Harold W., & Leighty, Robert (1988). Importance of specialized cognitive function in the selection of military pilots. *Journal of Applied Psychology, 73,* 38–45.

Gottfredson, Linda S. (1986). Occupational aptitude pat-
terns map: Development and implications for a theory of job aptitude requirements. *Journal of Vocational Behavior, 29,* 254–291.

Grandori, Anna (1984). A prescriptive contingency view of organizational decision making. *Administrative Science Quarterly, 29,* 192–209.

Guion, Robert M., & Gibson, Wade M. (1988). Personnel selection and placement. *Annual Review of Psychology, 39,* 349–374.

Harrison, E. Frank (1989). *The managerial decision-making process.* Boston: Houghton Mifflin.

House, Robert J., & Singh, Jitendra V. (1987). Organizational behavior: Some new directions for I/O psychology. *Annual Review of Psychology, 38,* 669–718.

Klein, Noreen M. (1983). Utility and decision strategies: A second look at the rational decision maker. *Organizational Behavior and Human Performance, 31,* 1–25.

Latham, Gary P. (1988). Human resource training and development. *Annual Review of Psychology, 39,* 545–582.

Lindblom, Charles E. (1965). *The intelligence of democracy: Decision making through mutual adjustment.* New York: Free Press.

Mabe, Paul A., & West, Stephen G. (1982). Validity of self-evaluation of ability: A review and meta-analysis. *Journal of Applied Psychology, 67,* 280–296.

McCaskey, Michael B. (1982). *The executive challenge: Managing change and ambiguity.* Boston: Pitman.

McGehee, William, & Thayer, Paul W. (1961). *Training in business and industry.* New York: Wiley.

Miner, John B. (1973). *Intelligence in the United States* (pp. 4–5). Westport, CT: Greenwood.

Pintrich, Paul R., Cross, David R., Kozma, Robert B., & McKeachie, Wilbert J. (1986). Instructional psychology. *Annual Review of Psychology, 37,* 611–651.

Reber, Robert A., & Wallin, Jerry A. (1984). The effect of training, goal setting, and knowledge of results on safe behavior: A component analysis. *Academy of Management Journal, 27,* 544–560.

Rowe, Alan J., & Mason, Richard O. (1987). *Managing with style: A guide to understanding, assessing, and improving decision making.* San Francisco: Jossey-Bass.

Salmoni, Alan W., Schmidt, Richard A., & Walter, Charles B. (1984). Knowledge of results and motor learning: A review and critical reappraisal. *Psychological Bulletin, 97,* 355–386.

Schwade, Stephen (1985). Is it time to consider computer-based training? *Personnel Administrator, 30*(2), 25–35.

Steiner, George A., & Miner, John B. (1986). *Management policy and strategy.* New York: Macmillan.

Sternberg, Robert J. (1985). *Beyond IQ*. Cambridge, England: Cambridge University Press.

Taylor, Ronald N. (1984). *Behavioral decision making*. Glenview, IL: Scott, Foresman.

Walter, Gordon A., & Marks, Stephen E. (1981). *Experiential learning and change*. New York: Wiley.

Weitzel, William, Dawis, Rene V., & Mason, Nancy (1981). Competence potential and organizational functioning. In George W. England, Anant R. Negandhi, & Bernhard Wilpert (Eds.), *The functioning of complex organizations* (pp. 1–23). Cambridge, MA: Oelgeschlager, Gunn, and Hain.

Wexley, Kenneth N., & Latham, Gary P. (1981). *Developing and training human resources in organizations*. Glenview, IL: Scott, Foresman.

Wortman, Camille B., & Loftus, Elizabeth F. (1988). *Psychology*. New York: Knopf.

CHAPTER 3

Adams, J. Stacy (1963). Toward an understanding of inequity. *Journal of Abnormal and Social Psychology, 67*, 422–436.

Adams, J. Stacy (1965). Inequity in social exchange. In Leonard Berkowitz (Ed.), *Advances in experimental social psychology*, Vol. 2 (pp. 267–299). New York: Academic Press.

Adams, J. Stacy, & Jacobsen, Patricia R. (1964). Effects of wage inequities on work quality. *Journal of Abnormal and Social Psychology, 69*, 19–25.

Alderfer, Clayton P. (1972). *Existence, relatedness, and growth: Human needs in organizational settings*. New York: Free Press.

Atkinson, John W. (1977). Motivation for achievement. In T. Blass (Ed.), *Personality variables in social behavior* (pp. 25–108). Hillsdale, NJ: Erlbaum Associates.

Atkinson, John W. (1982). Old and new conceptions of how expected consequences influence actions. In Norman T. Feather (Ed.), *Expectations and actions: Expectancy-value models in psychology* (pp. 17–52). Hillsdale, NJ: Erlbaum.

Bartol, Kathryn M., & Martin, David C. (1987). Managerial motivation among MBA students: A longitudinal assessment. *Journal of Occupational Psychology, 60*, 1–12.

Cook, Karen S., & Hegtvedt, Karen A. (1983). Distributive justice, equity, and equality. *Annual Review of Sociology, 9*, 217–241.

Greenberg, Jerald (1988). Equity and workplace status: A field experiment. *Journal of Applied Psychology, 73*, 606–613.

Griffeth, Rodger W., Vecchio, Robert P., & Logan, James W. (1989). Equity theory and interpersonal attraction. *Journal of Applied Psychology, 74*, 394–401.

Hatfield, Elaine, & Sprecher, Susan (1984). Equity theory and behavior in organizations. *Sociology of Organizations, 3*, 95–124.

Huizinga, Gerard (1970). *Maslow's need hierarchy in the work situation*. Groningen, The Netherlands: Wolters, Noordhoff.

Ilgen, Daniel R., & Klein, Howard J. (1988). Individual motivation and performance: Cognitive influences on effort and choice. In John P. Campbell & Richard J. Campbell (Eds.), *Productivity in organizations: New perspectives from industrial and organizational psychology* (pp. 143–176). San Francisco: Jossey-Bass.

Ilgen, Daniel R., & Klein, Howard J. (1989). Organizational behavior. *Annual Review of Psychology, 40*, 327–351.

Ilgen, Daniel R., Nebeker, Delbert M., & Pritchard, Robert D. (1981). Expectancy theory measures: An empirical comparison in an experimental simulation. *Organizational Behavior and Human Performance, 28*, 189–223.

Landy, Frank J., & Becker, Wendy S. (1987). Motivation theory reconsidered. *Research in Organizational Behavior, 9*, 1–38.

Lawler, Edward E. (1981). *Pay and organization development*. Reading, MA: Addison-Wesley.

Maslow, Abraham H. (1943). A theory of human motivation. *Psychological Review, 50*, 370–396.

Maslow, Abraham H. (1954, reprinted 1970). *Motivation and personality*. New York: Harper & Row.

McClelland, David C. (1961). *The achieving society*. Princeton, NJ: Van Nostrand.

McClelland, David C. (1975). *Power: The inner experience*. New York: Irvington.

McClelland, David C., & Burnham, David H. (1976). Power is the great motivator. *Harvard Business Review, 54*(2), 100–110.

Miner, John B. (1965). *Studies in management education*. Buffalo, NY: Organizational Measurement Systems Press.

Miner, John B. (1977). *Motivation to manage: A ten-year update on the "Studies in Management Education" research*. Buffalo, NY: Organizational Measurement Systems Press.

Miner, John B. (1980a). Limited domain theories of organizational energy. In Craig C. Pinder & Larry F. Moore (Eds.), *Middle range theory and the study of organizations* (pp. 273–286). Boston: Martinus Nijhoff.

Miner, John B. (1980b). The role of managerial and professional motivation in the career success of management professors. *Academy of Management Journal, 23*, 487–508.

Miner, John B. (1980c). *Theories of organizational behavior.* Hinsdale, IL: Dryden.

Miner, John B. (1981). Theories of organizational motivation. In George W. England, Anant R. Negandhi, & Bernhard Wilpert (Eds.), *The functioning of complex organizations* (pp. 75–110). Cambridge, MA: Oelgeschlager, Gunn, and Hain.

Miner, John B. (1982). The uncertain future of the leadership concept: Revisions and clarifications. *Journal of Applied Behavioral Science, 18,* 293–307.

Miner, John B., Smith, Norman R., & Bracker, Jeffrey S. (1989). Role of entrepreneurial task motivation in the growth of technologically innovative firms. *Journal of Applied Psychology, 74,* 554–560.

Mitchell, Terence R. (1982a). Expectancy-value models in organizational psychology. In Norman T. Feather (Ed.), *Expectations and actions: Expectancy-value models in psychology* (pp. 293–312). Hillsdale, NJ: Erlbaum.

Mitchell, Terence R. (1982b). Motivation: New directions for theory, research and practice. *Academy of Management Review, 7,* 80–88.

Murray, Henry A. (1938). *Explorations in personality.* New York: Oxford University Press.

Naylor, James C., Pritchard, Robert D., & Ilgen, Daniel R. (1980). *A theory of behavior in organizations.* New York: Academic Press.

Oliver, John E. (1982). An instrument for classifying organizations. *Academy of Management Journal, 25,* 855–866.

Pinder, Craig C. (1984). *Work motivation: Theory, issues, and application.* Glenview, IL: Scott, Foresman.

Porter, Lyman W., & Lawler, Edward E. (1968). *Managerial attitudes and performance.* Homewood, IL: Irwin.

Rauschenberger, John, Schmitt, Neal, & Hunter, John E. (1980). A test of the need hierarchy concept by a Markov model of change in need strength. *Administrative Science Quarterly, 25,* 654–670.

Remick, Helen (1981). The comparable worth controversy. *Public Personnel Management, 10,* 377–380.

Scholl, Richard W., Cooper, Elizabeth A., & McKenna, Jack F. (1987). Referent selection in determining equity perceptions: Differential effects on behavioral and attitudinal outcomes. *Personnel Psychology, 40,* 113–124.

Stahl, Michael J. (1986). *Managerial and technical motivation: Assessing needs for achievement, power and affiliation.* New York: Praeger.

Steers, Richard M., & Porter, Lyman W. (1987). *Motivation and work behavior.* New York: McGraw-Hill.

Vecchio, Robert P. (1981). An individual-differences interpretation of the conflicting predictions generated by equity theory and expectancy theory. *Journal of Applied Psychology, 66,* 470–481.

Vecchio, Robert P. (1984). Models of psychological inequity. *Organizational Behavior and Human Performance, 34,* 266–282.

Vroom, Victor H. (1964). *Work and motivation.* New York: Wiley.

Wanous, John P., Keon, Thomas L., & Latack, Janina C. (1983). Expectancy theory and occupational/organizational choices: A review and test. *Organizational Behavior and Human Performance, 32,* 66–86.

CHAPTER 4

Aldag, Ramon J., & Brief, Arthur P. (1979). *Task design and employee motivation.* Glenview, IL: Scott, Foresman.

Arvey, Richard D., & Ivancevich, John M. (1980). Punishment in organizations: A review, propositions, and research suggestions. *Academy of Management Review, 5,* 123–132.

Bandura, Albert (1977). *Social learning theory.* Englewood Cliffs, NJ: Prentice-Hall.

Berlinger, Lisa R., Glick, William H., & Rogers, Robert C. (1988). Job enrichment and performance improvement. In John P. Campbell & Richard J. Campbell (Eds.), *Productivity in organizations: New perspectives from industrial and organizational psychology* (pp. 219–254). San Francisco: Jossey-Bass.

Beyer, Janice M., & Trice, Harrison M. (1984). A field study of the use and perceived effects of discipline in controlling work performance. *Academy of Management Journal, 27,* 743–764.

Carroll, Stephen J., & Tosi, Henry L. (1973). *Management by objectives: Applications and research.* New York: Macmillan.

Cherrington, David J., & England, J. Lynn (1980). The desire for an enriched job as a moderator of the enrichment-satisfaction relationship. *Organizational Behavior and Human Performance, 25,* 139–159.

Dunham, Randall B., Pierce, Jon L., & Castañeda, Maria B. (1987). Alternative work schedules: Two field quasi-experiments. *Personnel Psychology, 40,* 215–242.

Earley, P. Christopher, Connolly, Terry, & Ekegren, Goron (1989). Goals, strategy development, and task performance: Some limits on the efficacy of goal setting. *Journal of Applied Psychology, 74,* 24–33.

Earley, P. Christopher, Wojnaroski, Pauline, & Prest, William (1987). Task planning and energy expended: Exploration of how goals influence performance. *Journal of Applied Psychology, 72,* 107–114.

Ford, Robert N. (1969). *Motivation through the work itself.* New York: American Management Association.

Fox, William M. (1988). Getting the most from behavior modeling training. *National Productivity Review, 7*(3), 238–245.

Fried, Yitzhak, & Ferris, Gerald R. (1987). The validity of the job characteristics model: A review and meta-analysis. *Personnel Psychology, 40,* 287–322.

Goldstein, Arnold P., & Sorcher, Melvin (1974). *Changing supervisor behavior.* Elmsford, NY: Pergamon Press.

Graen, George B., Scandura, Terri A., & Graen, Michael R. (1986). A field experimental test of the moderating effects of growth need strength on productivity. *Journal of Applied Psychology, 71,* 484–491.

Greene, Charles N. (1984). Effects of alternative work schedules: A field experiment. *Academy of Management Proceedings, 44,* 269–273.

Griffin, Ricky W. (1982). *Task design: An integrative approach.* Glenview, IL: Scott, Foresman.

Hackman, J. Richard, & Oldham, Greg R. (1980). *Work redesign.* Reading, MA: Addison-Wesley.

Haynes, Robert S., Pine, Randall C., and Fitch, H. Gordon (1982). Reducing accident rates with organizational behavior modification. *Academy of Management Journal, 25,* 407–416.

Herzberg, Frederick I. (1976). *The managerial choice: To be efficient and to be human.* Homewood, IL: Dow-Jones-Irwin.

Herzberg, Frederick I., Mausner, Bernard, & Snyderman, Barbara B. (1959). *The motivation to work.* New York: Wiley.

Hollenbeck, John R., & Brief, Arthur P. (1987). The effects of individual differences and goal origin on goal setting and performance. *Organizational Behavior and Human Decision Processes, 40,* 392–414.

Hollenbeck, John R., Williams, Charles R., & Klein, Howard J. (1989). An empirical examination of the antecedents of commitment to difficult goals. *Journal of Applied Psychology, 74,* 18–23.

Knoke, David, & Wright-Isak, Christine (1982). Individual motives and organizational incentive systems. *Research in the Sociology of Organizations, 1,* 209–254.

Kondrasuk, Jack N. (1981). Studies in MBO effectiveness. *Academy of Management Review, 6,* 419–430.

Kreitner, Robert, & Luthans, Fred (1984). A social learning approach to behavioral management: Radical behaviorists "mellowing out." *Organizational Dynamics, 13*(2), 47–65.

Kulik, Carol T., Oldham, Greg R., & Hackman, J. Richard (1987). Work design as an approach to person–environment fit. *Journal of Vocational Behavior, 31,* 278–296.

Latack, Janina C., & Foster, Lawrence W. (1985). Implementation of compressed work schedules: Participation and job redesign as critical factors for employee acceptance. *Personnel Psychology, 38,* 75–92.

Latham, Gary P., Erez, Miriam, & Locke, Edwin A. (1988). Resolving scientific disputes by the joint design of crucial experiments by the antagonists: Application to the Erez-Latham dispute regarding participation in goal setting. *Journal of Applied Psychology, 73,* 753–772.

Latham, Gary P., & Frayne, Colette A. (1989). Self-management training for increasing job attendance: A follow-up and a replication. *Journal of Applied Psychology, 74,* 411–416.

Locke, Edwin A., & Henne, Douglas (1986). Work motivation theories. In Cary L. Cooper & I. Robertson (Eds.), *Review of industrial and organizational psychology.* Chichester, England: Wiley.

Locke, Edwin A., & Latham, Gary P. (1984). *Goal setting: A motivational technique that works.* Englewood Cliffs, NJ: Prentice-Hall.

Locke, Edwin A., & Latham, Gary P. (1990). *A theory of goal setting and task performance.* Englewood Cliffs, NJ: Prentice-Hall.

Locke, Edwin A., Shaw, Karyll N., Saari, Lise M., & Latham, Gary P. (1981). Goal setting and task performance: 1969–1980. *Psychological Bulletin, 90,* 125–152.

Loher, Brian T., Noe, Raymond A., Moeller, Nancy L., & Fitzgerald, Michael P. (1985). A meta-analysis of the relation of job characteristics to job satisfaction. *Journal of Applied Psychology, 70,* 280–289.

Luthans, Fred, & Davis, Tim R. (1982). An idiographic approach to organizational behavior research: The use of single case experimental designs and direct measures. *Academy of Management Review, 7,* 380–391.

Luthans, Fred, & Kreitner, Robert (1985). *Organizational behavior modification and beyond: An operant and social learning approach.* Glenview, IL: Scott, Foresman.

Matsui, Tamao, Okada, Akinori, & Kakuyama, Takashi (1982). Influence of achievement need on goal setting, performance, and feedback effectiveness. *Journal of Applied Psychology, 67,* 645–648.

Mento, Anthony J., Steel, Robert P., & Karren, Ronald J. (1987). A meta-analytic study of the effects of goal setting on task performance: 1966–1984. *Organizational Behavior and Human Decision Processes, 39,* 52–83.

Meyer, Herbert H., & Raich, Michael S. (1983). An objective evaluation of a behavior modeling training program. *Personnel Psychology, 36,* 755–761.

Miner, John B. (1980). *Theories of organizational behavior.* Hinsdale, IL: Dryden.

Moses, Joseph L., & Ritchie, Richard J. (1976). Supervisory relationships training: A behavioral evaluation of a behavior modeling program. *Personnel Psychology, 29,* 337–343.

O'Brien, Richard M., Dickenson, Alyce M., & Rosow, Michael P. (1982). *Industrial behavior modification: A management handbook.* Elmsford, NY: Pergamon Press.

O'Reilly, Charles A., & Puffer, Sheila M. (1989). The impact of rewards and punishments in a social context. *Journal of Occupational Psychology, 62,* 41–53.

Pinder, Craig C. (1984). *Work motivation: Theory, issues and applications.* Glenview, IL: Scott, Foresman.

Podsakoff, Philip M., & Todor, William D. (1985). Relationships between leader reward and punishment behavior and group processes and productivity. *Journal of Management, 11,* 55–73.

Raia, Anthony P. (1974). *Managing by objectives.* Glenview, IL: Scott, Foresman.

Redeker, James R. (1983). *Discipline: Policies and procedures.* Washington, DC: Bureau of National Affairs.

Roberts, Karlene H., & Glick, William H. (1981). The job characteristics approach to task design: A critical review. *Journal of Applied Psychology, 66,* 193–217.

Ronen, Simcha (1984). *Alternative work schedules: Selecting, implementing, and evaluating.* Homewood, IL: Dow-Jones-Irwin.

Rosow, Jerome M., & Zager, Robert (1981). *New work schedules for a changing society.* Scarsdale, NY: Work in America Institute.

Russell, James S., Wexley, Kenneth N., & Hunter, John E. (1984). Questioning the effectiveness of behavior modeling training in an industrial setting. *Personnel Psychology, 37,* 465–481.

Schnake, Mel E. (1986). Vicarious punishment in a work setting. *Journal of Applied Psychology, 71,* 343–345.

Skinner, B. F. (1953). *Science and human behavior.* New York: Macmillan.

Skinner, B. F. (1971). *Beyond freedom and dignity.* New York: Knopf.

Skinner, B. F. (1974). *About behaviorism.* New York: Knopf.

Spector, Paul E. (1985). Higher-order need strength as a moderator of the job scope–employee outcome relationship: A meta-analysis. *Journal of Occupational Psychology, 58,* 119–127.

Szilagyi, Andrew D. (1980). Causal inferences between leader reward behavior and subordinate performance, absenteeism, and work satisfaction. *Journal of Occupational Psychology, 53,* 195–204.

Tubbs, Mark E. (1986). Goal setting: A meta-analytic examination of the empirical evidence. *Journal of Applied Psychology, 71,* 474–483.

Turner, Arthur N., & Lawrence, Paul R. (1965). *Industrial jobs and the worker: An investigation of response to task attributes.* Boston: Harvard Graduate School of Business.

Wagner, John A., Rubin, Paul A., & Callahan, Thomas J. (1988). Incentive payment and nonmanagerial productivity: An interrupted time series analysis of magnitude and trend. *Organizational Behavior and Human Decision Processes, 42,* 47–74.

Wood, Robert E., Mento, Anthony J., & Locke, Edwin A. (1987). Task complexity as a moderator of goal effects: A meta-analysis. *Journal of Applied Psychology, 72,* 416–425.

Zaccaro, Stephen J., & Stone, Eugene F. (1988). Incremental validity of an empirically based measure of job characteristics. *Journal of Applied Psychology, 73,* 245–252.

CHAPTER 5

Barbash, Jack, Lampman, Robert J., Levitan, Sar A., & Tyler, Gus (1983). *The work ethic: A critical analysis.* Madison, WI: Industrial Relations Research Association.

Bass, Bernard M., & Burger, Philip C. (1979). *Assessment of managers: An international comparison.* New York: Free Press.

Bazerman, Max H., Giuliano, Toni, & Appelman, Alan (1984). Escalation of commitment in individual and group decision making. *Organizational Behavior and Human Performance, 33,* 141–152.

Bergmann, Thomas J. (1981). Managers and their organizations: An interactive approach to multidimensional job satisfaction. *Journal of Occupational Psychology, 54,* 275–288.

Bhagat, Rabi S. (1982). Conditions under which stronger job performance–job satisfaction relationships may be observed: A closer look at two situational contingencies. *Academy of Management Journal, 25,* 772–789.

Blau, Gary J. (1985). Relationship of extrinsic, intrinsic, and demographic predictors to various types of withdrawal behaviors. *Journal of Applied Psychology, 70,* 442–450.

Brooke, Paul P., Russell, Daniel W., & Price, James L. (1988). Discriminant validation of measures of job satisfaction, job involvement, and organizational commitment. *Journal of Applied Psychology, 73,* 139–145.

Chaiken, Shelly, & Stangor, Charles (1987). Attitudes and attitude change. *Annual Review of Psychology, 38,* 575–630.

Conlon, Edward, & Gallagher, Daniel (1985).

Commitment to organization and union: The case of union members, non-members, and leavers. *Academy of Management Proceedings, 45*, 255–259.

Cook, John, & Wall, Toby (1980). New work attitude measures of trust, organizational commitment, and personal need non-fulfillment. *Journal of Occupational Psychology, 53*, 39–52.

Cressey, Donald R., & Moore, Charles A. (1983). Managerial values and corporate codes of ethics. *California Management Review, 25*(4), 53–77.

Davis, Mark A., & Bobko, Philip (1986). Contextual effects on escalation processes in public sector decision making. *Organizational Behavior and Human Decision Processes, 37*, 121–138.

England, George W. (1975). *The manager and his values: An international perspective.* Cambridge, MA: Ballinger.

Friedman, Lee, & Harvey, Robert J. (1986). Factors of union commitment: The case for a lower dimensionality. *Journal of Applied Psychology, 71*, 371–376.

Gerhart, Barry (1987). How important are dispositional factors as determinants of job satisfaction? Implications for job design and other personnel programs. *Journal of Applied Psychology, 72*, 366–373.

Gilmore, David C., Fried, Yitzhak, & Ferris, Gerald R. (1989). The influence of unionization on job satisfaction and work perception. *Journal of Business and Psychology, 3*, 289–297.

Hackett, Rick D. (1989). Work attitudes and employee absenteeism: A synthesis of the literature. *Journal of Occupational Psychology, 62*, 235–248.

Hollinger, Richard C., & Clark, John P. (1983). *Theft by employees.* Lexington, MA: D. C. Heath.

Iaffaldano, Michelle T., & Muchinsky, Paul M. (1985). Job satisfaction and job performance: A meta-analysis. *Psychological Bulletin, 97*, 251–273.

Kavanagh, Michael J., Hurst, Michael W., & Rose, Robert (1981). The relationship between job satisfaction and psychiatric health symptoms for air traffic controllers. *Personnel Psychology, 34*, 691–707.

Luthans, Fred, McCaul, Harriette S., & Dodd, Nancy G. (1985). Organizational commitment: A comparison of American, Japanese, and Korean employees. *Academy of Management Journal, 28*, 213–219.

McInnes, J. Morris (1984). Corporate management of productivity—An empirical study. *Strategic Management Journal, 5*, 351–365.

Michaels, Charles E., & Spector, Paul E. (1982). Causes of employee turnover: A test of the Mobley, Griffeth, Hand, and Meglino model. *Journal of Applied Psychology, 67*, 53–59.

Miner, John B. (1985a). Executive profiles. In *The Practice of Management.* Columbus, OH: Merrill.

Miner, John B. (1985b). *People problems: The executive answer book.* New York: Random House.

Mowday, Richard T., Porter, Lyman W., & Steers, Richard M. (1982). *Employee–organization linkages: The psychology of commitment, absenteeism and turnover.* New York: Academic Press.

Nord, Walter R., Brief, Arthur P., Atieh, Jennifer M., & Doherty, Elizabeth M. (1988). Work values and the conduct of organizational behavior. *Research in Organizational Behavior, 10*, 1–42.

Northcraft, Gregory B., & Wolf, Gerrit (1984). Dollars, sense, and sunk costs: A life cycle model of resource allocation decisions. *Academy of Management Review, 9*, 225–234.

O'Reilly, Charles A., & Caldwell, David F. (1981). The commitment and job tenure of new employees: Some evidence of postdecisional justification. *Administrative Science Quarterly, 26*, 597–616.

Parasuraman, Saroj, & Alutto, Joseph A. (1984). Sources and outcomes of stress in organizational settings: Toward the development of a structural model. *Academy of Management Journal, 27*, 330–350.

Petty, M. M., McGee, Gail W., & Cavender, Jerry W. (1984). A meta-analysis of the relationships between individual job satisfaction and individual performance. *Academy of Management Review, 9*, 712–721.

Pinder, Craig C. (1984). *Work motivation: Theory, issues and applications.* Glenview, IL: Scott, Foresman.

Posner, Barry Z., Kouzes, James M., & Schmidt, Warren H. (1985). Shared values make a difference: An empirical test of corporate culture. *Human Resource Management, 24*, 293–309.

Premack, Steven L. (1984). Prediction of employee unionization from knowledge of job satisfaction. *Academy of Management Proceedings, 44*, 279–283.

Pulakos, Elaine D., & Schmitt, Neal (1983). A longitudinal study of a valence model approach for the prediction of job satisfaction of new employees. *Journal of Applied Psychology, 68*, 307–312.

Purcell, Theodore V. (1960). *Blue collar man.* Cambridge, MA: Harvard University Press.

Reichers, Arnon E. (1985). A review and reconceptualization of organizational commitment. *Academy of Management Review, 10*, 465–476.

Rhodes, Susan R. (1983). Age related differences in work attitudes and behavior: A review and conceptual analysis. *Psychological Bulletin, 93*, 328–367.

Rice, Robert W., McFarlin, Dean B., & Bennett, Debbie E. (1989). Standards of comparison and job satisfaction. *Journal of Applied Psychology, 74*, 591–598.

Rokeach, Milton (1973). *The nature of human values.* New York: Free Press.

Spates, James L. (1983). The sociology of values. *Annual Review of Sociology, 9,* 27–49.

Staines, Graham L., & Quinn, Robert P. (1979). American workers evaluate the quality of their jobs. *Monthly Labor Review, 102*(1), 3–12.

Staw, Barry M., & Ross, Jerry (1985). Stability in the midst of change: A dispositional approach to job attitudes. *Journal of Applied Psychology, 70,* 469–480.

Swaney, Kyle, & Prediger, Dale (1985). The relationships between interest–occupation congruence and job satisfaction. *Journal of Vocational Behavior, 26,* 13–24.

Tait, Marianne, Padgett, Margaret Y., & Baldwin, Timothy T. (1989). Job and life satisfaction: A reevaluation of the strength of the relationship and gender effects as a function of the date of the study. *Journal of Applied Psychology, 74,* 502–507.

Vecchio, Robert P. (1980). The function and meaning of work and the job: Morse and Weiss (1955) revisited. *Academy of Management Journal, 23,* 361–367.

Walker, Jon E., Tausky, Curt, & Oliver, Donna (1982). Men and women at work: Similarities and differences in work values within occupational groupings. *Journal of Vocational Behavior, 21,* 17–36.

Wiener, Yoash, Vardi, Yoav, & Muczyk, Jan (1981). Antecedents of employees' mental health—The role of career and work satisfaction. *Journal of Vocational Behavior, 19,* 50–60.

Youngblood, Stuart A., Mobley, William H., & Meglino, Bruce M. (1983). A longitudinal analysis of the turnover process. *Journal of Applied Psychology, 68,* 507–516.

CHAPTER 6

Adler, Seymour, & Weiss, Howard M. (1988). Recent developments in the study of personality and organizational behavior. *International Review of Industrial and Organizational Psychology, 3,* 307–330.

Bandura, Albert (1982). Self-efficacy mechanism in human agency. *American Psychologist, 37,* 122–147.

Booth-Kewley, Stephanie, & Friedman, Howard S. (1987). Psychological predictors of heart disease: A quantitative review. *Psychological Bulletin, 101,* 343–362.

Boyd, David P. (1984). Type A behavior, financial performance and organizational growth in small business firms. *Journal of Occupational Psychology, 57,* 137–140.

Brockner, Joel (1988). *Self-esteem at work: Research, theory and practice.* Lexington, MA: Lexington Books.

Bruning, Nealia S., & Frew, David R. (1987). Effects of exercise, relaxation, and management skills training

on physiological stress indicators: A field experiment. *Journal of Applied Psychology, 72,* 515–521.

Byrne, D. G., & Reinhart, M. I. (1989). Work characteristics, occupational achievement and the Type A behavior pattern. *Journal of Occupational Psychology, 62,* 123–134.

Cohen, Sheldon, & Wills, Thomas A. (1985). Stress, social support, and the buffering hypothesis. *Psychological Bulletin, 98,* 310–357.

Day, David V., & Silverman, Stanley B. (1989). Personality and job performance: Evidence of incremental validity. *Personnel Psychology, 42,* 25–36.

Firth, Jenny, & Shapiro, David A. (1986). An evaluation of psychotherapy for job-related distress. *Journal of Occupational Psychology, 59,* 111–119.

Frese, Michael (1985). Stress at work and psychosomatic complaints: A causal interpretation. *Journal of Applied Psychology, 70,* 314–328.

Friedman, Meyer, & Rosenman, Ray H. (1974). *Type A behavior and your heart.* New York: Knopf.

Ganster, Daniel C., Fusilier, Marcelline R., & Mayes, Bronston T. (1986). Role of social support in the experience of stress at work. *Journal of Applied Psychology, 71,* 102–110.

Gaugler, Barbara B., Rosenthal, Douglas B., Thornton, George C., & Bentson, Cynthia (1987). Meta-analysis of assessment center validity. *Journal of Applied Psychology, 72,* 493–511.

Higgins, Nancy C. (1986). Occupational stress and working women: The effectiveness of two stress reduction programs. *Journal of Vocational Behavior, 29,* 66–78.

Hollinger, Richard C., & Clark, John P. (1983). *Theft by employees.* Lexington, MA: D. C. Heath.

Howard, Ann, & Bray, Douglas W. (1988). *Managerial lives in transition.* New York: Guilford Press.

Ivancevich, John M., & Matteson, Michael T. (1980). *Stress and work: A managerial perspective.* Glenview, IL: Scott, Foresman.

Jackson, Susan E., & Schuler, Randall S. (1985). A meta-analysis and conceptual critique of research on role ambiguity and role conflict in work settings. *Organizational Behavior and Human Decision Processes, 36,* 16–78.

Jackson, Susan E., Schwab, Richard L., & Schuler, Randall S. (1986). Toward an understanding of the burnout phenomenon. *Journal of Applied Psychology, 71,* 630–640.

Jamal, Muhammad (1981). Shift work related to job attitudes, social participation and withdrawal behavior: A study of nurses and industrial workers. *Personnel Psychology, 34,* 535–547.

Jamal, Muhammad (1984). Job stress and job performance

controversy: An empirical assessment. *Organizational Behavior and Human Performance, 33,* 1–21.

Kessler, Ronald C., Price, Richard H., & Wortman, Camille B. (1985). Social factors in psychopathology: Stress, social support, and coping processes. *Annual Review of Psychology, 36,* 531–572.

Kirmeyer, Sandra L., & Dougherty, Thomas W. (1988). Work load, tension, and coping: Moderating effects of supervisor support. *Personnel Psychology, 41,* 125–139.

Klimoski, Richard, & Brickner, Mary (1987). Why do assessment centers work? The puzzle of assessment center validity. *Personnel Psychology, 40,* 243–260.

Korman, Abraham K. (1974). *The psychology of motivation.* Englewood Cliffs, NJ: Prentice-Hall.

Krantz, David S., Grunberg, Neil E., & Baum, Andrew (1985). Health psychology. *Annual Review of Psychology, 36,* 349–383.

Krinsky, Leonard W., Kieffer, Sherman N., Carone, Pasquale A., & Yolles, Stanley F. (1984). *Stress and productivity.* New York: Human Sciences Press.

Lent, Robert W., & Hackett, Gail (1987). Career self-efficacy: Empirical status and future directions. *Journal of Vocational Behavior, 30,* 347–382.

Locke, Edwin A., Frederick, Elizabeth, Lee, Cynthia, & Bobko, Philip (1984). Effect of self-efficacy, goals, and task strategies on task performance. *Journal of Applied Psychology, 69,* 241–251.

Maslach, Christina (1982). Understanding burnout: Definitional issues in analyzing a complex phenomenon. In Whiton S. Paine (Ed.), *Job stress and burnout: Research, theory, and intervention perspectives* (pp. 29–40). Beverly Hills, CA: Sage.

Mathews, Karen A. (1982). Psychological perspectives on the Type A behavior pattern. *Psychological Bulletin, 91,* 293–323.

McDaniel, Michael A., & Jones, John W. (1988). Predicting employee theft: A quantitative review of the validity of a standardized measure of dishonesty. *Journal of Business and Psychology, 2,* 327–343.

Meier, Scott T. (1984). The construct validity of burnout. *Journal of Occupational Psychology, 57,* 211–219.

Miller, Danny, Kets de Vries, Manfred F. R., & Toulouse, Jean-Marie (1982). Top executive locus of control and its relationship to strategy-making, structure, and environment. *Academy of Management Journal, 25,* 237–253.

Motowidlo, Stephan J., Packard, John S., & Manning, Michael R. (1986). Occupational stress: Its causes and consequences for job performance. *Journal of Applied Psychology, 71,* 618–629.

Murphy, Lawrence R. (1984). Occupational stress management: A review and appraisal. *Journal of Occupational Psychology, 57,* 1–15.

Newton, T. J., & Keenan, A. (1987). Role stress reexamined: An investigation of role stress predictors. *Organizational Behavior and Human Decision Processes, 40,* 346–368.

Osipow, Samuel H., & Davis, Anne S. (1988). The relationship of coping resources to occupational stress and strain. *Journal of Vocational Behavior, 32,* 1–15.

Pervin, Lawrence A. (1985). Personality: Current controversies, issues, and directions. *Annual Review of Psychology, 36,* 83–114.

Pines, Ayala, & Aronson, Elliot (1988). *Career burnout: Causes and cures.* New York: Free Press.

Sackett, Paul R., Burris, Laura R., & Callahan, Christine (1989). Integrity testing for personnel selection: An update. *Personnel Psychology, 42,* 491–529.

Schmitt, Neal, Colligan, Michael J., & Fitzgerald, Michael (1980). Unexplained physical symptoms in eight organizations: Individual and organizational analysis. *Journal of Occupational Psychology, 53,* 305–317.

Schneider, Benjamin (1983). Interactional psychology and organizational behavior. *Research in Organizational Behavior, 5,* 1–31.

Schneider, Benjamin (1987). The people make the place. *Personnel Psychology, 40,* 437–453.

Selye, Hans (1976). *The stress of life.* New York: McGraw-Hill.

Somers, Mark J., & Lefkowitz, Joel (1983). Self-esteem, need gratification, and work satisfaction: A test of competing explanations from consistency theory and self-enhancement theory. *Journal of Vocational Behavior, 22,* 303–311.

Spector, Paul E. (1982). Behavior in organizations as a function of employee's locus of control. *Psychological Bulletin, 91,* 482–497.

Spector, Paul E. (1988). Development of the work locus of control scale. *Journal of Occupational Psychology, 61,* 335–340.

Spence, Janet T., Helmreich, Robert L., & Pred, Robert S. (1987). Impatience versus achievement strivings in the Type A pattern: Differential effects on students' health and academic achievement. *Journal of Applied Psychology, 72,* 522–528.

Spence, Janet T., Pred, Robert S., & Helmreich, Robert L. (1989). Achievement strivings, scholastic aptitude, and academic performance: A follow-up to "Impatience versus achievement strivings in the Type A pattern." *Journal of Applied Psychology, 74,* 176–178.

Storms, Philip L., & Spector, Paul E. (1987). Relationships of organizational frustration with reported behavioral reactions: The moderating effect of locus of control. *Journal of Occupational Psychology, 60,* 227–234.

Taylor, M. Susan, Locke, Edwin A., Lee, Cynthia, & Gist,

Marilyn E. (1984). Type A behavior and faculty research productivity: What are the mechanisms? *Organizational Behavior and Human Performance, 34,* 402–418.

Terborg, James R. (1981). Interactional psychology and research on human behavior in organizations. *Academy of Management Review, 6,* 569–576.

Thornton, George C., & Byham, William C. (1982). *Assessment centers and managerial performance.* New York: Academic Press.

Watson, David, & Clark, Lee A. (1984). Negative affectivity: The disposition to experience aversive emotional states. *Psychological Bulletin, 96,* 465–490.

Weiss, Howard M., Ilgen, Daniel R., & Sharbaugh, Michael E. (1982). Effects of life and job stress on information search behaviors of organizational members. *Journal of Applied Psychology, 67,* 60–66.

CHAPTER 7

Albanese, Robert, & Van Fleet, David D. (1985). Rational behavior in groups: The free-riding tendency. *Academy of Management Review, 10,* 244–255.

Alderfer, Clayton P. (1977). Group and intergroup relations. In J. Richard Hackman & J. Lloyd Suttle (Eds.), *Improving life at work: Behavioral science approaches to organizational change.* Santa Monica, CA: Goodyear.

Argyris, Chris (1962). *Interpersonal competence and organizational effectiveness.* Homewood, IL: Irwin.

Bond, Charles F., & Titus, Linda J. (1983). Social facilitation: A meta-analysis of 241 studies. *Psychological Bulletin, 94,* 265–292.

Cartwright, Dorwin, & Zander, Alvin (1968). *Group dynamics: Research and theory.* New York: Harper & Row.

Dorfman, Peter W., & Stephan, Walter G. (1984). The effects of group performance on cognitions, satisfaction, and behavior: A process model. *Journal of Management, 10,* 173–192.

Eddy, William B. (1985). *The manager and the working group.* New York: Praeger.

Eden, Dov (1985). Team development: A true field experiment at three levels of rigor. *Journal of Applied Psychology, 70,* 94–100.

Emery, Fred E., & Thorsrud, Einar (1976). *Democracy at work.* Leiden, the Netherlands: Martinus Nijhoff.

Feldman, Daniel C. (1984). The development and enforcement of group norms. *Academy of Management Review, 9,* 47–53.

Goodman, Paul S., Devadas, Rukmini, & Hughson, Terri L. G. (1988). Groups and productivity: Analyzing the effectiveness of self-managing teams. In John P. Campbell & Richard J. Campbell (Eds.), *Productivity in organizations: New perspectives from industrial and organizational psychology* (pp. 295–327). San Francisco, CA: Jossey-Bass.

Herbst, P. G. (1976). *Alternatives to hierarchies.* Leiden, the Netherlands: Martinus Nijhoff.

Luft, Joseph (1984). *Group processes: An introduction to group dynamics.* Palo Alto, CA: Mayfield.

Matsui, Tameo, Kakuyama, Takashi, & UyOnglatco, Mary Lou (1987). Effects of goals and feedback on performance in groups. *Journal of Applied Psychology, 72,* 407–415.

Miner, John B. (1982). *Theories of organizational structure and process.* Hinsdale, IL: Dryden.

Miner, John B. (1985). *People problems: The executive answer book.* New York: Random House.

O'Reilly, Charles A., & Caldwell, David F. (1985). The impact of normative social influence and cohesiveness on task perceptions and attitudes: A social information processing approach. *Journal of Occupational Psychology, 58,* 193–206.

Price, Kenneth H. (1987). Decision responsibility, task responsibility, identifiability, and social loafing. *Organizational Behavior and Human Decision Processes, 40,* 330–345.

Ritvo, Roger A., & Sargent, Alice G. (1983). *The NTL managers' handbook.* Arlington, VA: NTL Institute.

Schein, Edgar H., & Bennis, Warren G. (1965). *Personal and organizational change through group methods: The laboratory approach.* New York: Wiley.

Stevenson, William B., Pearce, Jone L., & Porter, Lyman W. (1985). The concept of "coalition" in organization theory and research. *Academy of Management Review, 10,* 256–268.

Wanous, John P., Reichers, Arnon E., & Malik, S. D. (1984). Organizational socialization and group development: Toward an integrative perspective. *Academy of Management Review, 9,* 670–683.

Woodman, Richard W., & Sherwood, John J. (1980a). Effects of team development intervention: A field experiment. *Journal of Applied Behavioral Science, 16,* 211–227.

Woodman, Richard W., & Sherwood, John J. (1980b). The role of team development in organizational effectiveness: A critical review. *Psychological Bulletin, 88,* 166–186.

Zander, Alvin (1982). *Making groups effective.* San Francisco: Jossey-Bass.

CHAPTER 8

Asch, Solomon E. (1951). Effects of group pressure upon the modification and distortion of judgments. In Harold Guetzkow (Ed.), *Groups, leadership and men* (pp. 177–190). Pittsburgh: Carnegie Press.

Ashton, Robert H. (1986). Combining the judgments of experts: How many and which ones? *Organizational Behavior and Human Decision Processes, 38,* 405–414.

Barrick, Murray R., & Alexander, Ralph A. (1987). A review of quality circle efficacy and the existence of positive-findings bias. *Personnel Psychology, 40,* 579–592.

Bass, Bernard M. (1983). *Organizational decision making.* Homewood, IL: Irwin.

Bazerman, Max H., Giuliano, Toni, & Appelman, Alan (1984). Escalation of commitment in individual and group decision making. *Organizational Behavior and Human Performance, 33,* 141–152.

Bordley, Robert F. (1983). A Baysian model of group polarization. *Organizational Behavior and Human Performance, 32,* 262–274.

Cosier, Richard A., & Rechner, Paula L. (1985). Inquiry method effects on performance in a simulated business environment. *Organizational Behavior and Human Decision Processes, 36,* 79–95.

Delbecq, Andre L., Van de Ven, Andrew H., & Gustafson, David H. (1975). *Group techniques for program planning: A guide to nominal group and Delphi processes.* Glenview, IL: Scott, Foresman.

Fox, William M. (1987). *Effective group problem solving.* San Francisco: Jossey-Bass.

Goldstein, S. G. (1985). Organizational dualism and quality circles. *Academy of Management Review, 10,* 504–517.

Greenbaum, Howard H., Kaplan, Ira T., & Metlay, William (1988). Evaluation of problem-solving groups: The case of quality circle programs. *Group and Organization Studies, 13,* 133–147.

Guzzo, Richard A., & Waters, James A. (1982). The expression of affect and the performance of decision-making groups. *Journal of Applied Psychology, 67,* 67–74.

Hill, Gayle W. (1982). Group versus individual performance: Are N + 1 heads better than one? *Psychological Bulletin, 91,* 517–539.

Huber, George P. (1980). *Managerial decision making.* Glenview, IL: Scott, Foresman.

Janis, Irving L. (1989). *Crucial decisions: Leadership in policymaking and crisis management.* New York: Free Press.

Jewell, Linda N., & Reitz, H. Joseph (1981). *Group effectiveness in organizations.* Glenview, IL: Scott, Foresman.

Leana, Carrie R. (1985). A partial test of Janis' groupthink model: Effects of group cohesiveness and leader behavior on defective decision making. *Journal of Management, 11,* 5–17.

Ledford, Gerald E., Lawler, Edward E., & Mohrman, Susan A. (1988). The quality circle and its variations. In John P. Campbell & Richard J. Campbell (Eds.), *Productivity in organizations: New perspectives from industrial and organizational psychology* (pp. 255–294). San Francisco: Jossey-Bass.

Libby, Robert, Trotman, Ken T., & Zimmer, Ian (1987). Member variation, recognition of expertise, and group performance. *Journal of Applied Psychology, 72,* 81–87.

Marks, Mitchell L., Mirvis, Philip H., Hackett, Edward J., & Grady, James F. (1986). Employee participation in a quality circle program: Impact on quality of work life, productivity, and absenteeism. *Journal of Applied Psychology, 71,* 61–69.

McGrath, Joseph E., & Kravitz, David A. (1982). Group research. *Annual Review of Psychology, 33,* 195–230.

Meyer, Gordon W., & Stott, Randall G. (1985). Quality circles: Panacea or Pandora's box? *Organizational Dynamics, 13:(4),* 34–50.

Miner, Frederick C. (1984). Group versus individual decision making: An investigation of performance measures, decision strategies, and process losses/gains. *Organizational Behavior and Human Performance, 33,* 112–124.

Morris, William C., & Sashkin, Marshall (1982). *Organization behavior in action: Skill building experiences.* St. Paul, MN: West.

Rafaeli, Anat (1985). Quality circles and employee attitudes. *Personnel Psychology, 38,* 603–615.

Richards, Max D. (1973). An exploratory study of strategic failure. *Academy of Management Proceedings, 33,* 40–46.

Schweiger, David M., & Finger, Phyllis A. (1984). The comparative effectiveness of dialectical inquiry and devil's advocacy: The impact of task biases on previous research findings. *Strategic Management Journal, 5,* 335–350.

Schwenk, Charles R. (1988). *The essence of strategic decision making.* Lexington, MA: Lexington Books.

Smeltzer, Larry R., & Kedia, Ben L. (1985). Knowing the ropes: Organizational requirements for quality circles. *Business Horizons, 28(4),* 30–34.

Sniezek, Janet A., & Henry, Rebecca A. (1989). Accuracy

and confidence in group judgment. *Organizational Behavior and Human Decision Processes, 43,* 1–28.

Steel, Robert P., Mento, Anthony J., Dilla, Benjamin L., Ovalle, Nestor K., & Lloyd, Russell F. (1985). Factors influencing the success and failure of two quality circle programs. *Journal of Management, 11,* 99–119.

Swap, Walter C. (1984). *Group decision making.* Beverly Hills, CA: Sage.

Tanford, Sarah, & Penrod, Steven (1984). Social influence model: A formal integration of research on majority and minority influence processes. *Psychological Bulletin, 95,* 189–225.

Tang, Thomas P., Tollison, Peggy S., & Whiteside, Harold D. (1987). The effect of quality circle initiation on motivation to attend quality circle meetings and on task performance. *Personnel Psychology, 40,* 799–814.

Taylor, Ronald N. (1984). *Behavioral decision making.* Glenview, IL: Scott, Foresman.

Vancil, Richard F., & Green, Charles H. (1984). How CEOs use top management committees. *Harvard Business Review, 62*(1), 65–73.

White, Sam E., Dittrich, John E., & Lang, James R. (1980). The effects of group decision-making process and problem-situation complexity on implementation attempts. *Administrative Science Quarterly, 25,* 428–440.

Wolff, Paul J. (1983). Quality circle intervention: Structure, process, results. Unpublished Ph.D. diss., College of Business and Management, University of Maryland.

Wolff, Paul J. (1987). Western problems—Eastern solutions: Mixed promise of quality circles. *Journal of Managerial Psychology, 2*(2), 3–8.

Yetton, Philip W., & Bottger, Preston C. (1982). Individual versus group problem solving: An empirical test of a best-member strategy. *Organizational Behavior and Human Performance, 29,* 307–321.

Yetton, Philip, & Bottger, Preston (1983). The relationships among group size, member ability, social decision schemes, and performance. *Organizational Behavior and Human Performance, 32,* 145–159.

CHAPTER 9

Bass, Bernard M. (1990). *Bass & Stogdill's handbook of leadership.* New York: Free Press.

Blake, Robert R., & McCanse, Anne A. (1991). *Leadership dilemmas: Grid solutions.* Houston: Gulf.

Blake, Robert R., & Mouton, Jane S. (1982). Theory and research for developing a science of leadership. *Journal of Applied Behavioral Science, 18,* 275–291.

Blake, Robert R., Mouton, Jane S., & Allen, Robert L. (1987). *Spectacular teamwork.* London: Sidgwick and Jackson.

Butterfield, D. Anthony, & Powell, Gary N. (1981). Effect of group performance, leader sex, and rater sex on ratings of leader behavior. *Organizational Behavior and Human Performance, 28,* 129–141.

Chemers, Martin M., & Fiedler, Fred E. (1986). The trouble with assumptions: A reply to Jago and Ragan. *Journal of Applied Psychology, 71,* 560–563.

Clark, Kenneth E., & Clark, Miriam B. (1990). *Measures of leadership.* West Orange, N.J.: Leadership Library of America.

Fiedler, Fred E., & Chemers, Martin M., (1974). *Leadership and effective management.* Glenview, IL: Scott, Foresman.

Fiedler, Fred E., & Garcia, Joseph E. (1987). *New approaches to effective leadership: Cognitive resources and organizational performance.* New York: Wiley.

Graeff, Claude L. (1983). The situational leadership theory: A critical review. *Academy of Management Review, 8,* 285–291.

Guest, Robert H., Hersey, Paul, & Blanchard, Kenneth H. (1986). *Organizational change through effective leadership.* Englewood Cliffs, NJ: Prentice-Hall.

Hammer, Tove H., & Turk, Jay M. (1987). Organizational determinants of leader behavior and authority. *Journal of Applied Psychology, 72,* 674–682.

House, Robert J., & Baetz, Mary L. (1979). Leadership: Some empirical generalizations and new research directions. *Research in Organizational Behavior, 1,* 341–423.

Howell, Jon P., Dorfman, Peter W., & Kerr, Steven (1986). Moderator variables in leadership research. *Academy of Management Review, 11,* 88–102.

Jago, Arthur G., & Ragan, James W. (1986a). The trouble with leader match is that it doesn't match Fiedler's contingency model. *Journal of Applied Psychology, 71,* 555–559.

Jago, Arthur G., & Ragan, James W. (1986b). Some assumptions are more troubling than others: Rejoinder to Chemers and Fiedler. *Journal of Applied Psychology, 71,* 564–565.

Kabanoff, Boris (1981). Critique of leader match and its implications for leadership research. *Personnel Psychology, 34,* 749–764.

Kennedy, John K. (1982). Middle LPC leaders and the contingency model of leadership effectiveness. *Organizational Behavior and Human Performance, 39,* 1–14.

Kenny, David A., & Zaccaro, Stephen J. (1983). An estimate of variance due to traits in leadership. *Journal of Applied Psychology, 68,* 678–685.

Kipnis, David, Schmidt, Stuart, Price, Karl, & Stitt, Christopher (1981). Why do I like thee: Is it your performance or my orders. *Journal of Applied Psychology, 66*, 324–328.

Latham, Gary P. (1988). Human resource training and development. *Annual Review of Psychology, 39*, 545–582.

Likert, Rensis (1961). *New patterns of management.* New York: McGraw-Hill.

Likert, Rensis (1979). From production- and employee-centeredness to Systems 1–4. *Journal of Management, 5*, 147–156.

Likert, Rensis, & Likert, Jane G. (1976). *New ways of managing conflict.* New York: McGraw-Hill.

Locke, Edwin A., Schweiger, David M., & Latham, Gary P. (1986). Participation in decision making: When should it be used? *Organizational Dynamics, 14*(3), 65–79.

Lord, Robert G. (1985). An information processing approach to social perceptions, leadership and behavioral measurement in organizations. *Research in Organizational Behavior, 7*, 87–128.

Lord, Robert G., DeVader, Christy L., & Alliger, George M. (1986). A meta-analysis of the relation between personality traits and leadership perceptions: An application of validity generalization procedures. *Journal of Applied Psychology, 71*, 402–410.

McGregor, Douglas (1960). *The human side of enterprise.* New York: McGraw-Hill.

Miner, John B. (1980). *Theories of organizational behavior.* Hinsdale, IL: Dryden.

Miner, John B. (1982). The uncertain future of the leadership concept: Revisions and clarifications. *Journal of Applied Behavioral Science, 18*, 293–307.

Ono, Kaoru, Tindale, R. Scott, Hulin, Charles L., & Davis, James H. (1988). Intuition vs. deduction: Some thought experiments concerning Likert's linking-pin theory of organization. *Organizational Behavior and Human Decision Processes, 42*, 135–154.

Peters, Lawrence H., Hartke, Darrell D., & Pohlmann, John T. (1985). Fiedler's contingency theory of leadership: An application of the meta-analysis procedures of Schmidt and Hunter. *Psychological Bulletin, 97*, 274–285.

Sashkin, Marshall (1984). Participative management is an ethical imperative. *Organizational Dynamics, 12*(4), 4–22.

Sims, Henry P., & Manz, Charles C. (1984). Observing leader verbal behavior: Toward reciprocal determinism in leadership theory. *Journal of Applied Psychology, 69*, 222–232.

Singh, Ramadhar (1983). Leadership style and reward allocation: Does least preferred co-worker scale measure task and relation orientation? *Organizational Behavior and Human Performance, 32*, 178–197.

Smith, Jonathan E., Carson, Kenneth P., & Alexander, Ralph A. (1984). Leadership: It can make a difference. *Academy of Management Journal, 27*, 765–776.

Strauss, George (1982). Worker participation in management: An international perspective. *Research in Organizational Behavior, 4*, 173–265.

Tjosvold, Dean (1984). Effects of leader warmth and directiveness on subordinate performance on a subsequent task. *Journal of Applied Psychology, 69*, 422–427.

Vecchio, Robert P. (1987). Situational leadership theory: An examination of a prescriptive theory. *Journal of Applied Psychology, 72*, 444–451.

Weiner, Nan, & Mahoney, Thomas A. (1981). A model of corporate performance as a function of environmental, organizational, and leadership influences. *Academy of Management Journal, 24*, 453–470.

Yukl, Gary A. (1989). *Leadership in organizations.* Englewood Cliffs, NJ: Prentice-Hall.

CHAPTER 10

Avolio, Bruce J., & Bass, Bernard M. (1988). Transformational leadership, charisma, and beyond. In James G. Hunt, B. Rajaram Baliga, H. Peter Dachler, & Chester A. Schriesheim (Eds.), *Emerging leadership vistas* (pp. 29–49). Lexington, MA: Lexington Books.

Bass, Bernard M. (1985). *Leadership and performance beyond expectations.* New York: Free Press.

Brown, Karen A. (1984). Explaining group poor performance: An attributional analysis. *Academy of Management Review, 9*, 54–63.

Crouch, Andrew, & Yetton, Philip (1987). Manager behavior, leadership style, and subordinate performance: An empirical extension of the Vroom-Yetton conflict rule. *Organizational Behavior and Human Decision Processes, 39*, 384–396.

Crouch, Andrew, & Yetton, Philip (1988). Manager–subordinate dyads: Relationships among task and social contact, manager friendliness and subordinate performance in management groups. *Organizational Behavior and Human Decision Processes, 41*, 65–82.

Dansereau, Fred, Graen, George, & Haga, William J. (1975). A vertical dyad linkage approach to leadership within formal organizations: A longitudinal investigation of the role making process. *Organizational Behavior and Human Performance, 13*, 46–78.

Drenth, Pieter J. D., & Koopman, Paul L. (1984). A contingency approach to participative leadership: How good? In James G. Hunt, Dian-Marie Hosking, Chester A. Schriesheim, & Rosemary Stewart (Eds.), *Leaders and managers: International perspectives on managerial behavior and leadership* (pp. 303–315). Elmsford, NY: Pergamon.

Duchon, Dennis, Green, Stephen G., & Taber, Thomas D. (1986). Vertical dyad linkage: A longitudinal assessment of antecedents, measures, and consequences. *Journal of Applied Psychology, 71,* 56–60.

Evans, Martin G. (1979). Leadership. In Steven Kerr (Ed.), *Organizational behavior* (pp. 207–239) Columbus, OH: Grid.

Fagenson, Ellen A. (1988). The power of a mentor: Proteges' and nonproteges' perceptions of their own power in organizations. *Group and Organization Studies, 13,* 182–194.

Field, R. H. George (1982). A test of the Vroom-Yetton normative model of leadership. *Journal of Applied Psychology, 67,* 523–532.

Fulk, Janet, & Wendler, Eric R. (1982). Dimensionality of leader–subordinate interactions: A path–goal investigation. *Organizational behavior and human performance, 30,* 241–264.

Gioia, Dennis A., & Sims, Henry P. (1986). Cognition–behavior connections: Attribution and verbal behavior in leader–subordinate interactions. *Organizational Behavior and Human Decision Processes, 37,* 197–229.

Graen, George, & Cashman, James F. (1975). A role-making model of leadership in formal organizations: A developmental approach. In James G. Hunt & Lars L. Larson (Eds.), *Leadership frontiers* (pp. 143–165). Kent, OH: Kent State University Press.

Graen, George, & Scandura, Terri A. (1987). Toward a psychology of dyadic organizing. *Research in Organizational Behavior, 9,* 175–208.

Grove, Andrew S. (1983). *High output management.* New York: Random House.

Harvey, John H., & Weary, Gifford (1984). Current issues in attribution theory and research. *Annual Review of Psychology, 35,* 427–459.

Hater, John J., & Bass, Bernard M. (1988). Superiors' evaluations and subordinates' perceptions of transformational and transactional leadership. *Journal of Applied Psychology, 73,* 695–702.

Heller, Frank A. (1971). *Managerial decision-making: A study of leadership styles and power-sharing among senior managers.* London: Tavistock.

Heller, Frank, Drenth, Pieter, Koopman, Paul, & Rus, Veljko (1988). *Decisions in organizations: A three-country comparative study.* Beverly Hills, CA: Sage.

House, Robert J. (1977). A 1976 theory of charismatic leadership. In James G. Hunt & Lars L. Larson (Eds.), *Leadership: The cutting edge* (pp. 194–205). Carbondale, IL: Southern Illinois University Press.

House, Robert J., & Baetz, Mary L. (1979). Leadership: Some empirical generalizations and new research directions. *Research in Organizational Behavior, 1,* 341–423.

Hunt, David M., & Michael, Carol (1983). Mentorship: A career training and development tool. *Academy of Management Review, 8,* 475–485.

Jago, Arthur G., Ettling, Jennifer T., & Vroom, Victor H. (1985). Validating a revision to the Vroom/Yetton model: First evidence. *Academy of Management Proceedings, 45,* 220–223.

Keller, Robert T. (1989). A test of the path-goal theory of leadership with need for clarity as a moderator in research and development organizations. *Journal of Applied Psychology, 74,* 208–212.

Kram, Kathy E. (1985). *Mentoring at work: Developmental relationships in organizational life.* Glenview, IL: Scott, Foresman.

Leana, Carrie R. (1987). Power relinquishment versus power sharing: Theoretical clarification and empirical comparison of delegation and participation. *Journal of Applied Psychology, 72,* 228–233.

Meindl, James R., Ehrlich, Sanford B., & Dukerich, Janet M. (1985). The romance of leadership. *Administrative Science Quarterly, 30,* 78–102.

Miner, John B. (1985). *People problems: The executive answer book.* New York: Random House.

Mitchell, Terence R. (1982). Attributions and actions: A note of caution. *Journal of Management, 8,* 65–74.

Mitchell, Terence R., Green, Stephen G., & Wood, Robert E. (1981). An attributional model of leadership and the poor performing subordinate: Development and validation. *Research in Organizational Behavior, 3,* 197–234.

Noe, Raymond A. (1988). An investigation of the determinants of successful assigned mentoring relationships. *Personnel Psychology, 41,* 457–479.

Paul, Robert J., & Ebadi, Yar M. (1989). Leadership decision making in a service organization: A field test of the Vroom-Yetton model. *Journal of Occupational Psychology, 62,* 201–211.

Roche, Gerard R. (1979). Much ado about mentors. *Harvard Business Review, 57*(1), 14–28.

Schriesheim, Chester A., & DeNisi, Angelo S. (1981). Task dimensions as moderators of the effects of instrumental leadership: A two-sample replicated test of path-goal leadership theory. *Journal of Applied Psychology, 66,* 589–597.

Shaver, Kelly G. (1983). *An introduction to attribution processes.* Hillsdale, NJ: Erlbaum.

Tannenbaum, Robert, & Schmidt, Warren H. (1958). How to choose a leadership pattern." *Harvard Business Review, 36*(2), 95–101.

Tichy, Noel M., & Devanna, Mary Anne (1986). *The transformational leader.* New York: Wiley.

Vecchio, Robert P., & Gobdel, Bruce C. (1984). The vertical dyad linkage model of leadership: Problems and prospects. *Organizational Behavior and Human Performance, 34,* 5–20.

Vroom, Victor H. (1976). Can leaders learn to lead? *Organizational Dynamics, 4*(3), 17–28.

Vroom, Victor H., & Jago, Arthur G. (1988). *The new leadership: Managing participation in organizations.* Englewood Cliffs, NJ: Prentice-Hall.

Wakabayashi, Mitsuru, Graen, George, Graen, Michael, & Graen, Martin (1988). Japanese management progress: Mobility into middle management. *Journal of Applied Psychology, 73,* 217–227.

Waldman, David A., Bass, Bernard M., & Einstein, Walter O. (1987). Leadership and outcomes of performance appraisal processes. *Journal of Occupational Psychology, 60,* 177–186.

Weber, Max (1968). *Economy and society,* trans. Guenther Roth & Claus Wittich. New York: Bedminster Press.

CHAPTER 11

Aiken, Michael, Bacharach, Samuel B., & French, J. Lawrence (1980). Organizational structure, work process, and proposal making in administrative bureaucracies. *Academy of Management Journal, 23,* 631–652.

Anderson, Roger L., & Terborg, James R. (1986). Managing employee beliefs in work redesign interventions. *Academy of Management Proceedings, 46,* 225–228.

Argyris, Chris (1962). *Interpersonal competence and organizational effectiveness.* Homewood, IL: Irwin.

Argyris, Chris (1982). *Reasoning, learning, and action: Individual and organizational.* San Francisco: Jossey-Bass.

Beer, Michael (1980). *Organizational change and development: A systems view.* Santa Monica, CA: Goodyear.

Beer, Michael, & Walton, Anna Elise (1987). Organizational change and development. *Annual Review of Psychology, 38,* 339–367.

Blake, Robert R., & Mouton, Jane S. (1985). *The managerial grid* (3d ed.). Houston: Gulf.

Bowers, David G., & Franklin, Jerome L. (1977). *Survey-guided development: Data-based organizational change.* La Jolla, CA: University Associates.

Bullock, R. J., & Svyantek, Daniel J. (1985). Analyzing meta-analysis: Potential problems, an unsuccessful replication, and evaluation criteria. *Journal of Applied Psychology, 70,* 108–115.

Burke, W. Warner (1987). *Organization development: A normative view.* Reading, MA: Addison-Wesley.

Chandler, Alfred D. (1962). *Strategy and structure: Chapters in the history of the industrial enterprise.* Cambridge, MA: MIT Press.

Cherns, Albert (1977). Can behavioral science help design organizations? *Organizational Dynamics, 5*(4), 55–63.

Dyer, William G. (1987). *Team building: Issues and alternatives.* Reading, MA: Addison-Wesley.

Emery, Fred, & Thorsrud, Einar (1976). *Democracy at work: The report of the Norwegian Industrial Democracy Program.* Leiden, the Netherlands: Martinus Nijhoff.

Faucheux, Claude, Amado, Gilles, & Laurent, André (1982). Organizational development and change. *Annual Review of Psychology, 33,* 343–370.

General Motors Corporation (1984). *Public interest report.* Detroit: General Motors.

Glassman, Alan M., & Lundberg, Craig C. (1988). In search of the right consultant: An OD fable. *Group and Organization Studies, 13,* 5–18.

Goodman, Paul S. (1979). *Assessing organizational change: The Rushton quality of work experiment.* New York: Wiley.

Greiner, Larry E., & Schein, Virginia E. (1988). *Power and organization development: Mobilizing power to implement change.* Reading, MA: Addison-Wesley.

Guzzo, Richard A., Jette, Richard D., & Katzell, Raymond A. (1985). The effects of psychologically based intervention programs on worker productivity: A meta-analysis. *Personnel Psychology, 38,* 275–291.

Gyllenhammar, Pehr G. (1977). How Volvo adapts work to people. *Harvard Business Review, 55*(4), 102–113.

Hermon-Taylor, Richard J. (1985). Finding new ways of overcoming resistance to change. In Johannes Pennings (Ed.), *Organizational strategy and change* (pp. 383–411). San Francisco: Jossey-Bass.

Hoskisson, Robert E., & Galbraith, Craig S. (1985). The effect of quantum versus incremental M-form reorganization on performance: A time-series exploration of intervention dynamics. *Journal of Management, 11,* 55–70.

Lawler, Edward E., Mohrman, Allan M., Mohrman, Susan A., Ledford, Gerald E., & Cummings, Thomas G. (1985). *Doing research that is useful for theory and practice.* San Francisco: Jossey-Bass.

Lewin, Kurt (1952). Group decision and social change. In Guy E. Swanson, Theodore M. Newcomb, & Eugene L. Hartley (Eds.), *Readings in social psychology* (pp. 459–473). New York: Holt.

Lippitt, Gordon L. (1982). *Organizational renewal: A holistic approach to organization development.* Englewood Cliffs, NJ: Prentice-Hall.

Massarik, Fred (1990). *Advances in organization development.* Norwood, NJ: Ablex.

McGregor, Douglas (1957). An uneasy look at performance appraisal. *Harvard Business Review, 35*(3), 89–94.

Miller, Danny, & Friesen, Peter H. (1982). Structural change and performance: Quantum versus piecemeal-incremental approaches. *Academy of Management Journal, 25,* 867–892.

Millsap, Roger E., & Hartog, Sandra B. (1988). Alpha, beta, and gamma change in evaluation research: A structural equation approach. *Journal of Applied Psychology, 73,* 574–584.

Miner, John B. (1990). The role of values in defining the "goodness" of theories in organizational science. *Organization Studies, 11,* 161–178.

Mohrman, Susan A., & Lawler, Edward E. (1984). Quality of work life. *Research in Personnel and Human Resources Management, 2,* 219–260.

Nadler, David A., & Lawler, Edward E. (1983). Quality of work life: Perspectives and directions. *Organizational Dynamics, 11*(3), 20–30.

Neuman, George A., Edwards, Jack E., & Raju, Nambury S. (1989). Organizational development interventions: A meta-analysis of their effects on satisfaction and other attitudes. *Personnel Psychology, 42,* 461–489.

Nicholas, John M., & Katz, Marsha (1985). Research methods and reporting practices in organization development: A review and some guidelines. *Academy of Management Review, 10,* 737–749.

Nurick, Aaron J. (1985). *Participation in organizational change: The TVA experiment.* New York: Praeger.

Randolph, W. Alan (1982). Planned organizational change and its measurement. *Personnel Psychology, 35,* 117–139.

Schein, Edgar H. (1987). *Process consultation: Volume II. Lessons for managers and consultants.* Reading, MA: Addison-Wesley.

Schuster, Michael (1984). The Scanlon plan: A longitudinal analysis. *Journal of Applied Behavioral Science, 20,* 23–38.

Sorensen, Knut H. (1985). Technology and industrial democracy—An inquiry into some theoretical issues

and their social basis. *Organizational Studies, 6,* 139–160.

Terpstra, David E. (1981). Relationship between methodological rigor and reported outcomes in organization development evaluation research. *Journal of Applied Psychology, 66,* 541–543.

Thacker, James W., & Fields, Mitchell W. (1987). Union involvement in quality-of-worklife efforts: A longitudinal investigation. *Personnel Psychology, 40,* 97–111.

Trist, Eric L., Higgin, G. W., Murray, H., & Pollock, A. B. (1963). *Organizational choice: Capabilities of groups at the coal face under changing technologies.* London: Tavistock.

Van de Vliert, Evert, Huismans, Sipke E., & Stok, Jan J. L. (1985). The criterion approach to unraveling beta and alpha change. *Academy of Management Review, 10,* 269–274.

Walton, Richard E. (1982). The Topeka work system: Optimistic visions, pessimistic hypotheses, and reality. In Robert Zager & Michael P. Rosow (Eds.), *The innovative organization: Productivity programs in action* (pp. 260–287). Elmsford, NY: Pergamon.

Whitsett, David A., & Yorks, Lyle (1983). Looking back at Topeka: General Foods and the quality-of-work-life experiment. *California Management Review, 25*(4), 93–109.

Woodman, Richard W., & Wayne, Sandy J. (1985). An investigation of positive-findings bias in evaluation of organization development interventions. *Academy of Management Journal, 28,* 889–913.

CHAPTER 12

Birren, James E., Cunningham, Walter R., & Yamamoto, Koichi (1983). Psychology of adult development and aging. *Annual Review of Psychology, 34,* 543–575.

Campbell, John P., Dunnette, Marvin D., Lawler, Edward E., & Weick, Karl E. (1970). *Managerial behavior, performance, and effectiveness.* New York: McGraw-Hill.

Ford, J. Kevin, Kraiger, Kurt, & Schectman, Susan L. (1986). Study of race effects in objective indices and subjective evaluations of performance: A meta-analysis of performance criteria. *Psychological Bulletin, 99,* 330–337.

Fossum, John A., Arvey, Richard D., Paradise, Carol A., & Robbins, Nancy E. (1986). Modeling the skills obsolescence process: A psychological/economic integration. *Academy of Management Review, 11,* 362–374.

Ghiselli, Edwin E. (1974). Some perspectives for industrial psychology. *American Psychologist, 29,* 80–87.

Halpern, Diane F. (1986). *Sex differences in cognitive abilities.* Hillsdale, NJ: Erlbaum.

Heller, Frank A., & Wilpert, Bernhard (1981). *Competence and power in managerial decision making.* New York: Wiley.

Hollenbeck, John R., & Brief, Arthur P. (1987). The effects of individual differences and goal origin on goal setting and performance. *Organizational Behavior and Human Decision Processes, 40,* 392–414.

Kaufman, Harold G. (1982). *Professionals in search of work: Coping with the stress of job loss and underemployment.* New York: Wiley.

Kessler, Ronald C., & McRae, James A. (1982). The effects of wives' employment on the mental health of married men and women. *American Sociological Review, 47,* 216–227.

Kleinberg, Jill (1989). Cultural clash between managers: America's Japanese firms. *Advances in International Comparative Management, 4,* 221–243.

Korman, Abraham K., & Korman, Rhoda W. (1980). *Career success/personal failure.* Englewood Cliffs, NJ: Prentice-Hall.

Maccoby, Eleanor E., & Jacklin, Carol N. (1974). *The psychology of sex differences.* Stanford, CA: Stanford University Press.

Matarazzo, Joseph D. (1972). *Wechsler's measurement and appraisal of adult intelligence.* Baltimore: Williams & Wilkins.

Miner, John B. (1976). Levels of motivation to manage among personnel and industrial relations managers. *Journal of Applied Psychology, 61,* 419–427.

Plomin, Robert (1988). The nature and nurture of cognitive abilities. In Robert J. Sternberg (Ed.), *Advances in the psychology of human intelligence, Volume 4* (pp. 1–33). Hillsdale, NJ: Erlbaum.

Rhodes, Susan R. (1983). Age-related differences in work attitudes and behavior: A review and conceptual analysis. *Psychological Bulletin, 93,* 328–367.

Schmitt, Neal, & Noe, Raymond A. (1986). Personnel selection and equal employment opportunity. *International Review of Industrial and Organizational Psychology, 1,* 71–115.

Shapira, Zur, & Bass, Bernard M. (1975). Settling strikes in real life and simulations in North America and different regions of Europe. *Journal of Applied Psychology, 60,* 466–471.

Waldman, David A., & Avolio, Bruce J. (1986). A meta-analysis of age differences in job performance. *Journal of Applied Psychology, 71,* 33–38.

Wanous, John P. (1974). Individual differences and reactions to job characteristics. *Journal of Applied Psychology, 59,* 616–622.

CHAPTER 13

Algera, Jen A. (1987). Job and task analysis. In Bernard M. Bass & Peter J. D. Drenth (Eds.), *Advances in organizational psychology: An international review* (pp. 137–149). Beverly Hills, CA: Sage.

Arvey, Richard D. (1986). Sex bias in job evaluation procedures. *Personnel Psychology, 39,* 315–335.

Ash, Ronald A., & Edgell, Steven L. (1975). A note on the readability of the Position Analysis Questionnaire. *Journal of Applied Psychology, 60,* 765–766.

Banks, Michael H., Jackson, Paul R., Stafford, Elizabeth M., & Warr, Peter B. (1983). The job components inventory and the analysis of jobs requiring limited skill. *Personnel Psychology, 36,* 57–66.

Cain, Pamela S., & Green, Bert F. (1983). Reliabilities of selected ratings available from the *Dictionary of occupational titles. Journal of Applied Psychology, 68,* 155–165.

Cain, Pamela S., & Treiman, Donald J. (1981). The *Dictionary of occupational titles* as a source of occupational information. *American Sociological Review, 46,* 253–278.

DeNisi, Angelo S., Cornelius, Edwin T., & Blencoe, Allyn G. (1987). Further investigation of common knowledge effects on job analysis ratings. *Journal of Applied Psychology, 72,* 262–268.

Doverspike, Dennis, Carlisi, Anne M., Barrett, Gerald V., & Alexander, Ralph A. (1983). Generalizability analysis of a point-method job evaluation instrument. *Journal of Applied Psychology, 68,* 476–483.

Gomez-Mejia, Luis R., Page, Ronald C., & Tornow, Walter W. (1982). A comparison of the practical utility of traditional, statistical, and hybrid job evaluation approaches. *Academy of Management Journal, 25,* 790–809.

Gunther v. County of Washington (1981). 101 S. Ct. 2242.

Hahn, David C., & Dipboye, Robert L. (1988). Effects of training and information on the accuracy and reliability of job evaluations. *Journal of Applied Psychology, 73,* 146–153.

Harvey, Robert J. (1986). Quantitative approaches to job classification: A review and critique. *Personnel Psychology, 39,* 267–289.

Harvey, Robert J., Friedman, Lee, Hakel, Milton D., & Cornelius, Edwin T. (1988). Dimensionality of the job element inventory, a simplified worker-oriented job analysis questionnaire. *Journal of Applied Psychology, 73,* 639–646.

Heisler, William J., Jones, W. David, & Benham, Philip O. (1988). *Managing human resource issues: Confronting challenges and choosing options.* San Francisco: Jossey-Bass.

Hill, M. Anne, & Killingsworth, Mark R. (1989). *Comparable worth: Analysis and evidence.* Ithaca, N.Y.: ILR Press.

International Labour Office (1975). *International standard classification of occupations.* Geneva: International Labor Office.

Jaques, Elliott (1961). *Equitable payment.* New York: Wiley.

Jenkins, G. Douglas, Nadler, David A., Lawler, Edward E., & Cammann, Cortland (1975). Standardized observations: An approach to measuring the nature of jobs. *Journal of Applied Psychology, 60,* 171–181.

Killingsworth, Mark R. (1990). *The economics of comparable worth.* Kalamazoo: Upjohn.

Lawler, Edward E. (1990). *Strategic pay.* San Francisco: Jossey-Bass.

Levine, Edward L., Ash, Ronald A., & Bennett, Nell (1980). Exploratory comparative study of four job analysis methods. *Journal of Applied Psychology, 65,* 524–535.

Levine, Edward L., Ash, Ronald A., Hall, Hardy, & Sistrunk, Frank (1983). Evaluation of job analysis methods by experienced job analysts. *Academy of Management Journal, 26,* 339–348.

Levine, Edward L., Sistrunk, Francis, McNutt, Kathryn J., & Gael, Sidney (1988). Exemplary job analysis systems in selected organizations: A description of process and outcomes. *Journal of Business and Psychology, 3,* 3–21.

Livernash, Edward R. (1980). *Comparable worth: Issues and alternatives.* Washington, DC: Equal Employment Advisory Council.

McCormick, Ernest J. (1979). *Job analysis: Methods and applications.* New York: AMACOM.

McCormick, Ernest J., DeNisi, Angelo S., & Shaw, James B. (1979). Use of the Position Analysis Questionnaire for establishing the job component validity of tests. *Journal of Applied Psychology, 64,* 51–56.

Mount, Michael K., & Ellis, Rebecca A. (1987). Investigation of bias in job evaluation ratings of comparable worth study participants. *Personnel Psychology, 40,* 85–96.

Olson, Howard C., Fine, Sidney A., Myers, David C., & Jennings, Margarette C. (1981). The use of functional job analysis in establishing performance standards for heavy equipment operators. *Personnel Psychology, 34,* 351–364.

Pearlman, Kenneth (1980). Job families: A review and discussion of their implications for personnel selection. *Psychological Bulletin, 87,* 1–28.

Rosen, Benson, Rynes, Sara L., & Mahoney, Thomas A. (1983). Compensation, jobs, and gender. *Harvard Business Review, 61*(4), 170–190.

Rynes, Sara L., Weber, Caroline L., & Milkovich, George T. (1989). Effects of market survey rates, job evaluation, and job gender on job pay. *Journal of Applied Psychology, 74,* 114–123.

Sparrow, J., Patrick, J., Spurgeon, P., & Barwell, F. (1982). The use of job component analysis and related aptitudes in personnel selection. *Journal of Occupational Psychology, 55,* 157–164.

Thompson, Duane E., & Thompson, Toni A. (1982). Court standards for job analysis in test validation. *Personnel Psychology, 35,* 865–874.

Treiman, Donald J. (1979). *Job evaluation: An analytical review.* Interim Report to the Equal Employment Opportunity Commission. Washington, DC: National Academy of Sciences.

Treiman, Donald J., & Hartmann, Heidi I. (1981). *Women, work, and wages: Equal pay for jobs of equal value.* Washington, DC: National Academy Press.

U.S. Department of Commerce, Bureau of the Census (1982). *Alphabetical index of industries and occupations.* Washington, DC: U.S. Government Printing Office.

U.S. Department of Labor (1977). *Dictionary of occupational titles* (4th ed.). Washington, DC: U.S. Government Printing Office.

Wall, Toby D., & Martin, Robin (1987). Job and work design. *International Review of Industrial and Organizational Psychology, 2,* 61–91.

Ziering, Barry A., & Raju, Nambury S. (1988). Development and validation of a job family specific Position Analysis Questionnaire. *Journal of Business and Psychology, 2,* 228–238.

CHAPTER 14

Benedict, Michael E., & Levine, Edward L. (1988). Delay and distortion: Tacit influences on performance appraisal effectiveness. *Journal of Applied Psychology, 73,* 507–514.

Brinkerhoff, Robert O., and Dressler, Dennis E. (1990). *Productivity measurement: A guide for managers and evaluators.* Newbury Park, CA: Sage.

Brush, Donald H., & Schoenfeldt, Lyle F. (1980). Identifying managerial potential: An alternative to assessment centers. *Personnel, 57*(3), 68–76.

Cash, William B. (1977). How to calculate an employee relations index. *Personnel Journal, 58,* 172–174, 183.

Cleveland, Jeanette N., Murphy, Kevin R., & Williams, Richard E. (1989). Multiple uses of performance appraisal: Prevalence and correlates. *Journal of Applied Psychology, 74,* 130–135.

DeNisi, Angelo S., Randolph, W. Alan, & Blencoe, Allyn G. (1983). Potential problems with peer ratings. *Academy of Management Journal, 26,* 457–464.

Dulewicz, Victor, & Fletcher, Clive (1982). The relationships between previous experience, intelligence, and background characteristics of participants and their performance in an assessment center. *Journal of Occupational Psychology, 55,* 197–207.

Farh, Jiing-Lih, & Werbel, James D. (1986). Effects of purpose of the appraisal and expectation of validation on self-appraisal leniency. *Journal of Applied Psychology, 71,* 527–529.

Farh, Jiing-Lih, Werbel, James D., & Bedeian, Arthur G. (1988). An empirical investigation of self-appraisal-based performance evaluation. *Personnel Psychology, 41,* 141–156.

Fay, Charles H., & Clark, Robert G. (1987). Work planning and performance review as a basis for merit pay decisions: An evaluation. *Journal of Business and Psychology, 1,* 276–290.

Gladstein, Deborah L. (1984). Groups in context: A model of task group effectiveness. *Administrative Science Quarterly, 29,* 499–517.

Goodman, Paul S., & Garber, Steven (1988). Absenteeism and accidents in a dangerous environment: Empirical analysis of underground coal mines. *Journal of Applied Psychology, 73,* 81–86.

Gupta, Nina, & Jenkins, G. Douglas (1982). Absenteeism and turnover: Is there a progression? *Journal of Management Studies, 19,* 395–412.

Harris, Michael M., & Schaubroeck, John (1988). A meta-analysis of self-supervisor, self-peer, and peer-supervisor ratings. *Personnel Psychology, 41,* 43–62.

Hinrichs, John R. (1978). An eight-year follow-up of a management assessment center. *Journal of Applied Psychology, 63,* 596–601.

Howard, Ann, & Bray, Douglas W. (1988). *Managerial lives in transition: Advancing age and changing times.* New York: Guilford Press.

Kanfer, Ruth, Crosby, John V., & Brandt, David M. (1988). Investigating behavioral antecedents of turnover at three job tenure levels. *Journal of Applied Psychology, 73,* 331–335.

Keller, Robert T. (1984). The role of performance and absenteeism in the prediction of turnover. *Academy of Management Journal, 27,* 176–183.

Landy, Frank J., & Farr, James L. (1983). *The measurement of work performance: Methods, theory, and applications.* New York: Academic Press.

Latham, Gary P., & Wexley, Kenneth N. (1981). *Increasing productivity through performance appraisal.* Reading, MA: Addison-Wesley.

Levitan, Sar A., & Werneke, Diane (1984). *Productivity: Problems, prospects, and policies.* Baltimore: Johns Hopkins University Press.

McEvoy, Glenn M., & Buller, Paul F. (1987). User acceptance of peer appraisals in an industrial setting. *Personnel Psychology, 40,* 785–797.

McEvoy, Glenn M., Beatty, Richard W., & Bernardin, H. John, (1987). Unanswered questions in assessment center research. *Journal of Business and Psychology, 2,* 97–111.

McGregor, Douglas (1957). An uneasy look at performance appraisal. *Harvard Business Review, 35*(3), 89–94.

McInnes, J. Morris (1984). Corporate management of productivity: An empirical study. *Strategic Management Journal, 5,* 351–365.

Merrihue, William V., & Katzell, Raymond A. (1955). ERI—Yardstick of employee relations. *Harvard Business Review, 33*(6), 91–99.

Meyer, Herbert H. (1987). Predicting supervisory ratings versus promotional progress in test validation studies. *Journal of Applied Psychology, 72,* 696–697.

Meyer, Herbert H., Kay, Emanuel, & French, John R. P. (1965). Split roles in performance appraisal. *Harvard Business Review, 43*(1), 123–129.

Mobley, William H. (1982). *Employee turnover: Causes, consequences, and control.* Reading, MA: Addison-Wesley.

Mohrman, Allan M., Resnick-West, Susan M., & Lawler, Edward E. (1989). *Designing performance appraisal systems.* San Francisco: Jossey-Bass.

Mount, Michael K. (1984). Psychometric properties of subordinate ratings of managerial performance. *Personnel Psychology, 37,* 687–702.

Muczyk, Jan P. (1979). Dynamics and hazards of MBO application. *Personnel Administration, 24*(5), 51–62.

National Center for Productivity and Quality of Working Life (1976). *Improving productivity through industry and company measurement.* Washington, DC: NCPQWL.

Pynes, Joan E. & Bernardin, H. John (1989). Predictive validity of an entry-level police officer assessment center. *Journal of Applied Psychology, 74,* 831–833.

Pynes, Joan, Bernardin, H. John, Benton, Arthur L., & McEvoy, Glenn M. (1988). Should assessment center dimension ratings be mechanically-derived. *Journal of Business and Psychology, 2,* 217–227.

Ritchie, Richard J., & Moses, Joseph L. (1983). Assessment center correlates of women's advancement into middle management: A 7-year longitudinal analysis. *Journal of Applied Psychology, 68,* 227–231.

Ryan, Ann M., & Sackett, Paul R. (1987). A survey of individual assessment practices by I/O psychologists. *Personnel Psychology, 40,* 455–488.

Sackett, Paul R., Zedeck, Sheldon, & Fogli, Larry (1988).

Relations between measures of typical and maximum job performance. *Journal of Applied Psychology, 73,* 482–486.

Staw, Barry B. (1984). Organizational behavior: A review and reformulation of the field's outcome variables. *Annual Review of Psychology, 35,* 627–666.

Steel, Robert P., & Ovalle, Nester K. (1984). Self-appraisal based upon supervisory feedback. *Personnel Psychology, 37,* 667–685.

Stockford, Lee, & Bissell, H. W. (1949). Factors involved in establishing a merit rating scale. *Personnel, 26,* 94–116.

Thompson, Duane (1981). Performance appraisal and the Civil Service Reform Act. *Public Personnel Management, 10,* 281–288.

Tsai, Shan P., Bernacki, Edward J., & Lucas, Lorraine J. (1989). A longitudinal method of evaluating employee turnover. *Journal of Business and Psychology, 3,* 465–473.

Walsh, James P., Weinberg, Robert M., & Fairfield, Marita L. (1987). The effect of gender on assessment centre evaluations. *Journal of Occupational Psychology, 60,* 305–309.

Wexley, Kenneth N., & Klimoski, Richard (1984). Performance appraisal: An update. *Research in Personnel and Human Resource Management, 2,* 35–79.

CHAPTER 15

Athey, Timothy R., & McIntyre, Robert M. (1987). Effect of rater training on rater accuracy: Levels-of-processing theory and social facilitation theory perspectives. *Journal of Applied Psychology, 72,* 567–572.

Baird, Lloyd S., Beatty, Richard W., & Schneier, Craig E. (1982). *The performance appraisal sourcebook.* Amherst, MA: Human Resource Development Press.

Barrett, Gerald V., & Kernan, Mary C. (1987). Performance appraisal and terminations: A review of court decisions since *Brito v. Zia* with implications for personnel practice. *Personnel Psychology, 40,* 489–503.

Beer, Michael (1981). Performance appraisal: Dilemmas and possibilities. *Organizational Dynamics, 9*(3), 24–36.

Berkshire, J. R., & Highland, R. W. (1953). Forced-choice performance rating: A metholodological study. *Personnel Psychology, 6,* 355–378.

Bernardin, H. John, & Beatty, Richard W. (1984). *Performance appraisal: Assessing human behavior at work.* Boston: Kent.

Bernardin, H. John, Carlyle, Jamie, & Elliott, Lee (1980). A critical assessment of mixed standard rating scales. *Academy of Management Proceedings, 40,* 308–312.

Bernardin, H. John, Orban, Joseph A., & Carlyle, Jamie J. (1981). Performance rating as a function of trust in appraisal and rater individual differences. *Academy of Management Proceedings, 41,* 311–315.

Bernardin, H. John, & Smith, Patricia C. (1981). A clarification of some issues regarding the development and use of behaviorally anchored rating scales (BARS). *Journal of Applied Psychology, 66,* 458–463.

Brito v. Zia Co. (1973). 478 F. 2d 1200 (10th Cir.).

Cardy, Robert L., & Dobbins, Gregory H. (1986). Affect and appraisal accuracy: Liking as an integral dimension in evaluating performance. *Journal of Applied Psychology, 71,* 672–678.

DeNisi, Angelo S., Robbins, Tina, & Cafferty, Thomas B. (1989). Organization of information used for performance appraisals: Role of diary keeping. *Journal of Applied Psychology, 74,* 124–129.

DeNisi, Angelo S., & Stevens, George E. (1981). Profiles of performance, performance evaluations, and personnel decisions. *Academy of Management Journal, 24,* 592–602.

Dipboye, Robert L., & dePontbriand, Rene (1981). Correlates of employee reactions to performance appraisals and appraisal systems. *Journal of Applied Psychology, 66,* 248–251.

Dorfman, Peter W., Stephan, Walter G., & Loveland, John (1986). Performance appraisal behaviors: Supervisor perceptions and subordinate reactions. *Personnel Psychology, 39,* 579–597.

Fay, Charles H., & Latham, Gary P. (1982). Effects of training and rating scales on rating errors. *Personnel Psychology, 35,* 105–116.

Fox, Shaul, Bizman, Aharon, & Hoffman, Michael (1989). The halo effect: It really isn't unitary: A rejoinder to Nathan (1986). *Journal of Occupational Psychology, 62,* 183–188.

Gordon, Michael E., Cofer, John L., & McCullough, P. Michael (1986). Relationships among seniority, past performance, interjob similarity, and trainability. *Journal of Applied Psychology, 71,* 518–521.

Guion, Robert M., & Gibson, Wade M. (1988). Personnel selection and placement. *Annual Review of Psychology, 39,* 349–374.

Hedge, Jerry W., & Kavanagh, Michael J. (1988). Improving the accuracy of performance evaluations: Comparison of three methods of performance appraiser training. *Journal of Applied Psychology, 73,* 68–73.

Ilgen, Daniel R., & Feldman, Jack M. (1983). Performance appraisal: A process focus. *Research in Organizational Behavior, 5,* 141–197.

Jacobs, Rick, Kafry, Ditsa, & Zedeck, Sheldon (1980).

Expectations of behaviorally anchored rating scales. *Personnel Psychology, 33,* 595–640.

Kingstrom, Paul O., & Bass, Alan R. (1981). A critical analysis of studies comparing behaviorally anchored rating scales (BARS) and other rating formats. *Personnel Psychology, 34,* 263–289.

Kozlowski, Steve W. J., Kirsch, Michael P., & Chao, Georgia T. (1986). Job knowledge, ratee familiarity, conceptual similarity and halo error: An exploration. *Journal of Applied Psychology, 71,* 45–49.

Krzystofiak, Frank, Cardy, Robert, & Newman, Jerry (1988). Implicit personality and performance appraisal: The influence of trait inferences on evaluations of behavior. *Journal of Applied Psychology, 73,* 515–521.

Landy, Frank J., & Farr, James L. (1980). Performance ratings. *Psychological Bulletin, 87,* 72–107.

Latham, Gary P. (1986). Job performance and appraisal. *International Review of Industrial and Organizational Psychology, 1,* 117–155.

Latham, Gary P., & Wexley, Kenneth N. (1981). *Increasing productivity through performance appraisal.* Reading, MA: Addison-Wesley.

Miner, John B. (1988). Development and application of the rated ranking technique in performance appraisal. *Journal of Occupational Psychology, 61,* 291–305.

Mount, M. K. (1983). Comparisons of managerial and employee satisfaction with a performance appraisal system. *Personnel Psychology, 36,* 99–110.

Murphy, Kevin R., & Reynolds, Douglas H. (1988). Does true halo affect observed halo? *Journal of Applied Psychology, 73,* 235–238.

Murphy, Kevin R., Martin, Carmen, & Garcia, Magda (1982). Do behavioral observation scales measure observation? *Journal of Applied Psychology, 67,* 562–567.

Nathan, Barry R., & Alexander, Ralph A. (1985). The role of inferential accuracy in performance rating. *Academy of Management Review, 10,* 109–115.

Piotrowski, Michael J., Barnes-Farrell, Janet L., & Esrig, Francine H. (1989). Behaviorally anchored bias: A replication and extension of Murphy and Constans. *Journal of Applied Psychology, 74,* 823–826.

Pulakos, Elaine D. (1986). The development of training programs to increase accuracy with different rating tasks. *Organizational Behavior and Human Decision Processes, 38,* 76–91.

Pulakos, Elaine D., White, Leonard A., Oppler, Scott H., & Borman, Walter C. (1989). Examination of race and sex effects on performance ratings. *Journal of Applied Psychology, 74,* 770–780.

Rosinger, George, Myers, Louis B., Levy, Girard W., Loar, Michael, Mohrman, Susan A., & Stock, John R. (1982). Development of a behaviorally based performance appraisal system. *Personnel Psychology, 35,* 75–88.

Russell, James S., & Goode, Dorothy L. (1988). An analysis of managers' reactions to their own performance appraisal feedback. *Journal of Applied Psychology, 73,* 63–67.

Saal, Frank E., Downey, Ronald G., & Lahey, Mary A. (1980). Rating the ratings: Assessing the psychometric quality of rating data. *Psychological Bulletin, 88,* 413–428.

Schoorman, F. David (1988). Escalation bias in performance appraisals: An unintended consequence of supervisor participation in hiring decisions. *Journal of Applied Psychology, 73,* 58–62.

Smither, James W., Barry, Stephen R., & Reilly, Richard R. (1989). An investigation of the validity of expert true score estimates in appraisal research. *Journal of Applied Psychology, 74,* 143–151.

Steiner, Dirk D., & Rain, Jeffrey S. (1989). Immediate and delayed primacy and recency effects in performance evaluation. *Journal of Applied Psychology, 74,* 136–142.

Tziner, Aharon, & Kopelman, Richard (1988). Effects of rating format on goal-setting dimensions: A field experiment. *Journal of Applied Psychology, 73,* 323–326.

CHAPTER 16

Arnold, John D., Rauschenberger, John M., Soubel, Wendy G., & Guion, Robert M. (1982). Validation and utility of a strength test for selecting steelworkers. *Journal of Applied Psychology, 67,* 588–604.

Barrett, Gerald V., Phillips, James S., & Alexander, Ralph A. (1981). Concurrent and predictive validity designs: A critical reanalysis. *Journal of Applied Psychology, 66,* 1–6.

Barrett, Richard S. (1980). Content validity: The impact of three recent decisions. *The Industrial-Organizational Psychologist, 17*(4), 43–46.

Bartlett, C. Jack, Grant, Donald L., & Hakel, Milton D. (1982). Comparison of the guidelines and principles. *The Industrial-Organizational Psychologist, 19*(4), 38–40.

Bray, Douglas W., Campbell, Richard J., & Grant, Donald L. (1974). *Formative years in business: A long-term AT&T study of management lives.* New York: Wiley.

Burke, Michael J., Raju, Nambury S., & Pearlman, Kenneth (1986). An empirical comparison of the results of five validity generalization procedures. *Journal of Applied Psychology, 71,* 349–353.

Cattin, Philippe (1980). Estimation of the predictive

power of a regression model. *Journal of Applied Psychology, 65,* 407–414.

Cronbach, Lee J., & Gleser, Goldine C. (1965). *Psychological tests and personnel decisions.* Urbana, IL: University of Illinois Press.

Dilla, Benjamin L. (1987). Descriptive versus prescriptive information in a realistic job preview. *Journal of Vocational Behavior, 30,* 33–48.

Dunlap, William P., & Kemery, Edward R. (1987). Failure to detect moderating effects: Is multicollinearity the problem? *Psychological Bulletin, 102,* 418–420.

Guion, Robert M. (1965). *Personnel testing.* New York: McGraw-Hill.

Guion, Robert M. (1987). Changing views for personnel selection research. *Personnel Psychology, 40,* 199–213.

Guion, Robert M., & Gibson, Wade M. (1988). Personnel selection and placement. *Annual Review of Psychology, 39,* 349–374.

Hunter, John E., Schmidt, Frank L., & Jackson, Gregg B. (1982). *Meta analysis: Cumulating research findings across studies.* Beverly Hills, CA: Sage.

James, Lawrence R., Demaree, Robert G., Mulaik, Stanley A., & Mumford, Michael D. (1988). Validity generalization: Rejoinder to Schmidt, Hunter, and Raju (1988). *Journal of Applied Psychology, 73,* 673–678.

Kemery, Edward R., Mossholder, Kevin W., & Roth, Lawrence (1987). The power of the Schmidt and Hunter additive model of validity generalization. *Journal of Applied Psychology, 72,* 30–37.

Lee, Raymond, Miller, Kenneth J., & Graham, William K. (1982). Corrections for restriction of range and attenuation in criterion-related validation studies. *Journal of Applied Psychology, 67,* 637–639.

Linn, Robert L., & Dunbar, Stephen B. (1986). Validity generlization and predictive bias. In Ronald A. Berk (Ed.), *Performance assessment: Methods and applications* (pp. 203–236). Baltimore: Johns Hopkins University Press.

Linn, Robert L., Harnisch, Delwyn L., & Dunbar, Stephen B. (1981). Corrections for range restriction: An empirical investigation of conditions resulting in conservative corrections. *Journal of Applied Psychology, 66,* 655–663.

Maier, Milton H. (1988). On the need for quality control in validation research. *Personnel Psychology, 41,* 497–502.

Mathieu, John E., & Tannenbaum, Scott I. (1989). A process-tracing approach toward understanding supervisors' SDy estimates: Results from five job classes. *Journal of Occupational Psychology, 62,* 249–256.

Miller, Edwin L. (1973). The international selection decision: A study of some dimensions of managerial

behavior in the selection decision process. *Academy of Management Journal, 16,* 239–252.

Miner, John B. (1992). *Role motivation theories.* New York: Routledge, Chapman, and Hall.

Mitchell, Terry W., & Klimoski, Richard J. (1986). Estimating the validity of cross-validity estimation. *Journal of Applied Psychology, 71,* 311–317.

Murphy, Kevin R. (1983). Fooling yourself with cross validation: Single sample designs. *Personnel Psychology, 36,* 111–118.

Orr, John M., Sackett, Paul R., & Mercer, Michael (1989). The role of prescribed and nonprescribed behaviors in estimating the dollar value of performance. *Journal of Applied Psychology, 74,* 34–40.

Potter, Edward E. (1989). Supreme Court's *Wards Cove Packing* decision redefines the adverse impact theory under Title VII. *The Industrial-Organizational Psychologist, 27*(1), 25–31.

Reilly, Richard R., Brown, Barbara, Blood, Milton R., & Malatesta, Carol Z. (1981). The effects of realistic previews: A study and discussion of the literature. *Personnel Psychology, 34,* 823–834.

Rusmore, Jay T., & Toorenaar, G. J. (1956). Reducing training costs by employment testing. *Personnel Psychology, 9,* 39–44.

Scharf, James C. (1980). Content validity: Whither thou goest? *The Industrial-Organizational Psychologist, 17*(3), 8–14.

Schmidt, Frank L., Gast-Rosenberg, Ilene, & Hunter, John E. (1980). Validity generalization results for computer programmers. *Journal of Applied Psychology, 65,* 643–661.

Schmidt, Frank L., Hunter, John E., Mckenzie, Robert C., & Muldrow, Tressie W. (1979). Impact of valid selection procedures on work-force productivity. *Journal of Applied Psychology, 64,* 609–626.

Schmidt, Frank L., Hunter, John E., & Pearlman, Kenneth (1981). Task differences as moderators of aptitude test validity in selection: A red herring. *Journal of Applied Psychology, 66,* 166–185.

Schmidt, Frank L., Hunter, John E., & Raju, Nambury S. (1988). Validity generalization and situational specificity: A second look at the 75% rule and Fisher *z* transformation. *Journal of Applied Psychology, 73,* 665–672.

Schmitt, Neal W., & Klimoski, Richard J. (1991). *Research methods in human resource management.* Cincinnati: South-Western.

Schmitt, Neal, & Noe, Raymond A. (1986). Personnel selection and equal employment opportunity. *International Review of Industrial and Organizational Psychology, 1,* 71–115.

Schmitt, Neal, & Ostroff, Cheri (1986). Operationalizing the behavioral consistency approach: Selection test development based on a content-oriented strategy. *Personnel Psychology, 39,* 91–108.

Schneider, Benjamin, & Schmitt, Neal (1986). *Staffing organizations.* Glenview, IL: Scott, Foresman.

Spector, Paul E., & Levine, Edward L. (1987). Meta-analysis for integrating study outcomes: A Monte Carlo study of its susceptibility to Type I and Type II errors. *Journal of Applied Psychology, 72,* 3–9.

Springer, James P. (1982). The importance of selection in public sector administration. *Public Personnel Management, 11,* 9–12.

Sussman, Mario, & Robertson, Donald U. (1986). The validity of validity: An analysis of validation study designs. *Journal of Applied Psychology, 71,* 461–468.

Wanous, John P. (1980). *Organizational entry: Recruitment, selection, and socialization of newcomers.* Reading, MA: Addison-Wesley.

Wanous, John P. (1989). Installing a realistic job preview: Ten tough choices. *Personnel Psychology, 42,* 117–134.

CHAPTER 17

Arvey, Richard D. (1979). Unfair discrimination in the employment interview: Legal and psychological aspects. *Psychological Bulletin, 86,* 758–759.

Arvey, Richard D., Miller, Howard E., Gould, Richard, & Burch, Phillip (1987). Interview validity for selecting sales clerks. *Personnel Psychology, 40,* 1–12.

Baxter, James C., Brock, Barbara, Hill, Peter C., & Rozelle, Richard M. (1981). Letters of recommendation: A question of value. *Journal of Applied Psychology, 66,* 296–301.

Breaugh, James A., & Dossett, Dennis L. (1989). Rethinking the use of personal history information: The value of theory-based biodata for predicting turnover. *Journal of Business and Psychology, 3,* 371–385.

Brown, Steven H. (1981). Validity generalization and situational moderation in the life insurance industry. *Journal of Applied Psychology, 66,* 664–670.

Brush, Donald H., & Owens, William A. (1979). Implementation and evaluation of an assessment classification model for manpower utilization. *Personnel Psychology, 32,* 369–383.

Campion, Michael A., Pursell, Elliott D., & Brown, Barbara K. (1988). Structured interviewing: Raising the psychometric properties of the employment interview. *Personnel Psychology, 41,* 25–42.

Carroll, Stephen J., & Nash, Allan N. (1972). Effectiveness of a forced-choice reference check. *Personnel Administration, 35*(2), 42–46.

Childs, Auralee, & Klimoski, Richard J. (1986). Successfully predicting career success: An application of the biographical inventory. *Journal of Applied Psychology, 71,* 3–8.

Dipboye, Robert L. (1982). Self-fulfilling prophecies in the selection-recruitment interview. *Academy of Management Review, 7,* 579–586.

Dougherty, Thomas W., Ebert, Ronald J., & Callender, John C. (1986). Policy capturing in the employment interview. *Journal of Applied Psychology, 71,* 9–15.

Dreher, George F., Ash, Ronald A., & Hancock, Priscilla (1988). The role of the traditional research design in underestimating the validity of the employment interview. *Personnel Psychology, 41,* 315–327.

Eder, Robert W., & Ferris, Gerald R. (1989). *The employment interview: Theory, research, and practice.* Beverly Hills: Sage.

Fleishman, Edwin A. (1988). Some new frontiers in personnel selection research. *Personnel Psychology, 41,* 679–701.

Gilmore, David C., Beehr, Terry A., & Love, Kevin G. (1986). Effects of applicant sex, applicant physical attractiveness, type of rater and type of job on interview decisions. *Journal of Occupational Psychology, 59,* 103–109.

Goldstein, Irwin L. (1971). The application blank: How honest are the responses? *Journal of Applied Psychology, 55,* 491–492.

Guion, Robert M., & Imada, Andrew S. (1981). Eyeball measurement of dexterity: Tests as alternatives to interviews. *Personnel Psychology, 34,* 31–36.

Hunter, John E., & Hirsh, Hannah R. (1987). Applications of meta-analysis. *International Review of Industrial and Organizational Psychology, 2,* 321–357.

Jones, Alan, & Harrison, Elizabeth (1982). Prediction of performance in initial officer training using reference reports. *Journal of Occupational Psychology, 55,* 35–42.

Koen, Clifford M. (1980). The pre-employment inquiry guide. *Personnel Journal, 59,* 825–829.

Mitchell, Terry W., & Klimoski, Richard J. (1982). Is it rational to be empirical? A test of methods for scoring biographical data. *Journal of Applied Psychology, 67,* 411–418.

Muchinsky, Paul M. (1986). Personnel selection methods. *International Review of Industrial and Organizational Psychology, 1,* 37–70.

Mumford, Michael, Stokes, Garnett S., & Owens, William A. (1990). *Patterns of life history: The ecology of human individuality.* Hillsdale, NJ: Lawrence Erlbaum.

Nash, Allan N., & Carroll, Stephen J. (1970). A hard look at the reference check. *Business Horizons, 13*(5), 43–49.

Owens, William A., & Schoenfeldt, Lyle F. (1979). Toward a classification of persons. *Journal of Applied Psychology, 65,* 569–607.

Paunonen, Sampo V., & Jackson, Douglas N. (1987). Accuracy of interviewers and students in identifying the personality characteristics of personnel managers and computer programmers. *Journal of Vocational Behavior, 31,* 26–36.

Paunonen, Sampo V., Jackson, Douglas N., & Oberman, Steven M. (1987). Personnel selection decisions: Effects of applicant personality and the letter of reference. *Organizational Behavior and Human Decision Processes, 40,* 96–114.

Peters, Lawrence H., & Terborg, James R. (1975). The effects of temporal placement of unfavorable information and of attitude similarity on personnel decisions. *Organizational Behavior and Human Performance, 13,* 279–293.

Raza, Susan M., & Carpenter, Bruce N. (1987). A model of hiring decisions in real employment interviews. *Journal of Applied Psychology, 72,* 596–603.

Robertson, Ivan T., & Makin, Peter J. (1986). Management selection in Britain: A survey and critique. *Journal of Occupational Psychology, 59,* 45–57.

Shaffer, Garnett S., Saunders, Vickie, & Owens, William A. (1986). Additional evidence for the accuracy of biographical data: Long-term retest and observer ratings. *Personnel Psychology, 39,* 791–809.

Simas, Kathleen, & McCarrey, Michael (1979). Impact of recruiter authoritarianism and applicant sex on evaluation and selection decisions in a recruitment interview analogue study. *Journal of Applied Psychology, 64,* 483–491.

Singer, M.S., & Sewell, Christine (1989). Applicant age and selection interview decisions: Effect of information exposure on age discrimination in personnel selection. *Personnel Psychology, 42,* 135–154.

Tubiana, Josef H., & Ben-Shakhar, Gershon (1982). An objective group questionnaire as a substitute for a personal interview in the prediction of success in military training in Israel. *Personnel Psychology, 35,* 349–357.

Tullar, William L., Mullins, Terry W., & Caldwell, Sharon A. (1979). The effects of interview length and applicant quality on interview decision time. *Journal of Applied Psychology, 64,* 669–674.

Webster, Edward C. (1964). *Decision making in the employment interview.* Montreal: Industrial Relations Center, McGill University.

Webster, Edward C. (1982). *The employment interview: A social judgment process.* Schomberg, Ont.: S.I.P. Publications.

Weiss, David J., & Dawis, Rene V. (1960). An objective validation of factual interview data. *Journal of Applied Psychology, 44,* 381–385.

Wiesner, Willi H., & Cronshaw, Steven F. (1988). A meta-analytic investigation of the impact of interview format and degree of structure on the validity of the employment interview. *Journal of Occupational Psychology, 61,* 275–290.

Wright, Patrick M., Lichtenfels, Philip A., & Pursell, Elliott D. (1989). The structured interview: Additional studies and a meta-analysis. *Journal of Occupational Psychology, 62,* 191–199.

Zedeck, Sheldon, Tziner, Aharon, & Middlestadt, Susan E. (1983). Interviewer validity and reliability: An individual analysis approach. *Personnel Psychology, 36,* 355–370.

Zima, Joseph P. (1983). *Interviewing: Key to effective management.* Chicago: Science Research Associates.

CHAPTER 18

Alexander, Ralph A., Carson, Kenneth P., Alliger, George M., & Cronshaw, Steven F. (1989). Empirical distributions of range restricted SD_x in validity studies. *Journal of Applied Psychology, 74,* 253–258.

Bass, Bernard M., & Barrett, Gerald V. (1981). *People, work, and organizations.* Boston: Allyn & Bacon.

Bureau of National Affairs (1983). ASPA-BNA survey no. 45—Employee selection procedures. *Bulletin to Management,* May 5.

Butcher, James N. (1985). Personality assessment in industry: Theoretical issues and clinical illustrations. In H. John Bernardin & David A. Bownas (Eds.), *Personality assessment in organizations* (pp. 277–310). New York: Praeger.

Cascio, Wayne F. (1991). *Costing human resources: The financial impact of behavior in organizations.* Boston: PWS-Kent.

Cornelius, Edwin T. (1983). The use of projective techniques in personnel selection. *Research in Personnel and Human Resources Management, 1,* 127–168.

Crown, Deborah F., & Rosse, Joseph G. (1988). A critical review of the assumptions underlying drug testing. *Journal of Business and Psychology, 3,* 22–41.

Distefano, M. K., Pryer, Margaret W., & Craig, Stella H.

(1980). Job-relatedness of a posttraining job knowledge criterion used to assess validity and test fairness. *Personnel Psychology, 33,* 785–793.

Elliott, A. G. P. (1981). Some implications of lie scale scores in real-life selection. *Journal of Occupational Psychology, 54,* 9–16.

Faley, Robert H., Kleiman, Lawrence S., & Wall, Patricia S. (1988). Drug testing in the public and private-sector workplaces: Technical and legal issues. *Journal of Business and Psychology, 3,* 154–186.

Fraser, Scott L., & Kroeck, K. Galen (1989). The impact of drug screening on selection decisions. *Journal of Business and Psychology, 3,* 403–411.

Frost, Alan G., & Rafilson, Fred M. (1989). Overt integrity tests versus personality-based measures of delinquency: An empirical comparison. *Journal of Business and Psychology, 3,* 269–277.

Ghiselli, Edwin E. (1973). The validity of aptitude tests in personnel selection. *Personnel Psychology, 26,* 461–477.

Gottfredson, Linda S. (1986). Occupational aptitude patterns map: Development and implications for a theory of job aptitude requirements. *Journal of Vocational Behavior, 29,* 254–291.

Guastello, Stephen J. (1988). A proper role for drug testing in the work place: Only if civil liberties are protected to their fullest. *The Industrial-Organizational Psychologist, 26*(1), 31–35.

Hartigan, John A., & Wigdor, Alexandra K. (1989). *Fairness in employment testing: Validity generalizations, minority issues, and the General Aptitude Test battery.* Washington, DC: National Academy Press.

Hunter, John E., & Hirsh, Hannah R. (1987). Applications of meta-analysis. *International Review of Industrial and Organizational Psychology, 2,* 321–357.

Lefkowitz, Joel, & Fraser, Alan W. (1980). Assessment of achievement and power motivation of blacks and whites, using a black and white TAT, with black and white administrators. *Journal of Applied Psychology, 65,* 685–696.

Matarazzo, Joseph D. (1972). *Wechsler's measurement and appraisal of adult intelligence.* Baltimore: Williams & Wilkins.

McClelland, David C., & Boyatzis, Richard E. (1982). Leadership motive pattern and long-term success in management. *Journal of Applied Psychology, 67,* 737–743.

McDaniel, Michael A. (1988). Does pre-employment drug use predict on-the-job suitability? *Personnel Psychology, 41,* 717–729.

McDaniel, Michael A., & Jones, John W. (1986). A meta-analysis of the validity of the Employee Attitude Inventory theft scales. *Journal of Business and Psychology, 1,* 31–50.

Miner, John B. (1985). Sentence completion measures in personnel research: The development and validation of the Miner Sentence Completion Scales. In H. John Bernardin and David A. Bownas (Eds.), *Personality assessment in organizations* (pp. 145–176). New York: Praeger.

Miner, John B. (1992). *Role motivation theories.* New York: Routledge, Chapman, and Hall.

Rabin, Albert I., & Zltogorski, Zoli (1985). The sentence completion method: Recent research. *Journal of Personality Assessment, 49,* 641–647.

Reilly, Richard R., & Chao, Georgia T. (1982). Validity and fairness of some alternative employee selection procedures. *Personnel Psychology, 35,* 1–62.

Robertson, Ivan T., & Downs, Sylvia (1989). Work sample tests of trainability: A meta-analysis. *Journal of Applied Psychology, 74,* 402–410.

Robertson, I. T., & Kandola, R. S. (1982). Work-sample tests: Validity, adverse impact, and applicant reaction. *Journal of Occupational Psychology, 55,* 171–183.

Robertson, I. T., & Mindel, R. M. (1980). A study of trainability testing. *Journal of Occupational Psychology, 53,* 131–138.

Robinson, David D. (1981). Content-oriented personnel selection in a small business setting. *Personnel Psychology, 34,* 77–87.

Sackett, Paul R., Burris, Laura R., & Callahan, Christine (1989). Integrity testing for personnel selection: An update. *Personnel Psychology, 42,* 491–529.

Schippmann, Jeffrey S., & Prien, Erich P. (1989). An assessment of the contributions of general mental ability and personality characteristics to management success. *Journal of Business and Psychology, 3,* 423–437.

Schmitt, Neal, & Noe, Raymond A. (1986). Personnel selection and equal employment opportunity. *International Review of Industrial and Organizational Psychology, 1,* 71–115.

Shackleton, Vivian, & Anderson, Neil (1987). Personnel recruitment and selection. In Bernard M. Bass & Pieter J. D. Drenth (Eds.), *Advances in organizational psychology: An international review* (pp. 68–82). Beverly Hills, CA: Sage.

Siegel, Arthur I. (1983). The miniature job training and evaluation approach: Additional findings. *Personnel Psychology, 36,* 41–56.

Tenopyr, Mary L., & Oeltjen, Paul D. (1982). Personnel selection and classification. *Annual Review of Psychology, 33,* 581–618.

Thornton, George C., & Byham, William C. (1982). *Assessment centers and managerial performance.* New York: Academic Press.

CHAPTER 19

Alliger, George M., & Janak, Elizabeth A. (1989). Kirkpatrick's levels of training criteria: Thirty years later. *Personnel Psychology, 42,* 331–342.

Argyris, Chris (1980). Some limitations of the case method: Experiences in a management development program. *Academy of Management Review, 5,* 291–298.

Baldwin, Timothy T., & Ford, J. Kevin (1988). Transfer of training: A review and directions for future research. *Personnel Psychology, 41,* 63–105.

Beatty, Richard W., Schneier, Craig E., & McEvoy, Glenn M. (1987). Executive development and management succession. *Research in Personnel and Human Resources Management, 5,* 289–322.

Berger, Michael A. (1983). In defense of the case method: A reply to Argyris. *Academy of Management Review, 8,* 329–333.

Billy, Christopher (1988). *Bricker's international directory: University executive programs.* Princeton, NJ: Peterson's Guides.

Briggs, Vernon M., & Foltman, Felician F. (1981). *Apprenticeship research: Emerging findings and future trends.* Ithaca, NY: New York State School of Industrial and Labor Relations, Cornell University.

Burack, Elmer H., & Mathys, Nicholas J. (1980). *Career management in organizations: A practical human resource planning approach.* Lake Forest, IL: Brace-Park Press.

Burke, Michael J., & Day, Russell R. (1986). A cumulative study of the effectiveness of managerial training. *Journal of Applied Psychology, 71,* 232–245.

Campbell, John P., & Campbell, Richard J. (1988). *Productivity in organizations: New perspectives from industrial and organizational psychology.* San Francisco: Jossey-Bass.

Casner-Lotto, Jill (1988). *Successful training strategies.* San Francisco: Jossey-Bass.

Ford, J. Kevin, & Noe, Raymond A. (1987). Self-assessed training needs: The effects of attitudes toward training, managerial level, and function. *Personnel Psychology, 40,* 39–53.

Gist, Marilyn, Rosen, Benson, & Schwoerer, Catherine (1988). The influence of training method and trainee age on the acquisition of computer skills. *Personnel Psychology, 41,* 255–265.

Goldstein, Irwin L. (1986). *Training in organizations: Needs assessment, development, and evaluation.* Monterey, CA: Brooks/Cole.

Gould, Sam (1979). Characteristics of career planners in upwardly mobile organizations. *Academy of Management Journal, 22,* 539–550.

Hall, Douglas T. (Ed.) (1986). *Career development in organizations.* San Francisco: Jossey-Bass.

Korman, Abraham K., & Korman, Rhoda W. (1980). *Career success/Personal failure* (Englewood Cliffs, NJ: Prentice-Hall.

Latack, Janina C., Josephs, Susan L., Roach, Bonnie L., & Levine, Mitchell D. (1987). Carpenter apprentices: Comparison of career transitions for men and women. *Journal of Applied Psychology, 72,* 393–400.

Latham, Gary P. (1988). Human resource training and development. *Annual Review of Psychology, 39,* 545–582.

London, Manuel (1985). *Developing managers.* San Francisco: Jossey-Bass.

McGehee, William, & Thayer, Paul W. (1961). *Training in business and industry.* New York: Wiley.

Miner, John B., & Crane, Donald P. (1981). Motivation to manage and the manifestation of a managerial orientation in career planning. *Academy of Management Journal, 24,* 626–633.

Morgan, Marilyn A. (1980). *Managing career development.* New York: Van Nostrand Reinhold.

Neider, L. L. (1981). Training effectiveness: Changing attitudes. *Training and Development Journal, 35*(12), 24–28.

Norris, William C. (1981). *Technology for company–employee partnership to improve productivity.* Minneapolis: Control Data Corporation.

Pintrich, Paul R., Cross, David R., Kozma, Robert B., & McKeachie, Wilbert J. (1986). Instructional psychology. *Annual Review of Psychology, 37,* 611–651.

Reynolds, John I. (1980). *Case method in management development: Guide for effective use.* Geneva: International Labour Office.

Rosow, Jerome M., & Zager, Robert (1988). *Training—The competitive edge.* San Francisco: Jossey-Bass.

Saari, Lise M., Johnson, Terry R., McLaughlin, Steven D., & Zimmerle, Denise M. (1988). A survey of management training and education practices in U.S. companies. *Personnel Psychology, 41,* 731–743.

Sprangers, Mirjam, & Hoogstraten, Johan (1989). Pretesting effects in retrospective pretest–posttest designs. *Journal of Applied Psychology, 74,* 265–272.

Storcevich, Matt M., & Sykes, J. Arnold (1982). Internal advanced management programs for executive development. *Personnel Administrator, 27*(6), 27–33.

Storey, Walter D. (1979). *A guide for career development inquiry.* Madison, WI: American Society for Training and Development.

Wexley, Kenneth N., & Latham, Gary P. (1981). *Developing and training human resources in organizations.* Glenview, IL: Scott, Foresman.

Williams, Richard (1981). *Career management and career planning.* London: Her Majesty's Stationery Office.

CHAPTER 20

Bacow, L. S. (1980). *Bargaining for job safety and health.* Cambridge, MA: MIT Press.

Boyle, A. J. (1980). Found experiments in accident research: Report of a study of accident rates and implications for future research. *Journal of Occupational Psychology, 53,* 53–64.

Cairo, Peter C. (1983). Counseling in industry: A selected review of the literature. *Personnel Psychology, 36,* 1–18.

Davids, Anthony, & Mahoney, James T. (1957). Personality dynamics and accident-proneness in an industrial setting. *Journal of Applied Psychology, 41,* 303–306.

Denning, D. L. (1983). *Correlates of employee safety performance.* Wilmington, DE: Employee Relations Department, E. I. duPont deNemours & Co.

Dickman, Fred, & Emener, William G. (1982). Employee assistance programs: Basic concepts, attributes, and an evaluation. *Personnel Administrator, 27*(8), 55–62.

Drake, C. A. (1940). Accident-proneness: A hypothesis. *Character and Personality, 8,* 335–341.

Eden, Dov (1987). Training. In Bernard M. Bass & Pieter J. D. Drenth (Eds.), *Advances in organizational psychology: An international review* (pp. 99–113). Beverly Hills, CA: Sage.

Foley, Robert J., & Redfering, David L. (1987). Bridging the gap between counseling psychologists and organization development consultants. *Journal of Business and Psychology, 2,* 160–170.

Frenkel, Richard L., Priest, W. Curtis, & Ashford, Nicholas A. (1980). Occupational safety and health: A report on worker perceptions. *Monthly Labor Review, 103*(9), 11–14.

Goodman, Paul S., & Garber, Steven (1988). Absenteeism and accidents in a dangerous environment: Empirical analysis of underground coal mines. *Journal of Applied Psychology, 73,* 81–86.

Hansen, Curtiss P. (1988). Personality characteristics of the accident involved employee. *Journal of Business and Psychology, 2,* 346–365.

Haynes, Robert S., Pine, Randall C., & Fitch, H. Gordon (1982). Reducing accident rates with organizational behavior modification. *Academy of Management Journal, 25,* 407–416.

Heisler, William J., Jones, W. David, & Benham, Philip O. (1988). *Managing human resources issues.* San Francisco: Jossey-Bass.

Heshizer, Brian, & Muczyk, Jan P. (1988). Drug testing at the workplace: Balancing individual, organizational, and societal rights. *Labor Law Journal,* 342–357.

Jones, John W., & Wuebker, Lisa J. (1988). Accident prevention through personnel selection. *Journal of Business and Psychology, 3,* 187–198.

Komaki, Judith L., Collins, Robert L., & Penn, Pat (1982). The role of performance antecedents and consequences in work motivation. *Journal of Applied Psychology, 67,* 334–340.

Komaki, Judith L., Heinzmann, Arlene T., & Lawson, Loralie (1980). Effects of training and feedback: Component analysis of a behavioral safety program. *Journal of Applied Psychology, 65,* 261–270.

Lawrence, A. C. (1974). Human error as a cause of accidents in gold mining. *Journal of Safety Record, 6,* 78–88.

LeShan, L. L. (1952). Dynamics of accident-prone behavior. *Psychiatry, 15,* 73–80.

Lofgren, Don J. (1989). *Dangerous premises: An insider's view of OSHA enforcement.* Ithaca, NY: ILR Press.

McBain, William N. (1970). Arousal, monotony, and accidents in line driving. *Journal of Applied Psychology, 54,* 509–519.

Merchant, Kenneth A. (1985). *Control in business organizations.* Boston: Pitman.

Miner, John B. (1985). *People problems: The executive answer book.* New York: Random House.

Miner, John B., & Brewer, J. Frank (1976). The management of ineffective performance. In Marvin D. Dunnette (Ed.), *Handbook of industrial and organizational psychology* (pp. 995–1029). Chicago: Wiley.

Mitchell, Terence R., & Wood, Robert E. (1980). Supervisor's responses to subordinate poor performance: A test of an attributional model. *Organizational Behavior and Human Performance, 25,* 123–138.

Mitchell, Terence R., Green, Stephen G., & Wood, Robert E. (1981). An attributional model of leadership and the poor performing subordinate: Development and validation. *Research in Organizational Behavior, 3,* 197–234.

Montag, I., & Comrey, Andrew L. (1987). Internality and externality as correlates of involvement in fatal driving accidents. *Journal of Applied Psychology, 72,* 339–343.

Oberer, Donna, & Lee, Sandra (1986). The counseling psychologist in business and industry: Ethical concerns. *Journal of Business and Psychology, 1,* 148–162.

Pence, Earl C., Pendleton, William C., Dobbins, Greg H., & Sgro, Joseph A. (1982). Effects of causal explanations and sex variables on recommendations for corrective actions following employee failure. *Organizational Behavior and Human Performance, 29,* 227–240.

Ryan, Ann M., & Sackett, Paul R. (1987). A survey of individual assessment practices by I/O psychologists. *Personnel Psychology, 40,* 455–488.

Sanders, Mark S., & McCormick, Ernest J. (1987). *Human factors in engineering and design.* New York: McGraw-Hill.

Schreier, James W. (1983). A survey of drug abuse in organizations. *Personnel Journal, 62,* 478–484.

Sheehy, Noel P., & Chapman, Antony J. (1987). Industrial accidents. *International Review of Industrial and Organizational Psychology, 2,* 201–227.

Siskind, Fred (1982). Another look at the link between work injuries and job experience. *Monthly Labor Review, 105*(2), 38–40.

Sonnenstuhl, William J. (1986). *Inside an emotional health program: A field study of workplace assistance for troubled employees.* Ithaca, NY: ILR Press, Cornell University.

Speller, Jeffrey L. (1989). *Executives in crisis.* San Francisco: Jossey-Bass.

Stein, Judith A., Newcomb, Michael D., & Bentler, P. M. (1988). Structure of drug use behaviors and consequences among young adults: Multitrait-multimethod assessment of frequency, quantity, work site, and problem substance use. *Journal of Applied Psychology, 73,* 595–605.

Terborg, James R. (1986). Health promotion at the worksite: A research challenge for personnel and human resources management. *Research in Personnel and Human Resources Management, 4,* 225–267.

Warr, Peter (1987). *Work, unemployment, and mental health.* Oxford: Clarendon Press.

Weiss, Richard M. (1987). Writing under the influence: Science versus fiction in the analysis of corporate alcoholism programs. *Personnel Psychology, 40,* 341–356.

Wuebker, Lisa J. (1986). Safety locus of control as a predictor of industrial accidents and injuries. *Journal of Business and Psychology, 1,* 19–30.

Zohar, Dov (1980). Safety climate in industrial organizations: Theoretical and applied implications. *Journal of Applied Psychology, 65,* 96–102.

APPENDIX

Ledvinka, James, & Scarpello, Vida G. (1991). *Federal regulation of personnel and human resource management.* Boston: PWS-Kent.

Miner, John B. (1973). *Intelligence in the United States.* Westport, CT: Greenwood Press.

Miner, Mary G., & Miner, John B. (1978). *Employee selection within the law.* Washington, DC: Bureau of National Affairs (BNA) Books.

Schmitt, Neal W., & Klimoski, Richard J. (1991). *Research methods in human resource management.* Cincinnati: South-Western.

Organization Index

Organization Index

Name Index

Name Index

Subject Index

Subject Index